Black & White

Black & White

THE BIRTH OF MODERN BOXING

BRIAN DOBBS

First published by Pitch Publishing, 2021

Pitch Publishing
A2 Yeoman Gate
Yeoman Way
Worthing
Sussex
BN13 3QZ
www.pitchpublishing.co.uk
info@pitchpublishing.co.uk

A CIP catalogue record is available for this book
from the British Library.

ISBN 978 1 78531 890 0

Typesetting and origination by Pitch Publishing

Printed and bound in India by Replika Press Pvt. Ltd.

CONTENTS

To Charlotte, David and James:
the very best seconds one could have in one's corner.

ABOUT THE AUTHOR

Brian Dobbs is the author of several books on sport and
other subjects. He was art editor of *World Sports* and
has written for several magazines and newspapers. His
acquaintance with boxing began when staying up with
his father to hear Freddie Mills, Bruce Woodcock and
Joe Louis fights on the radio.

PREFACE

MORE YEARS ago than I care to remember, I wrote a book about sport in the 1890–1914 period, placing sport within its historical context, then a much less fashionable approach. I was conscious that one major sport, boxing, was excluded. The omission was deliberate.

Boxing in the early 20th century was of such cardinal importance that a cursory treatment would not do. Other concerns then interfered. Only later was I able to give boxing the detailed attention it deserved. This book is the result.

Many readers will be astonished by the sight of royalty, the aristocracy and the middle classes flocking to glamorous fight nights, and even more by the ubiquitous coverage they commanded in serious newspapers. The glamour disguised a legal status that was highly dubious and controversially remains so.

Others will be shocked by the poisonous racism operating within boxing and disfiguring the sport and the society that contained it. Black and white applied to the newspapers and films of the period, also to the skin colour of participants, who were not boxers, but 'white' boxers and 'black' boxers, like different breeds of cattle. Modern senses of social justice were rare.

Today no witnesses survive to account for the fights they saw or fought. The last surviving veteran of the First World War of 1914–18, Florence Green of the WRAF, died in February 2012 aged 110, and the last man to serve in the trenches, Harry Patch, died in July 2009 aged 111. Even veterans of the Second World War of 1939–45, a rapidly diminishing band, tend to be in their 90s and over.

We are left only with the writings, films, documents and reports from the period. No one knows exactly what happened. We can only make informed guesses. My own biases and prejudices will have influenced my selections but sensitive readers will make due allowance for that.

The British, American, French and Australian contributions are covered. The fates of American boxers who visited Britain, and the fortunes of the British boxers who ventured across the Atlantic are also featured. The laws applied to boxing, both in Britain and in the USA, had major influences on both sides of the Atlantic.

Personal memories are notoriously subject to subconscious revision, self-editing and justification after the event. Take a famous fight from the 1960s. At Wembley Stadium on 18 June 1963, Henry Cooper fought Muhammad Ali, Ali then calling himself Cassius Clay. The result is not in dispute. Cooper, prone to cuts, was stopped in the fifth round when an ugly wound above his left eye, sustained in the second round, reopened and bled profusely. Referee Tommy Little called a halt.

Cooper, before the cut, had taken the fight to Clay but by round three, Clay was back in control and landing dangerous combinations. The closing seconds of round four and the interval before the fifth have been discussed endlessly. Cooper, knowing he would soon be stopped by the referee, threw a succession of his famous left hooks, punches that had given him an edge in rounds one and two. With seconds to go before the bell, one caught a complacent and clowning Clay on the jaw and felled him. (Clay had egotistically predicted that Cooper would be beaten in the fifth and, confident of a victory, was playing around to take proceedings into the fifth to fulfil his own prophecy.)

Clay went down, and as the referee counted one, the bell rang. With the stadium in uproar, Little continued the count. Little counted three and was about to add four when Clay got up and walked groggily to his corner. Had Cooper landed the punch a minute earlier in the round he *might* have completed a knockout, but that is speculation.

During the interval, Clay's corner pointed to a small tear at the base of the thumb on one of Clay's gloves, a tear tugged at by Angelo Dundee, Clay's second. The glove was *not* replaced

— 1 —

and round five began with a delay of possibly a few seconds as the tear was dismissed by the referee, determined to resume as quickly as possible.

Subsequently, this 'delay' increased significantly in the telling. Fresh gloves were fetched from the dressing room, according to Cooper in interviews late in his life. 'I was responsible for increasing the rip in the glove to guarantee my fighter a further recuperation period,' said Angelo Dundee in 1991. 'Maybe a minute, but it was enough.' 'It took nearly a minute to make the replacement,' wrote Ali in 1975.

Contrast this with contemporary coverage. *The Times* report mentions no delay. Neither does the *New York Times*. The BBC TV commentary by Harry Carpenter (1925–2010) mentions the referee's visit to Clay's corner but certainly not any time added to the interval. The BBC radio live commentary carried the traditional inter-round summary by the very experienced W. Barrington Dalby (1893–1975). As the referee went to Clay's corner, Dalby said, 'I say, now that is an extraordinary thing because if it means they've got to exchange the glove they're going to give Clay a rest, which I think would be an awful pity, awful rough luck on Cooper. No he's not going to change it now …' – circumstantial evidence that round five began promptly. Jim Wicks, Cooper's manager, in a post-fight interview, mentioned the split glove but not a delay. Neither did Cooper. Wicks wrote a few weeks later (12 July 1963) to *Boxing News*, but made no mention either of the glove or of a delay.

There are explanations for the discrepancies. Cooper, later Sir Henry and the most decent of men, dwelt on his bitter disappointment and its unlucky circumstances for years after (especially as he was again defeated by Ali on cuts in the sixth round on 21 May 1966 at Arsenal's Highbury stadium). He came to believe, wrongly, that he had been somehow robbed. His belief was further fostered by later pronouncements about the incident from Angelo Dundee, the man who had tampered with the glove. Dundee exaggerated his own role to enhance his reputation as the miracle worker who could magic victory out of defeat. The myth increased Dundee's Machiavellian reputation. It did little for historical accuracy and myth replaced history.

Commonly, 'histories' of boxing split the history into self-contained sections – 'The Heavyweights', 'The Welterweights', 'The Bantams', etc. Harry Mullan's *An Illustrated History of Boxing* (Hamlyn, London 1990 and later editions), and *A Pictorial History of Boxing* by Sam Andre and Nat Fleischer (Hamlyn London/New York 1959, and frequently updated) both follow this pattern, as does *A History of Boxing in Britain* by Frank Butler (Arthur Barker, London 1972), which devotes other chapters to individual boxer profiles. Though readable and useful, these approaches negate any view of proper context. To paraphrase the distinguished cricket writer C. L. R. James: how can we know about boxing if we know only about boxing?

There exists also a small army of meticulous boxing historians who modestly restrict themselves to researching and documenting minor details of results, career records and fights that might otherwise disappear into obscurity. Harold Alderman would be a shining example. This is a most valuable service. Any larger picture would be impossible without them. Anyone pursuing wider themes is overwhelmingly in their debt.

The years from 1909 to 1921 set the pattern for so much that was to follow. They featured some of the most brave and skilful men ever to pull on gloves, yet many others involved in the shark-infested waters of promotion and dishonest journalism. Over 50 of the legendary boxers and ancillary contributors appearing here were subsequently heralded and invested in the International Boxing Hall of Fame at Canastota, New York State. For all the importance of context and the operations of historical and economic forces, major fighters such as Jack Johnson, Jack Dempsey, Benny Leonard, Jim Driscoll, Ted Kid Lewis and Jimmy Wilde had a profound personal impact upon their profession, upon their sport and upon the public.

The ultimate history of boxing is what happened within the ropes. Among the hundreds of fights appearing in the following pages, included are some of the most dramatic and important ever to take place, honoured and discussed wherever the sport is taken seriously. They deserve to be seen against the background of their dramatic setting.

Grateful thanks are due to many institutions and organisations for their hospitality and the unfailingly helpful courtesy of their staff. They are the British Library; the London Library; the Chiswick Library; the Battersea Library; the Lambeth Library; the Hounslow Treaty Centre Library; the Lewisham Library; the National Archives at Kew; the Metropolitan Archives; the *Jewish Chronicle* offices; the British Boxing Board of Control offices (now in Cardiff but previously in London); the Cumbrian Archives; and in the United States, the New York Public Library; the Nyack Library; and the Finkelstein Memorial Library in Spring Valley.

Individuals who have been particularly helpful are Charles and Lois Goldsmith of Croton, New York (for the warmest hospitality, great company and legal advice and research); Judy Duncan of Walnut Creek, California; Paul and Jane Camillin of Pitch Publishing for their belief in the book; David Dobbs; Charlotte and James Lloyd, whose design and computer skills are formidable; and my late wife Judy who disliked boxing compared with her beloved cricket but whose wit, historical expertise and stimulating company were an inspiration for most things I have ever done.

BRIAN DOBBS
Chiswick, Spring 2020

THE BLACK AND THE WHITE
11AM SATURDAY, 26 DECEMBER 1908

In Which a Black Man Beats a White Man and Shocks the World

AT RUSHCUTTERS Bay near Sydney, Australia, it was 11am on Saturday, 26 December 1908. Two men sat under an overcast sky in opposite corners of a 24-foot roped square. The square, a boxing ring, was at the centre of an octagonal wooden stadium in the shadow of an unlovely gasometer and a few industrial buildings, on what had previously been a market garden. The site was readily accessible from the nearby city by tram, bus, car and buggy.

Among the 20,000 people crammed into the stadium, those at its outer limits were 360 feet away from the central square, of which they had merely a distant glimpse. Beyond them were the bay and the silver-grey Tasman Sea, and an unlucky 30,000 locked out of the stadium.

The two men were far from home. One came from the USA – nearly 10,000 miles away. The other was from Canada – nearly 12,000 miles away. This was long before the days of intercontinental air travel. (The Wright brothers' initial powered flight of a mere 12 seconds had taken place only five years before.) The two men had undertaken roundabout sea journeys of even more prodigious distances to be there. The Canadian was only 5ft 7in tall and usually weighed about 12st 12lb/180lb. This day he was at his slimmest and actually weighed only 12st 1lb/169lb. His chest, when he took a deep breath and adopted a characteristic pouter pigeon-like pose, measured 43¾ inches. His neck was 16 inches, short and set strongly within his powerful shoulders. His 14½-inch biceps bulged prominently on his arms, surprisingly long for a man so short and stocky, with a potential reach of 74½ inches.

The American's reach was fractionally shorter at 74 inches, and his expanded chest marginally narrower at 42¾ inches. In all other respects he physically dominated the Canadian. He was 6ft 1¼in tall and he weighed 15st 13lb/223lb – very close to his regular 15st 12lb/222lb. His biceps measured 16 inches and his neck 17½ inches. The length and breadth of his penis were not known, other than by rumour, although he had been known to swathe it in bandages to produce a phenomenally virile mound in the close-fitting genital area of his shorts.

No one, even the boxers' contemporary, Viennese doctor Sigmund Freud (1856–1939) had devised an instrument for measuring the sizes of men's egos. Neither was there a meter to record the sharpness of tongues finely honed for sardonic pre-fight comments and insults. Had such apparatus existed, both men would have notched high scores.

What was to happen between these men in the next hour would be followed avidly at first hand by the 50,000 people inside and outside the rough stadium, but subsequently just as eagerly at second hand by millions around the globe by telegraph, by newspaper and by newsreel film. The event would change the face of boxing – this particular 26 December was a Boxing Day in more ways than one. It would change permanently the face of sport. It would, in the words of author Jeff Wells who devoted an excellent book to the event, be the fight that changed the world.

These far-reaching consequences were because of one thing: the Canadian, Tommy Burns (born Noah Brusso, in Hanover, Ontario on 17 June 1881), and for the moment generally acknowledged as the latest heavyweight champion of the world, had a pale white

— 4 —

Thousands of Australians gather to see the Boxing Day clash between a black man and a white man. The result will foster racial prejudices across the globe.

Charles H. Kerry, National Library of Australia, nla.obj-136843728

skin. His challenger, the Texan Jack Johnson (born John Arthur Johnson in Galveston, Texas on 31 March 1878 and sometimes dubbed L'il Arthur), had a shining black one.

The immaculate Tommy Burns (1881–1955) of Canada. 'The Little General' was as competitive in his business dealings as he was in the ring.

PA/PA Archive/PA Images

As the length of Helen of Troy's nose supposedly provoked the bloody Trojan War, so Johnson's blackness was a major factor in the ugly and unworthy turmoil in Western society that followed the fight. To understand this lurid overreaction, it is necessary to know a little more about these men, and about the circumstances that had brought them to the eastern shores of Australia, so many miles from home.

Tommy Burns, known as Napoleon because of his small stature and pugnacious nature, referred to himself in the third person as the Emperor or the Little General. His other extravagant claim was to be 'the best damned puncher on the planet'. Like his Corsican model, he had a strong sense of his economic worth and took risks only when he believed the price was right.

Since 1900, when he began his professional boxing career across the border in Detroit, he had made 52 professional appearances in the USA, Canada and Europe. He had won 41 of those fights, and in 33 of them deposited his opponent on the canvas for ten seconds or more for clear knockout victories. Eight other bouts were drawn. He had lost a mere three, had never been knocked out nor been rescued by a referee from further punishment. These figures represent official fights. There were others too – for example, the March 1906 evening in Los Angeles when he took back-to-back fights and separated not one but two local heavyweights from their senses, one after another.

Burns had been recognised generally as world heavyweight champion since 23 February 1906. That day, in a mediocre 20-round fight in Los Angeles, he had outpointed Marvin Hart of Kentucky, who weighed 13st 8lb/190lb and stood 5ft 11¾in tall. Burns had adroitly jabbed, hooked and held the larger man. The uncomely Hart furrowed his battered eyebrows, puckered his facial scar tissue and peered at Burns from one eye (he was blind in the other). He chased Burns futilely around the ring for the last five rounds. Meanwhile, Burns, the matador tormenting an angry, frustrated and unseeing bull, brushed him aside with light but irritating punches. He added sarcastic verbal *banderillas* to lower Hart's morale, while preserving his own substantial points lead. Respect for a beaten opponent was not in the Little General's repertoire.

Burns was the new champion and richer both by the purse and by backing himself at the pre-fight odds of 17/11 laid against him. The bookmakers looked at the men's vital statistics and foolishly assumed the good big 'un (Hart) would beat the good little 'un. Since the Hart bout, Burns had cashed in on the title by defending it successfully 13 times against hand-picked opponents.

Having as keen an eye for plunder as Napoleon himself, Burns invaded other capitals looking for further spoils. On 2 December 1907, he was in London at the National Sporting Club in Covent Garden, to meet the plucky but limited Gunner Moir (British heavyweight champion 1906–09). Burns's failure there to observe the niceties of English etiquette was positively Bonapartean.

As a traditional London establishment at the heart of the British Empire, the club, of which we shall hear a lot more later, expected those who entered its portals to show gratitude for the privilege of being invited in, and to conform to the prevailing master/servant mores for the duration – with the boxers very much the servants. This was not to the gum-chewing Burns's taste.

He consented to appear only when the club agreed to put up a £2,300 purse with side stakes of £500, an unprecedented sum for the club but reflecting his attraction as the new world champion. At the premises in Covent Garden, he took over all arrangements. He chose the gloves and had them sealed away. He lined up the club's four principal officials and picked out a referee. He insisted the man should be present in the ring throughout the fight. (Normally, the club's referee sat on a high stool like a tennis umpire and issued verbal orders – 'Break!', 'Keep your punches up!', 'Don't hold!' and the like – from outside the ropes.)

All this they swallowed, but Burns's further demand that the £1,000 joint side stakes should be carried in the referee's pocket inside the ring throughout was deeply resented. The implication was that ultra-respectable tuxedoed English gentlemen would cheat him or abscond with the takings. Burns need not have worried. There was no danger of that and not much more that the heavily tattooed and clumsy Moir would beat him. Having 'carried' Moir for nine rounds (thus guaranteeing a respectable commercial length to the film of the proceedings), Burns knocked him out in the tenth.

After his adventures in London, Burns went to Dublin for some more easy pickings on St Patrick's Day (17 March) 1908, knocking out the Irish champion Jem Roche in less than two minutes. Burns then thoroughly enjoyed an April in Paris, swanning along the boulevards with his second wife, Julia Keating, whom he had married in 1906 after an unsuccessful six-month spar with his first wife, Irene Pepper. Julia transformed herself into 'Jewel', a new, elegant queen to the thoroughly dapper heavyweight king, and frequenter of the best Paris fashion houses. The couple popped champagne with *le beau monde*, including Baron de Rothschild. Burns and the baron shared a passion for owning and backing racehorses.

To sustain this elegant lifestyle, Burns took one evening off from merrymaking, 18 April 1908, swiftly to demolish the South African hopeful, Jewey Smith, in an untroubled five rounds.

The lovely Jewel did not attend fights, although many Parisian ladies did. A little later, on 13 June 1908, Burns climbed back into a French ring to delight his growing female fan club, and to replenish the funds for luxuries, by dealing with the Australian boxer, 'Boshter' Bill Squires. Squires's pugilistic tactics were as simple as his declared philosophical motto: 'I just 'its 'em!'

Squires had met Burns previously at Colma, California on 4 July 1907, and the only thing he had succeeded in 'itting was the floor within two minutes of the first round. As Burns became thereby $13,000 richer (an $8,000 purse and a $5,000 side stake) for less than two minutes' work, he was hardly reluctant to be rematched with Squires.

Burns v Squires II predictably lasted longer. With the film rights sold, another blink-and-you've-missed-it was to no one's advantage. Equally predictable was another Burns knockout victory. It came in the eighth, after a mildly embarrassing moment when Burns was knocked down at the start of the seventh.

A century ago, cynical promoters had no difficulty selling tickets to fights the cognoscenti knew to be hopelessly one-sided. Somehow, the Australian public was persuaded to forget that the

Boshter had been trounced twice by *le petit general* on foreign soil, and to part with good money to see Burns v Squires III in Sydney on 24 August 1908. The date and the place were chosen more meticulously than the matchmaking. The event coincided with Sydney Harbour's reception of the fleet of the USA, sent by President Theodore Roosevelt as a gesture of solidarity with Australia in the aftermath of Japan's victory over Russia in the Russo-Japanese War of 1905, a war perilously near Australian waters. On the day of the fight, 250,000 people crammed into Sydney's Centennial Park to see American sailors and Australian soldiers marching in harmony. But, just like the meeting of Tommy Burns and Jack Johnson a few months later, this seemingly innocent ceremonial had racist overtones.

Australian journals trumpeted the political meaningfulness of the junket. For one monthly journal (*The Lone Hand*), the US Pacific Fleet was 'the Great *White* Fleet' [italics added] defending white Australia against yellow- or brown-skinned Asiatic hordes looming across the ocean. Euphemisms had no place in the Australian public prints at this time – 'If there is one clear principle amidst the welter of wrongs and reprisals and deceits called "international politics", it is that *the supremacy of the white man must be maintained* … most will confirm without a moment's doubt, "*The White Race Right or Wrong*" … ' [Italics added].

Burns v Squires III was sold, both to the American sailors and to the Australian locals, as a topical friendly USA v Australia contest. For sports editors, the distinction between an American and a Canadian was a subtlety too far. In the Colma fight, Burns had shamelessly wrapped himself in the Stars and Stripes to gain local support, so was unlikely to object to the latest billing. It did not fool the US navy.

But Sydney's own residents convinced themselves that the Boshter just might be third time lucky against Burns and become an *Australian* world heavyweight champion. Some 40,000 people travelled out to the stadium, although it could hold officially a mere 15,000. The lucky 15,000 were exclusively male. Nearly 50 Sydney women, having socialised with the lovely Jewel and ogled the half-stripped Burns sparring and shadow-boxing at public training sessions, applied for tickets for the real fisticuffs. The promoter ignored their applications, clearly believing that Sheilas would be less resilient than Mariannes when genuine punches were thrown. The promoter's sole concession to female feelings was a promise to Jewel to install a ringside telephone so that she could be reassured of her husband's welfare after every round.

Whatever she was told, Burns suffered some superficial damage to nose, eye and mouth as he patiently waited for Squires to punch himself out. This the gallant Boshter had done by the 13th, when Burns knocked him down for two counts of eight, adding a final right to send him face down on the canvas for the end of the contest. So little real damage had Squires inflicted, that Burns was back in action in Melbourne within ten days on 3 September 1908, and treating a crowd of 19,000 unruly Australians to a sixth-round knockout of another domestic hopeful, Bill Lang.

Ever since Burns and Jewel had arrived in Western Australia in early August, Burns had run the smoothest of publicity campaigns, one worthy of a modern spin doctor. On all social occasions he launched a charm offensive, becoming the perfect gentleman, generous to defeated and to potential opponents, and gracing his world title with appropriate sartorial grandeur.

He wore a long camel-coloured overcoat with a velvet collar and gleaming buttons that could have served as saucers for Jewel's bone-china teacups, and he rounded off the outfit with a gold-topped walking stick. His dress suits were embellished with prominent TB monograms. Every time his fights were filmed, he had his second complete inter-round administrations by combing his hair before the next round commenced.

Appropriately conspicuous consumption and plenty of chutzpah accompanied Burns's elegant image – Havana cigars, vintage brandy, expensive his-and-her motorcars and generous charitable contributions to poverty-stricken turf accountants. When the Melbourne crowd turned a little ugly, he leaned over the ropes and treated them to flowery compliments on their sportsmanship.

Only in a fight did the real Burns appear. He was as ruthless as ever, boring in and upward with his head from his low crouch and hitting and holding. Psychologically, he was just as aggressive, taunting and demeaning opponents, and smiling sardonically whenever an opponent succeeded in punching him. Even Bohun Lynch, English boxing chronicler and one of Burns's champions, conceded, 'He went in for glaring balefully at his opponents, stamping on the floor to inspire terror, and worst, "mouth-fighting", pouring vituperation upon his man, and telling him exactly what he was going to do to him.' The gentler side of Burns also disappeared when a contract was on offer. No one was better at extracting the lion's share of a promoter's purse or guaranteeing the star's portion of the film rights. He insisted on being taken at his own high valuation.

'Modesty was not his strong point,' wrote Eugene Corri, the English referee who climbed into the NSC ring with Burns and Moir at Burns's request and reluctantly held the stakes in his pocket. 'I doubt if there was an ounce of that quality in his composition, and I am sure he would not have regretted the omission had his attention been called to it.'

Financial and sporting probity were not Burns's strong points either. On 8 May 1907, Burns had agreed to a third fight with Philadelphia Jack O'Brien, with whom he had previously drawn a 20-rounder in Los Angeles on 28 November 1906, and lost a six-rounder in Milwaukee on 7 October 1904. Burns v O'Brien III was less a fight than another crude fix. Even the original 20-rounder had been prearranged by Burns and O'Brien as a damageless ballet, more choreography than contest.

The third fight was just as inauthentic. Burns posted a secret $1,000 bond, having agreed to pocket the entire purse in return for not training for the fight, and for agreeing to keel over at an appropriate moment. This would have given O'Brien a prestigious knockout win on his record and Burns more possibilities for luxurious living. In the event, it was a double double-cross.

Burns put up the secret bond – in forged bills. Discreetly he trained hard and took the ring in tip-top condition against the complacent O'Brien, who was completely out of sorts, and expecting the pre-planned victory. Burns had the promoter and the referee announce from the ring at the last moment to the audience and to the flabbergasted O'Brien that all bets on the fight were null and void because there had been an attempted fix. O'Brien took a beating, and Burns's fists and impertinence took the decision and the money.

His more genuine victories in and out of Australia and his clever manipulation of the sports pages, plus his and Jewel's high profiles among Sydney's social elite, were the main reasons the Rushcutters Bay stadium was packed to its last wooden strut on Boxing Day 1908. Burns sat immobile in his corner – like many talented athletes he preserved his nervous energy for when it really mattered. His opponent could have been forgiven for wondering whether Burns was really there or been substituted by a clone in another of Burns's deceptions. Burns had been eluding his present challenger for years.

That challenger, Jack Johnson, was the best heavyweight in the world in the period leading up to the First World War; the best ever according to the doyen of American boxing writers, Nat Fleischer. Johnson had campaigned obsessively for an opportunity to fight Burns for the world heavyweight championship. He was 30 years old and had travelled a long way to be there in more ways than one.

His father Henry was born in the mid-1830s as a Maryland slave. By

'Jack' (John Arthur) Johnson (1878–1946) from the USA. 'Li'l Arthur' was never as carefree as his 'golden smile' for photographers might suggest.
Bain collection, Prints & Photographs Division, Library of Congress, LC-USZ62-29331

the time his son John Arthur 'Jack' Johnson was born in 1878, he was an emancipated but illiterate and physically challenged labourer of 42. His wife Tiny, 20 years younger than he, married him in the early 1870s. Together they produced six children, three girls and three boys, of whom Jack was the eldest. (Three other babies died at birth.) The home was pious, the parents using local church facilities to ensure that the children could do what their father could not – read and write. Jack became a well-read, articulate adult, although his prose style tended to the ornate. His authentic speech bore little resemblance to the grotesque black parodies white journalists persisted in placing in his mouth. His enemies were not inclined to credit him for his qualities, rather to dismiss them as the latest evidence of his uppitiness and of social pretensions to which he was not entitled. He declined to be patronised.

Full evidence about Johnson's early days is lost, although in its absence legends and fictions proliferated – amply fostered by Johnson's personal propaganda machine. Like Burns, he could feed a gullible journalist with an invented autobiographical titbit. His own book-length autobiography, possibly un-ghosted, was issued variously as *Jack Johnson Is a Dandy* and *Jack Johnson: In and Out of the Ring* and contains a bewildering mixture of fact with legends of Baron von Munchausen proportions. Documentary evidence for his claims – that, for example, he had privileged access to the private correspondence between the Tsar of Russia and the German Kaiser during the First World War – is lacking.

Inspired by contemporary newspapers, many at Rushcutters Bay believed he was a watermelon-sucking black giant, who trained for the fight by eating more chickens than the most rapacious fox, increased his speed by running down jackrabbits to catch them with his bare hands, and outlasted kangaroos on his roadwork so that the kangaroos, not he, suffered thrombotic collapse. Aided and abetted by the racist slant of that press, they believed more sinister things too, including the conclusion that a victory for Johnson over Burns would not be a sports result but the disintegration of Western civilisation.

Johnson's professional career started officially in Galveston, Texas in 1897, when he was 19, with a fourth-round knockout over Jim Rocks, but that official record does not include numerous encounters for which no written record has been found. Those encounters included examples of one

of the most repulsive spectacles ever devised by man – the Battle Royal.

The regal title glosses the squalid reality. Up to a dozen black youths, valued in the American South below fighting dogs or gamecocks, were placed in a ring before a white audience to fight, fair or foul, amongst themselves, with cents and nickels thrown into the ring for the last one standing. Refinements included blindfolding the participants, tying one of their hands behind their backs, tying two or more of them together, or having them fight naked. One such, featuring two fast-hopping, one-legged black youths, disfigured the undercard at the 25 February 1901 meeting between Johnson and Joe Choynski 'The Californian Terror'. (English readers cannot feel comfortably superior; a Battle Royal was enjoyed at The Ring, Blackfriars in 1900.)

Choynski (b. Joseph Bartlett on 8 November 1868) and also known as 'Chrysanthemum' because of his tousled hair rather than his aroma or his colouration, was Johnson's first serious opponent, and another man surrounded by legends. In his case, the legends were generally true.

He came from a highly intellectual Jewish household in San Francisco, his mother a lover of literature and a poet. His father, a campaigning journalist and editor, had been educated at Yale at a time when Jews were rarely admitted. Joe's resistance to anti-Semitism took more physical form.

He had an epic encounter in June 1889 on a barge tethered in Benicia Bay near San Francisco, to avoid police interference, and for which the Jew v Gentile angle was unworthily exploited. The match, fixed as a no-limit fight-

to-a-finish with minimal gloves, was against the great Irish American, James J. Corbett. They pummelled each other for 27 gruelling rounds until Joe had been downed for the count, and the barely vertical Corbett had been declared the winner, taking the $4,000 winner-take-all side stakes.

Choynski drew with the famous Bob Fitzsimmons in Boston in June 1894, and with the man mountain Jim Jeffries, 52 pounds heavier than he, over 20 rounds in San Francisco in November 1897. All these opponents had been, or would be, world heavyweight champions.

Even as a 32-year-old veteran of such punishing skirmishes, Choynski had enough ring-savvy, and enough remaining power in his fists to take care of the young hopeful, knocking Johnson out in the third round. Curiously, this did Johnson a favour.

Boxing in Texas was illegal; boxing between whites and blacks particularly so. As Johnson hit the canvas, five Texas Rangers hit the ring and arrested both boxers. Their contest was advertised euphemistically as a sparring exhibition. Exhibitions rarely resulted in one demonstrator flat out – 'He just found a soft spot and laid down,' pleaded Choynski vainly to the Texan judge who lacked any soft spot himself.

Choynski and Johnson spent a month in the Galveston jail.

There the two fighters became friends. They sparred together to keep fit and to pass the time. Thus, Johnson learned many of Choynski's hard-earned ring skills, which stood him in excellent stead later.

Subsequently, Johnson travelled east, west, north and south across the American continent, picking up

Joe 'Chrysanthemum' Choynski (1868–1943) was successively Johnson's opponent, his fellow prisoner and his friend.

Bain collection, Prints & Photographs Division, Library of Congress, LC-DIG-ggbain-04855

a solid *apartheid* that, post formal so-called emancipation, kept black people in the lowest stratum of their society. Sport has rarely been a leader in social practice; more often a field of human endeavour full of outdated practices and outmoded prejudices masquerading as immutable laws of the universe. Many examples will disfigure the pages of this book.

Where society has led, sport and boxing follow. For men like Johnson, a contest against a white opponent was a rare event. He and other highly talented black fighters of his day – Sam McVea, Joe Jeannette, Sam Langford, Denver Ed Martin and Harry Wills – were confined to roped squares that operated like black ghettos. More often than not they fought each other. Sam Langford and Harry Wills fought each other 22 times, possibly 23. Johnson touched gloves with Sam McVea on 26 February 1903, 27 October 1903 and 22 April 1904; and with Joe Jeannette on 9 May 1905, 25 November 1905, 16 January 1906, 14 March 1906, 20 September 1906 and 26 November 1906. There was a separate unofficial

Johnson knocked out Californian Sam McVea (1884–1921), 'The Oxnard Cyclone', in the last of 20 rounds in San Francisco on 22 April 1904. By beating Burns and becoming world heavyweight champion, Johnson escaped the norm where black fighters fought only each other.
BoxRec

small purses, now in California, now in Chicago, now in Denver, now in Vermont. The building of a reputation, the ability to challenge for a title; these were rocky roads for any young fighter. And Johnson was a black man in a white man's world.

Discrimination was formally enshrined in American state and federal legislation. Five years before Johnson and Choynski fell foul of the Texan authorities, the highest legal authority in the land, the Supreme Court, had firmly upheld segregation on so-called *public* transport, and in *public* schools. Backed by taboos and conventions and incorporated into the practical functioning of American society, was title of *black* heavyweight champion of the world.

Black Americans were expected to be content with this, just as they were expected to acquiesce in the situation in major league baseball where black players and teams were excluded from the late 1880s to the 1940s. Similar ideas prevailed in American football and basketball. All four professional sports would collapse in modern times *without* black participants.

The rough, tough and very white Irish American, John L. Sullivan (b. 15 October 1858), calling himself 'The Boston Strong Boy', had caught the American imagination for his bare-fisted exploits in prizefighting. He presided over the transition from bare-knuckle mayhem to gloved regularity, losing on 7 September 1892 in New Orleans to James J. Corbett in the first gloved heavyweight championship fight.

Sullivan's characteristic utterance, issued in many a packed sporting bar, was, 'I can lick any sonofabitch in the house!' He meant any *white* sonofabitch, and, as he declared in March 1892, 'I will not fight a Negro. I never have and never will.' His attitude encapsulated the shameful code upheld by his successors as heavyweight champion.

The code applied in the heavyweight division, slightly less often in the lighter weights. The heavyweight division appealed to a wide hinterland of public awareness beyond the inner circle of boxing aficionados. Sullivan's stance prevailed. As John Lardner wittily put it, 'Race honor became an issue when the scales reached one hundred and seventy-five pounds.'

'Ruby Bob', Bob Fitzsimmons, the red-haired Cornish New Zealander (title holder 1897–99) normally followed the Sullivan code of dishonour. He met Johnson in Philadelphia on 17 July 1907, contrary to his own prejudices, only because he was broke and coming to the end of his career. He may have believed Johnson would allow him a draw in gratitude for the match. He was sadly misguided. Johnson knocked him out in the second.

James J. Jeffries, b. 15 April 1875, the 'Californian Grizzly Bear', and undefeated heavyweight champion from 1899–1905, had seen his own less talented brother, Jack Jeffries, knocked out by Jack Johnson on 16 May 1902 in a rare black v white skirmish in Los Angeles. The result confirmed all his own prejudices on the subject: 'When there are no white men left to fight, I will quit the business.' He added, 'I am determined not to take a chance of losing the championship to a Negro.' It was also personal: 'I want it to go on record, however, to the effect that under no circumstances can I be prevailed upon to meet Johnson or any other colored man … so far as I am concerned Johnson is entirely out of the question.'

When Jeffries retired undefeated in May 1905, he treated the title as his personal property to be bequeathed as he saw fit. Fit meant in an all-white direction. On 3 July 1905, he refereed while two of his personal nominees, a short Kentuckian, Marvin Hart, and an Austrian-American, Jack Root, fought for his vacated title. Hart was Jeffries's anointed protégé but had to survive a long count in the seventh, before getting lucky with a right to the body in the 12th. Hart had actually fought Johnson on 28 March 1905 and been awarded a points win over 20 rounds. Johnson consistently claimed thereafter that the decision had been a robbery. Robbery or not, the bout was less decisive than Hart's boasts before the fight that 'before the 20th round is reached … there'll be a n****r on the floor'.

Once Hart was champion, his dislike of Johnson and all other blacks prevailed as with Sullivan, Corbett and Jeffries before him. A return with Johnson was out of the question. However, Hart on 23 February 1906 as we have seen, conceded his title to Tommy Burns in Los Angeles over 20 rounds.

Here was a new situation. Would the Canadian grant Johnson an opportunity to take the heavyweight crown? Would Johnson become the first black man even to contest the title? Would Burns be any less prejudiced against black opponents than his predecessors?

Burns's record suggested no change – 52 previous fights, 52 white opponents. Neither did his vulgarly and freely expressed racist opinions: 'All c**ns are yellow.' (This was meant as an aspersion upon the bravery of black fighters, not on their shade of skin tone.)

For the next two years, Johnson conducted a calling-out campaign to get Burns into a ring against him. As Burns toured the world exploiting his title in fights in California, England, Ireland, France and Australia, a dogged black shadow followed along behind, materialising at ringside to express his claims to anyone who would listen, or arriving in a country as Burns departed it and telling the local press that his entry and Burns's exit were not coincidental.

This global chase took Johnson to Australia twice. In early 1907 he was

The confident Burns was pursued across the world by Johnson, desperate to fight for the title.
Bain collection, Prints & Photographs Division, Library of Congress, LC-DIG-ggbain-08747

in Sydney to knock out Peter Felix, a fading black fighter, in the first round on 19 February, and then in Melbourne to knock out Bill Lang, an Australian Rules footballer turned boxer, in the ninth on 4 March. And, reading between the lines of the evidence presented in a curious New South Wales libel case of March 1908, it seems he more or less knocked out a Miss Alma Adelaide Lillian 'Lola' Toy as well.

She was a glamorous and affluent *white* Australian lady, and she sued local sporting paper *The Referee*, which had innocently repeated a quotation from a Californian newspaper to the effect that the boxer Jack Johnson planned to marry her. To be 'accused' of planning to marry a black man was, she claimed, a libel. It's an eloquent demonstration of prevailing attitudes that the case was not only brought and heard with due seriousness, but that the fragrant Miss Toy was awarded a court victory and £500 damages. (She had asked for £2,000.)

This verdict was particularly unjust in view of the evidence, dragged out of Miss Toy by *The Referee*'s barrister, that Lola was not quite the stranger to Johnson and his charms that she claimed. She had been happily photographed with Johnson's affectionate arm around her shoulders. He had escorted her around town in a horse-drawn carriage designed for one and she had frequently visited him in his room at the Sir Joseph Banks hotel to the detriment of his training schedule.

The barrister's innuendos, which stooped to phallic byplay about the implications of Miss Toy holding Mr Johnson's walking stick (hints that caused the sensitive Lola to collapse dramatically in the witness box), are relevant for two reasons. Johnson's predilection for white women would be used against him throughout his career. Also, the thousands of Australians packed into the stadium for the fight against Burns were familiar with the recent libel case, and much shrewder than the jury in picking up hints.

So, Johnson was attracted to white women. That was bad enough. But that lodged an even more subversive thought in their minds. *White women were attracted by Jack Johnson.* At a time of general sexual repression and prevailing racist taboos, no more frightening an idea could be grasped. The public newspapers retailed every juicy detail of the Lola affair. These coincided neatly with current Australian fears of *any* alien threats from abroad. The newspapers firmly connected the racial politics of the visit of the Great White Fleet against the 'Yellow Peril', and the half-grasped sexual implications of the boxing match about to take place at Rushcutters Bay. White supremacy trumped all other colours.

The Sportsman belied its title with a grotesque caricature of 'The Latest Manly Surf-Bather', i.e. Johnson, in a floral one-piece bathing suit, with a round-shouldered hunch Richard III might have sported, blubber-lips of pneumatic proportions, and saucer-like eyes staring maniacally as a small boy comments, 'My word. He's sunburnt.' Meanwhile, the *Australian Bulletin* adopted a new strapline. The old 'Australia for Australians' became 'Australia for the White Man'. The *Sporting and Dramatic News* editorialised shamelessly: 'Citizens who have never prayed before are supplicating Providence to give the white man a strong right arm with which to belt the c**n into submission.' The *Melbourne Herald*'s report on the day stated, 'Even at the Stadium, there was all the hatred of twenty thousand whites for all the negroes of the world,' and made a spurious claim for Australian tolerance by suggesting that had the event taken place in the USA, someone would have shot Johnson and been acquitted by popular acclaim.

To read the bile of the *Melbourne Herald*'s correspondent (who sounds as if he fancied carrying out the noble deed himself) is to be uncomfortably aware that the writer is not wholly wrong. Had the fight taken place before a white audience in the American South exercising their constitutional right to bear arms, some affronted redneck might have counted Johnson out for good from the barrel of his gun.

One tiny example will suffice to show the virulence of racial prejudice in the American South in the early 20th century. The black and ultra-gentlemanly American educationalist, Booker T. Washington (1856–1915), never a friend of Johnson, was invited by President Theodore Roosevelt to stay on at the White House to continue an interesting conversation over dinner in 1901. When the news of the hospitality leaked out, the prominent Mississippi politician, James K. Vardaman, pronounced the White House was now 'so saturated with the odor of the n****r that the rats have taken refuge in the stable'.

An intelligent man like Johnson had every reason to think that in Australia even the referee would be against him. In this case, the referee was the promoter who had built the arena, Hugh D. McIntosh. In his financial dealings with Burns and Johnson, McIntosh found Johnson quite an adversary. He told Johnson that Burns had been guaranteed £6,000, that the gate was a world record £26,000, and that he, Johnson would get only £1,000. (Burns entered the ring as odds-on favourite.) Rumours, probably highly embellished, spread that 'Huge Deal' McIntosh had pointed a gun at Johnson's head to get his cooperation. It was also said, with too many colourful details to be entirely true, that McIntosh kept a lead pipe wrapped up in a roll of sheet music

of 'Sing Me to Sleep, Mother' in case his relationship with Johnson turned even more rumbunctious. Johnson can hardly have believed that McIntosh would favour him in any close decision.

At a press conference, Johnson picked up on Burns's slur about his and other black fighters' courage. 'No one has yet found the yellow streak Mr Burns speaks of. That is a thing any man in the world would take offence at. When he steps into the ring we shall see where the yellow streak is.' To step into a boxing ring is at any time a courageous act. Even faith is insufficient at the critical moment. As the ex-bantamweight and trainer Harry Griver put it, 'You need more than a belief in Jesus to be a champion, much more. He ain't gonna stop some other guy tearing your head off when you start losing it in the ring.'

How much more courage Jack Johnson must have had on Boxing Day 1908. Imagine it. The long, lonely walk to the ring through rows and rows of Australians, many of them booing, hissing and screaming racist abuse and other demeaning epithets in Johnson's face – about the only black face among 20,000 white ones.

Would he get out alive if he defeated Burns? Would he be merely the 34th heavyweight to be knocked out by 'the best damned puncher on the planet'? (Burns had knocked out approximately 60 per cent of all his opponents.) As Johnson walked to the ring, he showed no doubts. His sangfroid in the crucible of fear and hatred that was the Rushcutters Bay arena was admirable. Such a façade made him formidable.

Note what Jose Torres, the 1960s Puerto Rican world light-heavyweight champion, had to say. He was actually

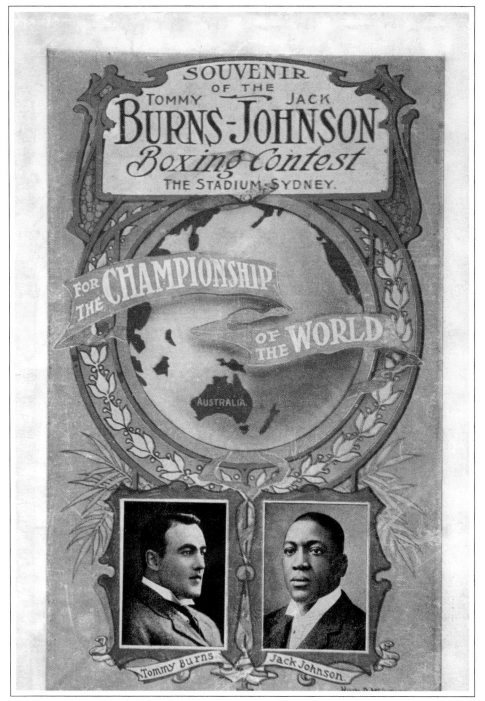

The souvenir programme for 'the fight that changed the world'.
Popperfoto via Getty Images/Getty Images

referring to Muhammad Ali, a man in limited ways a reincarnation of Jack Johnson 50 years on, but his words are apt:

Champions and good fighters are champions and good fighters because they can lie better than

the others. The first thing you learn in the gym is that you have to have a double personality if you are to become a good fighter.

As Torres pointed out, a feint, where a boxer pretends he will hit you in one place, and, as you cover up, hits you

in quite another, is the production of an outright lie. Elsewhere, Torres says that Ali's three and a half years of exile taught him 'more than Jack Johnson ever learned'. Difficult as it is to disagree with a man like Torres who has put his body on the line in championship fights, surely even Ali did not know how to be a better liar than Johnson on that ring walk in Australia.

Johnson's demeanour through all the anxiety-provoking preliminaries was a prodigious lie – a lie that deceived the spectators and his opponent alike. With every inward reason to be in fear and trembling, his body language conveyed the supreme confidence of a man strutting to the ring to claim what legitimately belonged to him: Burns's title. He climbed in through ropes supported quaintly by *eight* ring posts – four at the corners and four in the centres of the sides. On reaching his corner, he responded to the torrents of abuse with broad smiles and blown kisses. He ignored the wildly cheered arrival of Burns, until Burns stripped for action out of the natty blue suit he wore for his entrance. (Burns's own lie was to keep his opponents waiting while he casually removed his suit, folding it item by item, and packing it away into a suitcase as if he were soon to depart on an eagerly anticipated holiday.) Johnson then objected, quite legitimately, to the protective bandages wound around Burns's elbows. He put his robe back on and sat in his corner as impassively as Buddha, refusing to join the action unless the offending bandages were removed. He got his way and the fight started 15 minutes late. (It is symptomatic of boxing history that accounts differ on the time of day the fight actually began –

Burns takes a belligerent stance. Johnson ignores him.
BoxRec

1.30pm for Bill Beadle; 11.07am for Jeff Wells; 11.15am for Denzil Batchelor; scheduled for 11am and slightly delayed for Murray Greig; 1pm for the *Boxers/ Big Fights* video.)

When it commenced, Johnson was psychologically two rounds up – one because of his utter failure to be intimidated by a hostile crowd; the second because he had put the champion in the wrong. He then demonstrated his general opinion of boxing writers present by taking a swig of water and expectorating it across the press rows.

He was supremely ready to fulfil the promises he had made to the *Sydney Morning Herald* in October:

How does Burns want it? Does he want it fast and willing? I'm his man in that case. Does he want it flat footed? Goodness, if he does, why I'm his man again. Anything to suit; but fast or slow, I'm going to win.

Having waited years and travelled so many fruitless miles, a 15-minute delay was nothing.

What actually happened in the next 50 minutes or so was summarised in the *New York Herald* by Jack London (1876–1916), the American novelist and journalist, best known for his adventure stories (*The Call of the Wild; The Sea Wolf*) and his socialist writings (*The Iron Heel; The People of the Abyss*). London, who was at ringside on 26 December 1908, had spent the last decade vigorously attacking the evils of unrestrained capitalism, which he believed had placed the proletariat in the cellars and the abysses of human society, and had himself identified strongly with loners, outsiders and underdogs. He telegraphed:

The fight, if fight it might be called, was like that between a colossus and a pygmy. It had all the seeming of a playful Ethiopian

at loggerheads with a small white man – of a grown man cuffing a naughty child; of a monologue by Johnson, who made a noise with his fists like a lullaby, tucking Burns into his little crib; of a funeral, with Burns for the late deceased, Johnson for undertaker, gravedigger, and sexton.

Sadly, London's strong beliefs in the brotherhood of man did not extend to those with a black skin, and his identity with society's victims sat uneasily with his own deep-dyed racism. He was partly responsible personally for taking this fight beyond man v man into a drama of permanent significance.

The fight is worth detailed consideration, especially the first round, which encapsulated in microcosm the course of all 14 rounds. Johnson's height and weight advantages looked even greater as he towered over Burns, (Jack London's 'colossus' and 'pygmy' imagery). Burns placed his feet widely apart, one foot towards the opponent, weight on the balls of his feet, then settled down slightly on his haunches, meanwhile glowering up at his opponent and appearing even shorter than he really was. (There never was a shorter world heavyweight champion.)

Johnson kept his gloves very low, right glove at waist level and the left level with the bottom of his trunks. He moved those gloves round in short, circumscribed feints ready for instant attack or defence – he had very fast hands. He, like Burns, tended to lean back rather than forward, a pose from which he could sway away from a lead or launch himself aggressively with sudden swings, hooks and jabs.

Once he became champion, Johnson did more posing than fighting.
Bain collection, Prints & Photographs Division, Library of Congress, LC-DIG-ggbain-08094

He had confidently suggested that Johnson might not even turn up. He told a *New York World* reporter, 'I will bet a few plunks that the colored man will not make good! I'll fight him and whip him, as sure as my name is Tommy Burns.' His best hopes of beating Johnson lay in slipping inside Johnson's leads and pummelling away at his body. Burns may have been encouraged in this game plan by the prevailing white opinion that black fighters were particularly vulnerable to body blows. (When a young English toff outlined this racist thesis to the great black Australian fighter of the 1890s, Peter Jackson: 'They tell me, Jackson, that you black fellows do not like being hit in the stomach!' Jackson replied impassively, 'Can you tell me any white man that does?')

Myths apart, Burns had little chance of defeating Johnson from a distance, and needed to get inside those long arms to do any real damage. Stage one of Burns's master plan worked perfectly. He frequently got inside Johnson's first line of defence. Unfortunately for him, especially in the early stages of the contest, he got inside only to find all his aggression and ammunition neutralised by Johnson's ability to wrap up his arms and gloves as securely as if he had been coiled in adhesive black spaghetti. And, on his way in, he had to take sharp and damaging blows himself.

Barely had Burns left his corner at the first bell, avoided a Johnson long jab and failed to land his own left hook, when he was deceived by a Johnson feint and sidestep and left himself open to a carefully timed uppercut to the point of his chin. The 20,000 Australian hearts sank in their ribcages as Burns took an awkward backwards tumble to

In defence, Johnson used his long, strong arms to frustrate Burns by pinning his arms to his side, or gripping, hitting or pushing at Burns's biceps from the inside; in both cases preventing Burns from getting off effective punches. His other maddening line of defence was to hold his hands before his face, palms out, and use his speedy reactions to catch an oncoming glove as if it were a speedy baseball or cricket ball rendered harmless when plucked from the air. In the times Johnson had spent at the ringside of Burns's fights he had studied Burns's style meticulously.

Burns had a low opinion of Johnson's abilities and mental resilience.

the canvas. Pat O'Keefe, the old British middleweight and Burns's sparring partner and now his second, had no doubt that the blow was decisive:

Oh! That uppercut of Johnson's in the first round! I have never seen such a punch. It lifted Burns right off his feet, and dropped him like a sack of potatoes! On the floor he signalled to us that he was all right. But Lord, to have fought fourteen rounds like he did after that! Burns must be the gamest man who ever was.

Burns had enough resilience to get up after a count of eight and hang on to Johnson to recover. As O'Keefe suggested, Burns lacked neither courage nor resilience, but a template had been set for the fight. Burns was fated to take two more heavy head punches before the bell in return for one landed on Johnson.

Reminiscing later in life, Burns claimed the racist dimension to the fight had operated to *his* disadvantage:

Race prejudice was on my mind. The idea of a black man challenging me was beyond enduring. Hatred made me tense. It wasn't Jack Johnson who beat Tommy Burns but Tommy Burns himself.

Maybe, but it wasn't prejudice that dropped Burns like a sack of potatoes, nor Burns who then cuffed himself around the ring – it was a better fighter, pure and simple.

When he came out for the second, Johnson continued his assault with his fists – knocking Burns down again with another right – and freely exercised his tongue. 'Come right on,' he shouted to Burns to convey that he, Johnson, was enjoying every minute. More snappy punches connected with Burns's midriff and face, as Burns's left eye began to swell and blood seeped from his mouth. The crowd, especially those in earshot of the cutting words Johnson was throwing along with the cutting punches, howled impotently as the couple clinched at the bell.

In the third, Burns landed a solid right to Johnson's temple and got in some useful digs to his opponent's ribs. He had to take a succession of Johnson's chops to his kidney region – the dangerous kidney punch was still legal at the time. Johnson's ability to give and receive and *grin* about each action further stirred the crowd. He began to drop his hands even lower and taunt Burns's failures to hit him. In the fourth, Johnson landed on Burns's head and ribs, and the physical exchanges got fiercer, as did the dialogue.

Reports differ widely as to what was said and when. However, over the next ten rounds, Johnson certainly taunted Burns with remarks such as, 'I thought Tommy was an in-fighter,' 'Great blows, then,' 'Good boy, Tommy,' 'Can you fight at all?' 'Look, he's got me now,' to a photographer, 'Did you get that? No? Anyway, I'll give you a good picture,' 'Come on, Tommy, swing your right,' 'Poor, poor Tommy. Who taught you to fight? Your mother?' 'That was a good one, Tommy. Is that all you have?' 'Poor little boy, Jewel won't know you when she gets you back from this fight,' 'Go on, Tommy, hit me here,' (pointing to his midriff).

Burns's contributions were terser and uttered through clenched teeth:

'You big dog,' 'You yellow cur,' (to which Johnson's fastidious reply was, 'Oh dear! Oh dear! That's a nice expression for a little gentleman to use.'), 'C**n,' 'Come on and fight, n****r,' 'Why, you won't fight at all,' and – comically ironic in the circumstances – 'Fight like a white man!'

By the end of the fifth, Burns had several facial cuts and swellings but Johnson was reluctant to bring down the final curtain on the spectacle, preferring to play with his victim and cuff him relatively lightly while delivering further bons mots to ringsiders. They found it particularly offensive to be involuntarily acting as straight men to the pugilistic comedian, so shouted, booed and howled in the vain hope of upsetting Johnson's unruffled nonchalance.

Burns meanwhile was the punch bag, suffering many right hooks to the ribs in the sixth, mercilessly accurate lefts to his damaged eye in the seventh, and more of both in the eighth, which Johnson rounded off with a contemptuous 'ta-ta' wave of the glove at the bell. He was enjoying playing with the crowd's discontent as much as he enjoyed playing with Burns. The spectacle inspired *The Sportsman*'s correspondent to speak restrainedly of the ninth and tenth as mainly featuring 'the c**n … cake-walking vaingloriously'.

By the 11th, the only question to be resolved was how long the torture session would continue. Burns was, said *The Bulletin*, 'out-generalled, over-reached, overmatched in strength, insulted and treated like a helpless mouse by a great black cat'. Burns was limping in the 11th, reeling in the 13th and was felled again in the 14th for a count of eight. He had immeasurable reserves of bravery and willpower and was determined not to surrender. He told the white-capped McIntosh, the only referee in the southern hemisphere to look like an extra from *The Great Gatsby* years before the novel was written, not to allow anyone to stop the fight.

For Burns's own good, and in particular to deny Johnson the satisfaction of a final *coup de grâce*, the police entered the ring in the 14th round and halted the proceedings just as a groggy Burns was being nailed by blow after blow. It had previously been agreed by both men that a police intervention at any time would result in the referee awarding victory to whichever man was ahead on points.

As McIntosh later related it to his friend Norman Clark (a leading English referee and boxing administrator), the idea had come from an over-confident Burns:

'I knew', he said, 'that there was some chance of the police creating a bit of trouble; so, when, just before the fight commenced, I called the men together to give them their customary instructions, I said, "Now, if the police intervene, what do you want me to do – declare a draw or give the decision to the man leading on points?" And Burns at once answered: "Give it to the one leading on points" – thus showing, apparently, that he thought he was going to be very much in the picture.'

McIntosh, with the rigid glum look of a man employed as a professional mourner, raised Johnson's arm and declared him the winner on points. The crowd, having shouted and screamed until all their hopes were lost, filed away in a silence that would have graced a state funeral. The stadium, which had taken hours to fill, emptied in a fraction over ten minutes, all sounds evaporating along with destroyed white Australian illusions.

This present account, compiled from contemporary reports and the researches of meticulous historians, has concentrated upon what happened according to eyewitnesses. A film of the fight was shown twice daily in the Tivoli theatre at Sydney, at the Sydney Stadium and at the Melbourne Town Hall, and was presumably seen by many thousands in the first few days after the contest. Reports suggest that audiences were raised to further pitches of excitement, and, despite already knowing the result, responded with frenzied cheering, booing and hissing as the beloved Burns and the hated Johnson strutted their stuff on screen.

How can this be reconciled with the reactions of a modern observer confronted with the Burns v Johnson film today; a film about as exciting as a Victor Sylvester two-step in an old folks' home? The footage has been readily available on YouTube and will have been seen by many readers. It also features in, for example, Volume 27: Jack Johnson in the popular Marshall Cavendish video series *The Boxers* (VHS BXS 027) widely distributed in the UK. It has been shown frequently on cable and satellite channels on both sides of the Atlantic in, for example, the ESPN and Sky Sports series *The Big Fights*. Although the programming and packaging varies, the newsreel film is identical in most of these sources.

In fact, the film is so ruthlessly edited and cut as to constitute a lie in itself. This is not censorship on the part of the video publishers or the television companies. Many rounds do not appear at all and only abbreviated versions of others. As the action shown is usually restricted to a stately dance, with the partners linked in an affectionate clinch as they waltz back and forth across the ring, it is difficult to see how any serious damage short of foot blisters *could* have been inflicted.

Round eight lasts nearly two and a half minutes but shows none of Johnson's blows to Burns's ribs, with the exception of an abbreviated flurry in the middle of the round. It does include Johnson's fleeting bye-bye gesture at the end of the round. Round 11, or rather the 1 minute 50 seconds of the round to escape the scissors, has Johnson stalking Burns ominously, but more often the two protagonists merely link arms and push one another back and forth like two rutting but soporific stags. Only in the 25 seconds of round 14 is there real action, with Johnson very clearly landing damaging hooks and swings as he whirls around an off-balance Burns, a sequence stopped in mid-punch, supposedly as the police ordered the cameras to be switched off.

The discrepancy between the real and the filmed action can be explained. The police stopped the fight *after* Burns was knocked down in the 14th, but not before. It was stopped to spare white sensibilities the ultimate humiliation – Burns KO'd by Johnson. A fight between two excellent boxers, the first world heavyweight championship contested by a black fighter, and decided perfectly legitimately in favour of the challenger, *should* have lanced the boil of racism that so festered before and during the Rushcutters Bay event.

But boxing, with its unique capacity to reduce complex issues to crude polarities, had vested Burns with all the false values of white supremacy, and projected on to Johnson a role as the worst possible embodiment of white fears. It was now the victim of its own propaganda. It had created in Johnson's subsequent victory a nightmare from which it now desperately wanted to be awakened. The nightmare was to last six long years.

Burns's defeat at the fast hands of Johnson could not be forgotten nor reversed – neither Burns nor his backers suggested a return match – but it could be minimised. The film evidence – in black and white, so to speak – that had aroused almost as much passion in Australian cinemas as the fight itself, was thus an obvious candidate for censorship for white consumption. Whose hand wielded the scissors? No direct evidence exists but circumstantial evidence provides a candidate – the man who owned and profited hugely from the film rights, and who physically transported the film to the USA and Europe: Hugh D. 'Huge Deal' McIntosh. If he did not do the snipping personally (crude enough to suggest an amateur at work), without his permission and cooperation the film could hardly have been transformed from bloody epic to catwalk narcolepsy.

If he is the culprit, he did not cut the film immediately. The film version of the fight shown in London, and in several places in the USA in 1909, was the full-length one. For example, it was given a 'premiere' at the Broadway

Theatre, New York on 12 April 1909. The chairman of the proceedings was W. A. Brady, formerly manager of the retired world champion James J. Jeffries. Before the film, Brady introduced McIntosh to the audience as the promoter and referee of the fight they were about to witness. McIntosh then acted as a voice-over lecturer, talking the audience through the action on the film (silent, of course, as the talkies were another two decades from being invented). It showed Johnson and Burns in training, at social events and then through the *whole* contest. As the *New York Times* reporter present wrote:

> The pictures were remarkably clear and distinct, showing *practically every* move made prior to and during the fight.
> [Italics added.] *New York Times* 13 April 1909.

McIntosh was well aware of the worldwide interest his promotion had aroused and he travelled hopefully to cash in on that interest. He was, however, quite smart enough to realise that the potential audiences for his film in the USA and Britain were no more committed to racial tolerance than his own. In John Lardner's memorable phrase, the American public's attitude to pigmentation in high places was not unlike Goebbels's later. One chilling statistic suggests Lardner was not exaggerating. Over the six years that Jack Johnson retained the championship, 354 black men were lynched in the USA, 89 of them because they were accused of insulting, assaulting or raping white women. Can there be any doubt that there were, in the ranks of white bigotry, many who

would gladly have had Johnson push the total number of victims up to 355?

To such a constituency Jack London was appealing when he concluded his ringside report from Australia for the *New York Herald* with a supplication to the retired Jim Jeffries to return to the ring and give Johnson a moral and physical lesson in superiority:

> But one thing now remains. Jim Jeffries must now emerge from his alfalfa farm and remove the golden smile from Johnson's face.
> Jeff, it's up to you. The White Man must be rescued.

(The golden smile referred to Johnson's prominent gold fillings, a reference to which Johnson is said to have responded, 'Why doesn't Mr London like my gold teeth? Maybe, as a scribbler, he can't afford them, that's all.' A remark well calculated to win friends in press ranks.)

What was actually being said on the streets, or in the saloon bars of the public houses of Britain, on the touchy subject of Johnson and his threat to the 'White Man' (capital W, capital M), can only be guessed. However, there is concrete evidence that Britain also had its racists in boxing's high places. One of the most prominent boxing commentators of Edwardian Britain, author of several standard boxing texts and member of the National Sporting Club, was Bohun Lynch (1884–1928). What he had to say about black boxers in the privacy of the National Sporting Club bar can be readily surmised from the lurid fulminations he committed to print in his boxing books:

> … it is a thousand times better that he [Johnson] should not have

met Wells [the British fighter Bombardier Wells] or any other English champion. The swagger of the triumphant n****r is not pretty, and opportunities for triumphs of this sort should not be put in his way.

(*Prominent Pugilists of Today* p.27)

He [Johnson] was by no means unintelligent, and, not without good reason, was regarded generally with the greatest possible dislike. With money in his pocket and physical triumph over white men in his heart, he displayed all the gross and overbearing insolence which makes what we call the buck n****r insufferable.

(*Knuckles and Gloves* p.149)

He [Johnson] went to his corner grinning widely, as only a black man can.

(*Knuckles and Gloves* p.152)

Burns's mouth ... had been badly cut ... and round after round Johnson hit it again and

yet again, never missing, always with the fiendish desire to injure and give pain ...

(*Knuckles and Gloves* p.153)

... flashiness is so very characteristic of the Negro ...

... a black man is not made in the same way as a white man. He is far less sensitive about the head and jaw; he can take, almost without knowing it, a blow which would knock out the toughest and most seasoned white pugilist.

Any triumph, of whatsoever nature, turns the head of the average black. It is bad for him because he behaves like a spoiled child, which is just what he is. And when that triumph is a personal one, over a white man, the n****r becomes an appalling creature, a devil. His insolence knows no bounds. His preposterous swagger excites the passionate hatred of ignorant white men, the disgust of their betters.

(*The Complete Boxer* p.152)

These regular outpourings of bile show that for Lynch and others on both sides of the Atlantic there was *no* human being called Jack Johnson. There was only a grossly stereotypical construct compounded from ignorance and fear. Into that construct everything that Johnson did over the next decade was made to fit. A long and virulent campaign was launched to combat Johnson's supposed influence over his fellow blacks, and at all costs to wrest the prestigious world heavyweight championship away from him. So ugly did the Johnson affair become that boxing and Johnson together formed a virulent religious, political, legal and social issue.

Before that multifaceted campaign is considered, two other aspects of the Burns v Johnson contest need to be addressed. First of all, the meeting of the two set in motion a proliferation of publicity and popularity for boxing on a wholly new scale. Second, how could an event of such worldwide interest and importance be arbitrarily concluded by the local police before its natural close? The legality or illegality of boxing cannot be understood without some reference to its deep roots in English history and in English law.

CHAPTER 1

INTO THE DOCK
BRITISH BOXING AND THE LAW 1680-1891

In Which Boxing and the Courts Fight a Dubious Draw

SO LONG as men, and occasionally women, have quarrelled, so long have they progressed from angry words to trading blows. And when blows are struck, others have looked on with interest, egging on one combatant or both, and giving and taking odds on the outcome. Wherever these deeds were done, boxing in its crudest sense had been established, if not with quite the pomp and ceremony surrounding modern boxing. No specific origin for the activity can be pinpointed.

Many general boxing histories cite the inclusion of pugilism in the Ancient Greek Olympics in the 680s BCE, and the Imperial Roman gladiatorial exchanges between men wearing the *caestus* (a fearsome knuckleduster with spiked leather thongs bound to the hand), an activity that had died out by the 400s CE, as precedents for British boxing. This unlikely provenance was much talked about by young 18th-century aristocrats who had a classically based education and loved to put a scholarly gloss on their fondness for seeing blood spilled. Surely such remote historical perspectives were not uppermost in the minds of the English lower orders in their own undiplomatic exchanges?

English boxing grew rather out of good English precedents. For example, in the late 17th century (January 1681 to be precise), the Duke of Albemarle contrived a bare-fisted battle between his footman and a local butcher. A purse was involved, and side stakes and other bets. English gentlemen of the late Restoration period fostered horse racing at Newmarket and were notoriously prone to wager on anything that moved, from horses to cockfights and dogfights, so the footman and the butcher hardly knocked lumps off each other purely for His Grace's entertainment.

The *Protestant Mercury* of January 1681 in retailing details of the match – and thus becoming the first newspaper to report English boxing – specifically mentions a 'prize' awarded to the butcher for the win. It also reveals that the butcher already had a pugilistic reputation ('the best at that exercise in England') and a career record ('won … as he hath done many times before'). As the Romans had abandoned Britain by 420 CE, what realistically could the butcher have gleaned from his *caestus*-clad predecessors around 1,250 years before his own day?

Surely here was a purely domestic development? One step up from a violent quarrel between butcher and footman per se, was an arranged contest between two men known to be handy with their fists, with aristocratic backing and promotion, and a journalist at hand to record the event. It will have not been the first such, but over the next few decades, similar meetings became common. By 1719 it was worth James Figg's while to set up premises just off London's Oxford Street at Adam and Eve Court to offer instruction in the Noble Science of Defence.

James Figg (1695–1734) became England's first generally recognised bare-knuckle champion, though the main curriculum of his new 'Academy' composed instruction in fencing and the quaint arts of cudgelling (executed with a hefty wooden club) and quarterstaffing (executed with a hefty wooden pole). Figg's business card, once wrongly thought to have been designed by the contemporary artist William Hogarth, made no mention of his fistic prowess. Nevertheless, Figg had fought before political and literary celebrities such as Sir Robert Walpole and Jonathan Swift, as well as King George I, and the Prince of Wales (later King George II), and dined with the actor, Poet Laureate and playwright Colley Cibber. At

Jack Broughton (1705–1789) c.1767. Fame in the prize ring brought aristocratic patronage. Neither artist nor commissioner has been identified definitively but this image circulated freely. Broughton discards coat and shirt and poses beside an antique column with sculptured wrestlers – a sop to his classically minded fans.
Yale Center for British Art, Paul Mellon Collection

then cudgel. He won all three in front of an enthusiastic and distinguished crowd. He had come a long way for a lad from an Oxfordshire village and with no education. He never learned to read or write, though he could presumably count his cash. He is an early example of what became an observable pattern, the proletarian participant in a proletarian sport supported and patronised by slumming aristocrats.

As prizefighting grew in importance and popularity, and as more and more money was wagered upon it, the legitimacy of a contest was at a premium. A parallel case was horse racing, where similar needs brought forth the formidable Jockey Club from 1752 onwards to protect rich gamblers' money from illegitimately fixed results.

One of Figg's pupils, Jack Broughton (1705–1789), created an ambitious Broughton's Amphitheatre in 1748 near to Figg's old site. It was partly financed by his patron William Augustus, Duke of Cumberland (1721–1765), third son of George II. Cumberland's relish for Jacobite blood in the wake of the 1746 Battle of Culloden led famously to his nickname 'Butcher'. His enthusiasm for blood spilled between the ropes was equally intense, especially when he had a stake vested in the winner. Broughton himself, a part-time Thames waterman, was a skilful fighter and, unusually, matched it with business acumen.

He saw a market for instruction in the fistic arts among young toffs, always provided it was not their blood to be spilled:

> Persons of quality and distinction will be given the utmost tenderness, for which reasons mufflers [i.e. gloves] are provided, that

Figg's premises, the activities were not quite as didactic as the term academy suggests, and included cockfights, bearbaiting and 'female-fighting' (details disappointingly unspecified). A memoir of a later time links Figg's with fighting by cocks, bulls and Irish women.

There were several women fighters by the 1720s. The *Daily Post* of 1728 records a challenge by Ann Field from Stoke Newington to Mrs Elizabeth Stokes 'European Championess' to fight for a £10 purse. The challenge was accepted by Mrs Stokes, whose husband James conveniently ran a rival London amphitheatre to Figg's. Sometimes Mr and Mrs Stokes accepted challenges to fight other couples, an interesting version of mixed doubles.

In 1727, Figg engaged a prominent Gravesend rival, Ned Sutton, in a triple contest, firstly with sword, then fist, will effectually secure them from the inconveniency of black eyes, broken jaws and bloody noses.

The inconveniency of black eyes, broken jaws and bloody noses for the men fighting for real and for the aristocrats' indulgence, was a mere professional incidental. What *did* need proper protection was rather the money staked on the contests by gentlemen of quality. Rules of combat were therefore essential. The shrewd Broughton saw a need and provided a solution. Seven basic tenets known as Broughton's Rules were introduced in August 1743. They governed most prizefights for the rest of the 18th century. Some histories suggest the Rules were part-written by Captain John Godfrey.

The Rules show fights as a mixture of boxing and wrestling, with wrestling holds and throws permitted. They insisted upon a central square (as opposed to an ill-defined 'ring' formed by spectators holding a rope) – an area reserved exclusively for the combatants and their seconds. This prevented spectators interfering with events *inside* the ropes. Within the square, a loss could be signalled by a second or by the failure of one fighter to toe a line on the ground within 30 seconds of being felled. (This was a legacy of the previous practice where a stricken man was given time to recover and come up, or be brought up, to a line scratched on the turf – thus adding the expressions 'coming up to scratch' and 'toeing the line' to the English language.) A round was ended not by time but by one fighter going down, even voluntarily.

Here the rule makers had been naïve, failing to anticipate that a losing

Vanity Fair *10 November 1877: 'Spy' – Sir Leslie Matthew Ward (1851–1922) – captures Sir John Shelto Douglas (1844–1900), the eccentric ninth Marquess of Queensberry, friend of boxing and unbalanced enemy and persecutor of Oscar Wilde*
Hulton Archive / Stringer

fighter might appropriate a crafty recovery period by dropping to one knee. Other unexpected incidents could be judged by appointed umpires, with an agreed referee in the crowd ready to cast a deciding vote if the umpires were at odds.

Broughton's ideas were sufficiently influential to heavily influence their major successors. These were the 23 London Prize-Ring Rules of 1838, and the 12 Queensberry Rules of 1867 (named after, but not written by the 9th Marquess of Queensberry, Sir John Sholto Douglas [1844–1900]).

Broughton's contemporary fame lives on disguised in other contexts.

He was buried among the high and mighty in Westminster Abbey – in the West Walk of the Cloisters, where his monument is labelled 'Yeoman of the Guard', his greater claim to fame discreetly omitted. He is even more anonymously commemorated in the sculpture *Hercules* by John Michael Rysbrack (1694–1770) kept at Stourhead, the fabulous 18th-century landscape garden and Palladian mansion in Wiltshire. Rysbrack, looking for an impressively muscular model for his mythological hero, chose Broughton's sturdy forearms as being the most appropriate.

Broughton's literary collaborator, Captain Godfrey, left his own monument in the form of an instructional manual, *A Treatise Upon the Useful Science of Defence* of 1747. Dedicated to the Duke of Cumberland in sickeningly obsequious terms, the main part of the text was devoted to swordplay with small- and back-swords. Only a supplementary section covered prizefighting and included mini-profiles of contemporary fighters, including Broughton himself ('… undebauched Wind, and a bottom Spirit, never to pronounce the Word ENOUGH').

The semi-scientific instructional passages prove crude fisticuffs were giving way to increased skill and thought. Godfrey's own wise words, words that might usefully be pasted on the walls of every modern boxing gymnasium, were:

A less degree of Art will tell for more than a considerably greater Strength. Strength is certainly what the Boxer ought to set out with, but without Art he will succeed but poorly.

Daniel Mendoza (1763–1836) of Aldgate, the Sephardic prizefighter and inspirer of generations of Jewish East End boxers, captured in a striking 2008 relief by modern artist Louise Soloway Chan.

Source: Louise Soloway Chan/Philip Walker

Tom Sayers (1826–65), the short-lived but famous British champion of the prize ring.

Prints & Photographs Division, Library of Congress, LC-DIG-pga-04600

Mendoza's patron was Richard 'The Gentleman' Humphreys. They fell out and fought each other three times 1787–90. William Braddyll MP, Mendoza's new patron, commissioned royal artist John Hoppner (1758–1810) to paint this view of Humphreys and then cashed in with prints boosting the 9 January 1788 contest between them. Mendoza retired hurt.

The Alfred N. Punnett Endowment Fund, 1953

Strength, art and plenty of red stuff were freely on show in the square rings of England from about 1780 to the late 1820s – a period subsequently thought of as a golden age of prizefighting. The names and nicknames of the top prizefighters became known throughout the country, quite as widely as contemporary actors or politicians. These were men such as Daniel Mendoza (1764–1836) 'The Light of Israel', Jem Belcher (1781–1811) and John Gully (1783–1863), the latter going uniquely from the prize ring and the racehorse owners' winning enclosure (his horses won the Derby three times) to that other conflict-ridden cockpit, the House of Commons, as Member of Parliament for Pontefract in the Reformed Parliament of 1832. Tom Cribb (1781–1848) and, later, Tom Sayers (1826–1865) also achieved national recognition. Sayers's tomb in Highgate Cemetery features a sculpture of his faithful giant dog, which travelled to the graveside in a phaeton as the leader of 10,000 other mourners. The monument is still a minor tourist attraction.

These fighters and their deeds were elevated to cult status by contemporary journalists, none more so than by Pierce Egan (1772–1849), whose successive volumes of boxing writings,

When Sayers died, the 10,000 strong funeral procession to Highgate Cemetery culminated at an imposing grave now featuring his mastiff Lion, his chief mourner and faithful follower. The monument is still a tourist attraction.

Wikipedia

under the general title of *Boxiana*, were published in 1813, 1818, 1821, 1824 and 1828. Subtitled *Sketches of Ancient and Modern Pugilism: from the days of Broughton and Slack to the Heroes of the Present Milling Era*, these fat, closely printed volumes are a treasure trove, presenting lively and detailed round-by-round reports of every significant prizefight and perceptive mini-biographies of every major fighter. Egan's blend of racy fight talk, mixed readily with classical and literary allusions and collected in such expensive volumes, shows that pugilism had found an affluent and educated audience, eager to read about the bloody exploits of the bakers, butchers, costermongers, carters, labourers and blacksmiths who actually climbed through the ropes and fought each other. Egan's lively prose casts also a nostalgic glow over a robust rural world that seemed to be slipping away as Britain industrialised. Although the fighters' fellow workers and craftsmen formed the bulk of the attendees at the fights, the grandees still formed a significant minority.

These sociological reflections help to define the ambiguous status of boxing in the class-conscious society that was early 19th-century Britain. Around the rings, packed crowds enjoyed the sanguinary spectacle of two hardy men pummelling each other with bare fists until one or other of them was too senseless or too exhausted to continue. The audience for these marathon encounters contained relatively few middle-class or bourgeois elements, though this should not be exaggerated – more and more men and women in every social class liked boxing, just as many others found it offensive.

Well known to the point of becoming a cliché, the rise of the English middle classes resulted in a Victorian England strongly imbued with bourgeois values. Indeed, their determination to reform society's manners in the direction of sobriety, morality, punctuality and diligence was decisive. The rural peasantry and the growing urban proletariat were alike urged to sober up, abstain from sex, especially outside matrimony, turn up to work regularly and on time, and to busy themselves through every minute of the day as if their lives and souls depended upon it. Indeed, the faster the working classes could be persuaded to adopt middle-class mores and strive for middle-class respectability the better.

Admittedly, there were always evangelicals and self-improvers *within* the working classes. Similarly, among the Victorian middle classes there were some for whom a pint and a backroom punch-up were preferable entertainments to a Bible class in the vestry. No social class had a copyright on either pleasure or prissiness.

The middle-class reformers looked hard at the nobility and found their noble lords' manners disappointingly *ig*noble. Peers, by definition, monopolised the House of Lords. They also, by virtue of their nominees and placemen in rotten boroughs and the like, controlled the House of Commons and thus political power as well. On their vast landholdings were grown the crops that turned into the workers' beer. From every pint poured down the throat of a thirsty then drunken worker, came profits for the aristocratic landowner. Small chance therefore of milord promoting temperance legislation.

And what about morals? A scrutiny of Regency aristocrats would have produced plentiful examples of indulgence in the seven deadly sins – pride, covetousness, lust, envy, gluttony, anger and sloth. Reformers would have added a deadly eighth – gambling. Not only were the aristocrats rich and frivolous spenders on sinful pursuits, but they also threw their money away on wagers on the turn of a card, the speed of a horse or the damage caused by a clenched fist.

In France, the bourgeoisie had adopted a simple remedy for the unsatisfactory conduct of their aristocrats – cut their heads off. The English middle classes contemplated no such radical step. They did not want to destroy their betters and knew their own capacity fully to join their betters' ranks was limited. What they wanted was to mimic them. But first they had to get the aristocrat to shape up to their social responsibilities as a proper model, and to set a moral example to be imitated.

The existence of corrupt and restricted political franchises, an indifferent and unreformed Church of England, gambling clubs, high-class brothels, a crooked Turf, cock and dog fights did not present moral examples. All were subject to attack and to legislative amendment during the 19th century when middle-class reformers successfully increased their own Parliamentary representation.

Interestingly, the unstructured inter-village mass brawl that was the predecessor of association football had never found favour with central or local authorities. Banning orders and legislation specifically passed against football were perennial for centuries from the Middle Ages on. The damage done to property when two amorphous mobs pushed, shoved and hacked their way over valuable fields or down town high streets imperilling life, limb and windows, became increasingly unacceptable. With the advent of the Industrial Revolution, and the distinct trend for workers to leave the field for the factory, and the village for the town, control of folk football and its threats to property became more effective. In the early 19th century, while prizefighting was achieving unprecedented attention and publicity from Egan and his fellow scribes, football in its old crude form had almost disappeared. Unlike mass football, prizefighting, carefully organised and taking place at shrewdly chosen prearranged venues, did not constitute a threat to property and was generally tolerated; generally, but not invariably.

By its very nature, physical confrontation between two people may result in the unintended death of one of the protagonists. A satisfactory definition of such a death and the existence or absence of culpability were pressing legal issues. Even if there were no death, was a fight legal? Does a fight willingly entered into by its participants still constitute an assault? There were several relevant hearings on these matters during the 18th century.

At Abingdon in 1747, it was ruled that two protagonists had fought 'by consent', yet a contest at Gloucester in 1731 for five guineas (£5.25) a side had been ruled 'an illegal consideration'.

A Crown case published in 1762 seemed to confirm illegality. The judge suggested that friends who engaged by mutual consent in a trial of skill or manhood that ended unexpectedly in the death of one of them would be 'excusable'. He added a damning rider implying that had money been involved, his opinion would have changed:

> I would not be understood to speak here of prize-fighting and public boxing matches or any other exertion of courage, strength and activity of the like kind which are exhibited for lucre, and can serve no valuable purpose, but on the contrary *encourage a spirit of idleness and debauchery.*
>
> [Italics added]

Here is a clear shift from the strictest interpretation of legality inside the ring to the morality of the sport's effect upon the social ethics of spectatorship.

The 1762 case was incorporated into a legal commentary (*Buller's Nisi Prius*), which went through several editions over the next 50 years. Lawyers, as lawyers will, invented a colloquial ditty to serve as an aide-memoire to the general principle being applied:

> Parker, Chief Baron, held that Bruising,
> By some deemed healthful and amusing,
> Is an illegal, dangerous science,
> And practised in the Law's defiance.

An unfortunate Mr Ward fell foul of the interpretation in June 1789. He was brought to trial at the Old Bailey when his opponent Ashurst died at his hands. The evidence showed that Ward had been a most reluctant participant, only fighting when publicly challenged and taunted by the late Ashurst. He was still found guilty of manslaughter.

When the English middle classes determined to impose moral reform-ation, prizefighting was an obvious and convenient target. It was loved by the racier gambling elements in the other classes, it was visibly as brutal and bloodthirsty as a cockfight and seemed conveniently to be *already* illegal. To suppress it required no new legislation pushed through Parliament in the teeth of aristocratic opposition, merely increased pressure upon local authorities properly to apply the present laws against prizefighting. This despite the fact that the word 'prizefighting' appeared nowhere on the statute book.

There were plenty of precedents. For example, in October 1816, after an encounter at Moulsey Hurst with Ned Turner, young fighter Ben Curtis failed to come up to scratch after over 60 rounds and died soon after. Turner was charged at the Old Bailey with murder and was then confined to Newgate on the lesser charge of manslaughter.

By the 1820s and 1830s, prosecutions were frequent and verdicts ever more damning. In one among many, there was the *Rex v Bellingham* case at the Worcester Assizes of 1825. Bellingham had participated in a prizefight, and when a local magistrate had tried to intervene before the fight began, Bellingham had done his best to 'stop' the magistrate. In his verdict, Mr Justice Burrough condemned the fighters and promoters, and extended the guilt to everyone present. 'It cannot be disputed that all these fights are illegal … [because] … They are unlawful assemblies.' He further advised any local magistrate, hearing of a prizefight in his vicinity, to have the fighters brought before him in advance and to bind them over to keep the peace, with hefty sureties to be demanded of them

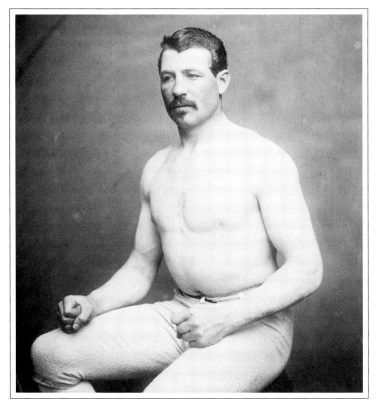 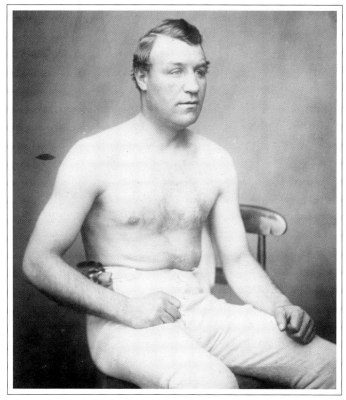

John Camel Heenan 'The Benicia Boy' (1834–73) of the USA (left) visited England to fight Sayers (right) at Farnborough Common on 17 April 1860.
National Portrait Gallery, Smithsonian Institution

to secure their compliance. Should they refuse, they could be committed on the spot. (Authorities have always loved the concept of a breach of the peace, a wonderfully elastic phrase applicable to anything of which they disapproved. It would be a useful precedent for future actions.) The changing climate brought other stark examples. At Oxford in 1831 in the *Rex v Perkins* case, not only were the fighters doubly guilty of assault and a breach of the peace, but the spectators were declared guilty of assault by their very presence. The same year, *Rex v Hargrave* suggested such spectators would be guilty of manslaughter in the second degree if a man died in the ring. By 1835 (*Rex v Murphy*), spectators could be found guilty of manslaughter 'although they say and do nothing'.

Underground, prizefighting continued to be popular with a large segment of the public, including the high and mighty, such as Prime Minister Lord Palmerston (1784–1865). Tom Sayers, the champion of England, met John Heenan, the champion of the USA, at Farnborough on 17 April 1860. *The Times* of London, Wednesday, 18 April 1860 provides a fascinating example of the public schizophrenia this caused.

The Times, widely considered by many abroad as the official organ of the government at the heart of the British Empire, devoted no less than three densely printed full columns and many thousands of words to acquaint the public at large with a detailed blow-by-blow account of the fight. It is a stirring piece worthy of inclusion in any sporting anthology. And it succeeds, incidentally, in capturing the strange anomaly of an illegal activity, officially disapproved of, yet unofficially loved by proles and peers alike:

There is no disguising the fact that this challenge has led to an amount of attention being bestowed upon the prize ring which it has never received before; and, much as all decent people disliked the idea of two fine men meeting to beat each other half to death, it was nevertheless devoutly wished that, as somebody was to be beaten, it might be the American. There is no doubt that Sayers *had the good wishes of nine-tenths of the community.* [Italics added]

Further anomalies were demonstrated as many distinguished and upright citizens, people who would normally have turned a miscreant unhesitatingly over to the police, aided and abetted in the conspiracy to deceive the peelers, and were happy to

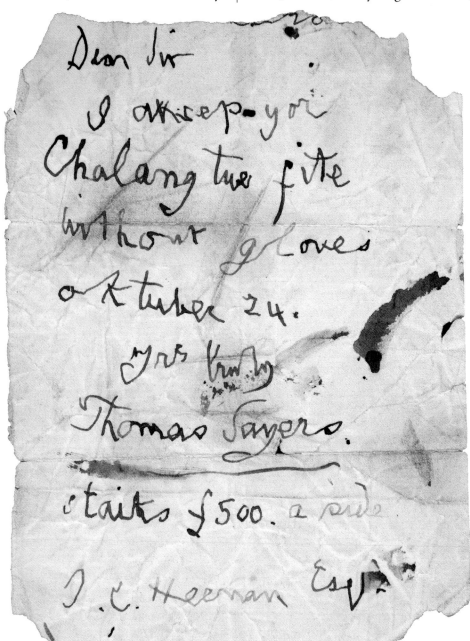

be first-hand witnesses to a crime being committed:

All relating to the day and place fixed for the match was, of course, kept a profound secret, as the police, to do them justice, left no means untried to prevent its taking place. Nevertheless, in spite of all precautions, a special train was hired, which started from London-bridge at 4 am yesterday morning. The train was one of immense length, containing *some thousand persons, all of what are called the upper classes* [Italics added], though each person was muffled up to the eyes in shawls and wrappers, so that it was hard to say whether your *compagnon de voyage* was or was not the redoubtable Sayers or Heenan himself. All along the line police were posted, with mounted patrols, at regular distances but the train turned off at Reigate, and after a long run came out in the Farnborough station, close to Aldershott [sic]. In an instant after, all were out in the fields, following the men who with ropes and stakes led the way across what turned out to be a most difficult piece of country.

These goings-on with upper-class parties, some members of the highest legislative chambers in the Empire, wrapped up in blankets and sneaking on to a secret unscheduled train, then sprinting across muddy fields to dodge the police, actually took place. It may sound like the plot from a farce, but it was a genuine piece of sporting and social history being enacted on the Surrey–Hampshire border.

It did evoke a legislative response. Before the decade was out, a Conservative government, Benjamin Disraeli's first administration, passed a new statute in 1868 about railway companies. This contained a clause to prevent a recurrence of the farce surrounding the Sayers v Heenan encounter (which resulted incidentally in an unsatisfactory and controversial draw when the police caught up with the event after 42 bloody rounds). The new statute used the word 'prize-fight' without defining what constituted a prizefight and provided for a railway company to be fined if it knowingly allowed persons to travel on its rails to a prizefight.

Boxing, especially in its bare-fist form, was technically illegal. However,

Sayers's acceptance letter replying to Heenan's challenge. Sayers was more adept with his fists than his pen.

it was very difficult ultimately to suppress something so firmly embedded in the popular consciousness and loved and supported by men of power and influence.

There were parallels in other sports. Football, as we have seen, had almost disappeared by the Regency period. Its remarkable recovery in the 19th century was due to a series of happy coincidences. The crude hundreds-a-side village shoving-match changed gradually into a more convenient and organised kickabout at English public schools such as Charterhouse and Winchester. Further clarification and codification took place at Cambridge University and other institutions of higher learning to allow boys from one public school to play with and against boys from another as undergraduates.

The modification process continued with the formation in October 1863 of a Football Association, a national controlling body, and with the spread of clubs for adult players anxious to carry on playing after graduation. Contentious practices like running with the ball tucked under one's arm or hacking with the boot at opponents' shins (not done with sadism in mind but an invaluable method for clearing a path for the ball through a forest of legs), were hotly debated and eventually eliminated. Advocates of a running, handling game formed a Rugby Football Union in January 1871, translating the local version of football played at Rugby School into a rival national code, and ultimately another successful national winter game.

There were significant differences between prizefighting and football. Football was a pastime, not a profession.

As is well known, the growth of professionalism within the amateur games of soccer and rugby in the 1880s and 1890s, as the urban proletariat began to reappropriate what had originally been *their* game, caused considerable agonies and rifts – professionals v amateurs; Football Association v Football League; northerners v southerners; rugby league v rugby union – strife lingering on for most of the 20th century as well.

Prizefighting was, by definition, a professional activity and flourished before being imitated by amateurs. So was rowing, done only by professional oarsmen and lightermen, until taken up for fun by public schoolboys in the 19th century. Like rowing, prizefighting could be imitated by participating gentlemen amateurs. Public schoolboys could do in the 19th century in padded gloves what the young gents at Broughton's had done in the 18th century in their mufflers.

A taste acquired at school or university is frequently a taste acquired for life. The 1860s saw the foundation of several rugby and association football clubs to perpetuate into adulthood the sport picked up as a schoolboy or undergraduate; for example, Blackheath founded 1858; Richmond founded 1861; Harlequins founded 1866. On a looser basis, many amateur boxing clubs existed by the 1860s. Some met together in 1866, and in 1867 held championships at three weights (lightweight, middleweight and heavyweight). The Marquess of Queensberry sponsored the relevant trophies (nothing so sordid as hard cash). The Marquess gave his name to the rules governing the contests. The association of the name Queensberry with boxing is so strong that it is worth

outlining the rather weak nature of the link.

An ever-present at the Regency ringsides had been the 4th Duke of Queensberry, William Douglas (1725–1810). Present, that is, when he could be persuaded away from gaming tables at White's club, or from his house overlooking Newmarket racecourse, or out of the beds of operatic divas. His passion for opera extended to more than auditory appreciation. He had helped arrange one of the most famous of prizefights in 1805 between the English champion Tom Cribb and the black American fighter Bill Richmond.

This was not the Queensberry of the Queensberry Rules and of Victorian times. That Queensberry was John Sholto Douglas (1844–1900), the 9th Marquess and no less controversial a figure. Indeed, he behaved generally like an unbalanced and unreformed Regency buck in a much soberer age, and plunged recklessly into everything he did, especially gambling, steeplechasing and adultery. In the course of these heady pursuits, he had acquired many a broken bone as well as the syphilis that took his wilder later actions into the positively insane. His contempt for polite public opinion was legendary. He was open about his multitude of infidelities. And when excluded from the House of Lords in 1880 because he refused to take the Oath of Allegiance, he professed himself an atheist who objected to such 'Christian tomfoolery'.

This might have been the act of a brave man determined to uphold his secular beliefs in a conventionally religious age. Unfortunately, his other opinions were an unholy mixture of anti-Semitism and homophobia. These led him into his infamous campaign

When the aristocratic crowd gathered for Sayers v Heenan and saw an artist, they posed for selfies.
Hulton Archive/Getty Images

against Oscar Wilde in 1895, at the time of the première of Wilde's comedy *The Importance of Being Earnest*. A series of Queensberry's public insults led Wilde, unwisely, to sue him for libel. The result was Wilde's eventual prosecution and conviction under the 1885 Criminal Law Amendment Act, a section of which made any form of private homosexuality illegal and turned homosexuals into the target of legal persecution until the 1960s. Queensberry's particular concern had been with the link between his third son (Lord Alfred Douglas) and Wilde, patently a sexual one.

Far less known is that Queensberry had previously, in 1893, pursued the English Foreign Secretary and later Prime Minister, Lord Rosebery (1847–1929), to Germany in the belief that Rosebery had given Queensberry's eldest son and heir, Francis, Lord

Drumlanrig, a job in the Foreign Office only to seduce him. Queensberry sent a series of intemperate letters to Rosebery using terms such as 'to the Jew Pimp' and 'dirty Jewry'. Only personal interventions from the local police and the holidaying Prince of Wales prevented him from physically assaulting Rosebery in Germany.

It would be pleasant to record that the later Queensberry marital and social travails could be balanced against a major contribution to British boxing. However, the inaugural 1867 amateur championships incorporating his trophies and the rules named after him should rightly be credited rather to an old Etonian and fellow Cambridge undergraduate, John Graham Chambers (1843–83). Chambers, a one-time lightweight champion, toured the USA with Queensberry and the Duke of Manchester in 1866. He had become

aware of the over-permissive nature of the London rules as they had tried to promote boxing in the USA. On his return to England, Chambers founded the Amateur Athletic Club (with a boxing section) in 1866. Chambers knew aristocratic names added to the prestige of any venture, which was why he had taken Manchester and Queensberry on the trip. He now persuaded Queensberry to donate the cups and his name to the new AA Club championships. (A marquess was, after all, only one step down from a duke in the hereditary title pecking order, and boxing in the 1860s was in pressing need of some social cachet.)

Chambers's championships lasted two decades until overtaken in importance by the Amateur Boxing Association (founded 1880), which has held its own national championships from 1881 to the present day. Chambers's organisational skills and energy were remarkable. He played a major role in the 1860s and 1870s in the administration of rowing and athletics. It is a pity for boxing that his involvement elsewhere made boxing the loser.

Nevertheless, in the misnamed 'Queensberry' Rules, Chambers left a lasting legacy without which modern boxing would have been impossible. The 12 rules introduced four new principles, departing radically both from Broughton's Rules, and from the London Prize Rules introduced in 1838 and amended in 1853 and 1866. The principles were: fighters to wear padded gloves; rounds to last three minutes with a minute's interval; wrestling throws to be banned; and a floored man allowed a mere ten seconds to rise or he would lose.

(The London Prize Rules had eliminated rougher past practices such as kicking, butting, scratching, hair pulling and low blows, but retained features of the multi-round epics of the past. A round still ended only when a man was thrown over or otherwise floored. He was permitted 30 seconds recovery period with another eight seconds' to come up 'to scratch'. He was no longer allowed to end the round prematurely by dropping down voluntarily. He was expected to be fighting throughout with his bare fists.)

Predictably, all the Chambers/ Queensberry Rules were designed for the part-time *amateur* boxer, not for the prizefighters. Only gradually would these innovations for amateurs make their mark upon the professionals. Furthermore, by the 1860s prizefighting was commonly under threat from the increased vigilance of an expanded and more professional police force. Local magistrates, who might once have looked away, became vigilant for potential breaches of the peace. Followers of prizefights became commonly regarded as thoroughly disreputable.

Four years after *The Times* had vicariously enjoyed the adventures of the upper classes journeying to Sayers v Heenan, the newspaper reported the attendees at a public execution as 'the incorrigible dregs of society', whom it defined as '[card] sharpers, thieves, gamblers, betting men, *the outsiders of the boxing ring …*' [Italics added]. What four years before had been solemnly declared to constitute 90 per cent of the population, was now apparently a socially disgraceful minority.

Whereas, in sexual matters, mid- and late-Victorians condemned prostitutes (professionals) and women of easy virtue (enthusiastic amateurs) alike, in sporting matters double standards applied. To play, to run, to row, to fight, if done by leisured amateurs, constituted a worthy attempt to create healthy bodies along with healthy minds and was to be encouraged. So encouraged indeed in the public schools by the 1880s and 1890s as to form an important part of the curriculum and to create a post-school taste for sporting activities catered for by a multitude of church, chapel and old boy associations. In many a church hall, young Christians were given gloves and encouraged not to turn the other cheek but to respond with a morally impeccable straight left to the smiter's nose. The young amateur boxer was having his soul straightened along with his jab. Boxing, in its amateur form, was to be encouraged.

Boxing in professional form was something else and should be suppressed. Attempts to take pugilists and their friends from the environs of the ring and place them in the dock became common. In 1882 (*Regina v Coney*), a token sample of the crowd at a prizefight between Jack Burke and Charlie Mitchell at Ascot was found guilty of assault as principals in the second degree. They had, as witnesses who had said and done nothing, supposedly encouraged the assault of one boxer upon another by their very presence.

The jury, at the direction of the judge, found the defendants guilty, though devalued their own verdict by saying that they had done so only because of the judge's direction. The case went on to the Court of Crown Cases Reserved, Queen's Bench Division, where eight of the 11 judges declared the verdict too harsh. All 11 judges, however, were unanimous that prizefights *were* illegal, and that any *positive* aiding and abetting, including promoting or match making, would constitute assault of the second degree.

After this case and others in the 1880s, a convention was followed that sparring and exhibition bouts with gloves were legal, providing there were no substantial purses. As in athletics and rowing, cups, prizes and medals were acceptable alternatives. Neither were the blows exchanged to be too hard. The fiction prevailed that two fit and healthy boxers would go into a ring and strive not to hit each other as hard as they might and that they would eschew an opportunity to knock an opponent out.

On this dubious basis, gloved boxing took place in many small halls, saloons, corporation baths and private clubs, and gained strongly in popularity throughout the 1880s and 1890s. While this rather vegetarian menu became commonplace, the red meat of bare-fist prizefighting became more difficult to find and attend. Matches that would have had half the population excited and cause traffic jams now took place discreetly, far from the eyes of the English authorities.

When Englishman Jem Smith fought New Yorker Jake Kilrain in 1887, it was on an island in the Seine. When Charlie Mitchell of Birmingham met John L. Sullivan, the Boston Strong Boy, in 1886, this also was staged in France. And the notorious 1889 encounter between Jem Smith and Frank 'Paddy' Slavin of Australia amid skulduggery, intimidation and flashing knives, was fixed at a venue near Bruges – 'fixed' in more senses than one. These were not places easily attended by the working man.

The police and local authorities tolerated some gloved fighting in the 1880s. Even the most arrest-happy inspector baulked at hauling off young Etonian bantamweights scrapping in the public school championships, or some young stockbroker lightweight competing in the Amateur Boxing Association championships. Early amateur boxing clubs were so socially exclusive, references could be demanded before entry, and even in one case a ballot of current members. A candidate could be blackballed as if the youth were up for the Carlton Club or White's rather than a recreational gathering.

Just as in rowing, where the gilded amateurs wanted no contact with anyone rowing for a living, and just as in athletics, where young gentlemen looked askance at runners who ran for money prizes, so in amateur boxing, the vested participants wanted no confusion with the pugilistic proletariat. (In athletics, the early winners of the AAA championships included working-class people such as barmen and coach drivers, but before the 1870s were out such men had been eliminated, not because they had competed for money, but because they came from the wrong social class. This is powerful evidence that the cult of amateurism was primarily *social*.) It is easy to set up social barriers. No one was better than an Englishman at distinguishing nuances of class, or what was and was not acceptable. Nothing need be written: he who knew, knew. To differentiate an acceptable boxing 'exhibition' legally from a real contest was much more problematical. Easy to see, but difficult accurately to define. Small wonder therefore that several small hall promoters and gentlemen's clubs staged gloved contests, labelling them 'exhibitions' and therefore legal, while knowing that the customers would revel in a real fight. Contrived exhibitions became indistinguishable from a fight.

Boxing would soon be back in court. On 3 October 1890 at the Lambeth Police Court, two boxers were arraigned for having 'assaulted and beaten each other against the peace' for the entertainment of the members of the Ormonde Club in Walworth. The Ormonde was a members' only club with a dark façade looking like an ordinary private house, but at the back it extended under a railway arch into a space large enough to accommodate a small boxing theatre.

The two boxers were Frank Slavin, the Australian champion who had barely escaped the Bruges fiasco with his life, and the fancied American Joe

Frank 'Paddy' Slavin (1861–1929), the Australian heavyweight whose fight against Californian Joe McAuliffe (1863–1926) in a private London club landed them both in the dock in October 1890.
National Library of Australia, nla.obj-148525544

McAuliffe (not to be confused with the better-known Jack McAuliffe), a fighter of toughness and talent in his own right, and the holder of the California and Pacific Coast heavyweight championship. Here was a match between two experienced foreign professionals, provoking ample publicity and public interest, staged on private premises before a limited members' and guests' audience behind locked doors.

Both sides saw this as a test case about the legality or illegality of boxing. A suit was brought, and a Treasury solicitor, Mr Poland, engaged to prosecute the boxers with the real intention of closing down professional boxing once and for all. Could the authorities show that the encounter *had* been a prizefight, there was an impressive list of precedents to prove illegality.

The boxers had been arrested in late September on a charge of *intending* to partake in a prizefight and were bound over to appear when called upon. The secretary of the Ormonde Club, Mr Temple, had supplied the police with a copy of the articles governing the event. Obviously aware of their own vulnerability, the club officials had hurriedly revised those articles to give them more of an exhibition flavour: the originally intended 30 rounds had been trimmed to 15; six-ounce gloves had replaced four-ounce ones; and to reduce possible overcrowding and disorder on the pavements outside the club from non-members, the fight was rescheduled for 4am.

The winner would receive a £1,000 purse, a valuable jewelled belt, and the so-called heavyweight championship of the world – handsome rewards for an 'exhibition'. Unusually, it was agreed to have two referees, B. J. Angle and G. Vize, a compromise reached when the fighters disagreed on which man should officiate.

If the police and the legal authorities were, so to speak, in the blue corner, the red corner had its own doughty and distinguished opponents, including Hugh Lowther the 5th Earl of Lonsdale, the Marquess of Queensberry, Sir John Astley, Lord de Clifford and several boxing experts who would later run the National Sporting Club in Covent Garden. It became the headquarters and primary venue of British boxing before the First World War. Some in the defence party knew a guilty verdict might bring further charges upon themselves for their part in the event.

Boxing would not be boxing without some upsets. Its history is littered with stone-cold certainties who finished stone cold all right, but stone cold and horizontal. This latest courtroom joust was another example.

Think for a moment what the prosecution needed to prove. If Slavin and McAuliffe were strutting their scientific stuff to show their sparring skills, they were innocent. If they were fighting for a substantial sum of money, or could win by overwhelming force, or if one or other was counted out for ten seconds and his opponent given the victory, or even if blows were delivered of sufficient force potentially to injure, then they were participating in a prizefight and were guilty. That is what the precedents suggest.

It sounds like a brief a clerk of chambers would give confidently to the most junior advocate as almost impossible to lose. Slavin, McAuliffe and their friends, and the future of British professional boxing, were all in severe danger. The only factors halfway in their favour were these: the incompetence of the police, who had sent to the fight men who knew precious little about boxing; and the blunders of the prosecution, who engaged solicitors equally ignorant of what they were supposed to expose.

The fight itself is easily described. It was witnessed by 150 lucky members packed in elevated rows around a smallish ring (c.18–20ft²). Slavin and McAuliffe traded enough blows to get the spectators up on their feet and yelling so loudly that the call of 'time' at the end of the first round was not heard, and the couple had to be parted by their seconds. At the preliminaries, the members had had the solemn words of referee Vize directed at them: 'The eyes not only of England but of Australia and America are upon you, and I hope you will keep order.' Order was one thing, silence quite another. As Angle, the other referee, wrote later: '… let me say … that there was a great deal of the primeval man about the Australian. All his boxing matches were fights, and fights with the object of proving his own superiority in the shortest possible space of time.' So much for scientific exhibition!

The American, initially on top, was weakened by Slavin's more solid punches, and in the second was floored three times – once by a hook to the ribs, then by one to the side of his head, and finally from a chopping right that left him inert on the canvas. Before he could be counted out, his seconds came through the ropes to rescue him.

Carried to the corner, McAuliffe was gradually revived on his stool, where he sat bemused for about 20 minutes, meanwhile suffering the added indignity of angry club members abusing him, some because they had paid premium prices for so few minutes' action and others because they had compounded the investment with heavy losing bets. Slavin, his £1,000 and his belt secured, shook hands with the groggy McAuliffe in a friendly consolatory gesture, then departed for the dressing room. Outside the premises, fans eager for first news of the result, despite the unseemly hour and the early morning chill, quietly dispersed to the relief of the 62 constables on duty and expecting far worse.

Had there been a prize? Yes. Had there been forceful blows? Yes. Had there been a count-out? Yes, begun if not completed because the seconds had intervened, making McAuliffe subject to disqualification. Had Inspector Chisholm, the policeman sent to the club, restricted his testimony to these salient facts, British professional boxing might have been defeated as speedily and decisively as poor McAuliffe.

Instead, Chisholm claimed that he had seen Slavin's seconds 'working' Slavin's gloves to push the stuffing into the finger and cuff regions and away from the knuckle area to increase the impact on his opponent's vulnerable chin. Perhaps Chisholm did this to convince the court he knew that of which he spoke.

Unfortunately, under cross-examination by Slavin's solicitor Mr Purcell, and by Mr Wood representing McAuliffe, he was forced to admit that he had been a full 25 feet away from the offending gloves, had not actually inspected them, had not seized them after the knockdown and would not know the difference between illegal tampering and a second's action designed to massage new gloves into an acceptable degree of pliability. He said that Slavin and McAuliffe had hit each other harder than they should have, had done so because of the size of the purse and would not have cared if the other had been seriously injured. (How did he know?) Blundering on, he conceded that he was unaware of the Queensberry Rule that 'if a competitor is knocked down, he must get up unassisted within ten seconds … [and] … failing to resume the contest at the expiration of ten seconds will be considered defeated'. Worse still, he had not realised that Slavin's victory was no knockout but awarded because McAuliffe's seconds had prematurely intervened. Whatever green pastures Inspector Chisholm visited in his leisure, ringside was not one of them.

Time ran out for the day and a week's adjournment was called. On the stand the following Friday, 10 October 1890, was Inspector Chisholm's colleague, Detective Inspector Harvey. Less clueless than Chisholm, or better briefed after the first day, he testified that he *had* seen quite as much crowd excitement at other boxing matches. He then undermined his supposed wider experience by admitting that he had never seen so quick a finish nor men so big as Slavin and McAuliffe fight (thus implying that he could be no judge as to whether they were hitting lightly, firmly or brutally).

New witnesses established that McAuliffe had not been injured by the knockout and that Slavin's gloves had been massaged yet the stuffing not displaced. Having taken the testimony of the police witnesses apart, Mr Poland and Mr Wood for the defence got somewhat complacent. Poland, instead of concentrating on the prosecution's blunders, claimed that Slavin v McAuliffe had been 'merely an exhibition of scientific boxing'. Wood insisted it had been 'an ordinary glove match such as amateurs frequently engaged in. If this was considered illegal, then … running, and other athletic sports would be so too.' So little did these claims ring true that Messrs Poland and Wood looked, in boxing parlance, as if they were neglecting meaningful point scoring for showboating. The boxers paid the penalty. The presiding magistrate brushed aside the shadow in favour of the substance – Slavin v McAuliffe had not been a mere scientific encounter, he said, violent blows had been used by both men, a disabling blow had decided the result, the rewards made it a prizefight. He was sending the accused on to the Central Criminal Court for trial in a month's time.

A retrial was arranged not for the Old Bailey, but for the County Court at Newington before Sir P. H. Edlin. On 14 November 1890, Mr Poland and his team reopened the prosecution against the defendants represented by Sir Charles Russell QC and Messrs Wood and Purcell.

The return bout, as returns sometimes do, followed the pattern of the first. Mr Poland opened by claiming that the charge was technically one of assault, even if the real guilt lay in participating in an illegal prizefight. He focused immediately upon the latter. 'It was said that the defendants were only fighting for points, but the main point seemed to be that one of them should get the £1,000 by so disabling his opponent that he could not come up to time. It was ridiculous to suppose that these men had come all the way to England for the purpose of showing their skill in sparring.' Quite.

Poland then called Inspector Chisholm to the stand, and Chisholm repeated most of what he had said at the first hearing about his visit to the Ormonde Club. Chisholm had not profited from his six-week opportunity to reflect upon his visit or upon his last court appearance. He persisted with the gloves episode (they had been 'twisted about' and one of Slavin's gloves before Slavin donned it had 'a hollow over the knuckles'). He still did not comprehend what he had seen when McAuliffe had lost. ('He appeared very much exhausted; his seconds gave him restoratives, applied ice to his head, and fanned his face, but he was not able to come up within ten seconds.')

Three other police witnesses, all inspectors, followed. Inspector Harvey supported most of Chisholm's evidence, but not all of it – 'the manipulation of gloves by the seconds', he thought, 'was intended to make them softer and easier to the hand'. Inspector Waddell agreed about the gloves and declared under cross-examination that 'it was a fair stand-up boxing match, fairly conducted, and like any other except in the strength and weight of the contestants', an answer more likely to favour the defence than the prosecution.

To this day, it is only possible from ringside, and certainly not on television, to grasp the force with which any skilled professional can deliver a punch, let alone a top heavyweight. Similarly, a trained boxer can take, with equanimity, a clout that would transfix an ordinary athlete. A policeman who had never seen a professional fight would readily believe that Slavin and McAuliffe were delivering blows of unparalleled brutality. Truly, they were not. Slavin, deliverer of the *coup de grâce,* had been conceding two stones in weight to the aggressive McAuliffe, who had been awarded the first round by 5pts to 2½ (5 points then being the score awarded to the winner of a round).

The other inspector, Darling, had registered the nature of relative force and 'had never seen a man hit harder than Slavin did'. The difference between this and other boxing matches at which he had been was that 'the fighting was much fiercer and quicker'. With the four policemen's testimony placed on record, the prosecution rested its case. Referee Vize then explained the rules governing the contest and described the actions of Slavin on behalf of the defence. At this point, proceedings were adjourned until morning.

Next day, Vize resumed his testimony. He did not minimise the force of punches given and received. He explained that, technically, McAuliffe had not been knocked out but disqualified as a result of his seconds' premature intervention. He went on: 'The blows were not struck with unusual force for heavy men.' He said it was usual for boxers to hit as hard as they could, such gloves as those used here being a sufficient protection against hard blows. 'The men were good-tempered throughout.'

Cleverly, the defence followed up with two fellows of the Royal College of Surgeons, Mr Bond and Mr Russell Harris, who had examined the fighters after the fight and pronounced them without serious injury. Bond dismissed reports that McAuliffe had vomited in his corner as a natural consequence of his having been punched in the solar plexus after an unwise pre-fight downing of calf's foot jelly, aggravated by a dose of brandy administered to revive him.

The second referee, B. J. Angle, supported Vize in every significant particular.

McAuliffe's indisposition had been strictly temporary as he had left the ring and negotiated three flights of steps without assistance. William Madden, McAuliffe's trainer and chief second, claimed that McAuliffe would probably have been able to continue the fight, but that he (Madden), registering Slavin's superiority, had entered the ring deliberately to bring a merciful close. By the end of the second day, the defence had been further boosted by several boxing experts, each asserting in turn that serious ring injuries even in fierce contests were actually rare.

After Sir Charles Russell had summarised these and other defence details, Slavin and McAuliffe must have felt more sanguine about the potential verdict than six weeks earlier. The prosecution had added nothing meaningful to the case against them. Even one of the policemen had conceded the propriety of the Ormonde's arrangements, and two distinguished medical men had confirmed on oath their post-fight health and fitness. However, their ordeal at the hands of English justice was not quite over.

Firstly, they had to wait out and worry over the weekend, before returning to court on Monday for the verdict. This they did, only for the jury to spend Monday morning locked away for another two hours, then emerge to say that they had been unable to reach a decision. The judge sent them back to reconsider, which they did for the rest of the afternoon, also in vain. Thus it would be necessary for Slavin, McAuliffe and their sport to go through the whole painful process of a third trial.

Only after another month of suspense were the two spared this unwelcome prospect. On 10 November 1890, the authorities conceded that it would be grossly unfair to put them through another trial. They were, therefore, formally acquitted.

Acquittal normally constitutes victory, but so far as professional boxing, the unnamed third party on trial, was concerned, the charges, hearings and procrastinations had led less to checkmate than stalemate; more temporary sufferance than vindication. In many ways that was to be its ambiguous status for the next century and more, and probably still is.

CHAPTER 2

CORINTHIANS OR CRIMINALS?
LONDON 1891-1901

In Which His Lordship and Friends Are Arraigned

WITHIN MONTHS of the Slavin/ McAuliffe second hearing, professional boxing took further steps towards respectability. On 5 March 1891, an historic building at 43 King Street, Covent Garden, a premises that had in its time housed Charles II's theatrical entrepreneur Thomas Killigrew, and later an early Victorian music hall and supper rooms, reopened as the National Sporting Club. The new club, often known by its initials NSC, had a grill room as well as a formal restaurant, but its prime purpose was to house a specially converted boxing theatre where members could watch club boxing nights as they digested their chops and their beer and wagered on the outcomes.

43 King Street, Covent Garden, London WC2. The façade and side entrance to the National Sporting Club, the heart of early British boxing and as respectable as a bank.

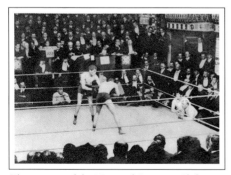

The interior of the National Sporting Club boxing theatre affording intimate and privileged views of championship fights for members and guests.

The modest music hall auditorium with its raised stage was simply and successfully transformed into an intimate and atmospheric small boxing hall with excellent sightlines. Where once there had been stalls was now a raised 16ft² boxing ring with metal posts and two ropes. The front stalls were replaced by a platform to accommodate a special chair for the club president with a rostrum for the timekeeper and his paraphernalia; and, quaintly for modern eyes, an elevated seat for the referee, who controlled ring proceedings by shouting and gesturing from *outside* the ring.

Behind these officials, the former stage now housed seven steeply raked rows of seats for pressmen and distinguished guests. On the floor of the auditorium, in the floor space remaining once the ring platform had been installed, were two rows of ringside seats, leaving space for any members who preferred to stand behind the seats. Above their heads, a gallery replaced what had once been boxes and circle seats and offered a close bird's-eye view of the canvas floor and the boxers.

Two men in particular had fulfilled their own ambitions when this new National Sporting Club opened its doors – John Fleming and A. F. 'Peggy' Bettinson. Fleming had long worked in boxing, originally as a publican and part-time manager, and then as organiser of boxing at the Ormonde Club. He had managed Jem Smith, the English fighter, in late bare-knuckle days. His involvement in the machinations and betting coups around the ugly 1889 Bruges encounter between Smith and Slavin was deeper than it should have been.

Bettinson was a successful and honest stockbroker with cash to spare and a passion for boxing. Nine years before his NSC venture with Fleming, he had won the 1882 Amateur Boxing Association Championships lightweight title. He now carried more pounds in his wallet and around his waistline. With some of his money, supplemented by gifts and loans and liberally extended credit, the King Street building underwent its latest transformation to a boxing headquarters. The partners had raised £11,500 – £8,500 cash and 1,500 £2 shares.

This odd couple, with little more in common than a passion for boxing and a joint aloofness and irritability when their autocratic ways were questioned, was giving British boxing itself a makeover. Both shrewd, and Fleming with a dodgy reputation to lose, they ensured the new venture was

Hugh Cecil Lowther, 5th Earl of Lonsdale (1857–1944), the free-spending 'Yellow Earl', sporting patron and autocrat of the NSC.
Bain Collection, Prints & Photographs Division, Library of Congress,LC-DIG-ggbain-01063

a manifestation of respectability. All that pillars, paint, plasterwork, linen tablecloths, carved staircases, brass lamps and leather armchairs could do to enhance the image of a club of some social standing was duly added. This was no dingy and disreputable backroom, rather another London gentlemen's club, like the Garrick (founded 1831) or the Athenaeum (founded 1824), with a billiard room and a boxing saloon. The membership lists, even with the ubiquitous Hugh Lowther, Lord Lonsdale as president, could not match others for royals, peers and assorted aristocrats. However, like Bettinson himself, they reeked affluence and middle-class respectability.

Barely a stone's throw away from King Street was the Theatre Royal, Drury Lane – another premises with 17th-century origins. It, like boxing, had suffered vicissitudes over subsequent centuries – royal and aristocratic patronage and national prestige in one era; disorder, riots and obscurity at others. The man in charge of Drury Lane in the 1880s and 1890s was Sir Augustus Harris (1852–96), also a Pelican Club member, who hit upon a brilliant formula to pack his theatre. He took two of the most disreputable forms of low entertainment – melodrama and music hall – and incorporated their essential elements into a new and highly dignified environment.

Melodrama was originally invented to evade the stringent licensing laws and monopoly applied to legitimate theatre. Dingy Victorian fleapits on the fringes of the metropolitan area found a working-class audience for lurid and sensational plays, with music added at exciting or pathetic moments. (The piano accompaniments to the silent movies of the early 20th century were a similar device.) Such musical underlinings might come from an out-of-tune piano or an abused violin, but the sounds enabled unscrupulous impresarios to claim they were staging not unlicensed plays but permissible musical entertainments.

Music hall, begun in the backrooms of London public houses in the 1840s, was just as aggressively proletarian. Music hall songs reflect the grimmer sides of working-class life – the slum landlord, the moonlight flit, domestic violence, over-frequent pregnancies – and reflect the concerns of the audience of the day. Sir Augustus Harris's brilliance was to repackage these dubious goings-on and sell them to the respectable late-Victorian middle classes. He devised annual Drury Lane seasons, which began with an autumn melodrama, but a melodrama staged with stunning and expensive theatrical effects, its lavishness accompanied by rigorous censorship of any line too risqué to be heard by a polite audience. His season continued with an equally lavish Christmas pantomime starring music hall personalities like Dan Leno, Vesta Tilley and Marie Lloyd – one-time bits of rough transformed into family entertainers. Harris's repackaging guaranteed class and respectability, and watched by dress-suited merchants, manufacturers and shop-owners of the posher kinds, made humble actors and one-time backroom artistes into names enthusiastically uttered even in vicarages.

In essence, Fleming and Bettinson served as an Augustus Harris for boxing. Extracted from the blood, spit and sawdust of the public house backroom and staged with care and solemnity before white-tied and toppered gents, boxing suddenly *looked* utterly legitimate. Even now, a century and more since the birth of the NSC, the legacy lives on whenever a dinner-jacketed master of ceremonies takes a microphone and announces to a glamorously attired ringside, 'My Lords, ladies and gentlemen …' (though 'ladies' is very much a later addition).

Had Fleming had his way, the atmosphere would have rivalled Drury Lane or even Westminster Abbey. Members were confined to a religious silence during rounds and extinguished their cigars and cigarettes for the duration of a bout. This was not respect for the linings of boxers' lungs, merely a desire to make the ambience as unlike boxing's murky past as possible. Even Fleming could not abolish gambling, so wagers took place in nods, winks, gestures and flurries of tiny notebooks, as if the Stock Exchange floor had been taken over by Trappist monks. As the 1890s wore on, this self-imposed silence became less effective, and a side-room (known inevitably as 'Tattersall's') was provided for the shouting and settling of odds. Order was strictly maintained. From the president's elevated chair, Lord Lonsdale had been known to lay his ornamental cane across the back of any middle-class oik temporarily forgetting his manners.

By creating a national and sometimes international temple of boxing, Bettinson and Fleming performed a huge service. Nevertheless, as anyone who has ever put on gloves and stepped into a ring knows, there is no gain without pain. Members of the NSC were well aware that the legal authorities, who had received a bloody nose and a disappointing draw over the Slavin v McAuliffe affair, would welcome a return contest given half a chance. The autocratic arrogance applied in the club, to bring over-boisterous members or stroppy fighters to heel, did not endear it to pressmen or other outsiders beyond the club doors.

(That blue-blooded collective, the Jockey Club, used its social prestige and unanswerability to quash crooked practices on the turf. It still alienated many by its disregard for the socially inferior jockeys who were, after all, risking their lives every time they climbed on to the back of a thoroughbred racehorse. In a class-ridden society, its high-handed administration survived sharp practice by some of its own members and kept racing out of the law courts almost entirely. Jockeys and trainers were licensed by the Club, which could withdraw a licence upon which livelihoods depended *without even giving a reason*. Anyone bold enough to suggest legislation on any aspect of turf affairs would be met in the Lords by some peer pronouncing, unchallengeably, that such matters were better left to the private machinations of the Jockey Club.)

The NSC could, by decree within its private fiefdom, keep boxing honest. It eliminated almost entirely common excrescences like the fix, the foul, the dive and the non-triers. What it could not do, for all the ceremonial and ethics, was to eliminate a basic biological fact. When two strong men rain blows upon each other, there is an outside chance that one of them might die. Modern boxing has come to terms with this tragic lottery and made strenuous efforts to do everything humanly possible to reduce the risks. The risks can be reduced. They can never be eliminated.

Late Victorian and Edwardian employers were not overly concerned for the health and safety of their employees. Every accident at work was placed in a catch-all category of unlucky occurrences. Dame Fortune had a perennial frown on her face at the NSC in the years at the turn of the century. Preceded by the sudden death of Fleming himself, who expired on a seat in the NSC lavatory, no fewer than four fights in a period of three and a half years resulted in the death of one of the boxers.

On 6 December 1897, Walter Croot of Leytonstone was knocked out by the American bantamweight James Barry

in the 19th round of a not particularly furious fight and never regained consciousness, dying in a coma in Charing Cross Hospital. Eleven months later, on 7 November 1898, a Holborn boxer, Tom Turner, was knocked out by a Paddington rival, Nat Smith, and he too expired at Charing Cross without coming round. On 29 January 1900, Matt Precious of Birmingham easily outpointed his flyweight opponent Mike Riley of Scotland, who later collapsed and died. To complete this dismal record, 'Billy Smith' (the ring name of Murray Livingstone) collapsed in the seventh round of a 15-round contest against Jack Roberts on 22 April 1901 and died, also in Charing Cross Hospital, two days later.

The record was grim and the NSC officials, not unlike their peers the Jockey Club, further alienated outsiders by a mixture of flippancy, evasion and irritability at legitimate questions. Bettinson's attitude was less about concern for the tragic loss of the lives of young men given in the course of entertaining his club members, than that the effect on *public opinion* would be 'deplorable' – a remarkably twisted view of moral priorities. His remark, made about the Croot tragedy, was hardly an unwary slip of the tongue uttered in the panic of the moment. It was made five years later when he reflected on events, and went on, 'An outcry was raised by everybody who was not present. A sect of people who are never happy unless they are hysterical, set up an insensate scream. It seemed at one moment as if a national pastime was to be vetoed by the outcry of a few irresponsible old women.' Irresponsible old women (of either sex) had not put poor Croot into a fatal coma.

The authorities levied charges against Barry (his opponent), Bettinson and other officials over the death of Croot, but it went no further than the Bow Street Magistrates' Court. Yet the club learned nothing by the tragedy. When Turner lay dying less than a year later, his lingering coma was accompanied not by humanity and fellow feeling for a sportsman in dire straits, but by false claims that he was merely convalescing.

Press hostility to the initial lack of information and subsequent deceit led to accusations that the NSC was guilty of licensed manslaughter. Bettinson thought this offensive hyperbole, but his callous dismissal of public concern as a 'second cyclone of Sentimentalism', due only to the 'clamours of Anti-Sporting faddists' was unforgiveable. His comments about Turner were merely that he was 'an expert boxer who had frequently performed with credit [but] … had the worst of a contest with Nat Smith'. He meanwhile quoted approvingly a press comment, printed *before* the seriousness of Turner's state became apparent, that 'A better night's sport could not be wished for, and Mr Bettinson, who, as usual, acted as M.C., is to be heartily congratulated on the continuation of his much-appreciated cards.'

This sickeningly inadequate response can be coupled with Bettinson's version of the Riley death. I give it in full:

> The *piece de resistance* of this moving evening was supplied by a contest between Matt Precious and Mike Riley. The putting of these two lads together was considered by experts as demonstrating the best quality

procurable at 7 stone 8lbs. Riley had the advantage in height, reach, and experience, but round nine saw the Birmingham boxer an easy winner.

'Best quality procurable' like so much meat; in Riley's case, Bettinson refrained from informing his readers that it was actually dead meat he had in mind.

With lingering resentments in legal and police circles over the Slavin/McAuliffe affair, it is not surprising that the fourth NSC death led to a criminal trial for 'feloniously killing and slaying Murray Livingstone, otherwise Billy Smith'. The presiding judge was Mr Justice Channell. Arraigned on the charges in the Old Bailey dock on 15 May 1901 were Jack Roberts (opponent); Bettinson, the club manager; J. H. Douglas, the referee; Eugene Corri, the timekeeper; Arthur Gutteridge, Arthur Lock and William Chester, Smith's seconds; and William Baxter, Ben Jordan and Harry Greenfield, Roberts's seconds. Again the shadowy co-defendant was British professional boxing itself.

This, the prosecutor, Mr R. D. Muir, made clear from the outset. He was not interested in punishing the defendants under the indictment; the prosecution was brought 'with a view of putting a stop to future competitions of this kind'. He conceded, 'Nothing was suggested to have taken place which was unfair. No precaution was neglected which could have been taken – subject to the rules under which the fight took place, to secure the safety of the combatants from serious injury.' He added, '… if the fight was lawful sport, the defendants were not liable

to any indictment at all, but if it was an unlawful fight the defendants were liable on this indictment'.

For the rest of the day, the jury was forced to listen to various witnesses, some hostile to boxing, others strongly in favour. The general impression emerged that Smith's death had been a tragic accident. Mr Justice Channell was not easily convinced that this necessarily mattered. He claimed to be the very last person to wish to discourage 'manly' sport. This did not prevent him from outlining the anomalies and ambiguities on show. His summing-up for the jury was designed to concentrate their minds on the real questions at issue:

The whole question was – Was this a contest or was it a fight? If it was a fight it was illegal. The question was not whether it was a fair fight, but whether it was a fight. To determine that, they must look at the rules and see what the real object of the contesting parties was. If it was a simple boxing contest, in which the object was not to administer blows, but merely to show how it could be done, it was lawful; but if it was a prize fight under the guise of a boxing competition it was illegal. If it was a mere contest of skill in which there was no intention by one party to injure the other, it was lawful and the defendants would be entitled to be acquitted.

No witness at a professional boxing match could ever honestly say they had seen an event 'in which the object was not to administer blows, but

merely to show how it could be done'. Small wonder, therefore, that the jury returned, after 90 minutes' private discussion, to declare no possibility of their agreeing upon a verdict.

Like Slavin and McAuliffe a decade before, the accused had endured weeks of uncertainty from the contest on 22 April to the 16 May hearing and were now told they had to return for a fresh trial before a new jury at the Old Bailey on 28 June 1901. The delay was devoted less to agonising over their dangerous vulnerability than to assembling an array of new witnesses, as distinguished as possible, and engaging – at the personal expense of Lord Lonsdale – as formidable a legal advocate as could be found; the glamorous and magnetic personality, Marshall Hall KC, MP (1858–1916), later Sir Edward Marshall Hall, a man rarely out of the headlines for his successful advocacy in major criminal trials, especially for the defence. In 1894 he had saved a sex worker from the gallows, although she had murdered an elderly client and stuffed his body in a trunk. And in 1907 he would clear a young artist on a murder charge, completely against the odds. His most famous cases lay still in the future but he was already an advocate to be reckoned with.

Marshall Hall, assisted by Charles F. Gill KC, led for the defence. Mr Muir was retained for the Crown but would face a much-strengthened defence team and a new judge, Mr Justice Grantham. Grantham, much less impartial than Channell, behaved as if he were a referee whose card had already been marked for a wide points victory for the defence. He treated defence witnesses with remarkable deference and pushed the jury towards the not guilty verdict he himself clearly favoured. But that is to run ahead of a fascinating day's proceedings worth recording in detail.

As in May, Muir opened his case with a long address, outlining the basic facts of the April contest as he understood them, then concentrating upon the major factors in the prosecution's favour: that the contest was clearly more a fight than a demonstration; that certain victory came only to a man who produced a knockout blow; that the fairness of the contest was irrelevant to its overall legality. As the defenders of boxing as a legal activity in the 20th century were frequently to quote this test case, *Rex v Roberts* and others in 1901, we should see what vindication it actually produced.

First up was the policeman who had attended the NSC on the fatal night. Police Inspector Boxall had visited the Covent Garden premises and, standard police procedure, had warned all the principals that in the event of a serious injury they might be held responsible. (By 1901, this must have received as much general attention as a modern airline stewardess preceding a transatlantic flight with a safety demonstration of life jacket procedures.)

Kitted out in six-ounce gloves and shuffling round a ring floor padded with a sheet of canvas and four thicknesses of felt, Smith and Roberts fought uneventfully for seven rounds with Smith building up a substantial points lead. Just before the end of the seventh round, Smith took evasive action, tangling up with Roberts, and both slipped down – probably not from a blow. In the fall, the back of Smith's head hit the lower rope and then the ring apron. As Smith got up, unassisted, Corri the timekeeper

John Herbert Douglas (1853–1930), referee, timber merchant, NSC committee man and a witness with very strong views.
Barratts/S&G and Barratts/EMPICS Sport

called time. After the minute's break, Smith left his stool but looked groggy, with one foot dragging behind him, and without receiving another blow, or possibly a very light one, sank to his knees and was counted out. He lapsed further into unconsciousness and was taken to hospital where he was diagnosed as suffering from a blood clot on the right side of his brain. In the

Portrayed on a cigarette card, J.W.H.T.Douglas (1882–1930), son of J.H.Douglas, England amateur cricket captain, Olympic gold medallist and all-round athlete pursuing a glittering sporting career supported by his father's money. He and his father were killed in an accident.
Popperfoto/Contributor

friendly spar with pulled punches and no knockdowns.

He [Mr Muir] submitted that, if it was a question of one competitor trying to knock his opponent out of time, so that he could not rise at the expiration of ten seconds, then this was in reality a prize fight, and as such illegal; but, on the other hand, if the parties were only trying to show how often, and on what part of the body, each could hit the other without intending to hurt him, then it was lawful sport, and they ought not to be held responsible for any fatal consequences which ensued.

This was Authorities v Boxing II, a rematch of the legal punch-up surrounding McAuliffe v Slavin, and turning upon the same dubious points. If the jury was convinced the encounter was really a prizefight in disguise, then 'in the interests of all true sport these contests ought to be stopped'.

Further witnesses were called and cross-examined, first John Troutbeck, the Westminster Coroner, who had taken statements at the inquest from three of those in the dock (Bettinson, Corri and Douglas).

He conceded that the jury at the inquest had defined Smith's death as 'accidental'. George Shepherd, the NSC glove attendant, took the stand and produced the six-ounce gloves used in the contest, explaining that the club had switched from four-ounce gloves to the heavier ones 'because the club thought they would be on the safe side'.

E. J. Churchill, an NSC member of three years' standing, was called

absence of any external signs of a blow, it was impossible to establish whether the internal laceration had been the result of a fist, the rope or the lightly padded floor.

The prosecution case, outlined by Mr Muir, focused upon the proposition that gloved boxing at the NSC or elsewhere was, like bare-fist pugilism, illegal. It differed in its very nature to a next and gave his own view of the fatal few minutes:

In the seventh round Smith invited Roberts to get in a blow; he was leading off with his left, and he avoided a blow from Roberts; he went like this [Churchill swayed his upper body backwards] and came back on to the ropes; his head struck the ropes, and he doubled up and came under the ropes on to the floor. As he got up time was called; he went to his corner a little bit *groggy*, but nothing unusual. After the usual minute interval the men stood up again – I did not notice anything about Smith till he turned round to face Roberts; then I saw that he was dragging his right foot after him; when Americans are boxing they have a way of dragging their feet in that way to get a firm hold on something. They got to the right side of the ring while sparring – Smith's back was to the referee; he went down on his knee – I cannot exactly say what caused that – I saw Roberts strike a blow, but whether Smith was struck or not I do not know; I believe he was; he rolled over – Roberts stood away – no other blow was struck. Smith was counted out – he got up with the assistance of his seconds and went to his corner – at the end of 10 seconds the referee called out, 'Out', and awarded the contest to the other man – the deceased became conscious; I see his seconds wipe him down and sponge him and help him to his room – I do not

think the blows exchanged in the contest were at all hard … it is usual in a boxing competition to strike hard blows. I should think they were striking as hard as they could to win the contest.

More than a century on, this account has a ring of truth. Rarely, in any of the regrettable ring tragedies since 1901, has it been possible to isolate any particular blow as *the* cause of the damage. And as Churchill added under cross-examination:

I do not think in the last round that Smith got a blow; if he did it was very light – if he was hit it was on the chin – he was defending himself. It could not be called a knockout blow by any exaggeration – in the seventh round he overbalanced himself in trying to get his balance. From first to last Roberts boxed perfectly fairly.

Throughout the hearing, the whole tenor of the defence was to demonstrate forcefully, and by their own lights, quite honestly, that *any* death in the ring in the course of a fight was wholly accidental. At times, they seemed close to demanding that the lower rope and the apron be put in the dock instead of the boxers and the NSC officials.

Next up was Lewis Darling, an NSC guest on the fatal night. He also drew attention to the rope:

… towards the end of the seventh round they both fell down in a corner of the ring, Roberts on top of Smith. I saw Smith's head on the rope for a second; then it

slipped to the floor. Smith lay down till Roberts got up, then he got up and time was called … when Smith left his corner for the eighth round he did not appear so well as he had been; he appeared to be lame, and drew one foot behind him. The round began, and one or two blows were exchanged. After a little while Smith sank down and held the ropes with one hand – he did not fall as if he was knocked down …

Darling was replaced in the witness box by the Charing Cross Hospital house surgeon, W. H. Dodd, the man who had examined Smith on his midnight arrival at the hospital, and who had been present at the post-mortem examination. He was clinically precise:

… on the right side of the brain and under the membranes there was some blood, which covered the whole of the right side – it came from the vessels of the membrane. There was a clot on the brain that had caused his death … the original cause of the bleeding was the rupture of some vessels on the surface of the brain … caused by some blow on the head … that might happen from a blow from the fist or a fall on the ropes or on the floor, but it must have been a padded object, because there was no mark.

Under cross-examination by Marshall Hall for the defence, Dodd repeated that the rope was as likely a culprit as any: 'If Smith fell in trying to avoid a blow, and in falling struck his head on the rope, that would cause the injuries.'

What followed was the most crucial episode in the court hearing – the appearance of John Herbert Douglas, boxing enthusiast, NSC member, and the man who had refereed the Smith v Roberts contest (from *outside* the ring). Douglas's son, J. W. H. T. Douglas – 'Johnny Won't Hit Today' Douglas – was incidentally the amateur boxer who would go on to win the middleweight gold medal at the 1908 London Olympics, but become better known as an Edwardian cricketer, captaining England several times against Australia. He also played international soccer as an English amateur. He and his father were a notoriously combative pair.

Douglas Snr was first questioned by the friendly Charles Gill, who swiftly established Douglas's right to testify from his experience of boxing spanning a quarter of a century and thousands of competitions. Together, they made several claims aimed at impressing the jury with the civilised nature of the NSC's proceedings. Smith and Roberts had supposedly responded to Douglas's cautionary preliminaries about fighting within the rules by declaring that 'we are the best of friends, and we only want to see who is the better boxer'.

The stilted words suggest a little *post facto* rehearsal. Nevertheless, no one familiar with professional boxers would doubt that camaraderie and mutual respect easily survives bloody mayhem between opening and closing bells of a contest and may be instantly resumed after the contest. It is in the very nature of sport for protagonists to have at one another with gusto for the duration, then walk into a warm, mutual and completely non-hypocritical embrace at the close. The Victorian novelist Anthony Trollope in one of his political novels, *Phineas Finn* of 1869, believed the bare-fist boxers of the 1860s to be just the same:

> How they fly at each other, striking as though each blow should carry death if it were possible! And yet there is no one whom the Birmingham Bantam respects so highly as he does Bill Burns the Brighton Bully, or with whom he has so much delight in discussing the merits of a pot of half-and-half.

In court, Douglas explained the scoring system in operation for NSC contests. Scoring by rounds, or by points, has undergone many changes over the years. The modern system operates a 'ten point must' mode, where one boxer is awarded ten points for his/her performance in a round, and the opponent ten for an even round, or nine, or eight (in the case of a knockdown) or even seven, for two knockdowns, or a markedly inferior performance. The earlier system used by Douglas at the NSC awarded a five points maximum to the winner of a round, and a pro rata four, three, two or even one and any fraction between these figures to the boxer adjudged to have lost the round. Douglas's card for Smith v Roberts, round by round, read as follows: 1st: S 5 R 4½; 2nd: S 5 R 4½; 3rd: S 5 R 4½; 4th S 5 R4; 5th S5 R4; 6th S 5 R 4; 7th S 5 R 5. So, at the point of the clever and elusive Smith's collapse, he had actually established a comfortable lead on points, 35 to 30½, having had distinctly the better of the contest and winning every round.

This is ample proof that Smith's tragic demise was not a case of a beating allowed by an incompetent referee. Unfortunately, Douglas, having made coherent and valid points, became more evasive when asked about two cardinal factors: the knockout rule and the force of blows given and received. Could a man hopelessly behind on points after 14 rounds win in the 15th round by a knockout? Genuine answer: unlikely, but yes. Douglas's answer: 'A Referee would not know his business who allowed a contest to go on while one man was getting the better. He would say, "I have seen sufficient," and would give the contest to the other man.' (Well known, to the point of a sporting cliché, seconds and managers are prone to urge their man on with the words, 'You're so far behind, you're going to have to knock him out!' According to Douglas, this situation would never arise.)

There was another awkward direct question: 'Taking your experience from the time that you were a boy, do men, boxing, hit each other hard?'

Douglas: I do not quite understand quite what you mean by 'hard'. If you mean by velocity—

Gill: Yes, velocity.

Douglas: Yes, by hitting your opponent quickly. That is what you want to do if you can, like that, and try to hit him a terrific blow. He may not do so. He may hit or he may not hit the man.

Apparently, the laws of physics were suspended within the NSC portals, and force no longer equalled mass times velocity. Hard had become merely quick. Recipients of punches from notoriously hard punchers like Earnie Shavers or George Foreman must have lost not from the force of the punches, merely by becoming discombobulated by their velocity. Amazingly, the judge was prepared to go along with this fantasy.

Mr Justice Grantham: Velocity makes up for weight?

Douglas: Yes, my Lord, it does.

Before the full absurdity of this exchange could stretch the court's credulity too far, Marshall Hall was on his feet and skilfully diverting attention to the points potentially awarded by a referee for clever defence, and to the contrast in speed between a three-round amateur fight and a 15-round professional one. He implied, without being specific, that professionals hit more softly than amateurs!

Marshall Hall: A man who goes the course in a 15-round competition, he must box more carefully?

Douglas: Yes.

Douglas then had the pleasure of being cross-examined by Mr Muir for the prosecution. Muir found it easy to irritate the irascible Douglas and have him contradict things he and other NSC officials had already put on record.

Muir: Do you say that without this ten-second rule [the knockout] you could not decide a boxing contest so that the best man should win?

Douglas: I could decide a contest up to the time that you are speaking of.

Muir: Why should not that show you which was the best man?

Douglas: Only up to that time. If they are going to box eight rounds, and you are going to decide by what has happened in the second, you cannot decide it.

Muir: But if you are going to be knocked out in the second round you do decide it?

Douglas: Yes.

Muir produced rule books governing boxing under the Amateur Boxing Association, the Army Boxing Competitions and the Scottish Amateur Boxing Association, and demonstrated the variety of practices about knockouts that prevailed – neither in the Army nor in the Scottish Amateur ranks did a knockout blow bring about anything other than the premature end of a round. Knockouts were even *discouraged,* as in the Public Schools Fencing and Gymnastic Club where a rule stated, '… if a competitor is seen to be working for a knock-out blow he will be cautioned'.

Douglas's responses to all this information were interspersed with irrelevant and offensive bluster or classic non sequiturs like this one:

Muir: It is a rule which prevents it being in the interest of either of the competitors to knock out his opponent?

Douglas: The Scottish men who lose are as hot-headed men as I have ever seen.

Elsewhere, Douglas parried and counter-punched more effectively:

Douglas: It is evident you have never seen a boxing competition, I should think.

Muir: I have never seen one at the National Sporting Club.

Douglas: Or anywhere else.

The main thrust of Muir's questions to Douglas was to show that professional boxing at the NSC and elsewhere was essentially different from its amateur equivalent. This could hardly be denied. When he pressed Douglas on the number of 15-round fights he had refereed that had not lasted the distance, either by being stopped or by dint of knockout, Douglas became surprisingly and conveniently amnesiac.

Muir: [At the NSC] … how many competitions did you judge?

Douglas: I cannot say – 15 to 20.

Muir: How many of those reached the 15th round?

Douglas: I cannot say.

Muir: I suggest to you about six?

Douglas: Six, or eight, or ten.

Muir: Did you hear the secretary of the club say that it was six?

Douglas: I did.

Muir: Is that correct?

Douglas: I do not know.

Muir: Is he likely to be right?

Douglas: I do not think the secretary really knew much about it, because he was really nothing to do with the boxing; I believe he was called as a witness for something utterly different.

Muir: Did not you yourself admit that on the question of the number of contests the secretary would be more likely to know it than you?

Douglas: I did.

Muir then returned to the vexed question of the severity of blows delivered by professionals, and, terrier-like, to the knockout:

Muir: Are all those that box in competitions at the National Sporting Club professionals?

Douglas: Yes.

Muir: Do they hit as hard as they can?

Douglas: They hit quickly.

Muir: Do they hit as hard as they can?

Douglas: What do you mean by 'hard'?

Muir: Have you said all boxers hit as hard as they can?

Douglas: Yes, but that means they get in quickly. If you mean hard by quick, they do.

Muir: As hard as they can hit compatible with their getting home?

Douglas: Yes.

Muir: Under your rules is not it the obvious interest of competitors to knock their opponents out?

Douglas: No, I do not admit that.

When the 15-rounder between the impatient middleweight Douglas and the suave lightweight Muir – in which Muir scored a points victory – was over, the court adjourned for lunch; much needed on all sides.

After the lively exchanges between Douglas and Muir in the morning, the afternoon started quietly enough with the President of the Amateur Boxing Association, George Henry Vize. Vize, often an NSC referee, had jointly refereed the Slavin v McAuliffe contest (see Chapter 1). In his youth he was a notorious Man About Bohemia, an ever-present at the music halls, always willing to join in the latest escapade having swum the Thames at midnight in full evening dress and pounded the nocturnal Haymarket pavements on horseback. In court, he was in sober and distinguished mode, painstakingly emphasising the care taken at the NSC and the authority and respect his fellow referee Douglas commanded in the sport.

Under cross-examination he did his best to support Douglas. He claimed a knockout blow was 'a most difficult thing to do … more often an accident than not'. He then almost gave the game away by conceding, 'If you want to hit quickly, you naturally hit hard – the only man I ever saw who could hit quickly and not hit hard was Jem Mace, and he is alone in the boxing world.' (Mace, 'The Swaffham Gypsy', 1831–1910, was an East Anglian heavyweight of the 1860s and 1870s who had progressed from bare-knuckle bruiser to skilful gloved boxing instructor.)

Next up was the Yellow Earl himself, Lord Lonsdale, President of the National Sporting Club. He had actively financed and organised this defence of boxing. His personal appearance as an expert witness came on top of the assembling and briefing of the defence team at his London house in Carlton House Terrace, and supplying from his personal fortune the funds that put a star advocate like Marshall Hall at the defence's disposal.

Lonsdale confined his testimony to his own long interest in boxing. Curiously, he claimed never to have seen a bare-knuckle contest in his life. His main thrust was skilfully to link boxing less with its bare-fist precedents, than with the Campbell/Queensberry gloved amateurs. In this context, he was able to describe the ten-second count as an act of mercy and a measure of safety. 'The National Sporting Club rules were instituted to substitute science for brute force.'

Two other distinguished NSC members – the Honourable Victor Montague, and the Earl of Kingston – followed Lonsdale. The collective presence of the three conveyed an unspoken claim – two peers and an admiral, how could they be involved in anything shady or illegal? Montague reinforced such thoughts: 'From what I have observed, they [the fights] are conducted in a thoroughly satisfactory manner and with every care.' Kingston agreed: 'I know the conditions under which they are carried out from what I have observed there, and I think they are carried out with every possible care.' Three aristocratic minds with a single thought, or perhaps with a single agreed briefing. The top of the bill heavyweights on the Old Bailey card were the main

defence barristers. In performance they did not disappoint. Mr Gill was the first. He opened with one of his strongest leads: how small a part any of Roberts's punches had apparently contributed to Smith's fall and eventual demise.

Gentlemen of the Jury, you have heard it given in evidence, and in evidence as clearly given as it can be, that the deceased man Smith met his death by stepping back to avoid a blow, losing his balance, and falling with the back of his head on the ropes.

(This line of defence might have saved Roberts and his so-called accomplices in this case. It would hardly have protected from prosecution the next boxer whose opponent perished as a direct result of a punch or punches.)

From the very first hearing in May, the prosecution conceded that the NSC procedures were commendable. Gill further emphasised the good order prevailing at NSC promotions: 'I tell you that this Sport of Boxing as carried on at the National Sporting Club *is* legitimate … Believe me, it is in safe hands.'

Much less persuasive were Gill's arguments on the knockout:

[It] … is a blow purely the result of accident, and one which cannot be brought off by intention, supported by skill, with any certainty whatsoever. To put the matter in a nutshell, these experts have declared that this knock-out blow (in cases such as the one under consideration where trained Boxers meet) is an impossibility except through the purest accident.

Were this to be true, then the master of ceremonies who announces a fighter into the ring with the words '20 wins, 20 within the distance – the perfect record', should really be saying '20 wins, 20 within the distance – the *most fortunate accidental* record'. No one would be impressed.

Gill paid a wholesome tribute to the ten-second count: 'A merciful provision on the part of Humanity itself!' – while his peroration made it appear that it was not a sport, but British imperialism and patriotism that would be threatened by a guilty verdict.

> I ask you this: Because there is an inseparable element of risk in this noble English Art of Boxing is it to be stopped; is it to be stopped by the judicial interference of well-meaning Busybodies, or a set of alternative rules more applicable to children at a Dame's School than to British Manhood holding World-Wide Empire?

These jingoistic references sound vaguely ridiculous, but Gill's address was made on 28 June 1901. At the same time, British 'Manhood' and 'Empire' were undergoing a severe test – the Boer War of 1899–1902 in South Africa. Only a few months before Gill's speech came the disastrous news of the proud representatives of British 'Manhood' and 'Empire' who now lay dead on the slopes of Spion Kop and the environs of Vaal Krantz, slain by a smaller but cannier enemy. Few patriotic appeals seem silly in fevered times of war.

The darker mood in the court suited Marshall Hall, whose strongest weapons were sardonic wit and biting sarcasm. He began seriously by reminding the court that Roberts was in the dock on a serious charge ('… the fact is sufficient that this man Roberts stands here indicted for Manslaughter'), but soon turned to mockery of the prosecution's motives for operating 'whether in the interests of Justice, Sport, or some Society for the Protection of Old Ladies, it is impossible to conjecture'. He went on, 'Either Roberts is guilty of Manslaughter or he is not, and that he is not guilty I have the utmost confidence that I shall convince you.'

Like all good advocates, Hall knew when to focus on a valid point (when it was to his advantage), and when to obscure one:

> … this contest had none of the objectionable features of a Prize Fight about it whatsoever. My learned friend, however, submits, and very insistently submits, that it was a Prize Fight, though he constantly calls it a Contest. He, in fact, alleges the deed and objects to the Word. But, Gentlemen of the Jury, *I* do not object to the word, though I submit that this was not the deed. The word 'Fight' is a good English word which everybody can understand.

Had these words been pronounced at the first hearing before Mr Justice Channell in May, the defence case would have collapsed. Channell had instructed the jury: 'If it was a fight, it was illegal. The question was not whether it was a fair fight, but whether it was a fight?'

As no one then or since has provided definitions adequately separating the terms prizefight, contest and fight, Hall's point was pure obfuscation. He used a similar oratorical trick over punches and their effects:

> I suggest … combatants should wear leather jerkins, under which bells should be concealed – electric if possible. The boxing gloves should be of the largest size and should be plentifully smeared with Chalk. For each chalk mark seen on an opponent's doublet the striker should be given a point. But if … he should happen to ring one of the bells, he should be instantly disqualified for unnecessary violence with the intention of effecting a knock-out, be rendered liable to an indictment for manslaughter.

None of the accounts discloses how Hall's flippancy impressed or repelled the jury in their deliberations. Ultimately, neither his nor Muir's eloquence can have been as effective as Mr Justice Grantham's. His mind was already made up and he used his final summing-up to tell the jury what they should think. The knockout and the ten-second count did not concern him:

> Now, I am bound to say, I do not think that it is necessary that the existence of that rule makes it a fight, and I think I might go further and say that the absence of the rule makes it a fight … I think the learned counsel put a little too much stress on this rule, and perhaps weakened his case by assuming it necessary to rely upon that.

Lonsdale appreciated deference.
Keystone/Stringer

When he turned to the cause of Smith's death, he had few doubts there either:

> I am bound to say that the evidence is not overwhelming, but more than that, it seems to point very strongly to the fact that the unfortunate man met his death from falling on the rope … I think your verdict ought to be that he died from a fall and not from a blow, but from his desire to avoid a blow, stepping back, or throwing his body back.

He was just as certain on the question 'whether the parties who were engaged in this combat were engaged in a legal or illegal act'.

Indeed he declared his sympathy for the weaknesses of the prosecution: 'He has no evidence to support him.' At this Muir and his team must have despaired, especially when his lordship pronounced the ten-second rule was 'to make sparring more scientific and less dangerous … it is certainly in favour of less injury than it is likely to create more'.

The judge then paid a warm tribute to Douglas ('I think he gave his evidence with very great propriety'), and to Douglas's authoritative experience. Douglas's evidence, to the effect that no boxer would dare to work towards a knockout, and that it would be impossible in any case so to do, was swallowed whole and regurgitated intact for the jury:

> He says he does not think it necessary to have the other words in, that if a competitor is seen to

be working for a knock-out blow, because he says no man could do it, and he says where you are deciding a contest between skilled men nobody could tell, therefore the language of the rules is different.

Grantham then wandered into irrelevant personal reminiscences of his experiences on the northern circuit where, he said, he had frequently advised men in altercations on the streets to use their fists (instead of knives):

It is better for a man to use the weapon that God has given him, namely his fists, because it is not so dangerous, and that is why it is that a great number of people are fond of boxing … it is very desirable that proper boxing under proper rules should be kept up; all people should not be afraid of using their fists when necessary.

The relationship between knife fights in seaport towns and Smith v Roberts was left to the jurors' imaginations. The verdict the judge expected of them was made more obvious:

… if you believe that this contest was carried on with the intention that the parties should fight, as it were, to a finish, and fight until one gives in from exhaustion, or from injury received through such fighting, then, Gentlemen, your verdict should be 'Guilty' …

This was certainly not the judge's preferred option:

… but if on the other hand you think it was simply a case of boxing or sparring, with rules proper for the purpose of preventing men going on or until exhaustion ensued or injury resulted, and with the desire to make it a pure question of science and as little injurious to the individual as possible, then, Gentlemen, your verdict will be 'Not Guilty' … [I] now leave it in your hands to say whether the death ensued from a knock-out blow or whether it did not, and secondly, whether this was a fight or a boxing or sparring contest as I have just described. Consider your verdict, please.

The jury, without leaving the box for further deliberations, showed they could take a broad hint; two minutes later, their foreman stood up and said that they had agreed their verdict:

Clerk of the Court: Do you find that the death was caused from a knockout blow?

Foreman: We do not, but that it was the result of an accident.

Clerk: Do you find that it was a fight or only a legitimate sparring contest?

Foreman: That it was a boxing contest.

Clerk: And you say that the defendants are 'Not Guilty'?

Foreman: That is so.

This old case demonstrates how the whole future of British boxing turned upon irrelevancies and fictions and the inadequacies of a legal system dealing with an activity it did not understand. Those on the inside of the sport feared that an unsympathetic and out-of-

touch judiciary would register the blood, violence, pain and danger of the ring, and fail to appreciate the skills, courage, thrills and even beauty. They compiled a defence that presented not boxing, but an ethereal construct where blows flew but barely landed; where ropes outpunched knuckles; and where knockouts occurred only when the victim accidentally threw his chin on to an opponent's glove. Afraid to present a fully honest case for boxing, they presented an artificial one and got away with it.

This conclusion should give no comfort to those a century and more later who would have boxing banned. Had professional boxing been made illegal in 1901, it would not have ceased.

It would, rather, have gone back to an underground, uncontrolled existence one step ahead of the police and the magistrates, more rather than less dangerous to its participants.

In any sport with elements of violent contact – boxing, obviously, but equally rugby, American football, karate and others – the appeal for most followers is *not* pure violence, but the creative and dynamic dualism between violent impulses, and the order kept by confining those impulses within the bounds set by rules and ritual. A fast bowler intimidating a batsman with a well-placed bouncer; a pile-driving tackle upon a rugby half-back by a flanker; the sacking of an American football quarterback; a boxer striving for a knockout – all these *could* disintegrate into squalid mayhem. When they do so disintegrate, there is no longer sport. Genuine sportspeople have always recognised the difference.

CHAPTER 3

STRONG BOYS AND SENATORS
AMERICA 1880-1911

In Which Politicians Take Their Gloves Off

THE *REX v Roberts* case at London's Old Bailey was closely scrutinised in the USA, in New York in particular. New York boxing had its own legal difficulties. Since 17 April 1896, the Laws of New York, Chapter 301 had grudgingly allowed sparring exhibitions with gloves 'of not less than five ounces each in weight'. Such exhibitions must be 'held by a domestic incorporated athletic association in a building leased by it for athletic purposes only for at least a year, or in a building owned and occupied by such association'. Any other kind of pugilistic activity was *illegal,* even within the premises of a private club.

The law was comprehensive:

A person who, within this state, engages in, instigates, aids, encourages or does any act to further a contention or fight, without weapons, between two or more persons, or a fight commonly called a ring or prize fight, either within or without the state, or who engages in a public or private sparring exhibition, with or without gloves, within the state, at which an admission

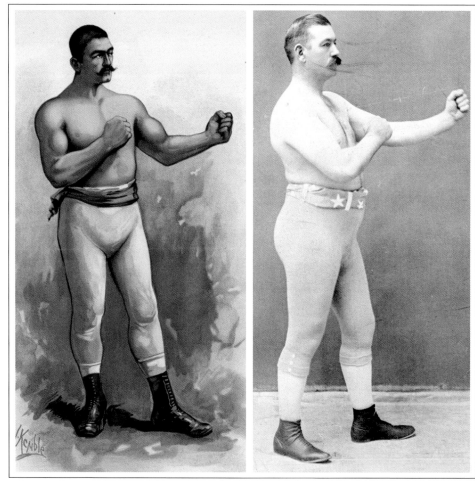

John L. Sullivan (1858–1918) 'The Great John L'. The bare-fist champion in 1885, moustache and biceps bristling. By 1898 the Stars and Stripes sash cannot quite contain the paunch. 'Fat as a pig with beer', said Johnson.
Prints & Photographs Division, Library of Congress, LC-USZ62-118653

fee is charged or received, either directly or indirectly … or trains or assists any person in training or

preparing for such a contention, exhibition or fight is guilty of a misdemeanour …

This quotation comes from a law sometimes called the Horton Act after the Senator George Horton who steered it through the State Legislature in Albany in 1896, having failed to do so in 1895. His central purpose was not suppression, but limited permission. Horton approved of sparring, he approved of socially prestigious athletic clubs, like the New York Athletic Club and the Manhattan Athletic Club, where members of gentlemanly standing contested for belts and medals in an activity that stretched the meaning of the word 'spar' beyond its conventional definition. (*Concise Oxford Dictionary*: 'Spar, 1. Make motions of attack & defence with closed fists, use the hands [as] in boxing, [often *at* opponent].')

New York was following precedents set 1,300 miles to the south in New Orleans. There, lax application of Louisiana state laws had notoriously allowed dubious underground pleasures to take place behind elegantly appointed façades; wickedness in dignified settings. Out of the brothels and street life of New Orleans came early jazz. Less famously, out of the gentlemen's clubs of New Orleans, came events that encouraged American boxing's transition from bare-knuckled anarchy to gloved respectability.

The chequered career of John L. Sullivan – 'The Boston Strong Boy' or 'The Great John L' – provides a convenient example. Born in Roxbury, Boston on 15 October 1858 to Irish immigrant parents, Sullivan strutted his stuff from coast to coast throughout the 1880s, challenging all-comers before twirling his luxuriant moustache and despatching them with his formidable bunch of fives, sometimes gloved, sometimes bare.

8 July 1889 Richburg, Mississippi: the last gloveless heavyweight fight for the championship. Sullivan stops New Yorker Jake Kilrain (1859–1937) in the 75th round.
Prints & Photographs Division, Library of Congress, LC-USZ62-98899

Sullivan's bread and butter, and an unprecedentedly generous spreading of jam, came from his 'picnic' tours. Sullivan travelled coast to coast, appearing in theatres, dance halls and any suitable space, and offering a cash prize for any man who could last four rounds with him under Queensberry Rules. If no such challenges were forthcoming, Sullivan would spar with one of his entourage instead. In 14 years of touring, these engagements pocketed him over a million dollars, rather more than the $100,000 or so he earned from genuine contests.

Sullivan was the first popular sports hero in the USA; one who could fight for the USA. He could drink and fornicate to international standards as well. Just under six feet tall and over 14 stones, he began the serious business with a hybrid contest against John Donaldson in Cincinnati, Ohio on 24 December 1880. Both men wore gloves of less than five ounces, but in all other respects followed prize ring conventions, including throws and rounds of unlimited duration. Donaldson's inability to continue after 21 minutes' intermittent pounding by Sullivan, made Sullivan 'champion' inasmuch as that title yet had any meaning. Post-fight, both men were arrested by the police but released without charge when spectators offered no evidence against them.

This led to other big fights – one against Paddy Ryan in February 1882 in Mississippi City also under prizefight rules; another against the Englishman Charlie Mitchell on a four-round exhibition basis, yet still halted by the police. The biggest was a return against Mitchell on 10 March 1888 at Chantilly in France over 39 rounds and three hours of general tedium. Sullivan also fought the last bare-knuckle championship fight on 8 July 1889, in Richburg,

George Wesley Bellows (1882–1925), an artist who produced many paintings and prints of the New York boxing scene, here depicts the MC assuring the audience The Great John L will take on all-comers.
National Portrait Gallery, Smithsonian Institution

Thus, in a very few years, a significant transformation had taken place. On 8 July 1889, as Sullivan pummelled Kilrain in their 75-round bare-fisted encounter, fighters and crowd alike had needed to have one eye on the ring and the other on possible incursions by the police. (A local magistrate threatened a reading of the Riot Act, but the receipt of a handsome bribe dissuaded him.) On 14 January 1891, 'Ruby Robert' Fitzsimmons and 'Nonpareil' Jack Dempsey, (not the later great heavyweight, but a middleweight from whom the later Dempsey borrowed a name), could meet unmolested by the authorities in a new arena built especially for the purpose in the middle of the city by the New Orleans Olympic Club.

Elaborate typography and high prices reflect boxing's bid for respectability.
BoxRec

Mississippi against Jake Kilrain over 75 rounds – two and a quarter hours of punch, clinch and throw.

The Kilrain fight, held outside the Louisiana state boundaries to avoid the temporary vigilance of state authorities, was attended less by Richburg residents than by thousands of New Orleans and New York boxing enthusiasts transported to the secret venue in special excursion trains provided by the clubs. The New Orleans clubs organised the affair and provided training facilities – Sullivan's at the Young Men's Gymnastic Club; Kilrain's at the Southern Athletic Club.

The fight staged in defiance of the law created interest across the continent, just as Sullivan's previous doings had created a national hero. Popularity for the man put pressure upon local politicians and officials who ultimately depended, at election time, on their own ability to please. Interfering with an activity celebrated by humble voters and potential rich patrons alike was not sensible politics.

Taking a hint from the English precedents, club officials stressed the difference between unlimited bare-knuckle fisticuffs and the gloved Queensberry Rules version. The New Orleans chief of police sensed the growing popularity and was discreetly acquiescent when the New Orleans clubs promoted professional encounters, adapting or constructing arenas to house a ring and spectator seating, and staging fully gloved contests. The local statutes were quietly amended by January 1890. By March 1890, the politicians on the New Orleans City Council had resignedly agreed to the holding of gloved professional fights, providing only that Sunday was avoided and that no alcohol was served.

On 7 September 1892, Sullivan (now aged 34 and weighing a bloated 15st 2lb/212lbs) returned to the Crescent City to meet 'Handsome' or 'Gentleman' Jim Corbett (13st/182lbs), a Californian who had just celebrated his 26th birthday. The promotion was an Olympic Club monopoly. The club put up the $25,000 purse and built yet another city venue to house the event. It took place as the climax of a three-day boxing festival, which included, unusually, a black champion (George Dixon) defending his featherweight title against a white challenger (Jack Skelly), and a segregated enclosure permitting black spectators to see him. The experiment was not repeated for many years. Symbolic of the change in atmosphere within boxing was the new challenger matched against Sullivan.

Corbett was an educated one-time bank clerk with carefully coiffured wavy black hair and impeccably genteel manners out of the ring (emphasised by boxing writers eager to enhance the new image). He was reportedly the man parents would have their daughters bring home to tea; Sullivan the man to have fathers reaching for their shotguns. Truthfully, Corbett's gentlemanly reputation was more image than substance, and his first wife, who divorced him after a stormy two years, ensured his dalliance with a contemporary actress earned him lurid headlines. That was in the future. In New Orleans, one reporter indiscreetly revealed that Sullivan, true to type, had preceded the tussle with Corbett at 9pm with an animated bout with Miss Mardi Gras in his hotel room in the early hours of the morning.

In the fight, Corbett, skilfully moving and jabbing, turned Sullivan's extra years and weight into disadvantages. In the 21st round of a bloody encounter, a slow and swollen-faced Sullivan took the latest clipping left hook on the jaw and collapsed to be counted out. The punch was 'audible throughout the house' and metaphorically echoed around the world. Sullivan and old-style pugilism were past; modern boxing was the future.

The victory was pyrrhic. The first gloved fight for the world heavyweight championship was transparently *not* a mere sparring exhibition. It provoked a legal reaction at state level. A new Louisiana governor, Murphy J. Foster, and his attorney general, Milton J. Cunningham, brought an action in November 1893 against the Olympic Club for their violations of the laws against boxing as currently understood. The case against the club was formidable: a long and bloody prizefight for a handsome purse, culminating in a knockout, had been publicly staged for a large paying audience, including many from out of state.

The prosecution's charge that the audience comprised thugs, conmen and criminals was untrue. The club's counter-claim that only highly respectable citizens were there convinced even less. As Cunningham pointed out, the club's committee had recently murdered its own president during a contentious club meeting.

The prosecution made much of bloody events *in* the ring. The defence paralleled the case that the NSC and friends would put at London's Old Bailey in 1901 as discussed in the previous chapter. The jury were treated to defence witnesses drawn from New Orleans's social elite. They played down the blood and violence, and emphasised science, aesthetics and skill, meanwhile suffering collective amnesia about cuts, knockouts and ring injuries. The jury obligingly bought the package. The Olympic Club and boxing were legal … temporarily.

The Attorney General promptly appealed the New Orleans jury's decision to the State Supreme Court, and a retrial was ordered for May 1894.

Doubly unfortunate for the Olympic Club, in a promotion just before the new hearing, George Kid Lavigne knocked out Andy Brown. Brown died the next day. The new trial before a less sympathetic jury produced much harsher decisions. What the Olympic Club was promoting was prizefighting. Prizefighting was illegal. The Louisiana state officials and the New Orleans City authorities would henceforward have no discretionary options – no real boxing.

Meanwhile, up in New York, Horton's 1896 Act, and the promotions of the New Orleans clubs, encouraged some clubs – the New York Athletic Club and the Manhattan Club and others – to extend similarly their activities beyond the letter of Horton's provisions.

In the 1880s, Madison Square Garden had successfully staged several of John L. Sullivan's four-round frolics, even if his fuller contests against Charley Mitchell (1883), Alf Greenfield (1884) and Paddy Ryan (1885) had all been subject to police interference. In New York, police interference and political interference were the same thing. The first two raids came during the reign of the Tammany Hall boss and city controller 'Honest' John Kelly. (The nickname was ironic, and his organisation Tammany Hall – the unofficial epithet for the New York County Democratic Party – was known best for political corruption.) The third incursion came during the even grosser era of Kelly's successor, Richard Croker, the notorious 'Boss Croker' (1843–1922). Croker was Irish (a prime local political requirement), had been a prizefighter himself and a gang leader prior to his political career. He, like most Tammany politicians, had found

Richard 'Boss' Croker (1843–1922), the corrupt Irish-American politician who ran New York's Tammany Hall and creamed fortunes from politics, brothels and gang warfare; in boxing nothing happened without his say-so.

Bain collection, Prints & Photographs Division, Library of Congress, LC-B2- 702-3

pugilistic connections an electoral asset. Before 1890, there was no secret ballot, and a few heavies who could canvass (i.e. intimidate) the electorate, and force timid voters to follow the party ticket, were invaluable. Kelly and Croker had no moral objection to boxing. They just wanted nothing to take place in Manhattan unless the right men got a piece of the action.

Close to New York was the pleasure resort of Coney Island – 'Sodom By the Sea' as its critics called it. Coney Island had the requisite attractions – a boardwalk, an aquarium, souvenir stalls, eating houses, a couple of racetracks, betting facilities and more than a dozen boxing clubs, including the Coney Island Athletic Club, founded 1892. The Democratic Party machine's Mr Big, John McKane, was, imaginatively, head of the town board, the health board, the water board *and* chief of police simultaneously. He had control of the Coney Island Athletic Club. When McKane was sweet, or sweetened, major contests were staged at the club.

In 15 months between 1892 and 1893, fights staged at the club took nearly a quarter of a million dollars at the box office. Purses were a more modest $75,000. A projected match-up between English Charley Mitchell and American James J. Corbett in the autumn of 1893 foundered only when the state politicians up in Albany got nervous about moral objections to boxing rocking the political agenda come election time. The more perspicacious politicians such as George Horton realised that the unregulated growth of dubious athletic clubs would do only gang bosses any favours in the future. His act aimed at encouraging American equivalents of London's NSC and discouraging less socially prestigious and less legitimate ones.

In practice his act provided a cover for many bouts for which the term 'sparring exhibition' was like calling the Battle of Gettysburg a family tiff. Territorial disputes between factions and rival clubs within New York Democratic circles having been temporarily resolved, the Coney Island Athletic Club looked to stage the bout most were eager to see – the 9 June 1899 return contest for the generally recognised heavyweight championship of the world between Bob 'Ruby Robert' Fitzsimmons, b. 26 May 1863 (one-time Cornishman, one-time New Zealander, one-time Australian and eventual American citizen), and James J. Jeffries, b. 15 April 1875 (one-time San Franciscan boilerman). Fitzsimmons had taken the title by knocking Corbett out in Carson City, Nevada in the 14th round on 17 March 1897.

For all his skill, and for all the shrill support of his wife at ringside, Fitzsimmons could not reasonably concede 12 years and 64 pounds to the very large 'Californian Grizzly'. He was counted out in the 11th. Despite the loss, Fitzsimmons made comebacks

Coney Island, 'Sodom By the Sea', offered every entertainment including professional boxing.

Bain collection, Prints & Photographs Division, Library of Congress, LC-B2- 702-3

17 March 1897 Nevada: Bob Fitszimmons knocks out James J. Corbett to become an unexpected and undersized heavyweight champion.

Bain collection, Prints & Photographs Division, Library of Congress, LC-USZ62-59410

over the following decade. Boxing in New York did not.

Like every heavyweight championship bout in history, every detail of the contest was discussed by the cognoscenti. Boxing's enemies animatedly discussed rather the legal context. The *New York Times* reported the fight in detail to boost its circulation, while calling elsewhere in the paper for a ban on boxing.

In 1899, the *New York Times* had a point. The Coney Island contest, which went far beyond Horton's permissiveness, had taken place with the corrupt New York Police Chief Devery giving as good an imitation of Pontius Pilate as was possible without a toga. He had even better reasons than Pilate to wash his hands. Devery – 'Big Bill' – was first among equals when it came to corrupt police chiefs. He and his pal, Frank Farrell – gambler, bookmaker and saloon-owner – lent their dubious services to the syndicate of another gangster, Boss Sullivan, so

loyally as to share generously in over *$3 million per annum* creamed off from prostitution, bribery and protection rackets. Devery retired from the police in 1903, and he and Farrell became owners of a modest little baseball club known as the New York Yankees, purchased from the dubious proceeds of their earlier careers. (They were at least more discreet than Police Captain Alexander 'Clubber' Williams, who commemorated his transfer to the lucrative mid-town 19th Precinct, a new job for which he paid a $15,000 bribe, with the blatant declaration, 'I've had nothin' but chuck steak for a long time, and now I'm going to get a little of the tenderloin!')

Early in 1900, M. E. Lewis, a Republican assemblyman, moved a bill to amend the New York penal code, section 458. By 2 April, he had succeeded. The section – the Horton Law – was repealed and replaced by a new Chapter 270, effective from 1 September 1900. The new section

repeated the Horton Law word for word, but then excised all the permitted qualifications about gloves, sparring and club buildings. In New York State, boxing was wholly illegal again.

The new version was approved and signed by the state's new Republican governor, the pugnacious Theodore Roosevelt (1858–1919), no mean amateur performer with the gloves while at Harvard. Like many godly advocates of muscular Christianity, he believed in a good punch to the nose. Why then would he endorse a measure to ban boxing? In fact, he had made his political reputation by breaking the corrupt links between the police and the criminal elements when he became the president of the board of the New York Police. The scale of the problem may be gathered from the damning report published on the New York Police Department by a New York Senate Committee just four months before Roosevelt took office:

Regular Appropriation	$5,139,147.64
Brothel Contributions	$8,120,000.00
Saloon Contributions	$1,820,000.00
Gambling-house Contr's	$165,000.00
Merchants, peddlers etc.	$50,000.00
New Members of Force	$60,000.00
Grand Total	**$15,354,147.64**

Some people thought boxers were criminal.

In signing the amended bill, Roosevelt confirmed his image as a corruption buster and man of moral stature and dished the Democratic Party machine. (The stance did him no harm politically – he was placed on the successful McKinley ticket as vice-president a few months later, and when McKinley was assassinated in 1901, he became the 26th President of the USA himself.)

Theodore Roosevelt (1856–1919), later the 26th President, was an enthusiastic amateur boxer but as President of the New York City Police campaigned vigorously against professional corruption.
Prints & Photographs Division, Library of Congress, LC-USZ62-41694

Where Assemblyman Lewis and Governor Roosevelt's political instincts were less sound was in failing to make New York boxing illegal *immediately*. The period of grace between the approval of the new law (2 April 1900) and its application (1 September 1900) stimulated a mushroom-like sprouting of seedy, unlicensed boxing clubs, plus a series of major promotions brought forward by the more established clubs, all before such activities became illegal. The Coney Island marathon at the Seaside Athletic Club between James J. Corbett and Jim Jeffries on 11 May 1900, when the large and ponderous Jeffries outlasted the speedy but ageing Corbett and knocked him out in the 23rd round, was a case in point. It represented one of boxing's most famous and dramatic reversals. Less well known is that it took place in the last few months of New York boxing's fading existence.

New York boxing did not disappear after September 1900. It resorted rather to an underground presence where unsupervised bouts, some gloved, some bare-fisted, some without limits and no legitimacy of results guaranteed, were held indoors and outdoors in out-of-the-way places before limited numbers of spectators in on the secret. Prohibition changed but did not halt the activity.

Rather, it thrust it into a seedy underworld of anarchy and confusion; it criminalised many guilty of nothing but a love of a particular pleasure. It fostered an environment where gangsters could provide, at inflated cost, a supply from which legitimate operators were banned.

There was a further parallel with the Prohibition era so misguidedly introduced to American life on 17 January 1920. Then the Anti-Saloon League predicted the new sobriety as 'an era of clear thinking and clean living'. In practice, the years after 1920 were notoriously the most alcoholic in American history. Indeed, for the 14 years after 1920, the USA suffered not temperance, but gang warfare, violence and political corruption. In the 14 years it took to rectify the error, in the speakeasies, dives and cellars normally law-abiding citizens drank illegally, sipping and listening out for police raids while mobsters flourished on the profits.

A lesson should have been learned from New York boxing, and Lewis's amendment to the Horton Law. In the 11 years after September 1900, boxing grew in popularity, checked only momentarily by the closure of many of the licensed athletic clubs that had been promoting fights. Boxing continued in a secret subterranean existence. For a New York boxer there were outlets. He could fight in backrooms outside the city limits or on barges tethered in the Hudson or East Rivers, financed by side stakes, betting and gate money. He could find remote locations in Long Island or New Jersey. He could find a private club staging bouts before a members' only audience, hoping the police would not interfere. Steven A. Reiss, who researched extensively New York boxing for the years 1896 to 1920, found that by 1905 about a dozen private clubs regularly staged three-round fights for members. Some of these clubs defined membership so loosely as to admit new 'members' on the basis of a single payment at the door on fight night. This 'illegal' entertainment was available almost nightly to a man who knew where to find it.

Better fighters looked for international competition and richer purses in places like Sydney, Paris and London, where they would be welcome. New York's temporary demise was London's and Paris's gain. This phenomenon increased popular demand for the reinstatement of proper professional boxing in New York. An American boxer's successes at, for example, Covent Garden's NSC or Paris's Cirque D'Hiver, and duly reported extensively in the *National Police Gazette* or even the *New York Times*, had readers asking the obvious question: I can read about him, why can't I see him for myself?

By 1906, promoters and clubs were using the membership device to stage boxing even at Madison Square Garden, and to appeal beyond the hardcore fans prepared to risk arrest to see a good match-up. In early 1906, there were well over a hundred arrests in connection with boxing. Precious few resulted in convictions. Even the New Yorkers who did not attend could read regular reports about boxing in their newspapers, and clubs proliferated. Many transcended the spit and sawdust category.

The National Sporting Club, a New York tribute to its London equivalent, was an exclusive institution founded in 1907. It included amongst its comfortable clientéle the millionaire philanthropist, James Buchanan Brady (1856–1917) – 'Diamond Jim' Brady – a man of gargantuan appetites for food and other pleasures, and the impresario Florenz Ziegfeld Jnr (1867–1932), who had just launched the long-legged lovelies of the Ziegfeld Follies on Broadway. A rival institution, the National Athletic Club (NAC), was even more prestigious socially and even more elegantly appointed. The new clubs had political clout to go with the Brady diamonds and the Ziegfeld glamour. Frank Farrell, owner of the Coney Island Club, ran the NSC. The NAC was beholden to Tim Sullivan, prominent Albany Democratic senator and a good friend of all those who agreed with him.

The hostile climate that had provoked Lewis's strict 1900 amendment of the original Horton Law was quietly changing. One dogged friend of boxing with political experience was the Democratic Senator James J. Frawley of Harlem (1867–1926), another Tammany Hall man. He pressed for more liberal laws for the sport and found himself pushing against a door that was opening gradually.

Frawley had unsuccessfully proposed new bills to cover both amateur and professional boxing in 1903–04. He had twice steered proposals through Assembly and Senate, only to have his initiatives vetoed by the Republican governor in April 1905 and again in 1907. That governor, Frank Higgins, was a determined opponent of boxing, undeterred by the favourable publicity surrounding the 1904 Olympics held in St Louis where American boxers had more or less monopolised the boxing medals. The USA had clinched gold, silver and bronze at featherweight; gold and silver at bantamweight; gold and silver at middleweight; and gold, silver and bronze at heavyweight. One American boxer, Oliver Kirk, won golds at feather *and* bantam.

Republican vetoes did not deter powerful Democratic Party bosses with boxing connections. The Fairmount Club in the Bronx promoted a much-anticipated bout in Manhattan in October 1908, one with ethnic connotations. The lightweight Leach Cross, who was Jewish, was matched against the Irish-American knockout specialist from Chicago, Packey McFarland. The meeting with McFarland at an arena on 137th Street drew 3,500 'members', including a heavy representation from the strongly Jewish Lower East Side.

The Police Commissioner decided that such blatant flouting of the law should not continue. Raids were made upon clubs electing 'members' on the door. Many clubs with rich and well-connected members were able to counter-punch against governors or commissioners interfering with their pleasures. By late 1908, the situation was farcical. The Fairmount AC was raided, probably as revenge for their cheek in successfully staging the Leach v McFarland contest. The club's retaliation was swift. On New Year's Eve 1908, the New York State Supreme Court granted an injunction to the Fairmount Club, restraining the police from entering the club premises without a warrant, and agreeing that the police had no right to interfere with private sparring, or with bouts conducted for the amusement of members.

On 4 January 1909, the police raided the Olympic Club. A fight was halted after two rounds. Both fighters were arrested, as was the referee. Two hundred well-heeled members suffered the indignity of being put out on the street on a chilly January night. A week later, the Olympic Club took out injunctions restraining the police from similar future actions and demanding $10,000 damages for the episode.

Just after the referee had halted a four-round exhibition between Joe Smith and Battling Sullivan, five armed officers arrested the ticket-taker at the door then burst into the auditorium to arrest the referee. They intended to arrest the boxers too, but the pair had wisely slipped away on hearing the commotion at the entrance. The members were less discreet. They took a spontaneous collective decision to expel the uniformed intruders forcibly. Faced with this unexpected resistance, one policeman panicked and fired his pistol into the crowd. That provoked a wholesale rush for the limited exits, the throwing of chairs at and by all and sundry, and further chaos when the fleeing members found that the police had covered all the exits including the roof. The police had also blockaded the street but that was partly to keep away casual spectators enjoying the free entertainment.

The members sullenly submitted to being lined up in the street and searched for weapons. Afterwards the police claimed that the club had provoked the raid by illegally selling tickets at the door. (Two plain-clothes policemen had obtained entrance by buying tickets.) The precipitate and dangerous police actions made the authorities look the guiltier party.

The temporary club membership device persisted over the next two years, if usually less blatantly. By 1911, approximately 30 New York clubs offered a weekly boxing evening. Raids continued. Yet even when police evidence looked overwhelming, they rarely led to convictions or closures. Despite the persistence of the authorities, New York, like London, was dealing with a sport whose popularity

Ad Wolgast (1888–1955). 'The Michigan Wildcat' was left with dementia after a series of savage beatings in the ring.

Bain collection, Prints & Photographs Division, Library of Congress, LC-DIG-ggbain-11250

Far from surrendering, the police were back in militant action on the night of 25 January 1909, this time at the Dry Dock Athletic Club on East 10th Street. The club had *already* taken out an injunction restraining

the police from interfering with their fights.

The police from the 17th Precinct ignored the order and conducted so heavy-handed an invasion that it provoked a riot.

could survive severe setbacks and a quasi-underground existence, and still capture the imagination of very many people.

Back in 1860, even *The Times* of London had been sufficiently sensitive to public interest as to print a blow-by-blow account of the illegal meeting of Sayers and Heenan. Similarly, the *New York Times* had vigorously editorialised against prizefights which 'put a stain upon [the city's] name' and condemned other newspapers for printing details about 'the repulsive features of these brutes and bruisers and their primal or inhuman instincts' (both quotations from June 1906). By 1911, the *New York Times* was giving round-by-round accounts of major fights in New York, London and elsewhere (e.g. Ad Wolgast v George Memsic in Los Angeles, March 1911). It also obligingly provided a bulletin board outside its offices where thousands of non-ticket-holders could gather for round-by-round news of sold-out bouts in Manhattan itself (e.g. Ad Wolgast v K. O. Brown, March 1911).

Newspaper editors are as swift as weather vanes to adjust to prevailing winds. Another body is even quicker – politicians. Senator Frawley, lone voice in the Albany Senate wilderness as a friend of boxing, gained support within his party for the legalisation of boxing in New York State. It helped that a Republican governor had been replaced by a Democratic hack, John A. Dix, and that both houses now boasted a Democratic majority. Frawley's bill, resubmitted in April 1911, became, with the approval of the governor, Chapter 779 of the Laws of New York, an 'Act establishing a State Athletic Commission and regulating boxing and sparring in the State of New York'.

This new legislation, popularly and rightly known as the Frawley Law, had two aims. It recognised boxing as a legitimate activity within the state. It found the activity worthy of regulation by a properly financed commission. The state governor appointed a commission of three expenses-paid commissioners and a salaried executive director for a five-year term. For its budget, the commission could collect five per cent of the gross ticket receipts from any promotion in the state. The commission had powers to issue subpoenas to witnesses, and to require those witnesses to give evidence under oath – 'subject to the same consequences and … subject to the same penalties as if … disobedience or false swearing occurred in an action in the supreme court'.

The new body could issue or revoke licences at its own exclusive discretion. Only boxing taking place under the commission's auspices would be legal henceforth. As Section Three of the act put it:

> The commission shall have, and hereby is vested with, the sole direction, management, and control of and jurisdiction over all boxing and sparring matches and exhibitions to be held or given within the state by any club, corporation or association; and no boxing or sparring match or exhibition shall be conducted, held or given within the state except pursuant to its authority and in accordance with the provisions of this act.

Its rights to inspect the books of bodies promoting fights could handicap crooked promoters. It could protect boxers and spectators by licensing only premises with adequate ventilation and proper fire escapes and exits. It provided proper penalties for the punishment of boxers involved in a fix: a six-month suspension for a first offence and a life ban for a second offence. It protected boxers' health by restricting contests to a maximum limit of ten rounds, and to gloves of at least eight ounces.

Admirable intentions do not always bring fully admirable results. Where this useful and imaginative act verging on municipal socialism in the heart of capitalism failed was in imposing the conditions of sparring exhibitions upon genuine contests. Sometimes a knockout blow would bring a decisive victory for one fighter before the ten-round 'spar' was completed. This possibility was completely ignored by the act as if it could not happen. The act also departed from reality by failing to acknowledge that the one question on everyone's lips following every sporting contest was this: who won?

By failing to provide a mandate for a referee, or a judge or judges, to pronounce upon that most cardinal of matters (the verdict), the Frawley Act undermined its own workings and created a vacuum. The vacuum would be filled by taking a consensus of the opinions of ringside pressmen – decision by newspaper. We shall see how open to corruption that was. Indeed, the act was actually repealed on 18 May 1917, within six years of its being passed. Its demise will fall in another chapter. First it is necessary to consider deeds within and without the ropes after Jack Johnson's victory over Tommy Burns in December 1908, with which we began.

CHAPTER 4
HALLS OF FAME AND SHAME
1909

In Which the NSC Takes Charge

IN THE early months of 1909, two British boxers were demonstrating their skills in the USA. Owen Moran, the current British featherweight champion, was at the National Athletic Club in New York on 29 January 1909 for a ten-round bout against the popular Harlem boxer, Tommy Murphy. Packed into the Athletic Club were boxing fans from Boston, New Jersey and Philadelphia alongside native New Yorkers, all eager to see if Moran was as good as claimed. Moran was given a surprisingly hospitable reception.

The background was unpromising. The 1908 Olympics recently held in London had seen ugly confrontations between American athletes – many of Irish descent – and the all-British

Owen Moran (1884–1949) of England and Abe Attell of the USA will need a giant referee in Jim Jeffries (1875–1953) to part them in their 1 January 1908 featherweight draw in Colma.
BoxRec

officials.[1] Halswell of Great Britain won the 400m track gold, but only after Carpenter, the American favourite, had been disqualified. The other American runners had withdrawn from the rerun race in protest. The marathon gold was awarded to John Hayes of the USA, on a controversial appeal. British officials escorted the first man home, the collapsing Dorando Pietri of Italy, helping him over the line just as Hayes, in second place, entered the new White City Stadium. Pietri was lauded in London as the 'real' winner and awarded a special silver cup by Queen Alexandra, thus robbing Hayes of the attention that belonged to the legitimate winner of the gold medal. (A little-known fact of athletics history is an epilogue. Pietri and Hayes were invited to rerun the marathon at Madison Square Garden in the autumn of 1908. The rerun, possibly the only marathon ever run *indoors in laps*, was attended by a sell-out crowd of Irish-Americans, come to cheer on Hayes, and Italian-Americans come to cheer on Pietri, who won by 60 yards in two hours, 44 minutes. The Tammany Hall boss Richard Croker fired the starting pistol.)[2]

Despite the previous Anglo-American misunderstandings, Moran (b. 4 October 1884) was granted a warm and sporting welcome. The tiny and spiky Moran was from Birmingham, of Irish immigrant stock, and as notoriously eager to fight outside the ring as furiously as in it. As one American sportswriter had written: 'That guy isn't British. He's an American. No Britisher ever fought like that.'[3] British Moran certainly was and determined to trounce all foreigners on principle. Foreigners, to him, were all who did not come from Birmingham.

His behaviour followed a discernible pattern. He would meet people and charm them with his impeccable courtesy. Then he drank. As the drink took hold, a fiery Irishman fulfilling every stereotype of the 'Foighting Oirish' replaced the genteel Midlander. He once attacked a whole troop of American soldiers just for the hell of it – and got beaten up as a result. One American correspondent ruefully recorded, half-admiringly: 'There will be many who will disbelieve the fact that the little Englishman was probably the heaviest drinker of his weight in the world. He

Abe Attell (1883–1970) 'The Little Hebrew': Attell's crafty ring deceptions were paralleled outside the arena. He helped bribe the Chicago White Sox to lose the 1919 World Series.
Bain collection, Prints & Photographs Division, Library of Congress, LC-DIG-ggbain-08235

certainly drank more in proportion than old John L. [Sullivan].'

Drink was the fuel behind a 1913 incident when Moran overheard the South African heavyweight George Rodel boasting of his intentions to put Moran's pal Jess Willard out of action in their coming return fight. Moran's objections were so piquantly expressed that only interventions by others prevented a Rodel v Moran fight breaking out on the spot. This feather v heavy street fight might have been a livelier encounter than any of the Willard v Rodel fights in 1913 and 1914.[4] (Willard knocked out Rodel in six in Atlanta on 28 April 1914 and previously in New Haven in nine on 29 December 1913; twin revenges for a boring ten rounds in Milwaukee on 17 November 1913 awarded to Rodel on newspaper opinions.)

Almost exactly a year before his 1909 match against Tommy Murphy, Moran spent New Year's Day 1908 in San Francisco pounding and being pounded by the American featherweight Abe Attell, 5ft 4in to Moran's 5ft 3in, for 25 rounds. Moran the Catholic and Attell the Jew, neither eirenic members of their faiths, conducted an unedifying theological disputation before the first bell. Moran came in two ounces over the 8st 4lb limit. Under the terms of their contract, he had to give $250 compensation to Attell. The payment was made but accompanied by unpleasant anti-Semitic remarks about Jews, pounds of flesh and the like. Attell replied with unworthy slurs about thick Micks who could not tell the time let alone read the scales.

The dialogue set the pattern for the fight. A 25-round bout means 75 minutes of action, yet even after 75 minutes and the final bell, the giant referee Jim Jeffries had forcibly to part them. Jeffries called it a draw. By most accounts it was a fair result. The scoring punches cancelled each other out, as did

the frequent blows delivered after the bell by Attell (duly hissed by the fair-minded American audience), which matched the illegal holding indulged in by Moran. Attell, years later, thought this the hardest of the five fights he had with Moran ('the toughest, meanest rat in the business') during their careers:

> In the first round he grabbed my Adam's apple … He choked me and I couldn't swallow … I called him a Limey so-and-so and told him if he choked me again I was going to bite off his nose … [so in the third] … I jumped off the ground, shoved my head against his and clamped my upper teeth down hard on the bridge of his nose …[5]

After this piece of dental infighting, Moran looked up, a long way up, at the 6ft 2½in referee and complained. Jeffries was unmoved. 'Bite him back!' he said. Jeffries knew the only ring language that Attell understood.

Moran's present opponent, Tommy Murphy, would later engage Abe Attell in another sanguinary 20-round draw at Daly City, California on 3 August 1912, and we will see Attell in other contests later. Moran faced Murphy on 29 January 1909, and the result was an altogether more cultivated spectacle – 'the prettiest and most scientific bout of the Winter in New York'.[6] Moran could touch the heights as well as the depths. Against Murphy, Moran was the more experienced, but Murphy boxed with the dedication and hunger of an up-and-coming featherweight given his best chance so far. When blows were exchanged after the bell for the end of the fifth round, there was no evil intent, merely two men so engaged that neither

registered the sound of the bell above the noise of the crowd.

Moran kept the fight at a comfortable distance, using his jab and ducking and sidestepping the attack-minded Murphy. Sometimes this worked very effectively. Two lefts in the second stopped Murphy in his tracks, and another in the fifth drew blood from Murphy's right eyebrow. Other times Murphy got in close and, in the eighth, dropped Moran to his knees with a flurry of hooks to the body, capped with a couple of uppercuts to the jaw. Ultimately, the Englishman deserved to win the newspaper decision because he had absorbed everything Murphy gave him and replied in kind. Moran indeed got the post-mortem print award, but on the night the whole audience stood and cheered both men through the tenth and mandatory last round. They stood toe to toe for three minutes and swapped hefty punches without flinching or retreating.

The *New York Times*'s boxing correspondent had to admit, in less than a fortnight, that his previous nomination, 'the prettiest scientific boxing bout that New York has seen in months', belonged not to Moran v Murphy, but to the even better Leach Cross v Jim Driscoll.[7] This Welsh-American contest topped the Anglo-American clash 13 days before. Cross v Driscoll, on 10 February 1909, was one of the most anticipated fights ever seen at New York's Fairmount Club – every member of the club wanted to see it, as did every non-member and guest. The result was an administrator's nightmare. Inside the club before the ten-round catchweight contest (Driscoll a trim 9st/126lbs and Cross estimated to be 12 pounds heavier), there were no less than 3,000 people. They stood in the aisles, they stood on the chairs and even on each other to glimpse the ring. Outside the club, held at bay by 150 of New York's finest, were another 3,000 people stretching back three city blocks, many of them waving membership cards or guest tickets or crisp green dollar bills or prayer cards, and all beseeching the cops to let them through to claim a seat. Remarkably, violent action confined itself only to the roped square.

Within that square, the event, delayed by the crowd confusion, and by Cross's successful request to have a second layer of bandages removed from Driscoll's fists, would be quite as fast, furious and exhilaratingly skilful as anticipated. No less was expected from either man.

'Jem' Driscoll, as he was often called in the USA, was a long way from his Cardiff home. Born 15 December 1880, he came out of a background with which the New York Irish policemen in the streets outside would have readily identified. He was Welsh by his Cardiff birth and Irish by parentage, his parents having settled in the fast-growing docks area of Cardiff, where the precious coal dug out of the Welsh mining valleys was loaded and shipped off to fuel the factories and engines of the world. The coal brought real prosperity to pit owners and to owners of land with mineral or docking rights; precious little to the miners and dockers who had to put their blue-scarred hands on the dark stuff.

The Driscolls were recent arrivals in a few predominantly Irish streets in the multi-ethnic melting pot of Cardiff's squalid Butetown. Though sociologists of a compassionate nature romanticise shared misery as a binding communal cement in proletarian solidarity, the depressing truth is that the deepest hostility to a new immigrant group comes from those most recently *in situ,* and little better off themselves. The Irish and their fellow Celts in Cardiff shared anti-English feelings yet mutual brotherly love was rarer. Butetown, named after the 2nd Marquess of Bute (1793–1848), was inherited in 1848 by his son, the 3rd Marquess, John Patrick Crichton-Stuart (1847–1900), who converted his millions of pounds of coal royalties into the nearby Victorian Gothic fantasies of Cardiff Castle and Castell Coch, magical fairyland interiors in the strongest possible contrast to the mean terrace dwelling that housed the six members of the Driscoll family.

The six Driscolls depended wholly upon the miserable wages earned by Jim's father as a railwayman in a docks railway goods yard. It got worse. When Jim was a mere six months old, his father Cornelius was killed aged 25 in a work accident. Six Driscolls were suddenly five, and the wages down to nothing. Adequate compensation for an industrial mishap was as removed from reality as one of Bute's fantasy ceilings. State provision was a wild idea fostered by fringe radical groups. All there was for a bereft widow like Mrs Driscoll was an arbitrary charity handout from the parish.

Just how arbitrary was shown when her original allowance of six shillings a week for the entire family was cut to four shillings in case her sterling efforts to feed and clothe Jim and his siblings disguised earnings on the side that the parish guardians had failed to trace. The guardians were usually Anglicans. Mrs Driscoll was a devout Roman Catholic.

Successful boxers could cash in with endorsements and advertisements like cigarette cards.
WF Images/Alamy Stock Photo

Underlying the religious prejudice may also have been racial intolerance as the Driscolls came of Irish travellers' stock.

Adequately to raise her brood, she undertook hard manual labour in the docks herself.[8] Her ambitions for Jim got him through a rudimentary schooling in Cardiff and into a job in the composing room of a Cardiff evening newspaper – a cut above the pit, the docks or the railways. However, this was a young apprentice with two extraordinary attributes: the fastest of hands standing him in good stead in street fights and an elasticity of neck and torso that made his head as elusive as a dancing unswattable gnat. In the print shop, he would stand on a sheet of newspaper and sway, bob and weave out of the way of his workmates' punches without moving his feet off the paper.[9]

These attributes led him successively to a local boxing booth, where he became a strong attraction, and inevitably into the professional ring by 1901. This was hardly the white-collar career for which his mother had hoped, but an excellent apprenticeship for a trade where to hit and not be hit were strong qualifications.

In the Fairmount Club on 10 February 1909, the slim, dark, tousle-haired, long-limbed featherweight, 5ft 6ins in his stockinged feet, had to use all his natural elusiveness just to get to the ring. Now 27 years of age, his skin showed some scar tissue and his once shapely ears cauliflower-like damage. He was a man on a mission.

He was in the USA, as Jack Johnson had been in Australia, to win fights over enough known opponents to shame a champion into giving him a match. In Driscoll's case, the target was the current American and world champion, the crafty Abe Attell. Driscoll was nine days away from a joust with Attell. (Fighters in the early 20th century showed productivity beyond the dreams of the manager of a Soviet Five-Year Plan.) Unless knocked out, Attell was guaranteed to retain his title as the law restrained fights to the ten-round maximum and the bout was not for the championship. Nevertheless, a demonstration by Driscoll of his superiority over Attell would create a demand for a future real championship match whenever and wherever that could be arranged.

Driscoll could not afford to be thinking about Attell, or nine days into the future. He had first to deal with the very real threat of Leach Cross in the opposite corner. The much-loved Cross had all the ring deviousness of Attell, without the malice, and a ready one-liner for all occasions, including defeat. 'Did I quit? Down 36 times and you ask that? If I quit I certainly took one helluva time making up my mind.'[10]

Cross was born Louis Charles Wallach, 12 February 1886, in New York's Lower East Side to Viennese Jewish immigrant parents. He strongly identified with his local heavily Jewish precinct. Like many others, he had taken full advantage of the social, economic and educational opportunities the USA had offered. 'Give me your tired, your

Leach Cross (1886–1957): the popular New York Jewish lightweight who combined boxing, dentistry and a ready wit.

Bain Collection, Prints & Photographs Division, Library of Congress, LC-DIG-ggbain-10655

poor,/Your huddled masses yearning to breathe free,' said Emma Lazarus in the verse inscribed on the Statue of Liberty. Taking her at her word, poor families such as the Wallachs had come, worked hard, prospered, breathed free and sent their children to college. Driscoll's opponent was a graduate of New York University and a fully qualified dentist practising in the Bronx. (His Lower East Side supporters joked that Cross could extract teeth the hard way in the ring, or the easy way in his surgery. Indeed he once loosened K. O. Brown's teeth in the ring and obligingly repaired the damage in his surgery the next day.)

Cross had adopted his ring name originally to conceal his boxing activities from his Orthodox father. When his ring earnings began to top his fees from dentistry, his father gave in and approved: 'I would have to yank all the teeth in the Bronx and put in crockery to make that much in a year!'

Conventionally, Cross stooped into a crouch, gloves up before his face as he advanced on an opponent, throwing swings, crosses and uppercuts from unusual angles, punches hard enough to finish 25 of his 43 victims by knockout. He adopted the same general tactics against Driscoll. He crouched, he threw swings, he crossed viciously with lefts and rights, and he brought up some savage uppercuts from the level of his boots. Unfortunately, most of his efforts landed only on the space Driscoll had vacated a mini-second before. Meanwhile, out of the newly occupied space, came counter-punches that landed firmly on Cross's face and ribcage.[11]

After three rounds of misses, without Driscoll needing even to block or parry his punches, Cross resorted to the straight left. Sometimes he succeeded in landing it, which was a distinct improvement, but he was landing it only on a target already receding away from him, thus taking the sting from the delivery. Only in the eighth did Cross land some real punches, but that was when Driscoll had slipped to his knees in a corner. Cross was barracked for the foul – another example of a New York audience expecting fair play for a visitor. The last two rounds were as one-sided as the others. In the ninth, Driscoll hit Cross as hard and often as he wished, leaving Cross staggering around the ropes at the bell. He recovered in the interval and rushed at Driscoll at the beginning of the tenth. The flurry was temporary, and normal service resumed with 'Driscoll landing blows wherever he directed them, and Cross, exhausted, swinging feebly and wildly at him'.

There was no decision, of course, but the journalists agreed the spoils were Driscoll's. Driscoll had had first and last blows. Cross, as usual, had the last word. He visited Driscoll in his dressing room where Driscoll lay on the massage table and tapped the Welshman on the chest with his fist: 'There,' he said, 'don't let anyone say that Leach Cross never hit Jim Driscoll.'

Nine days later on 19 February 1909 it was Driscoll v Attell at the New York Athletic Club, and the *New York Times*'s reporter had to revise his stock phrase again: 'The two cleverest featherweight boxers in the world … fought ten rounds of the prettiest and fastest sparring that any match has offered *in years* …'[12] [Italics added.] And so it was. They weighed in at 8st 13lbs/125lbs each at 6pm and, with every available seat in the club taken, took the ring to the relief of the spectators unsure whether the police might intervene. In fact, a local inspector, at the police commissioner's bidding, had *already* tried to stop the bout. He had spent that very afternoon in front of a magistrate pleading for a warrant to arrest Driscoll and Attell and the club officials. The magistrate, on the advice of the assistant district attorney (did they both have tickets, one wonders?), declared the evidence insufficient to justify a warrant. This was another battle won in the continuing war between the New York police and boxing.

This was pretty satisfying, if not as sweet as the Fairmount Athletic Club's further coup on 24 April 1909. Then, the police tried to circumvent a magistrate's order that the evening's bouts, including Young Corbett v Bert Keyes, constituted a perfectly legitimate activity. The club had the satisfaction of physically ejecting, one by one, a squad of plain-clothed policemen, who had infiltrated the club to stop the bout, but were unable to produce membership cards.

With the exception of some mutual holding and clinching from Attell and Driscoll, glad to grab some respite from otherwise continuous action, their contest was surprisingly clean; Attell was on his best behaviour. He was also at his cleverest, leading and countering with crisp, accurate punches, and blocking the snake-like jabs from Driscoll that any lesser fighter would not have seen, let alone countered. Attell's problem was that for all his guile and wit, Driscoll had more of both qualities.

The scenario was prefigured by the pattern of the first round. A tentative left from Driscoll fell short, so Attell landed to the body and crowded Driscoll to the ropes. Yet as he launched two swinging punches at Driscoll's ribs, Driscoll sidestepped, and Attell's gloves whipped harmlessly into thin air beyond the ropes. He had the good grace to grin at a manoeuvre he himself had often worked on others, although the smile vanished when Driscoll's left glove buffed up his temporarily exposed front teeth.

The second round was more even. Driscoll got in another left to Attell's mouth and three more to the face. Attell still scraped the round with his own lefts and rights to the head and a couple of wince-inducing leads to the veteran's solar plexus. From the third to the fifth rounds, Driscoll took charge, staggering Attell with right hooks to the jaw and following up with stiff lefts in the third and fourth. When Attell rushed in, Driscoll executed elegant little feints and planted a few painful punches into Attell's flanks as the little man rushed past him. (Kidney punches were legal and acceptable in 1909.)

Attell's right eye began to swell, was actually cut by a left in the fourth and sustained further damage in the fifth. But Attell had not won general recognition as a world champion without riding out adversity. Even in a no-decision ten-rounder, he was not going easily.

He took the sixth and seventh himself. Driscoll landed some more hooks to the kidneys but had to suffer a teeth-rattling uppercut at the end of the seventh when the referee separated the men from a clinch. Attell was repaid in kind with a Driscoll uppercut on the break in the eighth. With both of them landing so many punches, the eighth was too close to call.

With only two more rounds allowed, Driscoll could have been no more than one round in front. He could claim a strong psychological advantage in the rounds he had won. He had often landed two blows for Attell's one and made one of the most skilful boxers of the century look sometimes wild. In the ninth and tenth, Driscoll confirmed his superiority. Said one American writer, Driscoll 'went faster than a $20 bill'.

The ninth ended in a reciprocal flurry of body blows, but Driscoll's left had visited Attell's face painfully and often and set up the range for substantial rights to follow. Attell tried even harder in the tenth despite some heavy body blows at close quarters, and Driscoll's sharp lefts in his face whenever he kept his distance. He had fought his best, he had been beaten and everyone knew it, the no-decision fig leaf notwithstanding. Looking out of his one good eye, he knew that, and he, the shrewdest of punters, would not have put his money on retaining his championship against Driscoll in a return.

Attell being Attell, he did not continue to see it this way. In conversation with an American journalist in 1950, he claimed to have lost deliberately. He gave three reasons: he was boosting the odds for a $20,000 bet on himself to win in the return; he and his promoter Jim Coffroth had arranged the result in advance to their financial advantage; he had been intimidated by the Tammany Hall big shots at ringside who had backed Driscoll. As the claims were made 40 years after the event, Attell was deceiving himself. After all, he spent most of his life deceiving everyone else. Indeed, he played a major role

in 1919 in one of the most depressing episodes in the history of sport – the taking of bribes by the Chicago White Sox baseball team to throw that year's World Series. By that time, the retired Attell was on the payroll of a big gambler/mobster and profiting from his skills in deception outside the ring.

When Driscoll's American campaign culminated in his outstanding wins over Cross and Attell, the Welshman made a self-sacrificing decision that showed not all boxers were like Attell and prepared to do anything for money. He had promised to make a personal appearance at a Cardiff Catholic orphanage, Nazareth House, on St David's Day 1909 (1 March). He sailed for home and broke off negotiations for a return with Attell. 'I gave the Sisters of Nazareth House my promise that I would appear there on St David's Day, and I never break a promise.'[13] Unlike many who find rich pickings in the ring a balm to soothe memories of a poverty-stricken childhood, Driscoll never forgot who he was or where he came from.

He was the most open-hearted and open-handed of men, and many among the Cardiff poor had occasion to bless him in the future. Had his patronage not extended to swelling the funds of turf accountants by investing generously in losing favourites, still more would have gone in that direction. Back in Cardiff, he fulfilled his promise, and took many fellow pugilists along with him, raising over £6,000 for the nuns. To his embarrassment, he was chaired and cheered through the streets. The nuns presented him with an illuminated address as some compensation for the championship belt he might otherwise have brought home:

The Jews' Free School on Middlesex Street in London's East End in the early 1900s. It produced many young boxers and many fans at halls like Wonderland.

Lebrecht Music & Arts/Alamy Stock Photo

We can never forget, sir, how in the very zenith of your success, when fame of your prowess was on every tongue, you generously sacrificed pecuniary advantage and undertook a voyage of some thousands of miles in order to fulfil your promise of assisting Nazareth House.

Our earnest prayers are that He who never forgets a service done in His name, who promises a reward to those who aid even the least of His little ones, may grant you all the temporal blessings in this world and an imperishable, glorious reward hereafter.[14]

Historians lack evidence to speak of rewards in the afterlife, but tragically, Driscoll's temporal blessings were all too briefly enjoyed. He and the wife he married in June 1907 (b. Edie Wiltshire in c.1880) ran a public house, The Duke of Edinburgh, in Ellen Street in the Newtown area of Cardiff in his retirement. But at 4.25am on Friday, 30

January 1925, the 44-year-old Driscoll died there. He had contracted TB in 1919 and suffered further complications arising from a recurrence of stomach ulcers for which he had undergone a major operation in the spring of 1920. From all over the world, condolences and tributes poured in to Cardiff, including a sympathetic telegram from the touring New Zealand All Blacks rugby team as they departed from Wales for Canada.

On 3 February 1925, the streets of Cardiff saw a funeral to match a state or royal occasion, as many thousands of Welsh people bared their heads in the February gloom as one of the greatest ringcraftsmen the world had ever seen was escorted to his grave. The cortège carrying his coffin, draped with a Union Jack and topped with a floral bouquet, was escorted by a contingent of soldiers from the second battalion of the Welch Regiment bearing reversed arms, their rifle butts sticking up like ring posts. In honour of Driscoll's army service in the First World War as a boxing/

PT instructor, this was a military as well as civic funeral. At the back of the carriage was a large floral wreath formed around a giant boxing glove, courtesy of the Welsh Amateur Boxing Association – snobbish distinctions between gentlemen and professionals discreetly shelved in the solemnity of the occasion. Behind the soldiers, and behind a silver band playing the 'Dead March' from *Saul*, came a long line of mourners stretching from Custom House Street to Kingsway. The mourners covered all social classes from miners and labourers to businessmen and city dignitaries: boxers such as Johnny Basham and Owen Moran walking alongside priests and publicans. Spectators meanwhile lined the elegant St Mary Street six deep on either side and marvelled. No one had to ask whose funeral it was – Driscoll and boxing were by the 1920s universally recognised, a phenomenon in which Driscoll had played a major role.[15]

To return to 1909; while some of Britain's best boxers like Driscoll and Moran ventured across the Atlantic, the majority were content with domestic opponents and domestic purses. However, that British scene in 1909, still an activity of borderline criminality, was as rich and varied as could be imagined and is worth capturing in detail. Nothing on the statute book could ultimately protect the sport against an enthusiastic police chief or a strait-laced magistrate attempting local action against it. The Old Bailey decision of June 1901 (see Chapter 2) was a great relief to the men involved in British boxing; it was a long way from blanket exoneration. (Similarly, the raid on the Dry Dock Athletic Club in New York on 25 January 1909 – see Chapter

3 – left no room for complacency there either.)

There was a significant new factor. More and more people cared about big fights. More and more people were opening their newspapers, including the more prestigious ones like *The Times* and *Daily Telegraph*, and expecting to read about boxing and boxers. Typically, *The Times* of 28 December 1908 gave a 14-inch column to the Johnson v Burns encounter, including a round-by-round summary, and followed over the next few days with post-fight reports on the boxers, their physical condition, the takings and the like.[16] Furthermore, more people were attending boxing promotions in their own locality and creating a demand from which local promoters could make a profit.

The press, especially a national and local press that had as yet no radio or television or internet rivals, did not create this growing enthusiasm. Neither were canny promoters bamboozling ignorant and unsophisticated audiences. Surprised by the new fervour of the English masses and classes, the press barons and impresarios were not slow to respond accordingly.

The ancestor of today's long-standing and indispensable trade paper *Boxing News*, was the weekly journal *Boxing*, costing originally one penny and published every Thursday. It was well-written, carrying enthusiastic reports and knowledgeable features about boxing nationally and internationally, and excellently illustrated with black-and-white portraits, action photographs and lively cartoons and caricatures. It even carried occasional colour prints of contemporary boxers. Its first issue was dated 11 September 1909. The circulation of this imaginative

publication is not known, but it switched its publication day to Wednesday and then to Tuesday later on so as to bring reports of weekend bouts more promptly to its eager readers.

Hardly had the timekeeper rung the opening bell for *Boxing*, with its masthead boast 'The only Paper in the World solely devoted to Boxing', than it had a competent rival in the *Boxing World and Athletic Chronicle*, a similar weekly, one costing only a halfpenny and also out on the station bookstalls. The new weekly asserted:

> At no period in the fistic history of this kingdom has such a deep and universal interest been taken in the grand old sport, and almost every hamlet in the country can boast of a champion of more or less (generally less) prowess.[17]

The growing enthusiasm for seeing live boxing is proved also by the significant number of arenas and halls built or adapted for boxing over 1909. On Thursday, 2 September 1909, a new St James' Hall, Newcastle (later hosting a legion of significant fights in the north-east area) opened its doors. It could hold 3,000 people. Its first bill included a mini-classic between the elusive Tom Lancaster and the man with but one gear (forward), Young Johnson. Happily, unlike the baying crowds of Sydney's Rushcutters Bay stadium, the crowd was indifferent to the fact that, like his senior counterpart, Young Johnson was black.[18]

The growing French public was similarly disinclined to discriminate. As *Boxing World*'s Parisian correspondent put it, and full credit to him: 'For the life of me, I can't see how a man can call

himself a champion if he refuses to meet another boxer, whose skin, through an accident of birth, happens to be black.'[19]

The 27 November 1909 issue featured two black boxers (George Gunther of Australia and Hazel Fischer of South Africa) on its cover, so the magazine hardly thought of its domestic readers as white racists or English xenophobes.

Another upbeat message about boxing, and the new participation, came from *Boxing*'s Welsh correspondent from the South Wales valleys. A syndicate in Mountain Ash was putting up purses rich enough to attract good boxers to its local bills in Mountain Ash, Caerphilly and Pontypridd; this in the teeth of opposition from local Nonconformist chapel-goers, who hated boxing and demonstrated and prayed outside the halls in protest on boxing nights.

In London, other new ventures were launched. On the London Road next to the Elephant and Castle, W. F. Hurndall, the 'Dance King' impresario, opened, also in September 1909, the King's Hall, which held 2,000 people and featured 2,000 multicoloured electric light bulbs. This 'Palace of 2,000 Lights' was 'not only beautiful but in the best possible taste', and comfortably seated its clientéle at prices of 5s., 3s., 2s., and 1s., prices for which everyone was guaranteed a clear view of the ring for seven six-round bouts, one ten-rounder and a 126lbs competition involving *another seven bouts*. This is exemplary value for money and a luxurious indicator of boxing's cultural progress.[20]

New premises such as the King's Hall were being added to a large number of existing ones also staging boxing. In London in December 1909 alone, boxing could be seen also in the long-established Wonderland in Whitechapel Road; the Arena, Villiers Street; the National Sporting Club, Covent Garden; the Lambeth School of Arms; the Queen's Palace, Poplar; the South London Palace; the Myddleton Hall, Islington; the Forester's Music Hall, Mile End; the West End School of Arms, Marylebone Road; the Hackney Baths; the Euston Theatre; the Paragon Music Hall; the Canterbury Music Hall, Westminster Bridge Road; the Brixton Empress Theatre; and in the Olympia Theatre, Shoreditch. These venues do not feature in an official census; they are merely gleaned from advertisements and reports in the boxing papers. Not included are the many swimming baths and public houses accustomed to hold evenings of amateur or semi-professional boxing, or even some already famous venues.

British towns and villages from Brighouse to Market Drayton, or from Plymouth to Ipswich, could have told a similar story. These local audiences were not necessarily all male. Jack Goldswain (the Bermondsey lightweight and British champion from 1906–08) participated in a week-long Christmas boxing entertainment at the Canterbury Music Hall. The entertainment mixed an elimination competition with an exhibition spar featuring Goldswain and a different partner every day. It was said 'the bouts have been of the keenest, and have been thoroughly enjoyed by the whole audience; *in fact, the ladies seemed even more enthusiastic than the gentlemen present*'[21] [Italics added].

The infiltration of the music hall and even legitimate theatre by boxers, boxing and boxing-related activities had been going on for many years and had helped prepare boxing's latest expansion. John L. Sullivan had toured in the 1880s with jugglers, wrestlers and clowns.[22] James J. Corbett went from pounding Sullivan to pounding the boards in a play called *Gentleman Jack*, its plot deliberately devised to exploit Corbett's ring prowess and reputation. Corbett had previously appeared in a similar effort called *Sports Macallister* and came to find money more easily earned in mock fights than real ones.[23] Jim Jeffries also exchanged ring for stage in two crude theatre vehicles, *Eighty Minutes in New York* and *The Man from the West*, in 1899 and 1900, before going on tour eponymously as *Davy Crockett* – ring hero turned folk hero.[24] Theatre critics were not over-respectful of these dramatic invasions. What boxers and critics jointly failed to realise was that they were following a tradition that stretched back to the glory days of prizefighting. For example, the *General Evening Post*, an 18th century journal, was in December 1788 just as sniffy as any 20th century newspaper when Mendoza's rival Richard Humphreys 'The Gentleman Boxer' (c.1760–1799) dared to appear on the stage:

> … last Tuesday night, Humphreys, the celebrated bruiser, made his appearance at this Theatre in the Pantomime – He *sparred* for some minutes with Death, who is we understand, another practitioner of the same business. The usual term 'profession' we shall not in this instance apply.
>
> The combat, which was carried on with great dexterity, was received with a loud applause,

mixed in an inferior degree with disapprobation.

> We are not critics so squeamish, we confess, as wholly to condemn an exhibition of this nature. It is the duty of the manager to watch even the wildest of vicissitudes … The present is one of the new-blown bubbles of the day, and he has therefore introduced it in its proper place – a Pantomime.

A trawl through the music hall files in the old Theatre Museum (National Museum of the Performing Arts) in Covent Garden supplied many references to this continuing tradition, for example, the Oxford Music Hall in London's Oxford Street – 'The Brothers Horne in their Boxing Sketch' (18 March 1893); 'Harvey Boys … in their Boxing Act' (4 September 1897); 'Boxing Bantams' (14 August 1899). Also, the Canterbury Theatre of Varieties – 'The unprecedently Popular Production … THE FIGHTING PARSON by GEORGE GRAY & Powerful Company' (18 May 1903). The Brothers Horne were regulars at the Holborn Empire, later a major venue for professional boxing. The Empire, given a major refit in 1906, and holding 2,000 people, played a substantial role in fostering boxing's growing popularity. Its bills offered an eclectic mixture of entertainment at very modest prices; prices as low as 4d. for the balcony, 6d. for a pit stall, and, luxury of luxuries, 1s. 6d. for a front stall or grand circle seat.

In return for the minimal investment, the bill of fare on Monday, 8 August 1908 presented a heady mixture of sex and violence. Miss Irma Lorraine presented 'a series of exquisite Tableaux; also AN IDYLL OF SUMMER, Langorously Voluptious [sic] SALOME FASCINATING HEROD. THE VISION OF FAITH, from despair to salvation. Being an effort to present in an original manner a few impressions of various emotions.'

Whatever her charms and emotions, Miss Lorraine was a long way from the top of the bill. That particular spot, and by definition the main attraction, belonged to the man dubbed 'by the ENTIRE Press of America as the Greatest Coloured Fighting Machine in the World'.[25]

With an élan that exuberant boxing promoters of later days such as Jack Solomons or Don King might have envied, the management of the Holborn Empire was presenting in the flesh the top personalities of the ring including:

The Heavyweight Champion
of the World
the man they all dodge!!
JACK JOHNSON
(of America)
The Greatest Fighter the
world has known
The man that Tommy Burns
won't fight
Unless they guarantee him £6000.
JACK JOHNSON IS A FIGHTER
NOT A SHOWMAN.

During his engagement here
he will spar with the best men
in England. Pictures of the
World's Greatest Fighters will
be shown on the Bioscope at
every performance. JOHNSON
is open to fight any man in
the World and £1000 is at the
National Sporting Club for a
real match.

Here was Johnson in person sparring in front of men and women who might never have ventured into a boxing hall, and who in a pre-radio, pre-television era, could normally only read about Johnson, his fighting qualities and his headline-catching activities outside boxing. Johnson's physical charms for women, and some men, were quite as 'Langorously Voluptious' as those of Miss Lorraine.

Johnson was not the only pugilist illuminated by the Holborn Empire footlights. Boxers might crop up in the most unlikely of contexts. At the Empire for the week commencing Monday, 5 April 1909 (twice nightly at 6.20pm and 9.10pm, and at 2.30pm matinees on Thursdays and Saturdays) the top attraction was the latest hybrid offering devised by Fred Karno. Karno (1866–1941), the English impresario who invented the custard pie in the face routine, had launched the career of many comedians, including Charlie Chaplin.

His latest sketch for Holborn was entitled *The Yap Yaps* and featured at least 25 actors and dancers – 'in addition … the World-renowned Masters of the Fistical Art have been specially secured at an enormous expense, and will give an exhibition of the noble art of self-defence at every performance'. The two lucky fighters engaged at such 'enormous expense' were the popular Alf Reed (b. 31 October 1883), one-time holder of an unofficial British featherweight championship belt, and Johnny Summers (b. 21 January 1883), billed as the lightweight champion of the world. Summers was not actually world champion, and never would be, but he was only months away from an 8 November 1909 clash at the NSC with Freddie Welsh (of whom much later).

Welsh did become world lightweight champion five years later. Summers had recently beaten tough American opponent Jimmy Britt twice, once on points and once on a knockout, and was also very popular with London audiences.

The Yap-Yaps sketch climaxed with a 'Fight to a Finish' between its hero (The Hon. Charlie Chinn, the Yap Yap) and the villain (Ben Burley, alias 'Big Ben' the bruiser). Bookmakers wisely took no bets on the outcome. The Chinn-Burley denouement (Scene 3: Inside the [National Sporting] Club) took place after Summers and Read had sparred for the audience.[26] Fred Karno will have taught the two genuine boxers how to 'stage' a fight – plenty of loud open-glove slapping with a maximum of noise and a minimum of pain – methods one hopes they forgot when next in a real contest. Neither would they have benefited greatly in their regular profession from Karno's advice to knockabout comedians: 'When in doubt, fall on your arse.'

Posing, flexing the muscles, sparring, shadow-boxing, speaking a few stilted lines – what else could a fighter do to entertain a music hall audience? Fortunately, these basics were quite sufficient to attract and hold an eager audience. Shrewd theatre impresarios such as Jack Callaghan and George Edwardes at the Empire did not feature a Jack Johnson or a Johnny Summers because they wished to make boxers and boxing more widely known, or to foster an interest to make other men profits. They hired contemporary fighters, even expensively, because the fighters were *already* popular, and brought boxing fans into the house along with the curious.

Indeed, in the 1908–11 period, it became a paying proposition to add boxing to the Empire's other offerings, with another matinee – a Monday 2pm matinee boxing show. On 27 December 1910, for example, top of the bill was a 20-round catchweight contest between two decent middleweights, Arthur Harman (Lambeth) and Private J. W. Harris (Coldstream Guards) and the undercard offered another six contests, the whole bill available for prices from 1s. to 5s. The previous month, 21 November 1910, there had been a substantial undercard supporting the Bioscope film direct from the NSC, of the 14 November 1910 middleweight clash between Jim Sullivan of Bermondsey and Tom Thomas of Penygraig for the British championship.[27]

The fight seen seven days before only by members of the exclusive Covent Garden club was now on show for anyone who could scrape up a shilling to get in. (For the fight itself see Chapter 5.)

Though the Empire and other theatres used their facilities to stage boxing contests, the practice of adding top boxers to a music hall bill continued for many years. In *The Sketch* of 15 July 1914, a columnist called 'Rover' gave his eye-witness account of a visit to the Oxford Music Hall, where the handsome heavyweight Bombardier Billy Wells was on show. It is worth reading in full as, despite its satirical tone, it makes it quite clear that someone with no knowledge of boxing whatsoever could still be intrigued by the spectacle, and that the attraction of a muscular male body could make up for many a dramatic deficiency:

Boxing is now quite the vogue, and one night last week I felt myself impelled to pay a visit to the Oxford Music Hall to feast my eyes upon one of the heroes of the moment. For there, each of the evenings of last week, Bombardier Wells was permitting the British Public to gaze upon his magnificent proportions and to pay him the homage that is his due. So, after I had sat awhile listening once more to the humours of 'Mam'selle Champagne' – which, by the way, has settled down into a very substantial success – the curtain rose again, and there was displayed a series of animated photographs revealing the great man in his hours of training to the eyes of his admirers. One saw him boxing and running with his trainers, and beating the ball with all his might and main, and one also witnessed an amusing picture disclosing the great man engaged in a fistic contest with his little boy. After this, a well-dressed man advanced to the foot of the stage and volunteered a few remarks, in the source of which he led one to imagine that the Bombardier was now merely at the opening of his career, which was more or less certain to terminate in the downfall of those who had or had not already vanquished him. [The previous December, Wells had keeled over in one round to the equally handsome Frenchman Georges Carpentier to national mourning.] This duly raised the assembly to lusty cheering, and thereupon appeared the Bombardier, who proceeded to box three rounds with a smaller but very determined person [probably Seaman Smith, a regular sparring partner], the two retiring after their display amid a scene of great enthusiasm. The Oxford is to be congratulated on its enterprise in giving an opportunity of seeing this distinguished pugilist, for although the boxing is naturally not of a hefty order, it gives everybody a chance of seeing a fine figure of a man and of saying that they have done so. The sight is certainly as invigorating and as educational as is the vision of the now omnipresent revue. ROVER

As has been eloquently argued elsewhere, the strong emotions engendered by the sight of muscular male bodies had and have their appeal to women and to men.[28] Consciously felt or not, elements of exhibitionism, narcissism, sadism, masochism and homosexual attraction are bound to be present in a stage show like the above. They exert no less an appeal in a real contest.

In few other contexts is it common to gaze upon hyper-masculine bodies stripped to the waist, and on display throughout the ritualised flexing of biceps and pectorals for photographs; or upon the ceremonial disrobing of silken finery; or upon the salutes and thrusting gestures of a boxer to his fans; or upon the exhausted embraces of winner and loser sharing a unique and intense experience beyond the reach of most men. This is to say nothing of the climactic or orgasmic nature of the knockout. Post-Freud, it can hardly be denied that appreciation of the 'Noble Art' or 'Sweet Science' taps some very deep wells in our psyches.

Whatever the reasons, by 1909, in Wonderland in London's East End, and elsewhere, promoters were reversing Corbett's turn from ring to stage, and putting on fight bills *instead* of general entertainment. To tender consciences, this was definitely a turn for the worse. However, consider one of the offerings at Wonderland (J. Woolf prop.) in September 1909. This was a very full evening's boxing, with nine preliminary bouts for promising flyweights (8st/112lbs), a category only established in 1909 and the longer established bantamweights (8st 4lbs/116lbs), and followed by *eight* other major fights, including one between Bandsman Rice (Hounslow) and Jack Meakins (Battersea), in which Meakins was forced to retire in the third. The fights, all reasonable matches and adequately refereed, followed promptly one after the other. The punters, who had parted with 6d. to get in, and up to 3s. for a premium ringside seat, got full value for their money.[29]

On other evenings, Wonderland had been staging supposedly more elevated entertainment, 'all seen for one Price of Admission 6d.' Top of the bill was the Oriental Hebrew Operatic Company performing, in Hebrew, a sketch entitled *Rabbi Joselman*. Professional boxing supposedly represented a serious drop in class compared with this. In reality, *Rabbi Joselman* was more *schlock* than high art if the supporting acts are anything to go by. Would Bandsman Rice have been much less refined than Mr A. Broadhurst, whose act comprised standing on a chair to display his beard ('over 7 Feet long and a moustache

3 ft. in length')? Stand is all he did. And could the tottering Jack Meakins have been so much more a degrading spectacle than the 'wonderful living freak of nature, the Armless Midget Lady [who] Stands only 32 inches in height, born without Hands or Arms, and goes through a marvellous performance with her feet. Come and see her Knit, Sew, Cut out with Scissors Fancy Paper Designs, Pick up Pins, & c., & c.'? Neither do enthusiastic young flyweights seem so terrible compared with the Keyers, Abe and Clarissa, who were 'Up side-down Pedestal Dancers'. It is perhaps best not to speculate on what an upside-down pedestal dancer actually did.[30]

The common mental picture held of Edwardian theatre has dinner-jacketed, cigar-smoking gentlemen with comfortable corporations, alongside bejewelled and heavily perfumed ladies, immaculately coiffured and clad in elegant décolleté dresses and long gloves, sitting languidly in well upholstered plush seats and politely applauding the offerings put before them. The picture is authentic enough, but there are other versions too.

What was true in the West End, in, for example, George Alexander's luxury St James's Theatre, was not necessarily representative of seedy South London music halls where the expressions of disapproval might take the form not of silent apathy, but a hail of vegetables, bottles, seats and of whatever came to hand. Plenty of disreputable 'penny gaffs' and 'flea pits' still existed. Theatre had not in every form cast off its disreputable and disorderly past. Boxing, in its new polite guise, could not easily suppress its unmannerly side either.

In November 1909 alone, there were three occasions when it would have been preferable to be at home rather than in a boxing hall. At the Caledonian Athletic Club in Glasgow, an ugly foul-filled fight led to disorder in and out of the ring, because of the activities of a gang who were striving to control both the management of the hall and the referees' verdicts.[31]

Meanwhile, in London, in Upper Street in Islington, at the Myddleton Hall, a 20-round contest between the local hero Harry Greenfield of Camden Town and Coldstream Guardsman Private J. Harris, came to an abrupt end when a local mob hurled successively curses then bottles then themselves into the ring, and the referee sensibly abandoned proceedings.[32] And at Wonderland, a bout between Smith and Warren (no other details given) proceeded in fits and starts. Smith was disqualified for foul blows, yet when the referee left the ring, Smith continued to hit Warren in the corner. They were separated, but by popular acclaim from an audience who knew a grudge fight when they saw one, they were quite improperly allowed to continue with a new referee. The second referee (brave man) then disqualified both men for holding and wrestling, instead of boxing. Later it emerged that the first referee (Benjamin Cohen of the NSC) had not just disqualified Smith in the fourth round, but Warren as well. In sum, a farce in the *Rabbi Joselman* sketch class.[33]

The atmosphere at a Wonderland Saturday night's boxing in the early years of the 20th century was one of the marvels of London's nightlife. There would be up to 2,000 people packed into the hall, well before the first contest. Others, too poor to afford the tanner (6d.) to get in, and regardless of the weather, clustered on the pavements outside the hall to get for free the vicarious pleasure of receiving results by word of mouth from the luckier ones inside the hall.

The pavements had but one advantage – moderately fresh air. Inside, the aroma had many components, but fragrance was not one of them. The crowd was there to watch, but also to eat, drink and smoke. Vendors clambered in and out of the packed rows, proffering glasses of beer, oranges, jellied eels, cigarettes, cigars and shag tobacco, all for instant smelly and smoky consumption. Pre-purchased bottles and snacks smuggled in inside pockets supplemented the hall's offerings. Male toiletries and deodorants for the masses lay some years in the future, so the body odours of 2,000 or more men, packed sweatily together in a heated atmosphere, mingled with the perspiration, embrocation and testosterone emanating from inside the ropes, was a heady mixture. The living conditions of most East Enders – large families packed into single rooms, bathrooms as scarce as privacy, most men owning only the clothes they wore ubiquitously – ensured Wonderland on fight night would have left modern nostrils challenged. When packed to suffocation level, as it usually was, it was a rich combination of Turkish bath, prison cell and public urinal; a place where more odours and more quaint noises swirled around than almost anywhere.[34]

Late-19th century theatres and music halls had partly dealt with these and similar problems. Here is an extract from *The Era* of 5 August 1889:

The great middle-class of the suburbs, educated by the aesthetic movement, keenly susceptible to grace and beauty, and intolerant of dinginess and squalor, would not have been won over so quickly and thoroughly as it has been had not its tastes been appealed to as powerfully as possible by the comfort, cleanliness and grace of the modern suburban playhouse, which with its handsome outlines and spacious surroundings, reminds the travelled beholder of the municipal theatres in the smaller towns of the continent.

The standard London guidebook of the day had more reservations:

The entertainments offered by the Music Halls have certainly improved in tone during the last ten or fifteen years, and ladies may visit the better west end establishments without fear, *though they should, of course, abjure the cheaper seats.* [Italics added]

This source, the Baedeker guide of 1911, also shows that the cheapest seats at West End theatres cost generally 1s., as did the typical West End music hall, for example, the London Pavilion, prices from 1s. up to 5s.[35] So, the boxing at the King's Hall, Lambeth was exactly comparable to a West End theatre or music hall. But one visit to the West End was as expensive as two visits to Wonderland.

For a man on the breadline, boxing was no more on offer than tea at the Ritz, but for a working man in employment, an evening at the fights was one entertainment option among many, and boxing had to hold its own against rival attractions were it to prosper. (It is worth noting that even for soccer, the crowds were drawn from skilled workers and artisans, rather than from men at the very bottom of the social pyramid.)

Appeal to a working-class audience came mostly from the professional side of a sport, rather than the amateur. That boxing conformed to the pattern is obvious from the 1911 Baedeker entry on boxing. It gives the prices for the Amateur Boxing Association annual championships held every year just after Easter. The price for admission alone was 2s. and seats went from 5s. up to 42s (a whopping £2.10p), prices designed to appeal *only* to the middle and upper classes, and to keep the ordinary working man *out* along with any whiff of professionalism.[36] Naturally, there were many who could afford it, and so loved boxing that they would attend both ABA Finals and evenings at Wonderland. Unfortunately, they sometimes took their anti-Semitism along with them. Man about town Robert Machray attended Wonderland and observed closely the audience:[37]

Most of them are young – the great majority are between twenty and thirty, and nearly all of them are of the easily recognisable East End types, though there is to be seen a heavier percentage of Jewish noses than is usual in an East End assemblage. The proprietor of 'Wonderland', you see from the programme is a Jew; one of the boxers, to judge from his nickname, is a Jew; and, quite unmistakeably, your Hebrew of

Aldgate is well represented to-night, and takes a keen interest in the ring and its doings.[38]

Machray, however, did not quite match for prejudice Police Superintendent Sygrove who visited Wonderland and expressed his concern about overcrowding, and the lack of exits:

> This contingency is also likely to arise at any time in the case of fire, and *as the Jews are such a panicky race* it can be surmised what would be the result … [Italics added][39]

Presumably, in the case of fire, the Gentiles in the audience could be relied on to do the decent thing and sit quietly as they fried to a crisp.

Other official visitors expressed their concerns about the potential hazards of Wonderland – 'on 12th Dec. [1903] the house was packed to its utmost capacity, about 3,000 persons being present, and … the gangways are very narrow'; 'the *Lavatory* arrangements were disgraceful'. Still other visitors liked the quality of the Wonderland experience – 'The Boxing competitions were carried out with every care and fairness … I saw nothing objectionable in the entertainment and good order was kept among a decidedly rough audience.'; 'Everyone was well-behaved.'[40]

Boxing journalists usually took an equally positive stance:

> Sixteen couples, fighting for all that was in them, furnished a bill of fare such as has rarely been seen at the 'East End National' (as per advertisement), and for close on four hours the huge crowd enjoyed to the full the handiwork of Matchmaker Jack Woolf. It speaks volumes for the management when it was noted that many members of the N.S.C. as well as Army officers were present, and that this famous rendezvous is coming back to its old prestige is an assured fact.[41]

Wonderland and the narrow alleys that led to it were contained in an elongated triangle bound by Whitechapel Road to the north, Fieldgate Street to the south, and the northern section of New Road to the east.[42] This placed it in the very heart of the Jewish East End.

Much visited by sociologists and researchers in the early 20th century, the London boroughs of Whitechapel and Stepney *were* predominantly Jewish. The New Road section was calculated around 1900 as 95 to 100 per cent Jewish, as were the alleys around Wonderland. Whitechapel Road was up to 75 per cent Jewish; Fieldgate Street was anything from 75 to 94 per cent Jewish. Many of the narrow streets to the south of Fieldgate Street, such as Plumbers Row, Greenfield Street and the no longer existing Nottingham Place, were also calculated as being 95 to 100 per cent Jewish.[43] Small wonder then that Jack Woolf was drawing heavily upon local Jews for his audiences – for cinematographic films one night, for Yiddish music hall the next and for four- and five-hour bills of boxing on a Saturday night. Significantly for the Orthodox Jews among his patrons, boxing, taking place after sundown on a Saturday, was a perfectly permissible activity. Association football, the only sport to rival boxing in popularity and not yet subject to the demands of television ratings, was bound with almost religious timing to a 3pm Saturday kick-off and thus preceded the end of the Jewish Sabbath and was out of bounds for an observant Jew.

There was in any case a local Jewish boxing tradition stretching back to the 18th and early 19th centuries. The Sephardic Whitechapel-born Daniel Mendoza (1763–1836) was generally acknowledged as the bare-knuckle champion of England in the 1789–95 period. Samuel Elias, 'Dutch Sam' or 'The Terrible Jew' (1775–1816), was born in Whitechapel to Dutch immigrant parents, and later more often beaten by excessive consumption of rich food and gin than by others' knuckles. Elias was finally buried in the Whitechapel Jewish cemetery. At a less illustrious level, if J. B.'s *Pancratia* is accurate, 'a noted Jewess' of Wentworth Road, (close to the Upton Park Jews' Cemetery), fought a good fight against Miss Mary Ann Fielding for an hour and 20 minutes, undeterred by being knocked down herself 70 times.

By 1909, any young Jewish East End lad prepared to put on the gloves and climb into a ring had several small Jewish clubs and gymnasia available to him. Many Christian churches, chapels and settlements, convinced of the merits of Muscular Christianity and its healthy mind in a healthy body philosophy, incorporated boxing and sparring sessions into their youth club activities to broaden their appeal to the young. Clearly Muscular Judaism had its merits too.

Most famous of these clubs was the Judaean School and Athletic Club, in a defunct stable loft just off Cable Street, which could claim a sixpenny membership of over 1,000.[44] Few of the tiny scrappers seen there would eventually appear on a professional bill, let alone achieve the international fame of Gershon Mendeloff, a skinny 15-year-old who graduated from a first appearance at the Judaean to the world welterweight championship under his rather better known professional name – Ted 'Kid' Lewis. Lewis was also known as 'The Yiddisher Wonderman' or 'The Aldgate Sphinx'. (The early 20th century had no more appetite for tasteful nomenclature than we do.)

Even if Lewis was an exception, youthful participants in a sport are a powerful element in its popularity, so the Jewish boxing tradition was alive and well in the Edwardian East End. And Jack Woolf's Wonderland was perfectly placed to profit from it.

How deep that enthusiasm could be is difficult fully to comprehend without some sense of the likely experiences of London's East End Jewry. The 1880s and 1890s saw a virulent revival of latent anti-Semitism in areas of Russia and Russian-controlled Poland. Occasional riots such as a famous one in Odessa in 1871 became the norm, until there was hardly a political or economic difficulty for which the Jews were not blamed – the assassination of Tsar Alexander II in 1881, recurrent famines, the Russo–Turkish war of 1877–88, the Russo–Japanese War of 1904–05, the 1905 Revolution, Bolshevik agitation, disappearance of Christian children – if it happened, or even if it didn't, someone was to blame, so why not those traditional scapegoats, the Jews?

Popular prejudices form a fertile field for exploitation by unscrupulous authorities, and successive Russian governments indulged shamelessly. They passed anti-Jewish laws and organised pogroms, exclusions, forcible resettlements, compulsory recruitment for 25-year terms into the Tsar's armies, and the like. Meanwhile, Bismarck, the Prussian Junker heavyweight, was transforming Prussia and expelled Jews from Polish territories in 1886, pushing his victims back on to Russian territory – a classic case of fat and fire.

Unsurprisingly, there was a steady westward drift of Ashkenazi Jews out of the territories of the Russian Empire, heading for the new Promised Land – the United States of America. From 1900 to 1910, 400,000 European Jews settled in the USA.[45] With happy results for American boxing, theatre, music, science and many other fields, many settled in New York. Others, perhaps 100,000, did not make it the whole way and settled in Britain, usually in cities such as Leeds and Manchester and especially in London, in the East End in particular.

London had had an established community of about 20,000 Jews in 1850.[46] By the time of the 1901 Census, it had about 50,000 Jews, 43,000 of them in the borough of Stepney, where they constituted approximately 20 per cent of the local population.[47]

All the conventional episodes of immigrant experience can be guaranteed to have operated here. The need, in a strange land, to be in an area where one's fellows share a culture; the unifying bond of a shared language or distinctive clothing or a common ethnic or religious identity; the possibility of work for a boss who gives intelligible orders: these are the positive factors. The negatives were as powerful. Even if the Whitechapel High Street had no whip-cracking Cossacks on horseback, there were many resident and visiting anti-Semites ready with a fist, a curse and half a brick. There were many shysters and slum landlords ever eager to exploit others' poverty. And less recent immigrants were likely to see newcomers as a threat to their own hard-won status, rather than as fellow sufferers in need of help and sympathy.

A plethora of prejudices, amply fostered by local press and politicians, provoked the passing of the Aliens Act of 1905; the culmination of an ill-informed and virulent debate about the threat of the new.[48] During that debate, the Jewish immigrants were accused at various times of prostitution, white slavery, dope-peddling, unnatural vice and of spreading loathsome diseases. Secretly organising the Boer War was added to the trumped-up charges.

The years from 1905 to 1910 saw the summit of Eastern European Jewry settlement in the East End.[49] Against this background of immigration and hostility, it is easy to imagine the reactions of many in the Wonderland audience when a Jewish boxer climbed through the ropes to do battle. How could they not identify almost totally with such a figure, pitted against a rival regional, ethnic, national or religious representative? Woolf knew just how to add a certain frisson to a contest by matching, say, a Jewish boxer, with or without a Star of David on his shorts, against an Irish Catholic boxer who wore a green sash and a crucifix, and crossed himself and prayed before leaving his corner. In areas like Whitechapel, simmering resentments existed between the Irish – the earlier group of immigrants, who had previously suffered all the insults and prejudices themselves – and the Jews, the new kids on the block. Many

Jews and Catholics held street opinions about each other's religion some way from the truer spirits of Christianity or Judaism.

(At least Woolf, even at his most vulgar, did not stoop to the depths plunged by the American promoter who once sought unworthily to exploit ethnic difference by matching the great Jewish fighter Benny Leonard against the Chinese boxer Ah Chung in a hall in New York's Chinatown at the start of the Chinese New Year. 'Ah Chung' was actually another Jewish boxer called Rosenberg, who had been given an oriental makeover, with eye make-up and yellow skin dye to justify his new billing.)[50]

It was as if for three vicarious minutes every round, every punch thrown by the representative fighter transcends the particular moment and becomes the defiant answer to the slights of the world. Every man in the hall swayed his head, moving unconsciously in harmony with his boxer, clenching his own fists as if the gloves were on them, and the boxer's arms an uninterrupted extension of his own. The underdog has, for an exciting instant, become top dog, and a seedy hall temporarily an ethnic Valhalla.

These social and contextual factors behind the success of Jewish boxers are more convincing than those once put forward by a *New York Evening Journal* writer who claimed more mystical properties were at work:

The Jews have helped to teach the world how to fight cleanly, as they have how to live cleanly, morally and physically. It is to this heritage of centuries of clean living that they owe their wonderful endurance. The laws of hygiene that Moses laid down some thirty centuries ago have been followed faithfully as part of their religion.[51]

A kosher Moses might have been a powerful man to have in one's corner. Nevertheless, the experiences of the Jewish members of the audience at Wonderland were not unique. (Residents of Lower East Side New York would have felt completely at home.) They would be shared by other communities in other halls all over the world from Belfast to Albuquerque. The Irish, the Welsh, the Scots and other regional audiences in the British Isles; Afro-Americans, Puerto Ricans, Mexicans in the USA; Aboriginals in Australia; Algerians in France: all could have readily identified with the Wonderland menu, and recited similar encounters fulfilling their own fears, hopes and fantasies. A soccer team can readily encapsulate the hopes of an entire city or community. Yet because boxing is so directly physical, its victories and defeats so final and its psychological and physical scrutiny of its participants so raw and unforgiving, it provides an intense experience to which most sports can only aspire; effective because so basic – basic, but not necessarily simple.

That what happens in the heavyweight division is crucial is practically a cliché. So long as the laws of physics prevail, the heavier the man, the greater the power. Even the tawdriest match for a world heavyweight championship creates interest among viewers otherwise marginal to boxing. But boxing is about more than avoirdupois and crude slogging. The instant appeal of a round-arm swing connecting with an unprotected chin cannot be denied. The trouble is, in boxing as in other things, the instant appeal has a brief shelf life and soon palls.

The complexities and subtleties of boxing, its timing, its tiny variations, its psychological interplay, its cunning deceptions and its inspired improvisations are more frequently encountered at the lower weights than among the heavier men (not that history has not produced several highly intelligent and clever heavyweight champions). Its more subtle qualities are also more readily yielded to the regular follower than to the casual viewer. As that wise boxing journalist Harry Mullan put it: 'Don't be fooled into thinking that it [boxing] is an easy sport to understand, or to follow.'[52] His point is supported by the American novelist and fight aficionado, Joyce Carol Oates. She wrote: 'To the untrained eye most boxing matches appear not merely savage but mad. As the eye becomes trained, however, the spectator begins to see the complex patterns that underlie the "madness"; what seems to be merely confusing action is understood to be coherent and intelligent, frequently inspired.'[53]

The quintessential boxing experience enjoyed by the ethnic groups above was more likely to be found in the lighter divisions in the period. For one thing, the attainment of full growth in adulthood is heavily dependent upon adequate foetal nutrition in the womb and in the early months of independent life. Public concern about the health of the poor was common. It resulted in 1904 in a Parliamentary Committee on Physical Deterioration set up to investigate why so many potential recruits had been physically so feeble that they could not be sent off to the Boer War of 1899–1902. The statistics disclosed dreadful physical deficiencies.

In an underfed community where no one had enough to eat, the chances of children fulfilling their full growth potential were negligible. In many working-class homes, then and later, the male breadwinner was given the major share of what was available to keep up his strength for heavy manual labour. The mother, even when pregnant or suckling, and the children ate the miserable scraps left over or did without. Small wonder then that poor areas produced more than their fair share of flyweights, bantamweights and skinny featherweights. Particularly insidious was the fact that the very poor did not form a separate self-contained layer of society, but that most working-class people, because of illness or because of spells of structural or seasonal unemployment, could expect to suffer serious poverty, with the concomitant hunger, at some stage in their lives.[54]

Imagine then a young man from one's own topographical or ethnic community, looking as if a puff of wind might blow him over in his walk to the ring, engaging with a representative of one's supposed enemies and displaying toughness, power, courage, resilience and skill, ultimately to victory. This was to be transported from a prosaic world of defeat and misery, into a promised land where virtue outpointed vice and the lion was knocked flat by the lamb. In this feat, power and strength were but two elements; speed, wit, grace and beauty were also on show. The bull has as much power as can be imagined, beyond machines and motors; the

matador still wins, but is expected to win beautifully.

Other sports provide ready parallels. The diminutive Welsh outside-half feints, sidesteps and sends a lumbering back-row forward sprawling at his twinkling feet. The tiny Scottish winger, a soccer ball seemingly tied to his laces, evades a studs-first lunge of a towering full-back, then cuts back to do it again just for the hell of it. These are sportsmen not just admired by their community but also *loved*.

Boxing history is full of such mini champions, narrowly evading the ferocious rushes of a stronger opponent, and, when the moment arises, producing a deadly jab or a hook leading to victory. No period in boxing produced more such little assassins than the years covered in this book.

Jack Woolf presided over the multitudinous goings-on at Wonderland with the air of a benevolent rabbi temporarily relaxing his strictures while his flock let their hair down. Immaculately dressed, his curly hair pomaded, his military moustache waxed and curled at the ends, a large cigar in his right hand, a cute little terrier called Spider tucked under his left arm, he moved up and down the aisles exuding an aromatic effluvium a good deal more fragrant than the odours otherwise prevailing. He boasted that Wonderland had put on 11,000 fights in 11 years and no one could contradict him. 'Jack has done more for the boxing world, as represented by the East End, than any man I know,' confirmed *Boxing*'s correspondent.[55] He had come a long way since the setting up of the Wonderland company in October 1895 when he, the licensee of the East London Tavern, had joined

with a music publisher, a playwright, a painter, a solicitor and a gentleman with a private income, jointly to take shares in the new venture.[56] When the old company was formally dissolved in February 1909, he and a fellow promoter called Harry Jacobs emerged as the men responsible for the Wonderland boxing bills. Though the details and reasons are lost, there came a mighty falling-out between them in September 1909, 'and it is even reported that it hailed ledgers for a few moments although no fatal accidents are recorded'.[57] Jacobs the partner had become Jacobs the enemy.

Jacobs was not among the staff at Wonderland who expressed their appreciation of Woolf with the presentation of an illuminated address to him and a silver tray and tea service to Mrs Woolf on a Sunday evening in August 1909. The illuminated address:

> … was presented to Mr Jack Woolf by his employees at the Wonderland and his friends, as a mark of esteem and great respect for his manly and upright dealings to all those he came into contact with during his managerial career.

The *Jewish Chronicle* approvingly quoted the glowing tribute, its sporting columnist adding his own endorsement:

> Mr Jack Woolf has excellent personal qualities. It is not necessary to enumerate them; better call evidence of the fact, and that evidence is his remarkable popularity among all sorts and conditions of men, and the best test of all is that this popularity

is perhaps strongest among those who know him best, namely, his employees. Some have been with him since they were little boys, now being men in years with grown up families; in fact, it was said on Sunday evening that to be fairly sure of a situation under Mr Jack Woolf an individual should be entered on the list at birth, as though he were putting up for membership of the M.C.C.[58]

While Woolf presided so benignly over his East End sporting fiefdom, over in the heart of the fashionable West End, A. F. Bettinson and his colleagues at the NSC viewed boxing's new popularity with less than total delight. Their institution had stepped in at a crucial stage to replace boxing anarchy and borderline lawlessness with dignity and integrity. When the hostility of the authorities was brought to bear upon boxing, the club dignitaries had gone all the way to the dock of the Old Bailey to defend the sport.

The president of the club, Lord Lonsdale, had dug into his personal financial resources to underwrite the engagement of expensive advocates to win cases, and faced charges himself. The club had rigorously controlled the conduct of boxers in their ring and employed referees and timekeepers of experience and independence to keep it that way, meanwhile adapting the Queensberry Rules to modern circumstances. By operating as a private club restricted to members and guests, it had controlled the content and conduct of the audience at fights. Membership was a privilege, but it could be withdrawn if a member disobeyed the rules about silence during rounds

or behaved in any way likely to bring the club into disrepute.

The NSC, even at its inception in November 1891, was formed overwhelmingly by comfortable middle-class patrons. The original Articles of Association list the professions of some of those involved.[59] Preference shares were held by three 'gentlemen' (i.e. men with private incomes); one actor (symbolically his original designation as 'comedian' was struck out and replaced by the apparently more dignified 'actor'); an insurance manager; an agent; and a cement manufacturer who personally held 50 preference shares. They were all respectable citizens, but ones at some social distance from, say, the committees of the aristocratically loaded Jockey Club, or the distinguished Marylebone Cricket Club (MCC, where the presidents over the period of this book included one duke, four earls, one lord and two barons). A similar pattern prevailed among the 658 ordinary shareholders of the NSC, who included 300 'gentlemen'; two comedians; seven actors; 11 hotel proprietors; 21 licensed victuallers; and 31 solicitors (and one barrister).

Men such as these and committed officials such as Bettinson, Fleming and Corri had made significant contributions to the healthy and popular state of boxing by 1909. However, as all parents know, there is a gulf between controlling a small child and keeping a fractious teenager on the straight and narrow. Authority once obeyed without question becomes subject more and more to challenge, and who controls whom particularly contentious.

For nearly two decades, the NSC had used its power and prestige to control boxers and boxing. It had

decided who should fight whom and when. It had decided the size of purses. It had decided the relative values of one contender against another. But *all* the decisions were taken in the interests of the members of the club. Outside there were many who resented this.

Boxers, especially those in the preliminary bouts well down the bill, had to accept a miserably low fee for their efforts – 'When their expenses had been met they were left with just about enough to patronize a wayside coffee-stall,' said Trevor Wignall. And unless they *did* fight at the NSC, they were not considered when title or elimination bouts were arranged. So powerful was the hold of the club that a boxer who complained about his fee was about as likely to be accommodated as the kitchen skivvy who queried the downstairs wage structure to an upstairs Edwardian mistress. The blanket offer to a disgruntled wage slave in 1909 was 'take it or leave it'.

The more successful boxer, one with a title or a growing reputation, was obviously better placed to negotiate a more satisfactory fee for an appearance at the NSC. A top-of-the-bill slot still meant the bout took place at midnight or later when the actors, late diners and other men about town deigned to drop in after their other activities. The timing did not suit the gentlemen of the press, leaving them wandering along Fleet Street at ungodly hours with an important fight to report and precious little time to catch even the London morning editions.

Peggy Bettinson's attitude to journalists was heavily dependent upon their commenting on club affairs in favourable and even flattering terms. The merest suggestion of legitimate criticism would bring an explosion of Bettinson's wrath down upon a junior journalist's head along with the threat that their future presence at important club nights might well depend upon continuing club approval.[60] So long as the club was private, no non-members could be guaranteed entry. Veterans on the press benches could remember the unseemly case of R. P. Watson of the *Sporting Life*, who had been banned from reporting fights from the club by John Fleming after making hostile comments *even though* Watson was an NSC member in his own right.[61] Fleming's and Bettinson's pronouncements of decisions taken fundamentally in the club's interests as being purely for the good of the sport, reminded some of their critics of Disraeli's comment on Gladstone's more dubious manoeuvres – that he did not mind Gladstone producing the ace from his sleeve, but resented the pretence that the Almighty had placed it there for the purpose.

Others resentful of the club's monopoly were the professional promoters, able to offer a more commercial purse to bring two top men to fight each other, and willing to provide championship conditions quite as rigorous as those prevailing in Covent Garden, yet never able to stage a 'title bout', because the NSC was unwilling to recognise bouts beyond their premises.

Because professional boxing for so long lacked an authority to impose order upon an anarchic situation, the autocratic and often selfish decrees of the NSC were recognised by others and generally followed.

Even in matters so fundamental and so crucial to order and safety as the gloves to be worn, confusion could prevail. The weight of gloves to be used was always written into the articles drawn up before a major NSC contest. In minor bouts, there and elsewhere, improvisation or availability might affect the gloves chosen.

A 4oz minimum was set, yet manufacturers produced gloves in a bewildering variety of weights, from an outsize 16oz pillow to a lethal and skimpy 2oz glove. Such a pair, with curled hair stuffing, was reported to be in regular use at the Coney Island Club in the USA and elsewhere.[62]

The gloves from the Corbett v Sullivan fight sold at auction for over $40,000 in 1992, weight unknown, would look to modern eyes more like driving gloves than ones for boxing. Others, skin-tight and no more padded then modern golf gloves, had occasional use, especially at underground contests supported by audiences nostalgic for bare-knuckle days. As a comparison, modern middleweights would fight with 8oz or 10oz gloves, and the lighter weights with 8oz, or at least a minimum of 6oz.

Just as important for a boxer's safety was to be matched against opponents of a similar weight. In other circumstances, what the NSC decided on 11 February 1909, and the importance of its decision for the future of boxing, would have been emblazoned across the headlines of the sporting press and extensively discussed. Because of the NSC's decided ambivalence about publicity, the significance of their initiative gradually seeped out instead of being announced.

The club formally standardised the weights at which contests would be officially recognised. In ascending order, there were to be the following seven categories: flyweight – 8st/112lbs and under; bantamweight – 8st 6lb/118lbs and under; featherweight – 9st 4lb/130lbs and under; lightweight – 9st 9lb/135lbs and under; welterweight – 10st 7lb/147lbs and under; middleweight – 11st 6lb/160lbs and under; above and beyond the middleweight limit was heavyweight. A further category between middle and heavy, a light-heavyweight division of 12st 7lb/175lbs and under, was already operating in the USA, and had been since 1903, but it was not given full status in Britain until 1913, when it was introduced under the naval-sounding title of cruiserweight (appropriately intended to convey the idea of a speeding battleship with less than full armament).[63] This could not have come too soon for those unhappy fighters who could not make the 11st 6lb limit for middleweight, but who lacked enough poundage and firepower to challenge seriously a genuine heavyweight. There was also a significant 13lb gap between welterweight and middleweight.

Later decades brought further modifications – featherweights at 9st/126lbs, for example. The featherweight limit was particularly contentious and was often cited as evidence of the NSC's double standards. Bettinson had arbitrarily chosen various weights between 8st 8lb/120lbs and a full 9st 2lb/128lbs for his 'Featherweight Championships', conveniently tailoring the category to suit a particular man whom the club chose to promote. Americans regularly observed 8st 10lb as the limit.[64]

By the 21st century, categories have seriously proliferated, with 17 separately recognised by various sanctioning bodies. Though the safety of boxers is usually cited as the reason for such an outcrop, that more divisions equals more bouts equals more champions equals more sanctioning fees for more boxing authorities equals more profits for more promoters is as likely.

The majority of the weights sanctioned by the NSC in 1909 merely gave new force to prevailing conditions. One choice, however, was revolutionary, and indeed downright callous. Because of the nutritional deficiencies discussed earlier, there were, up to 1909, many small boxers in England at weights well below 8st/112lbs. Many fights had taken place for unofficial titles going up from the minute 6st 4lb/88lbs in two-pounds steps all the way to the 8st limit.[65]

By making eight stones the lower limit in 1909, the NSC in effect abolished these mini-categories, forcing men who had been tipping the scales at amazingly low weights to concede an impossible 20 pounds or so to an eight-stone man, were they to contest the newly authorised flyweight championship. No other title was now available. Kid Nutter of Workington, for example, who twice took the extraordinary Jimmy Wilde to the full distance in points losses over 20 rounds and 15 rounds in January and February 1914, weighed 6st 4lb/88lbs for the first contest and 6st 6lb/90lbs for the second.[66] Wilde himself sometimes came in at a barely perceptible 6st 10lb/94lbs and lower, but he was a physical phenomenon without parallel.

In 1909, other weights were, metaphorically, knocked out by the new NSC decree. All divisions between 8st/112lbs and 8st 6lb/118lbs were similarly abolished, creating further hardships for some. And 120-pounders suddenly had to fight over their own natural weight at 9st/126lbs or perish.

Along with the new weight classes, the club, just as discreetly if not positively stealthily, decided to award a presentation belt to champions who established their proper credentials by winning, on the club premises, a bout duly recognised *by the club* as being for a British title, and coming within the seven new categories.

Belts, official and unofficial, had been placed around the waists of boxers as prizes, as favours and as tributes throughout the previous century. In the early days of prizefighting, fighters were identified by a coloured silk handkerchief affixed to the stake post in their corner, and by another tied around the waistband. As a winner got to wear his own and his opponent's after the fight, the association of champions with a waist decoration became common. In 1810, King George III awarded Tom Cribb a belt after Cribb's defeat of Molyneaux. At the time of the 1860 Heenan v Sayers contest (Chapter 1), the ornamental silver belt that Sayers was given by his supporters after beating Percy the Tipton Slasher, was on offer for the winner as part of the side stakes. When a disputed draw resulted, both Sayers and Heenan appeared at the Alhambra Theatre in Leicester Square to receive twin silver belts in commemoration of their contest. The Boston public subscribed a grand $10,000 to commemorate the achievements of John L. Sullivan. This generous fund paid for a gold belt studded with diamonds. Sporting magazines, for example, the *Police Gazette* in the 1880s, and *The Ring* from the 1920s, continued the tradition,

both magazines presenting belts to chosen fighters. And no self-respecting sanctioning body would these days fail to seal a championship win without a monstrous plastic dustbin lid big enough to hide a flyweight.

The nine-carat gold belts inaugurated at the NSC in 1909 for their new British champions were more modest than Sullivan's dazzling jewellery, but tasteful, refined and eminently desirable. They are the ancestors of today's Lonsdale Belts, still awarded to British champions, now only part-gold, although still very covetable, and which carry at the centre of the waistband an oval medallion mounted by a prowling lion and showing an enamelled portrait of Lord Lonsdale. Smaller medallions at the side and back show the English rose, the Scottish thistle, the Irish clover and the Welsh daffodil. These design features were innovations made by the British Boxing Board of Control in the 1930s in tribute to Lord Lonsdale and his lifelong involvement in boxing. The anonymous boxers on the 1909 belts were replaced by the Lonsdale portrait and the national emblems.

It is a mystery why the belts were not announced as Lonsdale Belts from the very first. They were being so referred to by November 1909. Lonsdale consented to having them named after him and paid for the first one to be designed and made. Costing some £250, they were made by the firm Mappin and Webb, holders of Royal Warrants as silversmiths to every monarch from Victoria onwards, although the firm retains no records from the time. The significant original belt was won, as we shall see, in the lightweight class on Monday, 8 November 1909 by Freddie Welsh with a 20-round points victory over Johnny Summers at the NSC. A delay initiated by a successful appeal by Summers that Welsh's bandages were unsatisfactory and Welsh's temporary return to the dressing room to get them fixed, enabled the brand-new belt to make its first ring appearance:

> During his [Welsh's] absence the belt presented by Lord Lonsdale, to be worn by the holder of the lightweight title, was exhibited and generally admired.[67]

Curiously, the February 1909 NSC committee meeting, which inaugurated the radical changes in the weight categories and the circumstances in which British championships could be won, coincided with a rift between Lord Lonsdale, its president, and the NSC.

The NSC had accepted for membership a Mr Sievier. For some reason (snobbery? anti-Semitism?), this upset the noble lord to the extent that he threatened to resign. From his London home in Carlton House Terrace, he sent Bettinson an angry letter dated 22 February 1909:

> I received your letter re the election of Mr Sievier, and I confess that it has astounded me for the National Sporting Club is a sporting club not a Social Club, and if you look down the list of Members the difficulty is to associate them all with a Social club.
>
> I have reserved for myself a line that I must take what is obviously a hint that my Presidency is no longer required, and Although I have not been able to attend the Boxing Competitions as much as I should like I have on many occasions done everything that was possible and far more than the Committee of the Club know in the interests of the Club in many ways.
>
> I have spoken to a great many Members who assure me that if I withdraw my name they will all withdraw theirs at once.
>
> I look upon a sporting club as a club in the interests of sport, and I put on a par with racing clubs of similar description. However, I will decide nothing until after I have seen you and had a talk.
>
> Yours truly,[68]

Unfortunately, all other correspondence on the subject has been lost, so the true objections to the unhappy Sievier cannot be known – surely there were many members who were social rather than boxing members? It seems highly probable that Bettinson placated Lonsdale and rescinded Sievier's membership. Lonsdale, his income, his aristocratic status, and his behind-the-scenes influence at which his letter hints, and of which we will see further evidence, were all too valuable for the club to lose – as he well knew. He was mollified, perhaps by a request to have his name commemorated in the new belts, and coughed up accordingly. However obscure their origins, the Lonsdale Belts became one of the most prized trophies in British sport, and an appropriate tribute to Lonsdale's major role in the preservation of British boxing.

The gospel of the noble art was being received with enthusiasm in Britain. It was being transmitted to more and more people in France as

The image of Jack Johnson on a boxing booth banner typifies the grotesque caricature that passed for reality for many.

Collection of the Smithsonian National Museum of African American History and Culture

well, where it was making inroads into a Gallic sporting culture hitherto dominated by *la savate* or *chaussure*, folk combat sports incorporating blows with the fist and the foot that had undergone a refining process in the 19th century to produce a distinctive *Boxe Française*. Apart from isolated occasions such as the infamous Sullivan v Mitchell brawl at Chantilly in March 1888 (see Chapter 1) – an event on a private Rothschild estate watched almost exclusively by a British crowd – British-style boxing had barely appeared in France before 1900. Then, in remarkably few years, Paris became an attractive venue for British and American boxers to appear before British and American visitors to Paris in audiences swelled by native Frenchmen. By 1907, some of the best boxers in the world were fighting in Paris regularly.[69]

The reception accorded Tommy and Crystal Burns (see Prologue) was matched by the lionisation of the red-haired Philadelphian Jewish welterweight Harry Lewis (b. 16 September 1886 as Harry Besterman). Lewis could hardly saunter down a boulevard without being surrounded by French admirers. On his 1909 visit, French hospitality was his downfall. Whisked into a café by fans, Lewis was persuaded to try an attractive green cordial, and downed several to be social. The innocent-looking drink was the deadly French absinthe. Still under the influence at an exhibition bout that evening, Lewis shook hands with the referee and punched him to the canvas instead of his opponent.[70]

Before the First World War, Paris welcomed a host of foreign fighters, including Jim Jeffries, Sam McVea, Willie Lewis, Young Joseph, Frank Erne, Joe Jeannette, Frank Klaus, Jack Johnson and many others. French promoters were no slower to react to demand than their London and New York counterparts, and there was a mushroom growth of boxing halls in French provincial cities, and especially

The Los Angeles Herald *featured Jack Johnson's clash with Sam McVea in Los Angeles 27 October 1903 (w Johnson pts 20). It could not resist the demeaning racist graphics.*
BoxRec

in Paris with the Cirque de Paris, the Tivoli, the Doerrer Hall and, their names making maximum use of the new vogue for *la boxe Anglaise*, Wonderland and Premierland, all staging boxing shows and tournaments. La Salle Wagram followed at the end of 1909.[71] Most interspersed the appearances of foreign boxers with popular novice competitions. Soon there was a new crop of French boxers emerging, eager to test their prowess against the British at home and abroad. This was the best possible result for the future of European boxing.

On Monday, 18 October 1909, for example, Jack Goldswain of Bermondsey was defending the national honour at the NSC against one of the new breed of French boxers, the French middleweight champion, Marcel Moreau (b. 3 May 1888). Before the contest, contracted at a 10st 10lb/150lbs limit, Goldswain vigorously protested when Moreau weighed in at 10st 13lb – a protest less than convincing as he went nine ounces over himself.

Weight and Goldswain had a problematical relationship. In 1906 he had outpointed Jabez White in a 10st/140lbs match at the NSC, and thereafter claimed the British lightweight title as a result. White, the holder, had refused to concede, saying that because they had both been overweight, the title was not at risk. Goldswain, with some press support, continued to use the title until he was retired by Johnny Summers in the 14th round of another lightweight bout in November 1908. By the summer of 1909, he was fighting at welterweight (10st 7lb/147lbs) and was too relaxed about making the weight against Moreau in the autumn.

Goldswain was as popular at the NSC as he was at Wonderland or The Ring, Blackfriars, for not many would match his career over the 23 years he boxed from 1896 to 1919. Born 22 July 1878, he had close-cropped dark hair receding at the temples, black beetling eyebrows, and shoulder and neck muscles that even his docker father probably envied. (When not boxing, he worked in a dog biscuit factory, and had been known to climb in the ring straight from a late shift with biscuit flour still sticking to him.)

His French opponent Moreau parted tousled hair over his left eye, but his hair still spilled obstinately down over his narrow forehead. Chin on chest, he peered out at an opponent from under this unkempt fringe, ready to leap in at any opportunity. He rushed Goldswain vigorously in all the early rounds, landing crisp uppercuts at close quarters, and opening an old cut on Goldswain's eye in the second. Goldswain kept Moreau out on the end of his left jab and pummelled

Moreau's kidneys when Moreau rushed in. Goldswain finished the 15 rounds ahead on points.[72] Symptomatically, the courage, persistence and strength of a Frenchman such as Moreau could give even the best of British boxers an uncomfortable evening. The English audience, knowledgeable enough to appreciate how far French boxing had come in so short a time, gave the resilient Moreau a resounding ovation.

Paris, because of the new-found enthusiasm for boxing, soon produced an epic ('epic: of heroic type or scale', *OED*) that took place there on 17 April 1909. Not only was it a true heavyweight epic, it was actually the longest boxing contest of the entire 20th century. (A 41-rounder in June 1909 in California between Dick Hyland and Leach Cross, which ended with Cross being counted out came close.) It lasted 49 rounds and 3 hours 12 minutes, and only ceased at 3.45am because one of the boxers, Sam McVea, failed to come out for the scheduled 50th round.[73] It was arranged as a fight to the finish regardless of length. This barbaric idea, an anachronistic throwback to the days of Regency semi-slaughter, was possible because both fighters were black.

Sam McVea, the loser, and Joe Jeannette, the winner or at least survivor, were caught by the prejudices of the day on a vicious carousel not of their own making. They, and another black heavyweight, Sam Langford, were known collectively as The Big Four. The fourth member of that original quartet was Jack Johnson, who, purely because of his victory over Tommy Burns with which we began, was able to step off the roundabout and meet *white* opponents because he now held the world heavyweight title. Messrs

McVea, Jeannette and Langford lacked that invaluable accessory, but had too much skill to provide easy glove-fodder for lesser white fighters. They were therefore condemned to a repetitive cycle where they could fight each other or other black opponents. Record books vary but McVea, short (5ft 10½in) and stocky (14st 10lb/206lbs), fought Langford over four continents (North and South America, Europe and Australia) some 15 times in nine years. He also fought other black fighters – Jim Johnson seven times and Harry Wills four times.

Jeannette, taller (6ft) and lighter (13st/182lbs) met McVea at least four times, three of them in Paris. The second in Paris in February 1909 gave McVea an unpopular points verdict, so the April in Paris unlimited marathon was designed to prove which of them was genuinely better. Both men believed a win would get a title fight with Johnson. It did not, but that carrot, and a Cirque de Paris audience including the cream of Parisian society, spurred them on, round after exhausting round, until the handsome Jeannette outlasted McVea. Jeannette was knocked to the floor 27 times and illegally revived with water and oxygen in his corner. McVea was down 11 times, and bedridden for two weeks after the bout.[74] No one, least of all such brave warriors, should have been inveigled by false promises into a situation where only the limitations of the human frame could distinguish between them.

Two nights later in London, 19 April 1909, at the NSC, 'Iron' Hague (William Ian Hague) of Mexborough, Yorkshire was on show. His presence there was interesting. Had the question posed by irreverent modern crowds –

'Who ate all the pies?' – been levied then, the truthful answer would have been, 'Iron has!' Born 6 November 1885, the 23-year-old Hague had already shown all his boxing virtues and vices. At 6ft and a solid 14st/196lbs, he had a powerful pair of shoulders and a potential knockout punch in each horny fist. Put first into a glassworks at a tender age – the days of secondary education for working-class children being a long way off – he capitalised on his raw strength and swapped the factory for the coalmine for a few more pence, supplementing his meagre income by enrolling in that most demanding of academies, the boxing booth.[75]

Hague's educational deficiencies made him prone to the attractive pseudo-theorem that as productivity lay in profit divided by time, a two-minute knockout required much less preparation than a points victory. This sustained him through some spectacular demolitions of eager amateurs in the Yorkshire booths and for the early part of his career after he turned professional in 1903. Unfortunately, it convinced him further that it was unprofitable to train for a 20-round bout if he could win in one or two.

For the moment, his punch hard and train less strategy worked. Over went the quaintly named Corporal Sunshine in four rounds, and the veteran Big Ben Taylor, the Woolwich Infant, in two. As British heavyweights were then rare as orchids, these and other successes brought Hague a match with the reigning British heavyweight champion, the heavily tattooed and stocky Gunner James Moir (5ft 9½in and 13st 8lb/190lbs) at the NSC on 19 April 1909, with a purse of £900 to split (£650 to the winner). Also

Sam Langford (1880–1956) 'The Boston Tar Baby' came to the National Sporting Club to challenge British heavyweight champion Iron Hague (1885–1951) on 24 May 1909.

Historic Images/Alamy Stock Photo

at stake were side bets of £200, and Moir's title.

In an excessively productive 2 minutes 47 seconds, Moir was knocked down by powerful jabs and swings three times running, got up twice, and was content to stay on one knee for the third time until ten seconds had elapsed, and to be spared the taste of any more Yorkshire brawn. Hague's training (the only skimpy thing about him) had been sufficient, just, and his expanding waistline no serious handicap, although *The Times* (20 April 1909) was sniffily accurate – 'Hague's victory, which was hailed with enthusiasm, must be accounted a very cheap one.'

How cheap emerged a month later at the NSC on 24 May 1909. Hague was back, having set up a training camp at the Pier Hotel in the cosy seaside resort of Withernsea, near Hull on the north-east coast. Rolls of flesh over his waistband suggested Iron had spent more quality time in the Pier Hotel dining room than in the gymnasium. The purse was £1,400; the club was packed; expectations were even higher, for in the other corner was one of the formidable Big Four, Sam Langford, a man some authorities believe to have been the greatest boxer never to have won a world title, and that because of the prejudice against black fighters. When Bettinson spoke to Hague about his training, the complacent answer was, 'He doesn't weigh 12 stones, does he? Whatever chance has a man of that weight got with me?'[76] Hague failed to realise the quality and strength Langford packed into his compact frame.

Known ludicrously as the Boston Tar Baby, although actually born in Nova Scotia, Langford gained weight

Hague, clearly a chip off the old block, came to town with his father and supporter.
Dearne Valley/Alamy Stock Photo

Hague, unwisely contemptuous of Langford's power, suffered a stunning defeat.
BoxRec

over the years, but not by the Hague methods. Born in 1883, he boxed professionally first as a lightweight, and was good enough at the weight to beat the great Joe Gans in 1903. He grew to a muscular 11st 11lb/165lbs, a middleweight fighting heavyweights out of economic necessity, and trapped like his fellow black fighters in a restricted circuit.

Iron Hague, fat and white, loomed large in the other corner, half a foot taller than Langford's 5ft 6½in, and many pies heavier. Langford had been in London two years before. His comment on his experiences on London streets illuminated the treatment he expected at home: 'You really allow coloured folk to walk with white people?' The NSC audience greeted him enthusiastically. Whatever else could be said about them, they had no difficulty in accepting black boxers in the Covent Garden ring ever since the much-admired Peter Jackson (1861–1901), the West Indian/ Australian black heavyweight had appeared there in 1892.

Langford had previously stopped Tiger Smith in four rounds in the NSC ring in 1907, although film of the fight had been suppressed. This was not because of sensitivities about a black–white confrontation, but because the film had included a shot of two young royals,

the future King Edward VIII and the future King George VI, at the ringside.[77] The media, as remained true during the abdication crisis of the 1930s, saw their duty as being guardians of the public royal image in a way quite unknown in the early 19th century or the late 20th. They changed later, as did the club in its willingness to host black fighters, even those as blameless as Langford.

For their subscriptions, the club members got plenty of excitement. Those who had taken the longer odds on a Hague victory (Langford was a 4/6 favourite at ringside) gulped a little when Hague removed his robe and showed his ample belly. They were mollified when Hague launched fierce attacks from the bell in the first, the second and the third rounds. Hope turned almost to ecstasy when Hague caught Langford with a swinging right to the side of the head to put the Canadian down. Down, but by no means out, and Langford's skill, form and fitness reasserted themselves spectacularly in the fourth.

Langford's left glove buried itself in the Yorkshire man's ample midriff, and as Iron doubled up, his chin met a sweetly timed right hook precisely on the point. Even in the dressing room afterwards, Hague was unable to grasp the fact that he had been knocked out, and that a man so much lighter and smaller than himself could possibly have hit him so hard and so productively. Sam had no such doubts. As he confided to the ringsiders as he rested on the ropes listening to the count, 'He ain't gonna get up, boys. That baby's out for keeps!'[78]

Later in life, Iron would show, like a holy mediaeval relic, the gloves with which he had once floored the great

Sam Langford and point to two brown spots on one of them – blood from Langford's ear, he claimed. He never seriously mollified his lackadaisical attitude to training. Nevertheless, he did not defend his British title against a British contender at the NSC until 24 April 1911 (with what result we shall see later). Therefore, he was able to call himself the British heavyweight champion for the time being. Sadly, he found his brand of raw physical courage, undermined by token training, would not win him later battles. On the battlefield of Ypres in 1915, he sucked in lungfuls of German poison gas, seriously damaging even his abused but resilient frame. He eked out a painful post-war existence in a Sheffield steelworks, frequently falling ill, and he died in poverty aged 65 in 1951. His sole possession then was the gloves from the Langford fight, spots and all.

Sam Langford's end was also touched by tragedy. After a very long career record – over 250 official fights and probably over 600 unofficial ones – he retired in 1926 and was gradually forgotten by the fight fraternity. Old, blind and penniless in a Harlem tenement room in January 1944, he was rediscovered by Al Laney, a sports journalist. Details published in the *New York Herald Tribune* and in *Reader's Digest* pricked a few consciences and led to the setting up of a $10,000 trust fund donated by grateful boxing supporters who wanted to repay the man for the pleasure he had given in his prime. He was then properly cared for until he died in Cambridge, Massachusetts on 12 January 1956.

Unlike Langford, whom he had beaten in Boston in April 1906, but in a harder contest than he generally

Polish-American Stanley Ketchel (1886–1910) was a middleweight of uncontrolled passions. He died when shot in the back by a jealous farmhand.
Bain Collection, Prints & Photographs Division, Library of Congress, LC-DIG-ggbain-01676

at the signing of the contracts, the challenger wore built-up shoes and extra shoulder padding.

He was the infamous Stanley Ketchel (born Stanisław Kiecal of Polish immigrant farming stock in Grand Rapids, Michigan on 14 September 1886). Anything Ketchel lacked in physique, he made up for in aggression. Some thought him born angry and rechristened him the Michigan Assassin. Like other fighters of later years, Johnny Tapia of Albuquerque for example, his bristling hostility actually stemmed from childhood experiences as lurid as any a cheap novelist could have invented. As a 12-year-old, he had found his father in a barn with his throat cut. His mother was murdered a few months later. Small wonder, therefore, that in his short life, tenderer virtues were absent.

Before signing to meet Johnson, Ketchel shared in some memorably savage fights. There were four with Joe Thomas – 4 July, 2 September and 12 December 1907, and 18 August 1908 – that had ringsiders wincing in sympathy; and four with a rugged ex-miner from Illinois, Billy Papke – 4 June, 7 September and 26 November 1908, and 5 July 1909 – fights both men considered episodes in a personal vendetta. In the first seconds of the series, Ketchel set the tone by landing a full-bodied right when Papke went to touch gloves and went on to win on points in ten. Papke replied in kind in the second fight, stopping Ketchel in 12. In the third meeting, Ketchel knocked out Papke in the 11th, and then won on points in their last meeting over 20 bloody rounds.[79] Though Ketchel clinched the series 3-1, he was no mellower after

cared for, Jack Johnson, the world heavyweight champion, was enjoying the full fruits of his December 1908 victory over Tommy Burns. He had no intention of giving Langford a title chance when he could take easier lucrative outings against white

hopefuls. One such was undertaken on 16 October 1909 in Colma, California.

The new challenger was white, and physically no more than a middleweight – a mere 5ft 9in and 11st 6lb/160lbs. So that the discrepancy between the men should not be too apparent

When Ketchel met his hated rival Billy Papke (1886–1936) of Illinois at Vernon, California on 7 September 1908, he suffered a 12th-round knockout himself.
BoxRec

it. For him, in and out of the ring, life was a perpetual psychodrama. He was, said one of his heavyweight opponents, Philadelphia Jack O'Brien, 'tumultuously ferocious'.

A canny Californian promoter, 'Sunny Jim' Coffroth, heavily involved in the Ketchel series against Papke, next matched the battered and battering Ketchel against the man all white racists wanted to see beaten, Jack Johnson. Coffroth boosted the purse by selling the film rights. To ensure there would be enough ring minutes to film, Coffroth reached a secret agreement with both fighters – Johnson would not actually knock out Ketchel.[80]

In the era, fixed fights were not uncommon. Burns, for example, became a promoter frequently involved in convenient 'arrangements'. Johnson could, in any case, be a notably generous opponent, taking no pleasure in punishing inferior fighters for the sake of it. One such, Arthur Bennett of Walworth, quoted Johnson as saying to him, 'Jim, I want you to come into me, for if you stay away, I shall hit you more times than I want to.'[81] The merciless demeanour Johnson adopted for Burns in Australia, and for others who turned their meeting into a racist encounter,

was not permanent. A man who had taken part in degrading battles royal had little taste for knocking other black men senseless for the delectation of all white audiences.

Unconvincing sequences in Hollywood boxing movies demonstrate difficulties inherent in conforming to a predetermined script. Round 12 of the Johnson v Ketchel contest demonstrates another. Ketchel (supposedly now 12st 2¼lb/170¼lbs) was guilty of a double-cross, and tried to knock out Johnson (14st 9¼lb/205¼lbs). Perhaps he was incapable of restraining his instincts. Jabs from Johnson cut his face and kept him at a distance, and Johnson's gloves gripped his biceps frustratingly whenever he tried to close in. Suddenly, he felled Johnson with a round right arm swing, catching Johnson just behind the left ear. It was not Ketchel's cleverest ploy.

Johnson was up long before the count could be completed. He pounced on Ketchel with a long chopping right with all his weight behind it that left Ketchel twitching on the floor. So vigorous was the follow-through that Johnson had to hurdle over the recumbent Ketchel to avoid falling himself. His balance recovered, he leaned patiently on the ropes as the referee counted Ketchel out.[82]

Johnson's mighty punch provided the film with an ending more dramatic than any written screenplay and put Ketchel temporarily in hospital for dental treatment. Thirty-four seconds of decisive action, which had brought the crowd noisily to its feet, was followed by 60 seconds of sullen silence as the spectators, who had parted with $40,000 to be there, quietly dispersed.

The following spring and summer, 1910, Ketchel had another six bouts, including some against excellent opponents. He fought a no-decision six-rounder with Sam Langford in April and had knockout wins over Porky Dan Flynn and Willie Lewis in May. But then, outside the ring,

Ketchel the middleweight faced heavyweight Johnson on 16 October 1909 in Colma, California. He had the effrontery to floor Johnson in the 13th. The response was deadly – Ketchel out cold as Johnson relaxes on the ropes.
BnF

his wayward conduct had unforeseen consequences. While staying on a farm in Conway, Missouri, he seduced or probably raped the farm housekeeper, Goldie Smith. Her boyfriend Walter D. Dipley's reaction was positively Ketchel-like. He shot Ketchel in the back with a rifle, a revenge that cost him 24 years in prison, and Goldie Smith 12 as an accessory. Ketchel died in hospital from his wounds on 15 October 1910, slain as much by his own uncontrollable passions as by the bullets. He had died as violently as he had lived.

In London in late 1909, there were two outstanding contests emphasising the power of NSC control. At the weight limits the club had established in February, in the club outside of which no British championship fight would be recognised, and graced by the presentation of the first two of Lord Lonsdale's new belts, the British championships were decided at lightweight (9st 9lb/135lbs) and at middleweight (11st 6lb/160lbs). The fights were worthy of their enhanced status.

The lightweight fight took place on Monday, 8 November 1909 between Freddie Welsh of Pontypridd, South Wales, and Johnny Summers of London via Middlesbrough. It was a perfect match. Both weighed in comfortably at 9st 8lb/134lbs, although Summers stripped completely to do so. They looked quite different. The fair-skinned Summers, born 21 January 1883, had an unruly forelock bouncing about on his high forehead, not a chest hair in sight, and the shoulder muscles and biceps of a middleweight. He often brushed the irritating forelock back with his glove during rounds, and some feared Welsh might catch him with a damaging punch mid-grooming. He was the more naturally gifted fighter.

Welsh, the self-styled Welsh Wizard, was born Frederick Hall Thomas on 5 March 1886. He looked frailer in limb and torso but had trained himself to punch and move swiftly. The

Freddie Welsh (1886–1927) 'The Welsh Wizard', Tom Thomas (1880–1911) and Jim Driscoll, the Welsh triumvirate who dominated early Lonsdale Belt contests.
WalesOnline.co.uk

bronzed-skin athlete he had become was essentially a manufactured article, the product of years of physical culture, originally undertaken because he had been an undersized consumptive child. Application and nurture rather than nature brought Welsh's successes. Inside or outside the ring he did nothing instinctively; all was the product of a

high intelligence applied to his whole existence.

He was self-taught and no less intellectual for that. He was practically a one-man sweet science academy. He could not afford to be hit too hard or too often, so he cultivated elusiveness and a frustrating defence. He developed his legs so that he could travel twice or thrice as far around the ring as an opponent and still not flag. He needed a nutritious diet, so he devised an individual vegetarian programme with special vitamin supplements to give him strength and stamina without bulk. For close quarters, he developed a whole series of holds, hits and tie-ups (many illegal) to neutralise the other boxer, while landing debilitating hooks and chops to the kidneys to weaken him.

Welsh's defiance of boxing's contemporary conventions – a fighter who did not believe in good red meat? – brought him some unflattering epithets: the Snowflake Puncher, the Fruitarian Fighter, and the like. Yet his brain was not merely ingenious for its own sake, it gave him a mental edge, a boxing psychologist before his time. Below his dark unruly hair flopping down over the left side of his forehead, his pixilated features bore a frequent mocking and mirthless grin. This could drive even normally equable opponents to fury.

Opponents would look silly at a distance, then frustrated and hurt at close quarters where Welsh would craftily rub and poke with his head at their faces, while raising welts with whipping, short hooks to their kidneys. It was like fighting a man with three offensive limbs – a left, a right and a hard skull. He held an opponent by sliding an arm under his opponent's arm so as to make it appear that he was the innocent one. The other man suffered a double indignity – held by Welsh yet reprimanded by the referee for holding. And all the time there was that superior smile to make him feel worse. Half in admiration, that other master of dubious ring arts, Abe Attell, conceded, 'The guy showed me tricks about boxing I've never seen before.'[83]

Summers and Welsh were very experienced. Welsh had learned many of his nefarious niceties in American rings, having emigrated from Wales to Philadelphia as a boy when his estate agent father died. Back in London from 1907, he had taken useful British scalps – Young Joseph and Jack Goldswain included. Summers boasted his own victories over an American in Jimmy Britt, had fought in the USA himself, and at home beat both Spike Robson and Goldswain. The Goldswain victory allowed him to claim the unofficial British lightweight title now up for official NSC endorsement if he could defeat Welsh this November night.

The contest was a worthy one between two highly skilful but contrasting styles, between Wales and England, and between Church and Chapel. Summers was a devout Roman Catholic who knelt momentarily in prayer after each round and had the cloth strips of a Catholic monastic order tucked into his sock. Summers, with or without divine aid, stayed calm and controlled and inscrutable, no matter what provocation he received from Welsh. He won the first mental battle by challenging the legality of Welsh's bandages. He then sat impassively in his corner, while Welsh had the irritation of returning to the dressing room to be re-dressed.

The pattern established over the 20 championship rounds was for Welsh to land subtle, and sometimes heavy, punches to accumulate points, yet never to be sure that he had a beaten man before him. Summers sprang two surprises – he pressed forward time and again rather than standing off, and he pummelled Welsh's kidneys at least as often as Welsh did his. It took Welsh ten

rounds to achieve any kind of physical ascendancy. By then, Summers bled intermittently from the nose having suffered some stern left jabs full in the face. He found Welsh's smothering clinches difficult to counter.

Summers had the club audience generally on his side. Two of his attacks, fierce crosses to the head in the fifth, and a right hook to the ribs in the seventh, temporarily removed the sardonic smile from Welsh's face. Summers was strong. Summers was resilient. Even when Welsh rocked him back on his heels, he would shake his head like a dog recently emerged from water and go on looking to knock Welsh out. Yet when Welsh missed with a swing and nearly toppled over, Summers was either too slow or too apprehensive that this might be a cunning Welsh ploy to lure him in. When Summers's own swings missed as he tired in the later rounds, Welsh's responses were swift and punishing.

The 18th was conclusive evidence that Welsh would win, unless Summers could suddenly land a definitive right. Promisingly, Summers unbalanced Welsh with a left hook to the body as they emerged from a clinch. Welsh should have been vulnerable. Instead, before Summers could unload another major punch, Welsh was back on balance and driving Summers back to the ropes with three damaging hooks to the body, a swift left to the jaw, and, as the unlucky Summers bounced back from the ropes, catching him on the jaw with another straight and powerful left.

Most men would have been knocked out by this major attack. The resilient Summers was forced to clinch and hold, but he stayed on his feet. He did so again even when Welsh repeated the treatment in both the 19th and 20th.

Welsh could add more points for his inevitable victory. He could not finish the fight prematurely.

At the post-mortems, Welsh, ever the generous opponent *out* of the ring, acknowledged Summers's stubborn qualities: 'Johnny Summers is as clean and gentlemanly a fighter as ever put on a glove, and … his punch is a thing to be respected, and I am precious glad that I was able to keep myself clear of so many of them as I did.' Summers's dressing room reflections were just as apt: 'I don't feel that I have anything to grieve at more than ordinary, for, next to beating him, I think the next best memory I could have is to know that I have held my own so well as I did with such a flier at the game.'[84]

The quality of the Welsh–Summers contest for the very first Lonsdale Belt ever awarded, coupled with the attention it drew far beyond the walls of the NSC, added to expectations for the 20 December 1909 contest. This was another Anglo-Welsh encounter between Tom Thomas of Penygraig in the Rhondda Valley, and Londoner Charlie Wilson of Notting Hill, for the British middleweight title and the second Lonsdale Belt. Also on offer were a £400 purse and £200 a side in side stakes.

Thomas Thomas was born 19 April 1880 on a bare mountain-top farm at Carncelyn near Penygraig, a place suitably utilitarian for a man whose first and family names were prosaically indistinguishable. A man of few words, he preferred his own company to that of an entourage of parasites and flatterers. He was happiest when running along the lonely mountain tops or pounding a home-made bag in his barn. He left the farm, worked exclusively by him

and his father, only to take place in a contest, and he returned to the farm immediately the business was over. Not for him the nightspots of Covent Garden around the NSC, only the first possible train back to Wales. Once home, he bypassed the convivial valley pubs and clubs where he was such a local hero and went directly back to the lonely farm, perhaps to tell the sheep about his latest exploits. The Welsh valleys before the First World War, along with a large share of the world's coal, were producing a rich supply of hardy and accomplished boxers. They founded a tradition that sustained men like Welsh, Driscoll and Thomas, and would stretch to the Jimmy Wildes, the Dai Dowers and the Johnny Owens of the future.

The pale-skinned, dark-haired Thomas had a lozenge of black hair across his chest more luxuriant than anything that grew on his farm. Where Welsh had turned himself into a boxer from unpromising physical beginnings, Thomas had natural strength and talent, a sweetly timed punch in either hand and an instant attraction to the ring established by his first glimpse of a boxing booth. In most working-class areas of Britain, other than towns, a visiting boxing booth or a travelling fair were as near to entertainment as small communities ever got.

Thomas boxed regularly at the booths, preparation as rough and ready as his self-devised training programme. Later, he employed the eccentric Dai Dollings, a trainer who had a more eclectic collection of herbs than the Kew Gardens seed bank, a selection of which he carried in a shabby champagne bottle and administered in the corner, probably illegally, to cure ills

and injuries from cut eyes to leather-induced narcosis.

Hard work on the farm and rigorous dedication to training turned Thomas into a spare and muscular middleweight. Middleweights, remember, circa 1880 to 1910, before the new NSC codification, might be regularly matched against heavyweights – Ketchel against Jack Johnson, and the uncanny Bob Fitzsimmons (never more than about 12st 7lb/175lbs at his heaviest) against Jim Jeffries (15st 10lb/220lbs) for example.

Thomas had the potential to be another Ketchel or Fitzsimmons; he was just as strong at the weight and just as skilful. However, he was rarely at his fittest. His was not the indolence of a laid-back Iron Hague; rather, he suffered from a chronic rheumatic or arthritic inflammation of the joints. Between a strongly sculpted thigh and a taut resilient calf, both with strong muscles well able to carry Thomas around the ring for a full 20 rounds, was a knee joint that might cause him agony – agony akin to severe toothache, which left him barely able to hobble, let alone box. Behind his inscrutable facial mask lay his consciousness of major joints ready to flare up in crippling fashion.

His career, up to meeting Charlie Wilson, emphasised the stop-start pattern. He knocked out opponents with regularity at Wonderland and at the NSC, where in a much-discussed 28 May 1906 contest, he had defeated Pat O'Keefe on points in 15 rounds to become the generally recognised British middleweight champion. Thereafter, instead of enjoying profitable defences, he suffered periodic lay-offs with severe rheumatism and its painful effects. He took only one fight in 1907 and five in

1908. Resuming his career in October 1909 after another ten-month hiatus, he took two warm-up fights before the clash with Wilson. Though only insiders knew it, on a training run days before the Wilson fight, Thomas's knee had let him down again, and he had been carried home in a trap. A mystery mixture of Dolling's massages and magic potions had barely allowed him to walk again, let alone run and box.

Charlie Wilson would have been an odds-on favourite had the bookmakers been privy to knowledge of Thomas's interrupted run. Wilson was tall and elegant, his pale torso tapering to a tight waist, but he lacked Thomas's speed of thought and punch. He had often gone into the ring at 12 stone-plus to meet heavyweights, and some doubted whether he could any longer make the 11st 6lb limit. He proved them wrong by coming in at 11st 3½lb/157½lbs.

Wilson was neither slow nor clumsy, yet Thomas made him look so. Wilson believed his best tactic was to slow Thomas down gradually with blows about the body, and he used his longer arms to launch swings and drives towards that target. The tactic had two drawbacks. Thomas's surprisingly dainty and elusive footwork meant that the Wilson punches only landed weakly on a receding target. In addition, as Wilson moved towards Thomas, forceful stinging lefts to the face brought him to a painful standstill.

The second round confirmed the trend. Thomas landed his left leads regularly, Wilson struggling to reply with an occasional left hook. But there was a difference. The second round only lasted 2 minutes 27 seconds. At that point, Thomas switched from his punishing straight left to a strong

hook to the chin. As Wilson stumbled backwards, a lunge forward kept Thomas within range to follow up with a savage downward right to leave Wilson on his back, arms spread wide. Wilson bravely got up to a kneeling position, but his three attempts to rise in the remaining five seconds of the count were futile, and he toppled down again face first. Thomas, hoisted up on the shoulders of his supporters, was now the official champion and the Lonsdale Belt holder.[85] The NSC members who felt short-changed by paying championship prices for less than six minutes boxing were consoled by seeing film of the recent Langford v Hague and of Welsh v Summers bouts to round off an otherwise abbreviated evening.

Some time later, it was claimed that Wilson's rapid demise had been because of skulduggery at his hotel, and that a poisoned rabbit pie had robbed him of victory. Devotees of conspiracy theories spoke darkly of Dolling's magic potions being responsible. While not absolutely impossible, with Dolling cast as a Merlin able to infiltrate a hotel kitchen at will, the poisoning seems unlikely. In particular, Wilson, though deeply disappointed at losing so swiftly, made no mention of any problem *at the time*. Indeed, on his way to the ring from the dressing room, he told a correspondent he felt perfectly all right. And *Boxing*'s ringside reporter said quite graphically, 'There was no excuse for Wilson on the ground of lack of condition. If anything, he was a bit too fine; but there was no sign that his getting down to below weight had weakened him at all. He looked as fit as he has ever looked in his life, and confessed that he did so.' A man suffering even mild poisoning would hardly have presented so glowing a picture.

Between Thomas's receipt of the Lonsdale Belt, and the screening of the films, came a seductive little speech from Bettinson. He thanked Lord Lonsdale for his generous endorsement and the financing of his belts, and he expressed his conviction that the new NSC policy over weight categories and the official recognition of specific champions would soon be followed internationally. These were pious hopes.

The NSC and Bettinson could be just as short-sighted, obstructive and insular as anyone else. Victor Breyer, the French boxing journalist and enthusiast, came to London this very month of December 1909 to plead with the club officials to use their expertise to assist in the setting up of an international boxing control body. We have already seen how quickly and successfully the French absorbed British boxing. Breyer went away defeated and disappointed. The French, the Swiss and later the Belgians formed subsequently an International Boxing Union from 1912.[86] An important opportunity to advance the very standardisation Bettinson was supposed to believe in was lost.

It was no consolation to Breyer that previously the French Football Association had approached the English Football Association (November 1903) to ask them to lend their prestige to a projected federation of European football associations, to extend the English game further into Europe. The FFA received just as negative a put-down: 'The Council of the Football Association cannot see the advantages of such a Federation.'[87] In Paris, suspicions of perfidious Albion and predictable English Euro-scepticism were duly confirmed.

Endnotes:

1 Dobbs, B., *Edwardians at Play: Sport* 1890–1914 (London: Pelham Books, 1973) pp. 158–9.

2 Durso, J., *Madison Square Garden: One Hundred Years of History* (New York: Simon and Schuster, 1979) p. 96.

3 Quoted by Jersey Jones: 'Owen Moran, a Fighters' Fighter' *The Ring*, March 1949.

4 *Boxing*, 12 April 1913.

5 Blady, K., *The Jewish Boxers Hall of Fame* (New York: Shapolsky Books, 1988) p. 44.

6 *New York Times*, 30 January 1909.

7 *New York Times*, 11 February 1909.

8 Mullan, H., *Heroes and Hard Men: The Story of Britain's World Boxing Champions* (London: Stanley Paul, 1989) pp. 60–61. Driscoll entry in the DNB.

9 Myler, P., *A Century of Boxing Greats: Inside the Ring with the Hundred Best Boxers* (London: Robson Books, 1999) pp. 88–9.

10 See Blady, K., *Jewish Boxers Hall of Fame*, pp. 81–89.

11 *New York Times*, 11 February 1909.

12 *New York Times*, 20 February 1909.

13 Prestage, M., *Celtic Fists* (Derby: Breedon Books, 1997) p. 57.

14 Mullan, H., *Heroes and Hard Men*, p. 64.

15 *Western Mail*, 21 January 1925; 2 February 1925 and 4 February 1925.

16 *The Times*, 28 December 1908.

17 *Boxing World and Athletic Chronicle*, 2 December 1909ff.

18 *Boxing*, 11 September 1909.

19 *Boxing*, 11 September 1909.

20 Details drawn from *Boxing*, 18 September and 25 September 1909.

21 *Boxing World and Athletic Chronicle*, 23 December 1909.

22 Gorn, E. J., *The Manly Art: The Lives and Times of the Great Bare-Knuckle Champions* (London: Robson Books, 1989) p. 219.

23 Beadle, B., *Boxing's Mister President: The Story of the World Heavyweight Championship* (Dagenham: Wat Tyler Books, 1997) p. 44.

24 Blewett, B., *The A–Z of World Boxing* (Greenwich Editions, 2000) p. 393.

25 Handbill in the Holborn Empire box, Theatre Museum.

26 Handbill in the Holborn Empire box.

27 *British Boxing Yearbook* 1986, p. 340 – Jim Sullivan's record.

28 See, for example: Guttman, A., *The Erotic in Sports* (New York: Columbia University Press, c.1996) and Oates, J. C., *On Boxing* (London: Bloomsbury, 1987) p. 30.

29 Details drawn from *Boxing*, 18 September 1909.

30 Details from a bill reproduced in Willson Disher, M., *Pleasures of London* (London: Robert Hale, 1950).

31 *Boxing*, 27 November 1909 and 4 December 1909.

32 *Boxing World and Athletic Chronicle*, 2 December 1909.

33 *Boxing*, 27 November 1909 and 4 December 1909.

34 Wignall, T. C., *Thus Gods Are Made* (London: Hutchinson, n.d.) p.24.

35 Baedeker, K., *London and its Environs: Handbook for Travellers* (Leipzig, 1911 edition).

36 Baedeker, K., *London and its Environs*, p. 40.

37 Machray, R., *The Night Side of London* (London: T. Werner Laurie, n.d.). [Several editions were published in the early 1900s. Also drawn on for details about Wonderland.]

38 Machray, R., *The Night Side of London*, p. 260.

39 National Archives, Home Office File 45/18745.

40 Quotations drawn from reports and letters in the Greater London Archives: LCC Theatres Committee Papers LCC/Min/10,924.

41 *Boxing*, 15 January 1910.

42 Green, J., *A Social History of the Jewish East End in London 1914–39: A Study of Life, Labour and Liturgy* (Studies in British History Vol. 28, Lampeter 1991) p. 309.

43 Details shown in colour in Russell, C., and Lewis, H. S., *The Jew in London* (London 1900), but conveniently adapted for the endpapers of Gartner, L. P., *The Jewish Immigrant in England 1870–1914* (London: Allen and Unwin, 1960).

44 Green, J., *A Social History of the Jewish East End in London 1914–39*, pp. 305–307.

45 Boorstin, D., *The Americans: The Democratic Experience* (New York: Random House, 1973) p. 100.

46 Holmes, C., *Anti-Semitism in British Society 1876–1939* (London: Arnold, 1979) p. 5.

47 Holmes, C., *Anti-Semitism in British Society 1876–1939*, p. 5.

48 Gainer, B., *The Alien Invasion: The Origins of the Aliens Act of 1905* (London: Heinemann Educational Books, 1972) and Foot, P., *Immigration and Race in British Politics* (Harmondsworth: Penguin Special, 1965). [Foot's Chapter Five provides many depressing examples.]

49 Gartner, L. P., *The Jewish Immigrant in England 1870–1914*, p. 145.

50 Levine, P., *Ellis Island to Ebbets Field: Sport and the American Jewish Experience* (New York: Oxford University Press, 1993) p. 144.

51 Quoted in *The Jewish Chronicle*, 2 October 1908.

52 Mullan, H., *Boxing: Inside the Game* (Duxford: Icon Books, 1998) p. 5.

53 Oates, J. C., *On Boxing*, p. 100.

54 Harris, J., *Private Lives, Public Spirit: A Social History of Britain 1870–1914* (Oxford University Press, 1993).

55 *Boxing*, 25 September 1909.

56 National Archives File BT 31/6470/45578.

57 *Boxing*, 11 September 1909.

58 *Jewish Chronicle*, 27 August 1909.

59 National Archives File 1076133 / BT31/15196/ 35292.

60 Deghy G., Noble and Manly: T*he History of the National Sporting Club* (Hutchinson, 1956) p. 169.

61 Deghy G., *Noble and Manly*, p. 140.

62 Article on gloves in *Boxing World and Athletic Chronicle*, 5 May 1910.

63 Odd, G., *Encyclopedia of Boxing* (London: Hamlyn, 1983) pp. 172ff. [Helpfully lists the divisions with brief explanations.]

64 See the Jim Ruck article on Spike Robson, *Boxing News*, 10 May 1957.

65 For full details and a brilliant example of new perspectives arising as a result of painstaking research, see the Harold Alderman series, 'Early Gloved Championship Boxing: the True Facts' in successive editions of *The British Boxing Board of Control Yearbook* from 1999 onwards.

66 *The British Boxing Board of Control Yearbook*, 1999, p. 218.

67 *Boxing*, 13 November 1909.

68 Cumbria Record Office, Carlisle, Lonsdale Papers D/Lons/L1/2 Boxes 20 and 21 Jan–July 1909.

69 Schira, G., *De La Boxe* (Paris: Les Editions J. Suisse, 1943) pp. 45–49.

70 At least so says Bill Stern in *Boxing News*, 26 April 1957, p. 8.

71 *Boxing*, 8 January 1910.

72 *Boxing*, 23 October 1909.

73 *The Times*, 19 April 1909 says three hours and a half.

74 Details drawn from an article on Jeannette by John Jarrett, *Boxing News*, 9 March 1975.

75 See Hague's obituary, *Boxing News*, 29 August 1951; a profile by Gilbert Odd, *Boxing News*, 8 June 1979; Kent, G., *The Great White Hopes* (Stroud: Sutton Publishing, 2005) pp. 92–101.

76 Clark, N., *All in the Game: Memoirs of the Ring and Other Sporting Experiences* (London: Methuen, 1935) p. 84.

77 Deghy G., *Noble and Manly*, p. 198.

78 Sam Langford profile by John Jarrett, *Boxing News*, 28 February 1975. Butler, J., *Kings of the Ring* (London, n.d. [1936]) p. 29 has a slightly different version.

79 See among many accounts, Odd, G.,: *Great Moments in Sport; Boxing: Cruisers to Mighty Atoms* (London: Pelham, 1974) Chapter Five.

80 Roberts, R., *Papa Jack: Jack Johnson and the Era of White Hopes* (New York: Simon & Schuster, 1985) p. 82.

81 *Boxing News*, 11 January 1957.

82 Abbreviated film snippets of rounds one, two, eight and the decisive 12th can be seen in *The Boxers* video No.27: Jack Johnson; also findable on YouTube.

83 Quoted in Eddie Baxter's profile of Welsh, *Boxing News*, 14 July 1967. See also 'The Welsh Wizard' in the 31 July 1959 issue; Gallimore, A., *Occupation Prizefighter: The Freddie Welsh Story* (Bridgend: Seren Books, 2006).

84 A very full report and reflections on the fight were carried in the 13 November 1909 issue of *Boxing*.

85 Full reports in *Boxing*, 24 December 1909, and *Boxing World and Athletic Chronicle*, 23 December 1909.

86 *The British Boxing Board of Control Yearbook* 2000, p. 193.

87 Quoted in *The Oxford Companion to Sports and Games* (St Albans: Paladin, 1977) p. 303.

CHAPTER 5

DEATHS IN THE RING
1910

In Which Blood Is Spilled and Boxers Lose Out

AS 1910 began, the English political scene was as fraught as at any time throughout the turbulent 20th century. In January 1906, a Liberal Party promising extensive social and economic reforms won a landslide victory to replace a Conservative and Unionist government committed to the preservation of the status quo. When promise came to practice, the new Liberal government's radical ambitions were checked, not by the small rump (157 MPs) of Conservatives and their allies in the House of Commons, but by the unelected and overwhelmingly Conservative House of Lords. The fighting Welsh political bantamweight, David Lloyd George (1863–1945), had become the Liberal Chancellor of the Exchequer. A true contender, his challenge included a 1909 'People's Budget', aimed at landing some stinging punches on their lordships – income tax, supertax, death duties and land tax.

On 30 July 1909, the night before the third open-air contest between Jimmy Britt and Johnny Summers, in a speech at Limehouse, very adjacent to the small boxing halls of London's East End, Lloyd George had practically called out the Lords. ('No country, however rich, can permanently afford to have quartered upon its revenue a class which declines to do the duty which it was called upon to perform … I challenge them to judge the Budget.') Since July 1909, their lordships had not only judged the Welshman's budget, they had thrown it out of the ring. As a result, in January 1910, the country was in the middle of a General Election, called by the Liberal Prime Minister Asquith and designed to resolve the ongoing constitutional crisis. The election result – the Liberal government returned with a reduced majority – resolved very little.

Indeed, the result left the Liberals dependent upon Irish nationalists, themselves pressing for Home Rule for Ireland: a cause to which the Conservatives and Unionists were even more virulently opposed. The one man with enough experience and prestige to bring these warring factions to some compromise was the sportingly minded and diplomatically able King Edward VII. He died suddenly in May 1910. The crisis dragged on, not to be solved, merely to be overtaken by an even greater crisis when the great European war broke out in August 1914.

In 1910, other groups nursed legitimate grievances and resolved to wait no longer. From 1909 onwards, as the Liberals failed to ameliorate the distinctly second-class citizenship of women, the more militant women, the suffragettes, embarked upon more extreme forms of protest – civil disobedience, hunger strikes in prison, damage to male property. And as the Liberals failed to adjust the imbalance of power between low-paid workers and ruthless employers, industrial relations became ugly. Before 1910 was out, a Liberal Home Secretary (Winston Churchill) earned the long-standing hatred of the Welsh mining valleys by drafting in the 18th Hussars and the Metropolitan Police to Tonypandy to control striking miners. From 1910 to 1913, the number of strikes, many quite as bitter as the one in the Rhondda Valley, shot up dramatically.

What has all this to do with the noble art of boxing? Unfortunately, a great deal. Some people still believe the pre-First World War era to have been a time of peace and plenty, where all the manly Christian virtues were reflected in the flashing of a cricket bat or the sweet timing of a straight left, by handsome, young and strong if not over-muscular, English gentlemen. For some, boxing provided deep reassurance that whatever domestic or world disturbances were reported on the news pages, in the ring the old virtues would be upheld. The more elaborate and ritualised the ceremony, as at the NSC, or at Madison Square Garden on a fashionable New York evening, the more reassuring the spectacle. The crude brutality and ugly violence of the Regency period prizefight had been eliminated. The sense that power still rested with the dinner-jacketed employers at ringside, rather than with the two proletarian warriors punching each other for the pleasure of the audience, remained wonderfully comforting.[1]

When Tommy Burns had turned uppity colonial by asking for the money up front at the NSC (see Prologue), his behaviour called the social conventions into alarming question. A few Edwardian boxers and jockeys acquired enough affluence and charisma as to be seen at glamorous social events in their own right, but such privileges were rare and token in nature. (That celebrity and wealth can occasionally transcend humble origins drew the acid comment from the exceptionally talented black boxer Larry Holmes, b. 1949 and WBC/IBF world heavyweight champion 1978–85. 'I was black once – when I was poor!')

Boxing and football were textbook examples of industrial relations modelled on rigid servant/master, upstairs/downstairs templates. Boxers who fought hard or skilfully at the NSC were applauded and admired. They were not allowed through the front door like members and guests, only through the tradesmen's entrance at the back. When Jack Johnson defied the doorman, it was another embarrassing

Jim Jeffries dominated heavyweight boxing from 1899–1905, retiring undefeated. The 'White Hope' lobby persuaded him out of retirement.
Bain collection, Prints & Photographs Division, Library of Congress, LC-DIG-ggbain-08038

example of his failure to observe the expected social niceties.

Boxing as entertainment and comforting social balm flourished. Yet that tells at best half of the story. As we saw in 1909, boxing can raise the most intense of emotions and turn the ring into a raw theatre embodying deadly serious passions and commitments.[2] Any informed sports follower will think of appropriate examples, past and present.

Few, however, could find an example to rival the boxing contest

that took place on 4 July 1910 at Reno, Nevada, just on the California/ Nevada border, when the white James J. Jeffries, the former world heavyweight champion, came out of retirement to attempt to take the championship back from the black Jack Johnson. Where those adjectives 'black' and 'white' should be redundant, newspapers in 1910 used the words as often as possible, and employed capitals, italics, bold fonts, and triple underlining for them, lest any unsophisticated reader might mistake Jeffries v Johnson for a mere sporting event, rather than supposedly a mighty symbolic battle between two warring ethnic groups.

A full account of the contest will be found in its chronological place in this chapter. However, the long, intense build-up to that fight started with Jack London's demeaning words after Johnson's defeat of Burns in December 1908 ('Jeffries must emerge from his alfalfa farm and remove the golden smile from Johnson's face. Jeff, it's up to you!'). It culminated in the ugly repercussions in the aftermath of the July 1910 fight, but it was an unpleasant brooding presence hovering over the sport like a threatening cloud for the whole of 1910.

The more sensationalist newspapers were not the only culprits. As early as 1 November 1909, the *New York Times* included in its editorial pronouncements, a few unworthy paragraphs to insult black and white boxers alike:

… It is a really serious matter that, if the negro wins, thousands and thousands of other negroes will wonder whether, in claiming equality with whites, they have not been too modest. In too many cases the wonder will be followed by belief, and the result will be an acerbation of relations already sufficiently bitter.

Not a few white pugilists, from an instinctive feeling of ethnic pride founded on a deeper wisdom than they had the intelligence to realize, have refused to meet negroes in the ring. It were desirable, we incline to think, that all of them should

do so, for it is not well that the two races should meet … when the conditions are such that victory and defeat are decided by the possession on one side or the other of a superiority so trivial as that given by weight, strength, and agility.

Of course, prize fighting is not a mere matter of brute prowess, but the demands it makes upon the intellect are narrowly limited, and, while the sort of efficiency which avails in pugilism is in itself a valuable asset for the members of a dominant race, it is perilous to risk even nominally the right of that race to exercise dominance in a conflict which brings so few of its higher superiorities into play.

Therefore, as this fight cannot, or at least probably will not, be prevented, even those who have an absurdly exaggerated horror of prize fighting as a 'brutal' sport should gently warm in their sensitive minds a little hope that the white man may not lose, while the rest of us will wait in open anxiety the news that he has licked the – well, since it must be in print, let us say the negro, even though it is not the first word that comes to the tongue's tip.[3]

This thoroughly unpleasant piece hints hypocritically what it wants urban sophisticates to read between the lines. A Johnson win will make blacks feel unjustifiably superior; blacks may win in the ring by superior brawn where superior white brain power is at temporary disadvantage;

and we intelligent whites will not need the mystery word in the last sentence spelled out for us. When a so-called respectable newspaper of record could freely circulate these assumptions and linguistic niceties, it can readily be imagined what was said on the streets and in bars from north to south. Even the English publication, *Boxing*, normally balanced on the subject, pronounced a Johnson victory 'too awful to contemplate'.[4] From the moment Ketchel hit the canvas on 16 October 1909, to the fight between Jeffries and Johnson on 4 July 1910, the ugly tension about the outcome and its apocalyptic possibilities was an ever-present.

Elsewhere, boxing thrived. In February 1910 alone, there were three events worth recording in detail. Jim Driscoll reappeared at the NSC on 14 February 1910. His opponent, weighing in at 8st 12½oz/112.78lbs to Driscoll's 8st 13oz/112.81lbs, was Seaman Arthur Hayes. The new featherweight Lonsdale Belt was on offer. With the recent triumphs of Welsh and Thomas, it looked as if it was necessary to come from South Wales to win one of Lonsdale's belts. Hayes failed to break the sequence, defeated less by the tradition than by Driscoll's ring mastery.

Every ringside prophet predicted the course of the fight. Driscoll would keep Hayes out of range with his scintillating left, sometimes as light reproof, sometimes as strict chastisement. If that failed, Driscoll's consummate footwork would take him to places where Hayes's punches could not reach. Hayes, a stockier, bustling body-puncher with a shorter reach, would need to get inside and use short hooks, uppercuts and crosses. It was a classic boxer v fighter confrontation.

The prophets were only half-right. Driscoll dominated at a distance with the left, and he did use his ballroom quality footwork to avoid Hayes's punches. The surprise was that Hayes preferred to stand off and counter from a distance. It did not work. For the first nine minutes of action, the swarthy Driscoll hit the pale-skinned Hayes freely with his jab. When he got bored with his easy success, he switched to an over-the-top right or a passing right hook. By the fourth round, even Hayes grasped that his initial tactics were misguided.

Whatever tactics he had adopted, he would have been trounced. Yet the plucky Hayes could not stop trying. Reverting to type, he rushed out for the fifth, attempting to swarm all over Driscoll. But 'one of the wonders of the world at his weight' (as Hayes called Driscoll in the dressing room inquest) sent him reeling to the floor again with an exuberant combination of lefts and rights, culminating in a sickening left to the midriff. The gritty seaman survived the round, somehow, but even Driscoll looked relieved when Tom Scott, the referee, declined to continue the next count beyond three once Hayes was dropped again in the sixth. Driscoll, the all-round ring master, had clinched the featherweight belt with 14 rounds to spare.[5]

The second February event shows boxing challenging the barriers of class, gender and prejudice that had once confined it to seedy male realms in the English-speaking world. In Paris at the Cirque de Paris, there was a night to rival the opulent opera of the Second Empire or a French society ball for

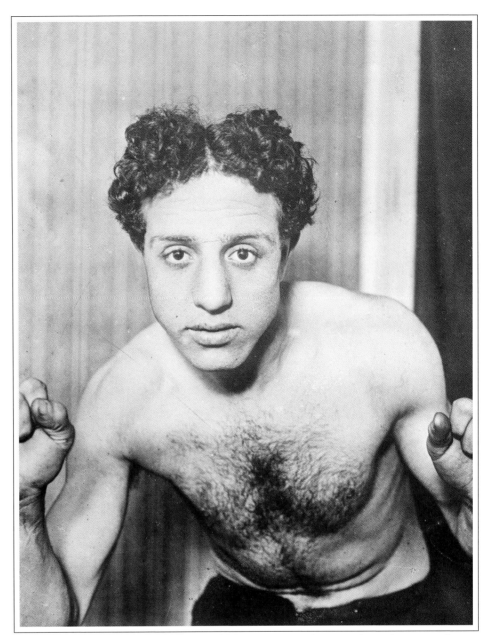

Harry Lewis (1886–1956): the Jewish Philadelphian was as popular in London and Paris as at home. When not posing as a Harpo Marx lookalike, he was a boxer to be feared.
Bain Collection, Prints & Photographs Division, Library of Congress, LC-DIG-ggbain-50006

glamour and social cachet. For the French equivalent of five guineas, a ringside seat could be obtained amidst a glittering array of French society – politicians of cabinet rank, millionaires, writers, painters and lawyers, and, in strong contrast to the audience in London's NSC, women of the highest social rankings, draped in jewellery and clad in the colourful creations of the Paris fashion houses.

They had gathered to see a world welterweight championship contest between two American boxers: Harry Lewis, the experienced 23-year-old champion from Philadelphia, who was as dapper and handsome as any of the French spectators there to see him, and his less seasoned but determined namesake, Willie Lewis. Harry Lewis was so popular in Paris he fought there no fewer than 14 times – a total boosted

Willie Lewis (1884–1949) shared his namesake's popularity in Europe.
Bain Collection, Prints & Photographs Division, Library of Congress, LC-DIG-ggbain-08232

by his exploits on 18 May 1910 when he beat Bert Scanlon (disqualified in round 2), Bert Ropert (knocked out in round 2) and Bill Davies (knocked out in round 1) in rapid succession all on the same day.[6] He was also a London regular.

Flamboyance was part of Harry's stock in trade. He was, as we saw, born Harry Besterman on 6 September 1886 to a New York Jewish family, whom he deceived about his boxing by adopting the ring name Lewis. The subterfuge was less about sparing an Orthodox family's religious sensibilities (a not uncommon motivation among many early Jewish fighters), than keeping his father Jacob out of his financial affairs.[7] When Harry's father found out about his son's lucrative gloved activities, he became so enthusiastic a supporter and amateur half-manager, he was dubbed Jake Pesterman. At Wonderland in London, where he was extremely popular for a bustling, aggressive style as distinctive as his flamboyant red hair, Harry sauntered to the ring in his colourful dressing gown and extinguished his cigar only when he had climbed into his corner.

Such insouciance did not impress Willie Lewis, who knew Harry well. They met five times between 1906 and 1910 and never reached a clear-cut verdict. Willie was neither as experienced nor as talented as Harry, but he was the one man whose style effectively countered Harry's virtues. On the big night in Paris, he would have to do this for a full 25 rounds to get a draw.

After ten minutes of exhilarating action, nothing seemed less likely. Barely had the reverberations of the first bell died away when Willie had been down twice for counts of three and five. To the consternation of the audience who feared their expensive evening finishing there and then, Willie was fortunate to survive the first round. The second round followed a similar course – Willie down again for a count of six, and scrambling and clinging for survival for the rest of the round. He was still there at the end of the third, but only at the cost of more heavy punishment.

Aided by his hard-working seconds, and reserves of energy engendered by the substantial chicken supper he had tucked away earlier, Willie survived the fourth and took the points himself. But for the next four rounds Harry walked through every one of Willie's counters, practically ignoring them in his determination to deliver the one punch that would finish Willie off. In the 11th, he almost succeeded with a rapid left-right, one-two, that put Willie down again for a count of seven. Harry had now abandoned all pretence of conventional defence with his gloves held low and contemptuously took punches on the jaw as if nothing Willie could do would ever cause him harm.

In the 14th, even Harry needed a breather, and the men clinched continuously as the English referee, his own stamina tested, forcibly parted them at regular intervals. Had the Lewises been fighting in the early 21st century instead of the early 20th, even a world championship bout would have lasted only *12* rounds, less than *half* of the 25 they were contracted to fight in 1910. And they fought *another* 25-round draw in Paris only two months later, on 23 April 1910, an accumulated 150 minutes of action.

The respite of a somnolent 14th round over, action resumed. Willie, partly refreshed, rattled up points in the 15th, and although Harry may have edged the 16th, he was himself beginning to flag, and took many of Willie's punches over the next three.

Nevertheless, he never looked likely to be floored, let alone knocked out, and more than held his own in the closing rounds. Indeed, in the 25th and last, he produced a swinging right that put Willie down yet again, if only briefly.

The referee's decision – a draw – must have done Harry Lewis some injustice. Putting an opponent down five times in four rounds (the equivalent of losing nine rounds in modern scoring), and still getting only a draw was harsh, especially as Harry shaded at least another seven rounds.[8] 'He usually belted my ears off in the early rounds but somehow I seemed to outlast him and finish off the stronger,' recalled Willie in later years, but in the February 1910 Paris meeting, outlasting should not have cancelled out all that early inferiority.[9] If Harry Lewis spent so much physical energy merely to get a draw, the two lightweights who met in Point Richmond near San Francisco to contest the Lightweight Championship of the World on 22 February 1910 might have dismissed his efforts as having it all too easy. One of the pair, Adolphus Wolgast, born of German-American stock in Cadillac, Michigan on 8 February 1888, fought regularly in a remorselessly fierce style that more than justified his lurid nickname, the Cadillac Bearcat.

Wolgast could be cited as the perfect professional prizefighter by three differing groups: by boxing fans as a model protagonist who never gave less than his best in the ring; by boxing managers as a client who never queried a purse or a piece of matchmaking, and would have gone into the ring to face a gorilla had the contract suggested it; and by the advocates of the abolition of boxing as a lurid example of the

lurking dangers of the most demanding of sports. Wolgast participated in two of the most gruelling contests in modern boxing – one versus Battling Nelson in February 1910, and one versus Joe Rivers in July 1912 – and took more blows than should ever be allowed.

He became prey to delusions, and having suffered a nervous breakdown, he took to the Californian hills where he lived in the open air as a supposed man (or bearcat) of the mountains. Eventually committed to a sanatorium for the insane, he spent his last decades before dying on 14 April 1955, frantically 'training' for a phantom bout against the famous Joe Gans, who had actually died in 1910. Even in the sheltered accommodation he did not find peace, and he died after a violent encounter with guards supposedly engaged to protect him.

Wolgast's February 1910 opponent was Oscar Nelson, born in Copenhagen, Denmark on 5 June 1882, and known predictably as Battling Nelson or the Durable Dane. He was indeed a battler, a very durable one who would use every scurrilous device possible to damage his opponent, including punches aimed at the testicles, forearm smashes, swinging elbows, gouging thumbs, kidney pummels and punches, mule-like kicks and a bony forehead used like a third fist. Over 132 fights, or brawls, his record read W.59 (39 KOs), L.19, D.19, no decisions 35, damage incalculable.

Lewis v Lewis before the Parisian glitterati suggested boxing's brighter future, but Wolgast v Nelson reverted to a rawer past; to a bloody Regency or backwoods pioneer culture, with all the savagery of a dogfight and as little redeeming skill or science as two pit bulls ripping lumps off each other. Why the lightweight division in particular should throw up in its adolescent years so many examples of boxing at its worst is unclear. A nine-stone man cannot deliver punches proportionally more damaging than ones at any other weight. Lightweight contests are not predetermined to outlast others. Joe Gans was world lightweight champion 1902–04 and 1906–08 and had 20 title fights, yet nearly half of them lasted eight rounds or fewer.

Forty-round marathons, where brave men, even in victory, took more punishing blows than any human being should, were by 1910 exceptional. After Wolgast v Nelson, no world lightweight championship fight ever exceeded 20 rounds. Perhaps the whiff of tragedy surrounding the division rests ultimately on the particular circumstances of these three contemporaries – Joe Gans (1874–1910), Ad Wolgast (1888–1955) and Battling Nelson (1882–1954). Wolgast's sad fate has been mentioned; Gans's was not dissimilar.

Gans, born 25 November 1874, came from Baltimore and became a genuine ring legend during his climb from obscurity. Many of his early fights were unrecorded when he became a professional aged only 16, yet his record still reads 156 fights, 120 wins, 10 draws and 18 no decisions.[10] By the early 1900s he had acquired the epithet 'the Old Master' in recognition of his fistic brilliance. A hard but accurate puncher, and the possessor of a defence difficult to penetrate, allied to a gliding elusiveness when he needed it, Gans had every quality to be an all-American champion but one. He did not have white skin. That he became the champion, despite being black, demonstrates how exceptional

Joe Gans (1874–1910), the dapper Baltimore lightweight. The brilliant Gans was used and abused by white promoters: 'the poor guy had to follow orders, otherwise he'd have starved to death'. Gans's fine physique was undermined by tuberculosis.
Prints & Photographs Division, Library of Congress, LC-USZ62-116814

his skills were. What he had to concede to unscrupulous white managers, promoters and fixers to have any sort of career can only be guessed at. One of his fellow professionals, Willie Ritchie, was interviewed in the early 1970s. He had no doubt what had happened: 'Poor Gans had to do what he was told by the white managers. They were crooks, they framed fights, and being Negro the poor guy had to follow orders, otherwise he'd have

Gans, dying, bade his multitude of fans goodbye from a stretcher in August 1910.

Chicago History Museum

starved to death. They wouldn't give him any work.'[11]

Against Frank Erne in New York City on 23 March 1900 in his first attempt at the lightweight championship, Gans thoroughly outboxed Erne for 11 rounds, only to retire tamely in the 12th at his own request, to the astonishment of the Bronx Athletic Club members. He lay down mysteriously in Chicago on 13 December 1900 in the second round of a contest against 'Terrible' Terry McGovern, the Brooklyn resident born in Pennsylvania on 3 September 1880. 'Gans took a dive. It was a fixed fight.'[12]

And on 12 May 1902, presumably when it suited the betting men to let his true form prevail, he knocked out Erne at Fort Erie in round one to become that glorious exception to the prevailing ethnic rule, a black world champion. His defences of the title were, for the next six years, worthy of the designation Old Master.

Unfortunately, where the original Old Masters in their renaissance studios could command fees commensurate with their stature before picking up a brush or a chisel, Gans, even as champion, was the victim of the golden rule of white promoters that black fighters would not draw white audiences. In 1906 he had been part recipient, part victim, of an early venture into boxing promotion by the flamboyant George 'Tex' Rickard, then owner of a gambling saloon in Goldfield, Nevada. Rickard, whose name will recur in later chapters, had grasped another golden rule of promoters – money can always generate more money.

To enhance the stature of Goldfield, a crude mushroom town that had sprung up in the Nevada desert as a

George Lewis 'Tex' Rickard (1870–1929), gambler, prospector, rancher and facilitator of big fights. He pitted Gans against Nelson in an obscure Nevada location.
Bain collection, Prints & Photographs Division, Library of Congress,LC-DIG-ggbain-18070

showdown for racial superiority between black and white; an apocalyptic struggle witnessed by anyone able to cough up $5 for general admission, and up to $25 for a ringside seat.[14] The stipulated limit of 133lbs was also discriminatory against Gans, who had to waste pounds and stamina to conform.

Show them the money and they will come. The $30,000 purse for Gans v Nelson was displayed in gold coins in a Goldfield, Nevada window.
BoxRec

The choice of referee was left to the Goldfield Athletic Club, theoretically the promoters of the bout. It fell upon George Siler of Chicago, upon the integrity of whom the fate of Gans belonged. In the blazing heat of the desert sun on 3 September 1906, Gans used all his manifold skills to punish Nelson and to keep away from the crude and dangerous illegalities that were Nelson's stock in trade.[15] For an hour and a half of sweaty action, Gans diverted the butts, kicks and elbows coming his way, and even put Nelson down in the 15th. In the 32nd round, he broke his right hand on Nelson's hard head, and thereafter had to keep the Dane away with his left, while Nelson aimed more and more stamina-draining punches at his abdomen. The body punches would have eventually overwhelmed Gans. However, two men lost their patience in quick succession. First, Nelson, once too often, swung a blatantly subterranean right full into

result of the discovery of gold deposits, Rickard devised a scheme to get the name of Goldfield into the smarter East Coast newspapers.

He put up a handsome purse of $30,000 (placing the amount in *gold* in a Goldfield shop window) to lure Gans to meet the notorious Battling Nelson in Goldfield, where Rickard

built an open-air wooden arena for 8,000 spectators. 'If you build it, he will come.'[13] Gans came, as did Nelson.

Even as champion, Gans was exploited. $20,000 of the handsome purse plus a bonus of $3,000 was going to his white challenger. Rickard had no scruples about shamelessly promoting the coming contest as a vital 133lbs poor Gans's sexual apparatus, leaving the black champion writhing on the floor. At this, referee Siler decided enough was definitely enough, and immediately disqualified the offender. Gans, on the floor, was still champion, and Rickard's epic was over with three official rounds still to go.

Rickard went on later to new ventures and to even greater profits than the $10,000 he cleared in Goldfield, Nevada. His building of a special wooden arena for a specific fight was a precedent for other important Rickard gambles in the future. Nelson continued on his gory path, and we shall see how he and Ad Wolgast matched crudity with crudity in their meeting. Gans lamentably began to make the weight limits more easily. His once-outstanding physical prowess was under triple attack: from age, from the accumulation of punishment from too many gruelling fights and from the full onset of the tuberculosis that finally killed him on 10 August 1910, less than four years after the Nevada epic. (He and Nelson fought twice more in the interim, both in San Francisco, both in 1908 [4 July and 9 September] and in both fights he was overwhelmed by the younger man's strength and was knocked out in the 17th and the 21st, respectively. He deserved a better fate.)

At Point Richmond on 22 February 1910 in a 40-round struggle against Ad Wolgast, Battling Nelson met his nemesis, an opponent as durable and as ruthless as he and six years younger.[16] The man closest to the action, the referee Eddie Smith, allowed things to take their natural course, saying:

Wolgast fought Nelson at his own game and beat him fairly and squarely. Nelson complained at times of Wolgast's butting, but I paid him little heed, as it was simply the case of one battler getting the worst of a game where both were equally guilty. Both men fought the same, but one had youth, the power to come back, vigour, life and all that goes with it, while the thirteen years of fighting through which Nelson had gone had sapped his strength and left him without the old snap, dash and stamina.

Nelson battled through another 40 rounds of savage punishment before succumbing to a knockout by Ad Wolgast 'The Michigan Wildcat' on 22 February 1910 at Point Richmond.
BoxRec

Out-boxed, out-hit, out-lasted and out-thought, Nelson's sole consolation was the major share of the purse (£2,500 to Wolgast's £750); a balm for taking a major share of the punishment. He stumbled from the ring after the 40th round, held up by his seconds, blinded, helpless and bleeding from most places it was possible to bleed from, and presenting a sorry and sanguinary spectacle. His only comment was, 'I was sorry they called the fight off when they did. I think I could have stayed the 45 rounds, but I have no complaint to make.' His stoicism did him credit, which is more than can be said for his seconds or the referee, none of whom acted when it was necessary to save the old battler from himself. From the 30th round onwards, all Nelson could do was to stumble forward, his weary arms too low to defend himself, his eyes too swollen to see his opponent, taking punch after unnecessary punch as he strove needlessly to survive to the end of the 45th.

His manager, John Robinson, asked the corner to retire him at the end of the 38th, but the over-enthusiastic corner declined to comply. The referee also warned the seconds in the 39th that if they did not stop Nelson, he soon would. In the 40th, that is what Smith did. As Nelson tottered helplessly on the point of collapse, Smith raised Wolgast's glove in victory and led the wounded Nelson back to the corner and to the seconds who had so eagerly seen pints of blood spilled that was not their own. Nelson tried to stumble over to Wolgast's corner to shake the victor's hand, when the seconds, uncomprehending, dragged him out of the ring. The world lightweight championship had changed hands, the transition had not been edifying.

The *New York Times* next day spread the sanguinary details over two and a half columns:

His eyes battered to a pulp, his eyes closed, covered with blood and staggering helplessly about the ring … The left side of his face had lost all semblance of its former contour …

The round-by-round summaries are similarly unsparing:

Nelson's lip bled slightly [2nd round] … brought the blood from Wolgast's nose [3rd] … both men bled from nostrils [4th] …

Nelson's face was a mass of blood [11th] … fearful punishment … the blood flowing from Nelson's face [12th] … Nelson's lips were puffed and his mouth and eyes swollen … spitting blood. Wolgast literally cut the Battler's face to ribbons [13th] … Nelson's face was badly swollen [14th] … uppercut in the sore mouth [15th] … received a hard uppercut on the jaw, causing the blood to flow afresh [17th] … peppering the champion's badly swollen face [20th] … went to his corner spitting blood [26th] … Nelson's left eye was almost entirely closed [27th] … left and right to mouth, starting blood [28th] … Nelson's left eye was completely closed [30th] …[17]

The ringside correspondent was not the Marquis de Sade, but in 1910 there was widespread ignorance about the inherent dangers of boxing, especially of the long-term neurological consequences of sustained blows to the head. There was also a robust attitude to the spilling of blood repugnant to more sensitive times. Accounts of Regency prizefights by Pierce Egan in the volumes of *Boxiana* (Chapter 1) or by others in the files of *Bell's Life* or *Sporting Magazine* show that, along with the picaresque prose and the admiration for men of extraordinary skill and pluck, went a sadistic relish for the inflicting of physical damage. Egan's elegant and witty euphemisms about 'tapping the claret' (i.e. spilling blood), or 'dislodging the ivory' and 'making a dice-box of his swallow' (i.e. knocking the teeth from a man's head or down his throat), cannot disguise the

fact that many at ringside were animated by the desire to see men suffer serious impairment; the ugly morality of the dog fight, or the bloodlust of the bear pit, sustained by callous human beings.

The *New York Times* report, unpleasant to read a century on, cannot disguise the fact that for 30 rounds, the extraordinarily resilient Dane was still in the fight with a chance of victory, and any who knew his record would have been reluctant to take that chance away. In the 21st he had Wolgast clinching desperately and back-pedalling. In the 22nd a right to the stomach and right and left hooks to the jaw put Wolgast down on the seat of his trunks. Some spectators left for the exits then, believing Nelson had yet again made a successful comeback from an early hiding.

After Wolgast's seconds had illegally anaesthetised their man with slugs of whisky, Ad recovered his senses and the initiative.

What made the subsequent course of the fight so degrading was that from the 30th onwards, Nelson had no chance of victory, and progressively less chance of seeing, let alone avoiding, the punches and butts raining in on him. For another ten rounds he was merely a stumbling punch bag, taking wholly unnecessary punishment. ('Both men were covered from head to foot from the Dane's blood and the arena soon became a shambles.') Nelson retired from the ring only after seven more full years of professional boxing and died penniless in his seventies in Chicago on 7 February 1954.

However irritating the autocratic behaviour of officials at London's NSC, neither the regular referees nor the smartly dressed members would have

allowed the Nelson v Wolgast contest to continue to its ugly conclusion had it taken place on club premises. The club had, however, its own controversies to deal with in the spring of 1910. One developed out of the decisive action of referee Tom Scott at the 21 March 1910 encounter between Jack Goldswain of Bermondsey (b. 22 July 1878) whom we last saw at the NSC in October 1909, and Young Joseph of Aldgate (b. 12 February 1885), a match made at welterweight with a newly minted Lonsdale Belt available for the winner. Both Jewish; East London v South London; old master v younger claimant; aspects of the contest would have made it a natural Wonderland spectacular. Only the NSC could offer a belt and official recognition as a British welterweight champion, so Goldswain was there to lay claim to both.

He was revisiting a ring where he had fought Moreau in October 1909 and where he first clinched the old British lightweight championship back in April 1906 with a points win over Jabez White over 20 rounds. For his win over White, he had reinvented himself, subduing his natural whirlwind aggression in favour of a newly refined left lead, and a defence much less profligate than the take-one-to-get-in-two tactics indulged by his younger self.[18]

That victory over White was devalued. White and Goldswain weighed in over the lightweight limit of 10st/140lbs so White had technically retained his lightweight title. There were other complications – Goldswain lost in November 1908 to Johnny Summers. He then won and lost against Curley Watson in less than three weeks in May 1909.[19] This made any linear progress (the man who beat the man who beat the man) impossible to decipher.

Now he was at the NSC against Young Joseph with the fourth of Lonsdale's belts on offer, and at a welterweight limit of 10st 7lb/147lbs. New title, new hopes, new limit – though even 147lbs was sometimes problematical for Goldswain. This time he accomplished 10st 5lb/145lbs to his opponent's 10st 6½lb/146½lbs. He had, however, lost twice before to Young Joseph, both on points, and both at contests restricted to *two-minute* rounds. Lately, he preferred punching bags on stage for the delectation of music hall audiences than live opponents who could punch back.

'Young' Joseph was properly Aschel Joseph, given the title Young by Jack Woolf on his first appearance at Wonderland as a diminutive flyweight. Such titles were common practice, though comic when applied to some grizzled and balding veteran evidently pushing 40. The not so young Joseph had become a Wonderland veteran of 25. Nevertheless, he was still lithe, handsome and very well equipped with speed of hands and tongue alike.

Goldswain v Joseph had, on paper, all the makings of a classic. In practice, it was a bore. Goldswain, pale and drawn, reverted to his earlier cruder self and chased Joseph, attempting to land a crude right swing. Joseph retreated, swayed and ducked, then, as Goldswain recovered his balance, delivered snappy and effective counter-punches to Goldswain's face and body. This happened throughout the early rounds, and more or less up to the fateful 11th.[20]

In the 11th, Scott, the very experienced referee, lost all patience with Goldswain and disqualified him for persistent holding. Weakening under Joseph's effective punches, Goldswain's defence of last resort had been to hang on and clinch when his desperate swings failed consistently to connect. Most agree that Scott was quite in order to call a halt. ('He [Goldswain] was warned repeatedly for this, and it is probable that his disqualification alone saved him from the most decisive form of defeat,' and 'Goldswain could not possibly complain at the decision, for he was warned often enough' – both quotations from the report in *Boxing*.) Scott, at the end of his refereeing career, was in a sad decline that resulted in a complete mental breakdown. Before his final retirement in 1910, he was to give some arbitrary and bizarre decisions.[21] Goldswain's disqualification was not one of them.

Goldswain had a more legitimate complaint in the peremptory and rather cruel decision the NSC made about his share of the purse. It was withheld, including all his training expenses. When he attempted, with Young Joseph's support, to prove in court that he had tried to the best of his ability, he came up against two formidable barriers: the NSC as a typical Edwardian employer, determined to hold to the letter of a contract if not to its spirit; and a typical Edwardian court, determined to uphold the rights of employers. Judgement, including costs, was awarded against Goldswain.[22]

The costs of boxing to an unlucky boxer could go far beyond the financial. On both sides of the Atlantic in the spring of 1910, boxers paid the ultimate price for following so dangerous a trade. On 5 March 1910, during a regular Saturday night bill at Wonderland, 'Curley' Watson, a popular middleweight (b. 5 October 1883 in Barrow-in-Furness in Cumbria, and one-time merchant seaman), was knocked out in the final round of a lively contest against Frank Inglis, a Birmingham boxer and West Indian immigrant. Watson had the upper hand for most of the contest, yet with a mere 30 seconds remaining was caught with a solid right to the body, went down, got up quickly, and received another legitimate punch to the jaw. Toppling forward, he may or may not have hit his jaw on the floor and was going down for the second or third time. Either eight-ounce or six-ounce gloves were used.[23]

Whatever the minor details, the consequences were fatal for Watson who died 90 minutes later without regaining consciousness. Much was made at the inquest of the scrupulous fairness of the fight and of the utterly unexpected collapse of Watson, so a verdict of accidental death was almost inevitable. The less than handsome purse for which Watson had died was a mere £7.

Neither reports nor court proceedings made much of the fact that Watson v Inglis had been a white v black contest. Nor did the fact that Curley was Jewish rate a mention. No blame was attached to Inglis, who merely participated in a match that, apart from its tragic outcome, operated just like a thousand others. Watson and Inglis had more in common as fellow combatants in an exploitative trade than they had anything to divide them.

The racist rancour simmering across the Atlantic as the Johnson v Jeffries showdown drew near was not operating in London. (Not so well known, even to boxing historians,

3 September 1906 Goldfield, Nevada: it took 42 rounds of heavy and painful fighting before a blatant low blow from Nelson earned Gans a harrowing victory by disqualification.
BoxRec

as the gory details about the Gans v Nelson fight at Goldfield in 1906, is that the disqualification of the white Nelson had also provoked incidents of racist violence across the country. A black bartender had his skull fractured in Flushing, New York by three white drinkers; a black doorman escaped in Manhattan by being well-armed himself; and the police reported parallel incidents in other states.)[24]

Owen Moran, another Birmingham fighter, found himself in a similar predicament to Inglis. His fight against Tommy McCarthy of the USA in San Francisco on 29 April 1910 reached a fateful 16th round. A Moran performance of skill and aggression culminated in a ferocious right-hand knockout punch. His opponent, like Curley Watson, struck his head on the canvas as he fell, and died in hospital without regaining consciousness. Unlike Inglis, Moran, along with the seconds and the officials, was arrested and charged formally with manslaughter. Moran, a toughie if ever there was one, was genuinely distressed when McCarthy failed to get up. He spent the night in his cell praying for McCarthy's recovery, unaware that the

man was already dead. The ring death, like every similar one, tarnished the reputation of the growing sport. So did Moran, by including in his defence the plea that the fight had been 'fixed' for McCarthy to lose but to stay the distance. Fortunately for him, the coroner's jury on 5 May 1910 found the cause to be 'accidental circumstances', and the manslaughter charges were dropped a week later.[25]

Owen Moran would have preferred to be in London that spring; specifically at the NSC on 18 April 1910 in the opposite corner to his great rival, Jim Driscoll. That privilege had fallen to another outstanding featherweight, Frank 'Spike' Robson. Born in the North East near South Shields on 5 November 1877, Robson was no young hopeful, rather an accomplished veteran with as many claims to the featherweight title as Moran or Driscoll. Moran had been the original choice for a meeting with Driscoll in February but refused the club's purse offer and opted for McCarthy and Californian gold. Driscoll took the match with Seaman Hayes instead. Robson could, and did, point to his own credentials as superior to those of either Hayes or Moran.

Back in 1906, Robson had beaten Johnny Summers to be widely thought of as the British featherweight champion. (Before the 1909 NSC revisions, what constituted a featherweight varied as widely as the championship claimants, with 8st 8lb/120lbs as a lowest limit and 9st 2lb/128lbs as the highest, with all the two-pound divisions between these figures prevailing on different occasions.) Since 1906, Robson had been back and forth to the USA and survived drawn no-decision bouts against quality opponents such as

Terry McGovern and Abe Attell. He had expected to meet Driscoll at the NSC, providing Driscoll had been able to raise a side bet of £200 a side to add to the official purse, a feeble £50. When Driscoll failed to raise the stake, Robson returned to the USA and met and lost to Joe Gans on 1 April 1908 by TKO in the third round. He was not best pleased to hear about the Driscoll v Hayes bout fought in his absence.[26]

Indeed, after the NSC awarded the Lonsdale Belt and the official featherweight title to Driscoll, the affronted Robson arrived at the NSC, £200 cash in his hand, and buttonholed Lord Lonsdale in person: 'It's a wonderful thing you are doing for boxing, my Lord, in giving these belts to be fought for and as the giver you probably have the right to choose who should fight for them. I have no objection to that bit. I would like to know who authorised the Club to give my title away with a Belt without first asking my permission?'[27]

For once, proletarian impudence, or perhaps the £200 cash, paid off. A Robson v Driscoll match was hurriedly rearranged. The 33-year-old Robson and the 29-year-old Driscoll met on 18 April 1910 and produced one of the most electrifying contests seen anywhere. 'It is safe to say that no big fight anywhere has been half as good as this for several years. For it was not only intensely and wildly thrilling at times, but positively sensational,' said *Boxing*.[28]

Before the sensations, Driscoll, Peerless Jim, acknowledged master of the straight left, and of an elusiveness that baffled some of the world's greatest fighters, was a heavy betting favourite. Few cared for the sensation of being made to look amateurish and silly.

Either by careful design, or perhaps upon the inspired improvisation of the moment, Robson declined to be so cast. As the fight warmed up, Driscoll began to wear the puzzled frown of a Sonny Liston confronted by Cassius Clay at Miami Beach on 25 February 1964 – a champion fazed by behaviour and tactics for which he could remember no precedent.

Unlike Liston, Driscoll could get off his normal barrage of punches. He could land them and land them well. Driscoll's problem was that the redoubtable and confident Robson seemed actually to enjoy every one of Driscoll's punches, and celebrated them by bouncing around the ring from rope to rope like a demented squash ball, or comically staggering like an actor giving an exaggerated impression of a punch-drunk fighter on the point of collapse. Whether Driscoll's punches were having their normal effect, or whether Robson's weird wobbles were craftily designed to get Driscoll close enough to suffer damaging counters, no one knew. For two rounds, Driscoll landed left leads, hooks, and heavy uppercuts, and Robson, though showing some superficial damage, danced, tottered and seemingly willingly invited more of the same.

At the end of the third, Spike confirmed that there was some method in the madness with a fast and clever rally in which three very firm and damaging lefts thudded painfully into the bridge of Driscoll's nose, making it swell and bleed at the nostrils. The master biter bit. Worse was to come for the Welshman in the fourth when he firmly punched Robson, yet, to his own dismay, received another driving left counter that almost closed his right

eye. A monocular Driscoll, unable to see punches coming to him from the right-hand side, would be only half a defensive master. This Robson well knew.

At the very beginning of the fourth, Robson rushed across the ring to Driscoll's corner and landed a punch before the Cardiff man was barely upright. In the fifth, he was there even faster, not too fast for the wary Driscoll, who, out of his one good eye, saw him coming and got out of the way, but much too fast for Driscoll's seconds, who were still lifting Driscoll's stool to pass it over the top rope. The shiny wooden seat and Spike's shiny shaven head met with the full impact of Spike's frantic rush behind it, causing a deep and sickening cut in the crown of his scalp. Robson slipped over in the confusion but jumped up immediately, a sure sign that he had trained assiduously to absorb anything Driscoll could throw at him. The stool was as hard as teak, but he continued to absorb that blow, and three more punches from Driscoll, as if nothing could ever stop him.

Apart from the serious inconvenience of blood trickling down his forehead and into his eyes for the next ten rounds, the severity of the blow must have had some effect on Robson's uncanny resistance. Yet there were times over the next five rounds when even Driscoll thought that had he used both stools to beat Robson over the head, Robson would still be there dancing before him. And not only dancing, but laughing and joking as well – 'You have the belt, have you? I'll *belt* you!' Driscoll landed on Robson's face. He pounded Robson's bruised kidneys. He was warned for butting Robson too, but even that failed to deter the oncoming

Robson, who came desperately close to closing Driscoll's left eye too ('at one time I thought he was going to beat me', recalled Driscoll). Driscoll's half vision was preserved only by some crude surgery in his corner.[29]

Had it not been for the collision with the stool, perhaps Robson's unorthodox tactics might ultimately have paid off. Even in the decisive 15th round, Robson was finally overcome, less by a particular blow (though Driscoll landed two rights to the jaw that would have finished most fighters) than by the repetitive effects of Driscoll's punches, added to the concussive effects of the collision with the ring furniture. Robson's inspired resistance concluded when he was floored for the second time in the 15th and tried to get up from his hands and knees at the count of six, only to stumble and fall back into an unconsciousness that lasted an alarming hour after the contest. No one could have given the NSC members better value for their money.[30]

London in the spring and summer of 1910 was graced with other contests almost as thrilling as Driscoll v Robson. One such was the latest international match-up, featuring another Welshman, Freddie Welsh, as much from that significant American boxing town Philadelphia as from his birthplace in Pontypridd. Welsh, whom we last saw at the NSC in 1909 v Johnny Summers, was back to meet the brilliantly gifted Irish-American from Chicago, Packey McFarland (b. 1 November 1888). Robson v Driscoll took its place in boxing history as a feast of the unexpected, Welsh v McFarland as a lustrous example of boxing to delight the connoisseur, a feast of skill and art. And, before it was over, it provided controversy and argument enough for any two normal contests.

McFarland, the American abroad, came out of the Irish Catholic community in the tough Stockyards quarter of Chicago.[31] He was tall, very dark-haired, swarthy of skin and ruggedly handsome. When he died in 1936 of a heart attack aged only 47, he was pushing the scales at almost double the weight limit of 9st 7lb/133lbs he made to meet Welsh in Covent Garden. (The 'lightweight' standard supposedly set forever at 9st 9lb/135lbs by the NSC from 11 February 1909 was still modified if it suited the club.) McFarland was hardly a man damaged by boxing. On the contrary, the youth who obtained his first job in a sweaty boiler shop invested one of his $4,000 boxing purses in an oil company. The company flourished, as did his capital account, whereupon he reinvested the profits in shrewd property deals. When he retired from the ring in 1915, the initial $4,000 had magically transformed itself into $300,000. His obesity and premature death were not the fruits of boxing, but of his wielding the knife and fork and glass and cigar in the environs of Chicago boardrooms, and the smoke-filled backrooms of Democratic Illinois politics. In 1910, few were advocating the abolition of such dangerous activities.

McFarland, whose fights were as clean and straight as his rhythmic and versatile left lead, was an innocent victim of the repercussions following the notoriously fixed Gans v McGovern fight of 1900 mentioned earlier. He was forced to ply his trade elsewhere by the closure by the authorities of the once flourishing Chicago boxing clubs, and he built up a considerable following on the East Coast, in the Midwest and in California. His London appearance against Welsh on 30 May 1910 was the third of four fights undertaken on his first visit to England, where his reputation preceded him. He and Welsh had met twice two years before – at Milwaukee on 21 February 1908 (won by McFarland on points over ten rounds); and in Los Angeles on 4 July 1908 (a 35-round draw).[32] The two did not warm to each other.

In addition to his better-known nickname, 'The Pride of the Stockyards', Packey was sometimes called 'The Chicago Flash'. Welsh, and the members sardined into the club in May 1910, were treated to an elegant demonstration of the aptness of the latter. He advanced swiftly on

Packey McFarland (1888–1936), the popular Chicagoan lightweight. Never a world champion, Packey ducked no one and pursued a successful business career with clever investments of his ring earnings.
Bain collection, Prints & Photographs Division, Library of Congress, LC-DIG-ggbain-10096

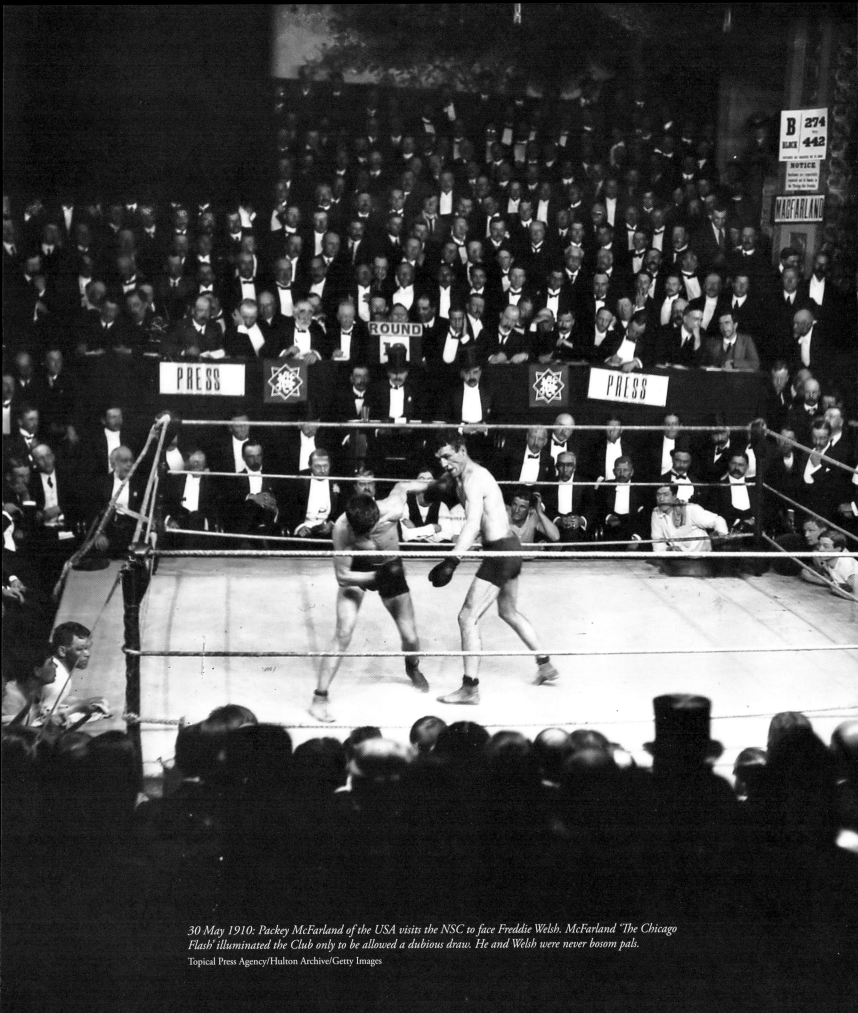

30 May 1910: Packey McFarland of the USA visits the NSC to face Freddie Welsh. McFarland 'The Chicago Flash' illuminated the Club only to be allowed a dubious draw. He and Welsh were never bosom pals.

Topical Press Agency/Hulton Archive/Getty Images

Welsh, using his dazzling hand speed against one of the cleverest defences in the world, the gratifying contrast of styles making this the most vintage of contests. Welsh was initially unable to do much except retreat, avoid and block, although Welsh's speed and intelligence applied to such normally passive defensive manoeuvres constituted a textbook demonstration in their own right.

McFarland at his best, which he was on this night, used left leads like fencing foils, lightly probing an opponent's guard to find a vulnerable chink through which to deliver a more damaging thrust. He was sometimes content to land lightly on the target with the flicked tip of an extended glove, as if the demonstration of precision was enough, rather than landing firmly with the knuckle part of a closed fist. The tip of a fencer's foil can gently caress the opponent's chest and register an electronic hit; only punches cleanly delivered with the knuckled ridge of the closed glove are meant to score in boxing. (Loud-sounding open-glove slaps may evoke ignorant responses from the far reaches of a large arena, but judges and referees are not supposed to be so fooled.) When he chose, McFarland could deliver as stinging a blow as anyone – by hook, by cross, by uppercut, or by piston-like straight drives.

His own defences were based on a cross-wristed, open-palm posture to protect chin and face, elbows down at the sides to protect the abdomen, and, mandatory against Welsh, to fend off round-arm assaults aimed at the kidney region. His stance was more upright than most Americans. Before the end of the exhausting 20 rounds, McFarland's guard was penetrated often enough to give him cuts to eyebrow and mouth, a bleeding nose, and bruised welts around his left kidney where Welsh's low right hooks had circumvented the elbow barrier. Welsh's nose also bled, and one of his eyes was distinctly bruised.

Most contemporary accounts suggest McFarland delivered more meaningful punches and was the major aggressor. The *Boxing* correspondent awarded but one clear round to Welsh before the 15th, as against the *nine* he credited to McFarland, and said that McFarland 'at the very worst scored a clear majority of the points in at least 14 of the rounds'. *Boxing World and Athletic Chronicle* told a similar story:

> I cannot possibly make out what the referee saw in Welsh's work to warrant him calling the contest a draw. In the minds of ninety-nine per cent of those present there was only one decision to be given, and that was 'McFarland the winner'. That was what we expected the M.C. to announce, and to say that we were surprised when Mr Bettinson said 'The referee's decision is a draw' is to put it mildly indeed.[33]

In some venues, a riot might have ensued among the disgruntled punters who had plunged heavily at the odds offered at ringside – 6/4 on Welsh before the first punch became 5/4 after the first round, even money halfway through the second, 1/2 on McFarland by the ninth, and 1/3 on McFarland by the tenth. By then some Welsh supporters cut their losses by laying large sums on McFarland before the books were closed on an obviously foregone conclusion. In their disappointment, dinner-jacketed members from the body of the hall, and from the overhanging balcony, so forgot themselves as to abandon the conventions of polite applause regardless of the verdict, and like a group of angry magpies hissed and booed the referee, the only man in the house to detect evidence of a draw. He was the unfortunate Tom Scott, never trusted with a major contest again. The strong integrity he had shown in disqualifying Goldswain in March had disintegrated into total lack of vision by May. Before the summer was out, he had been institutionalised.

McFarland, considering the personal dislike between he and Welsh, took the verdict well. Members knew a champion when they saw one and cheered him from the room. Being somewhere where unfair hometown decisions were actively disliked, and where his considerable skills were observed in appreciative silence during rounds, and thunderously applauded at the end of rounds, put him on his best behaviour and subdued his latent temper. (On 30 March 1909, in Boston, the vastly inferior fighter Dave Deshler had been awarded an undeserved draw against Packey over 12 rounds. McFarland was so incensed as to knock down the referee and fell one of Deshler's seconds. When general order was restored, and his ire brought under control, he apologised fully and handsomely, but who was to know when the volcano might erupt again?) The misbehaviour of NSC members at the verdict was firmly quashed by their mentor Lord Lonsdale. He quelled the turbulence with a glare from the centre of the ring and reminded the members of the principles of good sportsmanship. In the club, his word was law.

McFarland's English sojourn continued with a lucrative music hall tour and an easily won purse against Jack Goldswain at The Ring, Blackfriars on 18 June 1910. Goldswain took the Saturday night fight at short notice, looking podgier than usual, and still had his futile court case against the NSC hanging over him (the decision was made in August). Neither physically nor mentally up to the brilliant Packey, Goldswain was dumped on his shorts at the end of the second, the count interrupted by the bell. He was floored three times in the third, the last count also halted by the bell. The referee, Eugene Corri, wisely spared Goldswain the *coup de grâce* expected in the fourth by stopping the contest in the interval.[34] Packey returned to the USA richer than when he came and supposedly full of fond memories of his English experiences. Yet a statement he issued in September 1910, denying that he had ever called Lord Lonsdale 'a bum sport and a stiff', makes one wonder if the whole truth about the Welsh fight will ever be known.[35]

The Ring, Blackfriars had barely been open a month before the McFarland v Goldswain bout. Behind its official opening on 14 May 1910 lay a complicated drama, part sporting, part romantic, part theatrical. Blossoming in the music halls of the day was the gold-plated, 30-carat star, Marie Lloyd (1870–1922). Much better preserved than the ruins the 17th-century welterweight Oliver Cromwell had knocked 'abaht a bit', of which she sweetly sang, Lloyd made a lucrative living exploiting her ribald and extrovert personality and her

Rabelaisian Cockney wit. Aged 16, she commanded £100 a week, and by 1910 could demand her own price. (Never forgetting her own humble beginnings, she took part in the 1906 Music Hall strike to support much poorer artistes exploited by ruthless managers in a manner they would not have dared to treat her.) She was personally generous, and ever willing to give others a leg-up. Much taken with a young Leah Belle Orchard, a girl struggling to make a living on the halls, Marie had practically adopted her as a daughter, made her her dresser, shared stage duets with her and negotiated joint contracts for fees the young girl could never have obtained otherwise.[36]

In 1901, Marie and Belle, now dubbed Bella, took a joint engagement at Gatti's Music Hall in the West End. On the bill was Dick Burge, the boxer (b. 19 December 1865) just retired from the ring after an unfortunate fight against Jerry Driscoll in Gateshead (28 January 1901), when both were disqualified for not trying their best. Burge, looking to restore his dubious reputation, was as cheeky a chappie as the flamboyant Max Miller of later decades. He could flex the pecs and thump bag or ball before the footlights as to the manner born. He took the British lightweight championship from Jem Carney of Birmingham on a disqualification in 1891 but was a fighter happy to have a go at all and sundry, giving and taking beatings to and from middleweights and heavyweights. This was true only providing the price was right. The results of many of his bouts were preordained. Stage ventures spared him the agonies of sweating down to the lightweight limit. Backstage at Gatti's, Bella fell heavily for the ostentatious

Burge, aged 36. This new focus in her life brought her joy and trouble.

Burge was an inveterate gambler and a fervent juggler of funds from one account to another without much concern for the legality of the transfers. In February 1902, he was in the dock of the Old Bailey on fraud charges. Bella's savings of £300, her jewellery, and cheques she had signed were inextricably mixed up with his dealings. Ever loyal, Bella promised to wait for him when he was sent down on multiple charges for the next ten years. Meanwhile, she went back on the halls.

With remission, Burge was back out of jail in July 1909. Bella forgave him his past transgressions and, more trusting than most, gave him the money she had saved in the intervening years. She staked him to the lease of a building just south of Blackfriars Bridge on Blackfriars Road, and financed its conversion into a boxing arena. Dick Burge, ex-champ, ex-con, was now Dick Burge, boxing promoter of The Ring.

The building, approximately on the site where Southwark underground station now stands, had as varied a career as Burge himself. It dated from the vintage years of the prize ring, but its history was strictly other. Its inspirer was an enthusiastically evangelical minister, the Reverend Rowland Hill (not Sir Rowland Hill, 1795–1879, inventor of the penny post). Hill chose the site as central to what he called 'the very strongholds of the devil's territory'.[37] To reclaim the area for Christianity, Hill financed the building of a chapel, dedicated as the Surrey Chapel on 8 June 1783. An octagonal shape was chosen to eliminate any dark or popish corners where the devil, or any papist ideas, might lurk. Hill's was

Dick Burge (1865–1918): one-time British lightweight, one-time guest of His Majesty, one-time manager of The Ring.

PA Images/Alamy Stock Photo

a religion where atheism, devil worship and Catholicism were triple enemies.[38]

Hill was buried under his own pulpit in 1833. He cannot have rested in peace. In 1881, the Surrey Chapel became the Surrey engineering works, and the clergy house next door the Liberal and Radical Club. Hill must have thought the devil his posthumous conqueror when the engineers went out of business and his beloved building became a boxing stadium and part-time picture palace.[39] Dick Burge ensured the elegant pepper pot at the pinnacle of the round roof showed the word BOXING in all directions. The word was repeated on many of the eight sides. Over the main entrance, the new title THE RING appeared in distinctive typography (when Nat Fleischer's famous boxing monthly of the same name first appeared in the early 1920s, its logo was in almost exactly the same style).

Rowland Hill's inaugural sermon in 1783 included the words, 'What rivers of innocent blood have been shed to please the pride of tyrants!' The rivers of blood shed in fights to please innocent boxing fans, and not a few proud and tyrannical promoters, would have been ample proof to Hill that Blackfriars Road SE1 had gone over to the devil for good.

Proceedings at The Ring crudely shadowed those at the NSC. The MC, in a black morning coat and black-and-white striped trousers like the father of the bride, lent a certain pseudo-dignity to the affair with shouted introductions. His decibels penetrated not the aromatic blue smoke of expensive cigars but the

The Ring, Blackfriars, London SE1. Once an 18th-century chapel, the venue offered competitive fights at popular prices in a raucous atmosphere. An October 1940 German bomb brought about its demise.

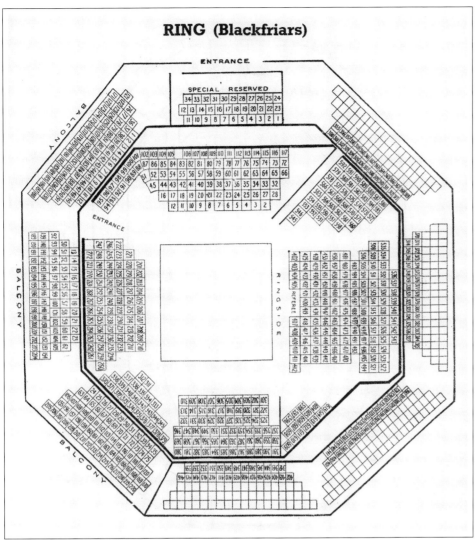

Every seat gave a close view of the action.
Antiqua Print Gallery/Alamy Stock Photo

dense cloud from a hundred Woodbines and home-made roll-ups. Meanwhile, the referee sat in a high chair outside the ring and shouted his own orders to the fighters from afar, not always effectively. Unlike the mock-religious decorum of Covent Garden were raucous ribaldry and dissenting comments hurled at the ring in the loud Cockney voices of men dressed not in dinner jackets but in their rough working clothes; their banter, obscene and witty, more reflective of the street than the drawing room. When they appreciated a good fight or a gallant loser, a cascade of copper and silver coins ('the nobbins')

flew on to the canvas, tangible rewards particularly meaningful for boxers giving their all for minimal cash.

The resilient Bella became proprietor herself in 1915 when Dick, technically overage, enlisted in the wartime army. When he died, not in action but of pneumonia while still in uniform on 15 March 1918, she ensured The Ring's valued role in boxing annals until its eventual knockout by a German bomb in October 1940. These developments were a long way off in 1910.

While the Blackfriars Ring acquired a formidable reputation for value-for-money fights at modest

prices, Wonderland packed its bills and its cramped arena with lively and sometimes distinguished action. One of Jack Woolf's most ambitious promotions took place there on 27 June 1910, a Monday evening. The NSC officials might try to monopolise Monday nights along with official titles and Lonsdale's new belts, but Woolf attracted good fighters and had them contest 'titles' in his ring, any night he fancied.

For £100 a side, and 70 per cent of the gate to be divided 65:35, winner:loser, the 70 per cent guaranteed to be of a £500 minimum, Harry Lewis of Philadelphia, the world welterweight champion agreed to put his title on the line against the East End favourite, Young Aschel Joseph, both men to weigh in at 10st 7lb/147lbs at 2pm on the day of the fight, and to fight over 20 three-minute rounds in the evening. Two months on from Lewis's second 25-rounder against Willie Lewis in Paris, mentioned earlier, here was Harry appearing, in the flesh, against their own man, Young Joseph, who had in March escaped from Goldswain's clutches and clinches at the NSC with a Lonsdale Belt and the British welterweight championship. It was a piquant piece of matchmaking – the hard-hitting American against the elusive East Ender, and two Jewish fighters clashing before a predominantly Jewish audience. The London newspapers, sensitive as ever, made much of phrases such as 'of the Hebrew persuasion', and 'representatives of the Chosen People'. *Boxing* devoted 44 column inches to a detailed report of the action and the audience reaction while abstaining from the 'J word' completely.[40]

Lewis soon proved that his reputation as a strong, hard-hitting and hurtful puncher was no promoter's hyperbole. He punched Joseph harder than the Aldgate man had ever been punched before. Joseph, in the dressing room later, speculated whether Lewis's hands had ever been wrapped in the obligatory bandages. They had, even if the bruises on Joseph's ribs and jaw suggested otherwise.

Lewis attacked from the start. He landed a left hook to Joseph's body. Joseph grasped immediately that Lewis was an opponent for whom discretion was the best antidote. He swayed out of range from a following right uppercut and used a few nifty sidesteps to take his ribcage away from left and right body punches aimed at him with serious intent. Joseph also ducked as an over-the-top right from Lewis grazed his scalp harmlessly, and he clinched hurriedly before the arrival of another. When Joseph tried a forward lunge of his own, he slipped and fell. As he got up, still slightly off balance, Lewis calmly clipped him on the jaw and sent him down for real. He got up at seven and showed that his head had cleared with some clever dodging and smothering, before landing three successive lefts to Lewis's head just before the bell. Ominously, Lewis declined even to blink.

Everything the Wonderland audience could do to help Joseph, they did. They cheered him when he punched. They cheered him when he glided out of Lewis's reach. They cheered him when he clinched. They cheered him when he rallied. Vicariously they suffered the power of Lewis's punches. But in the last resort it was Joseph who had to take the punishment. Despite the vociferous encouragement, he needed more practical help than the

crowd could give. Lewis continued remorselessly with short punches at close quarters, and full swings from a distance. A few of the swings floored Joseph in the third and the sixth and had him clinching at least as much as Goldswain had done against him – clinchee turned desperate clincher.

The seventh was a mercy. Sated, or bored, Lewis decided it was time to conclude. A strong left to Aschel's chin had the Londoner reeling. A repeat took him down for a count of nine. He got up only to be put down for seven, and then down for eight. As even his staunchest supporters were wondering whether another flooring and a fourth count in the round would be the last, the bell rang. Wisely, and to the great relief of all who cared for the welfare of the courageous young East Ender, discreetly Joseph declined to re-enter the fray for the eighth.

Packey McFarland had found the NSC audience very willing to grant him, an American, an ovation. (Packey was actually in the Wonderland audience for Lewis v Joseph, in the VIP seats, along with the Mayor of Stepney and every local dignitary who had been able to blag a ticket.) Now that the Wonderland devotees had seen Lewis smite their favourite so fairly and so often, they proved they were no less sporting a crowd than their supposed social betters in Covent Garden. They leapt to their feet, they stood on chairs, they clung to pillars, and they cheered the American world champion all the way down the aisle. They did the same for their man as he was helped away, barely knowing who or where he was.

No such sportsmanship and comradeship transcending national and ethnic divisions were on show as the

USA suffered the final fraught weeks of preparation for the long-awaited, half-dreaded clash between John Arthur Johnson, better known as Jack Johnson, current heavyweight champion of the world, and his latest challenger, James J. Jeffries, former heavyweight champion of the world, the bruising boilermaker who had retired as undefeated champion in 1905, having successfully defended his title seven times. Many Americans believed Jack Johnson the true champion – they tended to be black. Other Americans believed Jack Johnson a temporary usurper, one who had picked up Jeffries's crown off the battlefield and had no right to wear it – they tended to be white. All Americans, and boxing followers everywhere, believed victory on 4 July 1910 would settle far more than a sporting contest. In the words of a *New York Times* editorial (2 May 1910) it was 'a great contest of the Caucasian and Ethopian [*sic*] races'.

The pre-contest mating dance performed by all interested parties became a mini-saga. In New York, two days after Johnson beat Burns in December 1908, Jeffries responded negatively to an offer from Hugh McIntosh of the equivalent of £10,000 to fight Johnson. Jeffries 'said that he had definitely retired, and no amount of money would tempt him to re-enter the ring'.[41] As they say in boxing, never say never. Jeffries's resolve did not survive further offers. In Omaha in March 1909, prior to a lucrative theatrical engagement in New York, Jeffries further declared 'that after this engagement he will meet Johnson and will make an effort to reclaim the heavyweight championship of the world *for the white race*'[42] [Italics added].

As the Jeffries–Johnson clash loomed, the necessity to cast Johnson as pantomime villain intensified.
BoxRec

In New York in October 1909 the men agreed mutual terms.[43] The world's promoters then went into combat themselves. McIntosh, in November 1909, cabled an offer from Sydney of a £15,000 purse for the two to meet at Olympia in London.[44] Tex Rickard, in December 1909, offered a $101,000 purse and 66 per cent of the film rights.[45] Both men accepted Rickard's offer despite a McIntosh counter bid of £40,000.[46]

The preferred date was 4 July 1910; the preferred venue San Francisco. Work began on an amphitheatre big enough to house the event. At this stage, fate and Californian politics took a hand. So notorious a match was bound to provoke extensive debate even within circles where a ring was a commercial cartel, and a punch a spiced mixed drink.

First came the fatal outcome of the Owen Moran/Tommy McCarthy

fight in San Francisco in April 1910. This tragedy led many to plead for a ban on the upcoming July encounter. Typically, the Presbyterian General Assembly meeting in Atlantic City in May sent a vehement resolution to the Californian governor:

> Virtue, decency and patriotism demand that you save your State and our Nation's sacred birthday from the filth, the vulgarity and the brutality of a deformed prize fight on the Fourth of July.[47]

Initially, the Republican James Gillett (state governor 1907–11) resisted the agitation. So did the City's Board of Supervisors, who hustled through a confirmatory vote before too many church and secular groups got their opposition fully organised.[48] Federal opposition was more difficult to defy. Various congressmen let it be known that the next World's Fair due to be staged profitably in San Francisco in

commemoration of the Panama Canal might go elsewhere if the city persisted in its accommodation of the unwelcome prizefight.[49] Gillett, like any vulnerable politician, could take a hint. Nowhere in California would the big fight now be allowed.

If ever Tex Rickard, promoter extraordinaire, needed to confirm his genius, he could cite the enterprise he showed when, with the building of an amphitheatre in one state unexpectedly halted a bare 18 days before the fight, adding a £1,000 loss to his expenses, he not only found another site in another state, he had the new 300ft^2 arena up and ready on time in Reno, Nevada *at the expense of the citizens of Reno.*[50] The Reno authorities waived a licence fee in their anxiety to secure an event receiving such worldwide attention. Early spectators were coming through the entrances just as the last nails were hammered in and the last licks of paint added. Rickard, clerk of works, promoter and all-round dynamo, had,

Jeffries's entourage, including Mrs Jeffries, poses at a railway station, Jeffries as dominant a presence as he was in the ring.
Bain collection, Prints & Photographs Division, Library of Congress, LC-DIG-ggbain-08039

JAMES J. JEFFRIES

WE'RE PULLING FOR "JEFF" JULY 4, 1910.

Jeffries seeks canine assistance. Two rottweilers in the ring with him would not have brought him victory.
BoxRec

not for the first or last time, succeeded against heavy odds.

The spectators were admitted at noon, with 18,000 of them allocated seats, 2,000 standing at the top of the arena for $5 each, and 10,000 unlucky ones left outside when the gates closed. At an average price of $20 a time, Rickard took $360,000. Scalpers outside creamed off incalculable amounts as $50 ringside seats fetched a hefty $125 from anyone lucky enough to get one. Journalists commented on the presence of women. Rickard allocated a special muslin-shaded sanctuary for 500 women; for the more brazen Reno

divorcees, said the chauvinists. It was full, and dresses and bonnets to be seen elsewhere showed other women had foregone Rickard's sacred refuge to see the fight.

Male or female, spectators required stamina. Throughout the previous night, 15 special trains decanted passengers into a Reno unable to offer beds or meals for so many at any price. Even the lucky ones ushered into a good seat by noon were fated to sit in the hot sun before Johnson and Jeffries made their late appearance at about 2.30pm. No undercard was offered and the real business was preceded by an interminable hour of introductions and speeches. A century and more on, the roll call of ringside greats sounds like a distinguished Hall of Fame Annual Parade – Jake Kilrain; John L. Sullivan; Bob Fitzsimmons; Jim Corbett; Tommy Burns; Bill Lang; Joe Choynski; Sam Langford (all of the heavier persuasion); and, at the lighter weights, Billy Papke; Battling Nelson; Ad Wolgast; Owen Moran; Joe Gans;

Kid McCoy and Johnny Coulon. Abe Attell was there and would bandage Jeffries's hands, a task he had performed for Jeffries from boyhood, and a superstitious ritual on which Jeffries insisted. In the scorching heat, celebrity spotting was less tedious than a long eulogy delivered in honour of Nevada's Governor Dickerson for his defiance of the agitation that had so intimidated Governor Gillett.

The delay was not accidental. With an overheated, expectant and long-suffering audience packed in, and an arena-burning riot potentially close, Johnson was in his dressing room coolly renegotiating the shares of the proceeds. Originally scheduled as a 75:25 split, winner:loser, new terms had to be announced by Rickard before the men took the ring. The shares were now 60:40. $121,000 would be shared as $70,600 and $50,400. Rickard admitted he had paid a confirmatory bonus of $10,000 to each man a few weeks before.

These unprecedented sums were quite separate from the film rights (rights so carefully guarded that the crowd was searched at the gate not for weapons, but for unofficial cameras). The last-minute negotiations saw Johnson at his sharpest. On whether this was to be admired or condemned, *Boxing* was most ambivalent: 'Artha is such a simple specimen of credulous ebony that any ordinary white trash can beat him in a business matter – we don't think.'[51] Johnson, Jeffries and Rickard owned one-third of the film rights each, although Rickard was splitting his share with another promoter. Rickard and Jeffries actually pooled their one-sixth and one-third shares and sold the resulting half-share to a New York film

4 July 1910 Reno, California: in his corner, Johnson indicates that Jeffries holds no terrors for him.
Collection of the Smithsonian National Museum of African American History and Culture

MC Billy Jordan introduces a giant Jeffries, who takes a virile pose.

Bain collection, Prints & Photographs Division, Library of Congress, LC-DIG-ggbain-08565

company for $15,000. Johnson was offered £5,000 for his remaining share by another partnership, Hester and O'Day. If *Boxing* is to be believed, he switched into naïve mode, capable only of Amos 'n' Andy speak – 'Gemmen, I'm only a cullud brudder, an' don't know nuthin' about these things, but a man he come here yesterday and said he'd give me a hundred thousand dollars right away all in gold if I'd sell to him.' This generous offer came, he said, from an agent of the Sultan of Dahomey for the African rights in expectation of a Johnson victory. Hester and O'Day, convinced like so many other whites that Jeffries would win, took the bait and doubled their offer

to £10,000.[52] Poker-faced, Johnson accepted. Win or lose he would be rich for as long as his spending habits remained under control.

After the pompous preliminaries and such underlining of the bout's 'significance', how could the first exchanges be anything other than a tension-ridden anticlimax? How could either man not feel the hopes and fears of millions across the globe tightening his muscles and paralysing his nerve endings? By coincidence, Rickard's arena was built on the very spot where Jeffries had formally announced his retirement and presided over the feeble contest between Marvin Hart and Jack Root to be his successor.

It was the purple-trunked Jeffries who moved more comfortably towards his opponent, his huge thighs moving his bulky hairy torso through the shimmering atmosphere created by the afternoon sun and casting an ominous large shadow on the canvas and on his rival.

From the cheap distant seats, it was like a desert mirage peopled by two trembling giants. Johnson, looking the more apprehensive, was content to let Jeffries get close and exchange short punches, or merely clinch and smother, meanwhile testing the big man's strength by having Jeffries push him away as he leaned on. Jeffries's willingness to be the more aggressive

Jeffries, bleeding from his left nostril, clinches with Johnson.
Collection of the Smithsonian National Museum of African American History and Culture

won him the round, but little damage was done to either man.[53]

Jeffries also advanced in the second round, trying long lefts and rights on the retreating Johnson, who was naturally quicker of foot and head and thought. The best Jeffries could do was a right to Johnson's head as they emerged from another maul. More seriously, Johnson caught him with some ruthless counters – a strong left jab to the face, a right uppercut to the jaw, and another shorter left to the face that sent Jeffries's head back and provoked a puzzled frown. Some at ringside applauded when Jeffries pushed Johnson away or wrestled him around into the full glare of the sun.

Others, wiser, were sorry to see Jeffries expending valuable energy in such wasted work, rather than saving his impressive muscles for telling punches over the rounds to come.

By the third, nerves dissipated as both men warmed up. Johnson looked more relaxed despite a slight cut on his lip, a nick caused originally by a sparring partner and reopened by Jeffries. He advanced on the crouching Jeffries, openly and almost carelessly, feinting and throwing punches from long and middle distances, smiling if Jeffries missed with a counter, and cultivating an insouciance when Jeffries landed.

The Johnson smile flickered in the fourth, though the cut lip bled more

obviously. As it became visible beyond the immediate ringside, an infectious roar of 'First blood to Jeff!' was taken up as if Pierce Egan and his cronies were alive and present in Nevada. More acute observers saw that Johnson had even more to smile about in the fifth, when a short right delivered in a clinch brought blood from Jeffries's upper lip in turn. Jeffries had had further successes in the fourth, but the pleasure these evoked in the cheaper seats was misguided. Johnson's fewer punches were the more telling. He landed on the mouth in the fifth, sent a strong left lead to Jeffries's stomach, and followed it with a hurtful left-right combination to the head before the round ended.

Jeffries blocks Johnson's overarm right.
Bettmann/GettyImages

A new offensive pattern was set. Johnson could hurt Jeffries both on the attack and with counters. When Jeffries rushed in, he was met by a powerful straight left. If he avoided this and got closer, he was greeted with left and right hooks, short-arm punches that bloodied his nose, and brought bruising and swelling around his right eye, which began to close. At the end of the sixth, it was cut as well by a long stiff left.

Only the diehard believers in the Jeffries mystique could deceive themselves about the way the fight was unfolding. In his corner before the seventh, as his seconds worked to repair his bleeding brow, Jeffries no longer quite believed in his invincibility either. But he had every confidence in his own bravery and had no intention of surrendering. He irritably waved the administrations aside and lumbered out for the seventh.

Immediately, the tender eyebrow was targeted precisely by a right lead from Johnson, and Jeffries rubbed it with the back of his glove. Johnson, on the end of a Jeffries left hook, stayed off, content to pick away at Jeffries with left leads, landing some on that eyebrow and others on the bleeding lip. When big Jeff came boring in with his head down, he found his intended body blows cleverly blocked and smothered. He went back to his stool a worried man, visibly damaged in contrast to the smiling and relatively unmarked Johnson. Jeffries moved like a man with an Atlas complex – one believing he had the world's problems draped upon his shoulders. He had every excuse. The world had decided he was the man destined to solve *its* problems. That even his strong frame was now wilting under the strain of that burden, as well as the effects of the sedentary years spent on the alfalfa farm, were hardly his fault.

Over the next five rounds, the 8th to 12th, sobering reality spread from the ringsiders able to read the subtler signs, out to those many metres away. Cheers for Jeffries gradually subsided. He had met more than his match. When he closed on Johnson and threw his punches, Johnson blocked them. When he stood off and led, he was beaten to the punch. When he rushed, Johnson sidestepped him or swayed away, clipping him with stinging blows to head and body. Some diehards looked on, unable to shake off the belief that somehow Jeffries might yet land one all-conquering blow with one of those big fists and wipe out all that had gone before. Others, less optimistic, filed solemnly away through the exit. Many, men and women, stared compulsively down at their laps or their feet, unable to process the unwelcome message emanating from the ring. Hopes, momentarily raised by an early Jeffries rally at the beginning of the 11th, soon died, especially when Johnson sent Jeffries's head back with a jerk with a short left hook and followed it up with three rapid uppercuts in succession. Bookmakers stopped giving even the meanest of odds on a Johnson victory.

For those still watching as avidly as they had at the beginning, the bout was now like a classical tragedy where the denouement was predictable from the middle of the drama, yet inevitable. And just so, each protagonist was trapped within his role and could not avert his fate. Johnson's part was to continue to punish the helpless victim before him, as if every damaging clout and clip could eliminate every insult and injustice suffered by him and every black person over generations. Jeffries, in the full knowledge that he could not now do what the white world had asked of him, could only suffer as

The end is nigh – Jeffries clutches the rope. Johnson looks impassively on.
Bain collection, Prints & Photographs Division, Library of Congress,LC-DIG-ggbain-23084

stoically and as gloriously as possible on its behalf. As the bravest of sacrificial victims, round after round, he got wearily off his stool, barely able to lift his mighty arms in attack or defence and trudged towards his tormentor to take what Johnson cared to deliver. He had never surrendered before and he did not intend to do so now.

In his ring career, Jeffries had never been knocked down, but paper achievements are but poor defences against powerful punches. In the 15th round, the narrative changed. Johnson tired of playing the sadistic avenger and turned merciful destroyer.

Emerging from a clinch, he caught Jeffries with a long driving left brought up from hip level to Jeffries's jaw. The ringside reporter for the *New York Times* was a man who knew all about ring denouements, John L. Sullivan. Here he was, one ring titan recording the downfall of another, the perfect (ghosted?) eyewitness:

> Jeff tottered and went down on the west side of the ring. He fell on both knees, and as the timekeeper and referee yelled at him the number of seconds, he turned around and rested one foot on the

floor, looking the while toward the timekeeper. Johnson walked about the centre, craftily eyeing his big opponent. Jeff waited for nine and then arose. Johnson stepped in as he got on his feet and whipped another left full on the face, and Jeff went down again almost in the same place, but this time he crashed through the ropes. Several of his seconds and some newspaper men helped to get him back in the ring again, and Johnson coolly watched the proceedings from more than half way across the ring.

When Jeff landed inside again, he was reeling, but not nearly as far gone as lots of fellows who have been down twice for the count. He staggered over to the east side and Johnson stepped in to him as he came over and sent him reeling with a right on the ear. As he turned around, ready to close down, Johnson's left again found the already battered and beaten face. As Jeff sank sideways to the floor the immense crowd was on its feet, some yelling and some cheering. Johnson calmly walked around his big opponent toward his own corner. His seconds were already getting his chair ready to push through the ropes for him to sit …

Few would dispute Sullivan's accuracy here, but the next minute was full of confusion as the ringside and then the ring filled with helpers, hangers-on and mercy-pleaders who cried out desperately to Tex Rickard the referee to stop the contest before big Jeff was finally knocked out. Only Rickard, amid the general confusion, could pronounce definitively. He had expected Jeffries to win, but he said firmly and convincingly:

The fight was won and lost when Jeffries went through the first time. This is official. The other knockdown does not count. It was this way: Jeffries was brought to his knees and as he arose, dazed, Johnson hit him with a succession of lefts that sent him through the ropes. As he lay there several of his seconds caught hold of him and helped him to his feet. Under

the rules of the game, which I have read thoroughly, while certain people were saying that I would not referee the fight, this disqualified Jeffries, and Johnson was the winner.

I thought the seconds were going to carry Jeffries to his corner. Instead they shoved him into the ring again to be beaten further, while I was doing all I could during the confusion to stop the fight.

Then as now the referee's decision is all. Although many authorities, for example, the *Boxing Register* of the International Hall of Fame, record the result as 15th-round knockout; and the *Encyclopedia of Boxing* by the meticulous Gilbert Odd more accurately as 15th-round stoppage, perhaps a pedant could insist that the true record should read as a 15th-round disqualification.

Pedantry, however, cannot disguise the fact that Jeffries was beaten, and beaten quite as decisively as a man can be, and had Rickard neglected to intervene, he would have been down for longer than the magic and decisive ten. Though Rickard *claims* to have attempted to stop the fight after Jeffries was pushed back through the ropes, the extant film shows clearly that he did nothing of the sort. As Jeffries got up and tottered over to the other side of the ring, Rickard took up his conventional position a few yards away and followed the two big men to the other side. It was only *after* Johnson delivered the final blow that Rickard stepped in. His post-fight account betrays his own sensitivity about his position – he had never refereed even an amateur contest before – and his version was coined

without the benefit of a viewing of the film.

The preceding paragraphs have been devoted to the physical exchanges of two muscular men trying to establish physical domination over one another. But there was, as always, a profounder and more damaging struggle going on: the one to achieve psychological mastery. Jack Johnson had an overwhelming initial advantage: as he climbed through those ropes, he was entering a place he wanted to be. Despite his nominal title of champion, he knew he had acquired it on Australian soil with a victory over a lightly regarded Canadian. Most Americans regarded the undefeated Jeffries as the true champion. Only a victory over Big Jeff in the ring would produce a new real champion. (How many white Americans would accept such a victory if it came at the hands of a black man remained to be seen.) Jack Johnson could, therefore, be single-minded. Reminiscing many years later, he admitted this was not easy:

Strange as it might appear, the toughest fight I ever had, was not in the ring. It was one I had with my self over a long stretch, my idea of dethroning an idol of the people. I refer to the pre-fight days of the Jeffries-Johnson battle. Yes, that was my toughest.[54]

However tough Johnson found this pre-fight fight, he was a master at it. A week before, he was loftily dismissing the white veterans who were either advising or supporting Jeffries:

… the men who went in for pugilism five to 15 years ago were mere thumpers. Science to them was an unknown quantity. They went in for brute force, and the men who succeeded in getting in a genuine bullock-punch first generally carried off the battle. Jeffries has now around him a lot of the old scum of fighters – men who are uneducated to a degree, and have only one idea, and that is the asserting of the brutal element. Corbett, only a middle rater at his best; Sullivan, now fat as a pig with beer; Choynski, whom I regard as a 'has-been'; and others, all spar with my coming opponent daily. They have the poor blacksmith almost out of his senses telling him fairy tales.[55]

Johnson also scored a mental point in the immediate preliminaries by ignoring the toss for the choice of corners, claiming he would win whatever corner he fought from.

Poor Jeffries could not quite manage such mental single-mindedness. His poignant words post-fight betray his inner ambivalence:

I guess it's all my own fault. I was getting along nicely and living peacefully on my alfalfa farm, but when they started calling for me and mentioning me as 'the white man's hope', I guess my pride got the better of my judgement. At that I worked long and hard to condition myself, and I was fit, so far as strength goes, but the old necessary snap and dash, the willingness to tear in and crush were not with me.

Six years ago the result would have been different, but now –

well, *I guess the public will let me alone after this.* [Italics added]

On reflection, Jeffries felt that he had been coaxed and cajoled into leaving his fishing and his farming to take on the white champion role that ultimately overwhelmed him. He found it demeaning that although he had done what he believed his *moral* duty, it did not appear quite so noble to his fellow citizens. California's Governor Gillett, who had appeased protestors by banning the fight from his state, was anxious now to make sure he was on the side of the voting angels. His vocabulary, including words such as 'demoralising', 'corrupting', 'offensive', and 'public nuisance', was difficult to square with the supposed crusade on which Jeffries prided himself. Jeffries's reaction to Gillett's condemnation – 'I should tell them all to go to hell and go back home' – also lacked something in single-minded dedication.[56]

Johnson, a strength as well as a weakness, was very socially and politically aware, but not to be confused by complexities. Many blacks, in the USA and elsewhere, looked naturally to him as their representative. He was himself the representative, pure and simple, of the interests of Jack Johnson. Throughout his reign as champion from 1908 to 1915, black challengers were just as frozen out as if a white champion were operating a colour bar. Ever the pragmatist, Johnson saw no point in two black men beating each other up for limited purses before limited crowds.

Johnson presented himself as a well-read man of letters – another personality trait calculated to stir up the more philistine members of redneck America.

One wonders if he were familiar with the wise words of the English scholar and philosopher Francis Bacon (1561–1626) in *Advancement of Learning*: 'If a man begin with certainties, he shall end in doubts; but if he will be content to begin with doubts, he shall end in certainties.' He approached the Jeffries fight as if he did indeed know Bacon. The beating of Jeffries was the pinnacle of his career, yet his behaviour in and out of the ring thereafter suggests he should also have read Bacon's essay, 'Of Youth and Age', where the words 'And certainly, the more a man drinketh of the world, the more it intoxicateth …', might have been written with the excesses of world heavyweight champions in mind.

Johnson's frailties in human relationships outside the ring were rarely on show within it. On the contrary, he had an uncanny ability to obliterate self-doubts and exude superiority. Like a chess grandmaster, or a stony-faced poker player, he could intimidate mentally and silently, all his facial expressions and his body language united in conveying the image of a winner. To land, as Jeffries did in the second round, a solid punch, only to provoke a flashing smile and an audible chuckle, was to be the subject of coercion as disheartening as a firm counter-punch. Johnson could switch instantly from strong silent giant to wisecracking comedian with an armoury of witty remarks as cutting and hurtful as his uppercut. The verbal punishment taken by Burns in 1908 was duplicated by that suffered by Big Jeff in Reno, a phenomenon even Jack London conceded was 'golden repartee'. 'I thought you could punch,' 'Is that all you've got?' 'It's all over for you Jim,' 'I know you're a bear, but I'm a gorilla,' 'How do you like 'em, Jim?' 'Does it hurt, Jim?' 'Don't rush, Jim, I can go on like this all afternoon.'

Added to remarks aimed at his opponent were secondary asides directed to others in the ringside, but all too audible to Jeffries. 'I didn't show you that one in Sydney!' he shouted to Tommy Burns as he landed a left. 'John, I thought this fellow could fight,' he shouted to John L. Sullivan. And as Johnson wrote later:

New Yorkers gather at The New York Times *offices, desperate for the latest news from Reno.* WikimediaCommons/New York Times

In the gathering of spectators who saw the encounter was another huge group of newspaper writers and photographers, and round about us telegraph instruments clicked off a description of the fight blow by blow. I recall that occasionally *I took time during the exchange of these blows to suggest to telegraph operators what to tell their newspapers.*[57] [Italics added.]

When Bertolt Brecht, the German playwright (1898–1956), invented the alienation effect – of actors retaining a degree of critical detachment from the action in which they were performing, and commenting upon it – perhaps he was providing a theory for what Jack Johnson had already accomplished. Brecht was known to be an enthusiastic

follower of boxing. (Note again that Johnson's quaint prose style is some degree removed from the 'yes Massa' slang put into his mouth by racist white reporters.)

Prominent among white racists at ringside was the abusive and increasingly apoplectic 'un-Gentlemanly' Jim Corbett, John L. Sullivan's conqueror and the probable reason why the highly prejudiced Sullivan cast his report on the fight in terms surprisingly favourable to Johnson, especially after the champion had complimented him as being 'as fat as a pig with beer'. John L. concluded, '… the best man won, and I was one of the first to congratulate him …' Corbett acted as one of Jeffries's seconds and was the carrier not just of bucket and sponge but of a bundle of unenlightened prejudices. To Corbett, black fighters could look confident only because they were too unimaginatively stupid to anticipate the future. Black fighters were cowardly: 'Take it from me, the black boy has a yellow streak, and Jeff will bring it out when he gets into that ring.'

Black fighters were child-like, and so could be easily provoked into losing their tempers. Such crass crudities were echoed in more exalted places. As a preview to the Reno fight, *The Times* of 4 July 1910 carried an anonymous article, 'The New Prize Ring', over a column and a half. It provided some classic examples of rampant prejudice masquerading as scientific fact. Two quotations will suffice:

His [Jeffries's] courage cannot be questioned; whereas every negro, when the test comes, is apt to fall a victim to that nerve-storm which is called panic …

… like many negroes, he [Johnson] has an ill-balanced physique: his torso is admirably developed, but neither his ribs nor his abdominal muscles provide adequate protection for the lower part of his body, to which Jeffries will direct his most telling thumps, while refusing to waste energy on the negro's hard solid head, a racial heirloom …

Corbett decided to abuse and provoke Johnson during his ring walk, on the stool in his corner and throughout the action. In practice, Corbett found himself playing the hapless straight man to the accomplished jester in the ring. When Johnson arrived, he was loudly told by Corbett that he was a fool even to appear and was destined for the beating of his life. Corbett continued in the same vein: 'That left was a joke,' 'You big stiff, I always knew you were a faker,' 'Stand up and fight, you coward.' Johnson merely replied in kind: 'Did you see that one, Jimmy?' 'Too late to do anything, Jim, your man's all in.' And when Jeffries responded to Corbett's advice and went into his famous crouch: 'Don't worry, I will straighten him up in a minute.'

The longer the fight went on, the more damage showed on Jeffries's face, the angrier Corbett became. Corbett suffered two further humiliations, one as the butt for Johnson's irony ('I thought you said you were going to have *me* wild!'), and one as pleader with the hated Johnson for mercy on Jeffries's behalf ('Oh, don't Jack; don't hit him!'). Corbett should have learned a lesson that day, but as he appeared on the New York stage the following month duly 'blacked up' in a minstrel show, irony was presumably beyond him.[58]

By August even Corbett had changed his story to cast himself in a more tolerant light. According to *Boxing* (13 August 1910), he told the *New York American*:

I must admit that I have to admire Johnson's ready wit in the ring. It made him all the harder to whip for he combines his humour with his hitting and footwork that he never gets flustered, and simply throws his opponent into a frenzy.

I yelled to Jeff to hit him one good punch and the yellow streak would come out like a rainbow. Johnson clinched big Jim, and, flashing his gold teeth at me, said, smiling: 'That's what they ALL say, Mistah Co'butt.'

He used that famous line on me every time I tried to break up his wonderful display of self-control. Once I poked my head under the lower rope and said: 'Why don't you fight, Johnson? Please let yourself out for just one minute.'

He wheeled Jeff around until he could face me over Jeff's shoulder and, grinning, answered: 'I can't; I'm clever like you, Jim.' I tell you I had to hold my face straight then. I didn't dare let him see that he had really got a laugh out of the man who was trying to kid him.

The dialogue and the subtler aspects of the fight were lost on the majority of the people crammed into the expensive discomfort at the Reno arena. Nevertheless, they were in attendance, while right across the Western world others were jealously jostling for room on the sidewalks and pavements outside newspaper and telegraph offices for up-to-the-minute news at second hand. In London, the offices of sporting newspapers were besieged, as were hotel lobbies and anywhere news bulletins could be read. Paris and Berlin had similar experiences. In New Jersey, there were 15,000 at the Garden City airfield merely to hear fight bulletins read out. In New York, 30,000 people, including about 1,000 women, were crushed together in Times Square to read, word by word, an illuminated *New York Times* bulletin machine grinding out a report on the fight, information repeated on large blackboards on the other side of the building. Cheers for every reported blow from Jeffries were not propitious. A Johnson blow was marked by gasps or a sullen silence. About 1 per cent of the crowd was black. They stayed as quiet as a Glasgow Celtic supporter trapped unwittingly on a terrace reserved for fans of Glasgow Rangers.

Their discretion was wise. The New York crowd, like the Reno one, contained their disappointment and melted funereally away. Elsewhere, all the ugly and disgusting aspects of racism raised by the pre-fight publicity formed a gigantic boil that refused to be lanced by Johnson's decisive victory. It burst instead into riots, violence and running street fights across the USA, mostly in the east and south.

Page four of the *New York Times* of 5 July 1910 could reasonably have been printed with black edging as it recorded, place by place, a dark and humiliating day in the annals of sport and race relations alike. The following post-fight incidents appear in more lurid detail on that page.

In New York City, hardly had the huge Times Square crowd silently filed away, than reports came in of ugly incidents breaking out elsewhere in the city. Any city block where pleasure was shown at Johnson's victory became the site of violent assaults from disgruntled whites determined physically to assert the white supremacy they had expected Jeffries to demonstrate on their behalf. The West 37th Street police station became an ambulance centre for wounded blacks as a result of a Ninth Avenue white mob attacking any black who passed by. Another white gang took over Columbus Avenue and raided the mainly black tenements on the West 98th to 100th Streets. On Eighth Avenue, another group poured from a saloon calling loudly, 'Let's lynch the first n****r we meet,' and pulled an inoffensive middle-aged man off a streetcar and beat him badly. Many other blacks suffered similar indignities and at least eight died before the night was over, each a direct victim of the news from Reno.

In Uvalda, Georgia, three blacks died and many were seriously wounded when a celebration among the blacks in a construction camp led the whites in the camp to try physically to clear the camp of the blacks. Shots were exchanged on both sides. In Omaha, Nebraska, a black man who announced the result of the fight on a streetcar had his throat cut on the spot.

Elsewhere, passions spilled over in the opposite direction. A quarrel in Roanoke, Virginia, led to a white man being shot in the head. On a train in Tallulah, Louisiana, a ticket collector was shot by a black passenger. And in Pittsburgh, Pennsylvania, the Wylie Avenue area, mainly black, erupted first in joy and then in anger as old scores

Tom Kennedy (1884–1965), who knocked out Billy Wells in New York, embraces sparring partner and friend Joe Jeannette (1879–1958). They never met in the ring as black-white contests were as rare as such black-white friendships.

Bain collection, Prints & Photographs Division, Library of Congress, LC-DIG-ggbain-10000

against the Greek and the Russian communities were settled. Taxis, streetcars and private cars were seized and reckless joyrides attempted up and down Wylie Avenue. That few were seriously hurt and no one killed was a small miracle.

In Washington, fist fights between blacks and whites flourished after a black man shouted, 'Hurrah for Johnson, champion of the world!' and was promptly attacked by three whites. The shout, 'Hurrah for Johnson!' by a black in Atlanta, Georgia, was sufficient to provoke further fights and arrests. Meanwhile, in Louisville, Kentucky (the community that would one day produce Muhammad Ali, the most famous black boxer of all time), a white newsboy was beaten up by a group of blacks, and a white passer-by slashed with a knife. All this led to a full-scale riot with several thousand whites laying siege to a mainly black apartment block, and the air filled with flying missiles. Newsstands were also at the centre of running fights between whites and blacks in New Orleans.

St Louis, Missouri, and Macon, Georgia, were two other cities to see blacks celebrating in the streets; demonstrations followed promptly by police and white vigilantes 'restoring order' by clubbing the celebrants back indoors. In Norfolk, Virginia, the sailors from the battleships presently in port formed another vigilante group, attacking people in the street merely for being black.

Amid this grim catalogue, the actions of Mr S. I. Sawyer of St Joseph, Missouri should be remembered. Mr Sawyer, who was white, saw a black man attacked by another white on the street and bravely intervened on the black man's behalf. He personally had to be rescued from the clutches of an angry white mob by the police. On this night of evil deeds, many thousands of Americans of differing ethnic distinctions lost their heads, at least 13 people were killed and hundreds injured. Some 25 American cities suffered serious disturbances in which, said the London *Times*, 'the lynching of blacks was only prevented by the arrival of the police'. On the night, Mr Sawyer, at least, remembered he was above all else a human being.

How many, however, could be relied upon to behave like rational human beings in the aftermath of the fight, when the mere knowledge of the result had brought about such riotous consequences? As many American cities counted the cost of the night's disturbances, other questions arose. What would happen if the picture palaces of the world were to show, blow by blow, the film in which canny businessmen had invested heavily? Would the riots be distributed along with the celluloid? Many believed they would.

Cinema proprietors in many American cities were informed by police chiefs, mayors and other authorities that showings of the Jeffries–Johnson fight film would not be allowed – Washington, New York, San Francisco, Boston, Milwaukee and many southern cities. In sensitive corners of the British Empire where, like the Deep South, white minorities held power over black majorities, similar moves were made. Outright bans or strong recommendations against showings of the film took place in cities such as Cape Town, Bombay and Calcutta. There were others even in imperial cities where hardly a black face could be seen – Melbourne, Canterbury and Ontario, for example.

One of *The Times*'s correspondents in London wrote on 6 July that the 'gruesome spectacle of two men (black and white) mashing each other into a jelly, before a howling mass of spectators in this 20th century of the Christian era, is a sight ghastly enough to make angels weep over the hypocrisy of our modern civilization'. If the writer genuinely believed that boxing was inherently unethical, his sincerity can be admired. More likely was a different hypocrisy of early 20th-century civilisation: that boxing was perfectly acceptable; that contests

between black and white fighters were perfectly acceptable; but in both cases acceptable providing the white fighter won and confirmed prejudices about white supremacy.

The raw aftermath and the shock waves caused by the fight must be grasped in their political and sociological context; a context where every such event touched white nerves and stirred white fears. The *Boxing World and Athletic Chronicle* (28 July 1910) was being dangerously flippant in its cartoon cover (while insulting two American minority groups simultaneously). A crudely drawn Johnson in Native American dress executes a war dance, and displays scalps labelled 'Jeff', 'Burns', 'Ketchel' and 'Kaufman', while exclaiming, 'Whoop! dis chief get heap plenty pale face scalp'. To many, the threat Johnson represented was no joke, even one so unfunny and banal.

On 11 July, the film was the subject of a question in the House of Commons. The Liberal Home Secretary, Winston Churchill, did not know how Johnson and his exploits would be concerning him in the future, and gave a self-effacing answer: 'I am advised that I have no powers in the matter.'[59] Will Thorne, veteran trade unionist and a rare working-class Member of Parliament, raised the real issue: 'Does the Right Hon. gentleman think that if Jeffries had knocked out Johnson there would have been so much "slobby" talk about this subject as prevails at the present time?' Thorne apparently raised 'laughter and cheers'. Neither laughter nor cheers was much in evidence when the London County Council (LCC) debated the film on 13 July and passed by 45 votes to 29 the resolution:

That in the opinion of the Council the public exhibition, at places of entertainment in London, of pictures representing the recent prize fight in the United States of America is undesirable; and that the proprietors of London music-halls and other places licensed by the Council for cinematographic performances be so informed.[60]

The complexities of the laws surrounding boxing and the censorship of films encouraged this kind of broad hint. Proprietors of LCC-licensed premises were not banned from showing the film, but would hardly wish to risk losing in the future the licence on which their livelihood depended by showing a film that the licence-issuing body had declared 'undesirable'. The Ring at Blackfriars in the autumn of 1910 would supplement the regular Saturday night live fights with five weeknights devoted to boxing films; for example, the Battling Nelson v Ad Wolgast marathon.[61] They did not risk showing Johnson v Jeffries.

Pornography and sexually explicit material have always been obtainable by the rich and privileged, yet ruthlessly oppressed for popular audiences. Theatre, like publishing, suffered similar travails. In November 1910, Laurence Housman (brother of the Housman who wrote *A Shropshire Lad*) wrote a play, *Pains and Penalties* (about King George IV and Queen Caroline). It was refused a licence for public performance.[62] Yet Housman could publish the text in 1911 and have it performed privately to a select audience in November 1911.[63] A select audience at a price could see what was forbidden for the general public.

Battling Nelson (1882–1954), the Danish-American lightweight and possessor of a menacing left hook. His benign appearance belies the damage he suffered regularly. He 'battled' 82 rounds in just two fights.
Bain collection, Prints & Photographs Division, Library of Congress,LC-DIG-ggbain-23084

Similar double standards operated over the fight film. The 90-minute film was shown in Dublin to an audience drawn in for Horse Show week in August, an event drawing a distinguished and affluent audience.[64] It was also shown in full at the NSC premises on 12 September 1910, where *The Times*'s correspondent found it 'rather dull, and not at all like the highly-coloured word-paintings of it … A very harmless show; and anyone who could be demoralized by seeing it would certainly lose all his morality if he saw a car accident.'[65] Were you an ordinary boxing fan without membership privileges, you had to be protected from even this minimal risk.

At the beginning of 1910, *Boxing World and Athletic Chronicle* had pronounced that 'pugilistic fever is catching on everywhere'.[66] Far from alleviating the fever, the universal attention given to Johnson–Jeffries resulted in a burgeoning interest in ring happenings everywhere. Small hall promoters and sports editors benefited from the public's growing enthusiasm for seeing boxing in the flesh, and for reading more of the men with the courage to make a living from their fists.

Regrettably, this new passion could be channelled into less worthy ends too, none more so than the search for a 'White Hope' that disfigured the sport over the next few years. At the beginning of August 1910, Hugh D. McIntosh, the enterprising Australian promoter of the Burns–Johnson clash in Sydney, who was in Reno for the big fight despite losing out on the chance to stage it, sailed for Europe on the *Lusitania*. *Boxing* revealed:

> Mr MacIntosh [*sic*] does not believe that the negro is the superior of the white man in any department of physical excellence, regarding Johnson in the nature of a freak who has gone beyond his own kind.

In his dealings with journalists, including the writer of the *Boxing* article, McIntosh stressed the purity of his motives:

> He has no predilections or favouritism; his quest is an honourable one, guided only by his desire to bring back to his own people a title that is now, for the first time in ring history, reposing on the brow of the black.
>
> His friendship and admiration for Johnson shows that Mr MacIntosh is not moved by antipathy to the negro. He has given Johnson more honours than any other Caucasian, but he firmly believes that Johnson is only possible because a lethargy has seized the white heavyweights, and he wants to shake them out of it.[67]

The plea sounds like an anti-Semite explaining that many of his friends are Jews. It also places McIntosh in the role of the princess in the fairy tale who finds the search for a handsome prince involves the kissing of a lot of frogs. McIntosh and his fellow promoters were going to have to kiss a legion of white frogs before finding a white prince to beat Johnson.

A few weeks after the Reno fight, on 22 July 1910, a particularly handsome fair-haired British heavyweight made his Wonderland debut. He had impeccable credentials to be a new British hero. He was born on 31 August 1887 in Cable Street, Shadwell, one of the nine children born to a local bandmaster and his wife. Like many East Enders, he received a rudimentary education and was into his first menial job as a messenger boy at 14 years old. Big for his age in a time and place where many of his fellow teenagers were nutritionally challenged, he was drawn into the world of the Christian youth clubs for his recreation just when amateur boxing was encouraged. In the ring, he showed speed and skill beyond the ordinary for one of his size. And he had a punch.

For the moment, precious few local opportunities for social or professional advancement presented themselves. He responded instead to the siren call of King and Army. In 1906, he enlisted in the Royal Garrison Artillery. After a few months' basic training, he headed for the jewel in the British Empire's crown – India. His next three years were spent in north-west India. His regiment there took army boxing seriously and hired professional coaches to improve the team's chances in inter-regimental

Bombardier Billy Wells (1889–1967): the handsome and enigmatic East Ender was British heavyweight champion for eight years.
Bain collection, Prints & Photographs Division, Library of Congress, LC-DIG-ggbain-12208

competitions. From 1908 to 1910, he boxed in many a tournament and team matches in Poona, Quetta, Simla, Lucknow, Lahore and the like, always winning and usually knocking his opponent out. Such a talent could not be permanently confined to exotic locales and army boxing. In early 1910, he paid £21 to buy himself out of the army and he sailed for home. He left the regiment, he left India but he brought home with him the name and the rank he would make famous – Bombardier Billy Wells.[68] Not the least of his attractions was his white skin.

Unlike his more flamboyant rivals, Wells was reticent and modest:

He is as docile as a big dog that disdains to emulate the yelping and yapping habits of smaller canines. It is like extracting a double tooth to try and draw him upon the subject of boxing. He fights with his fists and not with his tongue. No man was ever less of a swaggerer or bragger.'[69]

This was the opinion of Eugene Corri, the referee. Corri, with his NSC connections was one of the men Wells first contacted on his return to London from India. Corri set up an exhibition try-out in a private club in early June 1910, followed by a genuine contest on 27 June at Shoeburyness against Gunner McMurray. Wells impressed in the exhibition and let his fists speak for him by knocking out McMurray in the first round.

Hardly had McMurray hit the canvas than McIntosh was on the *Lusitania* and on his way to London. Even Don King, the American promoter known to step over the inert body of one ex-champion to be the first to sign his conqueror, could hardly have moved faster. McIntosh had already matched Burns and his Australian rival Bill Lang against two Americans, Stanley

Ketchel and Al Kaufmann. He now planned to put Wells into the mix with the other British heavyweights of the day, including Petty Officer Curran, Gunner Moir, Jewey Smith and Iron Hague, with whoever came out top to be matched against the ultimate winner of the Australian–American contests. Thus, whatever happened, he had a white opponent to challenge Johnson. McIntosh got Wells's signature on a six-month contract for his next three fights once Wells had easily knocked out his Wonderland opponent Corporal Brown in the third round on 23 July 1910.

Hype, music hall engagements and a publicity campaign promoted Wells vigorously as the new boxing sensation. Wells, strictly a professional novice for all his promise, was elevated to the top of a bill at the Hugh D. McIntosh promotion at the King's Hall on 15 September 1910. The poster shamelessly proclaimed in bold type, 'The Search for a White Champion', adding 'The first of an eliminating series to find a real British Champion'.[70] Prematurely, it claimed 'Bomb. Wells' was 'Regarded as the best Heavyweight in England', and matched him against Sergeant Sunshine of the Royal British Fusiliers. (Sunshine had on 26 May 1910 lost to the perennially out-of-condition Iron Hague over 20 tedious rounds at the Liverpool Arena.) Considering Wells and Sunshine were matched over 20 championship rounds, when Wells had never previously been beyond six, with most of his contests over a maximum of three, this might have been disastrous.

In practice, Wells v Sunshine was extremely entertaining, although the entertainment was of roller-coaster unpredictability rather than skilled execution.[71] Wells the novice was still more scientific than the 33-year-old Sunshine. He profited from Sunshine's too-open style to land rights and lefts at will in the first from a safe distance. Sunshine did not go down, even when hit cleanly on the chin. People in the hall assumed he soon would in the second, which became a replay of the first, yet it ended rather with a wild rush from Sunshine, taking Wells back to the ropes undamaged yet looking discernibly nervous.

Had Jack Johnson been there, his smile would have been panoramic, especially when Sunshine decided in round three to change from target to attacker and landed some thoroughly unsettling left hooks on Wells. This was not to Wells's taste at all, especially when Sunshine stepped blindly through a flurry of tentative Wells punches and landed an impeccable right hook to the jaw that sent Wells down face first. As Wells scrambled around the floor on all fours like a man searching for a lost contact lens, the bell saved him a full count and an ignominious knockout.

Had Sunshine been calmer and cleverer, he would have knocked out Wells in the fourth. As it was, Wells survived by taking three more counts and clinching tenaciously and persistently. Indeed, his tactic was so blatant that referee Corri, hoarse from shouting 'break!' from ringside, climbed into the ring to enforce breaks physically. The delay enabled Wells to last the round.

The fifth had a punched-out Sunshine, and a punched-up and gradually recovering Wells, happy to lean on each other for as long as an impatient Corri would allow. How the slow waltz could have gone on for another 15 rounds is imponderable.

Fortunately, it did not have to. In the sixth, Wells's clearing brain recognised that one properly directed rally might finish it. A few classic straight lefts brought Sunshine upright and vulnerable. As he ducked his head down to avoid another, his jaw met a rising right from Wells. Down he went for the first time in the fight, and down for the necessary ten; sunshine turned to night-time. Wells, McIntosh's latest white hope, had lived to fight another day, just.

Wells kept McIntosh's crusade alive on 19 October 1910, also at King's Hall, when he met Private Dan Voyles of the Irish Guards and was again pasted all over the ring, kept up only by the ropes at one juncture, yet producing a saving body punch that did for Voyles in the tenth. McIntosh discreetly found him an easier opponent, Seaman Parsons, for 16 November 1910. Wells knocked Parsons out in the first, thus sparing himself, the promoter and his growing army of friends a further trauma like those of the earlier bouts.

During the next year, 1911, Wells would be making headlines in and out of the ring, but he had already demonstrated the defining elements of his boxing career. At his best, he looked the boys' comic picture of an English boxing hero – blond, handsome, with a chiselled torso. Not for nothing was he to grace the British cinema screens in later decades as the muscular hammermeister who solemnly struck the gong in the preliminary credits of J. Arthur Rank films.

He was a heavyweight who could move unusually quickly and gracefully on his feet, and he had a punch powerful enough to knock most men out – no powder puff tapper he. And yet there were signs that what one saw initially was not what Wells could necessarily deliver. The blond bomber could not always bring his full armour along; a certain fragility of temperament made him deliver less when the occasion demanded more.

Shakespeare's Henry V, before the battle of Agincourt, suggested, 'That he which hath no stomach to this fight,/ Let him depart … We would not die in that man's company,/That fears his fellowship, to die with us.' The text is traditionally interpreted as a call by the king to have physical cowards depart before their feebleness lets the army down. Perhaps, as ever, Shakespeare was being more subtle, and wanted to convey the duality of men like Wells who were certainly not cowardly yet had 'no stomach for the fight'.

Boxing history presents a long lineage of battlers who relished the ring, giving and taking punishment as if only in those bellicose moments were they at their happiest – Ketchel, La Motta, Freddie Mills, up to Arturo Gatti or Mickey Ward later, legendary participants in that fellowship of which Shakespeare writes. Yet there are others, more naturally talented, more skilful and perhaps more imaginative, who fought, and fought superbly in their day, yet gave the impression that ultimately professional boxing was not something they truly enjoyed, even when winning handsomely – Lennox Lewis, Roy Jones or Chris Eubank would be modern examples; Wells was one in his day.

Wells had 'no stomach' in another sense. Throughout his career, he was vulnerable to blows to the body. An opponent who could slip inside his stinging jabs and pummel him around and below the ribcage had chances of doubling him up, lowering his guard and knocking him out. It was not a great attribute for a potential world champion.

Meanwhile, 1910, so significant a year for boxing on both sides of the Atlantic, drew to a close with some other memorable contests. The NSC asserted its continuing importance, despite the flurry of public interest and private profit engendered by new promoters such as McIntosh, and new arenas such as the King's Hall and Olympia.

At Olympia, on Boxing Day, two years to the day after Johnson's defeat of Burns, the pathetic 'White Hope' series continued with the attempted resuscitation of the career of the Australian heavyweight Bill Lang (already beaten twice by Burns). Lang was matched with a Californian Jack Burns, whom he floored at the ends of both the second and the eighth rounds, but who clung on until the 12th when spared a final knockout by the referee.

That an Australian–American fight was taking place in London is clear evidence of how popular boxing had become there. Private promoters could offer big purses and big audiences. What the NSC could offer was a small but committed and knowledgeable audience, official championship status and prestigious hardware in the Lonsdale Belt. The belt was a fraction of the size of the beribboned synthetic monstrosities awarded across the globe in modern times by a multitude of 'world' sanctioning bodies. It was also a hundred times more elegant, and a significant factor in persuading many Edwardian boxers to forego the blandishments of commercial promoters in favour of Covent Garden exclusivity; cash trumped by cachet. If the modern light-welterweight Junior Witter (b. 10 March 1974) is to be believed, the tradition survives: 'To win the belt was brilliant … the amount of respect you get for a Lonsdale Belt is unreal. It definitely means a lot to me.'[72]

Meanwhile, two of England's cleverest boxers, Joe Bowker and Digger Stanley, met at the NSC on 17 October 1910 for the British bantamweight championship and the Lonsdale Belt. The purse was £400, small change to a Johnson or a Jeffries, and there were £100-a-side side stakes. Neither man was a novice – quite the contrary.

Bowker, a Mancunian born in Salford on 20 July 1883 as Tommy Mahon, could claim up to 1906 to be generally recognised as the *world* bantamweight champion.[73] He had beaten the cream of British challengers (Pedlar Palmer, Owen Moran, Spike Robson) and some top Americans including Frankie Neil. Since then he had lost twice to Jim Driscoll (on points over 15 rounds at the NSC on 28 May 1906, and to a 17th-round knockout at the same venue on 3 June 1907), and to a couple of Americans in the USA. Furthermore, he had been fighting after as a featherweight, with enough success to be recognised by the British as the world featherweight champion from 1905 to 1907.

Many doubted Bowker could make the new NSC weight limit of 8st 6lb/118lbs, but at the afternoon weigh-in, he surprised the sceptics by making the limit exactly; the full 118lbs was packed into a short, sinewy and tough frame, a fraction under 5ft 4in. He knew all about life's struggles, having fought as a teenager in the Manchester area's boxing booths, and all about poverty. He once turned up ten days late at the NSC for a novice competition. Reprimanded by Peggy Bettinson for his tardiness ('I told you to come at once'), he explained he had spent ten days *walking* the 181 miles from Manchester to London, sleeping rough on the way, having no money to travel any other way.[74]

Graduation from the university of hard knocks taught him a hatful of tricks. His speciality was to boost the odds laid against him by performing ineptly in training or in preliminary rounds, then turning on his razor-sharp skills. Sharp practice did not extend to his personal dealings, where he was warm and generous. Despite years without money, once he acquired some he forewent expenses to attend charitable events and found ways of making lavish contributions by stealth.[75]

His NSC opponent was no less a veteran. Digger Stanley, originally from Norwich, and boxing out of a caravan in Kingston, Surrey, came from a Romany family. He claimed to have been born on 28 February 1883, although Gilbert Odd thought the year was really 1876. When Stanley died on 7 March 1919, the tiny *Times* report next day indicated he was 42 years of age, so 1877 is another possibility. Had Stanley possessed such a thing as a birth or baptismal certificate, he could not have read it as he was illiterate and innumerate. Neither could he tell the time, although he made great play of opening and consulting the heavy gold watch he kept tucked in the pocket of his flamboyant waistcoat.[76]

Stanley played to the very limit of the rules and to what a referee would allow. Occasionally, he overdid it and got himself disqualified. More often he got away with practices that if done

less nefariously would have had him thrown out.

The Digger was taller than Bowker and, having longer arms, looked to keep him at a distance with left leads. Bowker had other ideas. With clever feints and a speedier delivery, he landed his own left with crisp regularity, drawing blood from Stanley's lip. Never one to stick to an ineffective plan A, the Digger by the second round was on to plan B. This was to slow the sprightly Bowker with close-quarter body blows, in particular with damaging hooks to the kidneys.[77] Punches delivered to the kidney region were, in 1910, legal *providing* they were delivered with the knuckle part of a closed glove – no easy feat as the fist had to come round almost 360 degrees before the knuckles could reach the soft tissue covering the vulnerable organs. Kidney punchers as canny as the Digger could adapt the delivery to a more powerful downward chop with the heel or the side of the glove, akin to a karate chop and just as painful and dangerous. The difference between legal and illegal was extremely difficult for a hard-pressed referee to detect, especially when delivered to the back of an opponent facing him. Ringsiders, better placed to see, were pretty vocal in protesting illegal blows, but what referee of integrity could rule on what he had not seen personally?

Bowker found the blows unpleasant, but he concealed their effects with an elusiveness and speed of punch all his own. Sometimes he rushed the taller man to the ropes and got in a few body punches himself. More often he landed flurries of lefts while avoiding Stanley's. Stanley landed occasional good punches to body or head, interspersed with the wicked kidney tattoo whenever

possible. After seven rounds, there was little between them and the furious initial pace dropped.

No one expected a premature end to this intriguing contest, yet the dramatic eighth produced one. Bowker straightened Stanley out of a crouch with a straight left, feinted to do the same again, and swung a right cross at the Digger's jaw. In doing so, he gave the artful counter-puncher an opening. A short heavy right thudded into Bowker's left temple and he fell, dazed, forward on to his knees. Referee J. H. Douglas was outside the ring and unable to see precisely when the next blow was delivered. A photograph taken at the critical moment and reproduced two weeks later in the 29 October 1910 issue of *Boxing* shows that the real finisher, another of those deadly kidney punches, was a powerful downward right delivered when Bowker was already on his knees with both gloves on the canvas and his back fully exposed.

In the confusion, Bowker's seconds erroneously claimed a low blow. Douglas had Bennison announce that his final decision would be postponed until a doctor had examined Joe's nether regions for evidence. A formal announcement declared the genitalia unharmed and Digger Stanley the victor by an eighth-round knockout, so he was now holder of title and belt. The punch *was* fair so far as the area and the impact of the glove were concerned. But it was *illegal* because delivered when Bowker was on the floor. The Digger should have been disqualified or severely warned and Bowker given an extended period to recover. Not for the first or last time, a dubious Stanley trick won him a major victory.

Neither boxer ventured abroad very often, content to mop up domestic opposition, and to eschew tough contests in the USA or elsewhere. Bowker visited the East Coast in March 1909 only to lose to Tommy O'Toole in Philadelphia in a second-round knockout, and on points to Al Delmont in Boston. Stanley met Frankie Burns in New York in January 1911 in an unimpressive ten-round no-decision bout. But one British boxer who, in a 17-year career, consistently spent more time in the USA than he did in the UK was the argumentative Midlander, whom we last met at the May 1910 inquest into the death of his opponent Tommy McCarthy in San Francisco: the extraordinary Owen Moran.

Moran, still in San Francisco and fighting all-comers, was about to enjoy one of his sweetest victories. On 26 November 1910, he met the durable Dane, Oscar Mattheus Nielsen, better known as Battling Nelson, the man who took such a clobbering from Ad Wolgast back in February, a defeat hard on the heels of his punishing part in the 1906–09 series against Joe Gans. A Nelson in decline, and it was a Nelson in decline, was as full of head-banging ruthlessness and crude action as ever, but his edge had blunted. He advanced as enthusiastically as a souped-up lawnmower, but a machine with only a rudimentary sense of where the lawn was.

Wild rushes would not do against Moran, who was as ruthless and determined as Nelson but much cuter. This left the Battler with only his durability to offer, and he had gone to that store more than once too often.[78] Although 20 rounds were scheduled, only 11 were needed.

For five rounds, Nelson chased Moran, who boxed brilliantly on the retreat, landing lefts and rights on the oncoming target almost at will. Nelson's face soon showed how many times his head had been snapped back by sharp Moran punches. By the sixth and seventh, Moran was sufficiently on top not to need to retreat. When Nelson rushed him, he coolly stepped aside and punished Nelson as he slid past. Even more ominously, he threw his weight on to his front foot, and punched his full weight to stop the baffled Dane in his tracks.

In the tenth, Nelson made one last flurry, a flurry matched in every way by Moran, more and more sure of victory and prepared now for toe-to-toe exchanges. Only part of the 11th was necessary for a finish. Not a knockout specialist – he mustered only a dozen over a long career – Moran did by repetition what others did by clean strike. He felled Nelson with a right to the jaw and repeated the treatment four more times in succession. Usually, the Dane somehow got back up to beat the referee's count. But down five times,

Nelson shows little facial evidence of the damage he suffered regularly.

Bain collection, Prints & Photographs Division, Library of Congress, LC-DIG-ggbain-04071

even Mr Durability could only get up four times. Moran, by knockout: Nelson prostrate on the canvas.

Sadly, after this decisive defeat, Nelson tried to prove his resilience again and again. After the Moran defeat, he boxed another 12 years and another 54 contests. He was said in 1910 to be boxing on, although he had no need of the money, having salted away his major purses. There is a sad inevitability about his fate. He died in poverty in Chicago in his seventies, misguidedly roughing up his helpers from force of habit.

The victory of Moran, who had fought at bantamweight and featherweight, over a lightweight champion in Nelson, brought him much attention in Britain even if it had taken place thousands of miles away. The news of such a British victory abroad came just after a major domestic concern: the deciding of the ownership of the next Lonsdale Belt and the official British middleweight title at the NSC on 14 November 1910. The holder was the Welshman Tom Thomas, conqueror of Charlie Wilson in December 1909 (Chapter 4) and the challenger 24-year-old Englishman, Jim Sullivan of Bermondsey. A middling £700 purse was on offer for the 20 rounds.[79]

Sullivan trained hard with the acquisition of Thomas's belt in mind but was the underdog. Thomas, surprisingly complacent, believed that his superior power would do. Sullivan, more upright in style and more scientific in approach – he was employed at Sherborne School as a boxing coach – was the more popular at the NSC. The fight was close. Sullivan used his excellent left, coupled with consummate balance, to keep Thomas and his stronger punches at a safe distance. Like many Edwardian boxers, he advanced by pushing his left foot forward, but putting his heel down first so that he could recoil into defence instantly rather like a fencer back-pedalling. In the early rounds, he built an early points lead. This eroded as Thomas gradually found his range and landed the heavier punches. By the 15th, the initiative was Thomas's, and Sullivan looked the worse for wear.

Thomas, sitting on his stool in the break, was secretly regretting the training sessions when he had taken pleasant horseback canters over the dunes of the picturesque Welsh coast, in preference to lonely marathon runs over the bleak local mountains. Just when he should have piled on the pressure and closed the show, he looked ponderous and predictable. Sullivan, recovering the quicker, used his left and all the space of the ring adroitly to foil the increasingly desperate Thomas. Thomas, to the considerable displeasure of members, roughed up Sullivan in every clinch and bored forward dangerously with the balding crown of his head. He was close to being disqualified for butting in the 19th. It was in vain. Sullivan had the ultimate compensation for his visible bumps and bruises – the first Lonsdale Belt to change hands, and a standing ovation at the end as his seconds hauled him up on to their shoulders in triumph. (Thomas had pronounced that he would never fight a black opponent. He should have extended the ordinance to white Londoners.)

In Britain, the year 1910 had begun, as we saw, in unseemly political turmoil, unresolved by an inconclusive General Election. Weighty issues and constitutional crises had dogged the whole year, exacerbated in May by the sudden death of the popular sporting King Edward VII. He was succeeded by his son, the 45-year-old King George V. Though the general public never knew it, the new king had all his father's sporting instincts, including an admiration for boxers, but none of his father's intellectual powers. He was singularly ill-equipped to deal successfully with a poisonous and complicated constitutional crisis.[80]

The second General Election of the year in December 1910 was inevitable. The campaign was a slanging match noted more for heat than light, although there was some wit in Lloyd George's comparison of the aristocracy to cheese – 'the older it is, the higher it becomes'. (One wonders how Lord Lonsdale took that.) The election results were even more inconclusive than the previous one: Liberals 272 seats; Conservatives 272 seats, and the Liberals thus only able to stay in office with help from Labour and the Irish Nationalists. There were some formidable statesmen and politicians on both sides – A. J. Balfour, Bonar Law, Lord Lansdowne, Herbert Asquith, Lloyd George, Winston Churchill, Joseph Chamberlain, for example – yet like two talented heavyweights cancelling each other out, the outcome was miserably negative and the event one in which no one enhanced their reputations.

What happened in Cardiff on 20 December 1910 was the pugilistic equivalent of the futile political election. Two of the finest boxers in the world met in the ring, misapplied their skills with venom akin to the worst political rhetoric, needlessly inflamed their many supporters, and left every issue about their relative merits hanging uneasily in the air.

The first was Freddie Welsh, pride of Pontypridd and Philadelphia, the scientific nutritionist, and holder of the lightweight (9st 9lb/135lbs) Lonsdale Belt ever since his 1909 victory over Johnny Summers. The second was Jim Driscoll, 'Peerless Jim', of the educated left hand, darling of the Irish community in Wales and holder of the featherweight Lonsdale Belt (9st/126lbs) since his victory over Spike Robson in April. Neither belt nor official title was at stake, even if the posters optimistically suggested the clash was for the British and European lightweight titles. The NSC monopoly prevailed.

This mattered not to those who packed out the American Roller Rink in Cardiff's Westgate Street on the Tuesday night when the two men met at a compromise of 9st 4lb/130lbs, as for the audience and for the boxers this was an unofficial Welsh championship, every bit as prestigious as a world title.

Both men had fought in the USA; both had met crafty and ruthless opponents such as Abe Attell. They had originally been good friends, but as the rivalry grew between their rival supporters, so did their own. Driscoll had the support of the Irish and Catholic community of Cardiff, and some of the Cardiff Welsh. Welsh, despite his transatlantic ways and affectations, had the overwhelming support of the Nonconformist Welsh valleys, and any Welsh resident hostile either to Irish immigration or to Roman Catholicism (regrettably many). Freddie affected an American demeanour – a cloak and hat more suitable to Broadway than Taff Street, Pontypridd – and swapped Welsh sibilants for American inflections, but the line in his CV reading 'born in Pontypridd' counted for more.

Many Welsh Nonconformists disapproved of boxing in any form and signed petitions to plead for the fight to be called off. Others interpreted the Lord's will as encompassing the physical chastisement of sinners, especially Catholics, and Welsh as just the prophet to carry out the Lord's work. The referee for this potentially explosive clash, and one who misguidedly opted to stay out of the ring and shout instructions against the yells of a fervent and noisy crowd, was Peggy Bettinson.[81]

Considering the consummate ring skills each man was capable of and the contrast of styles between Welsh's crouch and Driscoll's upright stance, the fight should have been an absolute classic. Disappointingly, there were tedious clinches and shapeless mauls as tension got to each man. Paradoxically, there was plenty of action but, especially from Welsh, action of the secretive underhand variety – the demeaning remark in the ear; the rubbing of head and bristly chin against the cheek; the lodging of the left glove under the opponent's right armpit accompanied by theatrical tugging as if it were the opponent doing the holding; the cuffing with the heel and lace of the glove; the almost accidental clip of the chin with an elevated shoulder on the exit from a clinch; the chop at the kidneys with the side of the fist on the blind side of the referee; and all such provocations accompanied by a broad smile or an audible chuckle from Welsh.

The kidney punches drew boos and hisses from spectators on the other side of the ring to Bettinson. When Driscoll slipped momentarily on to one knee in the fourth round, Welsh proffered a gentle gloved hand as if he were helping an old lady across the road. A sporting gesture said his supporters; a demeaning one said Driscoll's.

At intervals, there were crisp, clean punches from both men. Driscoll landed his famous left jab several times in the first but had to take a couple in the eye himself. Welsh landed well to head and body in the third and fourth and pounded Driscoll's kidneys legitimately as well as illegally in the frequent clinches. Driscoll flattened

20 December 1910, the American Skating Rink, Cardiff: the French magazine La Vie Au Plein Air *records the Driscoll–Welsh encounter. 1. Welsh covers his temple from a wild Driscoll swing 2. Welsh offers a helping hand after a Driscoll slip (sporting said some; demeaning said others). 3. Heads rub together. 4. Welsh often roughed up opponents. 5. Welsh crouches: Driscoll sways back. The bout ended in disorder.*

BnF

Welsh's nose in the second and again in both fifth and sixth.

What was really at issue was how long Driscoll could put up with Welsh's calculated provocations, all aimed at getting the peerless one to lose his temper. Driscoll's right eyebrow and forehead were swelling, partly from Welsh's punches and partly from a butt suffered in the second. He looked slightly odd, as he was wearing an unsightly plaster on his left ear where an abscess had recently healed. The plaster received its share of headwork from Welsh in the clinches, as did the other ear, in case Driscoll had been double bluffing and had cleverly decorated the undamaged one. The precaution was wise. Welsh would in the future bite a chunk of the ear off a crooked manager who, unasked, had put Freddie's purse on a losing favourite.

In round four, Driscoll appealed to Bettinson at ringside about Welsh's tactics. The appeal was ignored, as was a similar one in the fifth. To add to Driscoll's woes, he and Welsh were jointly reprimanded by Bettinson for a maul in the seventh. Driscoll, most unprofessionally, turned his head towards Bettinson to argue and received two stiff hooks to the head from Welsh for his lapse. Driscoll, deciding that disorder was better than order, got in a butt of his own in the fourth and delivered some blows to Welsh's kidneys in the sixth and eighth.

Driscoll's courage was not in question and by the end of the ninth he was reasserting his skills at legitimate boxing. Welsh, when he chose so to do, matched him skill for skill most of the time. Welsh led after five, with Driscoll seeming to flag, but from the sixth to the ninth Driscoll revived strongly and claimed the advantage in turn.

One question was whether Driscoll's stamina would last ten rounds and more of wrestling with a stronger man. An even more serious question was whether Driscoll's self-control could survive Welsh's smiles and niggles.

The tenth brought resolution. Driscoll delivered one of his best damaging straight lefts and followed up with a right hook to the head and several stiff body punches. Welsh's ripostes came in the clinches where he hit and held, bored in with the top of his head, pressed down on Driscoll's arms and roughed up his tender ears. These indignities, coupled with Bettinson's seeming indifference, made Driscoll lose control completely. He flew at Welsh, beating his ribs with heavy rights and lefts, and, thrusting his own head under Welsh's chin, butted him back across the ring like a furious Welsh regimental goat in full cry, adding lefts and rights to the jaw as Welsh reached the ropes. Only now did Bettinson decide that action on his part was necessary. Dragging his considerable bulk out of his chair and through the ropes, he pulled the men apart and disqualified Driscoll.

Driscoll, as the red mist in his eyes cleared, burst into tears as he realised he had been the one disqualified, and moved miserably back to his corner as Welsh, sore-jawed but victorious, returned jauntily to his own. They had stopped fighting. Others began.

Carried away by the emotions of the moment and by what he considered a grave injustice, Badger Brown, one of Driscoll's seconds, slung a punch at Boyo Driscoll, one of Welsh's seconds, who had just fought on the undercard and won a ten-round contest against Londoner Jack Daniels. Brown's punch

sparked a brawl in the ring featuring the seconds and groups of supporters from both camps who climbed through the ropes and joined in. Meanwhile, in the body of the hall, a three-sided rumpus began – Driscoll supporters versus Welsh supporters and both versus a large contingent of Cardiff police who laid about the other groups with gusto. While it lasted, the riot looked very threatening. Trevor Wignall, reminiscing 40-odd years later, thought it the maddest mob he had ever seen in boxing.[82] He crouched down near the ring, avoiding the flying fists and chairs. His unlucky colleague Fred Dartnell was flattened by a hurled chair, and when he got up dazed, was punched down again.

There were ugly incidents in the streets of Cardiff later. The disorder was not of the malevolent proportions that had disfigured the streets of American cities post Johnson–Jeffries but no more welcome. It cannot all be down to boxing, however. It cannot be completely coincidental that on the very day the favourite son of Pontypridd was fighting in Cardiff, a Glamorganshire police contingent had been operating up the valley against striking miners and creating much ill-feeling between the community and the authorities.

The man who supplied the spark that led to the conflagration, referee Bettinson, escaped relatively unscathed, although he did lose his new fur-lined overcoat in the ringside melee. His post-fight remark of 'Welsh, I admit, is a most exasperating man to fight, and I fully sympathise with Driscoll in losing his head' would have been little compensation to Driscoll, who had needed such sympathy, and a timely intervention, a few rounds earlier.

Endnotes:

1 See Hargreaves, J., *Sport, Power and Culture: A Social and Historical Analysis of Popular Sports in Britain* (London: Polity Press, 1986) for an extended and more sophisticated discussion of these ideas.

2 Hargreaves, J., *Sport, Power and Culture,* p. 11.

3 *New York Times,* 1 November 1908.

4 Editorial in *Boxing,* 23 October 1909.

5 Fight details in *The Times,* 15 February 1910 and *Boxing,* 19 February 1910.

6 Lewis's career record on the Boxing Records archive, www.boxrec.com

7 Blady, K., *The Jewish Boxers Hall of Fame* (New York: Shapolsky Books, 1988) p. 77.

8 *Boxing,* 26 February 1910.

9 Blady, K., *The Jewish Boxers Hall of Fame,* p. 79.

10 www.boxrec.com/Joe Gans

11 Heller, P., *In This Corner …! Forty World Champions Tell Their Stories* (London: Robson Books, 1985) p. 21.

12 Heller, P., *In This Corner …!,* p. 21.

13 A quotation from W. P. Kinsella's *Shoeless Joe,* the delightful 1982 sporting novel on which the memorable 1989 film *Field of Dreams* was based.

14 The article 'The Gold Rush' by Jersey Jones in *The Ring,* September 1956 gives many details and even reproduces the ungrammatical Articles of Agreement.

15 The normally reliable James Butler in *Kings of the Ring* p. 121 says Nelson 'always fought with scrupulous fairness' but this does not accord with most witness views.

16 *Boxing World and Athletic Chronicle,* 3 March 1910; *New York Times,* 23 February 1910; and 'In the Age of Great Lightweights' by Wilf Diamond in *Boxing News,* 9 January 1959.

17 *New York Times,* 23 February 1910).

18 See James Butler's *Kings of the Ring* chapter 5 for the change in Goldswain's style and an account of the match versus White.

19 'Jack Goldswain' in Maurice Goldsworthy's *Encyclopedia of Boxing,* many editions.

20 *Boxing,* 26 March 1910.

21 Deghy G., *Noble and Manly: The History of the National Sporting Club* (Hutchinson, 1956) pp. 170–171.

22 Harding, J., *Lonsdale's Belt: Boxing's Most Coveted Prize* (Worthing: Pitch Publishing, 2016) p. 23.

23 In the reports of the fight in *The Times,* 7 March 1910, and of the inquest on 9 March and 11 March, details vary.

24 Ashe, Jr, A. R, *A Hard Road to Glory: A History of the Afro-American Athlete 1619–1918* (New York: Amistad Press, 1988) p. 29.

25 See *The Times,* 2 May 1910, 6 May 1910 and 13 May 1910 for the death, inquest and dismissal.

26 *Boxing,* 26 February 1910.

27 Quoted in *Boxing News,* 10 May 1957.

28 *Boxing,* 23 April 1910.

29 Mullan, H., *Heroes and Hard Men: The Story of Britain's World Boxing Champions* (London: Stanley Paul, 1989) p. 64.

30 Details of the fight from *Boxing,* 23 April 1910; *The Times,* 19 and 20 April 1910; Harding, J., *Lonsdale's Belt,* pp. 30–34.

31 'Packey McFarland, master scientist' by George T. Pardy in *The Ring,* December 1936; Butler, J., *Kings of the Ring* (London, n.d. [1936]) Chapter 19.

32 www.boxrec.com/Packey McFarland; *The Boxing Register* 1998 edition, pp. 140–141.

33 *Boxing,* 4 June 1910 and *Boxing World and Athletic Chronicle,* 9 June 1910; Andrew Gallimore in his excellent biography, *Occupation Prizefighter: The Freddie Welsh Story* (Bridgend: Seren Books, 2006) takes a more favourable view of Welsh's performance, using American sources to suggest the British writers were prejudiced against Welsh and his 'American' style.

34 *Boxing World and Athletic Chronicle,* 23 June 1910.

35 *Boxing World and Athletic Chronicle,* 15 September 1910.

36 Bell, L., *Bella of Blackfriars* (London: Odhams Press, 1961).

37 Senior, B., *A Hundred Years of Evangelistic Work at Surrey Chapel* (n.d. but c.1895).

38 *Survey of London*; Vol. 22: Bankside, St Saviour and Christchurch, Southwark, p. 119.

39 Wilson, R. E., *Brown's Estate in Southwark* (n.d. but c.1967).

40 *Boxing,* 2 July 1910; and other details from *Boxing World and Athletic Chronicle,* 30 June 1910.

41 *The Times,* 29 December 1908.

42 *The Times,* 2 March 1909.

43 *The Times,* 30 October 1909.

44 *The Times,* 25 November 1909.

45 *The Times,* 3 December 1909.

46 *The Times,* 4 December 1909.

47 *New York Times,* 22 May 1910.

48 *The Times,* 2 June 1910.

49 *The Times,* 16 and 17 June 1910.

50 *Boxing,* 9 July 1910.

51 *Boxing,* 9 July 1910.

52 *Boxing,* 9 July 1910.

53 Details of the fight and events before and after have been drawn from *The Times,* 5 July 1910; *New York Times,* 5 July 1910; *Boxing,* 9 July 1910; *Boxers* video no. 27 'Jack Johnson'; and several secondary sources.

54 *The Ring,* July 1946.

55 Letter quoted in *Boxing,* 3 September 1910.

56 Roberts, R., *Jack Johnson and the Era of White Hopes* (New York: Simon & Schuster, 1985) p. 95.

57 Johnson, J., *Jack Johnson is a Dandy: An Autobiography* (New York: Chelsea House, 1968) p. 63.

58 Myler, P., *Gentleman Jim Corbett: The Truth Behind a Boxing Legend (London:* Robson Books, 1998) p. 180. [A sympathetic source that also confirms Corbett's dialogues with Johnson.]

59 *The Times,* 12 July 1910.

60 *The Times,* 13 July 1910.

61 *Boxing World and Athletic Chronicle,* 8 September 1910.

62 *The Times,* 17 November 1910.

63 Dobbs, J. E. '*The Response of London Theatre to Various Social and Economic Circumstances (1890–1914)*' p. 135.

64 *The Times,* 23 August 1910.

65 *The Times,* 13 September 1910.

66 *Boxing World and Athletic Chronicle,* 20 January 1910.

67 Frank Morley, 'The Search for a White Champion' in *Boxing,* 13 August 1910.

68 Shipley, S., *Bombardier Billy Wells: The Life and Trials of a Boxing Hero* (Tyne and Wear: Bewick Press, 1993).

69 Corri, E., *Thirty Years a Referee* (1915) p. 48.

70 Reproduced in *Boxing,* 10 September 1910.

71 Details from *Boxing World and Athletic Chronicle,* 22 September 1910.

72 Quoted in *Boxing Monthly,* October 2002, p. 15.

73 1883 according to Gilbert Odd's *Encyclopedia of Boxing,* but some contemporary accounts insist on 1882.

74 Mullan, H., *Heroes and Hard Men,* pp. 14–15.

75 Butler, J., *Kings of the Ring,* p. 67.

76 Deghy G., *Noble and Manly,* p. 183.

77 *Boxing World and Athletic Chronicle,* 20 October 1910; *The Times,* 18 October 1910.

78 *Boxing World and Athletic Chronicle,* 1 December 1910.

79 *The Times,* 15 November 1910. The British Film Institute No. 1530 has film of the edited highlights [44887A] where the credits trim the purse to £600.

80 James, R. R., *The British Revolution: British Politics 1880–1939* (London: Methuen, 1978) pp. 248–249.

81 Reports and subsequent debates about the evening appeared in *Boxing,* 24 and 31 December 1910; *Western Mail,* 20 and 21 December 1910.

82 *Boxing News,* 22 July 1953.

CHAPTER 6
PROMOTERS AND POLITICIANS
1911 (PART ONE)

In Which Promoters Seek a Mythical Beast

NEW PROMOTERS, new venues and significant fights had proliferated throughout 1910. *Boxing*'s first editorial of 1911 pronounced 1910 to have been the most important year in the *entire* history of boxing.[1] The sport grew even more in 1911, and over the next decade would reach heights beyond the imagination of any pugilistic prophet. Yet boxing, its eccentric perversity known well to its keenest followers, was never predictable, ever. Indeed, the most important fight of 1911 did not take place at all. We shall see why.

The 1911 Londoner who wanted to see boxing was spoiled for choice practically every night of the week. The fare varied from bread-and-butter promotions in East and South London, such as the Poplar Hippodrome or The Ring ('Dick Burge's cosy retreat'), to the champagne and caviar atmosphere of the Empress Theatre in the Olympia Annexe on the night of a major promotion. A Ring matinee cost 1s. 6d. top price; Olympia, perhaps ten guineas or more. At Olympia, women, especially glamorous society ones, were greeted and escorted to newly dusted seats by dainty usherettes and white-jacketed gentlemanly stewards. At The Ring, like the NSC, women were

formally discouraged. At Wonderland, they were grudgingly admitted, but restricted to their own small section on the stage.

Some of the new enthusiasm for the sport could be credited to Hugh D. McIntosh, now settled in the metropolis and pursuing his search for a white champion with all the monomania of Captain Ahab hunting Moby Dick. (At least the white whale existed.) Before the end of 1911, McIntosh gave up the lease of the Olympia Annexe, pronouncing it too far from the West End for his fashionable patrons, and extended Earl's Court to house 15,000 people, 12,000 of them in seats and 3,000 standing.

The rougher side of the trade also flourished. At The Ring, Blackfriars on 2 January 1911, Jack Goldswain participated in the latest controversy of many gracing his career. At some weight approaching welter, no weights announced, Goldswain looked a good ten pounds heavier than Joe Fletcher, his opponent. Their ignoring of weight categories was matched by their disregard for any other restrictions set by the Marquess of Queensberry.[2] On this occasion, Goldswain was more sinned against than sinning. He made a slow

start. Fletcher rushed at him, hooking in the clinches and pumping out left jabs from a distance. Goldswain's response was long and wild swinging rights as if he wanted to finish the fight with one blow. Nearly all missed widely. Fletcher asserted his superiority for the first four rounds, piling up points with lefts to the somnolent Goldswain's face, and opening a cut on his right eye. Fletcher went through a gamut of illegalities as well, pulling Goldswain's head down on to punches, and rubbing his nose and damaged eye with the inside laces of his glove.

Goldswain woke up, half-heartedly rubbing his head reproachfully against Fletcher's tender ear. When Fletcher held, Goldswain chopped away at his kidneys. R. B. Watson, the referee, had agreed to officiate at the last minute when the organisers had forgotten to engage anyone. What had he let himself in for? A packed and obstreperous crowd reminded him of his duties, casting severe doubts on the existence of his parents' marriage certificate.

By the fifth, Goldswain's lethargy disappeared and he and Fletcher swapped rounds regularly. Goldswain took the fifth, seventh and ninth, Fletcher the sixth and eighth. By the tenth, Fletcher looked woebegone, clinging to Goldswain like a limpet as Watson prised him off. He shamelessly pulled Goldswain's head down and raised his knee ominously near to Goldswain's softer reproductive organs. Chicanery continued until the 14th with Goldswain taking (mostly legal) retribution, and Fletcher much the worse for wear.

The 14th brought a shoddy denouement. With Fletcher still clinging on and Watson trying vainly to interpose his body between the fighters, Fletcher sank his teeth into Goldswain's left shoulder and hung on like a pit bull with lockjaw. Watson disqualified him instantly, although his words were drowned out by the shouts and screams of a raucous audience.

Legitimate boxing was as much the evening's loser as the dentally forward Fletcher. To the wits, this event in the middle of the pantomime season was a win by disqualification for the Principal Boy over the Cannibal King. *Boxing* also saw the contretemps as comedy. In a cod Personal Column, the following small ad appeared:

LOST – A sound set of teeth, last seen embedded in the juicy shoulder of Jack Goldswain. Finder will be suitably rewarded if returned to JOE FLETCHER.[3]

The Blackfriars rumpus, following the disorder surrounding the Welsh/ Driscoll fight in Cardiff weeks before, was a setback to the efforts of the McIntoshes and the Bettinsons to make the sport glamorous and socially respectable. Worse still, a mere 21 days later, also at The Ring, Aschel 'Young' Joseph lost on 23 January

1911 to Arthur Evernden on *another* disqualification.[4] Young Joseph, it will be remembered, was the Lonsdale Belt holder by virtue of Goldswain being disqualified *against* him in 1910. Joseph had subsequently acquired the European welterweight championship by beating Battling Lacroix of France in Paris on 19 November 1910.

Joseph and Evernden were matched over 20 rounds at 10st 7lb, a weight at which Evernden, a muscular ex-blacksmith, was much stronger than the faster Joseph. An alarming third round threatened a riot. The racing and betting fraternity present were strong supporters of the man they had backed heavily: Joseph, a 4/10 favourite. For two rounds, Joseph demonstrated his master plan: to dance, weave and duck Evernden's heavier punches, and notch up points with his foil-like left. When Evernden got close, Joseph tied him up and smothered any punches he could not dodge.

Twenty rounds is a long time to fend off a stronger man. As the crowd comfortably anticipated a full evening's entertainment, Joseph allowed his concentration to wander twice. At the end of the second, an Evernden right to the body had him wincing and clutching. Worse followed. At the end of the third, Joseph forgot the cardinal rule repeated thousands of times by thousands of referees in thousands of rings: 'Defend yourself at all times!' He turned his back on an Evernden temporarily on the ropes and walked back to the centre of the ring. Evernden instantly swung a heavy right to Joseph's unguarded temple and added two deflating drives just below the heart.

Grasping and gasping, Joseph clung to Evernden, deaf to the orders of

Eugene Corri, the referee, to step back and separate. Exasperated and bristling to the tips of his immaculately waxed moustache, Corri disqualified him. Robbed of a good night's boxing and hard cash, Young Joseph's supporters looked ready to riot. Trashing 'the best ventilated arena in town', and ventilating it further in the process, looked likely, followed by the lynching of a few stewards.

With commendable alacrity, Joseph saw the danger. Gloves held aloft for attention, he stepped to the centre of the ring and pronounced loudly, 'Gentlemen, there is no squarer nor straighter sportsman in the world than Mr Eugene Corri. All over the world he is respected, and though I am sorry that he has given the verdict against me, I know he must be right, and I abide by his decision.' A district commissioner quelling a rebellious colonial village mob could have been no firmer. Yet an ugly riot was only narrowly averted. Passions aroused at fights, like heightened emotions at soccer matches, are always potentially dangerous.

Hugh McIntosh, in partnership with the English Jimmy Britt, wanted no crowd disorder to disrupt his dedicated crusade to make London a boxing Mecca ('McINTOSH BOOMING BOXING IN LONDON' as the *New York Times* headline proclaimed admiringly, if ungrammatically).[5] McIntosh was successfully on course to 'boom' boxing, less so with his subsidiary purpose, to sell Bombardier Billy Wells as the new white hope.

McIntosh advertised a 20-round match between Wells and Gunner Moir for the British heavyweight championship for 11 January 1911 at the Olympia Annexe. Mention on match taking place outside the club, British heavyweights too had moved beyond the NSC reach.

McIntosh kept his prices at a reasonable level – from a £2 2s. ringside to a more distant seat for 10s. 6d., and general admission at 5s. and 2s. 6d. – but many small contributions make a formidable total. He had unerringly tapped the growing appetite for boxing. He could have raised those prices and still sold out. On the night, the doors had to be closed early, with thousands locked out in a freezing January offering many times the price of a ticket to be squeezed in with the warm and lucky ticket holders. The latter were rewarded by high excitement and fervour rather than skilful entertainment. In practice, the event offered comical vulnerability compounded with raw power, impetuous hostility along with dazed immobility, the action lasting a mere two and a half rounds.

On paper, the contrast was diverting. The new white hope, an East Ender and still a novice, matched against an older, more experienced Lambeth heavyweight in Gunner Moir (b. 17 April 1879). Moir had won the British heavyweight championship from Jack Palmer at the NSC back in October 1906. Like Wells, he had served in India, but unlike Wells, he boxed in Australia also.[6] He was dark-haired, large-eared and stocky, packing about 14 stones into an abbreviated frame under 5ft 10in tall. Moir, like Wells, packed a punch that when delivered correctly could render a referee's points score redundant.

In between sparring in the music halls, Moir dabbled with wrestling, taking time off from boxing to tour with the mighty Edwardian mauler,

Gunner (James) Moir (1879–1939), the Lambeth heavyweight who knocked out Bombardier Billy Wells in the third round at the Olympia Annexe on 11 January 1911.
Topical Press Agency/Getty Images

the posters of the NSC imprimatur on official British championships was there none.

Realistically, the NSC, restricted to a small membership-dominated theatre in Covent Garden, could not offer a purse of a magnitude to attract boxers whom thousands wanted to see in the muscled flesh. To the chagrin of the club and Lord Lonsdale its president, a new breed of commercial promoters waved larger chequebooks than theirs and attracted international boxers to new venues. With the Wells/Moir

George Hackenschmidt. From that master, he had picked up some bad habits. Confronted with an aggressive puncher, he coiled a prehensile left arm around the opponent's neck and pulled the head down on to his strong right. In Moir's 2 December 1907 bout at the NSC against the then world heavyweight champion Tommy Burns, Burns tolerated the treatment to prolong the contest for the film footage and exacted revenge with a tenth-round knockout.[7]

On 29 October 1906, also at the NSC, the then reigning British heavyweight champion, Jack Palmer, had countered Moir's Hackenschmidt-like tactics by placing two mighty uppercuts into Moir's testicles. As this was in full view of the referee, the act resulted in a disqualification, and the awarding of the title to Moir. The title, painfully won, was painfully relinquished at the NSC on 19 April 1909, when Moir misguidedly threw his chin on to Iron Hague's knuckles and was counted out in 2mins 47secs of the first round.

A new dawn in 1911 was implicit; newcomer Wells proves his potential by knocking out the still dangerous ex-champion Moir. It very nearly happened.[8] Throughout the first round, the Bombardier landed his elegant and forceful left hand – a punch at its best almost in the Driscoll class – and the head of the lumbering and slightly podgy Moir rocked back alarmingly. Moir's natural stance was an old-fashioned lean back on his right foot, and he leaned back further under attack. When Wells's left homed in so painfully there was no avoiding it. A swift conclusion seemed so imminent that hundreds of spectators abandoned

their seats and went looking for their carriages in the first interval to beat the homeward rush. Unlucky them.

Wells, eager to finish what he had skilfully and successfully begun, was the first to leave his stool for the second. After delivering a few more stinging lefts, he closed with Moir, ready to trade some blows on the inside. This was not a good idea. Moir landed a hefty right to the solar plexus and drew a startled moan from Wells. Seconds later, a short left followed to the same target, and Wells was down for a count of six.

Getting unsteadily to his feet, Wells was half-wrestled down for another count of six. He retreated hastily, trying to keep Moir away with his left. More damage resulted. As Moir clutched Wells with his left to pull him down on to his own right, he lost his balance, and the two men went down in a clumsy heap. Wells was at the bottom of the heap and took the collapsing Moir's knees in the middle of his chest, expelling even more precious air from his lungs. He had about eight seconds' respite as referee Corri pushed the recumbent Moir away.

Wells had trained assiduously and called on his accumulated reserves to go back on to the offensive, landing straight lefts and three chopping rights to the surprised Moir's chin. But Moir had powers of recovery too, and as Wells looked optimistically for a last knockout blow before the bell, Moir landed some more hefty body blows. In a desperate clinch he half-punched, half-wrestled Wells back to the canvas. It was touch and go whether Wells would beat the new count, but the bell sounded and saved him. Those of a nervous disposition in an audience seething with excitement felt similarly

at the end of their tether after one of the most eventful rounds in British boxing history.

The third round was no less fraught if abbreviated. Wells, still rocky, kept his left in Moir's face. Moir, none too steady himself, tried to push through the left and land more punches into Wells's vulnerable midriff. One good punch from either man would be the last needed. Moir landed it. A left hook to Wells's solar plexus sent the blond Bombardier back down. At nine, a distraught Wells was up and, on autopilot, still punching. In the next clinch, a glancing blow on the chin from the fast-fading Moir sent Wells back down. Wells rose again but only after the referee had pronounced the terminal ten. As Moir's seconds half-escorted, half-carried Moir back to his corner, Wells's overtaxed brain grasped the fact that he had actually lost. He promptly fell on his face, temporarily dead to the world as if Corri, not Moir, had delivered the final knockout.

This Olympia tumble-fest ended Wells's perfect professional record of five wins, five knockouts. There were still plusses, especially the sense that Moir had been so nearly knocked out by Wells. McIntosh's campaign to build Wells into the saviour of his skin types, and into a match with Jack Johnson, had been deflected, but not ultimately derailed. If other weaker opponents could be found and beaten, Wells would be back in line for a match against Johnson in front of a well-heeled London audience; a bout that would sell itself.

Meanwhile, many clashes at lighter weights had boxing followers licking their lips and dipping into their wallets. Within two weeks of Wells/Moir, there were two heady clashes between brilliant boxers who would have graced any age: one at the Olympia annexe for all-comers able to pay; and one at an NSC eager to demonstrate they could still persuade non-heavyweights to strut their stuff before members and guests.

On 25 January 1911, the Olympia Annexe was packed wall to wall for a fight billed as being for the world welterweight championship but made at 10st 4lb. Harry Lewis (USA), whom we last saw in East London against Young Joseph, met Johnny Summers (GB), whom we last saw at the NSC against Freddie Welsh. Modern research has revealed why the match, supposedly a world championship, was not at the standard 10st 7lb. Lewis had been struggling to stay a welterweight. (He would shortly move up to middleweight.) He stepped reluctantly on to the scales at 10st 8¾lb/148¾lbs. This gave him an overwhelming advantage over Summers, who was well below the unorthodox limit at 10st 0¾lb/140¾lbs.[9]

Few doubted the match would be a scientific one with skills in evasion and defence to the fore. Instead it was a spirited toe-to-toe struggle between two fired-up brave men happy to take punches provided they could give plenty back. It was just as the heavier, stronger Lewis might have planned, and as Summers might have planned to avoid. Yet it was Summers, more than punching his weight, who started as if he could overwhelm Lewis with out-and-out attack. For three rounds, it looked as if he could.

Lewis was shocked by half a dozen solid leads from Summers. ('Every time that left of his butted into my face I knew it.') He also got a tattoo of body punches in the clinches and a stinging Summers right hook that took him down for an early count. The storm continued in the second as Lewis fought, mostly legitimately, to keep Summers at a distance. Even a few unconstitutional head butts failed to stop Summers's onslaught. Again, Summers punched him to the floor, falling over him in the process. Lewis got up and, being Lewis, fought back vigorously. The fierce and unrelenting rallies had the ecstatic London crowd on their feet. Summers continued to come off the better. The third continued at the same hectic pace, both men exchanging punches without a break.

After nine minutes of tumultuous action, Lewis's heavier responses began to hurt Summers as much as Summers had hurt the iron-chinned Lewis. Middleweights who had previously declined to share a ring with Lewis knew something.

The fourth was decisive. Both men stood very close, punching away furiously as they moved collectively back and forth across the ring. Summers retained a slight edge and continued his rushes, sportingly restrained by Lewis when his momentum almost took him through the ropes. In another flurry, Lewis caught Summers with a clean right to the chin, and in the next maul put him on the floor for the first time with a heavy combination. Undaunted, Summers was up again, too fast, and throwing punches. The punches carried less weight than they had in the first three rounds and Lewis took them unblinkingly. Lewis sent Summers back down with a left hook, this time for a full count. Summers had never been knocked out before. He concluded correctly that he had lost to Lewis's extra poundage: 'He was just a shade too big for as good a boxer as he is.' Summers, the loser in this most gruelling fight, came out of it with credit.

On 30 January 1911, the NSC put up a £1,000 purse for the elegant Jim Driscoll and the resilient Spike Robson to recapitulate their stirring encounter of February 1910, when Robson had unsuccessfully fought Driscoll and Driscoll's stool. Would a return be any different?[10]

In practice, it was different, but not in Robson's favour. Painfully aware of the rock-like qualities of Robson's jaw, and the hurtful punches he had endured in the 1910 fight, Driscoll followed a master plan. He kept Robson at a discreet distance and piled up every point he could with speed and accuracy. Once he had landed, he was away again before Robson could respond. The plan proved itself in execution.

For six rounds, Robson tried pluckily to do the Welshman some damage the way he had previously. Driscoll remembered the Robson punches that had left him peering out of one open left eye and taking blows from angles he could not see from the closed right eye. The Cardiff brawl with Welsh had been only weeks before, so he had a double reason to keep his distance. (There were no extended 'rests' after major fights for Edwardian boxers; a luxury reserved for later, more affluent champions.)

Coolly swaying and leaning so that Robson missed by an inch rather than a foot, Driscoll landed two and three hurtful counters, then melted away. More and more, the crop-haired Spike was forced into the role of the bleeding victim, futilely charging the space the punisher had occupied moments before and being caught while doing so. Robson had lost some of his speed and power, but none of his bravado. With an insouciance he can hardly have felt, he dropped his guard and invited Driscoll to pepper his features some more.

Neither Driscoll, nor the audience, nor the all-important third man outside the ring, referee J. H. Douglas, was fooled. They knew Robson was constitutionally incapable of surrender. 'I may have looked all in,' he said later, 'but I did not feel it. It is my peculiarity to always look in a far worse state than I really am.' Robson was the man who says on his deathbed, 'Don't worry, I'll get up in a moment.' He was downed twice in the sixth as Douglas moved towards the ropes as if to halt proceedings. In the seventh, he staggered on until Douglas did actually call, 'That will do; stop it!'[11] By then, Robson had no defence against Driscoll or against his own bloody-mindedness. Every age has its humanitarians. The 1911 stoppage was wise.

On the NSC bill that night, in strong contrast to the skills shown by Driscoll and Robson, was a contest between two British heavyweights – one the up-and-coming Bill Chase, a Forest Gate butcher who had emerged from an NSC novices' competition. Chase had a long reach and a powerful punch. He was now up against the pride of Yorkshire, the more experienced but adipose William 'Iron' Hague.[12]

Between them, they proved two boxing truisms: that big men and sporting science are a rare combination; and that big men with big punches can please an unenlightened spectator no end. The first four or five rounds of funereal inaction could have been accompanied by the Elephant Section of Saint-Saens's *La Carnaval des Animaux*, played *lento ponderosa*. Then, as the members who had indulged themselves in the dining room before taking their seats began to slumber, the sixth brought action. A long, wild right from the tiring Chase caught the rather more skilful Hague on the chin and took him down for seven seconds. Woken rather than dazed by the blow and the indignity, Hague got up and took advantage of Chase's defensive inadequacies by knocking him out for real. Had a laughing Jack Johnson been present, he would have offered to fight both men simultaneously – at an inflated price.

The cumbersome pawings and wild swings of the Chases and Hagues of the world were proof that the genetic inheritance that had granted them the first of McIntosh's *desiderata*, a snow-like white skin, did not necessarily come along with the others – skill, strength and stamina. Those not blinded by spurious notions of biological determinism knew that Jack Johnson was the current heavyweight champion because he was the best heavyweight around, and that the Chases and Hagues were inferior also-rans. British boxing fans were better able to accept this fact of life than were their transatlantic cousins.

Nevertheless, as McIntosh pursued his White Hope London campaign, he sold tickets to the masses and the classes alike for his 21 February 1911 promotion at the Olympia Annexe by featuring the black v white theme strongly on his posters and press advertisements. He offered a handsome purse of £3,500 ('the largest ever offered in England') and priced seats from half a guinea up to ten guineas. The match was genuinely international with no British boxer involved. It pitted Bill Lang, heavyweight champion of Australia and conveniently white, against the great Sam Langford, long-time rival of Jack Johnson, a Canadian and for McIntosh's purposes now featured as 'The American Black Marvel'.[13] Both had been beaten previously by Johnson – Lang in Australia in 1908; Langford in the USA in 1906.

The event was a very hot ticket indeed and a fashionable one. Not since Regency times, or possibly since the Heenan v Sayers bare-fist classic of 50 years before, had so many Members of Parliament, professional men, dandies and peers of the realm been gathered at a ringside. One noble aged lord, Lord Grenfell, had actually *been* at the Heenan v Sayers clash, and looked frail but just as excited to be at this.

Langford had all the advantages skill could provide. He stood more upright than most North American fighters, he punched straighter and he could do serious damage with long rights and lefts, as he could with a short right uppercut. He lacked both inches (he barely topped 5ft 6in) and pounds (he was a lean 11st 12lb/166lbs – comfortably within even the modern super-middleweight limit of 12st/168lbs). He could still handle heavyweights, as Iron Hague had found out in May 1909 at the NSC (Chapter 4), and as did the up-to-135 men Langford knocked out in his too-long career from 1902–26. To Lang, the pride of Australia and the current holder of the Australian heavyweight title vacated by Tommy Burns, Langford was conceding the best part of 40 pounds in weight and nearly seven inches in height.

and swings, but no real jab. That is, no jab clean enough to hold off the pocket Hercules advancing purposefully towards him. Lang stopped more blows with his face than his gloves or his arms.

On his stool at the end of the first, in the 'lucky' corner, the corner from which Gunner Moir had beaten Wells, and Harry Lewis had beaten Summers, there was a panicky conference between Lang and his principal trainer Harry Nathan. Opposite, Langford merely sat and smiled. With the bell, the chase continued, until a wicked Langford right and Lang's prominent chin painfully collided, and Lang dropped to the floor. It took him a count of nine to recognise his whereabouts and to get unsteadily up again. He had to take more Langford punches before the bell rescued him. The third round was remarkably similar. A left jab and a right hook delivered by Langford in smooth combination dropped Lang again, for a count of seven, and by the end of the round, a cut Lang had suffered in training reopened over his left eye.

Lang landed a few more punches of his own in the fourth, to notch a few points. He did so because little Sam decided they could do him no real harm, and he could afford to take one or two as he looked for a knockout. Lang's flurries became ever more desperate. The audience gave Lang a loud and generous ovation at the end of the fifth, not because he had eased his way back into the fight, but because he had survived three long counts, two for nine. They were interspersed with desperate staggers and scrambles to keep away from the mini-assassin hunting him down.

Sam Langford was always challenging heavier men.
Bain collection, Prints & Photographs Division, Library of Congress, LC-DIG-ggbain-12254

In action, Langford was a blown-up version of the popular boxer of the 1990s, bantamweight Francis Ampofo, always in forward gear and always punching. Typically, Langford commanded the centre of the ring and drove Lang to the ropes, bewildering the Australian as punches flew at him from angles he did not expect. Lang had a left of sorts, some effective hooks

Langford beat Bill Lang (1883–1957) of Australia on a disqualification in the sixth round on 21 February 1911 at the Olympia Annexe. Similar black and white international contests became highly problematical.

Haeckel collection/ullstein bild via Getty Images

No one, including Lang himself, thought he could win. He made another determined flurry for the sixth, including a few swings below Langford's waistline. Wildness rather than malice was the culprit, as it was for the unexpected finish. As Langford slipped in avoiding another wild swing, Lang clipped him with a right hook, and Langford temporarily went down on one knee.

Lang, still out of full control, hit him with a swinging left to the head. Referee Corri instantly disqualified him for hitting a man who was down. Langford was the winner by disqualification, yet everyone present knew he had mastered his challenger in every meaningful department. Racists everywhere realised that another white hope had been eliminated. As a contemporary poem by Tom Akers put it:

> Whisper the news so sad
> Tell it with tears and sobs;
> Everything's to the bad:
> Men are a bunch of slobs.
> Gloomy and dark the day,
> Everyone's full of dope;
> Ne'er can our hearts be gay –
> There is no 'White Man's Hope'.

Only much later did it emerge that Lang's surprising survival of many of Langford's best punches owed less to his own durability than to the direct interference of the unscrupulous McIntosh. McIntosh made Langford wear a special pair of white gloves, supposedly to enhance the quality of the fight film.

The flashy gloves had been padded out with fur to reduce the impact of Langford's punches. As usual, a black fighter had to overcome unscrupulous handicaps.[14]

For all the glamour of McIntosh's Olympia promotions, the small theatre at the NSC could be the best place in the world for a boxing connoisseur. In front of the privileged few, on 27 February 1911, Freddie Welsh, first winner of the Lonsdale Belt and holder of the official

British lightweight championship after his win over Johnny Summers at the NSC back in November 1909, and impenitent about the shabby recent win over the Peerless One in Cardiff, defended his belt, his title and, perhaps, his reputation. The man who planned to take them away was the Londoner, Matt Wells.

Wells had been professional a mere two years, after a successful amateur career representing the Lynn Athletic Club and monopolising the Amateur Boxing Association's lightweight title from 1904 to 1907 before turning professional in 1909. Pressure to turn professional came as much from frustrated amateur lightweights as from greedy promoters. Once professional, Wells built his career in the paid ranks as thoroughly as he had his amateur one. From May to September 1910, he was in New York State, taking no-decision bouts against men like Eddie McMahon, Jimmy Howard (win for Wells on disqualification) and Paddy Sullivan (who would have outpointed him under British arrangements).

Born in Walworth on 14 December 1886, Wells had recently celebrated his 24th birthday. Physically he was at a peak. Throughout his amateur and professional careers, he consistently analysed himself and his varied opponents to build an impressive armoury of attacking and defensive skills. Self-study went along with the dissection of future opponents – every blow landed by Jim Driscoll in Cardiff on Freddie Welsh, before the descent into a brawl, had been quietly registered by Matt Wells taking notes at ringside.[15]

The photographic portrait most often reproduced of Matt Wells, clad in a sweaty black vest, thin-lipped and square-jawed, short thinning hair brushed forward and clinging to a taut forehead, makes him look like the grizzled veteran he became more than a decade after the first meeting with Welsh. (The British heavyweight champion of the 1960s, Henry Cooper, and his twin brother went as schoolboys to be trained by Wells. Cooper defined Wells's professional trademarks: 'He had two of the best cauliflower ears you've ever seen. Two lumps of gristle and little pinholes.') The young man who met Welsh at lightweight was much slimmer, sleeker and more handsome than the careworn welterweight of later years, dark slicked-back hair matched by a luxuriant growth of dark curls on his muscular chest. His bright responsive eyes hinted at the intelligence and natural wit lying behind the serene expression he assumed for the ring and for his dry remarks outside it.

Although Wells was a South Londoner, he was a favourite with all London Jewish communities; his fights covered extensively in the East End newspapers and the *Jewish Chronicle*. Sometimes known as The Wizard, his particular magic was not familiar to the NSC cognoscenti, who spurned the attractive odds of 3/1 and even 7/2 offered against him. The punters backed instead the Celtic Merlin, at a risk of £35 to win £10. The losses were a worthy price for the aesthetic privilege of seeing two such gifted boxers over 20 dexterous rounds.

The match had been made provisionally during Wells's American sojourn. A promoter's telegram urging him to come home and face Welsh had arrived at his New York address only after Wells had departed to New Orleans to act as a second for his friend Owen Moran. The first Wells knew of the title challenge was when the New Orleans master of ceremonies introduced him as the new British title contender. On his return to New York, he saw the confirmatory telegram, and caught the next available boat home. Over-eager for the opportunity, he signed an unequal contract that gave Welsh 75 per cent of the £750 purse. He even borrowed £100 to put down the side stake.

Welsh was assumed the speedier and more skilled of the two, qualities thought sufficient even if Wells was the stronger at the 9st 9lb/135lbs limit. This Wells made at an afternoon weigh-in, with Welsh a pound lighter. Welsh would surely use his speed and skill to keep Wells at a distance, but could get inside too, lay his head on Wells's doormat chest as if WELCOME were painted there, and, as he had Driscoll, uppercut and hook profitably between painful punches to the kidneys.

Astonishing to the audience on the night was that none of these tactics was possible. Wells beat Welsh to them on all counts.[16] Remembering Driscoll's best Cardiff moments had come with the jab, Wells out-jabbed him with a provoking left that sent Welsh's head halfway back to Pontypridd and wiped the trademark smile off his face every time it formed.

When Welsh retaliated and tried to get his head under Wells's chin, he found Wells had out-ducked him. He was forced to look vainly down on the top of Wells's head, his own uppercuts smothered in favour of his opponent's, and his round-arm swings at Wells's kidneys judiciously intercepted by cleverly placed elbows.

After 12 rounds, Welsh had shared only the 7th and 12th. Wells had won

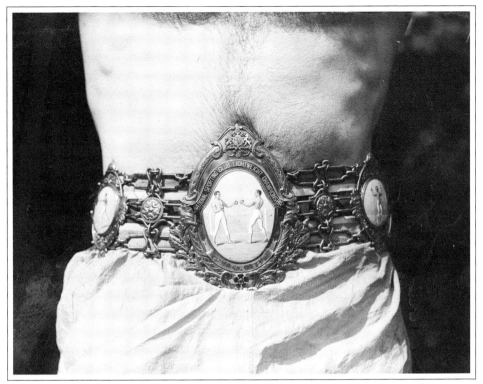

Wells was proud to show off the lightweight Lonsdale Belt he took away from Freddie Welsh at the NSC on 11 February 1911.

Bain Collection, Prints & Photographs Division, Library of Congress, LC-DIG-ggbain-09591

every other but 12 rounds of supremacy did not then win championships; in 1911, another eight rounds had to be endured. Like a five-day Test match in cricket, superiority in every individual session is rare. Welsh climbed back into the fight. With club members scrutinising his moves from every angle because of his reputation, and referee Douglas watching closely along with them, the tactics that had so frustrated Driscoll were no longer possible.

Knowing he was well behind, Welsh cut loose in the 13th, taking the jabs with which Wells strove to keep him away. Wells knew he had only to keep out of serious trouble to clinch the win. For the first time in the fight Welsh was landing more blows and won the round. In the next, his punches strayed below Wells's belt. As Wells continued to crouch and duck, and sometimes parry

blows downwards, Welsh got the benefit of the doubt, despite boos from sharp-eyed members. Welsh won that round too. In the 15th, Wells came back into it, using nifty footwork to have Welsh's wilder swings miss by some margin, and thrusting his own neat lefts into the torso of the off-balance Welsh.

Having completed, very competitively, the modern championship 12 rounds, and the previous limit of 15 rounds, these supreme athletes came dancing out of their corners and made the 16th the highlight of the entire contest for excitement if not for science. Welsh threw punches from all directions; Wells fended off and countered. As Welsh rushed headfirst into a fierce clinch, his head (accidentally?) caught Wells on the left eyebrow and gashed it deeply. Wells looked meaningfully at the referee. His looks, and his vocal protest, 'He's

butting, sir!', were ignored, as had been the low blows of the 14th. He would have to survive strictly on his own efforts. Meanwhile, Welsh ruthlessly secured the round with a flurry of rights on and around the wound.

Three rounds to go, with a desperate and fired-up Welsh looking for a knockout to win, against a crafty and part-dazed opponent needing to defend his cut eye and his chin for another nine minutes! In the 18th the pattern continued – Welsh striving to damage Wells, and Wells closing and clinching and fiddling as every second passing on the timekeeper's clock brought him closer to survival and victory. Again he lost the round, but he had kept Welsh from more serious inroads.

With increasing confidence, Wells edged the 19th, regaining some of the speed and crispness of punch he had commanded before that damaging clash of heads in the 16th. Barring accidents, or a real lapse of concentration, he was home and out-smiling Welsh. During the last, he fended off a desperate Welsh, hooked and jabbed himself, and clinched when he absolutely needed to. It was Welsh's round, but by too little and too late as the referee confirmed. Wells was the new lightweight champion, Lonsdale Belt holder and enjoying the standing ovation the members gave him. He had more than earned the £45-a-round he received for facing down one of the cleverest boxers of all time.

Two boxing phenomena might put a sparkle in a promoter's eye, and a few noughts on his bank balance: the emergence of a wholehearted new fighter like Matt Wells, and the refurbishment after a setback of a box-office favourite like his namesake

Bombardier Billy Wells. The time would come when promoters might go to the Wells too often, but that time was not yet. In the spring of 1911, Matt Wells went off to the USA to put some dollars into his meagre reserves. The other Wells underwent boxing's traditional resuscitation – bouts against lukewarm bodies he could actually beat.

McIntosh's first choice was blatantly inferior. Barely one-third of those who had shared the Bombardier's ups and downs against Gunner Moir at the Olympia Annexe showed up for his redeeming appearance against Dan 'Porky' Flynn (b. Daniel Francis Flynn 5 April 1888), the Irish-American from Boston via Killarney, on 8 March 1911.[17] They got unusually full value as the fight went its full distance. (Wells had 39 fights from 1911 to 1922 but, win or lose, only two of them went to the final bell.)

Porky was the perfect choice. He had skill without being anywhere near as good a boxer as Wells; he was game and could take punishment without looking for a convenient exit or getting knocked out. (Against that merciless middleweight Stanley Ketchel, Flynn suffered the double humiliation of being laid out cold in the third and revived by Ketchel dousing him with a bucket of cold water.) He was a light enough puncher so that a stray punch to Wells's vulnerable midriff would not necessarily fold Wells miserably in half. That midriff received great attention, not just from satirical journalists, but from a physical culture specialist, Thomas Inch, who pushed Wells through a remedial programme of weight-lifting and abdominal crunches supposedly to strengthen it.[18]

Matt Wells (1886–1953) of Lambeth was one of the cleverest boxers Britain ever produced.
Bain collection, Prints & Photographs Division, Library of Congress, LC-DIG-ggbain-11542

Wells's Inch-fortified six-pack went untested. He kept Flynn at a comfortable distance with rapid and hurtful jabs to Flynn's head. Wells's psychological uncertainties never surfaced, but then Flynn never seriously pressed him. Flynn, though, was staggering as early as the third; down twice for a count of nine in the sixth; down again for nine in the eighth; cautioned for hanging on; groggy in the 11th; staggering in the 14th; hanging over the ropes during yet another count of nine in the 19th; yet still trying to mix it bloodily in the last. Reporters wrote later of the Bombardier's improved skills and stamina, along with Porky's game survival. What they should have asked was how Wells was ever going to be an international heavyweight if an outclassed opponent could survive 20 rounds of target practice.

Promoters' hyperbole still worked its magic. The supposedly new and improved Wells was able in April 1911 to leapfrog two of his less glamorous rivals (Petty Officer Curran, who had already beaten both Iron Hague and Lang the Australian champion, and Gunner Moir, who had, after all, just beaten Wells). He, not they, challenged Ian 'Iron' Hague on 24 April 1911 at the NSC for the official British heavyweight championship and the Lonsdale Belt. The £700 purse, a mere 20 per cent of the Olympian pot of gold contested by Lang and Langford, was acceptable because the holding of the belt enhanced future earning power *outside* the club.

Iron, who wielded cutlery with more enthusiasm than dumbbells, and lifted pint glasses more readily than weights, was reported to be 'training hard' at Mexborough, his Yorkshire home. Perhaps he had cut his consumption of Woodbines by not smoking in the gym, for, as *The Times* drily reported on the night, 'It was evident … that Hague's friends had not persuaded him to make a drastic preparation.' More ambiguously, *Boxing World and Athletic Chronicle* suggested, 'Hague was far fitter than he had been for several years.' Wells at his Leigh-on-Sea headquarters trained assiduously and looked the very model of a well-prepared athlete.

Wells peppered his opponent with left jabs just as he had Flynn. The tactic was as effective in Covent Garden.[19] Every time Iron firmly planted his large feet to launch a heavy right to Wells's ribcage, or a big swing to his head, Wells pre-empted him with a crisp left. Once over his big occasion nerves, Wells took a few rights to the body without flinching. He was cool, disciplined and dangerous.

After a controlled second he looked even cooler and by the third had a flustered Hague bleeding slightly at the mouth. But would Wells do as he had against Moir, get caught and throw away a brilliant lead? That thought was uppermost in the mind of Jim Maloney, Wells's trainer. His voice cut through excited murmurs in the theatre when Wells rushed in during the third. 'Don't take any chances now. Box him!' His protégé obeyed and clipped Hague with more long lefts to leave the Yorkshireman unsteady at the bell.

The fourth was even more decisive: Wells prospered with controlled footwork and well-directed punches to have Hague down twice, for counts of eight and six, relieved to have survived at all. Hague had some skill, and more natural stamina than his skimpy preparations deserved. He took heavy punches from Wells in the fifth but landed one crisp right that took Wells temporarily aback. In the sixth, Wells reasserted his clear superiority and displayed the discerning ruthlessness he so often failed to show.

One combination dropped Hague for six. When he got up, another barrage of punches put him down for seven, including a whipped left catching Iron mid-fall. Somehow, he got up, but probably regretted it as Wells, looking every inch a genuine champion, finished him with a clubbing right that sent Hague down again and rolling over for a full count after an abortive and feeble attempt to rise at five. Wells was now the British heavyweight champion and the holder of the first heavyweight Lonsdale Belt. His chances of challenging Jack Johnson in a world title fight had been significantly enhanced.

The hype began immediately after the fight with the announcement from the ring by Bettinson that Wells would now meet, at the NSC, Fred Storbeck of South Africa. Storbeck was familiar to Londoners having won the ABA heavyweight championship in 1910. He was in the NSC audience and had just watched the Hague–Wells bout. Bettinson's announcement was clumsily premature, as terms had not been agreed with Wells and Jim Maloney, as Maloney was very quick to point out.[20] Storbeck would eventually get his chance, but for the moment it was the lighter divisions that were producing the most desirable match-ups and the most impressive results.

In the spring, a young English pugilist's thoughts turned to the USA, less to green shoots than to greenbacks. Owen Moran showed the way by fighting in the USA from 1908 to 1911. Always up for a challenge, he had faced a mighty one the previous month when he met Chicago's Packey McFarland at the Fairmont Club in the Bronx on 14 March 1911.[21] Skill for skill, resilience for resilience, aggression for aggression, this was a reasonable match. Pound for pound, a mismatch was more like it. The stocky Moran at 5ft 3in was a natural bantam; Packey a formidable lightweight. The match was made at 9st 9lb/135lbs, a limit Moran made with five pounds to spare, pugnacity not counting on the scales. He conceded about five inches in height and reach as well; all this to one of the most powerful boxers in the world at any weight. Win or lose, Moran stood to make $7,000 and get a severe trouncing for his money. Thus it proved.

The animated Moran went bravely at McFarland from the off, calculating that he might just sap his opponent's strength by mixing it in close and pounding away at his body. This was fully in accord with his promise to McFarland at the weigh-in: 'I'll buy you a drink, Packey, after I beat you.' McFarland's reply was measured: 'I'll go a long while thirsty if I wait for it!'

Coolness was the essence of McFarland. He met every Moran rush with precisely targeted lefts to put Moran off balance, then followed with neat stinging rights. What made an unequal contest exciting was that Moran never knew when he was beaten. He continued to throw fierce, dangerous swings. Even when an imperturbable McFarland combination put him through the ropes in the fourth, Moran stayed on the offensive, and he was still swinging furiously in the ninth and tenth despite the retribution McFarland was inflicting. The packed audience, who had paid more than $20,000 to be there, would have cheerfully parted with extra to see a rerun of that sporting rarity, an unequal contest of perpetual excitement. (McFarland by clear newspaper decision.)

On 12 April 1911, Freddie Welsh, anxious to rehabilitate his career on both sides of the Atlantic, sailed on the *Lusitania* to New York's National Sporting Club ready to face the 19-year-old Philadelphian prospect, Pal Moore, in a match at 9st 7lb/133lbs. (McFarland was at ringside.) Moore was a devout Quaker but little known for peace and love with his gloves on. Restricted legally to a no-decision ten-rounder, the bout resembled tactically the Moran/McFarland match of a few weeks before, with the Welshman the cool distance merchant and the American the rushing mixer. It too

was an uneven contest. Moore was unofficially outpointed in almost every round, sharing the first by virtue of a series of short uppercuts, and beating down Welsh's jabs in the eighth to land a solid right to the side of Welsh's head and a driving left to the midriff.

The tenth confirmed the expectations set through the fight. For all Moore's attempts at a big finish, Welsh struck often with jolting lefts that drew blood from Moore's nose and mouth from the second onwards. Moore's determined counters were avoided by Welsh's sways from the waist, or by Welsh ducking under the blows and landing short smacking hooks to Moore's ribs. Welsh, perhaps by eight rounds to one, had the referee been allowed to score.

At the Fairmont Club a week later, 18 April 1911, New Yorkers got another demonstration of Packey McFarland's skill and strength.[22] So did his fellow professionals, Welsh, Abe Attell, Ad Wolgast and the quaintly dubbed One Round Hogan, all at ringside while McFarland out-generalled, outfought and, had it been legally possible, outpointed the gallant and clever Harlem boxer Tommy Murphy. McFarland had weighed in at 3pm at 9st 8lb/134lbs, a comfortable pound under the 135lb limit. Because even at the best-appointed New York clubs arrangements were less than meticulous, Murphy was allowed to weigh in two hours later. Packey was as swift with his quips as with his gloves: 'I don't care if he weighs a ton, it's all the same to me … I can beat him anyway!' At 134lbs McFarland was one of the quickest men in the boxing world and he punched with every last ounce. Like Moran before him, Murphy found courage and

iron determination to take him to the final bell. Cuts and bruises were all he had left to show for it.

Despite to-ing and fro-ing to featherweight and up again, McFarland and his contemporaries formed a lightweight division that guaranteed glamour, heroism and drama. Any British promoter of our day would have relished matches with figures such as Freddie Welsh, Matt Wells and Owen Moran, not to mention a host of skilful Americans like Packey McFarland and Ad Wolgast. Truthfully, the lightweight division, from Australia's Young Griffo of the 1880s and 1890s to Panama's Roberto Duran of a century later, threw up continually outstanding fights and fighters, many of whom will feature in later chapters of this history. When Tex Rickard transformed Goldfield, Nevada, with the Gans/ Nelson promotion, he was exploiting a tradition already as valuable as a Nevada gold nugget.

Some of the boxers shaking hands in the ring during the introductions and preliminaries to the McFarland/ Murphy bout, were soon touching gloves in earnest. Ad Wolgast had lost none of his feline resemblance to the American lynx implied by his nickname, the Michigan Wildcat. He sighted his prey, the Californian One Round Hogan, across the ring of the Madison Athletic Club in Harlem on 26 April 1911.[23] All he had to do, he thought, was pounce. Hogan, as his ring name suggests, was not inclined to hold back his executionary powers until late in a contest.

The upshot was 4mins 40secs of boxing with more action than the average eight- or ten-rounder. There were fierce toe-to-toe exchanges with

Hogan landing blows to the head and Wolgast pounding away at ribs and stomach. Then a straight right to the chin from Hogan sent Wolgast tottering and clinching to survive the first round, which he barely did. After the break, Hogan, disappointed not to have delivered on his nickname, rushed out of his corner full of confidence and ready to complete what he had begun. He forgot that wounded wildcats are dangerous. Crosses from left and right stopped him dead. He, in turn, tottered backwards as Wolgast looked for a stoppage. Powerful blows to his midriff brought Hogan's chin down to waist level, only for a destructive uppercut to restore him painfully to the vertical and vulnerable. The counter-offensive continued with Hogan helpless until Wolgast, not famous for his compassion, looked enquiringly at the referee Charlie White. White took the hint and intervened in Wolgast's favour.

Wolgast's recent performances in New York against Knockout Brown (8 February 1911 and 3 March 1911) in no-decision bouts had been disappointingly tame. The Hogan result proved him a continuingly formidable opponent. His career lasted 14 years from 1906 to 1920 and about 140 fights. He would not surrender the world lightweight title so painfully won from Battling Nelson back in February 1910 without a struggle.

Despite the loss in March to McFarland, Owen Moran had alternative ideas about who should be the lightweight champion. He would meet Wolgast at San Francisco on 4 July 1911. In the meantime, he stopped off at Canton, Ohio, to meet the rugged Russian immigrant, 21-year-old Phil Brock on 2 May 1911.[24] The trouncing

Packey had given Owen had neither blunted his many skills nor ameliorated his belligerence. Brock had also been the target of McFarland's best attentions (knocked out in the seventh on 7 August 1908), but he was no pushover. He had twice taken Freddie Welsh the full distance (25 rounds in Los Angeles on 30 May 1908; 12 rounds in Boston on 25 May 1909) before losing both decisions.

In the event, so bemused was the stronger Brock by Moran's feints, sways and swindles, he pushed himself over in his desperation to lay a satisfying punch on the diminutive Midlander. While Brock puzzled how to locate the target, Moran rapped left leads into his face, caught him under the heart with crosses, and whipped in powerful hooks in mystifying combinations. After the fight, Moran claimed to have pulled his punches to save his hands for the title fight against Wolgast. Brock, still smarting from a smack in the mouth in the third and floored by a wicked body punch in the sixth, thought the claim to be one more Moran deception.

A very large and fashionable holiday audience, including women, assembled eagerly at San Francisco for the title fight between Ad Wolgast and Owen Moran on 4 July 1911.[25] They laid out some $40,000 to be there. Promoter Jim Coffroth had guaranteed Wolgast $12,500, win or lose, to get him to put his world lightweight title on the line. The large gate suited Moran, who was on a percentage, and he picked up a five-figure dollar sum.

In practice, the two earned every cent and put on one of the greatest fights of the decade. The match was made at 9st 7lb/133lbs. From first to last the two went at each other like two Tasmanian

devils quarrelling over the same burrow. That this was an Anglo–American clash added a further nationalistic spice to Independence Day.

Moran knew he was confronting a man as wily and strong as himself. There was no prospect of bamboozling Wolgast the way he had bamboozled Brock. Instead, he hit Wolgast every iota as hard as Wolgast hit him, and hoped to overwhelm him. The zealous Wolgast had exactly the same idea vis-à-vis Moran. If contrasting styles make distinctive fights, two men bent upon non-stop mutual destruction, regardless of aesthetics, usually have stadia erupting in excitement. This was the case with Wolgast and Moran.

Wolgast bored in, drawing a sharp protest from Moran for butting. He also swung legitimate but vicious left hooks and heavy short-arm jabs that drew blood from Moran's mouth and won him the round. In the second, he delivered more of the same, but in return took a staggering right from Moran that landed cleanly on his jaw, and a flurry of lefts and rights to his nose that left him bleeding in turn. One round each, and then a third in which both men landed heavily with big punches yet showed no inclination to ease off.

The fourth was just as lively. Wolgast glared out of a bruised eye. Moran oozed blood from his mouth. Moran's latest complaint was that Wolgast was using his elbow for rather more than forming a hook. He expressed himself volubly to the referee on the subject. The referee replied in kind. Wolgast's corner weighed in with their colourful contributions and Wolgast added a few gloved insults of his own. Punches continued to fly at the same furious rate in the fifth, sixth and seventh, first one man and then the other gaining a temporary ascendancy yet conceding it before the round was completed. Surely one of the two had to wilt soon?

By the eighth, Moran looked the weaker, if *Boxing World*'s reporter is to be trusted:

> Moran found Wolgast's face thrice with his left. They clinched, and Wolgast drove his right powerfully to the kidneys. Moran almost sent the champion through the ropes with a rush, and then went nearly through himself from the force of the onslaught. Wolgast drove a terrible left to the stomach, and followed it with right uppercuts to the jaw. Wolgast started the blood in a stream from the Briton's mouth, and Moran wilted like a leaf. Wolgast sent in a storm of blows, followed his man about the ring, and was using both hands with equal facility. Moran went to his corner with a bloody face, and appeared to be in sore straits.

Moran *was* in sore straits. After eight severe rounds and the round-closing battering from Wolgast, how could he not be? Yet Moran, the Midlander, was every bit as tempered by fire as a piece of metal in a Black Country forge. He not only survived the ninth, but rallied in the tenth as *Boxing World* registered:

> The champion then swung his left to the jaw, and almost sent the Englishman through the ropes with a right and left to the body and face. Moran brought

the crowd to its feet when he met Wolgast at his own game, beating him to the punch, and starting the blood from the champion's mouth. Wolgast slowed perceptibly, and they rested in a clinch. Moran swung a hard right to the jaw, and they were in another slashing rally when the bell clanged. It was Moran's round, and he was cheered to the echo.

Moran's rally was certainly striking, and he kept it going for the 11th and 12th, with the crowd stamping and cheering in appreciation. Yet there are limits to human endurance, even to that of the Moran/Wolgast calibre. Moran took another hard right to the mouth at the very end of the 12th and was seen spitting out a tooth in the interval. Still in some pain, he went back out for the 13th, unlucky for him.

Around the middle of the round, Wolgast slipped in a driving right to Moran's diaphragm, probably *the* punch of the whole fight. Moran winced as the smack of leather on muscle sounded above the noise of the crowd. He took two more in the same place before folding. That gave Wolgast the chance to whip over a left hook to the jaw to complete Moran's destruction. For the first time in over a decade, Moran was down and counted out. His inert presence on the canvas was in sad contrast to the bleeding but jubilant Wolgast, dancing around the ring and waving the Stars and Stripes above his head. On the Fourth of July, he ultimately had produced the more effective fireworks.

Wolgast believed he could beat anyone. He took a delight in dashing

the hopes of British lightweights in the USA to try their luck. Sadly, he never met the current British lightweight champion, Matt Wells, champion as we have seen by mastering Freddie Welsh in February. Matt Wells, remember, had gained valuable American experience in 1910 in several non-decision bouts before returning for the Welsh fight at the NSC. In 1911, his departure for a further USA venture was a much more lavish affair.

On 11 May 1911, he attended the Central Club in Tottenham Court Road for a dinner for 100 guests given in his honour to commemorate his win over Welsh and to send him off with a flourish. He was presented with a gold watch, a diamond ring and an illuminated address. In his speech of thanks he himself presented Dai Dolling, his trainer, with a commemorative medal. Dolling accompanied him to the USA.

The most useful assistant for a fighter to have in his entourage in 1911 would have been a lawyer as much as a trainer or a cuts man. Ad Wolgast probably thought so. The July epic against Moran was his seventh of the year. In February, he had been in Philadelphia for the first of two bouts against Knockout Brown. It took place at the American Athletic Club on 8 February 1911 in club conditions before members and guests, and was decided not by a referee, but by newspaper consensus. After the six-rounder, the newspaper decision was against Wolgast in favour of Brown. It was a similar story at the return in New York's National Sporting Club on 3 March 1911 over ten rounds.[26] Suffering an injury to his right arm already broken during 1910, Wolgast thought he had mauled, clinched and roughed up Brown quite sufficiently to earn at least two draws. Brown, the showier fighter on the outside, and hitting Wolgast's gloves quite as often as any real target, was again the newspaper winner.

Two weeks later, on 17 March 1911, Wolgast defended the world lightweight championship over 20 rounds against a local favourite, George Memsic, in the Vernon Arena in Los Angeles.[27] Memsic was merely his main opponent; the Californian State authorities the main threat. The fight was only allowed after referee Eyten had given a guarantee to the District Attorney that he would intervene should one man show marked superiority over the other. In practice, Memsic was a long way from Wolgast's class, and his equalisation tactics were essentially crude. Sometimes he punched Wolgast low, sometimes he wrestled Wolgast to the floor, and sometimes he followed in on a right or left swing with the top of his skull. These uncouth procedures increased Wolgast's determination to put him in his proper place with clean and hurtful punches. Memsic stayed upright but looked rocky. Before the end of the ninth, he was on the verge of a knockout. At this point, Eyten stepped in and declared that Wolgast had retained his title. He had not intervened swiftly enough for the District Attorney. Wolgast and the bruised and battered Memsic were arraigned 'on a charge of participating in a prize fight'.

March 1911 was a difficult legal time for professional boxing in the USA. While Memsic and Wolgast were suffering arrest in the west, East Coast boxers were suffering further police harassment. Frank Moran and

Al Palzer, the tough Pittsburgh Irish American and the New Yorker, both heavyweight contenders with white skins, were arrested and charged with being illegally engaged in a fight.[28] Palzer in May 1911 would come out top of an undistinguished heap of pudgy gladiators and be awarded the discreditable title of the World White Hope Champion.[29]

Meanwhile, at Coney Island, that noted centre for pugilism and pleasure, a local magistrate declared two other boxers (John Barrett and Eduard Powers) should answer to a charge of participating in a 'very brutal' contest in which Mr Barrett had knocked out Mr Powers in one round. At least Messrs Wolgast, Memsic, Moran, Palzer, Barrett and Powers were being arraigned for something they were paid to do. Twenty members of the New York Postman Athletic Club were also prosecuted for having *paid* to be spectators at a fight.[30] And a poor black hotel clerk, R. R. Salt, was found guilty of holding others' stakes for illegal bets struck on the Johnson–Jeffries title fight the previous July.[31]

This wave of prosecutions was not coincidental to the contemporary activities of Senator James J. Frawley in the Albany State Legislature. As we have seen (Chapter 3), Frawley steered his boxing bill into law over the spring and summer of 1911, beginning on 13 April. In the skirmishes over the bill, reformers who wanted boxing eliminated on political or religious grounds took every opportunity to obstruct the sport and to hamper its ever-growing popularity.

Matt Wells on his 1911 American trip would meet not Wolgast but an impressive array of American fighters:

Leach Cross (2 June in New York – no decision over ten rounds); Pal Moore (24 June in Boston – points win over 12 rounds); Dick Hyland (19 July in Albany – no decision over ten rounds); and Willie Moody (28 July in Philadelphia – no decision over six rounds). He did not know initially of the precarious legal status of American boxing. However, he certainly did when he appeared at Madison Square Garden on 30 August 1911 to meet Wolgast's supposed conqueror Knockout Brown over ten rounds. The bout was an excellent test of the relative strength of American and British styles, and the hottest ticket in town. It was also the first practical test of Frawley's new law as the first major bout to be held since its passing.

Frawley's law had set up a supervisory body, the State Athletic Commission, with wide-ranging powers to bring the random activities of promoters, clubs and boxers under control. To the extent that any control of the workings of the free market was bound to irritate the rich and powerful, Frawley's proposals were politically sensitive. The passing of the bill through the chambers and corridors of the Albany legislature took many months of skilful political sparring after its introduction in April, but there it was eventually on the New York Statute Book. (A logical extension to control boxing on a federal basis remained a pious hope. It foundered, as did other desirable proposals, on the sacred doctrine that a particular state's liberty to control or not control in its own way had to remain paramount.)

In New York State, the new commission of three had powers to license New York's boxing clubs on the basis of a $10,000 bond and a 5 per cent levy on receipts, such a licence to be forfeited in the case of serious misconduct or the staging of a fixed fight – relatively powerful deterrents. Boxers themselves were licensed, conditional upon their physical fitness judged by a commission-appointed physician, and upon being of 'good character'. Their licences could also be forfeited.[32]

The Wells–Brown bout, made at 133lbs and involving a half share of the £5,400 gate split between them (32½ per cent for Brown, 22½ per cent for Wells), met every expectation.[33] Wells, dark, powerful and elusive, boxing in an English upright style, looked to keep Brown at a distance. He hoped to use his speed to outwit Brown's southpaw style with which he was unfamiliar.

Brown, the blond and hyperactive Dutch-American, looked to catch Wells with the whistling left swing that had downed so many in the first. The first round was predictable. Brown rushing out intending to overwhelm the visitor with fierce flurries – range-finding right leads followed by the deadly left. The target declined to be engulfed. As coolly as if he were practising on a punching bag, Wells stepped aside and picked Brown off with punches to head and body.

Wells continued to sway, duck and slip Brown's punches, and punish him with accurate counters. Blood appeared on Brown's face. Brown landed with his trademark left and the odd left uppercut, but more often was tagged with the southpaw's nightmare, a crisp right over the top of his left cross. In the eighth, Brown landed a chopping right to Wells's mouth but was nailed, once with an uppercut and once with a short right. A late Brown onslaught brought only a

right hook to the side of his head and a thumping left that opened another cut, this one on his right eye. The ninth and the tenth were similar. Charlie White, the referee, and for most of the ten rounds a privileged spectator superfluous to proceedings, summed up: 'The contest was one of the finest lightweight fights seen in the city for years. Both Brown and Wells deserve great credit; they fought hard all the time, obeyed the rules, and broke directly I ordered them.' Still technically a no-decision bout, no one doubted a points verdict would have favoured Wells.

Under the eyes of White and the suffocatingly packed audience of 12,000, as well as assorted commissioners, police observers and civic officials, Brown and Wells passed every scrutiny. The organisers and stewards had not shown similar aplomb. With the audience still trying to get in, the management announced an arbitrary $2 hike in the price of tickets, passing on the new commission levy directly to the punters. This was not a psychologically astute manoeuvre.

So eager were New Yorkers to see Brown meet Wells, the streets outside the club were swamped with ticket holders and non-ticket holders alike.[34] Some non-ticket holders parted with their hard-earned dollars, paying scalpers 100 per cent mark-ups and more for the blocks of tickets cunningly acquired in advance. Other spectators, less affluent but just as eager to see the fight, broke the police cordon around the entrance and pushed their way into the arena, happy to stand in the aisles or to sit in someone else's seat to get a glimpse of the action. Possibly an illegitimate 3,000 got in that way; not adding to the $30,000 gate, or

to the $1,500 levy going to the new commission.

Sad to relate, any woman who tried legitimately to purchase an entry was refused at the ticket window. One lady slipped the *cordon sanitaire masculin* and took her paid-for seat, cheered on by her neighbours. This brought her to the attention of the stewards, who escorted her out again. She was presumed to be a greater threat to public order than the ranks of Tammany politicians, gangsters and gamblers crowded in the ringside seats.

The disorder featured heavily in the fight post-mortem, which dragged on through September, as the police, the fire department, the promoter (P. T. Powers), the attorney general and the new commissioners all put in their five dollars' worth. The upshot was the revoking of the licence of the Madison Square Athletic Club.[35]

A further safety measure for boxing halls was taken on 12 September 1911. It was announced that no New York City boxing premises could hold exhibitions without specific fire department approval. This was less a result of the Brown–Wells evening than lingering memories of the dreadful event of six months before (25 March 1911). That was the notorious fire at the Triangle Shirtwaist Company premises downtown when 146 workers, mostly women, had roasted at their work tables because an implacable management had locked all the exit doors in case an employee was tempted to take a crafty cigarette break on the back stairs.[36] Not even the shabbiest boxing promoter wanted an evening to end in similar fashion.

Wells meanwhile met Abe Attell at Madison Square Garden in New York on 20 September 1911. He successfully rounded off his American venture by outweighing (by 13 pounds) and out-fighting the American lightweight champion over ten rounds. Wells claimed afterwards that he could have knocked Attell out but declined to do so as there was no title at stake, and as the weight discrepancy would have diminished his victory, surely a spurious claim. Who forgoes a prestigious knockout? Attell, in turn, claimed he was foxing to build up the odds at a return. Spurious protestations aside, most agreed that Wells was genuinely the better on the night.

Back in London, while British boxers like Wells, Welsh and Moran chased dollars in American rings, there was plenty of action. In London, too, safety and good order were concerns. The NSC and a commercial promoter such as McIntosh viewed each other with suspicion, yet both were aware that a riot or a major conflagration would endanger them all. They trespassed on each other's territory regardless.

The NSC persuaded two current heavyweights to forgo the large crowds and the large cheques that McIntosh could offer and close the 1910–11 season with a 20-rounder. The Forest Gate butcher, Bill Chase, met South African Fred Storbeck on 29 May 1911.[37] This was the final Monday night fight of the season. Over the summer break, the club's boxing theatre would be rebuilt to increase its capacity the better to compete with promoters such as McIntosh. The necessary investment cost the club £11,380 16s. 7d.

McIntosh was not outdone. His response was to sign up two international middleweights.[38] On 8 June 1911 Jim Sullivan, English middleweight champion, officially

recognised as such by the NSC because of his win over Tom Thomas, met the formidable German-American Billy Papke for what was billed as a world middleweight championship. (Stanley Ketchel, Hugo Kelly, Cyclone Johnny Thompson, Harry Lewis and Leo Houck, all from the USA, laid claims in the 1910–12 period, so the posters were totally misleading.) The match was staged at the Palladium near Oxford Circus – a prestigious venue that would attract an impressive array of American singers and comedians from Jack Benny to Frank Sinatra in later decades.

Neither contest offered a surfeit of skill, and more comedy than song. Whether the converted amateur Storbeck could go 20 rounds instead of the three he was used to was never tested. The contest lasted three and two-thirds rounds but delivered the up and down tumults reminiscent of the yo-yo adventures of Bombardier Wells and Gunner Moir at Olympia back in January. Both men launched and missed with huge swings by sufficient margins as to cause small local gales. Both also landed from time to time. Storbeck landed three times on his taller opponent in the first, and Chase obligingly fell over twice for counts of nine and six. Round two saw a reversal. Chase, when he connected, had an effective punch too, and it was Storbeck's turn to collapse – three times running for counts of eight, four and two. Arithmetic alone was unlikely to decide this one. Chase chased in the third; Storbeck hastily retreated and took deep breaths to get his senses back. The fourth ended the fun. After two minutes, the recovering Storbeck caught Chase just above the heart with a straight left. Chase fell forward, rolled

over and stayed horizontal for more than a full ten. (On the undercard, Paul Til of France had been disqualified in a bantamweight fight with Joe Bowker for applying his patella to Bowker's scrotum, yet Chase's defeat was quite as painful as Bowker's win.)

For the big event at the Palladium, prices ranged from two guineas to ten guineas for a seat in a box; one guinea to 10s. 6d. for stall seats; and 5s. for the back of the upper circle. (To put these figures in luxurious perspective, in 1911 George Lansbury, the socialist MP, was pleading in the House of Commons on behalf of working men who had to feed large families on a mere 7s. a week.)

The Papke/Sullivan match was not likely to be settled on a surfeit of skills either. Papke had notched up victories over headcases such as Ketchel and artists such as Willie Lewis. But he had not outboxed them, rather swarmed irresistibly all over them. Fighting Papke was less like facing a conventional Roman gladiator than one of the *retiarius* kind who wrapped you up in an all-embracing net before despatching you. Papke's nickname was the Illinois Thunderbolt, but the Illinois Swarmer might have been more appropriate. Poor Sullivan was less than his usual equitable self. The taxi taking him from his Essex training camp to the 2pm weigh-in first took the wrong route, then broke down in the middle of nowhere, forcing him to jog many miles to a telegraph office, and he eventually turned up an hour late. He tipped the scales after the mishaps at 11st 2lb/156lbs. Papke made the time and the weight limit comfortably earlier in the afternoon.

The omen was unfortunate. Sullivan could have jogged to the Fleet Street weigh-in from his home in

Bermondsey with much less effort. And effort misapplied became his problem in the fight itself. He connected with the oncoming Papke with many a punch, but the punches, though piling up a useful points lead, failed in their real purpose – to keep the super-aggressive Papke away.

Papke was less clever than Sullivan even at his best, and often wild. In the third, he swung one erratic right that missed and left him, rather than Sullivan, on his hands and knees. When he had another spectacular miss in the eighth, Sullivan hit him twice on the jaw with big rights and followed the punches with a substantial attack that had his supporters on their feet, cheering, stamping their feet, shouting him on, and shaking the theatre to its foundations. Papke, utterly unfazed, replied with stiff lefts. The American's strength and powers of recuperation were ominous.

The ninth in retrospect was inevitable. Sullivan absorbed two heavy body blows and clinched. Foolishly he then broke the clinch by pushing Papke off with his gloves at shoulder level. This left his midriff temporarily exposed. A low driving right from Papke as they parted folded Sullivan nearly in half, and he dropped face forward before rolling over helplessly on his back as the count proceeded. As would be impossible under modern rules, the bell saved him mid-count when he looked as if he would be lying supine all evening.

The respite proved academic. His seconds dragged him back to his stool and tried every kind of resuscitation possible in 60 seconds. All was in vain. When the bell rang for the tenth, Sullivan could not stand up, let alone defend himself. Papke was the clear

winner, although Sullivan supporters in the audience judged some of Papke's headwork more severely than referee Corri.

Glamorous Anglo–American clashes in the lightweight division, such as the Brown–Wells classic in New York, and classy middleweight matches such as Sullivan–Papke, drew large crowds in London or New York, and evoked much press coverage on both sides of the Atlantic. Yet when enterprising promoters such as McIntosh or Rickard put their heads on their pillows and dreamed their dreams, it was not of lighter men they fantasised; it was of heavyweights. In Herman Melville's super-heavyweight novel, *Moby Dick*, the character Ishmael explains the obsessive search for the white whale:

> Therefore, in his other moods, symbolize whatever grand or gracious thing he will by whiteness, no man can deny that in its profoundest idealized significance it calls up a peculiar apparition to the soul.[39]

The grand and gracious symbol sought by boxing promoters, leading to some peculiar apparitions, was a new white heavyweight to defeat Jack Johnson and take his world crown. The heavyweight crown was the bauble that prevented the hated Johnson slipping back into the obscure fighting ghetto where he, Jeannette, Langford and McVea could punch each other and leave white racist prejudices undisturbed.

In an uncannily short time since Johnson's victory over Burns with which this book began, boxing achieved unprecedented popularity and importance, and London became *the*

place for big fights. Suppose the semi-rehabilitated young Bombardier Billy Wells could be matched against Jack Johnson in front of his own crowd in London for the title? The match had much going for it. Any American/British clash in London was a pre-determined sell-out. Any heavyweight contest transcended the cognoscenti and drew in even those who might never have seen a glove clenched with intent previously. Any clash sold as of dermatological significance fitted into the melodrama tradition where villains were black and heroes white: black v white = evil v good, QED, and Molyneux v Cribb revived.

In the promotional euphoria surrounding such a prospect – and mighty profits as good as in the bank already – reality was forgotten. Bombardier Billy Wells had no chance of beating Johnson or even lasting a respectable number of rounds. But when did a big promoter, from Tex Rickard to Don King, ever accept inequality of aptitude as a bar to a fight that could be sold to a gullible public?

A second factor was more ominous. A match transcending boxing's growing regular audience would be noticed by three other groups: those who hated boxing on moral or ethical grounds and wanted it banned; those who believed the sight of a black man beating up a white man would disturb a status quo where ethnic minorities did without question what they were told by white authority; and the authorities themselves, whose attitude to boxing was so ambivalent. As the very legality of boxing was problematical, a proposal that Wells fight Johnson in London, was, as Oliver Hardy might have said, a fine mess you're getting us into.

Endnotes:

1 *Boxing,* 7 January 1911.

2 *Boxing,* 7 January 1911.

3 *Boxing,* 21 January 1911.

4 *Boxing,* 28 January 1911.

5 *New York Times,* 23 January 1911.

6 Profile of Moir by Gilbert Odd in *Boxing News,* 25 May 1979.

7 See 'Burns', Volume No. 48 in the Boxers video series, Marshall-Cavendish.

8 *Boxing,* 21 January 1911.

9 This is one example of many such impeccable researches contained in Barry Hugman's indispensable and much lamented annual, *The British Boxing Board of Control Yearbook,* in this case the 1996 edition p. 213. The match was made at 10st 4lb as a compromise between the British 10st 7lb and the American 10st 2lb. For the fight details, see *Boxing,* 28 January 1911.

10 *Boxing,* 4 February 1911; Harding, J., *Lonsdale's Belt: Boxing's Most Coveted Prize* (Worthing: Pitch Publishing, 2016) p. 34; *The Times,* 31 January 1911.

11 A couple of sources, e.g. John Harding *Lonsdale's Belt* p. 34, and *The British Boxing Board of Control Yearbook 1985* p. 220 and p. 225, give the stoppage as happening in round 11, but the seventh is the accurate one.

12 *Boxing,* 4 February 1911; *The Times,* 31 January 1911; and film of the contest in the National Film Archive at the British Film Institute.

13 *The Times,* 22 February 1911; *Boxing World and Athletic Chronicle,* 2 March 1911; *Boxing,* 25 February 1911.

14 Kent, G., T*he Great White Hopes* (Stroud: Sutton Publishing, 2005) p. 169.

15 For details on Wells, see the obituary by Gilbert Odd in *Boxing News,* 8 July 1953, and Harry Mullan: *Heroes and Hard Men* pp. 40–43.

16 *Boxing World and Athletic Chronicle,* 2 March 1911; *Boxing,* 4 March 1911; *The Times,* 28 February 1911.

17 *Boxing World and Athletic, Chronicle* 16 March 1911.

18 Shipley, S., *Bombardier Billy Wells: The Life and Trials of a Boxing Hero* (Tyne and Wear: Bewick Press, 1993) pp. 42–44.

19 *Boxing World and Athletic Chronicle,* 27 April 1911; *The Times,* 25 April 1911.

20 *Boxing World and Athletic Chronicle,* 11 May 1911.

21 *Boxing,* 25 March 1911.

22 *Boxing World and Athletic Chronicle,* 4 May 1911.

23 *Boxing World and Athletic Chronicle,* 11 May 1911.

24 *Boxing World and Athletic Chronicle,* 18 May 1911.

25 Report in *Boxing World and Athletic Chronicle,* 13 July 1911, and a round-by-round summary in the 27 July issue.

26 *The New York Times,* 4 March 1911.

27 *The New York Times,* 18 March 1911.

28 *The New York Times,* 18 March 1911.

29 Robert, R., *Papa Jack: Jack Johnson and the Era of White Hopes* (New York: Simon & Schuster, 1985) p. 126.

30 *The New York Times,* 22 March 1911.

31 *The New York Times,* 23 March 1911.

32 *The New York Times,* 14 April 1911.

33 *Boxing World and Athletic Chronicle,* 14 September 1911; Jim Kenrick, 'How Matt Wells astonished New York', *Boxing News,* 17 January 1958; *Jewish Chronicle,* 8 September 1911.

34 *New York Times,* 1 September and 2 September 1911.

35 *New York Times,* 29 September 1911.

36 Zinn, H., *A People's History of the United States* (New York: Harper, 1995) p. 319.

37 *Boxing World and Athletic Chronicle,* 1 June 1911.

38 *Boxing World and Athletic Chronicle,* 15 June 1911.

39 Melville. H., *Moby Dick* or *The White Whale,* Chapter 42, 'The Whiteness of the Whale'.

CHAPTER 7

FIGHTS THAT NEVER WERE
1911 (PART TWO)

In Which Winston Spencer Churchill Outpoints Jack Johnson

A MINOR irritation for sports followers is to see normally rational people changing their behaviour radically when a television camera is in the vicinity. The waving, grinning and shameless gurning provoked by a lens can be remarkable. In that pre-television, pre-radio autumn of 1911, abnormal press coverage similarly provoked many affected by the projected Johnson/Wells clash to behave quite irrationally.

The promoter of the event, James White, after skilful negotiations with the two fighters and their managers, obtained the fighters' signatures on an Articles of Agreement of 15 July 1911.[1] The fight, over 20 rounds, under the Marquess of Queensberry's Rules, was planned for 2 October 1911 at Olympia, using four-ounce gloves (this was changed later to five-ounce, but four was the original agreement). Johnson's world heavyweight championship was at stake as well as a purse of £8,000 (a sum boosted by the film rights, and split £6,000 to Johnson, £2,000 to Wells, regardless of who won the fight). Decorum and good order would be ensured by the referee in the ring and by three judges positioned outside it.

This innocuous document was like a pebble dropped into a calm pond. The best part of a month after its signing, the spreading ripples turned into alarming tidal waves. Reactions, however slow, can be better understood in context. James White, for example, as promoter, hired the Empress Hall at the Earl's Court premises for the evening from the Earl's Court Company, and reached an agreement on 4 September 1911 with the company about the share of the profits.[2] Earl's Court Company was entitled to 10 per cent of all ticket revenue for the fight, and 40 per cent of the admission charges to the fighters' public training sessions at Earl's Court in the week before the fight. The company monopolised the rights to refreshments, drinks and the restaurant proceeds. White would get all the revenue from the sale of programmes, photographs and fight souvenirs.

White and the Earl's Court Company stood to make a tidy sum, providing enough people could be crammed into the hall. How many exactly became a matter of concern to the LCC Theatres and Music Halls Committee on safety grounds.[3] Seats for 5,793 and three rows accommodating another 880 standing football style behind metal barriers would make a grand total of 6,673. Unfortunately, as the supervisory architect was quick to point out, the existing exits could safely allow only 3,416 in and out. The Matt Wells/Brown August encounter at Madison Square Garden (Chapter 6) had made crowd control a hot issue.

White was not a man to be deflected by minor details. He submitted an amended plan; one which reduced the seating by 1,000 to 5,637. This would lose him no revenue, as the revised plan sneakily squeezed in three new standing areas for 2,400, 500 and 480, for a new grand total of 9,017! He did not get away with it, nor with a further proposal for 8,617 – 7,637 seated and 980 standing behind barriers.

By mid-September consultations with the London Fire Brigade brought further amendments, including an absolute limit of 5,000 on overall capacity. By then White had been selling tickets with abandon, so how the discrepancy between tickets sold and reduced accommodation would have been resolved is anyone's guess. What is beyond doubt is that White was being assailed on many other fronts than the inadequacy of entrances and exits.

Behind the sub-committee responsible for all public entertainments was the full London County Council (LCC), the elected ruling body for all metropolitan affairs. Its chairman was Edward White (no relation), a man who knew nothing of boxing, but who certainly remembered a resolution passed by the full Council on 12 July 1910 in the riotous aftermath to the Johnson/Jeffries fight in Reno. Passed by 45 votes to 29, it said:

> That in the opinion of the Council the public exhibition, at places of entertainment in London, of pictures representing the recent prize fight in the United States of America is undesirable; and that the proprietors of London music-halls and other places licensed by the Council for cinematographic performances be so informed.[4]

The resolution implied that any premises licensed by the Council ignoring the hint, having been 'so informed', would not be licensed in the future. If even a heavily censored film of Jack Johnson thumping the hulking Jeffries was 'undesirable' in 1910 for Londoners, how much more undesirable would be the sight of Jack Johnson in the flesh, thumping a handsome young Englishman in Billy Wells for real in 1911? On 13 September 1911, Edward White wrote to J. Calvin Brown, the chairman of Earl's Court Company, enclosing a copy of the 1910 resolution, and intimating his opinion that Earl's Court might be imperilling their future licence if they did not halt the 2 October contest.

Calvin Brown knew nothing about boxing either, but he was an adroit financial entrepreneur with extensive British and European entertainment interests. (He ran the White City in Manchester; the Magic City in Paris; was building La Babassada in Barcelona; and all this in addition to chairing the board of Earl's Court Company, which staged an extraordinary range of international exhibitions; military displays; circuses; menageries; ice skating; roller skating; epic plays and anything that would bring in the punters in large numbers.) He did not scare easily. By return of post, the LCC chairman got an uncompromising rejoinder.[5]

Brown reminded White that the Earl's Court Company had signed a contract with the promoter with no reason to believe that there would be anything untoward about the event; that to cancel at this late stage would make his company liable for damages; and that it would be quite contrary to natural justice for the LCC to oppose the eventual renewal of the Earl's Court licence merely because the company had fulfilled their contract. He added, truthfully, that great precautions were being taken to ensure good order on the night.

The political complexion of the LCC in 1911 contrasted interestingly to the make-up of the House of Commons. (After the second General Election of the year in 1910, the House was controlled still by 272 Liberals as opposed to 271 Conservatives, but their control was dependent upon the help of 42 Labour and 84 Irish Independents.) The LCC was first set up in 1888, and at the initial LCC elections fell into the hands of the Liberals (who called themselves the Progressives in the metropolitan context).[6] The Progressives, with a few Socialist allies, adopted radical measures aimed at ameliorating the manifold social and economic problems of a rapidly growing urban conurbation. The ratepayers (those with property) showed their gratitude for the using of their taxes to alleviate the problems of the poor by throwing out the Progressives in the 1907 London elections, and electing the Conservatives (called the Moderates at council level), who retained power for the next 27 years.[7]

In 1911, the LCC was therefore in Conservative hands, forming a natural target for Liberal agitation whenever an appropriate cause arose. On those sensitive territories where religion or morality overlapped with politics, it was predictable that the Nonconformists, the Free Churches and the more evangelical of Anglicans would identify with the Liberal Party and its traditional Gladstonian rectitude. Liberal v Tory; Chapel v Church; Temperance v Drink; Bible Class v Music Hall – such labels, even at their crudest, contained elements of truth. The determination of Victorian and Edwardian swells to have a bet on a sporting result was matched only by the tenacity of moralists who equated a flutter with the wages of sin, and a betting slip with a one-way ticket to Hell. As we saw in Chapter 1, the Tory aristocracy crowded Regency ringsides to bet and to idolise courageous prizefighters, to the disgust of the evangelical reformers who saw only blood, brutality and unearned rewards. Chapel-goers' attitudes were predictable when they came to hear of the projected fight.

The relevant Greater London Archive file contains the substantial sheaf of telegrams, petitions, resolutions and protests that poured into the LCC headquarters in the second half of September 1911 protesting against the meeting of Johnson and Wells.[8] There were 219 of them. They came from a rich variety of Nonconformist sources all over the country.

The Shirley Baptist Church in Southampton pronounced the coming event 'brutalising in character, demoralising in influence'. The Lincoln and District Evangelical Free Church Council dreaded the fight, 'not only for the Evil in itself but for its baneful effect on the Moral tone of thousands of people in the provinces who would see it through Cinematograph Exhibitions'. The Congregational Church in Ashton-in-Makerfield thought it 'calculated to foment the worst passions and to lead to degrading consequences among the lowest classes of our people'. The Harrow Wesleyan Men's Meeting believed it to be of 'incalculable moral harm'. The Kingston Brotherhood spoke of 'brute force, degrading alike to Christianity and civilization'. The Primitive Methodists of Morecambe worried about the 'great moral peril to the best interest of our national life'; and the Hebden Bridge Sunday School Union considered that the event 'would certainly exercise a baneful and degrading influence upon British young people'. The Calvary Welsh Baptists condemned it 'as a most barbaric movement, tending to create us an eyesore to the Nations … revolting in its Nature, marring the Character of our Christian land, brutalising to the Motives and well-being of the rising generations, inhumane … and justly bring[ing?] down upon [us?] the Wrath of Heaven'.

Jack Johnson drew crowds everywhere, here outside a New York Theatre.
Bain Collection, Prints & Photographs Division, Library of Congress,LC-USZ62-71758

The protests, nearly all dated within two weeks of one another and with words such as 'demoralizing', 'degrading' and 'disgrace' much in evidence, have all the signs of an organised and orchestrated campaign. The man whose own energetic opposition to the contest led to this nationwide anti-fight crusade was a prominent Baptist minister, the 64-year-old Reverend Frederick Brotherton Meyer (1847–1929). Meyer was twice the incumbent at the fashionable London establishment, the Regent's Park Chapel (1888–92 and 1909–15). He had been both President of the National Federation of Free Churches and the President of the Baptist Union.[9] In the First World War, he would campaign to have prostitutes compulsorily examined for VD.

Like many Free Churchmen, Meyer believed politics should uphold spiritual values; spiritual values, that is, as interpreted by the Free Church believer. No stranger to public campaigning, his

first spell as President of the National Federation coincided with missionary initiatives in Yorkshire and Lancashire that yielded many conversions and the mass taking of temperance pledges. Even more spectacularly, 1904 and 1905 had been the years of the great Welsh revival, when the chapels in the valleys had bulged with half a million worshippers, many of them newly converted to Christianity.[10] The fervour of the new converts had already been brought to bear against local boxing promotions, as we saw earlier. London, the great urban wen, was notoriously stonier ground for the sowing of spiritual seeds; pagan indifference as opposed to Welsh *hwyl*.

Considering the close identification of the Free Churches with the Liberal Party (the Liberal backbenches after the 1905–06 General Election had up to 200 Nonconformist bottoms upon them), men such as Meyer had so far had less impact upon politics than they

The Reverend Frederick Brotherton Meyer (1847–1929), the Baptist champion who organized a Free Churches' campaign against a projected London fight between Johnson and Bombardier Billy Wells.
Reinhold Thiele/Thiele/Getty Images

business, undertaken for less than worthy motives:

> The opposition to the Wells–Johnson contest is not one that is honestly inspired. It comes from a quarter that is notoriously opposed to all sports of the people, and is being agitated by those who were solely actuated by a desire for notoriety. They have not had, through experience, any knowledge of boxing, and are basing their opposition on the presumption that boxing contests of the present are similar to the prize-fighting of past generations. Should these few people succeed in this instance it would be the introduction of the wedge that might be used to part thousands of loyal British subjects from a manly, clean and honourable means of living.[14]

This was a valid and well-expressed argument, although the committee could not resist gilding the lily by claiming the average boxer quite the equal in moral stature of a Methodist lay preacher or Congregational deacon:

> No class in the community leads better lives than the boxers; they are compelled to eschew vices, intemperance, and many worldly luxuries if they have the ambition to succeed in their profession, and the police records prove that the boxer is above the average as a law-abiding citizen.

(The hyperbole can be forgiven from a small organisation fighting hard in a hostile environment. Organising

had wished and indeed expected.[11] By 1910, Meyer admitted he would support any party if he believed that it would do more for Free Church ambitions.[12] He needed a new public cause and, although he knew absolutely nothing about boxing, he saw one of James White's posters in the street advertising the Johnson–Wells contest.[13] He had found a new destination for a new crusade.

Within the narrower confines of boxing, attitudes to a new attack upon the sport were surprisingly ambiguous. Some were very predictable. The executive committee of the recently founded Boxers Union, a trade union open to all professional pugilists and allied to the Trades Union Congress, appealed to fellow unionists to resist the new agitation as an unreasonable restraint of a legitimate professional trade unions in scattered trades such as catering or retail is notoriously difficult, even in less divided societies than Edwardian England. The Boxers Union never had more than a shadowy existence. Indeed the Trades Union Congress's archives today have no papers surviving about the union. We will examine its demise later.)

The resolution also pointed out, reasonably enough, that:

Modern boxing became popular because it did away with the brutality of the old prize ring, and it is drawing to its ranks yearly thousands of the best blood of the land, all of whom are the better for its practice.

The one boxing institution that prided itself on incorporating the best blood of the land was, of course, the NSC in Covent Garden. It had, after all, been the main instrument in the creation and tight control of modern boxing and the abolition of prize ring brutality. What was the attitude of the NSC to the projected Wells/Johnson clash at Earl's Court? Answer: distinctly ambivalent. The willingness of the club and its aristocratic president Lord Lonsdale to defend boxing's legal status was legendary. At crisis points in the recent past (the Slavin/Jackson case of 1892; the Old Bailey trial of 1901), the club had been positively aggressive. NSC officials such as Bettinson and Douglas had stood in the dock to be counted, and Lord Lonsdale had opened his considerable coffers to pay the best barristers in the land to defend the sport. Continuity would suggest that the latest agitation against boxing should be resisted and fought with all

the vigour shown in 1892 and 1901. But now there were significant differences.

By 1911, new promoters such as James White and Hugh McIntosh, and their willingness to pay large purses to the best domestic and international fighters, were precisely why so many glamorous fights of the 1909–11 period had been staged *outside* the NSC. The handsome Bombardier was a case in point. It was McIntosh who had staged Wells's lucrative clashes against Gunner Moir and Porky Flynn at Olympia in January and March 1911, after the NSC boosted Wells's stature by matching him at the club with Iron Hague and granting him the official British heavyweight championship. Wells now had both the title and an opportunity to win the even more glamorous world heavyweight championship. He would be displaying his assets not for the sake of the NSC members but for the profitable balance sheets of James White and the Earl's Court Company.

Relations between the NSC and Jack Johnson were even more strained. Johnson first came to London in 1908 in pursuit of the elusive Tommy Burns, whose own ultracommercial attitudes had caused offence to NSC members and officials alike. Johnson was not invited into the premises but told to wait on the mat at the entrance like a trained Labrador, while his then manager, Sam Fitzpatrick, discussed his meeting Burns in the NSC ring.[15] The demeaning treatment, which offended Johnson, was also meted out to Burns.

The gulf between the £6,000 Burns was demanding and the price the club was prepared to offer, meant negotiations were not prolonged. Burns eventually got his price, but only from

McIntosh in Australia. However, a provisional arrangement that Johnson would return to London in early 1909 to meet Sam Langford in the NSC ring for a £1,000 purse and 33 per cent of any film rights was also agreed.[16] As a gesture of good intent, the NSC made a £500 contribution to Johnson's fare to Australia to pursue Burns.[17] Once Johnson had become the world champion by beating Burns and had acquired all the prestige and earning power that the title represented, he declined to accept any sum less than the £6,000 on which Burns had insisted for a title defence. Having climbed out of the black fighters' pool to which he, Langford, McVea and Jeannette had been confined for so long, he declined also to re-join it by fighting Langford. He repaid the £500 to the NSC but his failure to fulfil his supposed obligation to the NSC was bitterly resented in Covent Garden.[18] Indeed, on one of Johnson's returns to London, when he attempted to visit the club after his victory over Jim Jeffries, the jobsworth at the NSC door 'politely but firmly requested him to make himself scarce'.[19]

Thus, the very institution that had so stoutly defended boxing previously was unlikely to take the field in the interests of either a commercial promoter taking boxing further out of its own control, or of a man it had not allowed through its polished doors. Meanwhile, an even older and mightier English institution was reconsidering its attitude to the looming event and the growing agitation surrounding it. This institution was the Home Office.

Although the bulk of the petitions and protests from the Free Church ranks had been sent to the LCC as

Johnson loved to buy and drive expensive motorcars.
Topical Press Agency/Hulton Archive/Getty Images

we saw, a few strong ones had been sent directly to the Home Office to remind the Liberal government and the Liberal Home Secretary of their joint responsibility to make Britain a more Christian society; a Christian society moreover, where the moral response to whomsoever smote thee on the right cheek was not to turn to him a goodly right hook.

The Sheffield Primitive Methodist Council appealed to the Home Secretary to intervene 'against the growing vice of Prize Fighting'; the Second London District Synod of the Wesleyan Methodists believed 'that anything of the kind would outrage the best sentiment of this country and could only be attended with deplorable results'; and the Southampton Southern Baptist Association 'emphatically enters its protest against the proposed Fighting Contest between Messrs. Wells and Johnson', and specifically called upon the Home Secretary to use 'his great power to prevent it'.[20]

It is a safe bet that the dynamic politician who was the Liberal Secretary of State at the Home Office did not welcome these pleas. He was Winston Spencer Churchill (1874–1965), a man of dazzling oratorical gifts and pugnacious instincts, whose relish for a meaningful scrap saved his whole country in the 1939–45 war against Hitler. The trivial skirmish of 1911 over Wells and Johnson was less a challenge than an embarrassment.

He had been Home Secretary only since February 1910, a most elevated office for a man of 36 by Edwardian standards. He had been a member of the governing Liberal Party only since 1903, having abandoned the Conservatives in a quarrel over the freedom of trade issue. Remarkably, he returned to the Conservative fold in 1923, one of the very few politicians ever, as has been said, not only to rat but to re-rat and still prosper.

The Nonconformists on the Liberal benches were highly suspicious of this newly Liberal Churchill in their midst. He was the son of a renegade

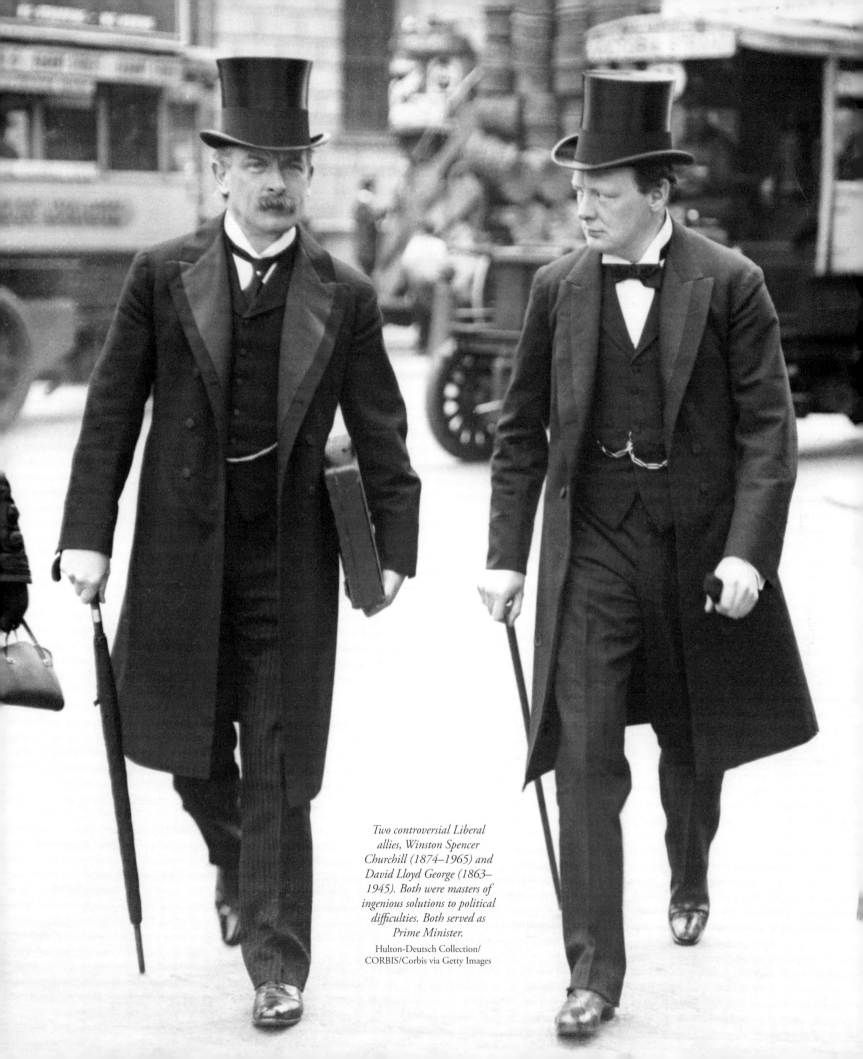

Two controversial Liberal allies, Winston Spencer Churchill (1874–1965) and David Lloyd George (1863–1945). Both were masters of ingenious solutions to political difficulties. Both served as Prime Minister.

Hulton-Deutsch Collection/ CORBIS/Corbis via Getty Images

Tory, Lord Randolph Churchill (1849–95), who died prematurely from degenerate syphilis and who delighted in provoking middle-class puritan fears in and out of Parliament: 'The aristocracy and the working class are united in the indissoluble bands of a common immorality,' he once said. Lord Randolph's son was continuing the family tradition.

Young Winston was, says historian David Cannadine, 'widely distrusted as a man of unstable temperament, unsound judgement and rhetorical (and also alcoholic) excess … there hung around him an unsavoury air of disreputability and unseemliness'. He formed friendships with a bizarre collection of louche and dodgy characters. He gambled freely in Continental casinos and absorbed a prodigious amount of alcohol at a sitting. His less than enthusiastic devotion to the Christian Church was summarised when he said, in an unguarded cynical moment, 'I could hardly be called a pillar of the Church, I am more in the nature of a buttress, for I support it from the outside!'[21]

Worse still, there had been the unseemly goings-on at the Empire Theatre, Leicester Square in November 1894. Mrs Laura Ormiston Chant, a campaigner for so-called 'purity', attacked the theatre for allowing a promenade and bar directly behind the dress circle, an area where young bloods and sex workers mingled and negotiated during performances. Under pressure from the formidable Mrs Chant, the Mary Whitehouse of her day, the Liberal-dominated LCC renewed the Empire's licence only on condition that the promenade section was modified. The theatre reopened with canvas screens separating the prom from the auditorium – those so minded could now watch the stage or cavort with the goods on show behind the screens; they could no longer watch and cavort simultaneously.

On the first Saturday night following the reopening, a party of undergraduates and cadets rioted and tore down the moralistic screens. The assault party was headed by a young Sandhurst cadet, none other than Winston Spencer Churchill. As he wrote proudly to his brother Jack, 'Did you see the papers? It was I who led the rioters.'[22]

Many Free Churchmen and Liberals read the papers too; and had long memories. Would a man with such inclinations really be the Liberal Home Secretary to deliver party and country from sin? Highly unlikely, surely? Left to his own devices, Churchill might have responded to the agitation about Wells/Johnson with a vigorous waving of the obverse side of his famous V-sign. But he was in no position to alienate the Nonconformist Liberal supporters when the party needed every vote possible to keep out the Tories, especially as the constitutional crisis over the House of Lords might bring yet another General Election in its wake. Were he to use what the Southampton Baptists called his 'great power' and call off the fight, White or McIntosh or others with commercial interests in the contest might challenge him in the courts, and he could be found to be acting *ultra vires*, a potential embarrassment for any Home Secretary.

Churchill did two sensible things. He accepted a social invitation that conveniently took him off to Scotland and not readily contactable by the press or the Meyers of the world. He also asked Sir John Simon (1873–1954) to draw up a secret report defining the laws of England relating to boxing and answering the vexed question of

Sir John Simon (1873–1954), the intellectual Solicitor General who in 1911 applied his forensic skills to the legal status of boxing.
Topical Press Agency/Getty Images

Lonsdale's declarations on the projected London fight were impossibly contradictory.
Fox Photos/Hulton Archive/Getty Images

whether Churchill *did* have any powers to stop the fight. Simon, the brilliant Liberal lawyer, served as Attorney General in the Liberal government from 1913 and became Home Secretary and Chancellor of the Exchequer in the 1930s. His intellectual powers were considerable. His report will be considered in its proper place below.

The tragic-comedy-cum-farce was acted out throughout September 1911. By Saturday, 16 September, the press was well aware that there was a good story in the fight and the campaign to stop it. *The Times* that day printed the appeal of Meyer's Free Church Council to the ministers of all Free Church denominations to use the next day's Sunday sermons to preach against the fight:

> We venture to ask all ministers
> of religion to refer to the matter
> on the coming Sunday with the
> view to arousing the conscience of

the nation against a spectacle in which two men do their utmost to batter one another, not in self-defence, nor to protect the weak, but for high stakes, and to gratify that craving for the sensational and brutal which is inconsistent with the manhood that makes a great nation.[23]

(This was the national Free Church appeal that produced the petitions duly received by the LCC and the Home Office.) Meanwhile, at the LCC itself, Edward White was attempting the impossible by trying to frighten Earl's Court into cancelling the fight, while admitting the Council's powers to force them to do so were distinctly feeble:

> The Council could do nothing;
> they had no control over the
> holding of such Contests. The
> Free Church Council and the
> members of other organizations

had imagined that the Council had some power, but this was not so. All they could do was to hold a threat that the licence would not be renewed, and if the majority of the London County Council, when they came to consider the question in November, decided against a renewal of the licence to Earl's Court (Limited), then the management of that concern would have no cause to grumble.[24]

One reporter secured a statement from Lord Lonsdale, whose motives were considerably more mixed in strong contrast to his normally automatic defence of the sport whenever it was under legal or popular attack:

> He [Lonsdale] would never
> believe that these large affairs,
> where money was the chief factor,
> were for the betterment of the
> sport. Boxing contests should be
> essentially and primarily a matter
> of science. The profit element was
> most undesirable. In the case of
> the Johnson–Wells contest it was
> like a three-year-old being pitted
> against a two-year-old, which was
> naturally considerably lacking in
> ripe experience.[25]

Like many rich men in the early years of the 20th century, Lord Lonsdale was fully imbued with the amateur spirit; sport for sport's sake, so to speak. But successfully to participate in a sport at the higher levels requires two things – the leisure freely to practise and participate; and the income to support that leisure. Lonsdale's multiple sporting activities – boxing, horse racing, hunting, shooting, coursing, and motoring – mostly highly expensive luxury enterprises, were sustained because he enjoyed a fabulous income from the lucrative Lowther estates. Few 18-year-olds (he was 18 in 1875) could command a £1,000-a-year allowance and a flat in the heart of fashionable St James's in London.[26] (Agricultural workers, like those on the Lowther estates, averaged 14s. a *week* in 1874.)[27]

By the 1880s, the trustees of the family estate were trying *in vain* to restrict Lonsdale to a modest £100,000 a year pocket money.[28] The cigars Lonsdale puffed at ringside in the NSC cost him £3,000 a year alone; the miners who dug the coal in the Whitehaven coalfields (mineral rights owned by Lonsdale) had to cut a full ton of coal to receive a handsome 1s. 9d. and in conditions so dangerous that 132 miners were killed there in May 1910. Lonsdale could well afford to be an amateur sportsman. There is something wonderfully ironic about his drawing a sporting parallel between the projected fight and horse racing (two-year-old matched against three-year-old), a sport where professionalism and gambling had controlled everything for centuries.

The NSC officials and committee men such as Eugene Corri, Peggy Bettinson and J. H. Douglas were comfortably middle class rather than wealthy aristocrats, but Corri's part-time dealings at the Stock Exchange allowed him many hours for his real passion, boxing. As Corri himself wrote, 'The great Gentlemen players like … Mr Douglas, have been able to devote quite as much time to cricket as any professionals.'[29] Douglas Snr, NSC member and referee, was a timber broker and made a fortune at it, allowing him

The ambitious Churchill became Home Secretary only to be faced with an embarrassing 1911 dilemma.
Bain Collection, Prints & Photographs Division, Library of Congress, LC-DIG-ggbain-04739

ample time for NSC business. His son, Douglas Jnr (J. W. H. T. Douglas), was thus born with the income and leisure to have an outstanding triple sporting career. He boxed as an amateur (ABA middleweight champion 1905; Olympic middleweight champion 1908). He played amateur soccer for Corinthian Casuals and England. He played cricket for England and Essex also as an amateur (23 Tests, including 18 as captain). He was captain of Essex from 1911–28, although his outstanding skills as an all-rounder did not always compensate for his aggressive and combative personality, much discussed when he was asked to stand down as captain in 1928. Many said that his long tenure at the county was at least partly sustained by the welcome funds, strings attached, put into the club by his father.

In contrast to the Douglases or Lonsdales of the world, a humble ex-soldier like Wells, or the son of an illiterate labourer and ex-slave like Johnson, were in no position to box purely for the betterment of the sport, and it would be disingenuous and hypocritical to suggest that they should. For some time, NSC officials had monopolised boxing, made matches to suit its members, fixed purses, issued unchallengeable edicts and expected boxers to queue up at the back door, and only at the back door, and express forelock-tugging gratitude for minimal rewards. Once boxing attracted followers worldwide and could fill arenas many times the size of the NSC theatre, it was all very well for Bettinson to go 'into a towering rage' at the effrontery of a boxer daring to have a manager to negotiate with the club on his behalf.[30] The world had changed. (It already had in professional soccer and rugby league, where the need of working-class players to be paid had led to significant breaks away from the ranks of the gentleman amateur.)

Another hypocrisy was on show in the early stages of the Wells–Johnson controversy: that this was just another contest, however unequal, between two ordinary boxers. In the wake of the riots after the Johnson–Jeffries fight of 1910 and the censoring of even the film of the contest, Wells–Johnson was inescapably and inevitably another clash between a black man and a white man. And a clash, moreover, where a black American promised a heavy beating for a white Englishman. This particular Englishman had recently spent three years in the army in India, keeping millions of brown men content with, or at least subservient to, the tiny white minority who ruled their country, a situation paralleled in many other countries in the Edwardian British Empire. Britain was a demonstrably less racist society in 1911 than the USA but there was still enough active British prejudice for many people to find such a potential beating publicly and privately disturbing.

Racism, stated or unstated, rather than issues of fair play, lay behind many of the protests. Had Wells been matched unequally with a black fighter whom he could be guaranteed to trounce, there would have been no such campaign. However, not everyone who signed petitions was a racist. Many Christians genuinely disliked boxing on the principle that hitting people was un-Christian; a principle to be upheld regardless of the skin colour of the participants. Of the 219 petitions received by the LCC, only 17 specifically mentioned the racial issue. The 17 were certainly not in accord with St Paul's words to the Galatians (3:28) that 'There is neither Jew nor Greek, there is neither slave nor free, there is neither male nor female; for you are all one in Christ Jesus.' Many another adjective repeated in the other petitions like 'barbaric', 'pagan', 'blasphemous', 'debasing', 'degrading', 'baser', 'baneful', 'evil', 'demoralising' and 'disgraceful' may still be coded references to emotions raised by the ethnicity of the contest in particular.

Across the Atlantic on 14 September, the *New York Times* took interest in the London controversy and repeated for its readers an editorial from an unidentified English newspaper to demonstrate the real issue:

> We have no sympathy with race antipathies, but the sight of a black man pounding a white man is far from attractive, and certainly cannot be considered as a public entertainment.[31]

(Presumably, the sight of a white man pounding a black man *would* be attractive and publicly entertaining.)

Two days later, the *New York Times* of 16 September specifically interpreted the petitions as made primarily on racial grounds:

> LONDON, Sept. 15 – A communication made public to-day by the National Free Church Council explaining that the Council is 'not attacking generally the art of self-defense' but only a specific contest, is taken as confirmation of the suggestion that the intervention against the Johnson–Wells battle is largely due to a fight between a colored man and a white man, which may lead to racial bitterness.[32]

In London, the Earl's Court press officer was also prepared to discuss the more awkward questions. How could the LCC, for example, threaten the Earl's Court licence for staging a prizefight when both Olympia and the Palladium had recently staged big boxing promotions unscathed? 'The only distinction between the Johnson–Wells contest and others was that this one might conceivably be complicated by the colour question. It might be urged that Imperial considerations rendered it undesirable that such a contest should take place at all.'[33]

There was no let-up in the campaign over the weekend of 16–17 September. On the Saturday, Meyer addressed a chosen audience at the Royal Albert Hall and explained that God (a powerful ally) had led him to try to stop the fight. Next morning, at his Regent's Park Chapel, he devoted his sermon to the theme 'The Temple of the Body', a further attack upon the fight, and prayed publicly for Johnson and Wells to be converted (converted to two white pacifists presumably).

Where did Meyer stand on the black/white issue? It was not his primary objection, but he did not hesitate to exploit it when it emerged as an effective factor in raising public consciousness. J. H. Shakespeare, his fellow Baptist and Secretary of the Baptist Union (President, F. B. Meyer), wrote to *The Times*, 18 September 1911, one day after Meyer's sermon, a letter which unhesitatingly tied the moral objections to the racial line. Meyer approved, if not actually dictated, the text:

It [the fight] cannot be separated from the racial animosities which are so perilous in the world today. The fight at San Reno cost scores of lives in subsequent riots. Whatever the issue might be, again black and white will be pitted against each other, in anger, revenge, and murder, especially in those lands like America in which the negro is the greatest of all problems. It is a dangerous responsibility to fan in any degree these smouldering fires.

Shakespeare then developed a further objection:

There can be no greater disservice to the negro race than to encourage it to seek a glory in physical force and in beating the white man. Booker Washington is incessant in the cry to his people, 'Educate, educate'. Slowly they are climbing the steep path, but every voice which exalts animal passion in them is that of an enemy. It matters not to us if an Englishman is beaten, for we have proved our place in the realms of courage, endurance, service, art, and learning. But to a race which has not yet achieved glory it is a crime to turn its ambitions to such glory as can be found in the Prize Ring.[34]

For all the apparent concern for the downtrodden Negro, it does not need a deep Freudian analysis to spot the transference of unconscious emotions going on here. The gravest American problem is not murderous intent towards blacks by whites; the problem is 'the Negro'. The classic white fears of 'anger, revenge and murder', and 'smouldering fires', and 'animal passion', all on the part of blacks, could hardly be more eloquently expressed.

The reference to Booker T. Washington in the letter is particularly interesting. Washington (1856–1915), son of a mixed-race slave mother and a white father, and born in Virginia, had claims to being white America's favourite black spokesman. Washington's gospel for blacks was patience, restraint and forbearance in the face of injustice and inequality; protest and agitation about their plight was useless until they attained economic equality by conforming to the white man's rules. Washington's formula for, for example, the black in the Southern States was to forgo the right to vote in favour of better job prospects, those prospects tied to vocational training for menial industrial jobs.

The other famous black spokesman of the day (and bitter opponent of Washington) was W. E. B. Du Bois (1868–1963) of Massachusetts, the founder of the National Association for the Advancement of Colored People (1910). Du Bois was the author of *The Souls of Black Folks* (1903), the quaintness of the title belying the fact that the book, like Du Bois's whole career, was geared towards the proper emancipation and equality of the black in American society. Towards Washington's gradualism, Du Bois was contemptuous.

Rivalry between Washington and Du Bois and their contradictory philosophies by 1910 spilled over into English Nonconformist circles, unsurprisingly in view of the strong part evangelicals had played in the anti-slavery movement of the early 19th century. Washington toured England in the autumn of 1910, appearing on many Nonconformist and evangelical platforms. His inbuilt conservatism meant he was particularly impressed by what he took to be English social deference and class order. He assured his English audiences that black adherents to his philosophy of advance by millimetres had already brought peace and harmony to American race relations. With breathtaking insularity, one English Congregationalist agreed with Washington, telling him that

Nonconformists in England were treated 'much as you are treated there'.

In the summer of 1911, Du Bois was in London at the First Universal Races Conference and gave the lie to Washington's comforting fantasies.[35] As a prominent Nonconformist and a vice-president of the Races Conference, Meyer shared the same platform and was very well aware also of Washington's speeches of the previous year. He gave no hint of absorbing Du Bois's contrary ideas, or of endorsing them. Meyer had lived for some time in South Africa, where ideas about race relations were hardly progressive, and where separate but equal theories about blacks and whites had been in practice as grotesque as in the Southern States. Even had Meyer been more liberally minded on the issue, endorsing the presence and lifestyle of Jack Johnson would have been a step too far.

Johnson frequented brothels for pleasures purveyed by white professionals, some of whom could be seen on his arm outside working hours. From 1910 he was frequently seen with the white Etta Terry Duryea, recently divorced wife of a racehorse owner, whom he married himself in January 1911. She, like many of his white lovers, found fidelity one of his lesser qualities.

He delighted in being the black cat ruffling the feathers of every WASP (White Anglo-Saxon Protestant) pigeon. He could be relied upon only to test tolerance to the limit. He was the living embodiment of all the secret racist fears of whites. He dominated all his white opponents so far, physically and psychologically. His muscular physique, before sybaritic pleasures took over from the ascetic discipline of the punch bag, was a thing of beauty. Just as he was attracted to white women, white women were attracted to him.

As some of his excellent biographers, Randy Roberts and Al-Tony Gilmore, for example, have argued, he became the living embodiment of the 'Bad N****r' syndrome, a stereotype offensively defined by whites as the black who refused to accept the humble role and subservient manners expected of an inferior.[36] Johnson behaved infuriatingly like an equal. His razor-sharp wit and intelligence made him a formidable verbal opponent and he consistently refused to be patronised. Gilmore's biography offers a wonderful selection of quotations from American newspapers to illustrate anti-Johnson opinions at work. The *San Francisco Examiner* of 1 July 1910 had a prize example of prejudice conquering perception:

> Johnson essentially African feels no deeper than the moment, sees no farther than his nose – which is flat and of the present … Incapable of anticipation … Johnson is safe in his soul shallowness and lack of imagination.[37]

As Meyer began his campaign in London, it is worth remembering that in the USA a similar crusade by the United Society of Christian Endeavour mobilised no less than *71,000* petitions, signed by over *four million* Christian members, and sent to the governor of every state where there was a possibility of the film of the Johnson v Jeffries fight being shown.[38] No such petitions were launched against the real barbarisms of time and place – mass lynchings of Johnson's fellow blacks. It was obvious that the coupling of the race issue with the agitation against Wells v Johnson would make that cause more effective.

Racist prejudices exist at all levels of society. The upper reaches of the Edwardian English establishment were not impervious. At what they took to be Johnson's effrontery, the NSC operated an unofficial ban thereafter against *all* black fighters. 'We have no prejudice against the fighting negro, but we would not run the risk of having to suffer another Jack Johnson,' in the words of Bettinson himself.[39] Bettinson ensured neither Johnson nor any other black fighter would appear henceforward at the NSC, nor, therefore, could ever contest a British title there.[40]

The difficulties the NSC had with other white boxers, Burns for example, did not result in a ban on all white fighters or all Canadians. The NSC's major historian puts it like this: 'The curious fact remains that Lonsdale Championship Belts were not available to coloured boxers – British though they might have been – up to a few years ago, when the British Boxing Board of Control altered that rule and awarded a Belt to Randolph Turpin.'[41] Turpin was awarded his (light-heavyweight) belt on 26 November 1956, when he defeated another black British fighter, Alex Buxton, at Leicester. For the record, when Turpin's brother Dick Turpin beat Vince Hawkins at Villa Park, Birmingham, on points over 15 rounds with the British middleweight title at stake on 28 June 1948, he was the first black fighter allowed to contest a British title for decades.

The fact about British boxing and black fighters was not so much 'curious' as ugly. For 37 years between the agitation over Johnson, and the emergence of the Turpins, black British fighters were continually denied the opportunities that were rightfully theirs. The characteristically impulsive reaction by Bettinson to Johnson's unreliability was the first in a series of decisions to eliminate black fighters from their proper place in the sport. The initial step was endorsed and perpetuated by the NSC's autocratic president, Lord Lonsdale. Lonsdale used his position as British boxing's most prominent and distinguished supporter to wield considerable influence behind the scenes. In the political world before the Great War, Parliament met for barely half a year. Inevitably, business was undertaken and far-reaching decisions made in drawing room conversations, in private letters, across dining tables and in the upholstered comfort of club armchairs. Many such decisions were, by their nature, left unrecorded.

Nevertheless, buried away in sundry forgotten files is plenty of evidence that Lord Lonsdale was personally involved in acts of discrimination against black boxers, including the one that got Wells v Johnson cancelled. In late 1922, plans were announced to match the British heavyweight Joe Beckett against Battling Siki, the world light-heavyweight champion and recent mauler of the glamorous Georges Carpentier (24 September 1922 in Paris by KO in round six).

Siki, from Senegal, was sufficiently flamboyant as to make Johnson appear a Benedictine monk. Wild in the ring and out, Siki emptied the boulevard *trottoirs* of Paris by parading with two lions on a leash and firing a pistol into the air to attract attention.

Siki was not thought to be the Home Office's most desirable visitor. Edward Shortt (Home Secretary 1918–22) knew

about the planned Siki v Beckett bout because Lonsdale had tipped him off but was out of office before he could take any action. On 1 November 1922, Lonsdale followed up with a visit and a private letter to Shortt's successor, Conservative William Bridgeman (Home Secretary 1922–24):

> As I told you when you were kind enough to see me, I was under an obligation to the late Home Secretary [Shortt] to inform the Home Office when a contest between a coloured and a white man was likely to take place: and I have no hesitation in saying that I believe this contest between a white and a black man is contrary to the interests of the Nation. At my interview with Mr Winston Churchill, and afterwards with Mr McKenna [Churchill's immediate successor as Home Secretary who served 1911–15], they were both very strongly of this opinion, and told me that they would on all occasions stop such contests as detrimental to the interests of the Nation.
>
> As I told you, I felt bound to trouble you, having made a definite promise to the late Home Secretary [Shortt] that I would report any such matches that are being made, and I assume from your letter that your feelings on the subject are the same as those of your predecessors, and they are certainly mine – that matches as between white and black men have a detrimental effect on their respective races, and they are michievous [sic] and of a far-reaching nature.[42]

Thus the secret cooperation between Lonsdale, Churchill and his successors began in 1911, as the above letter makes clear, and gives the lie to both men's public utterances that their objections were strictly sporting. Lonsdale, for example, said to the *Sporting Life* in late September 1911 and quoted in *The Times* 23 September 1911:

> I have been asked to join the movement to persuade the Home Secretary to take action in stopping the contest. I cannot see on what grounds the Home Secretary can possibly do so. For why should this special contest be more likely to cause a breach of the peace or a disturbance than one in the National Sporting Club or in any other sporting club in London?

In 1913, there was a projected match at the NSC between Sam Langford and the German-American Frank Klaus. It also fell foul of Lonsdale's secret alliance with successive Home Secretaries. As the relevant Home Office file says:

> The fight did not take place as Lord Lonsdale used his influence to stop it.[43]

The long private and confidential letter Lord Lonsdale wrote to the Home Office on 16 March 1913 is also extant and betrays his self-inflicted dilemma.[44] Langford v Klaus was an attractive boxing proposition.

There was hardly a more upright ring citizen than Sam Langford. Yet it would be another black v white contest, and that, since 1911, had wider implications:

The handsome French boxer Georges Carpentier (1894–1975) went from tiny flyweight to almost heavyweight, humiliating many British champions en route.

I feel bound to acquaint you of the proposed contest, and to ask whether you think there would be any objection to it taking place at the National Sporting Club, where I have emphatically refused to take part in, or allow to take place, any such competition pending enquiries.

Lonsdale was very determined that if the NSC could not hold the clash, the commercial promoters should not get their mercenary hands on it either. He was also at pains to keep his private relationship with the Home Office secret.

But if you think it better not to have the contest I would immediately say, without giving reasons, that the proposed match could not be proceeded with – that we could not expect it. At the same time if this were so, I think it would be very detrimental to the interests of Boxing if the contest were allowed to take place at any of these money-making establishments, where there might be trouble … The two men are particularly well-conducted and respectable, but still one cannot overcome the fact that the competition is a 'coloured' one.

In 1913, on the Home Secretary's desk alongside Lonsdale's latest letter was a supporting plea from the Director of Public Prosecutions dated 26 March 1913:

I much hope that the answer to Lord Lonsdale's very proper letter will be that the Secretary of State greatly deprecates physical contests of the description which is proposed between a white and a black man as being undesirable in themselves, demoralizing to the spectators of them, and as very far reaching in their mischievous consequences … were a tacit sanction to be given to the National Sporting Club, great difficulty might be treated to Police and other authorities in forbidding meetings when the consequences might be disastrous.[45]

Unsurprisingly, the contest was called off, as was a possible clash between Sam Langford and the white American Gunboat Smith in 1914. ('Lord Lonsdale, after obtaining the support of the Home Secretary, exerted his influence to stop the contest.')[46] The prevention of these high-profile international black v white contests created in turn an ugly and discriminatory tradition. The racism seeped into the very roots of British boxing, and poisoned the previously tolerant domestic scene where, as we saw in 1909 and 1910, most blacks were seen as boxers like any other.

Back then, *The Times* had reported black/white boxing perfectly objectively, and had even had a good word for Johnson:

In private life, however, the conqueror of Jeffries is an amiable person with a fund of quaint humour and a sportsmanlike trust in human nature … On the whole … he is a far more pleasant person to meet in a room than any of the white champions of complicated ancestry whom America exports from time to time to these unwilling shores.[47]

Contrast this with the virulent editorial *The Times* published in November 1922 about the Beckett/Siki proposal and referring back yet again to the disorder following Johnson v Jeffries. The tone would have gone down well in a local newspaper in Alabama.

These are risks which the British Empire in particular, with its vast coloured population in all parts of the world, cannot afford to run.
Boxing in itself is a fine and manly sport. But boxing matches between white men and blacks, to be photographed for the delectation of coloured races all over the world, have become a dangerous anachronism. To allow them to take place on English soil would in these days be an act of suicidal folly and the action of the Home Office in this particular case will meet, we are convinced, with the warm approval of the general public.[48]

Lord Lonsdale's determination to keep boxing white was also his main concern in March 1925, when a Conservative MP, Commander Kennedy, proposed sponsoring a Private Bill in the House of Commons to 'legalise boxing'. A note in the Home Office papers of the day, when the Home Secretary was the Conservative William Joynson-Hicks (1924–29), shows that Lonsdale had made one of his backstairs visits to put his case.[49] Lonsdale argued that boxing was already fully legal (as we have seen previously, it was not). His second point can be gleaned from the handwritten note added to the file by Joynson-Hicks, 'that nothing shall be done to prevent the occasional use by the Home Office of the powers of the Court to step in and prevent black and white contests. He is afraid, and I [Joynson-Hicks] agree with him, that the passing of that Bill [i.e. Kennedy's Private Bill] might render it more difficult than it is at present for the Courts to intervene.' Without government backing, such a bill was bound to fail and did.

The worst upshot arising from such reactionary opinions was that they were formally incorporated into the constitution of an English official sporting body in 1929. On an evil day for British sport, 15 February 1929, ten members of the British Boxing Board of Control, which was now running boxing, met at Anderton's Hotel in Fleet Street to consider the Championship Rules by which future titles would be decided. Under the chairmanship of Colonel R. E. Middleton, and the secretaryship of the autocratic Charles Donmall, whose high-handed ways became notorious, a significant decision was taken.[50] It can be read in the Board's minutes:

Regarding Paragraph 4, this was fully discussed, but before finally passing same, the Chairman was asked whether he would place before the President, the Rt. Hon. The Earl of Lonsdale, K.G., the suggestion that the paragraph should read as follows: –
'Contestants must be legally British subjects and *born of white parents*. Must be resident not less than two years in the British Isles.'[51] [Italics added]

Twelve days later, the Board formally adopted the amending paragraph and the Revised Rules, predictably given Lonsdale's thorough approval.[52] In other words, an official British sporting body deliberately incorporated a discriminatory racist clause into the heart of a formerly open sport. For the record, this had the further dubious distinction of preceding, by a few years, the Nazi regime's formal exclusion of Jewish boxers from German amateur boxing from 6 April 1933, a decree of parallel immorality.[53]

Having followed through to the ugly subsequent consequences, let us return to the agitation of September 1911, where the prevention campaign against Wells v Johnson was gathering further momentum. James White was understandably beginning to worry about the possible impact of Meyer's initiatives. White had not cared to be told that he was being prayed for, nor that he was planning a bout more brutal than any in history. His response was to emphasise that the rules drawn up to govern the event were stricter than any prevailing at the NSC, but that he might still cancel the event, providing Meyer indemnified him against potential losses.[54] Tactically, this was not astute – a public offer conceding that a promoter's cancellation was a possibility. White's naivety about the way things worked in English politics would feature again before Meyer's campaign was over.

Meyer, politically shrewder, suggested that if White cancelled, he, Meyer, would open a fund to reimburse White for out-of-pocket expenses and would contribute £25 himself. White was not so naïve as to believe that collection plates would be going around the churches and chapels on behalf of a needy boxing promoter. Nevertheless, he had been outmanoeuvred skilfully and made to sound much less public-spirited and open-hearted than Meyer in his reply: 'At present I am assured of a fair return for my risk, and to give up that would be too great a sacrifice.' He went on to claim, probably accurately, that about £12,000 would have been invested by the time Wells and Johnson climbed through the ropes. This gave more ammunition to those who believed sport and fair play disappeared when money and profits came in.[55]

White made a further offer to set up a committee of 12 (six from the sporting community, and six to be nominated by Meyer) to preview a film of the fight. If this motley gathering decided 'that it would be degrading or contrary to public morals', White would destroy the negative and open a fund to reimburse the owners of the film rights.

Meyer astutely turned this offer down. However, his reply to White amply demonstrates that he had learned nothing either. On ethnicity he was as unenlightened as Jack London:

The eyes of millions of the black and subject people are watching the issue of the contest ... as being in their judgment a decisive test in the matter of racial superiority ...[How did Meyer know this?]

and

... the present contest is not wholly one of skill, because on the one side is added the instinctive passion of the negro race, which is so differently constituted to our own, and in the present instance will be aroused to do the utmost that immense animal development can do to retain the Championship …[56]

On Wednesday, 20 September, in the USA, the *New York Times* was insufferably complacent about the debate taking place in London. It also indulged in a shameless historical rewrite of its own panic of the previous year:

Though the negro whipped his adversary with particular thoroughness and ridiculous ease, the consequences were nothing more terrifying than a few barroom brawls, and the race-fellows of the victor obligingly refrained from doing any of the terrible things which many professed experts felt sure they would do the moment news came that their champion had beaten the most efficient combination of strength, skill and courage the white race could produce.

The fact is that both races … appreciated the littleness and the unimportance of what the battle proved, and the elation of the negroes was as superficial and brief as was the humiliation of the whites. The pillars of the Republic stood as firmly after the fight as before it, and only failure to heed an American lesson accounts for the fact that the Britishers are having exactly the sort of panic we did and are making desperate efforts to save their WELLS from the defeat which they apparently think he is sure to suffer if he and the swarthy JOHNSON come

together in the only ring that has four corners.

To draw a color line in pugilism is a wild absurdity. The relative status of the two races cannot possibly be determined or affected in this way. Victor and vanquished are alike negligible in estimating racial superiorities and inferiorities.[57]

Unfortunately, the 'Britishers' in London declined to be reassured by the *New York Times*'s volte-face. Nowhere more so than behind the scenes at the Home Office, where letters from James White, J. P. Meyer and the Commissioner of Police of the Metropolis were all awaiting Churchill's attention. Telegrams were meanwhile going back and forth between the Home Office and the law officers, and back and forth between the Home Office and Home Secretary Churchill, presently up at Balmoral, and between Churchill and Prime Minister Asquith. Churchill's northern trip involved stays at Balmoral (the Scottish castle that served as the royal family's summer holiday home), and at Asquith's home at North Berwick. Churchill and Asquith (another trained and experienced barrister) thus had ample opportunity for off-the-record chats about the projected fight.

Meyer took it upon himself to pay a personal visit to the Home Office on Wednesday, 20 September 'to consult the officials there on procedure' and talked about taking a delegation up to Churchill at Balmoral to deliver his national memorial.[58] It was obvious that in these fraught circumstances the traditional English political solution to a difficult issue, procrastination, would not do.

By Friday, 22 September, the most important politicians and civil servants involved had the advantage of a five-page report from Sir John Simon, the legally acute Solicitor General. The report outlined the legal position as he understood it.[59] How tricky this really was will not have escaped anyone who has read Chapter 2 of this book.

Simon seized immediately on the distinction the law made between a sparring match won or lost on points (legal), and a 'prize fight' (illegal). Interestingly, what made a prizefight into a prizefight was *not* the money/stake/prize, *not* whether the fight was undertaken in anger, and *not even* the wearing/non-wearing of gloves. The fight was illegal 'if the object and intent of the combatants is to subdue each other by violent blows until one can endure it no longer'. The operation of Queensberry Rules, where a knockout is allowed – for example, Johnson v Jeffries at Reno – is what makes the event illegal. Moreover, 'We none of us think that there can be any question that what is contemplated on Oct. 2nd is illegal. It follows that Johnson and Wells and also Mr White, the promoter, of the contest, together with the referees, seconds and other officials are all contemplating a breach of the peace.'[60]

Simon anticipated the case the defendants would put up if White, Wells and Johnson, referee Corri and others were to be summoned to the magistrates' court at Bow Street and asked for large sureties that they would not commit such a breach of the peace:

No doubt they would make much of the fact that contests, less notorious, but somewhat

Carpentier's 1921 meeting with Jack Dempsey would be an unprecedented universal sporting and media event.

Bain Collection, Prints & Photographs Division, Library of Congress, LC-DIG-ggbain-50386

similar in character, regularly occur at the National Sporting Club and elsewhere in London, and that members of the Police Force officially attend some of such contests. They would also urge that the real reason why the Magistrate was appealed to was *because of the colour of one of the combatants.*[61] [Italics added]

There was another difficulty. White might put up the sureties and go ahead with the fight!

This would be a most unfortunate result, for it is plain that it would not be practicable or wise for Police Officers to interfere in the course of the contest itself in view of the number and character of the spectators. [!] Moreover, *the object of preventing a meeting in the Prize Ring of a black and a white man in the Capital of the Empire is only partially secured …* [Italics added]

Simon also pointed out that the showing of a film of an illegal assault was not in itself illegal, and possible 'consequential evils' might still ensue.

Simon's suggested solution was ingenious: prevent Johnson from entering the country by declaring him an undesirable alien. Johnson was training in Paris, and clearly no Johnson, no fight. A British citizen could neither be deported nor refused entry without appeal and possible legal redress. An alien already in the country had similar rights. But an alien prevented from entering could appeal only to his own government. And the US government would be unlikely to take offence at Johnson's exclusion, 'if it was made perfectly clear that the exclusion was entirely exceptional and was due to a desire to prevent the evil consequences of a black and white contest'. Even the notorious Aliens Act of 1905 could not be stretched to cover Johnson, and a refusal to accept him would have to be taken solely on the Home Office's initiative and would be without precedent.

It would have been quite in character for the impetuous Churchill to be attracted by the novelty and boldness of this idea, but wiser heads prevailed. Sir William Byrne, the Home Office official in charge of the affair, took soundings at the Foreign Office only to be told that nothing in the case could justify so drastic an action. Furthermore, Prime Minister Asquith, whatever he may have said to Churchill up in North Berwick in private, sent a telegram to Churchill at Balmoral: 'I am against exclusion.'[62]

The private letter Churchill wrote to his wife Clementine on 24 September 1911 from Balmoral contains the following sentences:

> I have made up my mind to try to stop the Wells–Johnson contest. The terms are utterly unsporting and unfair.[63]

This strongly suggests that Churchill's motives for deciding to intervene had nothing to do with race relations, nothing to do with concern for peace in sensitive areas of the British Empire, and everything to do with his concern for sport. Indeed, this is the comforting conclusion reached by Stuart Mews in his article on the subject previously cited (note 11 to this chapter). Mews

had not seen the Home Office files that make it crystal clear that Churchill's concern was all about what he saw as the undesirability of white men meeting black men in the ring.

For all his multitudinous talents, and for all the debts owed him by generations of British citizens, there is no doubt that Churchill was a racist. He was so, much more than Lord Lonsdale, whose public pronouncements in September 1911 similarly hid his private feelings behind the polite fiction that excess purses and inequality of matchmaking were his sole concerns. Lonsdale's difficulty was that much as he wanted this particular contest called off, he loved boxing and feared for its legal future. With the solitary exception of polo, the one sport he had tried himself, Churchill detested all forms of organised sport, team or individual. In the honest words of one of his present-day champions, Andrew Roberts: 'Churchill was more profoundly racist than most … He was a convinced white – not to say Anglo-Saxon – supremacist and thought in terms of race to a degree that was remarkable even by the standards of his own time.'[64]

Andrew Roberts, and other less favourably minded Churchill biographers such as Clive Ponting, have provided plenty of lurid examples of this uglier side to the national hero.[65] He was a disciple of the pseudo-science of eugenics and, had he been allowed to, would have introduced the compulsory castration and sterilisation of the 'feeble-minded' lest they dilute the national gene pool. (Shades of his arch-enemy Hitler.) His biological determinism took him into very dubious areas: 'Why be apologetic about Anglo-Saxon

superiority? We are superior,' he said, and he saw as a threat to this superiority, an 'ever-swelling sea of black humanity' and 'this black peril'. Decades later, he was claiming that no injustice had been done in history to the Native Americans or to the Aborigines of Australia: 'I do not admit that a wrong has been done to these people by the fact that a stronger race, a higher grade race, or at any rate, a more wordly-wise race, to put it that way, has come in and taken their place.' Even late in life Churchill refused to see the charming Otto Preminger film with Oscar Hammerstein lyrics, *Carmen Jones* of 1954, because he disliked 'blackness'.[66]

However virulent his private views, publicly stopping the fight was still a tricky proposition. Natural justice for Johnson was not the Home Office's first priority. But if Johnson's entry could not be stopped, resort to the riskier magistrates' court was still possible. Better still, perhaps the inexperienced White could be bluffed into calling the fight off himself if he thought that the Home Office had the powers to cancel the event forthwith.

Late on Saturday, 23 September, the Home Office received a long telegram from Churchill proposing a devious plan of action.[67] In conjunction with the Solicitor General, the Home Office officials were to announce that legal advice had found the proposed fight to be illegal, and a potential breach of the peace which the government was determined to prohibit. Should the promoters persist they would be threatened with drastic action. This was a bluff because straight prohibition was beyond Churchill's powers. True, the magistrates' court could always summon the fighters and officials and bind them over to give sureties *at the very time they were expected in the ring* – a clever if underhanded device. Or, as a last resort, Crown prerogative could be used to stop Johnson entering the country.

As it happened, James White, out of his depth in this moral, legal and political morass, was getting more and more worried. He had already written to the Chief Commissioner of the Police on 21 September 1911 pleading, 'I am further desirous of acting strictly in accordance with the authorities,' and asking for an interview on the subject.[68] The letter was sent on to the Home Office, and Byrne sent the eventual reply after the receipt of Churchill's telegram:

> I have received instructions from the Home Secretary to communicate to you the views of H. M. Government with respect to the contest in question, and I shall be glad if you will be so good as to call upon me here at 5 o'cl. or any later hour today convenient to you.
>
> If you wish to be accompanied by your legal adviser there will be no objection.[69]

White, two advisers in tow, went to the Home Office on Monday, 25 September 1911. He faced Sir William Byrne and two civil servants (Blackwell and Harris). Byrne opened the proceedings by reading out Churchill's planned announcement:

> He has instructed me to convey to you the decision of the Government, which I shall do in his exact words: –

> 'The Home Secretary, after full enquiry and having taken the best advice, has arrived at the conclusion that what is contemplated is illegal, and unless the promoters voluntarily abandon the contest, steps will be at once taken to prevent any such illegality taking place.'[70]

The transcript of the meeting makes for entertaining reading as the occasion turned more and more Kafkaesque. Poor White sought to cooperate with the authorities and to find an acceptable formula for the fight to take place legally. Byrne and his assistants might have been at Lord's cricket ground playing dead bats to every tricky delivery that spun towards them.

Their poker-faced ability to suggest mighty legal powers, without actually specifying any of them, was masterly and in the very best bureaucratic tradition. There was to be none of the cosy private gentlemen's agreement that the department clearly enjoyed with Lonsdale:

> Mr JAMES WHITE: The Home Secretary cannot compel us to abandon it altogether, I suppose?

> SIR WILLIAM BYRNE: No, not so far as the Secretary of State is concerned. His decision, as you see, is that unless the proposal is abandoned, steps will be taken to prevent it taking place if it is found to be illegal.

> Mr WHITE: I suppose the Home Secretary does not base his decision on any Act of Parliament, or give reasons for it.

> SIR WILLIAM BYRNE: Except that after full inquiry he is satisfied that the proposed contest is illegal.

Try as he might, White could get no constructive responses at all:

> Mr WHITE: … Are there no conditions that could be imposed upon me under which it could be allowed?

> Mr BLACKWELL: Any question of legality or illegality is a question for a court of law. The decision of the Home Secretary is that unless the contest is abandoned, he will have to get the decision of a court of law as to whether it could be permitted or not.

And shortly afterwards:

> Mr WHITE: This is what I want to get at. There must be some form of contest which is legal. If not, you cannot allow other contests to take place every night which are under the same conditions as mine.

> SIR WILLIAM BYRNE: That is a question which does not arise. If the other contests are illegal, that would be no defence for the illegality which the Secretary of State believes to be in contemplation.

None of White's appeals was going to make the slightest difference:

> Mr WHITE: … If a boxing exhibition is legal at all, how can

I make this legal? There must be a legal way of holding a boxing contest.

MR BLACKWELL: That is a question to put to the magistrate. If you wish to have a binding legal decision, that is an argument which you should put forward in support of your case.

When White pleaded correctly that this threat had not materialised except at the last moment, even though advertising for the bout had begun eight weeks before, and that he might now lose £12,000 in the event of cancellation, no compassion was forthcoming:

SIR WILLIAM BYRNE: I am very sorry; but I must point out that people who undertake the promotion of a contest which in the opinion of the Secretary of State is illegal, must not complain if they suffer inconvenience from it …

Significantly, from start to finish of this farcical session, reminiscent of a script for the television series *Yes, Minister,* not a word was said about the real Home Office objection – that London was planning to host a black v white boxing match.

Towards the end of the session, one of White's advisers (Woodhouse) suggested White took the initiative and went directly to the magistrates' court to establish the legality of the proposed contest. Had White indeed gone directly to Bow Street and pleaded his case, one wonders what the magistrate's response might have been. Furthermore, once White was outside the intimidating environment of the Home Office, he seems to have sensed that the oblique answers he had received concealed the limited options open to the Home Secretary. He decided to go ahead with the fight.

With the evident intention of strengthening his legal ground, he called in Johnson and Wells that very evening. Together they amended the Articles of Agreement – no longer would the fight be under Marquess of Queensberry's Rules but under NSC rules.[71] White was beginning to act with a little more political nous. He had been learning in a hard school but learning fast.

There were two significant implications to this seemingly minor change. The Queensberry Rules defined a knockout with brutal precision: 'Should the man fail to rise within ten seconds the referee to declare his opponent the winner.' The NSC rules had been adopted, remember, after the Old Bailey trial of 1901 (Chapter 2), which had threatened boxing's very existence. They had glossed the knockout thus: 'A contestant failing to continue the contest at the expiration of ten seconds shall not be awarded any marks for that round, and the contest shall terminate. The referee shall decide all contests in favour of the contestant who obtains the greatest number of marks [i.e. points].'[72] By adopting the NSC rules, White could argue that Wells v Johnson was not a prizefight and illegal (as Simon's report had indicated), but an exhibition of skill. Were it still to be found illegal despite the change, White could then reasonably argue that his event was an exact parallel to those taking place every Monday night at the NSC, and regularly tolerated by the Home Office and every other authority.

Where was the justice in tolerating one and banning the other?

As any American reader might confirm, litigation can become an infectious disease. Just as the promoter contemplated going to Bow Street to stave off the Home Office, and the Home Office contemplated going to Bow Street to avert the event, two wholly new and unexpected litigants entered the fray. The very evening that White, Wells and Johnson were amending the fight rules, Mr Justice Lush, the High Court judge, was entertaining at his Bexleyheath home a barrister representing the Variety Theatres Control Association. This barrister was seeking an injunction to prevent John Arthur Johnson, pugilist, from appearing in the Earl's Court ring on 2 October as he had previously signed a contract to appear that night at the Birmingham Hippodrome! Johnson's unreliability in such matters was notorious, and his music hall tours often left a train of angry theatre managers and impresarios in their wake. The Birmingham complaint was incidental, but almost certainly authentic.

The other unexpected litigant was the Metropolitan District Railway Company. The company were freeholders of the Earl's Court venue and alarmed by the possibility that their leaseholder, the Earl's Court Company, by allowing the unwelcome fight, might lose the premises' valuable licence. They sought an injunction to stop the event, particularly as the leaseholders had so clearly passed all control over order and propriety to the boxing promoter. The Earl's Court Company was duly served with a notice that the Railway Company would be at the High Court before Mr Justice Lush on Wednesday, 27 September seeking an injunction to restrain the company from allowing the contest, lest it endanger the renewal of the licence.[73] Lush was to hear the Birmingham Hippodrome case about Johnson the same day.

White's difficulties were multiplying. Because he had not yet been to Bow Street to pre-empt the Home Office, the Home Office went to Bow Street to pre-empt him. On Tuesday, 26 September, the Director of Public Prosecutions, Sir Charles Matthews, applied to Bow Street to have White, the boxers and their managers summoned as intending to commit a breach of the peace at Earl's Court on 2 October. No less than three relevant cases around the fight were up for decision on 27 September.

By far the best public spectacle was offered by the personal appearances of Wells and Johnson and their supporters at Bow Street court to show good cause why they should not be bound over to keep the peace on 2 October. Had it been possible, as many boxing supporters as would have been at the fight would have crowded into the public gallery to hear the fun. Unfortunately, only 100 spectators were allowed in (and that included Meyer and some of his supporters). Thousands of others lined the Covent Garden streets outside the court and cheered Wells and Johnson as they made their way through solid traffic to defend themselves.

Wells was his usual diffident self, politely acknowledging the crowd's cheers but looking somewhat embarrassed by the fuss. Johnson arrived in an open-topped car, immaculately dressed, smiling broadly and insouciantly raising a kid-gloved hand in response to the applause, like a king on the way to his coronation. He was no more fazed by his coming duel with the English courts than he had been intimidated by racist abuse in Sydney and Reno. He had decided to defend himself.

The defence opened with a request for an adjournment for two days. Had it been granted, they intended to brief F. E. Smith (later Lord Birkenhead) to represent them (all, that is, except Johnson). Smith's savage wit and forensic skill were already famous. Because the fight was a mere five days away, the magistrate Mr Marsham decided the hearing should not be postponed, but he conceded the defence's right to postpone their cross-examinations until next day or later.[74]

The prosecution began with their own heavyweight, Sir John Simon, the Solicitor General, and the author of the legal report prepared for Churchill. Unsurprisingly, he concentrated his attack upon boxing's legality, demonstrating that the wearing of gloves or limitations upon the number of rounds made no essential legal difference. He reminded the court that Johnson's fights with Burns, with Ketchel and with Jeffries had all come to an end before their scheduled number of rounds. (At this point Wells was heard to chuckle, but this was his way of showing that Johnson's record did not intimidate him, rather than a contribution to legal commentary.) Simon made play with White's late amendments to the original fight agreement – the expansion of the gloves from four to five ounces and the substitution of the original Queensberry Rules by the NSC's. He then made the telling point that a knockout, however scored, resulted in victory and was therefore a principal object of every fighter. This made such an event a prizefight (illegal), as opposed to a sparring match or exhibition 'which did not contemplate or involve the injury of one's opponent so as to prevent the continuance of the contest [and therefore] was clearly legal'.

Only one prosecution witness was called, Superintendent Duncan McIntyre of the Metropolitan Police, the officer responsible for the Earl's Court area. McIntyre brought cuttings from the *Sporting Life* and read out detailed accounts of Johnson's other title defences, supporting the accounts with recourse to a modest library of boxing record books in front of him. Johnson immediately objected – how could an *English* newspaper be authoritative on American events thousands of miles away? Johnson v McIntyre was as much a mismatch as Johnson v a flyweight. Johnson pounced on him as lethally as he had on Ketchel:

JAJ: Why did you say that I knocked Burns out in the 14th round? Don't look at the book! I object to your looking at a book every time I ask you a question. Did you say I knocked Tommy Burns out?

DMcI: Yes, but I corrected myself. I said at first that you knocked him out, but I find that the police interfered.

JAJ: Are you familiar with the Marquess of Queensberry Rules?

DMcI: No, not very familiar.

JAJ: The witness does not know what he is talking about. If

he only goes by the book, his evidence is very thin. How do you know that if Johnson and Mr Wells box on October 2 there will be a breach of the peace?

DMcI: I did not say so. I said I apprehend there will be a breach of the peace.

JAJ: I apprehend laughter in the court. Did you see Bill Lang and Sam Langford box?

DMcI: No.

JAJ: Did they commit a breach of the peace?

DMcI: I don't know.

JAJ: Did Langford and Hague break the peace?

DMcI: I don't know.

JAJ: Have you ever seen a championship contest?

DMcI: No.

JAJ: Have you ever seen a boxing contest?

DMcI: No.

JAJ: You have no idea what they are?

DMcI: No.

JAJ: So you know nothing about it?

DMcI: No.

JAJ: The witness may go; I am through.[75]

The magistrate must have contemplated stopping the contest to avoid the superintendent further unnecessary punishment. In any case, the hearing was adjourned at this point until Friday,

when the other defendants would have F. E. Smith at their disposal. One doubts Smith could have done much better than the world heavyweight champion in holding the prosecution up to ridicule. Between them, Johnson and Smith had a fighting chance of repeating Marshall Hall's success of 1901. (See Chapter 2.) Along with the Wells/Johnson fight, that possibility became one of history's great might-have-beens.

The Friday resumption never took place, because any Bow Street decision over the event was rendered redundant by the Metropolitan Railway Company's victory over the Earl's Court leaseholders in the High Court. Like most such leases, the relevant document barely conceded the tenants' right to breathe without special permission. Specifically, it insisted that:

> … exhibitions, entertainments, or amusements shall be of a high class … conducted with due regard to the maintenance of order, and shall be in no way contrary to decency or morality, *and shall not endanger or in any way injuriously affect any of the licences in force for the premises*[76] [Italics added].

The judge concluded that the freeholders had shown that Wells v Johnson *might* endanger the renewal of the licence and were therefore entitled to an interim injunction as a result. The implications were considerable, but there was no argument about one thing: Wells v Johnson was stone dead.

A reassembly of all the participants took place at Bow Street on Thursday afternoon, 28 September. White's solicitor stated that the event had been

cancelled because of the High Court decision over the venue and asked to have the proceedings against White formally withdrawn. Sir John Simon emphasised that the government's objections had been to this particular contest, not to boxing in general, and agreed that no useful purpose would be served by continuing the case.

A curious and little-known aspect of the whole affair was that various affidavits in favour of boxing had been laid before the judge from those concerned with the future of the sport. Astonishingly, one came from Lord Lonsdale, who was prepared to swear blatantly in public to opinions the absolute opposite of those he had urged in the privacy of the Home Office:

> In his opinion there could be nothing brutal or base in the proposed match. From his knowledge of the promoter (Mr White), he was satisfied that the contest would be carried out on proper lines. He failed to see in what particular the Wells–Johnson match differed from many that had gone before to none of which objection had been raised … He saw no reason why the Earl's Court licence should be objected to because the contest took place there …[77]

Lonsdale's new opinions were specifically rejected by the judge, who said that there was a strong case to be made for boxing contests, but not for this one, and that the very strength of opinion against it, and its subsequent notoriety, were strong confirmation of the freeholders' concern. One can only interpret Lonsdale's volte-face as a

Machiavellian public stance to conceal his private influence and real feelings, or as blind panic when it seemed that agitation about one particular contest might get the whole sport declared illegal.

The potential threat to professional boxing was of great concern to the *Boxing News and Athletic Chronicle*:

The Home Office has stated the Johnson–Wells contest to be illegal; there is no law on the subject, only the previous ruling of a judge, and we are left in the unfortunate position of not knowing how boxing stands in relation to the law. Had the case been fought through to a finish a decision would have been come to that would have clearly defined the position, and the trial would have been regarded as a test case, but we are left in the usual 'muddle', and completely in the dark, or, rather, no wiser than we were, about the legal position concerning boxing … The trouble was Johnson, but it might so easily have been the sport of which he is the champion!

Will it be the case one day?[78]

This editorial was very much to the point. Was there any difference between banning Johnson and banning the sport? Churchill had declared the sport to be illegal (while concealing his real motives), so it was unsurprising that his declaration had caused great concern within boxing. On 26 September 1911, the afternoon before the relevant legal hearings, several NSC members and other prominent well-wishers (including clergymen) gathered at the Hotel Cecil to express their concern at the implications of Churchill's pronouncement. (Continuing his tactics of playing both ends against the middle, Lord Lonsdale [further concealing his true motives] sent the meeting a telegram of regret for his absence, and a message of support that said deceitfully: 'Cannot understand Home Secretary, as when similar case occurred; "Slavin-McAuliffe", Judge decided in men's favour.'[79])

The protestors were not to know in their ignorance of all the backdoor political manoeuvres that nothing could have suited the Home Office and the legal authorities better than to have the position of boxing as ambiguous as possible. To have actually banned boxing might have pleased the occupiers of the plain pews of the Nonconformist chapels. But there were no political gains to be had from alienating the many followers of boxing, the immaculately dressed occupants of carriages rolling up to big promotions at Earl's Court, along with the mostly disenfranchised proletarian masses sweatily packed into The Ring or Wonderland.

Neither would it have been wise to go beyond the underground racism operating throughout the Wells/Johnson affair and openly adopt a legal device to make something permissible for a white man, yet illegal for a black man. (The turbulent course of 20th-century American social history provides evidence enough of what a folly that would have been.) Prime Minister Asquith saw immediately that to exclude Johnson from the country would have had mighty implications. Just so, legal discrimination against Johnson because of his skin would have undermined the operations of the law throughout the British Empire – a huge portion of the whole world.

Nevertheless, *Boxing World* and the Hotel Cecil protestors were correct to fear for the future of boxing. Before October was out, two stupendous new promotions were announced.[80] At the Empire Skating Rink in Sparkbrook, Birmingham, an arena potentially holding 12,000 people at prices from 5s. to five guineas, a contest was announced for the world featherweight championship, a gold belt, a purse of £2,600 and side stakes of £200 a man. The date, 2 December 1911; the boxers involved, the world's most famous Midlander, the dynamic and aggressive Owen Moran, and the Welsh hero, Peerless Jim Driscoll. For the first time since Moran's many triumphs in the USA, his local supporters would see him in the flesh.

Coupled with this major event was another: the winner would go on to contest a £4,000 purse at Olympia in Derby week (June) of 1912 against the Machiavellian American box of tricks, Abe Attell. (The Matt Wells no-decision bout with Attell, where Wells had demonstrated his clear superiority, had only just taken place on 20 September in New York, and gave an added piquancy to these projected fights.) Moran, Driscoll, Attell – between them, the events promised more collective sleight of hand than a Magic Circle convention.

Unfortunately, the next day's *Birmingham Post* (12 October 1911) published a letter from 'JEH' showing that what was prestidigitation for some was pure thuggery for others: 'Let me express the fervent hope that, whoever the authority may be, they will take such steps as will prevent our city or suburbs being a dumping ground for exhibitions of so debasing a character'. Following this first indication that not all the citizens of Birmingham wished to see Moran and his fellow boxers on his home ground, there were other protests too. Relevant cuttings from the Birmingham papers, and a three-page memorandum from a local coroner were duly sent to London to the Home Office on 14 October 1911 by C. H. Rafter, the Chief Constable of Birmingham, together with his own personal plea to have the fight banned:

> The Queensberry Rule as to the knock out blow seems to convert what would otherwise be a mere boxing contest of skill, into a prize-fight.
>
> I think this fight should be stopped; and I ask for the assistance of the Public Prosecutor in the matter.[81]

Churchill's and Simon's pinpointing of the dubious legal grounds on which professional boxing operated had created a context where such challenges were considerably more likely. Conveniently for Churchill, he was moved from his post at the Home Office before the end of October to become First Lord of the Admiralty, a role much more sympathetic to his temperament and inclinations. His successor at the Home Office, Reginald McKenna, followed the precedent set over the Wells/Johnson campaign. Having obtained the confirmation of the Director of Public Prosecutions that a magistrate could not actually stop the contest, but that the principals involved could certainly be bound over for

substantial amounts not to breach the peace, he advised accordingly. Rafter was told of the advice and took out the necessary summons.[82]

So, in the Birmingham dock on 13 November 1911 were those normally upright citizens Owen Moran, Jim Driscoll and Gerard Austin (the promoter).[83] Their defence of themselves and on behalf of their sport was argued by Marshall Hall, his expenses guaranteed by Lord Lonsdale, now anxious to put the genie back in the bottle and to preserve the liberties of white boxers.

Representing the police was J. E. Hill, who based his case upon two vital questions: Is a prizefight illegal, and, if so, is this contemplated fight a prizefight? The very questions unresolved at Bow Street in September were back on the agenda in Birmingham two months later.

In his opening address, Hill ran through the articles of agreement signed by Moran and Driscoll and read out in full the Marquess of Queensberry Rules. Uncharacteristically and surely unwisely, Marshall Hall interrupted him to point out that the original agreement had been amended to put the fight under NSC rules. (As we saw in the previous case, the difference between the treatments of the crucial knockout in the two sets of rules was relatively meaningless. Hall was misguidedly drawing attention to the weakest part of his own case.)

When Hill resumed his address, he drew the magistrate's attention to the four-ounce gloves to be used and to the fact that both Driscoll and Moran had knockouts to their credit:

> There was no doubt that heavy

blows would be dealt and that each of the men would fight for all he was worth, with a grim determination to win the battle and to secure the prize-money and the Feather-weight Championship of the World. Bodily harm was the sole motive of the contest, and there were all the elements of a prize-fight in the case.[84]

When it was the turn of the defence, a predictable phalanx of expert boxing witnesses was called: J. H. Douglas, Eugene Corri and Lord Lonsdale. Douglas argued that the more skilful the boxers, the less likely was a knockout, and that Driscoll and Moran were particularly clean and skilful boxers. Corri reminded everyone that under NSC rules six-ounce gloves would be used, not four-ounce. He also emphasised correctly that, like any other responsible referee, he would intervene in the case of one man outclassing the other to prevent anything approaching brutality. However, he also claimed: 'It was not absolutely necessary that the man who received a knock-out blow should lose the match, because he might and very often did, recover under the ten seconds.' This was ridiculous – if a man recovered in under ten seconds, he had not been knocked out. Lord Lonsdale, in turn, fell at the same place under cross-examination:

> HILL: The knock-out blow is, as a rule, of particular force?
>
> LONSDALE: I do not think it need be of particular force. It is the accidental position of the blow.

HILL: Do you mean to say that a light blow would knock a man out?

LONSDALE: It might.

HILL: More often it is a blow of considerable force?

LONSDALE: Yes. Naturally, it must be so when quick men are engaged.

At this point Hill moved in remorselessly and Lonsdale, his guard dropping, began to give answers out of touch with reality.

HILL: Is it not more by design and intention than by accident?

LONSDALE: No.

HILL: The man who deals the knock-out blow is probably the winner?

LONSDALE: I do not say that it is not so, but is not always the case if the man can respond within ten seconds.

The magistrate's final decision was that for all the guaranteed precautions about gloves, rules and referees, he could find no reason to define Driscoll v Moran as a mere exhibition of skill in boxing, rather than a prizefight. He bound Driscoll and Moran over to keep the peace in the sum of £50 each plus sureties of £25 each. (Promoter Austin was spared.) The great Midlands promotion was off. The law had stopped another contest.

During the hearing, Marshall Hall argued that if Driscoll v Moran were illegal, then there was no such thing as legitimate professional boxing. On that basis, all forms of professional boxing could be banned. Just as the supporters gathered at the Hotel Cecil, and the *Boxing World* editorial, jointly feared: any bout where a knockout meant victory was on the wrong side of legality.

In practice, professional boxing duly continued, in 1911 and thereafter. However, it did so only on the sufferance of the legal and political authorities. The establishment could afford to tolerate a highly popular activity, knowing that it could stop any particular bout of which it disapproved. This could be done openly – as in Wells v Johnson and Driscoll v Moran, both in 1911 – or behind the scenes as in Langford v Klaus 1913, Langford v Smith 1914, and Beckett v Siki 1922. Alternatively, local action might suffice. Also in 1911, on 20 November in Sheffield at the Attercliffe Hall, the police halted a heavyweight contest between Gunner Healey and Alf Langford (who was black) in the 11th round. Neither boxers nor spectators could prevent the interference.[85]

Despite the passing of another century, and the gradual assumption that boxers in gloves operating under strictly controlled conditions are entitled to an immunity that would not be granted outside the confines of the ring, this is more a convenient fiction than legally sound. Highly publicised cases arising from assaults in the context of rugby and association football matches demonstrate that the law cannot be ignored merely because players have freely assented to participate in the game. There was also the much-discussed Operation Spanner case of 1987 (*Regina v Brown* and others December 1990; decision upheld in the House of Lords in 1993) where it was found that adult sadists and masochists, operating in the privacy of their own homes, and eagerly joining in painful acts for their individual sexual gratification, could be found guilty of assault and grievous bodily harm, *despite* the agreement of participator and victim alike.[86]

Far from being discouraged in modern boxing, the win by knockout remains highly desirable, prized by boxers and spectators alike. As masters of ceremony love to announce: '15 wins, 15 by way of knockout … the PERFECT record!' Boxers, from 'K. O.' Brown to 'One Round' Hogan before the First World War, to James 'Lights Out' Toney or Bernard 'The Executioner' Hopkins or Harry 'Exterminator' Simon of modern times, all adopted their nicknames to advertise their ability to finish a bout early. The pretence that a knockout is an unanticipated accident has been long abandoned as a nonsense.

Fortunately for boxing, knockouts included, the legal anomalies that have remained ever since could only be sorted out by new legislation. It is much easier politically to suffer boxing to continue in ambiguity than to contemplate tackling the extremely complicated question of defining what should and what should not be allowed. Indeed, it is highly desirable that boxing should continue, and continue in roughly its present form. A government ban on boxing would not lead to the elimination of boxing, only the elimination of boxing in its best controlled and most responsible forms. A formal ban would produce inevitably a rash of unofficial, uncontrolled and underground contests, as dangerous and undesirable as the illegal bare-fisted contests to a finish that proliferated to the despair of the Victorian and Georgian authorities. A ban would be one of those measures theoretically aimed at progress and improvement that would, in practice, revive the reactionary and indefensible, thus encouraging the very dangers it was designed to eliminate.

Even without the two missing contests (Wells v Johnson and Driscoll v Moran), other match-ups distracted the punter from gloomy thoughts about the future of their sport. James White's ill-fated bill at Earl's Court on 2 October went ahead after a fashion, the main supporting contest moving to the top of the bill. Over 15 rounds, the rugged East End Jewish welterweight, Sid Burns of Aldgate, was severely trounced by a conspicuously handsome Frenchman from Lens, making his first appearance in England and his first outside France and Belgium. The Frenchman's elegant matinee idol profile, miraculously unspoiled for a young man who had become a professional boxer at the unripe age of 14, showed no corrugations or scar tissue as marks of his trade. He made the English and French women in the crowd very happy to be there. His name, which will recur often in subsequent chapters, was Georges Carpentier (b. 12 January 1894). Sid Burns did little damage to Carpentier's record or to the Frenchman's cultivated demeanour. Only one Englishman impaired Carpentier's image temporarily on this first visit. That was a Whitechapel tailor who clad him in a bespoke suit of such inaccurate measurements and so lurid a maroon colour that it had to be dumped before he returned to France.[87] The suit was scrapped, the win stood.

Three weeks later, *sans* suit, Carpentier fought at 10st 7lb/147lb at the King's Hall, London on 23 October 1911, for the European welterweight championship against another Aldgate stalwart, the very experienced and clever Young Joseph, whom we have seen previously in action against Arthur Evernden, Jack Goldswain and Harry Lewis.[88]

Carpentier began his professional career at a perfunctory 7st 2lb/100lbs and was already struggling to make the welter limit as his growth pattern continued. (He went up through the ranks to middleweight, light-heavy and almost heavyweight in turn.) When he met Joseph, he was only 17, but needed a crash diet, dehydration and Turkish baths to get down to 10st 6lb/146lbs. The two men were perfectly contrasted in looks – the rugged and seasoned 26-year-old British champion with the street appearance of a professional boxer, and the pale, youthful Frenchman, of whom the British press were using phrases like 'marvellous youngster who has shot up like some hot-house plant' (perhaps the beginnings of the nickname 'The Orchid Man' Carpentier would make famous) and 'wonderful little fellow'.

Emphasis on Carpentier's supposedly exotic qualities was seriously misleading. As many opponents were to find out, beneath the personable exterior lay a robustness of temperament and an executioner's dedication to concluding proceedings as efficiently and ruthlessly as possible. Lens, in northern France, was a tough and poverty-stricken mining community.

Even today now that the site that was once a major mine hosts a gleaming silver extension of the Louvre, a large coal tip can still be seen in the vicinity. Surrounding villages like Dourges and Billy-Montigny still look upon mounds formed by piles of earth and slag extracted from underground. In this area, as tough and unyielding as Tom Thomas's Rhondda Valley or Jim Driscoll's docklands, Carpentier learned quickly that his best hopes of renown and reward lay in the application of his fists to others' heads and torsos. He was also a very skilful boxer.

Round after round, Young Joseph retreated before a bewildering variety of painful and unanticipated punches. Carpentier used his superior hand speed to land left leads, right leads and left and right hooks whenever he cared to. Joseph damaged his own right hand when landing one good punch on Carpentier. Nobody believed the injury made a serious difference to the inevitable result. Carpentier won the last five rounds easily, dropping Joseph three times in the sixth, once in the eighth, three times in the ninth and twice more in the tenth. Before the 11th, Joseph's seconds showed the compassion that had so far escaped the referee and threw in a bloodstained towel.

The days when the English press and the English fans could patronise French fighters as game little fellows but no match for a determined Englishman were over. Not everyone grasped this. F. H. Lucas, in *Boxing* in an article entitled 'The Great Boom in France' (9 December 1911), could still write xenophobic rubbish:

The Frenchman's natural impetuosity and hot-headedness robbed him of the necessary qualities that form athletes.

Southern blood has always been considered thinner than that possessed by Northern peoples. The corpuscles are fewer in number, and the density of fluid less opaque. The medical fact established the superiority of Polar as against Equatorial races, and no doubt accounted for the racial superiority of England in its relation to athleticism.

Perhaps Carpentier was quietly conducting a scientific experiment on his first trip to England by showing how English blood looked when spilled on the canvas floor of an English ring. *Voila*, count the corpuscles in that.

Carpentier over the next decade acquired a very considerable and enthusiastic following in Britain, as passionate and devoted as that accorded most British boxers. Not all those fans were female.

Having beaten so convincingly two of England's top boxers, Carpentier went home to Paris. At the Gare du Nord, huge crowds met him. He was cheered and bodily chaired to a taxi. The surge of interest in boxing in France was topped by the pleasing notion that France had produced a convincing champion rather than ring fodder for more experienced Anglo-Americans. On 13 December 1911, Carpentier demonstrated his true class against one of the USA's finest, Harry Lewis, whom we last saw in London putting Young Joseph in his place.[89] The match, at the Cirque de Paris, was made at the middleweight limit of 11st 6lb/160lbs, yet Carpentier, still in his growth spurt, paid a forfeit for being a few ounces over on the day. It was his sole concession to his opponent.

In front of a huge and fashionable audience, who had paid collectively the equivalent of £5,000 to be there, Carpentier's ring entrance and the removal of his robe were greeted with the kind of awe and knee-trembling ecstasy his contemporary Vaslav Nijinsky the ballet dancer received during his appearances with Diaghilev's *Ballet Russes* in Paris and London. Like Nijinsky, Carpentier had aesthetic appeal for females and males alike. And, like Nijinsky, his sexy appearance was backed by a steeliness of intent and the physical strength to execute every chosen movement with power and purpose. This the red-haired Lewis found out at first hand.

Lewis relied on his strong punch and his aggression to back an opponent up and to slow faster men with draining body blows. Against Carpentier, his best punches were blocked or deflected; his strides forward neutralised in clever clinches; his head was the painful target for jolting lefts, right and left hooks; and his chin the recipient of whistling uppercuts to halt him. Nijinsky the Beauty was dancing rings around the hirsute Beast. He did so for all 20 rounds to get the decision and the cheers and tears of a crowd who could hardly have been more impressed if the referee had held up the hand of Joan of Arc.

Meanwhile, in London, Bombardier Billy Wells, having missed a mega-payday at Earl's Court (and maybe a mega-beating), looked to resume his erratic career. He must have reflected ruefully on what might have been when, on 4 December 1911, at The Ring, Blackfriars, two middleweights – 'Blink' McClosky and Young Johnson – put on a 20-round ding-dong battle before a packed and noisily enthusiastic crowd. No belt or championship was at stake; no headlines preceded the match-making; and the purse was of the regular Monday night pittance variety. No ministers of religion felt bound to pray for intervention; no politicians or police chiefs interfered. 'Blink' was given the narrow decision. Young Johnson was given a hearty welcome into the ring and a standing ovation after the bout as a plucky and possibly unlucky loser. (He had also lost at The Ring on 13 November 1911 to Charlie Knock in a conspicuously clean contest, giving good value to all and sundry.) Young Johnson was actually a black American but could have been a purple Martian for all anyone cared.

Before the year was out, the NSC invited Wells to revisit its remodelled and refitted boxing room on 18 December 1911 to meet Bill Chase's conqueror, Fred Storbeck. The NSC responded to the activities of the commercial promoters by expanding its own capacity from 2,000 to 4,000 to raise more money from members and guests to offer bigger purses, and to draw the likes of Wells. Though Storbeck was apparently more yellow in complexion than white, he could be billed as a white South African, so chances of official interference were minimal. He was big and clumsy, faster with his tongue than his fists. In the first round, as he and Wells clinched, he quipped to his seconds loudly enough to alienate the audience, 'Easy thing, this!' It was less an honest perception than a tactical gambit to get Wells to forget his boxing skills and get into a toe-to-toe slogathon in which one of Storbeck's clumsier punches might achieve a knockout.

Storbeck had other ploys to take Wells out of his mental and physical stride. He proffered his face, took a punch and smiled as if Wells's punch were a fleabite. More dangerously, he ducked under Wells's leads and plunged forward, shoulder first, as if he were a Springbok rugby forward tackling an opponent. The idea was clearly to contact Wells's midriff, that well-known area of vulnerability. Another wheeze was to feel tentatively with a range-finding left for Wells's head and lob a loaded right swing after it, like a man throwing a grenade over a wall. These stratagems were interspersed with heavy leans and smothers to tire Wells out. Occasionally, he 'forgot' the new NSC rule introduced for the 1911–12 season against the kidney punch and chopped away at Wells's kidneys in the clinches. The club members were not slow to refresh his memory, or to loudly condemn the ducks and crouches, even those that were legal.

Wells, sometimes embarrassed and once or twice rocked, especially in the seventh, was always the more likely winner. The win was laborious and took him 11 rounds. He hit Storbeck freely. Storbeck went down twice in the second, once in response to punches and once because he missed with a crude swing that spun him off his feet. He did the same in the third with an uppercut that went seriously awry. In both cases, he got up and smiled on. Only in the tenth did Wells secure another genuine knockdown. By then Storbeck was smileless and peering out of his left eye, the right closed by Wells's lefts. Three consecutive rights to the jaw felled him convincingly in the 11th, but even then he was within a millisecond of beating the count. Indeed some writers thought

he was counted out only because he had failed to pick up the count and could have risen in time. Storbeck never claimed so. Wells's stuttering career had resumed. The manner of his victory did not enhance it.

A much more aesthetically pleasing contest took place at the NSC two weeks before Wells/Storbeck. On 4 December 1911, a Lonsdale Belt and an official British championship were on offer for the smallest official division – the flyweight class of up to 8st/112lbs; the class specifically created by the NSC in 1909 to replace the myriad of 2lb and 4lb divisions previously existing. One invitation went, inevitably, to the extremely skilful, light-punching, 22-year-old Bermondsey boy, Sid Smith. Smith, one-time van boy, was as dapper a figure as a champion should be, with eyebrows that looked as if they had been created with a stroke of a calligraphic pen, and smoothly greased

Sid Smith (1889–1948), Bermondsey's Jewish flyweight who defied opponents and the NSC hierarchy.
BoxRec

hair swept back from a high forehead either side of a wide right-hand parting. He was such a master of ducking and weaving and poker-faced tranquillity under pressure that he was rarely pushed, let alone beaten. He started a hot betting favourite, especially in the South London Jewish community where he was loved and admired and believed to be better than anyone East London could produce.

Originally, he was to have met Bill Kyne, but he could no longer get down to the weight limit. The first replacement was Sam Keller of Aldgate (sometimes known as Kellar). He made the weight, but not the date, as he was stricken with appendicitis. Third choice was the tough and muscular Joe Wilson from Stepney (b.1889). So Smith v Wilson it was.[90] Quicksilver boxer v rugged puncher; a match more princely than the frugal purse suggested – £65 to the winner and £35 to the loser. The cruder blood and thunder of Wells and Storbeck paid £850 to the winner and £400 to the loser, with £260 side stakes.

For such lowly returns, Smith and Wilson laid on an epicurean feast of skill and courage; the nature of the two fighters guaranteed it. The speedy Smith danced around the ring on the retreat ('like a gnat at sunset' said *Boxing*), dabbing at the remorseless pursuing Wilson with fast and scoring, if less than truly damaging, punches. Wilson let Smith dab on, looking to land some of his own more solid punches to slow Smith down and to give an opportunity for a knockout. Smith could win, but only on points. Wilson could win, but only on a stoppage. The drama and suspense of the evening rode on whether Smith could stay out of Wilson's clutches for a full 20 rounds.

Or would Wilson get his opening and deliver the appropriate *coup d'état*?

In practice, Smith fought the opening rounds confidently, as if Wilson's power held no terrors, piling up points yet taking the occasional uncomfortable body blow. Worse still, he was trapped on the ropes in the fifth and floored by a sequence of Wilson's body blows, completed by a hard right hook to the jaw as he slumped down. He was up at nine, just, and back-pedalling unsteadily, only to be hit again and to go down again for an eight count. The rescue bell was a long time coming. Had Wilson been a little less eager and measured his punches coolly, the result would have been Wilson by a knockout in five.

Smith ducked, weaved and retreated, while regularly pecking away at the oncoming Wilson like a slim lady diner pushing a fork into a salad. His points accumulated. Wilson bided his time. In the 12th, he landed a straight right that knocked Smith over backwards with a surprisingly loud thump for an eight-stone man deposited on his bottom. Smith got up, too quickly, and suffered a repeat. Like a plastic toy in a budgerigar's cage, he bobbed back up again and was distinctly fortunate that the excited Wilson threw too many wild punches where one crisply timed one might have sufficed.

Thrice bitten, thrice shy, Smith belatedly learned his lesson. Using superior skill and plenty of pluck and resilience, he resumed his lead-and-move strategy to survive the next eight rounds and clinch a wide points victory. He had the Lonsdale Belt clicked around his mini-waist as Wilson cogitated on what might have been. The clean and thrilling contest had drawn involuntary gulps and gasps from members during the rounds, and hearty applause during the intervals and at the end, although the event was notably less well attended than Wells v Storbeck. Smith was there not for the miserable purse, nor because he appreciated the refined atmosphere more than the raucous ribaldry of the Blackfriars Ring, but because of the NSC monopoly on British titles and its Lonsdale Belt imprimatur. He lost the title on 2 June 1913, not at the NSC but at The Ring when he was stopped in the 11th by the New Cross battler Bill Ladbury. Before that, he declined the £100 the NSC thought fit to offer him to defend against Johnny Hughes, whom Bettinson considered the proper new challenger:

> *Bettinson:* 'You know you'll have to return the Lonsdale Belt if you don't accept the offer.'
>
> *Smith:* 'I thought you'd say that!'[91]

Smith accompanied his words with the handing over of a brown paper bag – in it was the flyweight Lonsdale Belt.

Aside from official recognition, a more natural venue for the Smith v Wilson fight would have been that East End palace of perspiring pugilistic claustrophobia, Wonderland. Alas, since 13 August 1911, Wonderland was no more.[92] At four o'clock in the afternoon, flames were spotted coming out of the first floor, and despite the attendance of some 20 assorted fire engines and tenders, fire gutted the entire boxing hall in ten minutes, apart from a fireproof box containing a film projector used for the Sunday evening pictures. Nearby houses and the neighbouring District Railway station St Mary Whitechapel escaped, but the centre of the conflagration was the boxing arena, of which only the walls and part of the roof were left. Of the memorable encounters that had taken place in Jack Woolf's punch academy, only smouldering memories remained.

What gave added poignancy to the mourning of ring deeds permanently departed (the uninsured Wonderland was never rebuilt) was the awareness that the fire was unlikely to have been an accident. Back in 1909, Jack Woolf shared his running of Wonderland with a partner, a prominent future promoter of boxing at venues like the Royal Albert Hall, the ruthless Harry Jacobs. By the autumn of 1909, a Wonderland sideshow, as spicy as many a bout on the undercards, was the simmering hostility between the quarrelling partners. 'There have been razors in the air for some time down East End way,' said *Boxing*, and a week later the journal referred to a lively Wonderland bill staged mainly by Jacobs as successful, 'despite war and rumours of war'.[93] By December 1909, the partnership had been dissolved and Woolf and Jacobs were staging rival bills at the Paragon Music Hall, at Wonderland and at the Olympia Theatre, Shoreditch, with double intent – to tap the Christmas holiday market and to dish each other.

. With Woolf in full charge at Wonderland, the rivalry continued over the next two years in the context of boxing's booming popularity and a willingness by less scrupulous promoters to harm their rivals:

> Some are resorting to the most contemptible methods of attack against their rivals. One man [Jacobs?] jealous of the success

achieved by another, has even gone so far as to threaten violence; the covering of one promoter's bills by another has become common; and one promoter has even gone to the extent of securing pills and potion posters wherewith to wipe out the publicity of his competitor. These are tactics that are neither fair nor square.[94]

(This Edwardian skulduggery seems remote, yet it is worth remembering that a Humberside boxing promoter had his fans' tyres slashed at a promotion in October 2002, and a rival promoter was at pains to deny any involvement.)

The victims are more easily identified than the perpetrators. (Dick Burge at The Ring was the main sufferer from the pills posters.) Nevertheless, Harry Jacobs's whole career shows him to have been 'neither fair nor square', and well capable of what American promoter Don King termed 'trickeration'. Indeed, the British Boxing Board of Control minute book No. 2, which covers the years 1925–29, records many of the Board's usually vain attempts to get Jacobs to pay outstanding debts and fines, and to account for other irregularities.

A Harry Jacobs fight poster came from the printers full of promised fights, fights whose sole reality was in the eye-catching typography. The lettering had to be eye-catching, because frequently the first a boxer knew about a match was seeing his name on the poster. All Jacobs's promotions depended heavily on a small army of unknown proletarians backstage, ready to step in when the headliners failed to show. If the takings fell below his expectations,

he would arbitrarily slash fees and purses on the spot.[95]

At the least Jacobs's distress at the Wonderland fire was less than total. When he opened a new boxing venue of his own called Premierland very close to the ashes of Wonderland within a few months of the fire, some asked pertinently whether Jacobs was in the habit of taking a Sunday afternoon stroll with a can of petrol and a box of matches in his hand.

So 1911 drew to a close, a year as full of thunderous themes and developments as a Beethoven symphony. There was also a lively coda. On Boxing Day 1911, precisely three years since the Burns v Johnson fight with which this account began, there was another fight at the Rushcutters Bay stadium; a fight that drew 18,000 people.[96] A Nova Scotian who had become an American citizen, and a trueborn American from Oxnard, California, contested a match for 'The Heavyweight Championship of the British Empire'. Even more surprising, remembering the racist hatred in the arena to Johnson in 1908, was that both fighters were black. Sam Langford, the Nova Scotian, was the pocket battleship at a modest 5ft 6½in and 12st 2lb/170lbs, and Sam McVea the more heavily armoured at 5ft 10½in and 14st 4lb/200lbs and with a longer reach. There were a few boos and catcalls at the end only because the sporting audience felt the eventual points decision to McVea unjust. Both men were loudly cheered into the ring and throughout 20 brave and stubborn rounds of fighting under a midday Australian sun.

The major black heavyweights of the day continued to travel the globe fighting each other. Langford fought

McVea 15 times. With intimate knowledge of each other's styles and the subconscious awareness that here were two black men punishing each other for white entertainment, not every one of the 15 encounters was an all-out cloutfest. But 26 December 1911 was just that, to the delight of Hugh D. McIntosh, the promoter with an uncanny knack of introducing new matches to new audiences successfully. (Like a profitable pantomime, he repeated the menu on Boxing Day 1912.)

In 1911, the two men went through the full array of their boxing skills, giving, receiving and countering with all the force and vigour they could muster. The smaller Langford put all his faith in aggression, bustling forward and landing heavily to McVea's head and body. In return he took McVea's skilful counters. Langford's eyes got puffier and puffier and were almost closed for the second half of the fight. His mouth bled from the fifth onwards. An over-zealous referee hampered Langford from close work in the clinches, an area where he was naturally strong. McVea landed a crisp left hook in the third, a heavy clout that took Langford two full rounds to shake off. Yet nothing stopped Langford coming forward. *Boxing*'s Sydney correspondent awarded ten rounds to Langford for his one-gear belligerence, and nine to McVea for telling jabs and hooks delivered cleverly on the retreat. The 20th began with a handshake and an embrace between two superb sporting athletes, and a standing ovation from the Australian audience amazed at the sustained action over the previous 57 minutes of sunny and sweaty endeavour. The referee compassionately allowed them to clinch more towards the final bell when he raised McVea's arm as the victor. The crowd audibly disagreed. In a large arena it is usually the obvious aggressor whom the crowd favours.

Really, there had been three winners – McVea, Langford and an enthusiastic white audience saluting two true sporting heroes regardless of ethnicity, in strong contrast to the ugly scenes of 1908. There was, perhaps, a fourth winner too – the sport of boxing, now a major draw in both northern and southern hemispheres, and one triumphing over official disapproval, a dubious legal standing, puritan and political opposition, and catching the popular imagination all over the globe. The astonishing thing was that its popularity was to wax even more strongly for many years to come.

Before we look at that sturdy growth, we must spare a thought for the eventual plight of James White, the promoter whose enterprise in matching Jack Johnson and Bombardier Wells had ultimately been bamboozled by an unbeatable combination of official and backroom politics, religious crusades and legal wrangles. Aged 34 in 1911, his career took off only to crash eventually to earth like a spent rocket. Wheeling and dealing from a suite in the Grand Hotel in Trafalgar Square, he used the money of the Beecham family as if it were his own. The Beecham fortune based originally on the ultra-successful laxative Beecham's Pills, had sustained their inventor Thomas Beecham (1820–1907), their developer his son Sir Joseph Beecham (1848–1916) and the glittering musical career of his grandson, the illustrious conductor, Sir Thomas Beecham

Sam McVea (above) and Sam Langford delighted white Australians in a series of stirring fights.
Bain Collection, Prints & Photographs Division, Library of Congress, LC-DIG-ggbain-12255

(1879–1961) in turn. It helped White expand his activities into property, industry, theatre production, oil, rubber and horse racing. His empire ended disastrously in 1927 when his dizzy tactics of spend now and pay later were rumbled. He took a fatal dose of prussic acid at his Surrey stud farm in June 1927, leaving many of his financial partners with burned fingers. (One of them, the boxer Jimmy Wilde, claimed to have lost well over £10,000 in one of White's less than glorious shows at Daly's, a misguided farrago called *Katja the Dancer*. Other trusting investors suffered even more.)

Endnotes:

1 Copy in Home Office file HO45/10487/110912 in the National Archives (NA).

2 Details in the London County Council file LCC/MIN/10,951 (1911) in the Greater London Archives (GLA).

3 See London County Council file LCC/MIN/10,952 (1911) in the Greater London Archives (GLA).

4 Text in *The Times,* 13 July 1910.

5 Original letter in LCC file/MIN/10,951 (1911) in the GLA.

6 Inwood, S., *A History of London* (London: Macmillan, 1998) p. 440.

7 Inwood, S., *A History of London,* p. 443.

8 GLA, LCC/MIN/10951 (1911).

9 *Who Was Who* 1929–40 p. 935.

10 Koss, S., *Nonconformity in British Politics* (Connecticut: Archon Books, 1975) pp. 42–43.

11 Mews, S., 'Puritanicalism, Sport and Race: a Symbolic Crusade of 1911' *Studies in Church History Vol. 8: Popular Belief and Practice* (Cambridge University Press, 1972).

12 Koss, S., *Nonconformity in British Politics,* pp. 118–119.

13 Green, J. P., 'Boxing and the 'Colour Question' in Edwardian Britain: the "White Problem" of 1911', in *International Journal of the History of Sport* Vol. 5, no. 1, May 1988, pp. 115–119.

14 The full text of the 18 September 1911 resolution is reproduced in *Boxing World and Athletic Chronicle,* 28 September 1911.

15 Bettinson, A. F. & Bennison, B., *The Home of Boxing (*London: Odhams Press, 1932) pp.95–97.

16 Bettinson, A. F. & Bennison, B., *The Home of Boxing,* p. 98.

17 Clark, N., *All in the Game: Memoirs of the Ring and Other Sporting Experiences* (London: Methuen, 1935) p. 99.

18 Clark, N., *All in the Game,* p. 99.

19 Bettinson, A. F. & Bennison, B., *The Home of Boxing,* p. 99.

20 Originals in the Home Office file HO45/10487/110912, National Archives.

21 Jenkins, R., *Churchill* (London: Pan Books, 2002) p. 49.

22 Mander, R. & Mitchenson, J., *The Lost Theatres of London* (London: Hart-Davis, 1968); Rose, N., *Churchill: An Unruly Life* (London and New York: Simon and Schuster, 1994).

23 *The Times,* 16 September 1911.

24 *The Times,* 16 September 1911.

25 *The Times,* 16 September 1911.

26 Sutherland, D., *The Yellow Earl: The Life of Hugh Lowther, 5th Earl of Lonsdale, KG, GCVO 1857–1944* (London: Cassell, 1965) p. 20.

27 Cole, G. D. H. & Postgate, R., *The Common People 1746–1946* (London: Methuen, 1956 ed.) p. 443.

28 Sutherland, D., *The Yellow Earl,* p. 65.

29 Corri, E., *Thirty Years a Referee* (1915) p. 170.

30 Deghy G., *Noble and Manly: The History of the National Sporting Club* (Hutchinson, 1956) p. 167.

31 *New York Times,* 14 September 1911.

32 *New York Times,* 16 September 1911.

33 Quoted in *The Times,* 16 September 1911.

34 Full text in *The Times,* 19 September 1911.

35 Mews, S., 'Puritanicalism, Sport and Race', pp. 324–326.

36 Roberts, R., *Papa Jack: Jack Johnson and the Era of White Hopes* (New York: Simon & Schuster, 1985) p. 69; and Gilmore, A-T., *Bad N****r: The National Impact of Jack Johnson (London: Kennikat Press, 1975)* p. 12.

37 Gilmore, A-T., *Bad N****r,* p. 37.

38 Gilmore, A-T., *Bad N****r,* p. 76.

39 Bettinson, A.F. & Bennison, B., *The Home of Boxing,* p. 99.

40 Butler, F., *A History of Boxing in Britain: A survey of the Noble Art from its Origins to the Present-Day (London:* Arthur Barker, 1972) p. 137.

41 Deghy G., *Noble and Manly,* p. 107.

42 Full text in National Archive file HO 45/11880/230,186/'Boxing (coloured v. white)'/24.

43 NA file HO 45/11880/230186/3.

44 Full text in NA file HO 45/11880/230186/3.

45 NA: HO 45/11880/ 230186/4.

46 NA: HO 45/11880/230186/3.

47 *The Times,* 4 July 1911.

48 *The Times,* 10 November 1922.

49 NA: HO45/18745/476,649/1.

50 Harding, J., *Lonsdale's Belt: Boxing's Most Coveted Prize* (Worthing: Pitch Publishing, 2016) Chapter 8 [for more details of the Board and of Donmall].

51 British Boxing Board of Control Minute Book no. 2, entry for 15 February 1929.

52 British Boxing Board of Control Minute Book no. 2, entry for 27 February 1929.

53 Information included in the Imperial War Museum section on the Holocaust.

54 *The Times,* 18 September 1911, although a carbon copy of the full letter to Meyer is contained in the NA file HO45/110917/33.

55 *The Times,* 19 September 1911.

56 The full Meyer–White exchange is reproduced in *The Times,* 22 September 1911.

57 *New York Times,* 20 September 1911.

58 *The Times,* 21 September 1911.

59 NA: HO45/10487/110912. It proved so useful, a copy was also placed in HO45/118880/230186 dealing with, for example, the 1922 affair about Beckett v Siki.

60 NA: HO45/10487/110912/ 41/f.1 & 2.

61 NA: HO45/10487/110912/ 41/f.2.

62 Byrne's note of the telephone conversation with the FO in 110912/37, and Asquith's telegram to Churchill 25 September 110912/37a.

63 Letter in full in Churchill, R., *Winston S. Churchill*: Companion Volume II Part Two 1907–1911 (London, 1969) p. 1128.

64 Roberts, A., *Eminent Churchillians* (Phoenix paperback edition, 1995) p. 211.

65 Ponting, C., *Churchill* (Sinclair-Stevenson paperback, 1995).

66 Quoted in Ponting, C., *Churchill,* p. 254.

67 Full telegram in NA: HO45/10487/110912/42.

68 Text in NA: HO45/10487/110912/43.

69 NA: HO45/10487/110912/43a.

70 A nine-page transcript of the meeting is in NA: HO45/10487/110912/43b.

71 *The Times,* 26 September 1911.

72 These rules and others can be found in the Appendices to Viscount Knebworth's volume XI of the Lonsdale Library, *Boxing,* London 1946.

73 *The Times,* 26 September 1911.

74 Court details in *The Times,* 28 September 1911, an issue that includes reports on the other two cases heard. Further details in *Boxing World and Athletic Chronicle,* 5 October 1911

75 Questions and answers derived from differing accounts in *The Times* and *Boxing World* as cited in Note 74, and the *New York Times,* 28 September 1911.

76 *The Times,* 28 September 1911.

77 Quoted in *Boxing News and Athletic Chronicle,* 5 October 1911.

78 *Boxing World and Athletic Chronicle,* 5 October 1911.

79 Meeting and telegram in *The Times,* 27 September 1911.

80 Full details in *Birmingham Gazette,* 10 October 1911.

81 NA: HO file 110912/92.

82 *Birmingham Daily Mail,* 4 November 1911.

83 Hearing reported in *The Times,* 14 November 1911.

84 Hearing reported in *The Times,* 14 November 1911.

85 *Boxing World and Athletic Chronicle,* 30 November 1911.

86 Points supported by a Radio Four discussion on 7 February 2003 in Marcel Berlin's *Law in Action* series.

87 *Carpentier: By Himself* (London: Sportsman's Book Club, 1958) p. 45.

88 Carpentier v Young Joseph reported in *Boxing World and Athletic Chronicle,* 30 October 1911.

89 Reports of the fight in *Boxing,* 23 December 1911 and *Boxing World and Athletic Chronicle,* 21 December 1911.

90 Report in *Boxing,* 9 December 1911.

91 Mullan, H., *Heroes and Hard Men: The Story of Britain's World Boxing Champions* (London: Stanley Paul, 1989) p. 27.

92 *East London Advertiser,* 19 August 1911, and *Jewish Chronicle,* 18 August 1911.

93 Interview with Woolf in *Boxing,* 18 September 1909, and report 25 September 1909.

94 'Friction Among Promoters' in *Boxing,* 17 September 1910.

95 Article by B. J. Evans, *Boxing News* 13 June 1951.

96 *Boxing* 30 December 1911 and *Boxing News* 31 December 1911.

CHAPTER 8

THE YEAR OF THE FRENCH
1912

In Which Fighters Fight in Foreign Fields

IN THE red and gold plush of the Royal Albert Hall arena, under the baton of the veteran conductor Sir Frederick Bridge, the formidable English contralto Dame Clara Butt (a six-footer with more heft than most British heavyweights) was thrilling a packed New Year's house with Handel's *Messiah*. The noble words of Isaiah promised much:

> O thou that tellest good tidings
> in Zion, arise, shine for thy light
> is come, and the glory of the Lord
> is risen upon thee.

Good tidings and shining lights featured all over the London West End as revellers buried 1911 and opened 1912 with enthusiasm. At the Waldorf Hotel, Father Time, accompanied by a gnome, wheeled in a giant cracker that exploded as midnight struck to reveal a glittering fairy holding up a signboard with the illuminated figures 1912.

Elsewhere in London, the frothiest of entertainment was available: two spectacular pantomimes, *Hop O' My Thumb* with George Groves, Violet Loraine and Barry Lupino at Drury Lane and *Dick Whittington* at the Lyceum; traditional music hall at the Tivoli with Marie Lloyd, Cinquevalli, Gus Elen and G. H. Chirgwin, or at the Palace with Vesta Tilley and Arthur Bourchier.

Musicals aimed at brows lower than those comfortable with Handel were equally plentiful: *The Follies* or *New York* at the Empire; Walter Monckton's *The Quaker Girl* with Gertie Millar at the Adelphi; *Nightbirds* at the Lyric (a version of Johann Strauss's *Die Fledermaus*), and a George Edwardes production of Franz Lehar's *The Count of Luxembourg* at Daly's. For those who preferred farce, the Whitney had *Charley's Aunt*; and for children, or for adults ambivalent about growing up, Pauline Chase was taking wired flight in *Peter Pan* at the Duke of York's.

Creeping doubts about Britain's imperial eminence could be dispelled at the Empire Theatre or the Palace Theatre at afternoon matinees where live entertainment was supplemented by Bioscope newsreels of the Delhi Coronation Durbar. In Delhi, the new King Emperor George V and his Queen Empress Mary sat beneath a golden dome on a dais on Tuesday, 12 December 1911 to receive a 101-gun salute and the obeisance of *over a million* of their Indian subjects stretching as far as the eye could see. Few Englishmen of the day doubted they too were on at least a metaphorical dais above the brown-skinned millions of the world. Estimates made the world land surface 55.5 million square miles and the global population about 1.62 billion. The British Empire in 1912 alone comprised 13.7 million square miles occupied by 426 million people, so 24 per cent of the earth and 26 per cent of its people came under British administration.

Boxing, like entertainment, had grown mightily, playing an ever-larger part in people's lives and commanding more column inches in a proliferating popular press. On 1 January 1912 alone, there were professional fights taking place from Santiago, Chile to Sydney, Australia; from Berlin, Germany to Hastings, New Zealand; and from Prince Rupert, British Columbia to Grasse, France. Just in the USA, there was boxing in California (Vernon and Taft), Indiana (Indianapolis and Jeffersonville), Ohio (Cleveland), Pennsylvania (Pittsburgh and Philadelphia), Louisiana (New Orleans), New York State (Buffalo and Rochester), and in and around New York City (Fairmont Athletic Club and American Athletic Association in Manhattan; Carlyle Athletic Club, Gowanus Athletic Club and Irving Athletic Club, all in Brooklyn; Olympic Athletic Club in Harlem). In Britain there was action from modest village halls like Pentre in northern Monmouthshire to the dedicated theatre in the NSC in Covent Garden, London.

Yet the glitz and glamour of the New Year's celebrations were misleading. All was not well beneath the jollities. Industrial harmony prevailed no more in 1912 than it had in 1911, a year when 864 strikes had meant 931,050 working days lost. In 1912 there were to be 857 more strikes, involving nearly 1.5 million employees. As *Whitaker's Almanac* recorded gloomily, 'Proletarian discontent seems everywhere.' Symptomatically, in Lancashire there was a dispute in the cotton industry, and Sir George Askwith, a Board of Trade official with a brilliant record in eirenic amelioration, was on his way to Manchester to do what he could to settle it. Equally symptomatically, the Lancashire cotton employers pre-empted him by provocatively announcing that 50,000 Lancashire cotton spinners were to be put on half-work and half-wages immediately. Happy New Year from the management.

Down in Swansea, supposedly respected labour leaders, J. H. Thomas the trade unionist elected to the House of Commons in 1910 as a man of the people, and J. C. Williams, the general secretary of the Amalgamated Society of Railway Servants, were howled down at a meeting of angry workers who suspected them of insufficient militancy in the workers' cause.[1]

When people went from aggrieved to positively angry, violence and strife were likely. Extreme militancy became the

new motif too in the struggle for women's suffrage. Women mobbed Prime Minister Asquith in Parliament Square in November 1910, and his colleague Winston Churchill was attacked with a whip on a Bradford train three days later. Hot political issues discussed relatively dispassionately in private over brandy and cigars got ominous when they reached the street and the victims who felt and were helpless.

The unpleasant twist to the last few years before the First World War was that these great issues (e.g. industrial relations, women's suffrage and above all Ulster and the status of Ireland) forced their way into the cosy drawing rooms and genteel debating chambers in new, alarming ways. As George Dangerfield memorably put it, 'For nearly a century men had discovered in the cautious phrase, in the respectable gesture, in the considered display of reasonable emotions, a haven against those irrational storms which threatened to sweep through them. And gradually the haven lost its charms; worse still, it lost its peace.'[2] Old Testament wisdom, and Proverbs in particular, seemed no longer to apply – soft answers, far from turning away wrath, rather fanned it into flames. Conflagrations broke out everywhere.

Men began to behave very badly. In January 1912, Ulstermen, backed by the Conservative Party under a new leader in Bonar Law, drilled a volunteer force, prepared for armed resistance to measures passed by a democratically elected House of Commons, hinting at civil war.[3] Bonar Law approved also military action on behalf of employers under attack from workers.

Theatres, music halls and boxing arenas carried reputations for tumult,

but in 1912 they were more genteel places than the Palace of Westminster where statesmen were howled down and missiles thrown across the chamber. (In boxing, disorder also occasionally resurfaced. In a Nottinghamshire meadow in January 1912, Dick Collier of Leicester and John Harvey of Liverpool participated in a secret £25-a-side bare-knuckle prizefight. Collier, who had broken his wrist in punching Harvey's head in the 17th, was himself punched down in the 18th and failed to come up to scratch. So did the police, who arrived only after fighters and spectators had melted away.)[4]

At the NSC in Covent Garden, violence was only allowed within the ring and, usually, the rules. On New Year's Day 1912, Fred Storbeck, two weeks after his failure to smile to victory over the Bombardier, faced the Irish-American Frank Moran.[5] Moran, born 18 March 1887 in Pittsburgh, was a major attraction; a handsome and sturdy athlete with an intellect some degrees higher than most fighters. He was a fully qualified dentist with his own flashing white teeth, which he displayed in a smile rather than a snarl. Even after a 12-year professional boxing career facing some formidable punchers (Al Palzer, Jack Johnson, Luther McCarty, Gunboat Smith and Jess Willard among them), he retained his teeth, his smile and his looks sufficiently to have a second career as a Hollywood actor from 1923 onwards. Like a ventriloquist who produces his most cutting lines through a dummy, Moran personified his right fist as 'Mary Ann'. When Mary Ann kissed men, they stayed kissed and the recipient usually had to sleep off the impact for at least ten seconds.

Both Storbeck and Moran were unpredictable. Moran's tactics varied from fight to fight, including a feigned stagger concealing the fact that Mary Ann would shortly be in action. Storbeck's head was a moving target; sometimes as high as a tall man on tiptoe could take it, and sometimes grazing the canvas in the lowest of ducks. Occasionally, Storbeck overdid the subterranean manoeuvres, leaving himself sprawling on all fours, or flopping down deliberately to avoid punches raining down from an upright opponent. Both men possessed knockout punches. In the circumstances, an exciting fight was practically guaranteed.

So it proved. Storbeck shaded the first. Moran won the second widely, punching Storbeck down twice, and only going to ground after swinging himself off his feet. Moran, hitting more often and more strongly, won the third. He punched harder in the fourth too but conceded the round as Storbeck rallied conspicuously. Storbeck took the fifth and sixth despite audible displeasure from crowd and referee Sydney Hulls at every shabby flop down. When Storbeck cut the antics and punched, the heavier Moran looked uncomfortable, though his mini-totters may have been contrived.

The aftermath to the seventh provided a semi-comic climax. Two thudding uppercuts to the body from Mary Ann provoked Storbeck to a flurry of punches, which in turn stimulated Moran into toe-to-toe exchanges interrupted only by the bell. Storbeck, deaf to the bell and blind to attempts by the referee and Moran's entourage to stop him, punched Moran all the way back to Moran's

corner, landing a further four punches, including a parting right hook when Moran's buttocks had already settled on his stool. Storbeck's disqualification followed automatically.

London had no monopoly on ring action. All over Britain, the sport found new audiences for more contests and more press attention. For example, in the Stadium in a snow-bound Liverpool on 18 January 1912, there was an all-American fight that would have graced equally New York, San Francisco, Sydney or Paris. The snow reduced the crowd, but many had willingly walked through a blizzard to see in the flesh the veteran Philadelphian who had recently lost to Georges Carpentier, the much-loved Harry Lewis. His opponent was Aaron L. Brown, born in Fulton, Missouri on 23 December 1883, a black American who had, like Lewis, often fought in England, but was better known under his ring name, the Dixie Kid.

Dixie was the nattiest of dressers. In his plush grey bowler hat, his grey-checked suit and his pristine white spats, he was as dazzling as a Scouse snowdrift. Heavy Liverpool snow penetrated the stadium roof and covered the ring. Had it not been already cleared, the snow on the canvas would have melted away in the heat of the action that the two were to sustain over a breathless eight rounds.

The fight is sometimes listed as for the world welterweight title. It was a catchweight contest within the middleweight limit of 11st 6lb/160lbs.[6] On the night, Lewis was up to a stone the heavier. Lewis and Dixie needed no belts to give of their best. The very experienced ringside witness, James Butler, recorded it as the most terrific battle and fiercest fight he ever saw.[7] The collateral form was confusing –

Lewis had lost to Carpentier in Paris on 13 December 1911, but the Kid had forced Carpentier into a fifth-round retirement a few months before, 29 August 1911 at Trouville.

Everyone knew how powerfully Lewis could punch, especially with a left hook to the body, and how resilient a chin he possessed – in over 170 fights he was counted out only twice. He was also a gifted counter-puncher. The Dixie Kid had pre-decided to plunge in anyway, prepared to take every Lewis punch for the sake of landing his own sharp hooks and short jabs. With this set-up, the first round contained more percussive action than many a full bout.[8]

After initial feints and prods, the Kid landed a solid left hook to the point of the Lewis jaw, a blow heavy enough to send Lewis reeling and have half the ringside gasping, including Lewis's entourage. Lewis's recovery powers were legendary, especially early in a fight, and he blocked and clinched before retaliating with fierce body punches of his own. Two Lewis swings that might have stunned Dixie were ducked, and then the Kid landed heavily with an arcing right swing followed by a right jab.

Lewis now lunged after Dixie, who stepped back and tried to fend Lewis off, never failing to look to counter. It was all Lewis for the moment – ducking, feinting and punching. He took three crisp counters from Dixie yet connected to Dixie's ribs with a left hook powerful enough to put his opponent down. Dixie was up before the word 'one' had barely formed on the referee's lips and he pushed Lewis back with drives and hooks from both hands. At the bell, the audience needed the break almost as much as the fighters.

The versatile Dixie Kid (1883–1954) in Paris. By 1911 facial marks betrayed his profession.
Branger/Roger Viollet via GettyImages

The second round was as intense as the first, both men feinting, ducking and slipping, both punching and landing accurately, and both willing to take punches to create an opening. Yet before the third minute elapsed, there were signs of how this exceptional affair would end. Bobbing and skipping backwards, the Kid kept his arms down at his side, inviting Lewis to lunge for his exposed chin. When struck, he stumbled and staggered as if in trouble. Then, just as his attacker poised to deliver a finishing punch, Dixie would throw instant combinations of his own, especially his favourite counter, a fierce right uppercut followed with a left hook to the head. In the 12 years of Dixie's

professional career, many tough fighters succumbed to the lure and collapsed under the response.

Initially, Lewis complied. As the Kid came apparently unhinged and staggered, Lewis leapt in to land two belligerent uppercuts and a cluster of straight lefts and rights. Dixie was foxing, and as Lewis lunged forward, he delivered his pre-planned uppercut to the body and four successive whistling hooks to head and jaw. Lewis, with the iron-chinned resilience of, say, a Mickey Ward of modern times, absorbed all five punches with no more than an impertinent wink to his seconds as he clinched with Dixie.

It was a significant psychological moment. The Dixie Kid had lured his opponent into his well-laid trap, delivered his best shots, and Lewis had refused to lie down. Worse still, Lewis was punching back more vigorously than he had at the beginning. What made the fight so outstanding in Britain's pre-war years was that Dixie absorbed this unwelcome turnaround but refused to accept it.

A speeding right grazed Lewis's chin and took Dixie down by its sheer force. When he got back up, his temporarily exposed face took three chopping left hooks, a Lewis speciality. Lewis then drove him back, only for the Kid cleverly to duck his punches and bring a long rising hook from his own waistband to Lewis's chin, sending Lewis staggering. Lewis still got in a parting right to put the Kid down for three at the very end of the round.

The Kid continued to land scoring punches but was outscored and outpunched by Lewis in the fourth. It was Lewis now landing the heavier and more damaging punches. The Kid's face showed that. In the fifth and sixth, Lewis eased back, conscious he might be in for 15 more rounds. Dixie advanced rather as if he were barnstorming the final championship rounds determined to annihilate an opponent, or at least to persuade a referee to give him the decision. The two-round flurry won the Kid both rounds but not the fight. By the end of the sixth he had landed nearly all his best punches and held the initiative for all six minutes. But Lewis was still upright and preparing to come back at him with both gloves.

Lewis, behind on points, was ahead physically and mentally. Throughout the seventh he chased Dixie from ring post to ring post, landing big single punches and pinning Dixie on the ropes or in a corner. Dixie's supporters were soon asking for a merciful stoppage for the man who had given and taken so much and was now kept vertical only by pride. Referee Douglas, mindful of Dixie's past resurrections from the brink of collapse, allowed him to come out for the eighth.

Lewis did not hesitate. He landed a left hook and right uppercut combination that left the Kid hanging on to the top rope. Another right hook to the left temple left him in a heap in the corner. Douglas declined to start the count and escorted Lewis to his corner. Behind him, the Kid got up again, but on legs so wobbly that his knees looked as if they might bend as readily backwards or sideways as conventionally. In that bemused state, he grabbed for the top rope for support, missed it and went down again. Meanwhile, the entire audience stood and stamped in appreciation, throwing hats, scarves and umbrellas in the air, and making enough noise to put the

temporarily repaired roof in danger of another collapse. They had seen two brave men operating to the limits and refusing to surrender whatever the odds against them.

The day before this epic fight, five other brave men – Wilson, Bowers, Evans, Oates and Robert Falcon Scott, the Antarctic explorers – had reached the South Pole, only to find their rival Roald Amundsen had beaten them to it a month earlier. All five men perished in the blizzard conditions; disappointment turned into tragedy. This is not to equate two boxers displaying skills and courage for a purse with an epic of scientific exploration that captured the British imagination like few others. Rather, the Liverpudlians, standing on their chairs and cheering two American boxers were responding at a deep humanitarian level. That Lewis was Jewish and the Dixie Kid black mattered not. In an increasingly complicated world, where morals and ethics were problematical and the gap between rich and poor so alarmingly wide, two men of extraordinary fitness and consummate skills had pushed each other to the limit in a contest where each man was absolutely isolated and wholly reliant upon his own inner resources for victory. A boxer might become the embodiment of a whole community, yet ultimately he was a mere man, and a man alone in circumstances bringing unmistakeable and painful defeat, or victory. (For the explorers, it brought a lonely death.)

Most major sports offered a little of the same, but boxing offered it in a simple, concentrated and stark fashion. To boxing, Edwardian crowds responded with unprecedented enthusiasm. Their obsession cannot be comprehended without this emotional

identification with the protagonists as human beings first, as well as representatives.

Before January 1912 was out, the focus was back in London and on the NSC ring for the 1912 version of Peggy Bettinson's benefit. Bettinson was able to supplement his funds like a professional cricketer awarded a benefit match. The date was 29 January 1912; the bill of fare as long as one for an Edwardian state banquet.[9] The hors d'oeuvres included exhibition bouts between noted amateurs and famous professionals. (Amateur/professional apartheid, sacred in the Amateur Boxing Association, could be ignored in the cosy comfort of the private club. Indeed, currently serving as president of the ABA was J. H. Douglas; a vice-president was G. H. Vize; treasurer was B. J. Angle; and recently elected to the ABA committee was J. W. H. T. Douglas, currently out of the country serving as a substitute amateur captain of the mostly professional cricket team touring Australia for the 1911–12 Test series. All these 'amateurs' served professional boxing in some capacity as NSC members and officials.)

On Bettinson's January night, several British professionals – Digger Stanley, Pat O'Keefe, Jim Driscoll, Pedlar Palmer, Matt Wells and Gunner Moir – sparred in exhibition bouts against amateur opponents. They escaped physical damage and the opponents escaped morally unsullied by professional contamination.

The next course had more of solid professional food about it. Kid Logan (Islington) hooked Bat McCarthy of Cardiff to some effect over six rounds but conceded a points victory to a stronger and more versatile boxer.

A six-rounder had Charlie Dixon (Southwark) and Tom Danahar (Bethnal Green) holding, hitting, wrestling and slugging with lots of noise and little skill for one and a half rounds, and ended prematurely when two wild swings connected with Danahar's jaw and left him helpless.

Top of the undercard and tasty entrée was a solid middleweight clash over 15 rounds between Welshman Dai Thomas and the promising Jack Harrison of Rushden, Northants. Both weighed in a pound below the middleweight limit of 11st 6lb/160lbs. This suited Harrison, not the taller Thomas, who gradually outgrew the division and squeezed into it only at the cost of strength and stamina. Thomas used a straight left to keep Harrison away. Harrison was tough enough to take a few to the head as a quid pro quo for belabouring Thomas's ribs and kidneys. Both forgot the changed rule outlawing the old response to an unwelcome clinch, a quick hook into the unprotected kidney region. Thomas's other strays into illegality were low punches, delivered to Harrison's visible and understandable distress.

From the fifth to the terminal eighth, the traffic was all one way. Thomas went backwards, poking out the left with less and less power, as Harrison punched his lower ribcage, mixed with hooks to the softer region below it. A wincing Thomas took three counts of eight in the seventh and barely got through the round. When he went down again in the eighth, the referee called a sensible halt.

For a purse of £225, Harrison had given good value as had the evening. There was still more to come. The main course was the latest Anglo-French

Charles Ledoux (1892–1967) 'The Little Apache'. The French bantamweight made Driscoll regret a decision to emerge from retirement.
Bain Collection, Prints & Photographs Division, Library of Congress, LC-DIG-ggbain-11077

contest at the bantamweight limit of 8st 6lb/118lbs. The Englishman was the irrepressible Joe Bowker. When the Digger knocked out Bowker at the NSC back in 1910 (Chapter 5), some had wondered whether the prize was the Lonsdale Belt or the Central Casting Award for Best Artful Dodger.

Now the sprightly veteran was plying his magic wiles against an exceptionally tough 19-year-old Frenchman, Charles Ledoux, who, influenced like many French boxers by American visitors, fought out of a crouch. Many thought him a boiled-down version of Harry Lewis.

Talking to pressmen a few days before, Bowker assured them that all the advantages were with him: age and experience over relative beginner; Anglo-Saxon consistency over supposed fitful Gallic élan. Ledoux had a weighty punch in each hand, especially the right, but what good was that if he were unable to land them?

From the first bell, Bowker, up on his toes, set a furious pace, dancing around the solidly planted Ledoux, landing and ducking and swaying away from Ledoux's swinging responses. Before the round ended, Bowker made Ledoux look out of his depth, and already puffy and swollen about his dark, deep-set yet prominent eyes.

Ledoux's frustrations continued subsequently. He rushed in merely to punch the air, or to be tied up, or to be stopped mid-rush by another stinging left jab to his reddening complexion. Bowker grew visibly more confident, indulging in showy and extravagant ducks and dives and taking avoidable body blows, including one very low one that had him wincing and Ledoux apologising.

Not one of nature's intellectuals, Bowker had never seen a Greek tragedy and was unfamiliar with the concept of hubris. It and its successor, nemesis, followed in the ninth. A smug grin on his face, Bowker held the top rope, ready to make a sliding lunge out of harm's way when Ledoux tried to catch him. Unfortunately for him, he was a fraction late and was duly impaled on a probing left to the midriff. Folded in half, grin turning to grimace, this was not part of Bowker's extensive repertory of deception. A right hook to Bowker's chin sent him sprawling. The worm had turned. The biter bit.

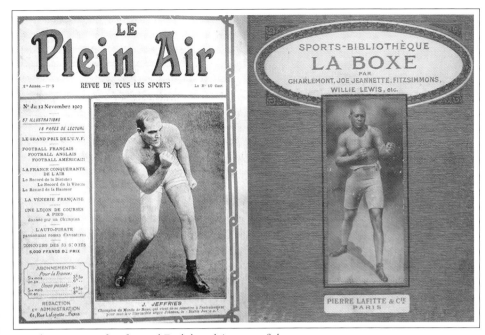

French magazines often featured English and American fighters.
BoxRec

The ninth-round twist put Ledoux in control and Bowker the butt of all Ledoux could throw at him. Up at eight, Bowker took further counts of eight, nine, eight and seven respectively – 40 seconds on the canvas wondering what on earth had gone wrong. A further 60 seconds on his stool between the ninth and tenth left the enigma unsolved, and he tottered out for the tenth round. Down again for two and then for six, Bowker recovered fleetingly and got off some token jabs at the poker-faced Frenchman. They served merely to irritate, and more powerful body blows sent him back to the floor for further counts of seven, eight and nine.

Robbed of a 'certain' victory over the French, the members were still relieved when the referee decided to stop the contest. No one could say they had not been privileged to share a fine evening, as entertaining as the music hall, as sensational as a melodrama, and as over-caloried as a stodgy supper in the club's dining room. Like Harrison and Thomas, Bowker and Ledoux had put on a superb show for a relatively modest purse of £225.

The rise of French boxing was paralleled by the rise in French interest in English football of both codes. France's first ever rugby international was lost against the New Zealand touring All Blacks on 1 January 1906, then they took on their neighbours – England 1906, Wales 1908, Ireland 1909 and Scotland 1910 – losing in all cases but showing what a formidable rugby nation they would become by beating Scotland in Paris in 1911. The French took up association football even earlier, sending two (unsuccessful) teams to the 1908 London Olympics, yet were prominent in the formation of the first Federation Internationale de Football Associations (FIFA) in May 1904. The British stood aloof from any such European sporting alliances. The French took the hint and very much got on with it themselves.

They did much the same in boxing. Indeed, they got on with it in boxing so speedily that in 1912 there were no fewer than nine major Parisian venues catering for *la boxe*: Premierland, Wonderland, Boxeland, the Arena, the Boxing Palace, the Wagram, the Colisee, Le Ring de Paris and the Cirque de Paris. The choice or adaptation of English titles helped French promoters make clear that boxing, British and American style, was on show rather than French kick-boxing (a sophisticated form of combat refined in the 19th century from Le Savate, a folk combat of earlier centuries, but like its predecessor restricted generally to domestic consumption).

In the USA, the other National Sporting Club, in New York, was packed to the limit on 18 January 1912 (the same night as Dixie v Lewis in Liverpool) for a bout that promised everything and delivered very little. Standing room only prevailed as 3,000 people crammed in, many having paid scalpers hugely over the odds.[10] Billed as a featherweight contest between Knockout Brown and Abe Attell over ten rounds, Attell weighed in at 8st 9lb/121lbs with Brown scaling 9st 2lb/128lbs. Brown's scant regard for the nine-stone limit was cynically designed to enhance his strength over the slighter Attell. It was utterly untypical of Attell to concede poundage, or anything else, unless there was money in it.

This evening, Attell was not his normal self, despite winning a mini-psychological battle during the preliminaries when, absurdly, Brown and he sat in their respective dressing rooms, both refusing to be the first boxer into the ring. Meanwhile, 15 minutes passed as the uncomfortably packed crowd grew more and more restive until Brown conceded and agreed to lead the parade to the ring providing Attell and his entourage followed in immediately.

Once the fight began, Brown aggressively advanced on Attell, swinging a variety of punches, some crisp and neat, others clumsy and painfully predictable. Attell held off, but for once his legendary elusiveness and cleverness of counter had been left in the dressing room, and he took several heavy Brown punches to the head. This was disappointing all round – disappointing to Brown's supporters who saw KO's best weapons thudding in to relatively small effect; disappointing to Attell's supporters, baffled to see the impact of crude punches that would normally have failed to land on the crafty Abe in a month of trying; and doubly disappointing to the neutrals who had so relished the prospect of a classic encounter between a puncher and a ring scientist.

After ten rounds, everyone knew Brown a worthy but tame winner, whose supposedly lethal left hook was more ponderous than deadly. The newspapers' decision was still unanimous that Brown had won. In view of Attell's dubious reputation and the considerable sums wagered on the outcome, there was bound to be an inquiry. The New York State Athletic Commission conducted one over the next few weeks.[11]

Attell got his retaliation in first. He testified that he could beat Brown any time he chose. However, that particular evening he had been physically out of sorts because the National Sporting Club doctor, Dr Joseph Satian, a man previously unknown to Attell (a lie), had treated his painful hand with an overdose of cocaine (!) Having dropped the little bombshell – it ain't me, it's the NSC to blame – Attell left the state and was back in California before his version of events could be challenged. The ploy did not work. Having taken statements from everyone else, the Commission absolved the club and its officials from blame and suspended Attell and his chief second, Danny Goodman, for six months.

Because of the anarchic structure of American boxing, with no overall federal control, the New York ban carried no jurisdiction outside New York State. Weeks later Attell was back in the ring and on 22 February 1912 met Johnny Kilbane of Cleveland, Ohio at the Vernon Arena, Los Angeles, California.[12] The two had met twice previously. Attell had outpointed Kilbane over ten rounds at Kansas City on 24 October 1910 but withdrew after four rounds with a broken shoulder blade in Cleveland, Ohio on 30 January 1911. Both were eager for the decisive rubber match, which drew a $3,500 gate. Kilbane boxed on until the 1920s, only retiring after being stopped in six rounds by the toughest of Frenchmen, Eugene Criqui.

Attell, the Little Hebrew as the posters called him, had boxed professionally since the turn of the century, and was feeling his years as never before. Age, rather than funny chemicals, was the real culprit in the New York fiasco. Attell, born in San Francisco on 22 February 1884 as the 16th child of Russian Jewish immigrant parents, 16th of 19 that is, was involved subsequently in many unofficial fights as well as recognised ones (165 official ones when he retired in 1917). Two of his brothers, Monte and Caesar, also boxed professionally. Neither against Brown, nor now against Kilbane, was

Abe able to give of his considerable best. He was, though, well able to give of his considerable worst.

Unable to keep Kilbane off with legitimate punches, he clinched, grabbed and held shamelessly. He indulged in other idiosyncrasies such as rubbing Kilbane's face with the rough heel of his glove, grabbing and bending Kilbane's left arm back painfully in the eighth, and splitting Kilbane's left eyebrow with a blatant headbutt in the 16th. He further upset referee Charles Eyton by emerging for the 16th so liberally covered with protective grease that Eyton vigorously towelled it off himself. Cocaine in New York, grease in Vernon, enough substance abuse already one would think, yet Kilbane claimed that Attell had also used some chloroform body rub in the hope the fumes would stupefy his opponent.[13]

The moral qualifications of Kilbane, the younger man in the ring, were impeccable. He was a model husband to his wife Mary, the model father to baby daughter Mary Coletta, and a model caring son to his blind father. His virtuous standing was well known to the huge crowd (10,000 in the arena; 5,000 turned unluckily away) with whom he was extremely popular. He was cheered home to victory over the 20 rounds with quite as much vigour as Attell's antics were booed and hissed. Kilbane was the new world featherweight champion. (Perhaps not all about Kilbane was quite as simon -pure as his newspaper hagiography suggested. On 29 October 1912, he knocked out the lightly regarded Tommy Dugan in the fourth round of a so-called world championship bout. He, his sparring partner, his manager and his promoter were all charged with

In 1912, lightweights were ubiquitous. This consortium includes many all-time greats. From left to right: Freddie Welsh; Frankie Conley; 'One Round' Hogan; Ad Wolgast; Johnny Coulon; Abe Attell; Harlem Tommy Murphy; Johnny Kilbane; Mexican Joe Rivers.
BoxRec

conspiracy and fraud. Nothing could be proved; doubts remained.)

Looking back in 1950 on the Kilbane fight, Attell was respectful of Kilbane with reservations:

I think Kilbane had the best one-two punch of all us little fellows. Yet he seldom made a sensational fight. That was because he wouldn't take no chances. Nobody ever hit him when he was good, you know – and he never started a punch until he was sure it was going to land first. Over-cautious.[14]

Excess of caution was not a charge laid often at Attell in or out of the ring. In the same interview he freely admitted to gambling heavily on fights in which he was involved, to holding up inferior opponents or to making them look good merely for the sake of a lucrative return. In the subsequent return, Attell, having backed himself heavily, could cut loose and win easily.

The trick was to let the yokel hold you even. In those days the newspapers gave the decisions. I always felt I'd turned in a bad job when they gave me a shade. The line I liked to read was: 'The champion was entitled to no more than a draw'.

From carefully negotiated purses (he got a guaranteed $15,000 for purse and film rights from his loss to Kilbane), and his betting coups on boxers and horses, Attell had seen anything from $250,000 to $300,000 pass through his hands by 1912. 'Pass' is probably the operative word. And 'pass *to*' the bookmakers the direction. The first Mrs Attell, Ethel, who divorced him, saw the Kilbane earnings converted into sparkling rings and necklaces to grace her fingers and neck on a temporary basis, only to go to cover his gambling debts soon after.[15]

Just over a fortnight after the Kilbane fight, and during the suspension period, his gambling debts had him dragging his body back into a ring on 9 March 1912 in Daly City, California for an exceptionally bloody losing encounter against Harlem Tommy Murphy over 20 rounds. The ring canvas was stained scarlet and the fighters' torsos turned red as if they were wearing red vests – the blood was Attell's. He took more and more punishment until, as *Boxing* graphically put it: 'At the end of the 20th rd. Attell groped his way to his seconds, a bruised, bloody, indescribable piece of beef. He was dazed and licked.'

The sordid sight of a man of once superlative skills being trounced by a heavier and clumsier man he might once have laughed at did not have the tragic consequences that might have been predicted. The feisty Attell did not suffer permanent damage or develop Alzheimer's later. He fought the occasional bout until his retirement in 1917. He was an ever-present at ringsides for many decades after that. The great A. J. Liebling of the *New Yorker* in 1951, at the time of the Rocky Marciano v Joe Louis fight, records the aged Attell amusing himself in bars and clubs by shooting lead airgun pellets with a bamboo toothpick through the gaps in his teeth at unsuspecting bartenders, or at lady hostesses with impressive cleavages; a clear talent to annoy.[16] Attell's conscience was as resilient as his skull and his gambling with his own and others' money, plus operations in and out of legality, would yet land him back in the dock.

The other great maverick of American boxing, the world heavyweight champion Jack Johnson, was, in 1912, enjoying the prestige of the title with relish. He had not felt it incumbent upon him to defend the title

Jack Johnson and his wife Etta, a glamorous but doomed marriage.
Prints & Photographs Division, Library of Congress, LC-DIG-ppmsca-31941

once during 1911, and he did not enter the ring competitively from 4 July 1910 to 4 July 1912. From any champion this was a dubious proceeding. His reign was still regarded by many whites as a foreign occupation of territory rightfully theirs, fear and hatred accompanying the grudging recognition of the *force majeure* that had placed the belt around his waist.

Some believe only Johnson's arrogance and frequent misbehaviour left

him lonely and detested, and had he shown the charm of a Floyd Patterson, or the lip-buttoned deference of a Joe Louis, all would have been well. This is pure fantasy. Johnson would have been bitterly resented, whatever he did to ameliorate it. Even the saintly Peter Jackson, whose gentlemanly mien so appealed to NSC members ('this finest of boxers and *finest of men*'[17] [italics added]), was also publicly humiliated when he tried unwittingly to book into a hotel where blacks were unwelcome.[18]

Resentment against Johnson might have lessened had he adopted the forelock-tugging obsequiousness of an ex-slave demonstrably grateful to be freed. Johnson, being Johnson, reserved the right to behave as badly as he wished, just like Corbett and Sullivan before him. In Johnson's case, this took many forms.

His consumption was legendarily conspicuous and he dressed and behaved in ways calculated to draw attention. Speed limits were there merely for him to exceed once behind the wheel of whatever new speedster he had just acquired. Anecdotes, not always fully documented, circulated freely about his motoring career. These included a traffic cop who levied a $50 fine for speeding given a $100 bill and told, 'Keep the change, I'll be back this way in a minute.' There was the four-block tailback caused by Johnson's car parked in the middle of the street as he stopped to shop. A Chicago policeman was advised, 'Stand back, Mr White Offisah, and let dem coloured peoples hab a look at me.'[19] Note that the articulate Johnson had his words conveyed in mock black minstrel-speak, although he could turn on the irony and satirise white expectations anyway. That such incidents were calculated on Johnson's part is highly likely, if his autobiographical account of his presence in London for King George V's Coronation in June 1911 is to be believed:

Despite the fact that the King and his coronation was [sic] the center of attention, when my car travelled along London streets and

it was announced that I was in sight, the attention of the crowds was turned upon me, and as long as I was in view the coronation ceremonies were forgotten while crowds milled and struggled for a glance at me.[20]

Such ego trips were Johnson's counter to the hatred and discrimination he, like other black American citizens, faced regularly. It was his uglier side, one that left a sordid trail of broken contracts, non-appearances, debts, violent confrontations and damaged property behind him as he and his entourage moved on to the next engagement. Worse still, his violent side spilled over into his complicated relations with women.

His ring record amounted to over a hundred bouts and included, especially in his early days, many quite obscure, as well as no-decision and exhibition bouts later in life that it would be futile to record in detail. His encounters in bed were even more complex for he was a serial husband, a serial adulterer and a serial server of sex workers and amateur chorus girls alike. The title Mrs Johnson was bestowed indiscriminately on the latest lady on his arm regardless of ceremony and documentation. Some hotels boasted the registration of two 'Mrs Johnsons' simultaneously.[21] In *Jack Johnson is a Dandy*, Johnson claims a black Texan lady called Mary Austin was 'my first wife'.[22] Yet, as Randy Roberts's researches disclose, he later entered a marriage contract claiming never to have been married previously.[23]

Another of his biographers, Denzil Batchelor, demonstrating an amazingly intimate knowledge of private conversations and actions taking place

behind closed doors, proffers a long liaison with 'Sadie', who supposedly loved then dumped him, and finished in prison on a murder charge.[24] 'Sadie' and her tragedy sound suspiciously like a garbled account sometimes told of Clara Kerr, a black sex worker whom Mr Roberts links to Johnson from January 1902, and with whom Johnson says 'I became greatly infatuated'. Clara did leave Johnson, but whether she ran off with a racehorse trainer, or was charged with the murder of her own brother, or whether Johnson financed her legal defence or set her up in the hotel business when she was acquitted, as he claimed later, are more dubious. Along with the myths that journalists created about Johnson, he spun many himself – that he was a crack sprinter who chased down chickens and ate them by the coopful before fights; that he dictated copy to telegraph operators over Jeffries's shoulder in the 1910 fight; that he was merely a musical philosopher who put down his bass viol only to immerse himself in a volume of improving literature.

Once Johnson became world heavyweight champion in December 1908, he was rarely seen without a white lady companion in the background or the foreground. On 18 January 1911 he married a white French American called Etta Terry Duryea, claiming her to be his second wife in succession to Mary Austin, although, thanks to Mr Roberts, we know her to be the first genuine Mrs Johnson. Etta was married previously to a racehorse owner, Charles Duryea. Her second marriage was no smoother than her first. On good days she was installed in luxury hotels and bought expensive clothes and jewellery by an attentive husband. At other times she was ignored or cast aside like a once fashionable accessory superfluous to need. Theirs became an abusive and violent relationship. Reliable witnesses to ugly incidents between them include the veteran boxing writer Nat Fleischer. He saw a sorely provoked Etta take up a hotel chair to hit her husband.[25] According to Gunboat Smith, who was a sparring partner, friend and guest at their wedding, 'he treated her like a dog'.[26] Like a dog, she was sometimes beaten.[27]

Etta's humiliations included sharing her husband's favours with many white sex professionals, some on a one-night stand, others, like the German-American Belle Schreiber and the New York Irish Hattie McClay, on a more frequent visitor season ticket. Their turbulent marriage was in a particularly unsatisfactory trough in the spring of 1912 as he exploited the full fruits of the prestigious crown. He signed a profitable contract to defend his title against the latest 'white hope', Fireman Jim Flynn of New Jersey, on 4 July 1912 in Las Vegas in a $100,000 promotion. Earnings from this were reinvested in a superior Chicago Cabaret de Champion, which opened, with silver cuspidors, mahogany furniture and 'a few real Rembrandts', a week after the fight against Flynn.[28] The contrast between the sumptuous public display and the sordid reality of domestic life in private seems to have tipped Etta over the edge. On 11 September 1912, as the Cabaret customers partied downstairs, she shot herself in an upstairs bedroom.[29]

Another provocation behind Etta's despairing act of self-destruction was Johnson's sexual involvement with an 18-year-old employee at the Cabaret, Lucille Cameron, whom the press and the authorities categorised as a white, wide-eyed innocent bemused by the Svengalian black Johnson. The labels did not concur with reality. Lucille was, said Gunboat Smith, 'altogether different … a bum right out of the house'.[30] The 'house' meant brothel, and Lucille, despite her tender years, was an experienced brothel worker.[31] She became the second genuine Mrs Johnson on 4 December 1912, less than three months after Etta's suicide.

This marriage lasted at least technically until 1924 when Lucille divorced him. He married another glamorous white divorcée, Irene Marie Pineau, in 1925, when approaching 50 himself. Johnson claimed in his 1926 autobiography: 'The heartaches which Mary Austin and Clara Kerr had caused me, led me to forswear colored women and to determine that my lot henceforth would be cast only with white women.'[32] Three marriages to, and countless liaisons with, white women constitute a trend, yet the concept of Johnson as victim hardly convinces. As Randy Roberts says, 'He made love to his white women, but he also beat them up.'[33]

There are two highly Freudian motifs to be detected here. Johnson flaunted his marriages and affairs with white women to demonstrate his right to be a full member of a white man's world. This was as clear as when he drove his latest open-topped racer down streets where other blacks stepped into the gutter to give precedence to whites, and where an ordinary black man who looked into the eyes of a passing white woman risked a lynching. Remember also his delight at proving himself at least the equal of white legal minds in a London magistrates' court in 1911. Nevertheless, Randy Roberts surely overstates his case when he suggests Johnson wanted subconsciously to defile and humiliate white women as much as elevate them.

Most boxers of any ethnic origins confine their aggression to the roped square and remain model citizens outside it. Yet there has always been a minority who resort to violence when placed under stress in their private lives. The well-known excesses of the American heavyweight Mike Tyson and his ugly out-of-ring behaviour, the lightweight Diego Corrales guilty of beating his pregnant wife, and the volatile relationship between Vera and the less than Gentlemanly Jim Corbett are but a few examples.

All that Tyson, Corrales and Corbett have in common is that they are all *boxers*. Their ethnic identities, even so crudely defined as Afro-American, American Latino and white Irish-American respectively, are irrelevant. Boxers have been trained to respond with their fists at moments of crisis. It is less than astonishing that some fighters – the word *some* is crucial – are unable to control such responses when the contest is over. Such impulses are inexcusable, especially when directed at targets more vulnerable than themselves. It is also utterly unprofessional because every good trainer insists from lesson one that it is *controlled* aggression that wins fights, and that losses of temper and control produce only losers, in and out of the ring.

Regrettably, some modern promoters and editors perceive antisocial behaviour as selling points. The excesses of Tyson stimulated ticket and pay-per-view sales for his contests and the coverage he commanded. The more the man misbehaved, the more people wanted to see him. In the 1990s, Tyson gave calculatedly outrageous performances as Big Bad Mike as if that were what was expected of him. The more virulent the nonsense he spoke, the more eagerly editors filled their spaces with verbatim quotations or lengthy condemnations. When Tyson visited Britain in June 2000, *The Guardian*, which prides itself on ethical stands and has called editorially for professional boxing to be banned, devoted hundreds of column inches to Tyson's out-of-ring activities from his Brixton walkabout to his remarkable retail therapy. Tabloid newspapers are not alone in their application of double standards.

To what extent do spectators bear collective guilt for such excesses? The holder of a £25 unreserved arena ticket did not rape Desiree Washington as did Tyson. Neither did the man in the $2,000 ringside seat bite off a chunk of Evander Holyfield's ear as did Tyson. Nevertheless, many in boxing helped Tyson's career to flourish even *after* these misdeeds. Others persisted in seeing Tyson as a black victim of a white racist society. This seems as crass as the misjudgement of Tyson as an unredeemable black monster. Michael Gerard Tyson remains a complicated human being, entitled to much compassion on the basis of his horrendous childhood (as even the crassest of his biographers concedes), yet also to condemnation for a profligate and irresponsible lifestyle, and for the use of his uncanny physical strength for dubious ends.

Jack Johnson raises similar ethical questions. Johnson was a flawed human being, well capable of irresponsible social and financial misbehaviour. He used his physical prowess to abuse his wives and sexual partners, and to win arguments in and out of his entourage. He still has more claims than Tyson to be seen as a victim of white racist society. As his story unfolds over the next few years, we will see him severely punished by American officialdom, less for his misdeeds than for his stubborn breaking of two discreditable American shibboleths – that a man with a black skin had no right to accompany let alone marry or sleep with white women; and that he had no right to contest physical superiority with white men, let alone hold the world heavyweight championship.

In the spring of 1912, Johnson signed to meet Fireman Flynn in July, thought vaguely about training, and was, unknown to him, being monitored by agents of the Federal Bureau of Investigation. FBI reports, especially about his relationships with white women, were accumulating in voluminous official files.[34]

Other name fighters took the next steps in their careers. The NSC wanted to host a return bout between the large South African Fred Storbeck, and the Mary Ann-wielding Frank Moran, a fight to resolve the questions unanswered by Storbeck's January disqualification. Instead, on 5 February 1912, The Ring at Blackfriars staged the next instalment, and confirmed that Moran had Storbeck's measure over a full distance.[35]

Storbeck's intentions were simple: to teem all over Moran, landing as often as he could. Moran, less profligate, landed less often, but weightily and more painfully. Moran's sole extravagance was the odd whistling left hook that grazed Storbeck's scalp as he launched one of his eccentric jack-knife ducks towards the canvas. These weird bobs got Storbeck out of one difficulty and into another. On his return to the land of the vertical, he met a straight Moran left over his lowered guard and colliding painfully with his right eye. Moran, in this pre-video era, had done his homework. As rounds went by, Storbeck's right eyebrow and cheekbone swelled and hampered his vision.

Storbeck was not as strong as Moran, nor as strategically adept. But he was just as game. Seconds after the latest visitation to the right side of his face, he lunged forward after Moran, trying to do with flurries what Moran could do with one good punch. Storbeck had anticipated visits from Mary Ann, but her sister in the left glove was doing the major damage.

Forward went the gallant Storbeck in the eighth, ninth and tenth rounds, throwing punches as best he could and taking more. He barely survived the 11th. He got off his stool for the 12th, somehow, and was floored twice, once by a weary slip, once by a punch. When he got up again and tottered towards Moran, Mary Ann smooched him and he crashed to the boards too comatose to hear the bell ringing a second too late to rescue him: Moran by knockout.

Storbeck's double failure to beat Moran was symptomatic of a trend established by 1912. In a contest between an American in one corner and a Briton, a European or a representative of the extensive British Empire in the other, the American usually won. French boxers, who had come late and enthusiastically to the sport, lost more bouts to British fighters than they won. No country has a monopoly on misguided nationalism. There were cracker-barrel philosophers in all three countries eager to equate the failure of any one boxer as evidence of growing national decadence. Neo-Darwinian gloom and dubious racial theories about genetic decline were ten a penny in the early 20th century. They were just as misguided as the lauding of a ring success as certain proof of inherent national superiority – a testosterone-loaded guarantee of virility awarded along with a passport.

Often enough, fighters defied general trends or won against the odds. When British boxers showed real prowess in American rings – as did Driscoll and Moran and a few other illustrious fighters we will meet in the next few years – American journalists and American crowds received them enthusiastically. When an American of the calibre of a Harry Lewis or an Eddie McGoorty did the business in British or French rings, they were also noisily and admiringly cheered.

Top French performers such as Jean Poesy and Charles Ledoux became very popular with British audiences and the relationship of the British with Georges Carpentier became an all-out love affair.[36] At a Ring matinee on the same afternoon and in the same ring as the second Moran/Storbeck fight, the popular English featherweight Charlie Dixon was cleverly outpointed over ten rounds by the Frenchman Charles Legrand and, said *Boxing*, 'Dixon tried his uttermost to turn the tide in his own favour, but without avail, the visitor coming in for a great reception upon being proclaimed the winner.' No misplaced xenophobia there it seemed.

Admittedly, the British continued to regard a gallant losing performance by a home boxer against strong American opposition to be as commendable as a victory. Tommy Farr stayed the distance for 15 rounds with Joe Louis in New York on 30 August 1937. Don

Cockell resisted the considerable force of Rocky Marciano for nine rounds in San Francisco on 16 May 1955. Henry Cooper knocked down Muhammad Ali (then Cassius Clay) on 18 June 1963 before losing. All three British performances lodged themselves more fondly in British hearts than other domestic boxers who actually won world titles.

The first half of 1912 saw many Frenchmen in British rings, including Charles Legrand. Legrand weighed in at 9st 1½lb/127½lbs, a pound heavier than his opponent, the stockier, shorter and very tough Englishman Seaman Arthur Hayes, on 19 February 1912, two weeks after Legrand's success over Charlie Dixon.[37] Seaman was not a showy fighter, more content to set a stately course around the ring, keeping his big guns under wraps while fleeter opponents circled around him. Oddly, Legrand chose to circle Hayes clockwise, in the risky direction of Hayes's damaging right hook. Hayes had a left lead but landed it less often. When Legrand tapped him swiftly three or four times with a left, Hayes riposted with a shuddering straight left that jolted the Frenchman's head back, and a right hook delivered with force to the ribs. The contrast in pace and style was intriguing, and 15 absorbing rounds sped swiftly by. Legrand edged ahead, only to be overhauled. As *Boxing*'s reporter saw, Hayes 'had reduced Legrand's speed to only about twice his own'. Hayes the tortoise beat the French hare on points.

Another Anglo-French fracas was decided over 15 rounds at the NSC a week later on 26 February 1912.[38] The veteran Romany fighter Digger Stanley (whom we last saw in action in

Jean Poesy (1889–1955), the Marseilles featherweight dubbed 'The Third Musketeer'.
BnF

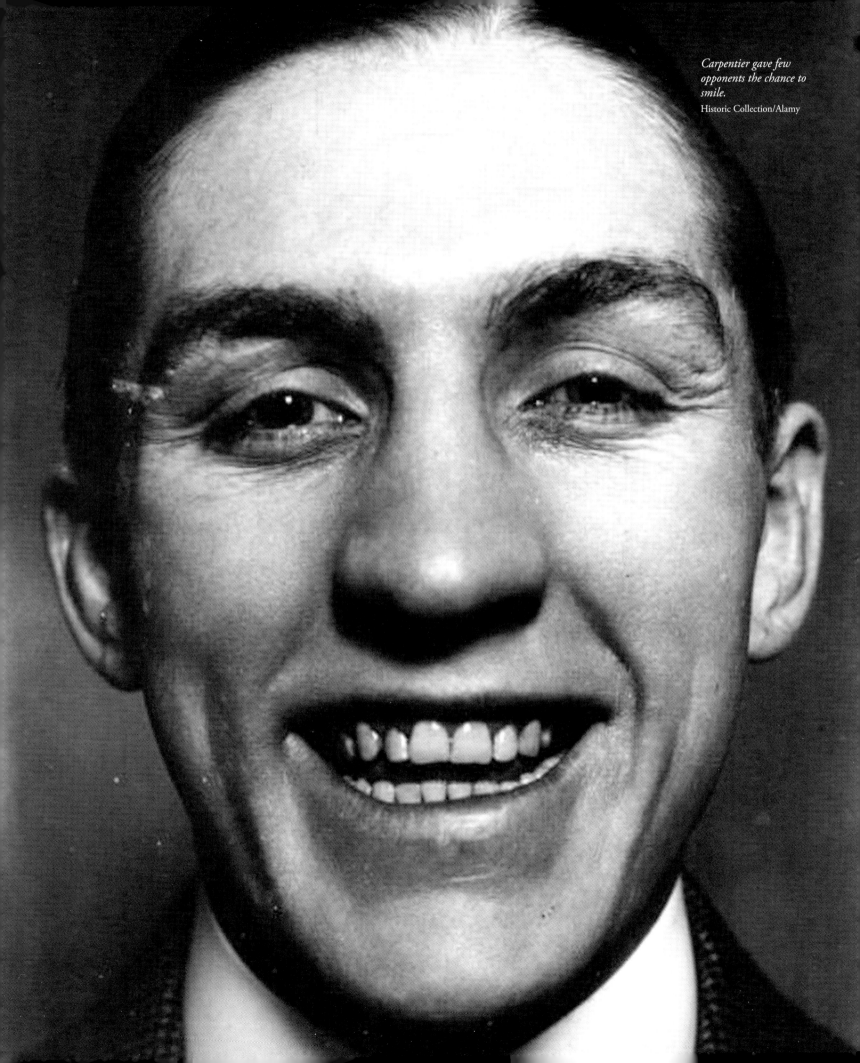

1910 against Joe Bowker in Chapter 5) gave away some six pounds to another talented French featherweight in Jean Poesy (b. Marseilles, 26 January 1889, the same year Digger made his professional debut). This time Digger's immaculately greased quiff was more prominent than his swindles. The perceptive NSC audience remembered the dubious ploy against Bowker two years before. Members itemised loudly illegalities tried on the referee's blind side. Chicaneries aside, Digger was as brilliant as they came, as courageous as a little terrier tackling a rat, and as full of wiry speed and stamina as a trained whippet. Had he heard of Anno Domini, he would have thought him an Italian bantam easily beaten.

Poesy was as fast and clever as Stanley, and stronger physically. Both were cool thinkers, eager to mix it and go toe to toe in rallies, yet strategically savvy. Poesy hinted he would win by knockout, more ploy than serious prediction. (Poesy's ability to sell a fight had him recruited by Hugh McIntosh to fight in Australia before 1912 was out.)

The encounter was vintage. From the first bell, Poesy forced the pace and countered fiercely. An early clinch turned into a mini-wrestle, a trial of strength won by Poesy, who pushed Digger off so vigorously that the Englishman touched down with his gloves to keep himself off the canvas. That bit of nonsense over, both settled to give of their skilful best.

In the early rounds, a favourite Digger tactic – a range-finding left followed instantly with a right from an unorthodox angle – worked. Poesy merely blinked. Digger took punches on gloves and forearms and swayed and ducked fractions of an inch away from a punch. Poesy was also a clever escapee. At the end of the sixth, a bob of his head met a Digger right hook with the hardest part of his skull. The skull survived the encounter better than the Digger's knuckles. Stanley was left with nine more rounds to fight against a stronger man with a right now capable of only token punches.

It is symbolic of Stanley's sangfroid that nothing in his Buster Keaton-like features, relieved occasionally by a grim smile, hinted that he was seriously handicapped. Only gradually did Poesy realise that Stanley's thunderous rights were not thudding home as they had in the first five rounds.

The next six rounds had members on the edge of their seats, gnawing at their moustaches, the handles of canes and umbrellas, and anything that came to hand, as Poesy went hunting his opponent, eager to fulfil his pre-fight prediction and become the first man to beat the veteran by a knockout. Digger declined to be caught, boxing, slipping, feinting and keeping Poesy away with a left and half a right. Poesy, now fully aware of Digger's injury, stormed after him, prepared to absorb Stanley's lefts to land himself.

Despite the trend from eighth to 13th, Poesy took more and more sharp lefts coming back from Stanley and looked weary himself. When these two great boxers came out for the 15th, they shared the warmest double glove handshake in mutual respect before resuming the frenzied action. *Boxing*'s ringside reporter conveys the climax:

> [Poesy] … breaking loose, charged furiously at Digger. Stanley tried to stop him with his

left, but was driven into a neutral corner and severely hammered on the stomach. Digger got away from this smartly, however, and well held his own for a while in some particularly hot rallies which swayed backwards and forwards across the ring. It was plain now that much of the power had gone out of Poesy's punches. Stanley, however, took no risks, but clinched at every opportunity, and though Poesy continued to force matters to the final gong, he was unable to do any serious damage. The verdict in the Frenchman's favour met with a tremendous ovation.

Again an English audience received a French success over an English champion in London sportingly. However, having lost to one Frenchman in Poesy, Digger Stanley put his nominal title as world bantamweight champion (not recognised as such in the USA) on the line against another in Charles Ledoux at the NSC on 22 April 1912 over 20 rounds for a £500 purse. Ledoux, the heavier by fight time by about six pounds and with a real dig in his right hand, hoped to repeat his January win over Bowker when he had allowed a clever opponent to dance all around him then produced the great equaliser the first chance he got.

Stanley, quite as clever as Bowker, was a slowish starter. In the first half of the fight he landed fewer scoring punches than Ledoux. Stanley would never match him for power but knew how to hurt an opponent. Only in the last three rounds did Ledoux revive to have Stanley on the verge of a knockout. Stanley stayed elusive and countered effectively. Effectively enough, that is, to win narrowly on points. An observant audience and a competent referee had kept him on his best behaviour.

In strong contrast, a return between the two on 23 June 1912 in Dieppe as part of a week-long International Boxing Festival was a disgrace. In essence, Stanley boxed himself to a comfortable lead for six rounds then came out for the seventh, gloves down at his knees and his chin out front. Ledoux, the qualified pastry chef, could spot a free cream puff when he saw one and caught Stanley with a volley of hard punches, none defended against. Over and out went Stanley. Much later, he admitted to James Butler that he had been bribed to throw the fight.[39]

The defeat of another British boxer, Fred Delaney, disqualified against the French welterweight Marcel Thomas for persistent low blows when well ahead on points, was similarly dubious. Another British welterweight, the blacksmith Arthur Evernden, was in serious difficulties in the second round against Bernard, his French opponent. He resolved the crisis by knocking out not Bernard but the French referee. The local gendarmerie cleared the ring but not before one of Evernden's seconds had knocked the referee down again.[40] The behaviour of British boxers at the Dieppe festival enhanced neither *entente cordiale* nor their integrity.

Tolerance for foreign boxers had already been tested in Monte Carlo back on 29 February 1912 when the English middleweight champion Jim Sullivan travelled there to meet Georges Carpentier in a specially constructed open air ring on the front. Sullivan was accompanied by a small group of English supporters less

than disappointed to leave a wet and windy London for the Mediterranean. They were a small section within a largely French crowd of 10,000. In a preliminary bout, the French lightweight Bernstein was thoroughly outboxed by another Englishman, Alf Spenceley. Wrote an English journalist: 'The verdict was received by the somewhat surprised French spectators with positive enthusiasm. No one will ever have any ground for denying that our neighbours are as genuine sportsmen as can be found anywhere.' The English had no monopoly over sporting generosity and Sullivan's delayed ring entrance was, rather to his surprise, warmly applauded.

The extended preliminaries to the main contest, purse £1,800, were as contested as the fight itself, and lasted longer. Colourful heraldic devices and national flags fluttered in the sea breezes, as did two huge banners proclaiming 'GRAND COMBAT INTERNATIONAL DE BOXE'. Before the two boxers appeared there were mini-eruptions over sundry details. The black Australian boxer George Gunther, long anxious to fight Carpentier, pleaded his cause in and out of the ring. M. Descamps, Carpentier's manager, and Sullivan's representatives disputed ownership of the picture rights up to the last possible moment. Descamps had already vented his anger spectacularly over some trifle during the weigh-in four hours earlier and his equanimity was not fully restored. (At that weigh-in, Sullivan was 11st/154lbs and Carpentier a surprisingly light 11st 1lb/155lbs.)

Descamps threatened another explosion. The bout, unlike those in Britain, was not to be decided by the

referee but by a panel of three judges. Two experienced English referees, J. T. Hulls and Jim Pratt, had been chosen, along with M. Emile Maitrot from Paris. M. Maitrot never appeared. The Sullivan camp refused to allow M. Vienne, the promoter, to replace him. Only when Descamps agreed to accept the verdict of the two English judges alone was the fight back on.

Descamps's patience was tested further. Carpentier took the ring and stood to attention as a hatless standing audience fervently sang 'La Marseillaise', and, with less gusto, 'God Save the King'. Sullivan was still sulking in his tent over the initial delay. Carpentier, wrapped in a snazzy blue-and-grey robe, jogged, shuffled and shadow-boxed until Sullivan deigned to join him.

Two can play these games. Once Sullivan reached the ring, Carpentier suddenly found his gloves did not fit, and only when another 20 pairs had been tried did he find a satisfactory one. When the first bell rang, he challenged the loose bandages around Sullivan's cuffs and another delay ensued while they were trimmed.[41]

Sullivan was a slow starter, and apprehensive of Carpentier's well-known uppercuts, adopted an unusual stance with his gloves low and his torso leaning away from his opponent. It was a reasonable posture for swaying back or withdrawing, not for delivering swift counter-punches, the one way the young Carpentier (barely past his 18th birthday in February 1912) could be beaten. Few boxers could face Carpentier with an elevated chin and escape the consequences. ('I preferred to meet boxers, feeling that I should always be able to find their weak spots, rather than those tough slogger types with about as much sensibility as a doorpost,' he wrote later in life.)[42]

A long-range right probing for Carpentier's lower ribcage brought Sullivan's chin within range a minute into the round. Carpentier met it with a well-timed left hook that seriously shook Sullivan. The fight was already really over. Carpentier caught Sullivan again with a straight jolting left and followed it with punches that would have floored Sullivan had the bell not rung.

So fuddled was Sullivan that he failed to take full advantage of the minute's break. A tiny noise at ringside convinced him the bell had gone and he pushed aside his seconds and stumbled towards Carpentier's corner. He was dragged back to his stool, precious seconds of rest lost. When the bell did ring, he had still not fully recovered.

He went into a clinch to smother Carpentier's opening sally. Unfortunately, he again fell for the Carpentier two-card trick that had fooled him in the first. Again Carpentier left a midriff seemingly exposed, tempting Sullivan to let go a low right. Before the punch could land, Carpentier again landed a wicked left hook over Sullivan's low right directly to Sullivan's exposed chin. A right hook followed instantly. Outclassed and outthought, Sullivan went over backwards, hitting the back of his head solidly on the unpadded boards. He was out for a full five minutes, as jubilant French supporters invaded the ring and hoisted Carpentier up on to their shoulders. To Carpentier the glory and a glittering future; to Sullivan the eventual recovery of his senses, but the bitter realisation that he had done his own talents scant justice. 'It's not that I mind being beaten, but to have made such a can [sic] of myself and to be beaten before I'd started.' Later, illness intervened and he was forced to hand back his Lonsdale Belt to the NSC without defending it.[43] Not for Sullivan the luxury of a Jack Johnson, holding a title and being idle for two years.

With Sullivan left post-Carpentier to lick his wounds and his wounded pride, and with Tom Thomas lying in a Welsh grave, the focus shifted to other middleweights. On 20 May 1912, two men were invited to the NSC to decide over 20 rounds to whom the British championship, the Lonsdale Belt and a £400 purse would be awarded. The two were an Englishman, Jack Harrison of Rushden and an Irish-American, Private Pat McEnroy.[44] Harrison had all the credentials. He claimed to be a descendant of the mighty prizering fighter, Tom Sayers, and he had Jim Driscoll as a second. In genetics and ring culture he was theoretically already a champion. After 20 rounds, he was awarded the verdict and the championship, a decision undisputed even by a disappointed McEnroy. Yet the event was never fully satisfying.

Harrison was the more skilful, manipulator of an educated left and normally a swift seizer of momentary opportunities. McEnroy was a scrapper and a swarmer, all glares, elbows, forearms and backhanders, and non-stop aggression. On the night, neither performed to his potential. Seldom had a belt and a title been so tamely won. The unlucky Sullivan must have been particularly chagrined.

Carpentier, well informed about British boxing, could reflect ruefully two days later about fights lost and won so easily. On 22 May 1912, he was back at the Cirque de Paris for his third bout since crushing Sullivan. (He outpointed the patient George Gunther over 20 rounds in Paris on 3 April 1912, then despatched fellow Frenchman Hubert Roc in six rounds down at Marseilles on 10 May 1912.) His new opponent was almost as well known in Paris as himself – American middleweight Willie Lewis, a man who would celebrate his 29th birthday next day, and who had been

Monte Carlo: Sullivan discovered Carpentier's virtues at first hand when knocked out in the second.
BnF

a professional boxer since 1903. Since his debut Lewis had shared a ring with opponents of the calibre of Honey Mellody, Joe Gans, Harry Lewis and Billy Papke.

Over 20 rounds, Carpentier could be reasonably sure of finishing the fresher, but Lewis was at least as skilful as he. Both liked to win, and win gracefully and legitimately. Neither was under the illusion that to lose gracefully took precedence over a victory. Carpentier and Lewis, both weighing in at 11st 4lb/158lbs, would do what they had to do to win.

The fight drew one of the most glittering French audiences ever previously assembled ('all sporting, literary and fashionable Paris was there'). Carpentier was confidently expected to confirm the arrival of French boxing on the international scene by beating Lewis, the man who besotted the French public before the emergence of their own hero.[45] Disobligingly, Lewis did not see it that way. Barely had the contest begun when a piston-like Lewis left landed smack in the middle of Carpentier's forehead raising a lump, drawing blood and sending the pale-skinned Frenchman a few degrees paler.

Carpentier was more circumspect for the next few rounds, defending skilfully and getting off his own punches when he deemed it safe to do so. Lewis landed several good scoring punches, shading the fourth and clearly winning the fifth and sixth. The audience, which had cheered Georges all the way to the ring and cheered any of his half-decent punches, now fell into anxious silence. They knew Carpentier was having an off night and it would get worse before it got better.

In the eighth, Carpentier dropped his left hand as they parted from the latest clinch. Lewis, none too scrupulous about punching on the break whenever a referee tolerated it, caught Carpentier on the borderline between left temple and left cheekbone with a fiery right hook. Down went Carpentier, dropping like French spirits. Fortunately for him, down went the timekeeper's arm before a full count could be administered. Lewis, magnanimous as a man on the verge of victory, helped Carpentier's seconds pull the dazed Georges back to his feet. He wanted the Frenchman sufficiently restored to be finished off in the ninth.

In the ninth, Carpentier survived by dint of frantic holding, retreating, clinching and dodging. It took three rounds to recover his wits. Then it was Lewis's turn to suffer despite his extensive points lead. As Carpentier got back into the fight, Lewis felt the draining effects of having a younger opponent on the brink of defeat and failing to clinch the win. In the 13th, the crowd grew in confidence and fervour as Carpentier looked more like his old self.

Lewis, who had earlier tried out a few old pro tricks – tapping his neck or pointing to his boots and whipping over a punch while his opponent was distracted – now strayed into other more blatant illegalities. He held and hit; he roughed up with head and glove; he hit on the break. The referee, M. Cuny, who had tolerated liberties from both men in the heat of the early action, issued Lewis with a public warning in the 15th. With the pragmatic shrug of an old pro rumbled, Lewis conformed for the rest of the fight.

The tide had changed. From the 15th to the 20th, it was Lewis looking to survive. In the last round he clinched so desperately that he took both men down to the floor in an exhausted heap. Against every early trend and with uncanny psychological and physical resilience, Carpentier clinched the narrowest of points victories.

Carpentier's career in 1912 was as up and down as the fight against Lewis. His next two fights (24 June and 23 October 1912) were against formidable German-American middleweights – the short and stocky Frank Klaus (b. 30 December 1887) otherwise known as 'The Pittsburgh Bearcat', and Billy Papke (b. 17 September 1886), 'The Illinois Thunderbolt'. Both Americans were one-time holders of the world middleweight title. Carpentier lost both fights and both in odd circumstances. In the June fight, Klaus was severely punishing a reeling Carpentier in the 19th round. Carpentier's manager Francois Descamps leapt into the ring anxious to save his protégé and friend from further damage. Shouting volubly at the referee, he grabbed a tearful and resistant Carpentier by the waist and tried to drag him from the ring. Meanwhile, Carpentier's seconds threw in a sponge. Already incandescent at Klaus's illegal use of an elbow to Carpentier's stomach in the 18th, Descamps had lost all self-control. Nevertheless, in an age when many managers permitted their charges to be flogged as long as their pulses weakly throbbed, Descamps's righteous passion does seem excusable. Better a fight conceded by disqualification than a career ruined. At the time, Carpentier thought the intervention premature but admitted subsequently that he had been helpless.

(Loss of control and ring excesses can be infectious. The next fight on the bill

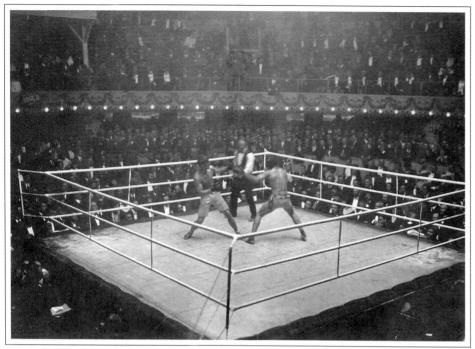

23 October 1912, Cirque de Paris: against Papke, Carpentier was overmatched until his manager compassionately intervened.
BoxRec

featured Arthur Evernden of England against the Parisian welterweight Georges Bernard. The referee pulled Evernden back in the second round only for the Englishman to turn and punch him to the floor. His neutrality invaded, the referee got up and swung punches at Evernden. Seconds and spectators joined in heartily, as did the gendarmes, the ultimate victors in the brawl. Evernden was disqualified.)

For the October meeting with Papke, the town of Dieppe generously boosted the purse to 80,000 francs to attract tourists; the municipal beneficence had not extended to accurate scales. Even with some leniency, Papke exceeded the 11st 6lb/160lbs limit and forfeited his title chances. Carpentier was finding it difficult to contain his growing frame within the middleweight limit and would soon move up to light-heavy and heavyweight categories.

Half-starved and parched, he made the limit against Papke, and

took the loser's share of the enhanced purse of 110,000 francs. It was utterly predictable that he would run out of stamina by the 17th.

Carpentier's right eye was closing by the end of the eighth and he could not see, let alone avoid the savage left hook to the jaw in the 17th that stunned and dropped him. He barely survived the round. Wisely, Descamps supervised his retirement during the interval before the 18th. (Papke had once fought a notoriously sanguinary series with Stanley Ketchel, winning one and losing three, and had the potential to give Carpentier a career-threatening beating. Descamps was wise to intervene.) In Carpentier's own words, 'Quite suddenly, my strength gave out and I was no longer firm on my pins, although I had not suffered any really damaging punches. I went on for another couple of rounds and then Descamps quite properly conceded the fight.' He did not come out for the

18th. There would have been no mercy from Papke, a ruthless man who ended his own life in 1936 with a gun, having already shot his ex-wife dead.

Even with the 1912 setbacks to Carpentier, the advance of French boxers was impressive. There were many piquant meetings in the summer of 1912. The most eagerly anticipated took place at the NSC on 3 June 1912 for what the club inaccurately billed as the 'Featherweight Championship of the World'. The USA and Abe Attell in particular strongly disagreed. The contestants were Digger Stanley's French conqueror, Jean Poesy, and the outstanding Welshman, Jim Driscoll, last seen in action in early 1911 against Spike Robson (Chapter 6). The purse of £1,200, two and a half times that contested by Stanley and Ledoux, had lured Driscoll back into the NSC ring. Poesy was two pounds lighter than Driscoll though bigger and a full decade younger. Driscoll looked trained up to the minute and ready for serious business.[46]

Poesy, expected to hustle and bustle the scientific Driscoll, declared his intention to knock the Welshman out in the 12th. Prediction was one thing, execution quite another. In the fight, Poesy granted Driscoll the respect lacking in his press interviews and stood off, moving away from the Driscoll left, a punch delivered with the power and accuracy of a billiards master driving through the cue ball on a long pot. (Like boxing, billiards reached great popularity in the Edwardian era with the famous manufacturers Riley selling 4,000 tables a year by 1910.) The punch, beginning roughly from Driscoll's left eyebrow, was accompanied by a transfer of his body weight over his advancing left thigh. When properly delivered it would have given a charging bullock pause for thought. It is still discussed with awe by boxing historians a century later.

Driscoll gave Poesy frequent demonstrations of its efficiency as Poesy sought to slow him down with attacks to the body. He was meeting a Driscoll at the height of his powers. Poesy launched his hooks, drives and swings. They were brushed aside by a Driscoll glove or an elbow or forearm. And each failure brought that resolute and stinging left back painfully into Poesy's face. Poesy had grown the stubble on his chin to nail brush length with the intention of roughing up the glowing Driscoll cheeks in the clinches. The bristles did nothing to offset the impact of that infuriating left. He had but one legitimate complaint when Driscoll, who had not fought since the rule had been amended, punched him in the kidneys.

After referee Douglas warned Driscoll for a perfectly legitimate hook to the soft tissue below the ribcage, Driscoll discreetly eschewed any more kidney punches. Poesy's illegal use of the head in close quarters escaped Douglas's attention. Douglas's powers were actually in decline, not enhanced by his seat outside the ring. This was fortunately not a close contest. By the tenth, the whole audience including Douglas had Driscoll miles ahead.

In the 12th Poesy rushed to clinch only to be met with half a dozen short, sharp punches. In desperation, he grabbed Driscoll and brought the top of his skull under Driscoll's chin ready to butt the Welshman. Driscoll put him in his place with a few sharp uppercuts. As Poesy staggered, Driscoll

hooked him to the floor. Poesy's prediction had been a knockout in the 12th. Perhaps mindful of his own prediction being precisely reversed, he got up again, much too quickly, at the count of two. Driscoll got in a sighting left to the Frenchman's bristled chin and followed with a measured right, leaving Poesy face down, unsuccessfully trying to beat the count. Driscoll lifted him up and tenderly escorted him to his corner.

Driscoll, Peerless Jim, had lived up to his epithet against Poesy, and indeed looked capable of beating any opponent anywhere. Three years before he had gone to New York and shown his abilities against Attell and others (Chapter 4). Other boxers such as Matt Wells and Owen Moran had also crossed the Atlantic to try out with mixed fortunes their collateral form in American rings. The trend continued in 1912.

On 26 April 1912, Matt Wells met Packey McFarland of Chicago at the Madison Square Garden arena in New York over the obligatory ten rounds for an obligatory no-decision.[47] In practice, McFarland, the press agreed, was a clear points winner. Some 9,000 people attended, including an abundance of impresarios, film actors, stockbrokers and assorted celebrities. McFarland and Wells jointly weighed in at 9st 12lb/138lbs. Had they weighed again after the bout they would have been very much lighter, dried out almost to a husk by 72 intense spotlights installed directly above the ring by a film company determined to maximise their investment in the film rights. So bright was the illumination that there were more green eyeshades at ringside than in the *New York Times* newsroom.

When the roof was opened to let out some of the heat generated by the lights, a sharp shower added fluid ounces of spring rain to the perspiration-soaked shirts and dresses in the front rows. It raised enough steam as to make the fighters wonder whether they were in a contest or a sauna. Even in such trying conditions, two of the cleverest lightweights in the world put on a fierce and unyielding battle.

Wells believed his best hopes lay in rushing in to close range with McFarland. McFarland clinched and smothered, biding his time. Wells got in and hooked fiercely to Packey's ribs, and, until warned by referee Sam Austin, Packey's kidneys. The tactics were moderately effective, but McFarland was a fast and elusive opponent. When Wells's hooks dissipated into the steamy air, he was open to punches from McFarland from unanticipated angles. Wells received painful uppercuts drawing blood from his nose and chin, and gulps of air from his open mouth when they connected to his solar plexus. By the fourth and fifth, McFarland had his measure and picked him off with jabs and swings. Wells's cauliflower ear bled throughout the second half of the fight, and the post-fight photos showed conclusively who had been the main recipient of punches. Only at the end of the eighth did Wells manage a straight left to McFarland's face, suggesting that on another day another result might have been possible.

The resilient Wells, who never knew when to stop, was back in an American ring at the Clermont Rink, Brooklyn on 5 June 1912 for a ten-rounder against the New York lightweight Young Brown.[48] Wells's confidence dipped when Brown, leaving his stool as if it were red hot, landed many punches on Wells, including a left swing to the temple that sent him sprawling across the ring and almost through the ropes. Brown was not McFarland. Wells recovered his poise and used his better ringcraft and greater hand speed to win most of the following rounds. He punched Brown about the body to slow him down and caught him with stiff jabs to the face, causing visible damage. There were angry shouts from ringside when his grizzled head conveniently collided with Brown's chin. Brown fought on, sustained by stamina and mental resilience, just, to the weary and bloody end.

This Matt Wells newspaper victory prefigured the summer visit to New York of his namesake, the handsome Bombardier Billy Wells. The controversy over the 1911 Johnson fight that never was, made Wells already a name in the USA. Billy had all the box office desiderata – the weight, the skill, the right shade of epidermis – added to matinee idol looks. Unfortunately, like many a man mountain before and after him, he had a propensity to play mental games with himself in which he usually turned loser. Mountains can defy assault only if they are not undermined from within. Wells had physical courage yet suffered a certain psychological fragility that reasserted itself embarrassingly at crucial moments. But then, promise mixed with unpredictability has rarely damaged the box office returns.

Once Billy and his entourage stepped off the SS *Mauretania* and set up a training camp outside the city, the New York sporting press awarded him extensive coverage further to boost the box office. Conventional wisdom suggested adjustment to a new climate and a new time zone, and a warm-up fight against inferior opposition were wise. Regardless, Wells was in the ring on 28 June 1912 at Madison Square Garden against the unbeaten blond Iowan farmer of German extraction, Al Palzer, no minor challenge.[49] The winner could expect to be matched with Johnson for the world heavyweight championship, providing Johnson beat Fireman Flynn a week later on 4 July.

Broadway is always a magnet for the British. Every so often, a British playwright, actor or entertainer will transfer a West End success to New York. Many succeed; many do not. Would the personable Bombardier be chaired and cheered from the Garden ring or escorted away in silent embarrassment like a British comedian whose wit has withered on stony American soil? The arena was as packed as a sardine tin by those eager to know the answer to the question.

Fireman Flynn (1879–1935) (in the light suit) in his Las Vegas training camp before meeting Johnson.
Bain collection, Prints & Photographs Division, Library of Congress, LC-DIG-ggbain-12201

Both men stripped to their muscular best – Wells to 13st 6½lb/188½lbs, Palzer to a heavier 14st 4¼lb/200¼lbs. What Wells lacked in mass, he hoped to make up in skill and speed. Within seconds of the first bell, this reading was seemingly confirmed. Palzer accelerated out of his corner, flailing punches like some Midwest agricultural instrument thrashing the imported English corn standing before him. Wells sidestepped, delivered a painful left to Palzer's prominent nose and added a couple of neat hooks as Palzer stormed past. This was no early fluke and the belligerent Palzer suffered three or four replays, quite enough for the damage to show on his face. Wells, now all adrenalin, had seized the initiative and continued on the offensive. Off a strong left lead and his front foot, he delivered the neatest of combinations, culminating in a crisp right hook to the jaw that dropped Palzer into a heap on the canvas. Palzer got up at six, clutching and clinging in desperation.

Experienced watchers marvelled at the novel sight of a good-looking white heavyweight who could actually box, and box at speed – shades of Gentleman Jim Corbett at his best. Wells began the second as a man who had a fight won and would soon prove it. He moved on to Palzer, jabbing and hooking to head and body. This brought him within Palzer's reach, the reach of a man whose punches had already knocked out strong men like Tom Kennedy (3 August 1911) and Al Kaufmann (28 December 1911). In the midst of a cluster of Wells's punches, Palzer caught him on the left temple with a looping right. Wells paused with the puzzled air of a DIY enthusiast bitten suddenly by a nail he had just been hammering

into a wall. Palzer added a jolting right uppercut to Wells's chin followed by a left hook. It was Wells's turn to inspect the ring floor at close quarters.

Wells took a full nine seconds to get up. For the rest of the round it was the weakened Englishman boxing on the retreat as Palzer, scowling under the shock of fair hair that flopped over his right eye, looked for one more good punch to add Wells's name to the long American mental list of horizontal Brits who had come, seen and been conquered. Wells survived the second, barely. He later said he had been affected by the New York climate ('I have had it hot in India, but never anything like the heat in New York'), and a bout of dysentery that had lost him over six pounds by the day of the fight. If either is true, he had no business being in the ring unprepared for so major a fight. There had been precious little listlessness about his first-round performance.

The new traffic pattern continued in the third, Wells on apprehensive retreat, Palzer confidently stalking him. One rush was met by Wells's jab but with none of the power of that exciting first round. Palzer walked through it untroubled and delivered a right hook to Wells's jaw. Wells needed every second of another nine count to get up, and then only on trembling legs. Barely was he vertical than Palzer delivered a malevolent right just under the heart. Wells's exhalation of all the breath he had left in his lungs was audible even above the cheers of the excited crowd, as he folded up and fell face down. Before the count was complete his English seconds threw a sponge into the ring. For the Bombardier, New York had so far been

much less than a wonderful town, for all the initial excitement.

Palzer left immediately after the fight to catch a cross-country train to California to see the Johnson–Flynn showdown. Wells stayed on the East Coast to rehabilitate his and British boxing's reputation with a further appearance at Madison Square Garden on 18 July 1912 against an earlier Palzer victim, the tousle-haired and affluent Tom Kennedy.[50] This was a more even match as to skill and weight (both men registering 13st 9½lb/191½lbs).

In the first round they went down together in a disorderly tangle of arms and legs, mostly because Kennedy, caught with a good Wells punch, had grabbed on to his opponent. Wells's skills were marginally better. He should comfortably win the newspaper victory over ten rounds, but as he often began wonderfully, only to suffer some serious lapse of concentration and get caught with a stray punch, nothing was certain. (Kennedy landed a right-hand swing in the seventh that shook Wells for a moment.)

Wells had displayed a strange reluctance to finish Palzer when, having dropped him with a clean punch, he stood back watching big Al collect his wits. His seconds *had* shouted to him to have a care. In fact, Wells later admitted that the crowd noise at Palzer's toppling had drowned out the call. The fastidious pause was all his own work. This penchant of allowing beaten opponents back into the fight brought his downfall against Palzer and Moir. So even when Wells had Kennedy down for a count of nine in the eighth, the Kennedy supporters had not given up hope. As Kennedy slowly got up, the gentlemanly Wells allowed him to regain his full balance and to restore his guard. Only after that did Wells move in and finish the despatch with an overhead clubbing right. Before the count was over, Kennedy's seconds did what Wells's had done in the Palzer fight, compassionately throwing in the sponge to stop the count and succour their man.

The latest great white hope had come to the 'Great White Way' with 50 per cent success. He had demonstrated his skills and his mental vulnerability. He was an enigma – even to himself:

> I looked at him [Palzer] and knew that I had only to go in and finish him. One punch would have done it. But somehow I couldn't. Something held me back … I knew I was doing wrong, and yet I held back. Perhaps some of you may be able to explain it.

No one then or since has been able genuinely to explain it. He could be conned by an opponent mentally more robust than he.

> I felt positive that no man could stand up against a hammering like that, but he [Palzer] did, and, what was more, he kept coming on. I landed half a dozen more real smashers, and then he suddenly stopped and winked at me. I had to laugh, I couldn't help it.

This was Wells falling for one of the oldest tricks in the old pro repertory – when hurt yourself, make the opponent think the opposite. ('Is that all you've got?')

One thing was certain about the clash between Jack Johnson and Fireman Jim Flynn in Las Vegas on 4 July 1912: there would be no over-sensitive fragility, in or out of the ring.[51] Johnson's ability to psych out adversaries was proven. Rumours from Flynn's camp suggested that the rough, tough railway fireman was rehearsing a succession of illegal moves especially for Johnson. (Flynn's trainer, Tommy Ryan, resigned days before the fight. He, the ex-middleweight, said he had quit because he believed Flynn to be outclassed. Unofficially, he did not wish to be associated with illegal methods of combating Johnson's superiority.) Johnson had physical advantages – 17st 2lb/240lbs against Flynn's 13st 10lb/192lbs and thee inches in height and reach. The formbook revealed similar discrepancies. On 2 November 1907 in San Francisco, the men had met before. Johnson had knocked Flynn out in the 11th, fracturing his jaw in the process.

Optimists for Flynn pointed out that Johnson had not defended his title in two years since taking it from Jim Jeffries in July 1910. Some degree of ring rust could be expected and the two stones that Johnson had gained since (he had weighed in at 15st 2lb/212lbs against Jeffries), were more flab than muscle.

Flynn met Sam Langford twice in early 1910: on 8 February in a no-decision ten-rounder, and 17 March, when Langford knocked him out in the eighth. Since then Flynn's record had improved. He had taken ten fights and won eight by knockout. Thus, he was an active fighter, a year younger than Johnson and one punching a bag, while Johnson exercised in bar and brothel.

Flynn had popular support on the day. Johnson had received a death threat at his training camp. It read starkly: 'Lie down tomorrow or we string you up – Ku Klux Klan.'[52] Past threats had not intimidated Johnson, but what black victor could ever feel wholly safe before a frustrated white audience, possibly with fringe lunatics in their midst? In return for the $30,000 purse, both men agreed to a fight to a finish – no limit to the number of rounds. If Flynn could avoid a knockout, perhaps he could outlast the podgier Johnson. Ringside odds had Johnson 10/3 on. This underestimated Flynn's chances. Curiously, most subsequent reports also seem ungenerous to Flynn.

Johnson had the reach, the hand speed and the skill to fight Flynn from a comfortable distance, using the long, raking punches of the sort that had rattled and hurt men as small as Burns and as big as Jeffries. Flynn, gloves up in front of his chin, advanced in a lopsided crouch, left shoulder held slightly lower than the right, looking to get under Johnson's long arms and slow the champion down with short, heavy body blows.

The crowd, as meagre as 3,000 according to some,[53] was three times that number according to at least one other reporter.[54] Reuters put it at 'some 8,000 persons'.[55] Many women were present, eager for action and in holiday mood.

One aspect of Johnson's complex personality – the showman – was perfectly in keeping with the Independence Day atmosphere. He refused the conventional handshake, playing up the role of villain. As he had against Burns and Jeffries, he interspersed his punches with gestures, comments and expressions. He clipped Flynn around the head and grinned his

Las Vegas, 4 July 1912: Johnson beat Flynn with some dubious tactics but the local police made the final decision.
Bain Collection, Prints & Photographs Division, Library of Congress, LC-DIG-ggbain-11306

grin. He allowed Flynn to punch him amidships and grinned some more to show how little harmed he was – a rope-a-dope tactic preceding Muhammad Ali's mock passivity against George Foreman by 62 years. Meanwhile, he addressed remarks over Flynn's shoulder to all and sundry – to his seconds, to Mrs Johnson at ringside, to referee Ed Smith and to any spectator who caught his eye.

Flynn, irritatingly patronised, received many more punches than he delivered. To his credit, he did his courageous best to turn the movie back into a fight. But from the first round, discouraging counters met his storming rushes at Johnson. One rush stopped dead on the end of a straight left jab, a painful left hook deflected another and a third petered out on a sharp right uppercut. Before the end of the round, a looping Johnson right inflicted a cut under Flynn's left eye. Things were not going well for the Fireman.

As he sat on his stool at the end of the first, he had much to contemplate.

He had been out-sped, outpunched and outclassed. He was no quitter, and as an experienced pro he might still outlast Johnson long term. An unlimited number of rounds was, by definition, potentially very long term.

In the second round, Flynn rushed, and matched Johnson verbally with some choice epithets of his own. Some rushes were met with clean punches, and damaging ones at that. Yet what began visibly to upset him was that Johnson used a blatantly illegal tactic designed to stop Flynn punching at all. Stretching out those long arms, open gloves palm forward, Johnson rested his gloves on Flynn's biceps, pushing against them and squeezing, sapping the strength in Flynn's arms and frustrating his attempts to get off punches. Johnson mixed the treatment with a variation where he curled his gloves around the back of Flynn's arms and pulled them hard to leave Flynn wriggling in pigeon-chested impotence. The twin ploys began in the first round and became blatant in the second and

fourth. Flynn appealed to the referee and to all others within earshot. He appealed in vain.

Insultingly, Johnson used his reach in another novel way. He plonked his left glove on Flynn's forehead to keep him at a uselessly flailing distance and to give himself a sight-finder for his own right. More often, he just held Flynn's biceps. Flynn, his arms trapped to his sides as surely as if he were in a straitjacket, had only one weapon left to hurl at Johnson – his head. Clumsily, he tried to clip Johnson under the chin with the top of his head. When that failed, he jumped completely off the floor in an attempt to drive his head into Johnson's face and to demonstrate even to the complacent referee that Johnson was preventing him from punching. His sole rewards were a lecture from the referee and more punches from Johnson. His frustration was considerable.

In the third, Flynn got his arms free temporarily and landed a solid right hook on the Johnson smile. He got a flurry of well-aimed punches as a riposte. Johnson indicated that he could have ended it all there, but thinking of profitable film rights, strung out the action. For another five rounds he punished Flynn. In the ninth Johnson decided there was enough film in the can and he need exert himself no further. When Flynn made one last desperate lunge with his head, Johnson unleashed a devastating right uppercut that lifted Flynn up on tiptoes before dropping him in an untidy and bleeding heap in the centre of the ring.

Before Ed Smith could count Flynn out, the substantial figure of Captain Fred Fornoff, the Governor's Representative, accompanied by the police, entered the ring and loudly declared the contest over because an 'exhibition' had disintegrated into a brutal prizefight. (Only naivety could have supposed a clash, rounds unlimited, between the ruthless Johnson and the wayward Flynn could ever have been an 'exhibition'.) Technically, the intervention was a nonsense even if Fornoff had a moral point. Ed Smith promptly awarded Johnson a victory by technical knockout – perhaps the only thing he got right in nine rounds.

On this very day, 4 July 1912, at Vernon in California, another referee, Jack Welsh (Welch in some accounts, Walsh in others) was making Ed Smith look like Solomon with as bizarre a third-man performance as any in boxing history.[56] The open-air contest, for the world lightweight championship, was between the current champion Ad Wolgast and a 19-year-old challenger from Los Angeles, the Mexican Joe Rivers. For this, 11,000 eager spectators had paid $41,465. The bull-necked Welsh in natty striped trousers, watch-chain and waistcoat stretched over his substantial corporation, looked big enough to lift the two lightweights off their feet simultaneously. This is almost what he did.

Welsh had refereed previous Wolgast bouts with notable tolerance for Wolgast's more erratic target areas, all outside those envisaged by Queensberry. A year ago to the day, Welsh had obligingly counted out Owen Moran against Wolgast, swiftly pronouncing the fateful ten as Moran lay on the canvas trying with a gloved hand to count up to two to check how many bruised testicles he had left. Were Rivers to take a low punch from Wolgast, Welsh was likely to be temporarily blind.

On paper, Rivers looked a safely inferior opponent for a formal title defence. Unfortunately for Wolgast, Rivers was not. Quite as good at the rough and tumble as the champion, he was faster and stronger. After three relatively even rounds, the fiery Rivers took over. Wolgast, crouching behind a cross-armed defence, was on the back foot, his face showing plenty of traces of Rivers's punches winging over, under and through his guard. Wolgast clinched. Wolgast cast aspersions on Rivers's Native American/Mexican heritage. Wolgast wrestled and tangled. (In the 11th, one such mesh had both men falling through the ropes and having to be helped back in.) Still Rivers came on. That is, until the notorious 13th.

Wolgast in the corner had a furious row with his second, Herman Stitzel. Wolgast wanted Stitzel to throw in the now bloody towel. Stitzel threatened to hit Wolgast with a beer bottle and made him continue. Wolgast, seeing Rivers temporarily as the lesser evil, went out for the 13th. At the end of the round what happened was this.

Rivers launched two big left hooks, one to the body followed by a heavier one to the jaw. Both landed, the second to stunning effect, but in that momentary interval between them, the latest of Wolgast's subterranean piledrivers buried itself in Rivers's groin. Down Rivers went, and down went a semi-conscious Wolgast on top of him.

This novel situation brought a desperate piece of improvisation from Welsh. With his left hand, he hauled the floppy Wolgast half-upright and, holding him there like a sack of potatoes, used his right arm to count out Rivers, who was squatting on his haunches clutching his lower abdomen and staring uncomprehendingly. In the midst of this farce, timekeeper Al Harder rang the bell for the end of the round *before* Welsh finished his count. Harder said later, 'I don't know how many seconds Welch [*sic*] had counted before I rang the bell, but I do know that after I had rung the bell ending the round, Welch gave the decision to Wolgast.'

Welsh's decision was a win for Wolgast by knockout, a verdict so outrageous that he had delivered it and fled before most people had truly registered it. Some angry punters pursued him but by then Welsh was ensconced in a private compartment of a fast train home. Ad Wolgast seemed destined to be world lightweight champion in perpetuity, providing he could rely on employing Welsh as the referee.

Life in and out of the ring was not normally like that. Many, therefore, chuckled when, in his next major title defence on 28 November 1912 in Daly City, California, without his pal Welsh, Wolgast lost his title to a promising young fighter from San Francisco, Willie Ritchie. Irony of ironies, Wolgast lost on a disqualification for a low blow. The referee, Jim Griffin, a more scrupulous performer than Welsh, gave Wolgast a final warning and refused to have his bluff called. Ritchie (b. 13 February 1891) thus acquired the title by a strict application of the rules. He never forgot it. In later decades he was a notably upright and incorruptible Chief Inspector for the California Athletic Commission through the scoundrel years when organised crime and professional boxing were synonymous. Ritchie reminisced about the Wolgast fight many years later in a fascinating interview:

> … I went along boxing my usual style, watching that I didn't get hit or get hurt, and tied him up in the clinches as best I could, because he was a rough fighter inside – arms, shoulders, head, everything went. I tied him up as best I could but I got a black eye doing it. I got messed up defending myself. Along about the twelfth round I hit him a punch in the body and he stopped and grabbed me. That was a signal that I'd hurt him. I thought, *Well, now, brother, I know your number.* Then in the sixteenth round … I feinted at his body, crossed with a right to the jaw, and he went down like a log.
>
> He got up and came at me and I couldn't get a punch at him, but when he came punching he came at me and hit me in the groin. I had a cup on so I wasn't hurt a bit, but I was frightened, naturally,

28 November 1912, Daly City, California: Ad Wolgast is disqualified in the 16th against Willie Ritchie (1891–1925) after repeated low blows.

Bain Collection, Prints & Photographs Division, Library of Congress, LC-DIG-ggbain-11009

and I dropped my hand to my groin and stood there because it was a clear foul blow and the referee, Jim Griffin, came over and said, 'Be careful, Ad. Don't do that again or I'll disqualify you.' So I stood there holding my groin, and bang! Right in the groin again. Griffin stepped right in and disqualified him for a deliberate foul. He admitted later that he wasn't going to let 'that son of a bitch' knock him out. He'd rather foul out than get stopped.[57]

The man who would rather foul out than get stopped is usually the man coming knowingly to the end of his career. Ritchie was Wolgast's 12th opponent of the year. Tragically, Wolgast was the last to recognise that he had already had sufficient gruelling contests to last a lifetime. After this loss to Ritchie at the end of 1912, he fought at least another 56 times before he retired finally in 1920. Ritchie spent a long and rewarding life after his boxing career (he became the father-in-law of the brilliant Hollywood actress-singer, Jane Powell, and moved in interesting West Coast circles). Wolgast was confined to a mental institution, preparing assiduously in his confused mind for a phantom return against Joe Gans, who had actually died in 1910.

The undignified scrambles of Johnson and Flynn, and the 1912 Wolgast Follies, did little for boxing's prestige. The last third of 1912 in Britain also suffered several poor contests, along with a few extremely good ones. Even the poor ones had the virtue of unpredictability. That boxing often provides a shock exit for a complacent champion, or a surprise win for an obvious underdog, or the falling apart of a seemingly evergreen champion helps sell tickets.

Gunner Moir's supporters, for example, suffered many ups and downs, including the many such in spoiling Wells's record on 11 January 1911. On 2 September 1912, a fitter looking Moir at the Blackfriars Ring faced another master of the unforeseeable, Petty Officer 'Nutty' Curran.[58] Rarely has so much action been contained within one minute, 25 seconds total. Both men swung, both men missed. Curran landed one right and one left to the jaw, and down went Moir. He got up but staggered. Referee Corri tried to intervene as Curran rained punches on him. As Corri pulled Curran away, Moir obligingly collapsed again. End of fight and perhaps of Moir's chequered career.

But no, Moir was back at the NSC on 18 November 1912 and losing the dullest of six-rounders against Hawker Wilson on points. We will meet him again in September 1913. Curran, his latest conqueror, went on fighting until 1920, but his waistline expanded faster than his biceps. (In June 1913, the *Mirror of Life* published

an unkind but accurate caricature of Nutty shown from the side and labelled A, B and C: – 'A = superfluous tissue; B = fat; C = plain bingey'.) Three weeks after the win over Moir, Curran faced, for the third time in the year, the slimmer and lighter South African heavyweight, George Rodel – 12st 10lb/178lbs against the shorter Curran's 14st 2lb/198lbs. The clash was at The Ring on 23 September 1912 in a bout described as 'funereal' and 'one of the worst apologies for a boxing bout between prominent exponents of the science … ever seen'.[59] Speculation that a contest between a tortoise and a limpet would be more animated was rife. Sixteen soporific rounds decided only how many times Rodel could metronomically butt Curran in the face in every clinch and get away with it. In the 16th, Dick Burge, at last, stepped in and saved Curran, bleeding from cuts on his forehead, his cheeks and both eyes, all from Rodel's head, by disqualifying Rodel. Said Nutty, 'My face must have looked like a butcher's shop.' Disqualification on the basis of terminally boring Burge's patrons would have been quite as appropriate.

Boxing's saving grace was that such dross was interspersed with bouts of sufficient quality to wipe the Rodel nutfest from the memory bank. Also at The Ring, on 19 September 1912, was a meeting between two highly skilled and fast-moving local Bermondsey flyweights, Sid Smith and Curley Walker. The match was billed as for the 'World and British Championship' at 8st/112lbs. The weight was the one fully recognised by the NSC but they, as usual, denied their imprimatur to a championship fight outside their auspices. This did not concern the

Bermondsey crowd packed into The Ring to see it.

The tiny Smith did not punch even his limited weight. In over 100 fights, the referee pronounced the full count over a mere four of his opponents.[60] He still had three major assets. He could deliver his light punch and have the glove back defending his chin faster than the average chameleon could catch and swallow a fly. He could control his lugubrious expression in the most dubious circumstances with the persistence and skill of a professional actor. (He pursued a successful post-ring career in music hall as the deadpan foil to the popular comedian Harry Weldon.) Even for a flyweight his balance and speed of foot were legendary.

Against Walker, he showed all these traits and was loudly applauded for sustaining his rapid-fire punching and his dazzling footwork over a tiring 20 rounds to outpoint comfortably his rival. Whatever they said at the NSC, all South London seemed to be in the hall to see Smith confirmed as King of Bermondsey and all points north.

Intense local interest was one thing. The boxing aficionados who picked up their copy of *The Times* on Monday, 16 September 1912 read the remarkable news that a British featherweight, Harry Thomas, had spent the previous Friday night (13 September) in the Madison Square Garden ring with the Little Hebrew of all the tricks, Abe Attell, and not only survived the ten rounds, but had been awarded a clear newspaper victory. The critics agreed that Attell looked the older and heavier at 9st 3¾lb/129¾lbs and slower than Thomas, who was 9st 5lb/131lbs. He even looked older, heavier and more ponderous than his old self and was expected to go up to lightweight in future.

Thomas's victory was still being discussed when another packed crowd assembled at The Ring to see two international lightweights: Matt Wells, just back from the USA, and the less skilful but very robust Australian Hughie Mehegan.[61] Mehegan was born on 26 August 1886 in Melbourne and a formidable opponent. His eventual ring record from 1905 to 1916 read: won 63 (37 by KO), lost 28, drawn 3, having fought his last fight only weeks before his early death, aged 30. He died, in uniform, of a severe inflammation of the kidneys in a French casualty station on 28 November 1917.

The Wells/Mehegan 15-rounder seemed a natural for the NSC. Dick Burge secured it by offering both men a percentage of the gate instead of a flat fee. Thus, the hundreds locked out on the pavements of Southwark contributed nothing to the fighters if much to the atmosphere. The lucky ones inside got their money's worth.

Wells showed his talent for skilful boxing at a distance. He used every inch of the ring to run laps around the crouching, black-shorted Mehegan, catching the slower Australian with lefts and long right crosses almost at will as he loped past on one of his circuits. He dropped Mehegan for a count of six in the second. His tactics were paying off handsomely. However, Mehegan had seen plenty of Fancy Dans in his career (a category into which he mistakenly placed Wells). He scowled and bided his time. At the halfway point, the contest began to turn. Mehegan, feet firmly planted and still in a crouch, began, like a rugby prop-forward engaging in a fiercely contested scrum, to advance menacingly and remorselessly forward, catching Wells with short fierce blows to head and body to slow the Englishman.

The later rounds were almost unbearably exciting as Wells, who could mix it with the best, refused any longer to retreat. Instead he went toe to toe with Mehegan, both men now more macho than maestro and striving for straight physical dominance. The 13th and 14th would have strained the capabilities of Compubox for an accurate count of punches thrown and landed. Gilbert Odd tells us that one spectator counted up to 200 and then gave up in despair long before the round had ended. The decibel count also went off the scale, and this was, quaintly, a decisive factor at the end of a torrid 14th.

When the bell sounded, Mehegan broke off and moved towards his corner. Wells, deaf to everything, went on punching and sent Mehegan tumbling down. From his sitting position, the Australian made a caustic remark. Wells reached down and gave him a sharp right uppercut to shut his mouth. It would not do. Wells was instantly disqualified.

When Wells had recovered his sangfroid and his sportsmanship, he rearranged the terms of the contracts to share his profits with Mehegan. (The original percentages had made Wells, the loser, a financial winner, and Mehegan, the winner, much the poorer.) Hardly ever was a return fight so obviously desired, yet it would take until 1913 to arrange it.

Smith v Walker was an aesthetic counterpoint to the melodrama of Wells v Mehegan. The fight that took place at Madison Square Garden in New York on 23 September 1912 between Jack Harrison and Eddie McGoorty rivalled Moir v Curran for brevity; ring introductions taking longer than the fighting.[62] Full of hope, Harrison had travelled from England to New York to meet the impressive and experienced McGoorty, the Wisconsin middleweight. Harrison weighed in at 11st 9lb/163lbs; McGoorty marginally heavier by two pounds. For the man from Rushden, Northamptonshire, it proved better to travel hopefully than to arrive. The boring victory over McEnroy bringing him the British middleweight title was no preparation for McGoorty.

McGoorty's reputation was patchy. He preferred the drinking den to the training camp and was erratic in the ring – deadly when in the mood but irritatingly tentative when out of sorts. Harrison was unlucky. On the night, McGoorty was sharp, sober and looking to punish someone. The result took little reporting. Harrison advanced. McGoorty hit him. No one argued for a return.

In London, the new season 1912–13 started late as the NSC was given a refit. The club reopened on 6 October, but the biggest date of its and many people's year was 11 November 1912, when it hosted the long-desired return fight between the two lightweights so much admired on both sides of the Atlantic: Matt Wells and Freddie Welsh. Ever since Wells's unexpected win over Welsh at the NSC on 27 February 1911, the members, the sporting press and the public had animatedly discussed the relative merits of the pair. Only another match-up could settle the arguments.

Returns after one-time epics are often routine confirmations of the original result minus the fireworks. Boxing history has many examples. Wells v Welsh II was, to the contrary, eminently worthy of the occasion and at least as warmly contested and skilfully fought as the original.[63]

There was one change; no one yet knew how significant. The veteran trainer, Boyo Driscoll, a prominent member of Wells's original camp at the Black Bull in Whetstone, Essex, was now in Freddie Welsh's corner. Welsh in any case prepared himself mentally and physically differently according to the opponent. His tactics were not always endearing, but he knew how to win. Georges Carpentier, in the NSC audience, approved.

Tagging Wells or Welsh were achievements in themselves. Wells's nifty footwork took him away from dangerous punches and his fast hands blocked others. Welsh had a magical ability to duck, sway and slip out of danger. Here comes the punch, yet, like McCavity, Welsh is not there. He conjured other strange varieties of Celtic magic. He rematerialised at the closest of quarters, head on his opponent's chest, delivering short and painful punches to the body. One of the surprises of the first fight had been Wells holding his own close in to Welsh, normally the Clinchmaster General.

In the first of 20 scintillating rounds, Wells swaggered like a man with a Lonsdale Belt as safe around his waist as if deposited in the Bank of England. With the sharpest of straight jabs, he rocked Welsh back on his heels within seconds of the opening bell, and moving all around the ring at speed, he caught Welsh with a significant percentage of the punches he threw. Welsh ducked some, dodged others,

but had to take many. His own punches sounded like open-glove slaps rather than the effective thuds of a closed fist. The second round was more even. Welsh quietly reasserted himself, yet it was Wells who punched with more solidity.

Wells took the third and certainly the fifth and sixth. In a 20-round fight between two such experienced men, these were merely preliminaries. Both expected to be there at the finish. Welsh was biding his time. The sharpest observers registered that he was taking only the lighter leads. He blocked with gloves, elbows and forearms the more damaging body hooks. He himself got home with short blows to and below the ribs, mixing in some short uppercuts to chin and nose.

From the sixth, Welsh launched a fresh variation learned in some American ring. He flicked out an open-gloved left, too light to damage, to Wells's chin, and as Wells brushed it aside, followed it up with an over-the-top right from a completely novel angle to connect painfully with that chin. The speed and the force coming from an unanticipated compass point troubled the Londoner from then on. This clever ploy was only part of a strategy aimed ultimately at long-term success.

Wells had moved fast early on, while Welsh was less profligate. Welsh had saved stamina for initiatives in the crueller middle rounds. (How many modern boxers would cope, if after nine heavy rounds of action, they were told that they were not yet halfway through the full 20 rounds of a championship fight of the early 20th century?) Of the seven rounds from the seventh to the 13th, Wells took only the tenth as Welsh wiped out his early lead and piled

up points himself. In each round, Wells landed two or three eye-catching lefts, only to find that over the three minutes, Welsh had moved less yet economically delivered more.

Wells, as consummate a professional as he had been an amateur, knew the score as well as anyone. From the 14th he launched a sustained rally. He had no desire to see his Lonsdale Belt disappearing over the Welsh border or across the Atlantic. He showed his true class in the 16th when Welsh drove him back with a barrage of long-range punches. He feinted with his left, then caught Welsh with a full-bodied right cross that stopped and staggered the gleefully advancing Welsh. Welsh smiled his nonchalant smile, although everyone knew it as the smile of a man hurt and disguising it. He had to force another grim smile in the 17th when a Wells left and a right uppercut in swift succession tested him again.

Welsh was still the master of ring psychology who had undermined even Driscoll. He was biding his time for a barnstorming finish. The Londoner looked for a knockout in the 18th and 19th rounds, sensing that Welsh was sufficiently ahead to win on points. Welsh did everything to keep Wells at bay – ducking, swaying and slipping out of danger effectively as Wells's swings and drives grew wilder. He landed his own punches often, including that flicked left/over-arm right combination that Wells never truly fathomed. After the exciting 20th, Welsh was pronounced the new official British champion.

Such dicta were particularly irritating just across the Thames at Dick Burge's Blackfriars Ring where, on that very same evening, 11 November

1912, there was an equally skilful and dramatic fight between two significant British fighters. It lacked the NSC imprimatur and the seal of approval represented by a Lonsdale Belt. The journalists present nevertheless were full of praise for the quality of boxing on show. The two flyweights involved, Bill Ladbury of New Cross and Sam Keller of Aldgate, were responsible for what *Boxing* called 'the best fly-wt. battle seen in England for the last 20 years … one of the fastest, cleverest exhibitions of clean boxing put on at any hall for years', one in which Ladbury was the winner on points over 20 rounds. The NSC had no monopoly on fine boxers. Yet in early 1914, Ladbury accepted a miserable purse offer turned down by Sid Smith and participated in another outstanding flyweight epic on the NSC premises.

Dick Burge wanted to stage the natural match-up created by recent results. Hughie Mehegan of Australia had beaten Matt Wells at The Ring but only on a disqualification. Freddie Welsh had beaten Wells at the NSC. Mehegan v Welsh would draw a full house anywhere. The big question was whether a Burge or a Jimmy White could offer a purse big enough to attract these two with no title at stake, or whether the NSC's unique standing could still tempt the best and have cachet trump cash.

Other commercial promoters were providing attractive match-ups. On Friday, 6 December 1912, at the King's Hall, Bombardier Billy Wells, still Britain's biggest draw, met the South African heavyweight George Rodel on a Jimmy White bill. White's posters proclaimed that the 'British Empire Heavyweight Championship' was at

stake. Wells's first appearance on home soil after his mixed New York venture, this was superficially an appealing fight. (Wells had appeared at the NSC once; that was on 24 April 1911 when he had won the official British heavyweight championship against Hague [Chapter 6].) Rodel had lost narrowly to Fred Storbeck back home in Johannesburg. He had neither the skill nor the speed to keep a boxer like Wells at bay for long. Wells, in one of his more focused appearances, knocked him out in the second round.

Enhanced prices in South London for five minutes' heavyweight action hardly represented value for money. In December 1912, the NSC members got better rewards for their subscriptions. Six months before, on 17 June 1912, with a £400 purse, a Lonsdale Belt and the British welterweight championship at stake, the popular Johnny Summers had disposed of the ex-blacksmith, Arthur Evernden of Erith, by knocking him out through the ropes in the 13th round. As Evernden's seconds tried desperately to push him back into the ring from his recumbent position, head dangling over the apron's edge and his legs tangled with the bottom rope, Summers had knelt down and tried to punch *them*. With the club in uproar, Summers's seconds joined in. Only the ringing of the bell brought both official and unofficial fights to an end.[64] The chaotic finish was more exciting than the rest of the fight. The wits suggested that £50 of Evernden's purse should have gone to the referee for the throat lozenges necessary after his ringside shouts to break had punctuated every round. Back at the club in December, Summers might prove that against a less negative opponent he could put on a real show.

He was matched over 20 rounds, for his welterweight championship and belt and a £450 purse, against his London rival, Sid Burns of Aldgate, another contender out of the Jewish East End. The younger (b. 26 May 1890) and stockier Burns had a good pedigree. On 2 October 1911, he had lasted 15 rounds against the glamorous Frenchman then passing through the welterweight division – Georges Carpentier. Not many English boxers could claim that. Although squat, Burns was taller than Summers and had a longer reach. At this fight on 9 December 1912, Summers was still the heavier puncher.[65] He looked to get inside, to hit and to hold when necessary. In referee J. H. Douglas, the pair had a man who would not allow extended clinches at any price. After a particularly fierce lecture to both men in the seventh, they kept the practice to a minimum.

Douglas was too ready to call for a break while two such skilful inside fighters were contesting the action vigorously at close quarters. In contrast, he seemed oblivious to either man landing punches on the enforced break. Despite calls from the crowd, punches on the break persisted.

Summers was a 6/4 on favourite and behaved like one. He smiled pleasantly at crowd and opponent alike and moved around easily. He landed right hooks into Burns's ribs and sometimes into his kidneys – a calculated attempt to weaken his opponent. It was effective, leading to a detectable slowing on Burns's part in the third quarter. Yet Summers had no easy defence. Burns landed long targeted left swings, mixed in with crisp hooks on the exit from clinches. Burns had the edge in at least the third, the seventh, the ninth, and probably the fourth and sixth as well.

After the 13th, the scores were roughly level. Burns moved marginally ahead when he opened the 14th with more of his long lefts and closed out the round with a fierce rally. On the other hand, the pounding his ribs and kidneys had received weakened him and the advance looked like the last throw of a tiring man. After a pacific 15th, when both men discreetly took a breather, Summers took over, strongly and productively, edging out the 16th, 17th and 18th over a feebler and sometimes tottering Burns.

Takers of the short odds on Summers gleefully anticipated a payout after the 19th as Summers left his stool, eager to complete an early finish. The winnings looked to be in the bag as Burns took more heavy lefts and wobbled back to the ropes. Summers pulled back his right and aimed a final cross to the chin. Just as he did so, Burns lashed out with a right of his own. Both connected. Both men were stunned. Shades of Rivers-Wolgast, and almost a double knockout. Referee Douglas, outside the ring, was in no position to help either man even had he wished to. Instead he shouted impotently, 'Break! Break!', a command two comatose men were unable to obey as they clung to each other to avoid a joint collapse. A slow, staggering waltz was all they could manage.

After the minute's rest, and frantic rehabilitation from the seconds, they survived the last round with Burns poking out a few token lefts. It was insufficient to wipe out the lead that Summers had built up before the surrealistic 19th. Summers got the points decision and another notch on

his Lonsdale Belt. He had earned it the hard way.

Minutes after the extraordinary fight, which nearly outdid *The Sleeping Beauty*, the Drury Lane pantomime, by providing *two* sleeping beauties, an exciting announcement was made. The NSC management had agreed terms with Freddie Welsh and Hughie Mehegan. They would meet at the NSC on 16 December 1912; an enticing climax to a brilliant domestic year.[66]

Glittering prizes were proffered: a purse of £1,000; a side-bet of £1,000-a-side; an individually designed £300 trophy; and, supposedly, the world lightweight championship. No one denied the world status of the fighters. But all Americans knew the current lightweight champion was Willie Ritchie, the man against whom Ad Wolgast had been disqualified in the recent (28 November 1912) fight at Colma, California. Wolgast's low blow in the 16th had produced a champion. Freddie Welsh had beaten Ritchie (30 November 1911 in Los Angeles) over 20 rounds, but Ritchie had not been champion then. The NSC's fiefdom might prevail over Blackfriars or Newcastle or Liverpool. The USA had no such client status.

Niceties about the championship did not concern those desperate to see the Welsh–Mehegan fight. 'Not since the historic meeting of Frank Slavin and Peter Jackson [May 1892] has any contest in this country created so much interest,' said *The Times*. On the night, national flags were waved in the audience. Both men were as different from each other as their national emblems. The Australian Mehegan fought from an American-style crouch, packing almost middleweight power

into his punches. Welsh, more versatile, dazzled at a distance and was up to every ploy at close quarters. He would do what was necessary, even if that meant infuriating an opponent (e.g. Driscoll) or irking an audience. All Welsh wanted, and usually got, was a referee grudgingly lifting his arm in victory at the end of a contest. His craft had been keenly honed in American rings against tough American fighters, and under the forgiving eyes of American referees who tolerated a degree of sharp practice.

Welsh also did what an opponent least expected. Where Mehegan might have anticipated Welsh's 'English' skills, that is, points scoring with left leads and the keeping of a safe distance, Wells plunged in immediately, testing his strength against Mehegan's and showing he had no intention of being outmuscled. He laid his head comfortably on Mehegan's hairy chest, using gloves, elbows and forearms to frustrate Mehegan. More often than seemed accidental, the top of his head collided with Mehegan's bristly chin.

Another Welsh trait was to come into the ring in tip-top condition. In 1912, most boxers thought Nutrition a quaintly named racehorse rather than a training aid. And being in excellent condition, Welsh husbanded his resources through a fight, rarely wasting punches and conscious that 20 championship rounds meant 60 minutes of action. Mehegan was more profligate, throwing punches often and from all angles, trading pleasure from the ones that landed as compensation for those that missed.

Surprised to find Welsh so close early on, Mehegan caught him with a bruising left to the right eye in the second and landed a few heavy blows to the body in the second and third. He shaded a close second round but Welsh's clever tactics took Mehegan over three-quarters of the fight before he could win other than an isolated round. Admittedly Mehegan hurt Welsh in the 13th.

It was not in Mehegan's nature to resign a struggle. He rallied strongly in the 15th and 16th, commendably for a man who had been hit frequently at close quarters and at a distance. Even as he tagged Welsh with some strong body punches, he suffered some lusty responses from the Welshman, who just shaded those rounds too. Whatever adrenalin flowed through Welsh's system in the heat of the battle, nothing short-circuited his cool and calculated tactics.

Mehegan's agenda was simpler. He might win the last three rounds. He might catch Welsh again with his dangerous body punches. But unless he knocked Welsh out, he had lost by a wide margin. No one knew that better than Welsh, and he had blotches on his ribs to remind him. There were no such blemishes on that other vital organ – his brain.

Welsh saw no need to treat the spectators to a grandstand finish by going toe to toe with the still dangerous Mehegan and risk one of his swings exploding on his chin. Rather he stayed away and boxed on the retreat or clinched and smothered.

The 20th was a digest of the whole fight. Mehegan threw three big rights. None did more than glance off Welsh's head. A fourth switched to the body, and as Welsh lowered his guard to intercept it, a big right uppercut got through. Welsh winced, tottered and, as ever, kept his cool. Into a clinch he went,

and in the clinch he stayed to the limit of referee Douglas's tolerance. After that, every desperate Mehegan punch was slipped and Mehegan found himself wrapped up like a present. Victory went to Welsh by some distance. As Mehegan generously conceded: 'The best man won and I am perfectly satisfied with the result. He is the toughest and cleverest man I have ever met.'

The fight and the verdict rounded off a boxing year that, in Britain, had been fuller and more rewarding than any before it. The sport had advanced everywhere, was stronger domestically and internationally. Glamorous fighters, new and old, had found fame even among non-boxing crowds in their own and others' countries. British and French fans could discuss intelligently the merits of a Harry Lewis or a Jack Johnson or a Georges Carpentier. American fans were familiar with Bombardier Billy Wells and Freddie Welsh and Jim Driscoll. Column inches in serious newspapers reflected a sustained and serious interest in these men and others.

On Boxing Day 1912 in Sydney, Australia, four years to the day since the Burns v Johnson clash with which we began, two very talented black American fighters, Sam Langford and Sam McVea fought each other, drawing large enthusiastic white crowds. This latest encounter resulted in a win for McVea by a knockout in the 13th round. There were several surprising things about this event. It was the *fifth* of a current series of six such fights held on Australian soil over 16 months. (For the record: 26 December 1911, Sydney, Langford pts 20; 8 April 1912, Sydney, Langford pts 20; 3 August 1912, Sydney, Langford pts 20; 9 October

1912, Perth, Langford TKO 11; 26 December 1912, Sydney, Langford KO 13; 24 March, 1913, Brisbane draw 20.)

A 4,000-strong crowd, including Prime Minister Scaddan and half his cabinet attended the Perth match. The April meeting in Sydney drew a full 15,000 and the first in 1911 no less than 18,000. The series had been arranged under the auspices of Hugh McIntosh, whose usual flair was paying off. It demonstrated that white Australian crowds would turn out to see black fighters. The underlying tragedy was that McIntosh would match black v black, or white v white, yet baulked at the prospect of any black v white contests. Boxing was flourishing, but an apartheid of the ring was flourishing with it.

Boxing was now a major world sport, a phenomenon barely comprehensible to those who remembered all too well that the previous year, 1911, had seen grave threats to its very existence. Equally unanticipated as 1912 drew to its satisfying close was that the next year, 1913, would actually top it in every way. 'The Boxing Boom that hit Britain in the year before the First World War,' was how Guy Deghy described it.[67] He accounts for the boom by mentioning several contributory factors: new handsome boxers, more matinee idols than traditional bruisers; the growing attendance of women; the ringside mixing of royalty and the multitude unmatched since Regency days; and ambitious producers selling glamorous fights. His conclusion describes 1914 as better than 1913. Nevertheless, the trends are clear and no boxing follower of today would refuse a time-travelling opportunity to visit the glamorous fights to come in 1913.

Endnotes:

1 *The Times,* 1 January 1912.

2 Dangerfield, G., *The Strange Death of Liberal England* (London: Paladin, 1970) p. 134.

3 James, R. R., *The British Revolution: British Politics 1880–1939* (London, Methuen, 1978) p. 269.

4 *The Times,* 26 January 1912.

5 *Boxing,* 6 January 1912.

6 *British Boxing Board of Control Annual,* 1996, p. 213.

7 Butler, J., *Kings of the Ring* (London, n.d. [1936]) p. 20.

8 *Boxing,* 27 January 1912.

9 *Boxing,* 3 February 1912; *The Times,* 30 January 1912.

10 *New York Times,* 19 January 1912.

11 *New York Times,* 23 January, 24 January, 25 January, 1 February and 22 February, all 1912.

12 Reports in *New York Times,* 23 February 1912 and *Boxing,* 9 March 1912.

13 Blady, K., *The Jewish Boxers Hall of Fame* (New York: Shapolsky Books, 1988) p. 46.

14 Interview with Joe Williams reproduced in *Sports Illustrated Book of Boxing* ed. W. C. Heinz and Nathan Ward. New York, 1999, pp. 347–348.

15 Blady, K., *The Jewish Boxers Hall of Fame,* p. 46.

16 Liebling, A. J., 'Broken Fighter Arrives', in *The Sweet Science*. Many editions, inc. The Sportsmans Book Club, London, 1958.

17 Deghy G., *Noble and Manly: The History of the National Sporting Club* (Hutchinson, 1956) p. 123.

18 Sammons, J. T., *Beyond the Ring: The Role of Boxing in American Society* (University of Illinois Press, 1990) p. 33.

19 Farr, F., *Black Champion: The Life and Times of Jack Johnson* (London, MacMillan, 1964) p. 80.

20 Johnson, J., *Jack Johnson is a Dandy: An Autobiography* (New York: Chelsea House, 1968) p. 64.

21 Roberts, R., P*apa Jack: Jack Johnson and the Era of White Hopes* (New York: Simon & Schuster, 1985) p. 9.

22 Johnson, J., *Jack Johnson is a Dandy,* pp. 45, 46 & 71.

23 Roberts, R., *Papa Jack,* p. 9.

24 Batchelor, D., *Jack Johnson and His Times* (London: Phoenix Sports Books, 1956) pp. 35–52.

25 Fleischer, N., *Fifty Years at Ringside* (New York: Fleet Publishing, 1958) p. 77.

26 Heller, P., *In This Corner* (London: Robson Books, 1992) p. 42.

27 Roberts, R., *Papa Jack,* p. 140.

28 Johnson, J., *Jack Johnson is a Dandy,* p.67.

29 Roberts, R., *Papa Jack,* p. 141.

30 Heller, P., *In This Corner,* p. 42.

31 Roberts, R., *Papa Jack,* p. 143.

32 Johnson, J., *Jack Johnson is a Dandy,* p. 76.

33 Roberts, R., *Papa Jack,* p. 75.

34 Roberts, R., *Papa Jack,* p.264, gives the reference: National Archives, General Records of the Department of Justice, File Number 164211, Record Groups 60 and 165, and FBI microfilm reel 33749 – files that Roberts used in his biography.

35 Report in *Boxing,* 10 February 1912,

36 See 'The Progress of French Boxers' in *The Times,* 29 February 1912.

37 Report in *Boxing,* 24 February 1912.

38 *Boxing,* 2 March 1912.

39 Mullan, H., *Heroes and Hard Men: The Story of Britain's World Boxing Champions* (London: Stanley Paul, 1989) p. 27.

40 *The Times,* 25 June 1912.

41 Report in *Boxing,* 9 March 1912.

42 *Carpentier: By Himself* (London: Sportsman's Book Club, 1958) p. 56.

43 Harding, J., *Lonsdale's Belt: Boxing's Most Coveted Prize* (Worthing: Pitch Publishing, 2016) pp. 28–29.

44 *Boxing* 25, May 1912 and *The Times,* 21 May 1912.

45 *Boxing* 1 June 1912; *Carpentier: By Himself,* pp. 60–61.

46 *The Times,* 14 June 1912; *Boxing,* 8 June 1912.

47 *New York Times,* 26 April 1912.

48 *Boxing,* 22 June 1912.

49 *New York Times,* 29 June 1912; Shipley, S., *Bombardier Billy Wells: The Life and Trials of a Boxing Hero* (Tyne and Wear: Bewick Press, 1993) p. 63; Soderman, B., 'The American Invasion of Bombardier Billy Wells' in *The British Boxing Board of Control Yearbook* 1998, pp. 227–232; *Boxing,* 6 July 1912.

50 Shipley, S., *Bombardier Billy Wells,* p.64; Soderman, B., 'The American Invasion of Bombardier Billy Wells', pp. 229–30; *Boxing,* 27 July 1912 (report), 3 August 1912 (retrospect), and 10 August 1912 (Wells's own account).

51 *The Times,* 5 July 1912; *Boxing,* 13 July 1912 and 27 July 1912; Johnson, J., *Jack Johnson: In the Ring and Out* (London: Proteus 1977) p. 58; Roberts, R., *Papa Jack,* pp. 133–137; film of rounds 1, 2, 4 and 9 in *Boxers,* No. 27 'Jack Johnson'; extracts on YouTube.

52 Carpenter, H., *Masters of Boxing (*London: Heinemann, 1964) p. 103.

53 Roberts, R., *Papa Jack,* p. 135.

54 *Boxing,* 13 July 1912.

55 *The Times,* 5 July 1912.

56 *Boxing,* 13 July 1912; *The Ring,* September 1945; Kent, G., *Boxing's Strangest Fights* (London: Robson Books, 2000) pp. 75–78; Suster, G., *Lightning Strikes* (London: Robson Books, 1994) pp. 34–5.

57 Heller, P., *In This Corner …!,* pp. 18–29.

58 *Boxing,* 7 September 1912.

59 *Boxing,* 28 September 1912.

60 Mullan, H., *Heroes and Hard Men,* p. 29.

61 *The Times,* 17 September 1912; Odd, G., 'How Matey Matt Pulled a Fast One', in *Boxing News,* 18 July 1980; *Boxing,* 21 September 1912. For Harry Thomas's win, *New York Times,* 14 September 1912.

62 *The Times,* 25 September 1912. This is a Reuters news report giving the weights as shown here in the text. Hugman, B., *The British Boxing Board of Control Yearbook* 1997, p. 237 uses a different source to credit both men with 158lbs.

63 *Boxing,* 16 November 1912; 'The Welsh Wizard' in *Boxing News,* 31 July and 7 August 1959; Gallimore, A., *Occupation Prizefighter: The Freddie Welsh Story* (Bridgend: seren Books, 2006) pp. 163–4, although Gallimore mistakenly dates the fight to 16 December 1912.

64 See Odd, G., 'The Iron Man Who Showed His Mettle', in *Boxing News,* 4 July 1980.

65 *The Times,* 10 December 1912; *Boxing,* 14 December 1912.

66 *The Times,* 17 December 1912; *Boxing,* 21 December 1912.

67 Deghy G., *Noble and Manly,* p. 189.

CHAPTER 9

LITTLE AND LARGE
1913

In Which Small Men Miss Out

IN BOXING 1913 brought little genuinely novel, but plenty that was the successful development of the familiar. New names emerged but the tried and tested monopolised attention. The sport continued to flourish.

On New Year's Day, *The Times* published an anonymous article by 'A Correspondent' on 'British Professional Boxing: the Present Situation'.[1] Clearly a man who thought himself in the know, the unknown writer made interesting points. He suggested that an ordinary professional boxer in 1913 had a better chance than ever of earning an honest living. Improved refereeing, and the banning of the dangerous kidney punch, had made the ring a safer place. Outside the ring, he detected the elimination of crooked promoters. (He was being too sanguine. A century on, the shysters, like the poor, are still with us.)

The journalist was unaware of the squalid conditions in which the lesser fry operated. A more accurate picture of life at the bottom of boxing can be pieced together from an obscure file in the National Archives.[2] The small envelope records the melancholy demise of the first Boxers Union established on 7 July 1910 as 'a union founded to benefit professional boxers'. It was dissolved formally in late 1912, said a letter from its secretary and joint trustee Frank Ward to the Registrar of Friendly Societies, because of 'the laxity of members & general non-payment of subscriptions'.

It had foundered, like many such in the catering and retail trades, upon the difficulties of organising a collective identity among the full-time, part-time and occasional fighters taking fights where and when they could get them from promoters and managers to whom their welfare was hardly a top priority. The declared objects of the union were hardly radical:

> The objects of the Union shall be to improve the condition, and protect the interests of the members; to amicably arrange differences with and regulate the relations between promoters and others, and boxers; to grant assistance to distressed members and provide for the payment of a sum of money upon the death of a member.

The union divided boxers realistically into four classes, A, B, C and D. The A class constituted the elite – the champions, the belt-holders, fighters selected by its committee (comprised of active boxing journalists and boxers). Others were admitted once they had won at least 12 fights in category B. The lowest category D was for winners of novice competitions and those who had engaged in any professional contest of a stipulated number of rounds. Progress to category C was open to any winner of six D bouts. Category B was achieved by winning nine C bouts.

After an entrance fee of 1s., weekly subs were 3d., sums suggesting the operation was run on a shoestring and able to pay only modest benefits. The widow of a member of three years' standing killed in the ring would receive a princely £3, and one of five years standing £5.

Proof that the union was fighting an uphill battle, and that shockingly inadequate rewards often prevailed, can be seen in the union's instructions to its members to insist upon specified minimums (minimums clearly often *not* achieved). These were 3s. a round for D fights, 5s. a round for C fights, 10s. a round for B fights and 15s. a round for category A. Members were also instructed to expect the correct sum for the *whole* fight, regardless of the result and regardless of an early finish. (Many unscrupulous promoters paid boxers knocked out or stopped in, say, two rounds *only* for the two rounds, not the whole four, six or eight.) Even top fighters might be fighting 12 rounds for less than £9.

The Army and Navy Boxing Associations had been long aware that many a boxing bill (and some major championships) had featured six-round fillers where the ranks of fighters had been emphasised – *Bombardier* Wells, *Petty Officer* Curran, *Bandsman* Blake, etc. Because the associations believed the publicity a useful boost to service morale and to recruitment, they encouraged the practice. However, as employers concerned about their soldiers, they compiled a warning list of rogue promoters. Any promoter who ignored contracts, or disappeared with the takings, or paid miserably poor purses, or all of these simultaneously, was duly listed, thus potentially obstructing his supply of rough and ready fighters. The necessity for such a list proves such parasites had not yet been eliminated.

The services had actively encouraged boxing as a valuable ancillary activity in the barracks and on the ships. (There was as yet no air force.) With coaching and frequent practice, stamina and useful manual dexterity had been added to combat fitness. Regimental or fleet boxing champions were no longer round-arm swingers obligingly thrusting their chins out to meet a right uppercut. And so-called unsophisticated matinee audiences, once made familiar with the good, were less inclined to tolerate the crude and primitive.

Outside the services, some British regions – Wales was mentioned specifically – continued to supply useful, talented fighters inspired by the successes of men such as Welsh and Driscoll. *The Times* writer was a great admirer of Driscoll:

> … one of the finest boxers of all time, certainly the finest seen in this generation on either side of the Atlantic. With the exception of Gans, the negro boxer, who died not long ago, there is nobody who could be compared with our feather-weight champion for grace of execution, accuracy, pace and power – and even Gans had not Driscoll's knack of putting leg-drive into the most casual jab …

The writer, like most genuine followers of Driscoll in 1913, hoped their idol would stick to his declared intention to retire from active combat and concentrate on coaching into others his superlative ring skills.

Other men and other weight categories were thought worthy of specific mention – Matt Wells, Digger Stanley, Johnny Summers, Young Joseph, Jack Harrison – but the article concluded with those hardy perennials, the sad state of British heavyweight boxing and the erratic form of its principal practitioner, Bombardier Billy Wells. Wells was the one and only good British heavyweight but 'still the X in the equation'. It hardly needed algebra to weigh Wells's pace, skill, physique and his ability to dazzle Al Palzer in the first round of their New York bout, against his miserable capitulation in the fourth round and on similar occasions.

On the very day that *The Times* published this analysis, thousands of miles away on the West Coast of the USA, Al Palzer was back in action. Around him, as around Wells, there floated the desperate hopes of white racists, that he would prove the Right White One; the One, that is, to beat Jack Johnson and reclaim as they degradingly put it, the heavyweight crown for the so-called White Race. In Los Angeles, at the Vernon Arena, on 1 January 1913. Palzer's own vulnerabilities, hinted at in that first round against Wells, were more elaborately demonstrated over 18 rounds by the slighter but effective

Nebraskan Luther McCarty (1882–1913), the talented and fast-rising heavyweight.

Bain Collection, Prints & Photographs Division, Library of Congress, LC-DIG-ggbain-11977

cowboy puncher Luther McCarty (b. 17 March 1892, Nebraska).[3]

Palzer had every physical advantage over McCarty. He was taller, substantially heavier and had a longer reach. He was 16st 3lb/227lbs against McCarty's 14st 4lb/200lbs. Of course, no weight advantage means too much unless it translates into heaviness of punch. This conversion was something Palzer was unable to accomplish. Of the 18 rounds the bout lasted, Palzer lost probably 15 and merely shared equally the other three. McCarty's manager, Billy McCarney, had not anticipated so uneven an outcome when he had settled, pre-fight, for an anaemic half-share of 55 per cent of the gate receipts and refused a suggestion that they should be split 35 per cent to the winner and 20 per cent to the loser. Tom O'Rourke, Palzer's manager, was no shrewder – he conveyed all his instructions to his fighter during the fight with a megaphone, obtusely ignoring the fact that McCarty could therefore also hear them and react accordingly.

Palzer was an easy, large and soft target, soon showing damage to eyes, nose and mouth, and incapable of an effective counter. Only pride and stamina kept him going. The *New York Times* report of the final two rounds makes sad reading:

ROUND 17 – Palzer was groggy as he came up for the seventeenth round but there was no doubt of his courage. His ability to assimilate punishment appeared to be his sole asset. McCarty put two terrific rights to the jaw and followed with straight lefts to the injured eye. A short uppercut to the jaw almost finished Palzer and the Iowan hung on with his eyes half closed. Palzer hit McCarty low and the referee cautioned the big fellow. Palzer could hardly find his corner at the bell.

ROUND 18 – Palzer stumbled into a terrific left hook and hung onto McCarty's shoulder. McCarty shot a hard left to the jaw and played a terrific tattoo on Palzer's body. The blood flowed from Palzer's eyes and mouth as McCarty shot two terrific straight lefts to his head. As Palzer staggered about blindly with his guard down Referee [Charles] Eyton rushed to McCarty and held up his right glove. Palzer was so weakened that only the intervention of the referee saved him from being floored. He had to be assisted to his corner.

With this demise of one white hope and the rise of another, the presentation of a diamond-studded belt to McCarty by the promoter Tom McCarney was intended as a symbol of the awarding of the title of heavyweight champion of the world. Perhaps McCarty and Palzer had been led to believe that they were genuinely contesting such a title. The public at large in the USA and Europe made no such assumption. There would be no new heavyweight champion until someone had met Jack Johnson in the ring over a championship distance and clearly defeated him. Could Luther McCarty be the one? (Johnson's last serious outing had been his 4 July 1912 match against Fireman Flynn. We will be seeing his further battles since that less than glorious defence.)

McCarty's 1912 rise had not gone unnoticed. 'In his two years of boxing McCarty has made what is undoubtedly the most impressive ring record in the history of pugilism,' said the *New York Times* hyperbolically in January after this latest win over Palzer.[4] McCarty's progress since his professional debut against Watt Adams (7 January 1911, Culbertson Montana, won by a KO in two rounds) *had* been impressive. Having won mostly by knockouts in his early bouts, by May 1912 he was taking on serious opponents and still winning convincingly. On 3 May 1912, in Springfield, Illinois, he met another of the promising 'White Hopes' in Carl Morris of Oklahoma and produced another big right to knock out Morris in the sixth. On 19 August 1912, in New York, he met the 6ft 6¼in giant from Potawatomie, Kansas (and future genuine world heavyweight champion 1915–19) Jess Willard, in a ten-round no-decision bout and was generally adjudged the better. He closed out 1912 with two other decisive victories.

On 12 October, his San Francisco meeting with the home-grown Al Kaufmann came to a dramatic end when McCarty knocked Kaufmann down twice in the second and then through the ropes on to the row of typewriters on the press bench. Journalists, eager to reclaim their machines and anxious for more copy, tried to push Kaufmann back through the ropes only to be preempted by the local police chief calling a halt there and then. Fresh from this bizarre triumph, McCarty rounded off 1912 by knocking out Fireman Jim Flynn (Johnson's recent victim) in the 16th round of a bout at the Vernon Arena, Los Angeles on 10 December.

McCarty had thus proved himself thoroughly worthy of a crack at Palzer, although his manager, interviewed at the end of the Kaufmann fight, had suggested a match with Bombardier Billy Wells, somewhere in the USA on the glamorous 4 July date in 1913.[5] In the meantime, McCarty cashed in on his image as the fighting Montana cowboy by landing an undemanding engagement in vaudeville in New York, where he was paid $2,500 a week for swinging a lariat instead of punches.

Boxing apartheid continued. The all-white McCarty v Kaufmann on the West Coast coincided with an event at the Irving AC Brooklyn on the East Coast. Here two black boxers, Jim Johnson of Galveston, Texas and Joe Jeannette of Hoboken, New Jersey, had brought 4,000 white club members to their feet, stamping and whistling their appreciation of a breathtaking ten rounds club matinee.[6] Jeannette won the newspaper decision by the narrowest of margins, both men having been pummelled to the floor during the course of the fight. A natural sequence to these two events should have been an eliminator between the two victors, McCarty and Jeannette, for a challenge to Jack Johnson for the real title. Boxing politics, alas, was not so simple.

Legal doubts about the sport persisted and the half-life of an artificially limited existence was an American norm. The inflammatory issue of inter-racial bouts was guaranteed to provoke threats of official action. In January 1913, a bill introduced into the Californian State legislature suggested the making of any fight between a white and a black boxer should be made illegal, with fines of up to $3,000 and three-year prison sentences envisaged

for violations.[7] The bill was not enacted but raised serious threats that a similar one might be. As had been found on the East Coast, and in Britain, the threat of legislation could be just as effective as an out-and-out ban. The New York State Athletic Commission had previously discussed a similar move but backed out at a later stage.

Nevertheless, the New York boxing clubs, which had once frequently staged black v white bouts, now avoided them. By the end of 1912, mixed contests were rare. Soon enough, convention turned into formal rule. On 5 February 1913, the New York State Athletic Commission formally decided mixed bouts were no longer permissible anywhere in New York State.[8] When Joe Woodman, the manager of that other wonderful black boxer, Sam Langford, applied to arrange an attractive ten-rounder in Madison Square Garden between Langford and Gunboat Smith, permission was refused.[9] Smith knew only too well what was what: 'I was the White Hope Champion of the World. But still, I knew in my heart that I wasn't the champion of the world. White, yes – but there was Jack Johnson.'[10]

In Britain, in contrast to the tightening of a legal grip upon the sport by American authorities, there were signs of a new liberality. An all-white fight between the brilliant Welshman, Jim Driscoll, and the rough, tough Midlander Owen Moran – the very match that had been cancelled in late 1911 in conjunction with the Home Office in the aftermath of the Wells–Johnson fiasco (see Chapter 7) – was, after four years of trying, back on. It would be held, not in the open air in the Midlands or in Wales, where huge crowds would be expected, but in the

select and controllable environment of the NSC on 27 January 1913.[11]

The attractions underlining this ludicrously delayed clash, sustained by the club's highest-ever priced seats (the cheapest seat in the house costing £3. 3s.), were a purse and side stakes totalling £1,700; Driscoll's British and European featherweight titles and Lonsdale Belt; and his partially recognised claim to the world title. Sometimes, elements in so anticipated a contest – a strong contrast in fighting styles, a certain edge to the relationship between the protagonists, the hopes of entire communities – can make for the most memorable of occasions. At others, all the hopes and latent talents can be smothered by the intensity of expectations and die an anticlimactic death.

In practice, the result of the so long postponed meeting between Moran and Driscoll lay somewhere between the extremes: too much mutual respect for an uninhibited contest and too much skill to disintegrate into an undistinguished maul. 'A most unsatisfactory fight', said *The Times*; 'an unsatisfactory contest', said *Boxing*; yet plenty of good judges found it absorbing from first to last and at least one man (H. Robertson) spoke of 'an exceedingly clever exhibition by both men'.

At the 2pm weigh-in, the taller Driscoll was exactly on the 9st/126lbs limit, and the stockier and shorter Moran comfortably down to 8st 12½lb/124½lbs. Both looked extremely fit, as well they might with 20 rounds to fight. Driscoll had just celebrated his 32nd birthday. Moran was 28. Moran was in sombre black trunks. Driscoll was in green shorts with a multicoloured waistband, choosing to emphasise his Irish roots as well as his Welshness. The odds shouted at ringside had Driscoll the favourite, hovering from 1/2 to 4/9.

Moran chose unexpectedly not to rush out and crowd Driscoll, beating down that infamous Driscoll left lead to get in close. Rather he began circumspectly, willing to swap leads with the master strategist at a Driscoll-like distance. Consequently, out snapped the Driscoll left leads and back went Moran's head. Out flew long Driscoll rights and Moran's lower ribs reddened. However, cannier spectators noted that the early Driscoll powerhouse punches seemed to sting and torment less than usual. Neither the lefts to the face nor the rights to the ribs wiped the thin half-smile from Moran's lips. Moran was scarcely inferior either at ducking punches or swaying economically away from a hook or a swing aimed at his chin.

Once the fighters had felt each other out, the fight settled into an unexpected pattern. Driscoll was eager to get in close and short jab, hook and uppercut Moran, while cleverly blocking, holding and frustrating Moran's best efforts to do the same. In the post-mortems, Moran claimed to have broken his right hand in the seventh. The firm right-handers he landed in the later rounds suggested this an exaggeration and not, in practice, a serious handicap.

Driscoll's problem was different. He was landing freely outside and inside, but he had to avoid, for a full hour, the heavier punching of a younger and stronger opponent. He had to clinch and smother and retain any points lead accumulated in early rounds. He had also to do what he had failed to do against Welsh in Cardiff, keep his head if his opponent adopted illegitimate subterfuges. A few of these – the head

up under the chin, the suddenly raised shoulder, the elbow that followed a swung punch – were duly hissed by the NSC audience. Both men were cautioned, but Moran was the chief offender.

The meat of the fight came in the second half when Moran caught Driscoll more often. In the 11th, Driscoll landed four clean lefts in succession, yet he was barely a whisker away from a Moran right swing whizzing past his chin. Just after this, Driscoll put in a pretty left and right combination. Before he could admire its effects, he was caught by a Moran left hook that travelled the width of the Bristol Channel and sent Driscoll tottering back on his heels. Involuntary staggers were not normally part of Driscoll's immaculate footwork.

Cautiously, Driscoll shaded the next five or six rounds by the tiniest of margins as Moran began to force the pace, landing heavy lefts in the 13th and formidable rights to Driscoll's body in the 16th. One of the rights landed precisely on the spot already tenderised by an illegitimate shoulder charge half a round before. Another right landed painfully on Driscoll's gradually swelling left eye. Fears in Driscoll's corner that Moran might yet stop the master grew rapidly.

Moran again visibly hurt Driscoll in the 18th. Driscoll went on landing punches but could not keep Moran away. He received more Moran attention to his eye and to his body and sank gratefully on his stool for the minute's break at the end. Part of his pain lay in knowing he had two more full rounds to neutralise the now rampant Moran.

He needed all his experience and all his waning reserves to survive the penultimate round as Moran launched

attack after attack. Driscoll landed some neat counters and one clubbing right that was as good as any in the fight. Nothing deterred Moran. The final round was even worse for Driscoll.

As the sounds of the starting bell died away, Moran attacked Driscoll to the body with a painful right hook and followed it with a swinging left to the jaw. Driscoll's legs went too rubbery to steady him for a serious punch in return. All he could do was wobble and cling. And cling he did; a Welsh limpet succoured on a Black Country rock as the rock did all it could to detach him. Whenever Moran could actually withdraw an arm and a glove from the tangle, he hit Driscoll. He could not do that often enough to finish his weak opponent. A tottering, clinching Driscoll hung on to the final bell.

The last word, therefore, rested with referee J. H. Douglas. He had MC Bettinson declare the decision – a draw. To many this was a verdict as unsatisfactory as the fight. Driscoll's victory in at least half the rounds was clear; Moran's in two or three. Driscoll shared at least a few of the eight other close rounds. Some observers, including *Boxing*'s correspondent, awarded him the whole of those eight rounds. Moran's jubilation at the announcement suggested he knew his desperate attempts to finish Driscoll in the one-sided last rounds had not wiped out Driscoll's accumulated lead. Enough of the old Moran was left for him to threaten physically a boxing writer daring to suggest Driscoll had been marginally superior.

Driscoll's reflections were more gracious. He believed he had won but conceded, 'But there you are, age will tell and I'm not anything like as youthful as I used to be,' and that he was 'nothing like so fit as I was when I boxed Poesy', (June 1912). To his real friends and admirers, the first serious signs of decline were there.

That mighty sign of power and beauty, the famous Driscoll left lead, had been launched at Moran with its old pace and precision, yet with less than its old percussive effect. The right cross he had landed on Moran's chin in the 19th had neither stunned Moran nor even slightly discombobulated him. Those economically calculated head movements, which had once had opponents' punches wafting harmlessly fractions of an inch past his chin, had let him down dangerously late on in the Moran fight. The unplanned totters and wobbles of January 1913 were embarrassing substitutes for the bewildering sidesteps and swift retreats that had once flummoxed opponents and preserved Driscoll's urbanity under fire. Grabs, holds and clinches had not been his style. It was definitely time to retire. One week later, Driscoll admitted that he had never felt against Moran the sharpness and vigour he had felt against Robson (1910 and 1911) or Welsh (1911) and he formally announced his retirement.[12]

Driscoll began his professional career in 1902, and give or take a few obscure exhibitions and early forays in Welsh boxing booths against all-comers, his encounter with Moran had been his 50th contest. He had faced serious opposition – George Dixon, Harry Mansfield, Johnny Summers, Joe Bowker, Leach Cross, Abe Attell, Spike Robson and Freddie Welsh among them.

His record contrasted with that of the young Frenchman who had just (12 January 1913) celebrated his 19th birthday. Georges Carpentier, for this was he, began his professional career at an unlikely #14 years of age and was experiencing a transition from middleweight up to light-heavyweight as he matured physically. He had already had 50 professional fights by the spring of 1911 and fought another ten times in 1912, including five where a title was at stake. The most acute interest in Britain in his fortunes continued remorselessly throughout 1913.

The British boxing papers all reported his catchweight bout against Marcel Moreau at the Cirque de Paris on 8 January 1913.[13] He was coming off two consecutive defeats at the hands of American opponents, against Frank Klaus and Billy Papke, where too rigorous attempts to get down to the middleweight limit had cost him dearly. Against Moreau (11st 8lb 13oz/162.93lbs), Carpentier looked fit and strong, tipping the scales at an almost identical 11st 8lb/162lbs; the more liberal allowance making a visible difference. Carpentier's skilful lefts penetrated Moreau's rudimentary cross-hands guard and jolted his head back. By way of elegant variation, Carpentier brushed down the guard with his left and landed aggressive right crosses to the jaw over the lowered barrier. Long before a compassionate referee declared enough was enough in the eighth, Carpentier's technical superiority had been amply demonstrated.

The result boosted Carpentier's next appearance before 5,000 customers at the Cirque de Paris on 12 February 1913.[14] No one thought it excess productivity to take another fight five weeks after the last. Having dominated Europe at two separate weights, welter and middle, he was ready to add the light-heavyweight category (introduced by the French-dominated International Boxing Union at 12st 7lb/175lbs) to his fiefdom. The obstacles were 20 three-minute rounds, and an apprehensive British opponent, Bandsman Dick Rice. Rice coolly viewed a smiling Carpentier take the ring, ignored the jokes swapped between Descamps and Carpentier's seconds, and shrugged his shoulders at the heavy odds quoted against him.

What Rice later admitted had astonished him was a row of private boxes where beautifully dressed and glamorous French ladies flaunted their jewellery and flashed their tiaras in the spotlights at the sight of Carpentier doffing his robe to get down to business. Wonderland or the Old Cosmo, Plymouth, where sweat and embrocation had been the prevailing perfumes, had never been like that. (The previous year, Ted Kid Lewis had met Leon Truffler of France at the Cirque de Paris [3 April 1912] and been similarly astonished by Truffler's equally glamorous appearance. Lewis looked at Truffler's silk robe and pomaded hair, sniffed Truffler's aftershave, and asked his second, 'Am I meant to fight him or ask him to dance?')

After a rousing 'La Marseillaise', Carpentier and Rice touched gloves, feinted and led tentatively in turn, looking evenly matched. Returning to his corner, Rice felt pleasantly surprised that the French hero was human after all, and no quicker nor cleverer than the British top professionals. Alas, it was amidst such complacency, and in such unguarded moments, that the French Faust had a nasty habit of turning into a French Mephistopheles. In the second,

Carpentier gave Rice a glimpse of his exposed chin. Rice went instantly for the tempting target with a right of power and venom and all his weight behind it. Carpentier fastidiously moved his jaw a studied fraction out of reach, then put all his new poundage into a counter that sent Rice flat on to his back, wondering why the lights in the roof of the Cirque had so proliferated without warning. It took him considerably longer than ten seconds to work out an answer.

Just as Carpentier benefited from going up a division, so one of Britain's best boxers, Matt Wells, who had celebrated his 26th birthday in December 1912 a few weeks after losing his British and European lightweight titles to Freddie Welsh, enjoyed the transition from lightweight up to welterweight. His loss, on disqualification, in the frenzied overweight bout against Hughie Mehegan of Australia at The Ring in September 1912, still rankled. On 24 February 1913, for a £900 purse, split £625:£275/winner:loser, and sidestakes of £100 each, the NSC persuaded Wells and Mehegan to settle the arguments arising out of Wells's disqualification.[15] The match was made at 9st 9lb/135lbs. Wells, the stockier, weighed in at 2pm at 9st 8½lb/134½lbs, and Mehegan at 9st 7¾lb/133¾lbs.

For the first three rounds, two clever men tried eagerly to overawe one another. Wells out of his characteristic crouch bustled in looking to catch Mehegan about the body. Mehegan was cool and collected, using his reach and his skilled footwork to pick off Wells from a safe distance.

From the fourth, Wells concluded that Mehegan's leads and counters were too hurtful to take with indifference. He looked to close in and clinch and

maul. Both men were reprimanded for holding, but Wells was the major offender. He wanted to break up Mehegan's rhythms and use his own strength close in to weaken the Australian. The intention sustained him the best part of 15 rounds. In the 16th, both men decided independently that a grandstand finish was necessary to win.

Mehegan commanded the centre of the ring, sometimes leading, sometimes countering, always looking to knock Wells out. Wells put his mauling behind him and also looked to lead and counter promptly and precisely, if never with the raw power of Mehegan. It worked. Wells got a narrow points victory, much to Mehegan's disgust. 'I thought I won nineteen rounds out of twenty, and think the decision a robbery.' Two fights, two tumultuous scraps, two controversial decisions – small wonder therefore that Mehegan went off to Australia in high dudgeon and that Australian promoters thought it worthwhile to import Wells for two more fights against Mehegan (one in Sydney and one in Melbourne) in the summer, supposedly to see justice done. We shall see later if it was.

By staging the first return bout between Wells and Mehegan, the NSC had poached a fight that would have fallen naturally to The Ring, host of the original match. Mehegan v Wells II would have packed out The Ring and made money. By way of retaliation, The Ring put on, *the very same evening*, a most attractive clash between two top British flyweights, Sid Smith of Bermondsey and Sam Keller, another Jewish East Ender from Aldgate. Keller had spent two periods in the USA (1907–08 and 1911) honing his sharp skills in its rings.

Edwardian England was no less divided about smaller weight divisions than modern audiences. Some responded to skill, courage and resilience in the ring no matter who demonstrated such qualities. For those spectators, no boxer had to carry a minimum of poundage to be of interest. Others, at the announcement of a flyweight fight, preferred the bar to the ringside. *The Times* correspondent, quoted at the beginning of this chapter, was in the latter ranks. He showed a lofty distaste for tiny titans: 'We are well off for flyweights,' he wrote, 'but nobody is very much interested in the doings of such microbes of the ring.'[16]

The contemptuous dismissal of flyweights, along with what became light-flyweights, straw-weights, paperweights, gnat-weights and minimum weights, as lower forms of ring life, was as unworthy then as now. It was particularly ungenerous in 1913 when a rich crop of small fighters graced many a bill. Apart from Sid Smith and Sam Keller, there flourished Percy Jones from the Rhondda Valley, Johnny Hughes who fought out of Bloomsbury, Bill Ladbury of Deptford, Joe Symonds of Plymouth, Tancy Lee of Leith (b. 31 January 1882), Edinburgh (not Glasgow as is sometimes claimed), and an even greater name than these who will shortly feature in this history.

Everyone with the slightest interest in boxing is in the debt of Harold Alderman for his painstaking research into the chaos that surrounded the lower weights from the 1870s up to the controversial decision of the NSC to recognise *no* category below 8st/112lbs (Chapter 4).[17] The decision was painful for many a small fighter because there had previously been a full *12* divisions between the lowest (6st 4lb/88lbs) and the full 8st, going up in two-pound steps with championships to be claimed at each – 'Joe Blank, champion at 7st 8lb', 'John Doe, champion at 6st 6lb', and the like. The 1909 NSC decree punished particularly a fighter who could, for example, make so rigorous a limit as 6st 6lb/90lbs. He would now have to give away an impossible 22 pounds to contest the 8st/112lbs title.

The anarchy in the lower weight divisions prevailing up to 1909 was a trivial symptom of a serious problem: the nutritional ravages wrought in the working-class population by poverty and miserable standards of living. Ill-fed populations produce many small men. Early sociologists such as Charles Booth (*Life and Labour in the People of London* completed in 17 volumes by 1902–03, including four volumes specifically on 'Poverty' in 1902) and Seebohm Rowntree (*Poverty: A Study of Town Life*, 1901) had provided the most damning evidence about the true nature of urban working-class life; for example, that a full 30 per cent of Londoners lived in poverty. Poverty brought in its wake hunger, inferior accommodation, poor hygiene, vulnerability to disease, a predictably shorter lifespan than that enjoyed by the well-off, and because of child malnutrition, the failure to reach true growth potential.

As Marghanita Laski once eloquently pointed out:

Even allowing for the dietary deficiencies imposed by ignorance, the differences between the physical conditions of rich and poor children were gross, as a few statistics show. The average height of working-

class was five inches below that of public school-boys, and the average weight of working-class boys at the age of 13 was eleven pounds less than that of boys from wealthier families. At the beginning of the period [1901], 18 per cent of children born in the west end of London died before the age of 5; in the east end, 55 per cent did so. Though the infant mortality rate fell by one-third between 1900 and 1910; it remained largely unchanged in poverty areas. In Blackburn, for instance, in 1911, the infantile death-rate in the wealthier area was 96 per 1,000, in the poorer areas 315 per 1,000.[18]

Should it be mistakenly thought that the damning figures she quotes were out of date by 1913 after a decade of progress, it should be remembered that in the British Army of the First World War, officers, overwhelmingly public-school products, were on average *five inches taller* than their men, overwhelmingly working class – making the term 'look down on' as true physically as metaphorically.

In 1913, fewer working-class children survived. Yet for those who did, the harshness of their stunted lives honed their tiny frames to a toughness unknown to a healthier child of a century later. The child of 1909 might walk or run everywhere, play outside in all weathers from sunrise to sunset (in preference to being cooped up in one tiny room with all too many other family members), and put to work early, filled a job involving long hours of hard, physical exercise. Add an aggressive temperament fostered by the

childhood scraps so often on offer, and the potential for a good flyweight was obvious. Live hard, fight hard, prosper in the ring, die early – a magic tragic formula. Such experiences deserved better than cursory dismissal by a well-fed *Times* journalist.

Boxing in early 1913 offered some brilliant British flyweight bouts. On Monday, 17 February 1913, The Ring at Blackfriars (again cheekily staging a contest on the NSC's traditional Monday night) had an overfull house and an unlucky overspill out on the pavements for the London debut of Johnny Best of Glasgow ('one of the classiest that has ever been brought up on porridge') who was matched against Johnny Hughes ('The Bloomsbury Bearcat').[19] Scotsmen who did not eat porridge were presumably as rare as bearcats in Bloomsbury, but such niceties did not deter a 4,000 capacity crowd levered into the building. Hughes was confidently expected to win, and Hughes himself, who had skipped a few days' training because of illness, assumed he could beat Best anyway. He was due to be disillusioned.

Hughes started complacently and aggressively, head forward, chin on chest, letting his opponent stare him straight in the immaculate parting. He delivered straight short punches, coupled with neat left and right hooks to the body. Many in the hall applauded, yet more discerning patrons registered that Best's elbows and forearms tight to his sides kept Hughes's gloves away from any damaging targets. Some hissed Hughes for blows that circumvented Best's tight defence and plunged into the Scotsman's kidneys. Hughes also was aware of his failure to land the hooks effectively.

He did better in the third and fifth but landed nothing to ruffle Best's composure. Best kept him off with his left and rocked Hughes with a straight right in the sixth. When Hughes launched a similar punch in the 11th, he raised not a bruise but a laugh, as Best slipped away and the punch hit only the top rope. Best, on top and piling up points, was giving a masterclass in flyweight tactics, picking off his opponent with lefts, sidestepping, swaying and melting away, leaving Hughes angrily chasing shadows. The doubt was whether Hughes might outlast Best and then make him pay for his early successes.

Unfortunately for Hughes, by the 18th he was the one feeling the strain induced by the missed days of training, and the accumulated effects of punching the air. These counted for more than the energy Best had expended in his twinkle-toed travels all around the ring. Hughes caught up with him twice, once in the 18th and once in the 20th, leaving Best twice on the canvas, yet in each case it was more push and slip than genuine knockdown. Best was soon up and away again. Best's points victory was clear and its confirmation drew warm applause, even from an audience packed with Hughes's supporters. Hughes graciously conceded that Best had indeed been better.

The staging of the Monday fight was a snub to the NSC, the result another mini-humiliation on top of mini-humiliation. In December 1911, it will be remembered that the first Lonsdale Belt awarded in the flyweight division went to Sid Smith after his victory over Joe Wilson. Smith was, eventually, invited by Bettinson to defend his belt and his title against Johnny Hughes at the club. As Smith saw it, the offered purse of £100 (£5 a round) was insultingly small, and he turned it down. To emphasise his disappointment at the club's autocratic take-it-or-leave-it attitude, he looked Bettinson straight in the well-filled waistcoat and handed him a paper bag – in it was the Lonsdale Belt.[20]

Bettinson, less than impressed by a fighter showing a degree of independence, promptly arranged for Johnny Hughes and Bill Ladbury to box for the belt and the title, which the club declared vacant, at the NSC on 10 March 1913. (Smith's point must have penetrated Bettinson's bluster for the purse for the new fight was raised to £175.) However, and it was a very big however, how could a Hughes/Ladbury title fight have any credibility when the Scot Best had just trounced Hughes over the championship distance? The NSC, embarrassed, called the new fight off.

Into the vacuum moved The Ring. On 24 February 1913, the Blackfriars venue staged Sid Smith – still flyweight champion in the eyes of everyone but the NSC – versus Sam Keller.[21] Smith and Keller both weighed in at an indulgent three pounds over the 8st/112lbs championship limit. This did nothing to impair the attractiveness of the match-up. The popular Sam Keller had, like Smith, gained useful experience in American rings.

He had visited New York in 1907 and 1908, and again in 1910 and 1911 with mixed fortunes. He had won a newspaper decision over the talented Tommy Houck but outstayed his welcome for his share in a fight at the Fairmont Athletic Club in the Bronx on 6 February 1911 against Jimmy Dunn. The fight was memorable only for the mysterious unwillingness of either boxer ever to throw a punch. No one believed such apathy would prevail at Blackfriars, especially as Keller's return from the USA in 1911 had been specifically to box against Smith at the NSC, a golden opportunity he had lost by falling ill on the eve of the fight.

At Blackfriars against Smith, Keller was in forceful mood and he took Smith to the limit over the 20 rounds. Smith's speed around the ring was at its swiftest, as was his rapier-like left lead. These had been expected. What surprised both sections of the crowd (the Bermondsey Jewish contingent there to support Smith *and* the Jewish East Enders crossing the river to cheer the Aldgate man) was the extent to which Keller had held his own, move by move, punch by punch. The post-mortems pronounced the event worthy of the title and the belt it had been officially denied.

Smith's superb skills had been hard won. Since his debut in early 1907, he had fought upwards of 70 professional contests and would fight over 30 more. So when Keller coolly swayed his head milliseconds before Smith's left glove could land, Smith's answer was to double his work rate and throw more and more lefts until they *did* land. At other times, when lefts as hard as Smith ever threw went harmlessly over Keller's delicately lowered shoulders, Smith had to reorganise his own defences as Keller's hooks and counters thudded into his ribs.

After ten rounds, Smith was marginally ahead, but Keller was far from discouraged. Keller won rounds himself, for example the 14th, by moving in close to Smith and landing scoring punches under and over Smith's guard. True champion that he was, Smith went back to his corner after the painful 14th to consult his extended team of seconds (six in all) and to respond in the 15th by redoubling his efforts to keep Keller at a safer distance with ever more left leads. The climactic 20th was accompanied by shouts, screams and cheers as Keller, knowing he needed a big finish, went ferociously for Smith. Smith used all his evasive skills to keep him away. When Dick Burge gave Smith the verdict, no one in the house, including Keller, seemed like a loser.

Smith v Keller was a delightful treat for the Blackfriars patrons. The 20-round contest at 8st 6lb/118lbs that took place on 28 March 1913 between Johnny Hughes, the Bloomsbury Bearcat recently tamed by Johnny Best of Scotland, and the up-and-coming Bill Beynon of Taibach, South Wales, was another for South Londoners at the Canterbury Music Hall, Lambeth. Each man made the limit (Beynon 8st 4¼lb/116¼lbs and Hughes 8st 4½lb/116½lbs). The bout was over a championship distance and of championship quality. Each man claimed physical and mental ascendancy for a few rounds, then conceded both to his opponent for the next few. After 20 scintillating rounds, the bout was declared a draw. Sid Smith, despite the much discussed win over Keller, was only on the Canterbury undercard (a ten-round points win over Charlie Ward).

Barely two weeks later, Sid Smith, the tiny beetle-browed rebel who had spurned the NSC, demonstrated his true box office potential in Paris at Premierland Français on 11 April

1913.[22] A huge crowd gathered to see him and the tough little Frenchman Eugene Criqui contest the European flyweight title, and to English and French minds if not American ones, the world title as well. Both men were comfortably within the eight-stone limit. Criqui, although still a teenager, was compact, muscular and as resilient as a rubber punch bag. He had quite a dig in each hand. Smith, no heavy puncher, was as fast, elusive and accurate as ever, although his left was inclined to be an open-gloved slap rather than a punch.

All French supporters hoped Criqui's front-foot aggression could overwhelm Smith's superior skills. In the event, Criqui tried desperately, yet Smith's elusiveness on the retreat frustrated all his attempts to make his superior reach and strength tell. Smith, prompted by Georges Carpentier, who was acting as referee, remembered to close his fist and punch with the left, peppering the oncoming Criqui with painful scoring punches. Occasionally – in the seventh, ninth and last two rounds – Criqui got close and landed effectively. This was insufficient to wipe out all the other Smith successes. The Criqui camp generously conceded that Carpentier's decision in favour of Smith was thoroughly justified.

Smith's declaration of independence from the NSC had paid off. Few could deny he was the real British champion even if he had no NSC imprimatur or belt to go along with his European title. Smith, and Dick Burge at The Ring, rubbed the point home on 2 June 1913. The NSC had announced for Derby week, a Monday night's boxing, including the defence of the British bantamweight title and

Lonsdale Belt held by Digger Stanley against the challenger, the young Welshman Bill Beynon. At the time, the Derby, the premier classic race for three-year-olds at Epsom Downs, was held on a Wednesday afternoon. It was therefore an attractive proposition for sporting gentlemen on their country estates to take the first few days of June in town to see the race, and to precede it with a Monday night's boxing at the NSC.

In the event, the 1913 Derby was won by a horse called Aboyeur. As the horses emerged from Tattenham Corner, Amner, the much-fancied horse belonging to HM King George V, led only to be intercepted by Miss Emily Davison, a member of Emmeline Pankhurst's Women's Social and Political Union, formed in 1903 to promote female suffrage in the face of male hostility and indifference. At the cost of her own life, Miss Davison ran on to the course, grabbed Amner's reins and brought horse and jockey down in a heap on top of her. This, the first and by no means the last political demonstration held at a sporting event, captured the headlines just as Miss Davison had intended. (She had probably not meant her intervention to be suicidal as she had a return ticket from Epsom in her pocket.) Less well known is that Jones, the King's jockey brought down in this dramatic and dangerous fashion, was retrospectively so impressed by the martyr's physical courage that he attended Mrs Pankhurst's funeral in 1928, bearing a wreath to honour both women.[23]

Far from deterred by the NSC bill, Burge announced, *also* for the Monday night, 2 June, the latest challenge to Sid Smith's flyweight dominance with a fight between Smith and the heavy-punching Bill Ladbury of Greenwich. So, as the Derby week began, two of the most attractive fights of the year were staged in direct competition with each other, making it impossible for even the most dedicated fan to see both. The outcomes were unexpected.

At the NSC, Digger Stanley had a mixed reputation. There, both sides of Digger, the admirable and the shabby, had showed. He, boxing's equivalent of the music halls' Dan Leno, had originally been asked to fight Welshman Eddie Morgan. Were he to beat Morgan, the Lonsdale Belt he had won against Joe Bowker and defended against Alec Lafferty would be his personal property along with an eventual pension. When Morgan withdrew because of illness, Bill Beynon replaced him.[24]

Beynon was taking a big risk. He had been walking around, out of training, at about 9st 6lb/132lbs, and had hardly recovered from a damaged left eye, an unwelcome legacy of his defeat by Johnny Hughes over 20 hard rounds at the Canterbury Music Hall on 2 May 1913. Shedding weight at the drastic rate of three pounds a day, he trained demonically for this unanticipated chance of a title. He would go all out for an early knockout and surely run out of steam over a championship 20 rounds. Both he and Stanley weighed in at 8st 5½lb/117½lbs.

Stanley used his longer reach, fought brilliantly off the back foot and pulled out every trick in his repertoire to keep the advancing Beynon away. Beynon came in. Stanley hooked and jabbed him. Beynon moved in again. Stanley uppercut him. Beynon bore in again. Stanley slipped inside and hooked him around the body. The pattern pleased

Stanley and his many supporters as he was a big betting favourite.

The treatment did not deter the ultra-determined Beynon for a second. He took the punches from all angles with the indifference of a lump of anthracite. In between them, he got off some good scoring punches of his own.

Stanley suffered the discouragement that comes from landing five, six or seven good left leads on an advancing opponent, only to find him undaunted, undeterred and unweakened. Whatever Stanley did, Beynon kept on coming.

Digger never stuck to a tactic if it seemed ineffective. If to win meant to go in for a toe-to-toe scrap, so be it. And if he could not win with his masterly repertory of legal defensive and offensive ruses, he would dip into his magic box for more nefarious ones. At the end of the seventh, he ignored the bell and landed a severe clubbing right as Beynon obediently dropped his arms and made for his corner. He was booed for these incidents, and reprimanded by the referee frequently for holding, and in the eighth for hitting and holding simultaneously. In the 14th, he followed in a right cross with his head, and 'accidentally' butted Beynon on the closed and swelling eye. He also sprang up so vigorously from a low duck as to bring his head into painful collision with Beynon's chest.

Nothing, however fraudulent, was going to stop Beynon on the best night of his whole career. By the late rounds he was taking less and delivering more, even knocking the Digger clean off his feet with a big left in the 19th. Had Beynon's unrelenting aggression outscored the many legitimate punches Stanley had landed for three-quarters of the fight? Would referee Douglas, well

familiar with Digger's shabbier ploys, and having given him seven separate warnings during the fight, dock points? Was a champion allowed to keep a title and a belt when they had not been clearly taken from him?

Douglas, in the twilight of his career as a referee, to the surprise of many, and to the anger of those who had backed Stanley heavily, had Bettinson announce the name of the winner – Beynon! Noisy protests, encouraged by Stanley's seconds (including the less than eirenic Owen Moran), echoed around the hall until Lord Lonsdale stepped into the centre of the ring. The noble lord, aristocratic pillar of the boxing establishment, reminded the turbulent middle classes of their sporting duties: 'We must abide by the referee's decision.' The noise turned to sulky silence. Lonsdale would have been the perfect casting for the Lord Chancellor in Gilbert and Sullivan's *Iolanthe* at the Savoy Theatre close to the NSC. And only Gilbert and Sullivan could have done justice to the scene at Aberavon station when Beynon brought his Lonsdale Belt home. A silver prize band playing 'See the Conquering Hero Come' greeted him, as did a triumphant procession led by a Welsh regimental goat, its horns stuffed into a pair of boxing gloves.[25]

Just as Lord Lonsdale was quelling the mini-rebellion at the NSC, another army of boxing enthusiasts was packed into the Blackfriars Ring to back Sid Smith, the people's flyweight champion if not the NSC's, against his tough neighbour, Bill Ladbury of Greenwich.[26] Ladbury was billed as coming from Greenwich because his amateur career had been launched with the Greenwich Amateur Boxing Club. His home was less the elegant Greenwich of Wren and Nelson, rather the rougher, tougher environs of New Cross.

Smith was the punters' favourite, especially after his defiance of the NSC establishment. Much of his support was drawn from the Bermondsey dockers, a community whose members stood daily at the dock gates wondering whether the gaffer would employ them for the day or send them away payless. Smith was the worker who had sent the boss packing, something dockers only dreamed of.

Ladbury was a coarser fighter of power rather than finesse. Against Smith's skills, Ladbury offered endurance. While Smith demonstrated his aesthetic superiority, Ladbury could last 20 rounds, and give the crowd their money's worth. The ring walks were in character: Smith, head high, walked in like a champion, graciously inclining his head to the applause and the cheers that followed him all the way to the ring. Ladbury, 5ft 2in of lolling indifference, ignored the shouts of his supporters and shuffled forward as if he already knew his role in the night's proceedings was to be the punch bag while the star showed off. For six thrilling rounds, Ladbury was indeed the obligatory punch bag and Smith the demonstrator of every pretty punch in the boxing textbook.

In the second, a bewildering succession of left leads from Smith connected with Ladbury's flattening nose, and a follow-up left hook to the jaw put Ladbury on the seat of his trunks. He was down again at the start of the third and spent the last 30 seconds of the fourth retreating before an onslaught that had Smith landing his lefts at will without serious reply. At this

stage, Smith's fans elevated their hopes for an early finish and doubled their stakes with any layer of odds in the hall willing to proffer much shortened odds.

Only experienced observers could detect the discrepancy between the light impact of Smith's sparkling punch combinations and the exaggerated reactions with which Ladbury was receiving them. Ladbury was soaking up the Smith attacks with very much more comfort than he was indicating and was biding his time.

A chance came in the seventh. Smith sped out of his corner, eager to keep up the one-sided onslaught and was met with a thumping right cross from Ladbury that sent him sprawling across the boards and down with a mighty clatter. He was so astonished he got up quickly and very unwisely, only to be met by another that took him back down. As his supporters blanched, the carrier of all their hopes took six counts over the three minutes. And Ladbury's carefully contrived *coup de théâtre* was not over yet.

Smith's jaw was a lot harder than most of his punches, and he had courage in abundance. After some frantic restorative work between the rounds, Smith spent the eighth in full retreat, landing light punches on Ladbury, keeping his distance from him. After the damage he had done in the seventh, Ladbury was prepared to wait. The ninth showed why. Another hurtful right put Smith back down, and he got groggily up at nine only because he had to. This time he moved desperately away from the dreaded Ladbury right. This merely brought him into the target area of the Ladbury left. Five times was Smith hit with the left; five times was he down again.

No conscientious modern referee would have failed at such a stage to call a compassionate halt. Referees in 1913 were commonly afflicted with EDS, or Empathy Deficiency Syndrome, just as 1913 audiences lacked apparently a Fastidiousness Gene. So the gallant and doomed Smith had further to suffer – five long counts in the tenth, plus a cruel 11th round when he spent more time on the boards than on his feet. Only when he had been down another nine times in the round was the referee, Mr E. A. Humphreys, prepared to spare so gallant a loser more punishment. By then the timekeeper needed an abacus as much as a clock. Smith, unsurprisingly, was never the same fighter again. He still did not make his last ring appearance until late 1919.[27] By then, his conqueror could no longer fight anybody, having been killed in the First World War in France on 27 June 1917.

The two men who won so unexpectedly on that memorable June night in 1913 (Beynon at the NSC over Stanley, and Ladbury at The Ring over Smith) were not allowed the rest of the year off. Beynon, the new bantamweight champion, was rematched at the NSC on 27 October 1913 with the aggrieved Digger Stanley.[28] This was Beynon's opportunity to prove that he was truly the champion, not dependent upon the frailties of a faltering referee. For Stanley, it was the last hurrah of a veteran a decade older than his opponent and a final chance to own a Lonsdale Belt outright and qualify for the concomitant pension.

The Digger was too canny an operator to get into toe-to-toe exchanges while conceding strength and youth. He suffered damage to his knuckles when he punched too hard with either hand. Without undue risk he controlled virtually every round of the 20. The members who remembered the injustice of the June decision now gave him a forgiving ovation, the hoots and hisses of June forgotten. He cancelled Beynon's aggression by subtle clutches, clinches and evasions while piling up points with rapid light punches from a distance. Beynon's intent to close in and punish came to nothing. His tiring swings evaporated short of or beyond their targets or glanced off a hedgehog-like defence. Sometimes they thudded into the soft and forbidden kidneys to Stanley's great discomfort, more pain to suffer along with his tender knuckles. Referee Angle, severe on clinching from either man, ignored the kidney punches. (Beynon's kidney punches, as even Stanley later admitted, were really the result of the Digger stepping inside swings aimed legitimately at his ribs.)

The feel of the Lonsdale Belt around his waist again was as good to Stanley as embrocation. The Digger being the Digger, the belt was soon out of the trophy cabinet and on its way to the pawnshop but enjoyed for the moment. For the disappointed Beynon, that first win against Stanley subsequently proved a career highlight. Before 1913 was out, on 27 December 1913 at the American Ice Rink in Cardiff, he suffered another significant loss against Stanley's one-time conqueror, Charles Ledoux of France.[29] One of Ledoux's devastating rights split Beynon's left eyebrow so significantly it led Beynon to retire. (The punch was similar to the one that had knocked out Stanley in the seventh on 23 June 1912 in Dieppe, the firmest possible reversal of Stanley's points win over Ledoux on 22 April 1912 at the NSC.)

Before the unfortunate cut, the two men had gone at each other so ferociously – all attack and no discernible defence – that the Cardiff crowd gave Ledoux as hearty a standing ovation as if he had been decorated in daffodils. At the particular request of the Beynon camp, both fighters had dispensed with hand wraps. Some French fighters it was believed overdid the bandages. After the cut, Beynon must have regretted the request. Ledoux's manager, Descamps, the very same who managed Georges Carpentier, could have told them that a good French puncher could do damage whatever the hand protection – a fact others in the UK were learning the hard way.

Meanwhile, Bill Ladbury, coming off the shock win over Sid Smith in June, had mixed fortunes over the rest of the year. He won comfortably a 20-round points decision against Tommy Harrison in London on 24 November 1913 but was knocked out cold in the tenth by Jimmy Berry of Newcastle on 15 December 1913 at New Cross. During 1914 he would defend his title at the NSC but against another outstanding small fighter, Percy Jones of Pentre.

The last few years before the outbreak of the First World War in August 1914 were not a period, like modern times, where men with a modicum of talent could glove up, win half a dozen fights against mediocrities, and fight for a spurious world belt within months of their professional debut. On the contrary, the way to the top in pre-war boxing was hard; many were called, as St Matthew's Gospel has it, but few were chosen.

When Percy Jones made an appearance in a six-rounder at the NSC

on 28 April 1913 against Gus Govaerts, he had an unbeaten record of 23 fights (21 wins and two draws) acquired locally – apart from one venture to Cardiff. In 1913 alone, he fought 24 times, meeting and beating many good men – Alf Mansfield three times, Joe Wilson twice and Sam Keller once. By the time he fought for the championship against Bill Ladbury in January 1914 he was practically a veteran. By contrast, the Welsh flyweight title was won in 1989 by David Afon-Jones of Neath from Phil Dicks of Ammanford, an exciting ten-round contest by all accounts but contested by two men who could previously muster only 11 professional fights between them.[30]

Poor Percy Jones not only had to struggle against many talented and experienced rivals, but he was also never comfortable at the 8st/112lbs limit. Rigorous dieting and occasional fasting made his career even tougher, and his weight-reducing efforts not always effective.

A second Welshman coming to prominence in 1913 was one with, rarely enough, connections to North and South Wales. He was born in Newport, Monmouthshire (later Gwent) on 13 September 1889 to a mother with Irish connections (shades of Driscoll). In 1911, aged 21, he enrolled in the army as a Royal Welch Fusilier, a regiment with an HQ at Wrexham on the Wales–England border. Afterwards he fought often at the Liverpool Stadium, Liverpool, having both a long-established Welsh community and a large number of Catholics eager to support a co-religionist. The soldier was Johnny Basham.[31]

Early on, Basham gave scant indication of how formidable an

opponent he would become. The two named opponents he had faced – the great Matt Wells (26 December 1912 at Swansea) and the obstinate Yorkshireman Gus Platts of Sheffield (20 November 1911 at Cardiff) – had beaten him convincingly, Wells by a seventh-round knockout and Platts on points over 15 rounds. Nevertheless, Basham, who spent most of his career in the highly competitive welterweight division, was no novice. As his enthusiastic biographer Alan Roderick reveals, his meeting with Wells was at least his 59th appearance in the ring if novice encounters and exhibitions are counted. Boxing experience, paid for in hurts and bruises, does not come cheap. But no substitute is adequate to replace it.

Private Basham's perky happy-go-lucky approach to life and sport was as attractive to his followers as his ready smile and his clean punching. They did not spare him a dreadful experience in 1913. On 21 August 1913, at the Liverpool Stadium, he met the South African Harry Price over 15 rounds.[32] By the 11th Basham was narrowly in front and moving in to bring the contest to a premature end. A left cross to Price's jaw sent the South African down for a count of nine. As he got up, unsteadily, Basham, as he was perfectly entitled to do, followed in with a hard right. Down went Price again, hitting his head on the boards and lying absolutely inert.

As soon as it was realised he was not coming round, he was taken to the Liverpool Royal Infirmary but died overnight without regaining consciousness. Instead of being chaired from the ring and back to the barracks by jubilant comrades, Basham was attended only by the police and spent a sleepless night in a cell. He was there when the news of Price's demise was brought to him. Next morning he was at the magistrates' court, charged formally with grievous bodily harm and manslaughter and remanded on bail. The heavy-handed treatment of Basham was matched by the farcical burial service for Price conducted by a hastily summoned priest and only halted when it was realised that Price was actually Jewish and needed a rabbi instead. (When the correct ceremonial was observed, Basham made it his business to be in attendance.)

Basham attended the formal inquest held on Thursday, 4 September 1913. He was formally cleared of the manslaughter charge only when the jury was given the medical evidence that the death had been caused by the fall and not one of Basham's punches, and brought in a verdict of death by misadventure. What would they have done if the post-mortem *had* concluded a punch had done the deed? A rare and tragic but always possible outcome. As has been discussed earlier, the legal position is highly ambiguous. The jury, sensing this perhaps, took their duties very seriously and insisted on having a not guilty verdict accompanied by a 'strong protest' against the practice of ever awarding a victory by knockout.

In practice, the jury's protest was ignored. Where was the logic in holding a contest where a man is encouraged to strike an opponent, yet penalised were he to be too good at it? By 1913, boxing had claims to be a genuinely national sport, as popular as football or cricket. A major fight commanded as many column inches in quality newspapers as a Test match or an FA Cup final. Asquith's Liberal government in 1913 was being assailed on all sides – by militant suffragettes on the women's vote; by militant trade unionists over a multiplicity of industrial grievances; by angry Northern Irishmen on the future of Ulster. The prospect of banning formally a highly popular and tacitly legitimate sporting activity would have been a political altercation too far. Whatever hostility to boxing prevailed in some circles, a formal attack on boxing would have done the vacillating Liberal government of 1913 more harm than good.

The British press treated the death of Basham's opponent with restraint. It is rarely mentioned in standard boxing histories. Not so the ring death that occurred in Calgary, Canada in the spring of 1913. The Calgary incident was subject to intense discussion and subsequent mythologising.[33] It was the terminal event in the career of Luther McCarty. In 1913, McCarty became the USA's most upwardly mobile cowboy until Will Rogers (1879–1935) rocketed from Oklahoma cowpoke to Hollywood's best-paid actor and popular natural philosopher.

As most candidates on the 'White Hope' trail in 1913 waltzed, stumbled and fumbled their way to oblivion, McCarty remained a serious prospect. He topped 6ft 4in, had a comparable reach and moved around a ring with balance and purpose. He cultivated a strong left jab and supplemented it with an over-the-top right and an effective uppercut. He celebrated his 21st birthday in March 1913 knowing that he had personally overseen the demise of many other hopefuls. He had given Al Palzer a severe trouncing, knocked out some 'names' such as Carl Morris, Jim Flynn and Al Kaufmann,

McCarty's image as cowboy and 'White Hope' was assiduously polished by his manager Billy McCarney. He was in actuality of Native American pedigree.

Bain Collection, Prints & Photographs Division, Library of Congress, LC-DIG-ggbain-11845

and been Jess Willard's clear superior in a no-decision contest in New York (19 August 1912).

McCarty had acquired a sympathetic promoter/manager – the veteran Bill McCarney. McCarney had handled the unsuccessful Carl Morris and was well acquainted with the nuances of a 'White Hope' campaign. Consequently he knew how to make a silk purse out of a pig's ear. With a flair for publicity in the McIntosh or Rickard class, and knowing how to suborn and sweeten boxing correspondents, McCarney underlined the pig's ear side of the equation. He exaggerated the amenable Luther's cowboy background and flooded the newspapers with staged photographs of a lassoing, bronco-riding McCarty under a sombrero the size of a giant satellite dish. McCarney acquainted everyone with McCarty's Scottish-American breeding, an excellent pedigree for a white hope, if a little at odds with reality. Luther's

father was a Native American called White Eagle. McCarty himself cooperated fully with the campaign by taking several New York vaudeville engagements as a stage cowboy with a rope-twirling and lassoing act. He obligingly told the boxing writers that his vaudeville earnings were going to pay for his heart's desire, a bespoke saddle with genuine silver trimmings.

Another ancient master of hype was at hand in the sturdy frame of our old friend Tommy Burns, whose defeat by Johnson in 1908 had stimulated the whole racist enterprise. Burns boxed when it suited him and the price was right. Money and inclination had coincided only twice in the five years since 1908. Nevertheless, Burns turned an eagle eye to money-making opportunities. Operating in Calgary, Canada, he acquired a financial interest in the local boxing arena (renamed the Tommy Burns Arena). Burns, still the horse racing maven, controlled two possible runners in the white heavyweight stakes – himself (still aged only 30), and the 28-year-old French-Canadian Arthur Pelkey (real name Arthur Peletier).

Quite as skilfully as McCarney had built up McCarty's prospects, so Burns dangled intriguing possibilities. Perhaps he himself would go back into the ring with Johnson and reverse the Sydney verdict. That got the sporting citizens of Calgary actively discussing the issue. Simultaneously, Burns promoted Pelkey, his protégé, born 27 October 1884, gratifyingly taller at 6ft 1in, if much less skilful. On 2 April 1913, Pelkey and Burns met in Calgary in a less than genuine six-round no-decision bout. What manager would put a blemish on the record of his own

protégé? Or damage his own reputation by losing to a young pretender?

With all the artificial highlights of a pre-scripted stage fight, Pelkey and Burns met and reportedly thrilled. Burns was knocked down once and Pelkey three times. In between, the action was fast and furious. That could all have been anticipated, as could the post-fight announcement by Burns that he was renouncing his own chances to match Pelkey with Johnson. Until that happy day, he would himself promote a meeting in Calgary between Pelkey and the new Nebraskan, Luther McCarty.

In front of an enthusiastic Calgary audience of about 3,000, who paid up to six dollars each for their seats, Pelkey and McCarty met at Burns's arena on 24 May 1913. The entire fight lasted less than two minutes with no significant action whatsoever. The two men shuffled around, feeling each other out and closed a few times. McCarty stepped back from a clinch, tottered and fell to the canvas to the astonishment of Pelkey, who had barely thrown a

Calgary, 24 May 1913. McCarty falls to the canvas when Canadian Arthur Pelkey (1884–1921) has barely thrown a punch. A cynical photo editor added a supposed heavenly beam of light.

Cyberboxingzone

punch, and of referee Ed Smith who had not seen one either but began to count McCarty out. The audience, just as taken aback but thinking they were being robbed of their dollars, began to boo and chant 'Fix!' McCarty lay there completely inert, a state that continued as he was carried outside and subject to frantic attempts to revive him. He was pronounced dead eight minutes later. Then even the angriest protestor realised this was no con but an irreversible catastrophe.

Pelkey, visibly distressed in the ring and after, found himself arrested and arraigned on manslaughter charges. He was discharged only after the medical evidence showed that a previous blow or accident inflicting a broken

All attempts to revive McCarty are in vain.
Cyberboxingzone

neck had caused the haemorrhage in McCarty's brain. The fatal blow was not struck by Pelkey but by an earlier opponent or during a fall from one of McCarty's horses.

The whole surrealistic calamity was deeply unfortunate, even more so as the Burns arena burned down the day after the death. It did not need mythologising by writers eager to suggest divine retribution rather than plain arson was responsible for the fire. Neither did it need the cynicism of a photo editor responsible for retouching a photograph of the fight to suggest that a shaft of sunlight had illuminated the figure of McCarty at the moment of death. Only the credulous could interpret this as the Great Promoter in the Sky calling the young Golden Hope prematurely to Heaven. The episode was too awful in reality to need such callous embellishments.

Completely exonerated by the coroner's findings and by the legal hearings, Pelkey found it hard to exonerate himself. From a pretty successful fighter, he became a regular loser, usually by knockout. Before he eventually retired in December 1920, he took 26 more fights, winning five, drawing two, and losing to stoppages and knockouts no fewer than 15 times. (He had only ever been knocked out once before, in his second fight of a total of 33 before meeting McCarty.) Surely this was a man of sensitivity at least subconsciously punishing himself for his part in the Calgary tragedy. The real victim was McCarty, but Pelkey was a serious secondary sufferer.

Basham, who had been fighting two or three times a month, did not resume his career until the October after the death of Harry Price. He was not a man

of complexity but who is to know what mental scars remained after the Price tragedy? He outpointed Eddie Beattie, a Scot who fought out of Liverpool, at the Liverpool Stadium on 16 October 1913 over 15 rounds. As he floored Beattie four times in the third round in the very same ring in which Price had died in August, he seemed, consciously or unconsciously, to be holding back after the knockdowns. It would be December 1914 before he next knocked an opponent out.

As an incidental light on the inherent risks of sport exposed by the deaths of Harry Price and Luther McCarty, it is worth noting that a few weeks after Basham returned to the ring, the 1913 American football season ended with the Army v Navy game plus a frightening casualty bill – 14 deaths and 147 serious injuries, including fractured skulls, broken necks and other grave spinal injuries.[34] Boxing was not the only sport with dangers.

The third Welshman climbing gradually up the professional ladder was arguably the greatest of them all, William James Wilde, to be known universally as Jimmy Wilde. On 21st-century golf driving ranges one sees purple-faced men of 18 stones and more, on the verges of a double hernia, straining to hit one small white golf ball into the distance, only to have the tiny object squirt mockingly away from their feet. Meanwhile, on US tournament tees, Michelle Wie, a 14-year-old schoolgirl was driving a golf ball consistently 300 yards. The contrast is between misapplied brute strength, compared with the correct application of force sweetly timed. Only in such terms can one understand the punching power of Jimmy Wilde, the

Jimmy Wilde (1892–1969), the tiny Welsh flyweight who knocked out men much bigger and stronger than he. Was he Britain's greatest ever fighter?
Bain Collection, Prints & Photographs Division, Library of Congress, LC-DIG-ggbain-30538

Mighty Atom, the Welsh Wizard, the Tylorstown Terror, the Ghost with a Hammer in his Hand; all epithets coined to convey the formidable power of this tiny man.

Wilde fought over 860 times, including early encounters in boxing booths.[35] His fight record, restricted to official appearances, has been variously counted by authoritative sources as 132 victories (including 101 KOs), two draws, six losses and 13 no-decision bouts;[36] and alternatively as 130 victories (including 99 KOs), one draw, three losses and 11 no-decision bouts.[37] The knockout percentages are 76.5 per cent and 76.15 per cent, respectively, figures comparing very favourably with the powerful Jack Dempsey, whom Gilbert Odd credits with 52 per cent, and Muhammad Ali, whom Odd calculates at 66 per cent. And these were heavyweights.

In 1913, Wilde's greatest victories lay in the future but he gave hints of what was to come. He first left the Welsh valleys for one London appearance at The Ring, Blackfriars on 20 January 1912 against Matt Wells's Nipper (novices with no drawing power of their own were given a spurious authenticity for billing purposes as Young _____ or _____'s Kid to associate them with a more famous fighter). Pale-skinned and with a childlike innocence in his seemingly guileless grey eyes, Wilde was almost prevented from fighting by Dick Burge. The Ring promoter feared being accused of child abuse if he allowed this poor waif actually to box. Wilde, with dignity, pointed out that he was already a husband and father and a full consenting adult. He proved it by knocking out his opponent in the first. One wag called out to Wilde's opponent in the preliminaries, 'Hey, Nipper, don't swallow the leek in one mouthful!' Nipper had to swallow, metaphorically, Wilde's whole right glove.

Others paralleled Nipper's rude awakening. Jimmy Fitzpatrick of Birmingham met Wilde in Tonypandy over 20 rounds for a purse of £25 and a side bet of £25 a side on a Saturday night bill on 15 February 1913. The account in the *Mirror of Life* is worth an extended quotation:

> The first round both lads used the ring. Wilde was the first to draw blood.

As Fitzpatrick went to his corner and had a good look at Wilde, wondering, no doubt, as to where did the latter possess his hitting power.

The second round the 'Brum' boy was not long before he took a count of six. He was, however, seen to much better advantage and forced Wilde to the ropes, where he landed once or twice. He made a great mistake in being over-confident, and Wilde drove in two successive rights downstairs which nearly doubled up his opponent. The third and last round Fitzpatrick came up, and it was evident he had not recovered from the effects. He was again quickly down for another six seconds, and Mr Lile wisely stopped the bout.

Speaking to Fitzpatrick later, he told me that he was only 6st 4lbs, and could not afford to give weight away to such a man as Wilde. He declared that Wilde was the champion of the world. He possesses the punch of a 10 stoner, and there were but few flyweights which he could not beat. He finished up the chat by declaring that 'Blimey, he's a marvel.'[38]

Many accounts romanticise Wilde's appearance as a tiny refugee from a TB ward, starved ribcage, pipe-cleaner arms and the like. The films and action photographs do not support this.[39] He was very small – 5ft 2in tall – and comfortably made 6st 10lb for major contests, fighting at many weights between 6st 10lb and 7st 4lb. Nevertheless, he had conventional athletic musculature and proportions. The innate deception in his appearance lay rather in the discrepancy between initial impression and subsequent execution – a bit like an angelic choirboy who poisons the chalice. Wilde could, better than almost anyone alive at the time, condense every last ounce of his frame into a devastating punch like a stiletto heel digging into a wooden floor. He was a phenomenon but not a freak.[40]

Born in Quaker's Yard, Merthyr Tydfil on 12 May 1892, Wilde grew up in the Tylorstown area of the Rhondda Valley in South Wales. To be born there was not to be born with a silver spoon in one's mouth, rather with a pick and shovel in one's hands. Precious little employment other than the local mine was available. Like many other poorly educated youngsters, Jimmy, aged 13, got his first job down the pit as a boy helper earning 2s. 6d. a day. Tiny but strong, (probably 4ft 6in and 5st at this age), he was at a premium underground for one job in particular. He could crawl into coal-bearing seams too narrow for fully grown men and still wield a pick with enough force to extract lumps of coal. Even in maturity, he was comfortably outweighed by the hundredweight sacks of coal that were the results of his early labours. Lying in the dark in hazardous conditions swinging heavy tools is no task for an early teenager in a civilised society. When the adult Wilde turned his socks down, an ugly gouged scar was revealed just above his right ankle. The mark showed where a flying metal cable had shown steel to be harder than flesh, even of the well-honed Wilde variety.

The legacy of this dreadful apprenticeship was physical strength accurately applied. A blow with a pickaxe on unproductive rock rather than a coal deposit is a blow wasted. The accuracy and power built into Wilde's back and arms at work he duly put to use in a local boxing booth, as many a flattened opponent found out.

The mine was a harsh place, with quarrels between men and management, and between man and man. One altercation led to a bare-fist fight on a mountaintop between Wilde and a fellow miner. The other man sustained such damage as to lose three weeks' work, which had Wilde paying him a percentage of his own meagre wages until the man recovered. The miners might quarrel among themselves, yet readily rallied round in solidarity with their own in times of trouble. Times of trouble just about defines industrial relations in the coal trade in the early 20th century. Wilde and his friends and enemies were as likely to be on strike or locked out, and have their wages drop from low to nothing, as to be in work.

In hard times, a man needs allies. Wilde found two. Dai Davies, a workmate who acted as a second in Wilde's mountaintop fight, had been a bare-fist mountain fighter himself. He took Wilde home with him and installed him as his lodger. Wilde had found a sympathetic landlord, and in Davies's daughter, Elizabeth Anne, a formidable future wife. However, unlike most of his early opponents, 'Lisbeth' was not giving in easily. Remembering her mother's experiences of her home turned into an ambulance station when Dai lost a fight, she declined to marry another fighter. Wilde could put the ring on her finger only if he gave up boxing. Reluctantly, Jimmy agreed, although he still sneaked off to the boxing booth in secret. They married in 1910.

The domestic ban on his boxing lasted until a long pit strike. When the couple scoured the valley, scavenging to stay alive, Wilde persuaded Lisbeth that with his talent he was better off boxing in the booths for money. When he brought home his next purse, a princely five shillings, even she saw the sense of the argument. Once convinced, she dedicated her energies to furthering her husband's career, becoming his financial manager and a shrewder negotiator of contracts than he.

Rarely did Tylorstown see anything odder than Wilde's early morning training runs; a polo-necked Wilde preceded by Lisbeth in her Sunday best frock and hat, pedalling furiously on an ancient bicycle to set a pace for her protégé. Behind the lace curtains of the Wilde bedroom was another bizarre sight – Jimmy honing his punches on his sparring partner, Lisbeth, clad in an appropriately stuffed corset like a Michelin Man in drag. Until he could afford a proper sparring partner, this would have to do. In later life, he was scathing about any professional boxer who skimped training even for a day. He did not necessarily conform to the ideal himself.

As his career progressed, he trained with other professionals, including Jim Driscoll, but he never came to adopt Driscoll's orthodox stance or model straight left. He stood rather with his feet wider apart than was usual, weight mainly on his right foot and the ball of his left foot lightly touching the ground. His guard was surprisingly low, his left forearm resting on his left thigh and his right arm low across his body. His real skills came into play when an opponent

tried to hit this seemingly easy target. He coupled a dancer's swiftness of foot with controlled movements of his head that took it out of range a fraction of a second before a punch arrived. As the punch barely grazed the head and its bobbing dark forelock, Wilde simultaneously launched a heavy and accurate punch in return from some unanticipated angle. (This was a trait Wilde shared with Naseem Hamed of the 1990s.) Similarly, Wilde's speed of thought and deed were such that he could pull off ploys such as long right leads that would have landed a slower man in trouble.

This description applies to the finished fighter he became, rather than the Wilde of 1913 before his true genius emerged. Of his eventual stature there is no doubt. Experienced observer Patrick Myler wrote: 'No one can seriously dispute that Jimmy Wilde was the greatest British fighter of them all.'[41] Many agree. Extraordinarily, in 1913 there was an Englishman who had his own claims to be the greatest British fighter of them all. Unlike Driscoll, Basham and Wilde, he did not come from Wales, despite assuming a Welsh-sounding ring name. He came rather out of that other fertile boxing breeding ground, the Jewish East End. His name was Gershon Mendeloff, better known across the world as Ted Kid Lewis.

Which man, Wilde or Lewis, should ultimately be considered the best ever seems a sterile and unrewarding academic question. Here were two mighty champions, good enough and successful enough to be admired and heralded in any era in any century. Happy would be the modern era that could claim their like. As Patrick Myler also wrote: 'Only "mighty midget" Jimmy Wilde could seriously dispute

Ted "Kid" Lewis's right to be recognised as the greatest fighter ever produced in Britain.'[42]

Born 24 October 1894 in Aldgate and fighting professionally from the age of 14, Lewis was in action at the NSC on 6 October 1913, three weeks before his 19th birthday, against Alec Lambert of St James's for the British and European featherweight championships, a Lonsdale Belt and a £350 purse. Lambert was practically the house fighter – his father was an NSC official – with an immaculate amateur record, including the 1909 ABA featherweight championship. The unfashionable Kid was not strongly fancied against him. Lewis had lost on a disqualification to Lambert's ABA successor, Con Houghton (ABA featherweight champion 1910), in the sixth round of a Premierland contest on 5 October 1912. His first showing at the NSC on 1 April 1912 had been even less impressive – knocked out in the first round by Duke Lynch of Camberwell, an inferior opponent he had outpointed over ten rounds less than two months previously at Premierland, and would outpoint again on 26 July 1913 over 20 rounds at The Ring, just before meeting Lambert for the title.

Lewis had appeared also at the NSC, well down the bill, on the night of 2 June 1913 when Bill Beynon and Digger Stanley had met for the bantamweight title. He faced Joe Starmer of Kettering at featherweight, outpointing him over a scrappy 15 rounds. Lewis put Starmer down for six in the second and for eight in the third, then got rather wild and unfocused and allowed Starmer to survive the distance.[43]

Whatever doubts he felt as he got into the ring against Lambert, the unfancied Lewis did not show them. He was a notoriously poker-faced fighter, expression-free, a calm mask of utter indifference whatever the circumstances. His skin was tough and taut, a leathery product of soakings in brine to prevent cuts. With a mop of unruly hair, hollow cheeks, high cheekbones and imperturbable expression, he was the very model of a serious fighter.

He expressed his emotions purely through his fists, which he threw at a furious rate from all directions. His modus operandi was reflected in the epithet added to his naming in the headlines – 'The Dashing, Smashing Kid'. Others have added to it – 'Crashing, Bashing, Dashing' (Patrick Myler); 'Crashing, Bashing, Smashing, Dashing' (Harry Carpenter); 'Dashing, Slashing, Smashing, Bashing, Crashing' (James Butler). Lewis's modern sponsor would have been Roget's Thesaurus or a publisher of rhyming dictionaries. The compulsion to add yet more adjectives is a natural desire to do proper justice to an extraordinary boxing phenomenon.

The packed NSC theatre saw the Lewis v Lambert bout on 6 October 1913.[44] Lewis proved a worthy new champion, taking the first major step on a 20-year career that would take him from London to Montreal, and from Boston to Sydney, involving over 280 fights.

The original belt was Driscoll's property, so a newly commissioned one costing £1,000 awaited the new champion. Lewis earned it in the ring. When Lambert at 8st 13½lb/125½lbs and Lewis at 8st 13¾lb/125¾lbs weighed in almost identically, Lewis looked bigger and stronger. From the first, he proved the more powerful.

Both men tried speculative left leads in the trying-out period. Lambert threw a genuine left from which Lewis backed away and retaliated with one that connected painfully with Lambert's nose. As Lambert blinked and winced, two more solid punches, one left and one right, thudded into his ribs. The odds shouted at the end of the round were distinctly in the underdog's favour.

Lewis carried his right arm low across his body, with the left even lower, rather like Wilde. His feet were wider apart than was conventional and he was poised on the balls of the feet, ready to move swiftly away, or closer to the opponent.

Lambert was swift and sleek, and, like Lewis, full of fight. He was not strong enough seriously to disturb Lewis. The fifth was typical. Lambert moved around, well balanced, and landed light lefts to Lewis's head before Lewis could intercept them. Unfortunately for Lambert, these mini-successes merely provoked sterner rejoinders – heavy lefts to heart and head and swinging rights to jaw and temple. The sixth was similar. By the tenth Lewis was 10/1 on. In the 15th Lambert was caught badly by a heavy right. After that, his determination was admirable but insufficient.

Lewis danced sprightly out for the 17th, feinted elegantly, then landed a measured right to Lambert's jaw that toppled the St James's Club man forward on to his face for a count of nine. He got up, somehow, and staggered away from the pursuing Lewis, who was swinging away with both hands, over-eager to finish it. (The maturer Lewis knew well how to pause a second and measure a final punch to a weakened opponent.) Lewis landed more punches. They, and the accumulated 16 rounds

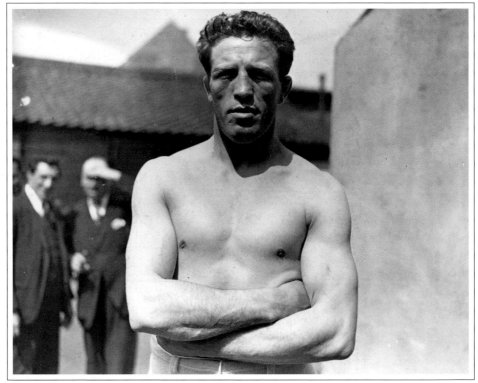

The rugged Ted Kid Lewis (1894–1970), idol of Jewish East London and the only rival to Jimmy Wilde's claim to be Britain's greatest fighter.
Topical Press Agency/Getty Images

Ted Kid Lewis: the tender father spars his son Morton.
Topical Press Agency/Getty Images

of punishment, told. Lambert's knees buckled and he again toppled forward. A count was superfluous so referee J. H. Douglas intervened, declaring Lewis the victor and sparing the gallant Lambert further pain. 'I thought it was raining boxing gloves tonight,' Lambert said ruefully in the dressing room post-fight. The members gave him a standing ovation for his gallantry in a lost cause. Lewis was applauded respectfully rather than enthusiastically, many members believing Driscoll-style textbook stances and punches were de rigueur for all other featherweights. Actually, Lewis's future extensive experiences in American rings made him ever less the upright British boxer, and more a dangerous American-style fighter, crouching and throwing punches from all points of the compass.

Lewis was not given to deep self-analysis.[45] The new belt was fastened around his waist, yet for all his brilliance, he never won one outright at any weight. (Dai Dollings could claim this represented his personal fifth

championship win as a trainer.) Lewis had, however, transcended the most unpromising pugilistic circumstances to become the British featherweight champion while still a teenager.[46]

Although Reg Gutteridge, the veteran boxing commentator, insisted Lewis was born a year before, his official birth date was 24 October 1894.[47] He was, by any reckoning, an exceptionally young champion and younger than current rules would allow. He was born, the third of eight children, into a Russian immigrant family at 56 Umberston Street, Aldgate, one of a series of undistinguished streets sandwiched between Commercial Road and Cable Street. His father was a cabinetmaker, Solomon Mendeloff, with whom his son Gershon had a continually fraught relationship. Like many of his generation, Solomon had a hard life – leaving his Russian homelands to escape pogroms; reaching London where new arrivals were not guaranteed a red carpet greeting; humiliated by an unsuccessful attempt

to better himself in South Africa in the two-year period before the Boer War of 1899–1902. He returned from South Africa as penniless as when he had left his family behind to go. He turned into a hard and harsh father and a hard and harsh employer. In both roles he was more than his eldest son and sometime employee Gershon could always take.

The feet that scuffled in and out of Lambert's reach had once scuttled along filthy London pavements without decent footwear to protect them. One of the joys of a place secured at the Rothschild-financed Jewish Free School was charity extended beyond the mere waiving of tuition fees – 'no more would I go ragged nor wear boots through which my toes peeped out on a cold hard world'. The fists that had pounded Lambert to the floor had been honed in early street fights against Gentile gangs anxious to supply Jewish kids with a hot rather than warm welcome. Lewis's first appearance in a ring had also come from Jewish charity – at the Judaean Club in Prince's Square, Cable Street, an organisation set up by the Jewish Stitcher brothers in 1902 as a calculated response to the many Christian settlements flourishing in the East End. The Judaean had over 1,000 members.

Father Solomon had no compunction in lying to the school authorities about Gershon's age to turn the young scholar illegally into a poorly paid apprentice in his workshop. He held to the managerial philosophy that hits and curses were preferable to reward or praise and was a parent who thought the showing of affection morally corrupting. Adequate wages, leisure time, sport and especially boxing were all anathema.

Ted Kid Lewis was utterly ruthless in the ring. He overdid it against Marcel Thuru of France 8 October 1925 in the Royal Albert Hall and was disqualified. He mercilessly knocked out Tom Gummer 16 February 1922 at Brighton.

Topical Press Agency/Getty Images

The wonder is that the fractious relationship of domineering father and spirited son survived later in life. The apprenticeship began in 1906. Young Gershon first appeared at the Judaean in September 1909, losing a six-round points decision to a Johnny Sharp. This was the initial step in a new apprenticeship, the one necessary to become a master of boxing. Morton Lewis's biography lists (pp. 258–66) the 63 bouts undertaken by Gershon up to December 1911 as he learned his new craft, this one as exacting as fine cabinet making and as tough and intractable as a rough plank of teak. He was very successful – after the initial loss he lost only another three throughout his Judaean career. Unfortunately, such experience can only be bought at the cost of the occasional cut, contusion and swelling – signs as unwelcome to a strict employer as a morning hangover.

To conceal from Solomon what he was up to in the evenings, Gershon adopted the ring name Ted Kid Lewis (inspired by his boyhood hero, the American Jewish fighter Harry Lewis, whom we saw to be as popular in the streets of Aldgate as he was on the boulevards of Paris). Gershon could disguise his name; he could not, even with his mother's active contrivance, disguise the physical evidence on his face of his previous evenings' activities. In September 1911, a domestic fracas worthy of a B movie boxing biopic took place when the angry Solomon ordered the pale 16-year-old from home and workshop unless he gave up boxing. The ambitious youth had once walked to James Butler's Fleet Street office, and politely asked the boxing writer to mention him in his column as a future champion.[48] The incident is believable, if not Butler's colourful detail of Young Lewis twisting a yarmulke in his fingers. If Lewis as a teenager were still wearing one, he would hardly have doffed it like some young Gentile removing his cap to tug his forelock. Only one course of action was now possible. He walked out of home and out of the apprenticeship – better to be a new Mendoza than a new Sheraton.

In later years, he put his hidden anger against his father to more constructive use. Out of the ring he had no intention of becoming either a petty-minded domestic tyrant like Solomon or of reproducing Solomon's penny-pinching ways. On the contrary, he became the most open-handed and generous of men, spending every penny he earned in the ring. (Estimates range from £150,000 to £250,000 over his career, figures that would have to be converted into millions for their modern equivalent.)

His largesse was legendary, extending even to the undeserving Solomon and his relatives, close and distant, and showered upon beggars, parasites, children in the street and practically anyone happy to use him as a perennial meal ticket. He was as generous with his affections – a loving father to his son Morton who idolised him, and a loving husband to his American wife Elsie whom he met and married in New York in September 1915. The Lewis family album had many photographs of Elsie in elegant furs, and Morton in Little Lord Fauntleroy or sailor suits, no less expensive than those worn by contemporary royals. He himself was the snappiest of dressers, quite a sight at the wheel of the latest gleaming roadster in well-tailored suits and gleaming handmade shoes. Only a churl would have begrudged him a penny.

While the new generation of fighters such as Lewis, Wilde and

Basham emerged in 1913, how did the more established names fare? With mixed fortunes, it has to be said. The heavyweight division pursued its eccentric path, its world champion even more at odds with the authorities than he had been over the last five years. The significant happenings in Jack Johnson's life since his 1912 victory over Fireman Flynn were all outside the ring.

Johnson reinvested that purse in a Chicago saloon named, pretentiously enough, the Cabaret de Champion, or Café de Champion, a place where men and women could congregate, eat, drink and dance in some luxury. It was given a gala opening on 11 July 1912, one week after the Flynn fight, for maximum publicity.[49] It was a major bid by Johnson for a new respectability and a public demonstration that he was personally a man of impeccable aesthetic taste:

> In the furnishing and decoration of the cabaret, I had spared no expense nor effort. Having travelled extensively, I had gained a comprehensive idea of decorative effects; I had viewed some of the most notable amusement centers of the world, both as to their exterior and interior arrangements. I also had collected many fine works of art, curios and novelties. These I used in providing the attractive features for which my cabaret gained considerable distinction. In addition, I had engaged artists and decorators of undisputed talents, whose ideas, *combined with my own* [italics added], resulted in an array of artistic creations which put to shame many similar establishments … which have attained world-wide prominence … I displayed a few real Rembrandts which I had obtained in Europe … Only the very best of material had gone into the equipment. The bar tables and other pieces of furniture were of solid mahogany … The appearance of the interior was neither gaudy nor vulgar. I had striven to make it distinctive and attractive, but also had combined it with real beauty and dignity. Another feature … was the silver cuspidors, decorated in gold.[50]

Behind the glittering surfaces (and the characteristically *faux-elegant* prose), all was not well at the palace. Johnson installed Etta upstairs in a comfortable room, but supplied adjacent accommodation for mistresses, long and short term. Just 55 days after the opening gala, on 11 September 1912, Etta took one of Johnson's ornamental guns and shot herself dead in the room she had come to think of as a luxurious prison. She was not mentally stable and had tried to kill herself on previous occasions. Four weeks previously she had locked away a letter to her mother written in suicidal terms, although significantly *not* blaming Johnson or his infidelities – 'Jack has done all in his power to cure me but it is no use.'

Johnson wrote, 'This tragic event laid me low.' He was low only temporarily, finding more than adequate consolation in the arms of Lucille Cameron, an 18-year-old sex worker with whom he had been sleeping before Etta's death and whom he had also installed in the Cabaret for stenographic and presumably more personal services. Publicity about this new black/white old/young relationship alerted Lucille's mother, Mrs Cameron-Falconet, who went to the police and had Johnson arrested on charges of abduction.

The charges were inherently ridiculous. A mother allowing her daughter to sell her body is hardly in a strong moral position to argue that a big black abductor has ruined her child's pale-skinned innocence. She was encouraged to press a suit by state and federal authorities to whom Johnson's every act was an irritant. The more he defied convention, the fatter became the official files and agents' reports upon him. The accumulated evidence paid dividends.

The story of Johnson's year after the Flynn victory is complicated.[51] Essentially, the authorities, aided and abetted by Johnson's enemies, were out to get Johnson, one way or another. If one legal move did not work, another would be tried until the man was safely behind bars. Johnson fought Flynn knowing that a serious charge of smuggling a valuable diamond necklace through customs was pending. Johnson and Etta bought the $6,000 jewellery in London and foolishly concealed it on their re-entry. One or more informants made the act known to the authorities. (The charge also strained Etta's mental health.) Johnson was potentially liable to a $9,000 surcharge. And if more serious charges could be levied, a prison term could be secured.

Conveniently, on the statute book was the White Slave Traffic Act, a controversial and repressive piece of legislation known popularly as the Mann Act. It was passed in 1910 to prohibit the inter-state transportation of women for immoral purposes.[52] The Supreme Court confirmed it as constitutional in 1913 on the grounds that prostitution was reasonably a matter of federal concern. Although passed in a hysterical fit of moral rectitude, it was aimed not unreasonably at vice organised by criminal gangs. It was not designed to indict a New York businessman taking his secretary to Newport or Cape Cod for a recreational weekend, although such voluntary pleasures became technically illegal. However, if a hated figure like Johnson had had sex with a lady with whom he had crossed a state boundary, perhaps the Act could be used to nail him.

In October 1912, Lucille was taken away from Johnson and called before a grand jury for evidence to justify charging Johnson with an offence under the Mann Act. Lucille declined to join the plan. She admitted to being a prostitute but firmly asserted that her relationship with Johnson was simply as a lover, and payments for sex or transportation aimed at immoral earnings did not come into it. It was not what the authorities wanted to hear and she was kept away from Johnson in the hope she would change her testimony.

More promising was another of Johnson's sex worker lovers, Belle Schreiber. She was persuaded to come forward in late October 1912 to speak about their former relationship. On 7 November 1912, she repeated the details to another grand jury. As her and Jack's love affair had been at its height at the time of the Ketchel fight in October 1909, *before* the Mann Act became operative from 1 July 1910, her evidence would have been ignored in calmer times. But these were not calmer times, and Johnson was assailed on all sides

with dubious legality. On 1 November 1912, the Chicago licensing authority refused to renew the liquor licence for the Café – a spiteful deathblow to its future continuance. On 7 November 1912, Johnson was rearrested for supposed offences under the Mann Act with Belle Schreiber as the victim. Johnson had generously paid Belle's rail fare in October 1910 (conveniently just *after* the Mann Act) and given her money to set up as a madam in Chicago but not for his own profit. So, at the beginning of December 1912, Johnson and Lucille were kept apart on dubious legal grounds. However, he was out of detention within a week by virtue of paying a $30,000 bond, and she before the month was out.

Promptly and defiantly they reunited. At a private ceremony in the Chicago house on 4 December 1912, they married. What white Chicago thought of this was symbolised by the residents of the upmarket Lake Geneva neighbourhood, who virulently opposed the couple's attempt to purchase a house there. The press treatment of the marriage was even more poisonous. Johnson's old enemy in the Senate, the racist S. A. Rodenberry of Georgia, was typical: 'this slavery of white women to black beasts' made it necessary to 'uproot and exterminate now this debasing, ultrademoralizing, un-American, and inhuman leprosy'. Fuelled by the hysteria, over 20 bills seeking to ban inter-racial marriages were introduced to Congress in 1913. None succeeded but the proposals reflect the emotional climate around Johnson.

On 4 January 1913, Johnson was indicted on 11 separate charges framed (the operative word) around violations of the Mann Act, based on testimony

from Belle Schreiber. The hearing was delayed until 7 May 1913, when the Supreme Court had confirmed that the Mann Act was constitutional. In the meantime, the smuggling case was heard at the end of April 1913 and resulted in an anticlimactic fine of $1,000 with $740 costs and left Johnson at liberty. A guilty verdict in May under the Mann Act would carry much severer penalties.

Johnson's previous court appearances, in London in 1911 for example, had been notable for his sangfroid under attack and his razor-sharp forensic questioning of others; the legal parallel to a brilliant boxer absorbing blows on his gloves and arms, then going lethally on to the attack. This time, whatever his self-confidence and articulate wit, the odds were heavily against him. The jury, hand-picked, was all male and all white. Randy Roberts picks out William Ulrich as typical of the 12 chosen men – a Republican-voting Episcopalian who hated sports and was 'strongly prejudiced against negroes'.[53] How could an Ulrich *not* find Johnson guilty when he had listened to lurid details from a succession of low-life witnesses, prostitutes, a self-claimed madam in Belle Schreiber and parasitic hangers-on in the champion's entourage?

Five days of testimony about Johnson's lifestyle was sufficient. Four of the 11 counts relating to so-called sexual perversions were tacitly not argued by the prosecution, who realised that the evidence relating to them would damage the standing of the witnesses quite as much as damaging Johnson's. To the Ulrichs of the world, Johnson was guilty – guilty of being Johnson, black lover and abuser of white women, black challenger to white authority. Technical details as to whether Johnson had knowingly transported Belle or anyone else across state boundaries, or ever intended to finance her career, or had profited personally from her labours, were glossed over.

After four ballots, the jury decision was unanimous – Johnson guilty as charged. The words of Harry A. Parkin, Assistant District Attorney, who had prosecuted the case against Johnson, demonstrate conclusively that Johnson had not been given a fair trial:

> The negro, in the eyes of many, has been persecuted. *Perhaps as an individual he was.* But it was his misfortune to be the foremost example of the evil in permitting the intermarriage of whites and blacks.[54] [Italics added]

The logic was justice at its most Kafkaesque – a man punished for violating a law that had not existed at the time of his violation. Johnson was expected back in court on 4 June 1913 for sentencing. His punishment was a fine of $1,000 and imprisonment for one year and a day, although he was given leave to appeal. As the maximum sentence under the Act was five years, he had got off more lightly than he might have feared. However, he had no intention of losing his liberty at all. Flight, rather than fight, was a better bet.

His exit from the USA, arriving in Paris on 10 July 1913 via Canada, provoked some tall tales after its accomplishment. In one of his autobiographies, he says he disguised himself as a member of a black baseball team to get to Hamilton, Ontario.[55] It

may be true. He met up with Lucille in Toronto for them both to sail on the SS *Corinthia* to Paris. The Canadian officials could not retain Johnson on behalf of the USA as the couple were holding tickets that involved passing *through* Canada; that is, they were not immigrants attempting to stay. Johnson's sole undertaking was to turn up for the appeal hearing. He was free to travel in the meantime. He became a guilty absconder only *after* his failure to return, thus becoming liable to arrest if he stepped on to American soil. He claimed that bribes had eased his passage, and it is possible that a few corrupt officials aided and abetted his departure.

Thousands of miles away in Paris, arrest was less a problem than another dilemma. How was he to sustain his extravagant lifestyle without lucrative American fights to sustain it? He tried to resume tours of the English music halls. However, in London in late August 1913, owners, wary of the hostile reception a fugitive from justice might receive from audiences, cancelled a contract for appearances at the South London Music Hall and the Euston Theatre.[56] His old foe, the Reverend J. P. Meyer, sought to prevent any managements employing Johnson: 'Surely our variety stage will not stoop so low as to engage him. All that makes for national decency appeals to the variety managers to save us from the threatened disgrace.' When Johnson appeared in a box at the Euston, he was snubbed by the patrons in the stalls yet cheered from the crowded gallery where the punters had a different view of men who challenged authority.[57] Johnson's offer to debate publicly with Meyer was declined.

He then, like Joe Louis, Muhammad Ali and Mike Tyson after him, resorted to that degrading refuge of declining boxers, the wrestling ring. At the too-aptly named Nouveau Theatre Cirque, on 25 November 1913, he grappled with a German wrestler called Ulrich.[58] It was a lively occasion, invigorated by Ulrich's failure to follow the script. (Ulrich's grasp of English or French was less impressive than his wrestling holds.) He assaulted Johnson with vigour using means fair and foul. The French crowd, women and all, with one war against Germany lost and another possibly pending, saw it as their patriotic duty to howl abuse at Ulrich, following in with a hail of oranges and coins when he failed to understand them either. Losing his own temper, Ulrich resorted to boxing, clouting Johnson on the jaw. At this, further fist fights broke out in the hall, and the scene descended to utter confusion with gendarmes rushing in and arresting all and sundry. Despite this farce, Johnson agreed to another wrestling bout on 17 December 1913, and was thrown twice by a wrestler called Jim Essen in more decorous circumstances.[59]

The unsatisfactory ten-round boxing match on 19 December 1913 between Johnson and Battling Jim Johnson was not too distinguished either. This bout at the Premierland Française on the Boulevard Rochechouart in Montmartre was Johnson's first proper fight for two years.[60]

A lurid yellow poster printed for the fight shows prices from standing room at eight francs up to a ringside seat at 150 francs, a policy aimed at attracting all classes of society. Heavily overprinted in black over the yellow background were images of both Johnsons, bare fists raised and aggressive looks on their faces, with the background showing through – the only authentic example of Papa Jack ever showing a yellow streak.

Jim Johnson had been more active than the champion, meeting Joe Jeanette four times previously (no-decision results on 19 July 1912 in Philadelphia, 30 October in New York, and 1 January 1913 in Brooklyn [the thrilling bout recorded early on in this chapter]; and losing on 21 January 1913 in Providence RI). He would have another four no-decision bouts with Jeannette in the future. He was no more than a reliable opponent, condemned to fights down the bill in small halls or slotted into the mix as Jeannette, Langford and McVea took their perennial circus around the world.

Despite his average record, and having no real claims to a title fight, Battling Jim tried to make a real fight of it. Jack Johnson, ring rusty and following a pre-fight programme around bars and nightclubs, was content to clinch, clinch and clinch again, neutralising Jim's efforts with superior defensive skills. As maul succeeded maul, the French audience, including many women, booed, whistled and demanded a refund (those still awake, that is). The final three rounds were conducted quite as soporifically, accompanied by boos, chants and slow handclaps, a ground bass that continued up to the verdict – that the passive contest was null and void. The proffered explanation, that Jack Johnson had broken his arm in the third, was greeted with a burst of derisive laughter. It was true. A post-fight examination revealed Johnson had broken a radial bone in the left arm. The damage to his ego and his reputation was less easily treated.

Johnson's descent from proud champion to exiled criminal to participant in French farces, focused more attention on potential white successors to his title. In Europe that meant the English and French heartthrobs, Bombardier Billy Wells and Georges Carpentier. Both had their triumphs and their embarrassments over the year, and their career paths crossed dramatically during 1913.

In 1922 or thereabouts, the London publisher T. Werner Laurie issued a book with a bright yellow binding. It was called *Physical Energy: Showing How Physical and Mental Energy May Be Developed by Means of the Practice of Boxing*. It was supposedly written by Bombardier Billy Wells. A major sales feature of the book was glossy black-and-white plates, including five of a completely nude Wells posing artistically as 'The Gladiator: a study' and delivering, for example, 'The Straight Left'. Even with Wells's genitalia carefully airbrushed into shadow, the plates carried enough sex appeal to boost sales. The glamour does not extend to the turgid pseudo-scientific ghostwritten prose:

> Not only does the ability to put up a fight with or without the gloves at any moment give a man self-confidence when dangerous situations arise: his whole preliminary preparation also plays a very large part in making him a good and useful citizen by inculcating self-control, equanimity in misfortune, rapid judgment, quick decision, rapid perception, prevision, initiative, moral courage, and other mental qualities.[61]

With Wells's mixed fortunes over 1913 in mind, the real doubt is not whether he wrote *Physical Energy*, but whether he ever read it.

In the spring of 1913, he and his wife and his entourage boarded the

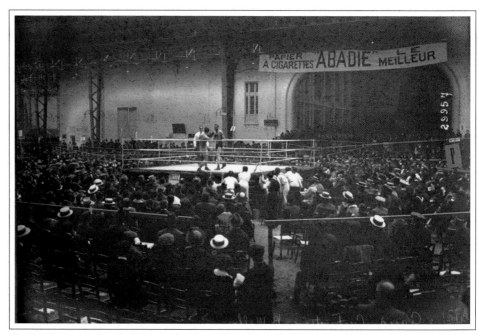

Georges Carpentier knocked out Bombardier Billy Wells in the fourth round of their first encounter in Ghent, Belgium.
BnF

Carpentier v Wells II, 8 December 1913 at the NSC. The return engendered huge attention, minimal action and an even swifter result. Wells was knocked out in seconds.

Topical Press Agency/Hulton Archive/Getty Images

Mauretania for a luxury Atlantic crossing to New York in hopes of lucrative fights in the USA, including one against Luther McCarty. The upshot was an appearance at Madison Square Garden on 14 March 1913 against the ex-naval heavyweight Gunboat Smith.[62] (The nickname Gunboat was not coined in admiration of his firepower, but because he had once been forced to fight in size-15 boots, although his feet were only size 12. The epithet coined at the sight of spray-legged Smith shuffling across the canvas like a clumsy catamaran stuck to him thereafter.)

Only in the footwear department could Smith lord it over Wells. Wells was heavier (13st 10lb/192lbs against Smith's 13st/182lbs) and had a longer reach. He was also more skilful. Both men were fair-haired and blue-eyed, but only Wells fitted the Nordic hero stereotype. Smith was the bruiser, deep-set eyes beneath a long ridge of forehead and one long bushy eyebrow serving for two, while his nose was bridgeless, a relic of being flattened in previous fights. Wells looked more the matinee idol than a prizefighter.

A smartly dressed Manhattan audience assumed this pale handsome Englishman was their best hope of a 'white' champion. They greeted Wells rapturously, to the disgust of Smith, who thought he was entitled to a little more patriotic support:

> The house was packed to the rafters, and when I came out there one fellow was sitting way up in the balcony clapping, and that's all I got when they introduced me. When that lousy Englishman came out, I thought the building fell in. It made me sore how they let me down and think so little of me and make a big fuss over this bum … I said, 'Why that dirty limey, I'll break his goddam neck if it's the last thing I do.'[63]

Anger in the ring is rarely a fighter's ally. Smith surged out of his corner, guns blazing. Wells, uncharacteristically calm and collected, stood off and delivered classic straight lefts firmly into Smith's stomach and face, hurting and spreading Smith's nose still wider ('… he broke my nose, I think twice, with straight lefts. Bang! Whang! Jesus, if it goes 10 rounds like this, my God, they'll pick me up in a vacuum cleaner!' Smith recalled). The pre-fight odds had been 5/8 Wells. Although ringside betting was technically illegal, unofficial wagers among the businessmen, men-about-town and Supreme Court judges at ringside at the front of the 6,500 crowd, flourished. As the blood trickled from Smith's nostrils, the odds-on Wells became even less

generous. When Smith swung a punch so wildly as to topple over from his own momentum, Wells's backers smiled the smiles of legatees coming into a fortune.

No one had explained to Smith that revenge was a dish best served cold. He plunged into a second round every bit as hotly as his start – head down, left and right punches dispensed as wildly as before. The results were different. One of his looping rights thudded into Wells's stomach. As the Bombardier gasped and lowered his head, a left hook caught him on the right temple and a clubbing right to the jaw dropped him to the canvas. His senses floating somewhere in the cavernous space above the ring, he very unwisely staggered up at the count of five straight into another flurry of hooks, the last connecting to the back of his head as he subsided again. Few thought he would or could get up, yet at nine he did. Calmly, Smith spied out his target, then hit Wells with a powerful stunning right cross. Over and out went Wells, not only for the regulation ten seconds, but for ten minutes on floor and stool before recovery. Smith was as inconsistent as Wells, but when he was on song, formidable. Jack Dempsey said that the hardest punch he received in his entire career came from Gunboat.

Having contributed to the thesis that British heavyweights flattered only to fold in practice, soon exchanging the elegant vertical for the comatose horizontal, Wells sailed back home. His entourage and British journalists made much of his first-round treatment of Smith, relatively little of his demise – the anyone-can-be-unlucky syndrome. His personal version of his fall from grace lacks all conviction. He says he

hesitated because 'I didn't know which part to hit and then Smith's right came over.' (Really?) Domestically, where he was greeted enthusiastically wherever he appeared, many still believed he was the man who would soon be world champion. His relative inexperience was ignored. As Stan Shipley accurately points out, in 1911 and 1912 Wells took seven fights, Smith, his conqueror, 31.[64] Wells's next opponent, Georges Carpentier, had taken 27. The redoubtable Frank Moran fought 42 times in 1919 and 23 times in 1920.

The Wells–Carpentier clash was arranged for 1 June 1913 at the Floral Palace at Ghent in Belgium to coincide with an international exposition, thus guaranteeing an international audience. The original date was 25 May 1913 and changed at the personal request of the King of Belgium, King Albert I (reigned 1909–34). He was attending a horse show on 25 May and determined to see the fight. Many British journalists assumed Wells had only to turn up to win. The editor of *Mirror of Life and Boxing World* was typical. He looked at the heights of the two men – Carpentier at 5ft 7in and Wells at 6ft 2in – and concluded: 'A good big man can always beat a good little one.' He continued:

> 'I do not for a moment think that Carpentier will beat the Bombardier; I fail to see what kudos Wells will gain by beating a man so much his inferior in size.'[65]

The writer seemed prescient for fully half the ensuing contest. That meant a mere two rounds.[66] Wells towering over the Frenchman, outfought him ruthlessly. Carpentier, too eager to get inside Wells's reach and attack him about the body, rushed out of his corner. He was met with majestic straight lefts, pretty as a textbook illustration and delivered with real venom, so as to stop the Frenchman dead in his tracks. After three such episodes, there was worse to come. Wells followed another left with a right cross that sent Carpentier sprawling across the ring and down for a count of nine. To shouts and cheers, he got up groggily at nine, and grabbed and held to survive the round.

As Carpentier proved on many occasions, he had depths of bravery and resolution, and powers of recuperation that restored his senses remarkably quickly. His strengths, and the assiduous attentions of his seconds, had him back on the offensive at the beginning of the second. It made no significant difference. Again Wells picked him off ruthlessly before he could get within reach of Wells's body. He delivered two hooks to Wells's torso, and they merely provoked an attack from Wells that drove him back across the ring where a culminating right to the head dropped him again. Foolishly, Carpentier got up after four and swung wild punches without a trace of his normal power and precision.

Back on his stool at the end of this torrid second round, Carpentier needed all the sponging, towelling, stimulating and exhortation from his seconds to return to action in the third. In this context, his Orchid Man nickname is particularly misleading. Far from being a tropical exotic, Carpentier, had he any botanical attributes, had the strength and persistence of a robust weed remorselessly springing back up even when cemented over. He had taken a full six minutes of everything that Wells could throw. He was still there. Had the two rounds gone the other way, with Carpentier severely testing Wells's

powers of recovery, would Wells have survived physically and mentally?

From the start of the third, Carpentier continued to attack. Wells countered with more long lefts and a crisp right uppercut. They had visibly less impact on Carpentier than those of the first two rounds. Moreover, Wells had to take a vicious right hook into the region around his heart. Both before and after this particular blow, which resounded throughout the hall, the now open-mouthed Wells began to breathe heavily. Carpentier landed further punches to his ribs and finished the round with a right uppercut every bit as good as Wells's earlier in the round. The tide had turned and was now flowing towards France.

The fourth round proved that the change was permanent. Carpentier, back to his near-best, provoked Wells into leads, which he then slipped to land more powerful body punches before Wells could cover up. Now it was the lighter man driving the heavier across the ring and on to the ropes. Bewildered by this transformation, Wells gasped and suffered.

Carpentier, a congenial gentleman out of the ring, extended no unnecessary courtesies to weakening opponents. A short left doubled Wells forward to meet a super-efficient Carpentier combination – right hook to the jaw, left hook to the body – that had Wells like a tall classical column with its base removed toppling and slowly falling. For a few seconds, Wells lay on his side, stricken and helpless. He stirred only to roll over on to his back and stay there. He alone could truly know whether he had skimped his training, confident that his size and strength could be used to stop Carpentier

early. Or had the physical and mental vulnerabilities he had demonstrated against Al Palzer and Gunboat Smith reasserted themselves? Again he had flattered only to deceive. Always the boxer, he was never quite the fighter, and his resilience seemed regularly to decline readily into resignation. Meanwhile, the French celebrated all over Ghent and Carpentier was chaired from the building to the predictable sounds of a French band playing 'La Marseillaise'. The English supporters melted silently away.

At home, the English have always had a penchant for French vocalists delivering in charming French accents and quietly murdering English songs. Carpentier was no singer, but in his case an English welcome was extended for a supreme athlete who spoke a rudimentary but charmingly accented English, and quietly murdered English welterweights, middleweights and heavyweights in turn. On the heels of his Ghent triumph came a three-week engagement at £1,000 a week at the London Opera House in Kingsway, to do a turn comprising a few spoken lines and an ample display of his handsome profile and torso. First appearing in a gorgeous silk dressing gown, he disrobed to his trunks to spar with Marcel Ludo, a regular sparring partner, for three rounds in an unusual ring comprised of scantily clad chorus girls holding hands. The action, warmly applauded by a packed house, climaxed in a brief finale where Carpentier, MC Arthur Deacon, and the self-effacing Marcel joined hands with *les girls* and hoofed it up in a dancing line as the curtain fell.

One night during the run, there was a 'surprise' interruption to Carpentier's act. From the wings strode an immaculately dinner-jacketed Bombardier Wells, who stiltedly told the audience, 'Ladies and gentlemen. I am here to issue a challenge to Carpentier. My friends think I can turn the tables on him in another contest, and they are willing to back me for £1,000.' At this Wells and Carpentier shook hands and bowed, the audience clapped and cheered, and Wells made a dignified exit.[67] Of course, there was going to be a return bout between them, but it is doubtful that even an Edwardian Don King could have pulled off a better stunt to promote it.

Before that return took place, there were two other significant fights. On 9 August 1913, in Sydney, Australia, in front of a large Australian crowd of 17,500 and dependent upon an Australian referee, Matt Wells outpointed his old rival Hughie Mehegan over 20 rounds. A fast and furious bout, in which Wells's penchant for counter-punching did not preclude plenty of toe-to-toe action, showed that British boxers could perform on foreign fields. Neither were they beholden to English referees for success. Mehegan's claim that English officials had previously robbed him at Blackfriars in February was neutralised.

The Bombardier himself redeemed the reputation tarnished in Ghent in August, meeting and beating strong domestic rival Gunner James Moir at the Canterbury Music Hall on 10 September 1913.[68] With Jack Johnson in the audience and with the spice of an all-London clash (Moir from Lambeth and Wells from Stepney), the pair produced 15 minutes of exceptionally focused action. Moir was a slightly crude but often effective swinger. Wells,

as he had against Carpentier, looked to keep his opponent away with his left and to cover up and neutralise Moir when he could not. Moir landed some of his right swings to Wells's body for which Billy showed little relish, but they never had the paralysing effect of Carpentier's. The referee spoke to Moir unfairly for kidney punches when his swings landed round the corner. The fault was Wells's for his tendency to twist his torso inwards to protect his vulnerable midriff.

In the fifth, Moir was looking discouraged by the referee's displeasure coupled with his own failures to reach the right target. A short sharp left hook on the break caught him. Before he could adjust, a fierce Wells right hook put him down for the full count and beyond.

Despite the stunning win in Ghent, Carpentier's form in the second half of 1913 had been patchy, and there had been other distractions. On 11 October 1913 in Paris, he met the American Jeff Smith and outpointed him over 20 rounds. In the fight, Carpentier had looked half-trained and dissipated a reasonable lead over the third quarter, only recovering when Smith in turn had run out of steam.

Worse still, Carpentier was involved in a thoroughly disreputable matter in Switzerland organised by Descamps, his manager. The event was a well-paid exhibition bout in Geneva against James Lancaster, a champion boxer from Scotland – or so the posters said. The opponent was not Scottish, not a champion, and not even 'James Lancaster'. He was a suspended boxer called Max Abbat. Predictably, the French Boxing Federation and the Council of Boxing Federations took

a dim view of Carpentier's role in the scam, as they should have. A year's suspension loomed. It did not come to that. In November, Carpentier and Descamps were leniently treated and fined a nominal £20 each for the deception. The referee *was* suspended.

Wells v Carpentier II would have filled a football stadium. By offering a record purse of £3,000 and £500 side stakes, and selling out its limited capacity at record prices, the NSC secured the plum engagement for 8 December 1913. At news of Carpentier's possible suspension, the NSC showed its regard for ethics held only when it suited them. They issued through Bettinson a statement that the Wells fight would take place anyway, as the French authorities could not 'possibly interfere' with a match on private premises.[69] Profits and members' privileges outweighed consciences.

Even the Covent Garden streets around the club were packed to capacity by ticketless enthusiasts, unable to get in but willing to stand in the December cold to get early news of the result. The result was bound to be a sensation, whatever happened. A sensation it duly was.[70]

The physical differences were not as obvious as when they had met in Ghent. The French teenager had grown in height and bulked out. There were still discrepancies, with Wells at 13st 10lb/192lbs to Carpentier's 12st 4lb/172lbs, and Wells at 6ft 3in to Carpentier's 5ft 10in, if the estimations in *The Times* are to be believed. Was Carpentier really three inches taller since April?

On the night, members were given as a preamble a mock exhibition of old fashioned bare-knuckle fighting by Billy Ross and Jack Collinson. Shortly after this, a calm and collected Carpentier strolled to the ring, smiling and waving to his supporters in the audience. He climbed into the ring and waited for Wells … and waited … and waited, as did everyone else. The delay was variously blamed on Wells's desire to lay another £100 on himself to win and on the club's officials failing to call him. Neither explanation convinced, especially when Wells took a further five minutes and resorted to other subterfuges such as challenging Carpentier's bandaging, taking an age to get his own gloves on and calling for fresh water to swill his dry mouth. If these were ploys to make the Frenchman nervous, they failed spectacularly.

Pale on entrance, Wells looked thoroughly ill at ease while Bettinson the MC and B. J. Angle the referee completed the preliminaries. After the fight, Wells's state of mind was much discussed. He wrote later:

> It was only natural that previous to my second meeting with Carpentier I should be a little nervous at the outcome. I was desperately anxious to repay the public for the fidelity they had shown during all my ups and downs.

It was indeed natural but Wells's tragedy was that he was unable to leave these thoughts behind in the dressing room when the action commenced:

> Then suddenly, how I can never tell, I became overwhelmed with a sense of the wiliness of my adversary, the importance of the fight and the responsibility …

One recalls that Wells's concentration had been similarly distracted when Palzer had conned him in June 1912. In Wells's own words:

> Another punch there and then would probably have finished him, but he winked at me, and somehow I began to fancy that I could not really have hit him as hard as I thought I had.[71]

There is a parallel here to the 'stage fright' suffered by even distinguished actors waiting, sick with worry, in the wings before stepping out into the play.

The Russian stage director Constantin Stanislavski (1865–1938) famously devised circles of attention, encouraging the most nervous of actors to concentrate on the matter in hand within a narrowly focused circle, eliminating irrelevancies and distractions *outside* the circle. Wells, bothered by thoughts of Carpentier's wiliness, of the importance of the fight, and of public expectations, could truly have benefited from a Stanislavskian focus on the point of danger – the Frenchman's fast-travelling fists. The professional actor survives by concentrating exclusively on speaking and listening within his role in the play – or he will not be a professional actor for long. Contrast Wells's apprehension with Carpentier's approach:

> … the sight of that big, powerful fellow [Wells] with his big square shoulders should have been quite enough to inspire misgiving. But as big and powerful as he was, I had already sent him down for the count once so why should

I worry? All I had to do was to administer the mixture as before.

(A very simple and effective circle of attention!)

The fight is the least interesting aspect of the evening. As it lasted a mere 73 seconds it is easily recorded, with Carpentier executing physically the resounding victory he had already won psychologically.

Wells came from his corner lethargically and looked astonished when Carpentier did what everyone except Wells expected, rushed in under Wells's left (proffered much more tentatively than usual) and beat Wells about the body. Instead of moving away and keeping Carpentier at a safe distance with his superior reach, Wells defended his vulnerable solar plexus by doubling over into a crouch and crossing his arms over the target.

Carpentier backed away, apprehensive that so clumsy a defence must be a cunning plan to lure him to destruction. Wells was as disoriented by Carpentier's retreat as by the first onslaught. He stayed rooted to the spot in his odd crouch. The pattern – rush, crouch, retreat – was repeated twice over with but a minor variation when Wells retaliated with an uppercut that missed, but also with two hooks to Carpentier's body. Effectively these constituted his whole offensive during the fight. Next time, Carpentier decided Wells's vulnerability concealed no hidden purpose and could be taken at face value. He delivered a triple combination: left swing to the temple; long right to the jaw; and deadliest of all, a driving left sinking into Wells's torso just above the waistband of his shorts. Wells folded and suffered two more token punches as he sank miserably to the floor. *Boxing*'s reporter recorded the scene as the club members looked on in silent embarrassment and the French contingent jumped to their feet ready to chair their champion from the ring:

> Carpentier stepped away and surveyed his prostrate antagonist with an air of the utmost confidence.
>
> Wells writhed, groaned, raised himself, say, half an inch, and then went back to more writhings and the word 'Out!'

Until he was restrained personally by Lord Lonsdale and quietly escorted away, Jim Driscoll, who had watched the proceedings with disbelief and was moved to frustrated tears, hissed the insulting word 'Quitter!' at the recumbent Wells, who had the further indignity of hearing shouts of 'Cur!' and 'Coward!' from disgruntled members. Writers later have been no more forgiving. Bettinson and Bennison in *The Home of Boxing* written in 1922, nine years later, were just as scathing:

> Wells was frightened of himself; he was a man without an ounce of confidence, and absolutely unmindful of his immense physical superiority. Wells beat himself, as he had done many times before. He was muddled; he lived in a whirl; he was as a blind man; he groped. He was a great big fellow without strength and no boxer at all – just a stiff-limbed giant, positively scared. His request for water before the contest began, the inordinately long time he took in fixing his

bandages and putting on his gloves, was an index to the state of his mind … Never have we seen a man so obviously beaten in any fight, great or small, before a blow was struck. Wells knew that he was doomed …

Sir Arthur Conan Doyle, author, sporting enthusiast and NSC member, shared his feelings with *The Times*. He 'had never imagined he would come away from a fight so miserable as the meeting between Wells and Carpentier made him. He admired Wells as a boxer and as a man, but there could be no doubt that he had not the temperament for the prize-ring.'

It is true that Wells was on the night truly pathetic ('exciting pity or sadness': *OED*). He knew it himself and when he had been brought round on his stool by his seconds he made a halting and mournful speech from the ring, audible only to those in the immediate vicinity:

> I should like – I want to say something about my defeat. It was unexpected. I don't know how it happened. I suppose – I suppose Carpentier found my weak spot. My body has always been my weak spot. I wanted to win. I hoped I could. But Carpentier – has knocked me out. That's all.

His words were received in embarrassed silence and Wells walked funereally back to his dressing room accompanied by his equally melancholy entourage of mourners. Meanwhile, the thousands outside in the street cheered Carpentier, who waved to them from one of the club's windows. A week later he would be at the Palladium, paid £500 a week

to thump a punch ball and spar a few rounds before an enthusiastic audience – including the women automatically excluded from the all-male NSC.

Before Carpentier took up his lucrative Palladium engagement, he found out how much his second victory over Wells meant back in France. When his boat train reached the Gare du Nord in Paris, thousands greeted him. The gendarmerie attempted to smuggle him discreetly out of a side entrance. They were out-thought by the throng who hoisted Descamps and his prodigy on to their shoulders and paraded them around the station shouting 'Vive La France!' until Carpentier's eventual escape into a taxi.

The double triumph of a French sporting hero in a sport his country had only just taken up, over an English idol Billy Wells, successor to the English prizefighters of previous centuries, did not lead to domestic apathy in England. On the contrary, the following year, 1914, saw boxing more popular than ever. The august *Times* devoted hundreds of column inches to boxing; important fights received ever more extensive coverage. Boxing news and views invaded the news pages as if no longer containable in the sporting columns. On 1 January 1914, Bandsman Blake of Great Yarmouth and the Dixie Kid of the USA met at The Ring, Blackfriars over 20 rounds. *The Times* that day carried a 12-inch preview of the fight and followed it with a half-column report on 2 January 1914 (it would have been more had the fight not taken place after 9.30pm and so close to printing deadlines). *The Times* knew that the British classes would want the latest information about boxing along with their breakfast.

Endnotes

1 *The Times,* 1 January 1913.

2 National Archives: FSA7/28/1467.

3 *New York Times,* 2 January 1913.

4 *New York Times,* 5 January 1913.

5 *New York Times,* 5 January 1913.

6 *New York Times,* 2 January 1913.

7 *New York Times,* 2 February 1913.

8 *New York Times,* 6 February 1913.

9 *New York Times,* 11 September 1913.

10 Heller, P., *In This Corner …! Forty World Champions Tell Their Stories* (London: Robson Books, 1985) p. 42 (an interview conducted with Smith in 1970).

11 *Boxing,* 1 February 1913; *Mirror of Life and Boxing World,* 1 February 1913; *The Times,* 28 January 1913; Bettinson, A. F. & Bennison, B., *The Home of Boxing (*London: Odhams Press, 1932) pp. 147–150; Deghy G., Noble and Manly: *The History of the National Sporting Club* (Hutchinson, 1956) p.186.

12 *Mirror of Life and Boxing World,* 8 February 1913.

13 *Mirror of Life and Boxing World,* 18 January 1913.

14 See 'Wrecker of British Championship Prospects' in *Boxing News,* 2 September 1953.

15 *The Times,* 25 February 1913; *Jewish Chronicle,* 28 February 1913; *Mirror of Life and Boxing World,* 1 March 1913.

16 *The Times,* 1 January 1913.

17 See in particular, 'Early Gloved Championship Boxing: The True Facts – Part One' in *The British Boxing Board of Control Yearbook,* 1999, pp. 215–240, the series continuing in subsequent yearbooks.

18 Laski, M., 'Domestic Life', in Nowell-Smith, S. (ed.), *Edwardian England 1901–1914* (Oxford: Oxford University Press, 1964) p. 205ff.

19 *Mirror of Life and Boxing World,* 22 February 1913.

20 Mullan, H., *Heroes and Hard Men: The Story of Britain's World Boxing Champions* (London: Stanley Paul, 1989) p. 31.

21 *Mirror of Life and Boxing World,* 1 March 1913.

22 *Mirror of Life and Boxing World,* 19 April 1913.

23 Cowles, V., *1913: The Defiant Swan Song* (London, Weidenfeld and Nicolson, 1967) p. 51.

24 *Boxing,* 5 June 1913 (partly reproduced also in *Boxing News,* 12 August 1953); *Mirror of Life and Boxing World,* 7 June 1913.

25 Harding, J., *Lonsdale's Belt: Boxing's Most Coveted Prize (*Worthing: Pitch Publishing, 2016) pp. 44–45.

26 *Boxing,* 6 June 1913 (partly reproduced in *Boxing News,* 5 August 1953); *Mirror of Life,* 7 June 1913.

27 Mullan, H., *Heroes and Hard Men,* p. 31.

28 *Boxing,* 1 November 1913; *The Times,* 28 October 1913.

29 *The Times,* 29 December 1913; *Boxing,* 3 January 1914.

30 Hugman, B., *British Boxing Yearbook 1990,* p. 60.

31 Roderick , A., *Johnny! The Story of the Happy Warrior* (Newport: Heron Press, 1990); Butler, J., *Kings of the Ring* (London, n.d. [1936]) pp. 101–107; Deakin, F., *Welsh Warriors* (Stone, Staffs: Crescendo Publications, 1990) pp. 40–46.

32 *The Times,* 23 August 1913.

33 Greig, M., *Goin' the Distance: Canada's Boxing Heritage* (Toronto: Macmillan, Canada 1996); Kent, G., *The Great White Hopes: The Quest to Defeat Jack Johnson* (Stroud: Sutton, Publishing, 2005) pp. 147–158; 'When White Hopes Were the Rage – How Luther McCarty was Exploited' by Professor (*sic*) Billy McCarney, *The Ring,* March 1930.

34 *The Times,* 24 November 1913.

35 Guesstimate by James Butler – see Deakin, F., *Welsh Warriors,* pp. 48–49.

36 Odd, G., *Encyclopedia of Boxing* (London: Hamlyn, 1983) pp. 117–118.

37 *The Boxing Register: International Boxing Hall of Fame Official Record Book* (London, Robson Books, 1998), pp. 174–175.

38 *Mirror of Life and Boxing World,* 22 February 1913.

39 The British Film Institute for example has film of his loss to Tancy Lee.

40 Biographical accounts of Wilde include Mullan, H., *Heroes and Hard Men,* pp. 48–53; Carpenter, H., *Masters of Boxing* (London: Heinemann, 1964) pp. 23–32; Deakin, F., *Welsh Warriors,* pp. 47–54; Butler, J., *Kings of the Ring,* pp. 108–114; Butler, J & Butler, F., *The Fight Game* (Kingswood: World's Work, 1954) pp. 52–60; Myler, P., *A Century of Boxing Greats: Inside the Ring with the Hundred Best Boxers* (London: Robson Books, 1999) pp. 378–382; an article by Gilbert Odd, 'So Good They Paid Him in Diamonds' in *Boxing News,* 27 July 1979 is worth finding, as is an article Odd ghosted for Wilde and carried with other interesting material on the website www.johnnyowen.com.

41 Myler, P., *A Century of Boxing Greats,* p. 378.

42 Myler, P., *A Century of Boxing Greats,* p. 214.

43 *Mirror of Life and Boxing World,* 7 June 1913.

44 *Mirror of Life and Boxing World,* 11 October 1913; 'Peerless Jim's Mantle Falls on the Kid', *Boxing News,* 24 August 1953; *The Times,* 7 October 1913.

45 See a moving filial account of Lewis written by his son Morton in 1990, Lewis, M., *Ted Kid Lewis: His Life and Times* (London: Robson Books, 1990).

46 Butler, J., *Kings of the Ring,* pp.219–225; Butler, J & Butler, F., *The Fight Game,* pp. 101–112; Carpenter, H., *Masters of*

Boxing, pp. 163–178; Mullan, H., *Heroes and Hard Men,* pp. 18–23; Myler, P., *A Century of Boxing Greats,* pp. 214–220; Marshall Cavendish video collection, *Boxers,* No.67.

47 Morton Lewis also gives an earlier 28 October 1893.

48 Butler, J., *Kings of the Ring,* p. 219.

49 Roberts, R., *Papa Jack: Jack Johnson and the Era of White Hopes* (New York: Simon & Schuster, 1985) p. 139.

50 Johnson, J., *Jack Johnson: In the Ring and Out* (London: Proteus 1977) p. 59.

51 See Roberts, R., *Papa Jack,* pp. 141–184; and Ward, G., *Unforgivable Blackness: The Rise and Fall of Jack Johnson* (New York: Knopf, 2004) pp. 296–349 for much more comprehensive accounts. Ward p. 290 quotes Etta's letter in full.

52 Boorstin, D. J., *The Americas: The Democratic Experience* (New York: Random House, 1973) p. 80.

53 Roberts, R., *Papa Jack,* p. 170.

54 Quoted in Roberts, R., *Papa Jack,* p. 178.

55 Johnson, J., *Jack Johnson,* p. 72.

56 *Mirror of Life and Boxing World,* 30 August 1913.

57 Roberts, R., *Papa Jack,* pp.186–187.

58 *The Times,* 26 November 1913.

59 *The Times,* 17 December 1913.

60 *The Times,* 20 December 1913.

61 Wells, B.. *Physical Energy: Showing How Physical and Mental Energy May Be Developed by Means of the Practice of Boxing (*London: T. Werner Laurie, n.d.) p. 20.

62 *The Times,* 17 March 1913; Shipley, S., *Bombardier Billy Wells: The Life and Trials of a Boxing Hero* (Tyne and Wear: Bewick Press, 1993) pp. 68–71; Heller, P., *In This Corner …!,* pp. 31–45 [interview with Smith in March 1970, although the date of the Wells fight is wrongly given there as 1912]; *New York Times,* 15 March 1913.

63 Heller, P., *In This Corner …!,* p. 37.

64 Shipley, S., *Bombardier Billy Wells,* p. 74.

65 *Mirror of Life and Boxing World,* 26 April 1913.

66 *Mirror of Life and Boxing World,* 7 June 1913.

67 *Mirror of Life and Boxing World,* 14 June 1913.

68 Reports in *The Times,* 11 September 1913 and *Boxing,* 20 September 1913.

69 *The Times,* 19 November 1913; 20 November 1913; 26 November 1913.

70 *Boxing,* 13 December 1913 and 20 December 1913; *The Times,* 8 December, 9 December, 10 December and 11 December 1913; Shipley, S., *Bombardier Billy Wells,* pp. 86–89; Bettinson, A. F. & Bennison, B., *The Home of Boxing,* pp. 152–7; *Carpentier: By Himself* (London: Sportsman's Book Club, 1958) pp.79–81.

71 *Boxing's New Year Annual 1913* p.12.

CHAPTER 10
MASSES AND CLASSES
1914

In Which Britannia Fails to Rule

STRONG HISTORICAL empathy is necessary to grasp just how important boxing became in Britain by 1914. Two specialised boxing weeklies covered bouts at home and abroad for the many aficionados. Six days a week in every week, bills were presented somewhere in the country. Boxing's claims to have become perhaps *the* national sport are supported by the very substantial contemporary coverage in serious newspapers like *The Times* and the *Daily Telegraph*. A fight for a British championship, or an international contest between a Briton and a Frenchman or an American, were of major concern and were discussed ubiquitously. In the USA, expanding column inches awarded by the *New York Times* told a similar story. The *New York Times* in January 1914 confidently predicted another boxing boom because so many promoters had contracted halls with capacities of thousands.[1]

This is in such contrast to the 21st century when serious newspapers routinely ignore major contests or relegate them to the media margins along with badminton, hockey and cycling, all competing for survival outside the hegemony of soccer. The one weekly journal still devoted to boxing,

the admirable *Boxing News*, refers to itself as a 'trade' paper, humbly accepting its restricted role and focusing on the already committed. What modern British heavyweight could receive the devotion awarded Bombardier Billy Wells in all his vicissitudes? What French boxer could stop the traffic in the Strand like Georges Carpentier? Or paralyse Paddington station like Gunboat Smith?

Edwardian boxers, such as the Bombardier, Matt Wells, Jim Driscoll, Jimmy Wilde and others, had names that transcended sport and were as well known to the general public as music hall artists, politicians or actors. A century on, they are arguably still as famous as, say, an actor-manager such as Herbert Beerbohm Tree, or a politician such as F. E. Smith, equally eminent in their day.

The average boxing follower of 1914 was not necessarily grateful. Like the gloomy observer of naval affairs in 1914 worried about the serious growth of the German navy, or the pessimistic academician who saw English art threatened by avant-garde European ideas, he dwelt on the uncomfortable fact that English superiority had taken some severe knocks in 1913.

Bombardier Wells, trying to obliterate his embarrassing loss to Al Palzer in New York in the summer of 1912, had been humiliated three more times in 1913 – in two rounds by Gunboat Smith in New York in March; and twice by the much smaller Georges Carpentier – in four rounds in Ghent in June, and, worse still, in a mere 73 seconds at the NSC in December. That 1913 had promised much and delivered little, made John Murray of *Boxing* mindful of sexual parallels:

> 1913 was a coquette, a jade of the worst description all the way. She emerged from an atmosphere golden with hope and promise. She came wreathed in smiles – and then before January was through she began to flout and jeer at us.[2]

That entertaining mirror of middle-class opinion, *Punch*, not a boxing magazine despite its title, ruefully reflected on the bare-knuckle giants of the past in contrast to Wells's dismal 1913 record. In December 1913, it published 'The Boxiad', a long anonymous poem. Twenty-nine lines of this epic outlined the mighty deeds of Cribb, Bendigo and Sayers. It continued with cautious optimism about the future:

> At last the Spirit of British Boxing
>   spoke,
> And he was cheerful, on his open
>   brow
> No frown was seen, nor sadness in
>   his eyes:-
> 'If hearts ye have, lift up,' he said,
>   'your hearts;
> Let not your manly minds be
>   steeped in woe,
> 'Tis true CARPENTIER beat the
>   BOMBARDIER,
> Jabbing him six times shortly in
>   the stomach,
> So that he fell and swift was
>   counted out.
> But this CARPENTIER is a
>   proper man;
> And you, old heroes, you may well
>   be proud
> To own a hero, though he comes
>   from France.
> And it may hap that on another day
> Some beef-fed British boxer shall
>   arise,
> Cool in his guard and crafty in
>   his blows,
> Lithe and enduring as
>   CARPENTIER is,
> And turn the changing tables on
>   the Gaul.
> Dame Fortune shifts her smiles,
>   but gives them most
> To those who by their toil deserve
>   them well.'
> So spoke the Spirit, and the
>   thronging Shades,
> Won o'er to cheerfulness,
>   acclaimed his words.[3]

As 1914 continued, there were few not 'won o'er to cheerfulness' as boxing flourished, with a proliferation of fights as competitive and exciting as any other year, before or since. Previous chapters have shown how the sport became respectable and indeed glamorous.

Theatre too had shaken off its dubious antecedents. An Edwardian first-night audience, all dinner jackets, gowns and glitter, were highly respectable in contrast to their rowdy, duelling, orange-throwing and tumultuous ancestors. The ultra-fashionable and glamorous audiences, stepping from their carriages for the Olympia ringside on international boxing nights, thoroughly transcended every trace of the roughs and toughs who had once packed the squalid backrooms of public houses.

In 1915, Eugene Corri, self-proclaimed veteran of three decades of boxing, reflected on the previous year:

> … I can remember few more remarkable events connected with the sport than the boxing boom of 1914. For three months, roughly – May, June and July – all England was in a ferment over boxing. It was *the* topic of the hour. Hundreds – nay thousands of recruits were brought into the game. Some of them, no doubt, were fickle, attracted by the latest sensation, but there were others who have remained lovers of boxing, thanks to their 'baptism of fire' in the memorable year 1914.[4]

The Olympia shows were brilliantly organised and promoted with panache by Charles B. Cochran, an impresario with flair and experience. He was not the inventor of the new boxing, rather the inheritor of a long-term trend in the sport's development.

As always, the clashes of heavyweights stirred most pulses and sold most tickets. If the Bombardier could not fulfil national hopes, would another British contender take his place? What about Bandsman Blake? On New Year's Day 1914 at the Blackfriars Ring, the undefeated young Great Yarmouth musician was matched over 20 rounds with an American headline name – the Dixie Kid.[5]

In fact, Dixie was now a veteran in decline. His actual age was a mystery, although he was certainly 20 years older than Blake. He was a natural welterweight so conceded over 20 pounds. By 1914, Dixie was a 'shot' fighter, a shadow of his former self with diminished speed and stamina. He kept only his ringcraft. He was cunning enough to force less experienced men into mauls, escaping relatively unhurt with at least a loser's share of the purse. Blake could add a famous American to his win record without excessive effort. The only risk was having Blake's limitations exposed.

Youth and strength prevailed over the last third of the fight. Dixie, for all his guile, took hurtful punches and endured some long counts. Dixie's counter-punches, that once rocked aggressors back on their heels, were now too light to deter. The verdict went to Blake while perceptive observers registered glumly the naiveties Dixie exposed.

Many thousands of miles away in Dale City, California, another heavyweight contest was widely noted. On New Year's Day 1914, two heavies fought to top that distasteful pyramid labelled the 'New Great

Frank Moran (1887–1967) of Pennsylvania frequently toured Europe carrying his powerful right ('Mary Ann') along with him. He was to knock out two British champions, Wells (1915) and Beckett (1920) but lost to Johnson in Paris in 1914.

Bain Collection, Prints & Photographs Division, Library of Congress, LC-DIG-ggbain-21194

White Hope', or, as the *New York Times* euphemistically called it, 'a solution of the heavyweight question'. Defending over a potential 20 rounds was Arthur Pelkey of Chatham, Ontario, holder of the 'white' heavyweight championship of the world. Pelkey had deep-seated reservations about boxing at all, ever since May 1913 when Luther McCarty had so suddenly collapsed and died in front of him.

His new challenger was the robust Gunboat Smith, who had stopped Bombardier Wells in Madison Square Garden in March 1913. He had beaten an impressive number of other hopefuls over the last two years.[6] Al Palzer, Frank Moran, Jess Willard, George Rodel, Sam Langford, Fireman Jim Flynn – all had been knocked out or outpointed after suffering Smith's formidable right hand. In his defeat of Wells, and in his outpointing of Sam Langford (17 November 1913 over 12 rounds in Boston), Smith added a useful left jab and a reasonable defence. He was no longer so dependent on his erratically swinging right.

Never one to oversell himself, Smith modestly downplayed his big right: 'They used to call it the flopper, or hospital punch [but] … in the Navy, it was just an apple-knocker.' (Some apple! Some knocker!) The US Navy nurtured the Philadelphia-born Smith (b. 17 February 1887), a child dumped untutored and illiterate into an orphanage. It gave him self-respect and developed his innate talent. He left the navy in 1909 and gradually climbed the professional boxing ranks. By the end of 1913, he was tough, powerful and aware he could win fights without propelling his right fist wildly into orbit. The advice shouted from his corner by Jim Buckley, his manager, rarely varied from 'Box 'im!' Smith learned to take notice when the Willards and the Langfords took the big right hand but disobligingly failed instantly to fall over.

When Smith, a congenial companion to other boxers including Jack Johnson, manned a friend's corner, he gave advice himself. On 16 December 1913, he seconded the ultra-aggressive British Midlander, Owen Moran, in Oakland, California. Moran was fighting Joe Azevedo. The veteran Moran took a beating over the first five rounds. At the end of the fifth, Smith advised Moran to cool his growing anger and frustration, and to out-think Azevedo: 'Take your time and use your head!' The volcanic Moran took the advice literally and was disqualified by referee Griffin for using his head not to think but to butt Azevedo under the chin four times in succession.[7]

Against Arthur Pelkey, Smith fought a canny fight, softening up the big French Canadian with skill and economy. In the 15th of the possible 20, Smith landed his big right directly on Pelkey's chin for a clean knockout.

Poor Pelkey's inherent decency hampered his fighting qualities. He was never the same fighter after May 1913. Luther McCarty's death was followed by a sleepless night in a hotel, an arraignment for manslaughter and a distressing inquest to suffer. His innocence was publicly established; his private reservations lingered.

A grim reminder of Pelkey's trial took place on 8 January 1914 in Los Angeles. Jess Willard, his manager, his seconds and others in his entourage, were prosecuted because Willard's opponent, William 'Bull' Young, died from a broken neck when knocked out in the Vernon Arena on 22 August 1913. On 13 January, Willard was found innocent (although it took the jury all night to reach its verdict) and resumed his career unscathed. Willard was a less imaginative and sensitive man than Pelkey. Pelkey's later career was dogged by his masochistic desire to suffer for his part in McCarty's demise.[8] Willard went on to greater things.

Boxing in California took a severer punishment. As a result of the Willard/Young case, a State Amendment 20 (The 'Anti Prize Fight Act') was passed, eliminating California as a venue for major boxing (only amateur-style four-round bouts were subsequently permitted). Pittsburgh and Indianapolis also banned serious boxing.

In Britain, Smith's other victim, Bombardier Billy Wells, underwent his latest rehabilitation. Such was his phenomenal popularity with the British public that they turned out in large numbers, at enhanced prices, hoping mistakenly for great things. The muscles might ripple, the limbs move athletically, yet the brain failed on a big occasion.

Wisely, his return was a modest affair against a determined scrapper from Dundalk, Gunner Rawles. The venue was the Theatre Royal, Belfast. Wells was metaphorically sticking his head into a lion's den of a claustrophobically crowded theatre on 14 January 1914.[9]

Rawles lost every round but he was a man full of spirit. In a small ring, one of his left swings and hooks might have landed on the Wells chin or in the vulnerable Wells midriff. Wells's usual left leads delivered while moving to the right would have brought him towards Rawles's best punches. Improvising well, Wells avoided the Rawles lefts and delivered mid-range uppercuts. He leaned as heavily on Rawles as Rawles sought to lean on him.

In the fifth, Wells slipped and a Rawles glove grazed his forehead. It was merely a slip and Wells was immediately back on his feet and defending himself. Wells was clearly on top. Rawles took several combinations in the seventh and eighth without serious reply. At the end of the ninth he was nearly stopped.

In the final minute, Wells landed a long left and a long right just above Rawles's belt. Rawles doubled over and fell. He hauled himself up at nine and caught another right in the same region to return him to the canvas. Gamely, he struggled up after another nine seconds and the gong intervened. Sixty seconds on his stool, despite his seconds' best efforts, were not sufficient genuinely to revive him.

He tottered out for the tenth, an open target, grabbing at Wells for support. A short Wells right had him clutching at Wells's legs as he slid down. Full of obstinacy, if nothing else, he again got up at nine, and a forlorn but

welcome towel floated in before Wells could hit him again. It was over.

Both men emerged with credit. Rawles displayed determination and grit. Wells conquered with dignity and skill. The Rawles victory looked even better when Wells was back in the ring at Cardiff ten days later on 24 January 1914 to meet French heavyweight Gaston Pigot.[10] Taking *any* fight just over a week after the Belfast venture suggests that the Wells camp had at least partly identified his past failures with the relatively few fights he took.

Pigot, shorter but heavier, looked tough; his extra poundage packed into a muscular frame. Later, Wells claimed his right hand was unusable because he had damaged it against Rawles. Why then did he appear in Cardiff? An ignominious one-handed failure against another Frenchman would have put even his yo-yo career beyond redemption. In practice, the right was barely tested.

Pigot rushed in, swinging at Wells's diaphragm. Wells slipped aside leaving the swings dissipating into the empty Cardiff air. The Welsh crowd chuckled appreciatively. Showing who was boss, Wells connected with three or four crisp lefts from a safe distance. As Pigot paused to rethink, Wells moved menacingly forward and put in three more lefts to Pigot's jaw and one to the stomach that sank Pigot to his knees. These details are taken from *Boxing*'s reporter and fit the damaged right hand theory. It was done at speed and *The Times* reporter saw the sequence quite differently. 'Several left jabs reached his [Pigot's] face – they came over smoothly enough, but were evidently full of sting – two *right* upper-cuts shook him sadly, and a glorious *right* drive to the stomach put him down in a neutral corner.' [Italics added.] Not for Edwardian ringsiders were there slow-motion replays to settle discrepancies.

Pigot, on one knee, suffered a full count delivered by referee John Murray in French and failed to rise before *dix* had been called. Up at about *douze*, he claimed to have misunderstood the count. Even had Murray's French been impenetrable, Wells could have repeated the dose if necessary. From start to finish 109 seconds elapsed; exciting but hardly value for money.

In early 1914, many British fighters were attracted by Australian or American purses, and foreign experience. The opponents were not necessarily foreign. Johnny Summers, who by 1912 went from lightweight to welterweight, spent much of 1913 and 1914 in Australia where Sydney became a major venue. Summers had successfully defended his British welterweight title against Sid Burns at the NSC on 9 December 1912 (Chapter 8). Summers v Burns II – an almost identical win for Summers on points over 20 rounds – took place in the stadium at Rushcutters Bay in Sydney on 21 June 1913. Summers's old opponent Arthur Evernden, whom he had beaten in an ultra-dramatic 13th round in London on 17 June 1912, was rematched with Summers twice in Australia – in Melbourne on 11 October 1913 (Summers winning on points over 20 rounds) and in Sydney on 31 January 1914 (Summers winning similarly).

Summers also lost twice to a sturdy Dundalk fighter, the worthy Tom McCormick (b. 8 August 1890). Both bouts took place in the Sydney arena and brought wins for McCormick (10

January 1914 on points over 20 rounds; 14 February by a first-round KO). No modern welterweight would, whatever the purse, take major fights so close together. McCormick's productivity was equally impressive – in January 1914 he fought 20 rounds against Summers, but also beat Waldemar Holberg, a Dane currently claiming to be the world welterweight champion, on a disqualification in the sixth in Melbourne on 24 January 1914, before the February return against Summers.

McCormick, born in Northern Ireland, spent much of his early life in Lancashire and became a regular soldier in his late teens.[11] When his regiment was based at Plymouth, he discovered a talent for boxing and fought often at the Old Cosmo. His ring technique was a product of self-tuition. Jim Driscoll was then attracting much publicity. McCormick, a young man with an enquiring mind, bought Driscoll's book on boxing. Not many professionals taught themselves the rudiments by shadow-boxing in front of a mirror with a textbook in one hand. For McCormick it worked. In his climb up the ranks, he beat good fighters of more orthodox schooling, such as Gus Platts, Young Joseph and Albert Badoud. When he was experienced enough to challenge top fighters such as Summers, Summers had already left for Australia.

Too impatient to await Summers's return, McCormick and his manager, an affluent Plymouth caterer called Sid Alger, left for Australia themselves. Celebrating their departure at a lavish public dinner financed by McCormick's Plymouth supporters, they reached Sydney by early December 1913. Australian promoters drew up the fine print on contracts for the McCormick/

Summers bouts and added a Holberg/McCormick fight at Melbourne. (Two other British welters, Sid Burns and Sid Stagg, also met in Sydney in January 1914, Sid B outpointing Sid S over 20 rounds.)

McCormick and Summers II in February was a clincher twice over. Frustrated in January by his inability to nail McCormick over 20 championship rounds as McCormick followed Driscoll's literary advice (to hit and not be hit) to the letter, Summers tried in February to overwhelm McCormick the moment the Plymouth man left his stool. It was unwise. McCormick took the onslaught on his gloves and arms and slid away, Summers in frantic pursuit. McCormick then stood his ground and stopped Summers with two powerful body punches. Summers halted and instinctively lowered his guard. McCormick delivered two hooks, one right and one left, to the chin. Summers dropped instantly to his knees and folded at the waist, his face to the canvas like a supplicant at prayer. No divine help came and he was counted out.

At the first bout, Summers pronounced McCormick's points victory a fluke and predicted the return would not last the distance. Two minutes and 20 seconds proved him right; he just got the winner wrong. This was the moment when Summers, a talented veteran, began to decline. Though his career lasted until 1921, he never again notched a major victory.

Curiously, McCormick, who had sailed halfway round the globe to defeat both Summers and Holberg, never had another major triumph either. Worse, he was denied a long and happy retirement when a German shell exploded at his feet in France in the summer of 1916 and killed him instantly.

Australia as a new goldfield for British boxers was partly due to the British trainer Jack Goodwin. Goodwin's legacy included a very readable book of memoirs, *Myself and My Boxers* (London: Hutchinson, 1924). He handled at various times Harry Mansfield, Sid Burns, Sid Stagg, Harry Stone and Matt Wells. Somewhat down on his luck and his funds in Britain in the winter of 1912–13, although never short on enterprise, he worked his passage on a ship bound for Australia in January 1913. Not one to shrink away from betting opportunities, he visited Melbourne and increased his resources with some skilful punting at the Melbourne races. When he reached Sydney, he accumulated his wages, his winnings and his *en voyage* tips, and supplemented them by working as a docker. He then clinched lucrative deals with eager Australian promoters and imported British boxers to fulfil them. First Burns, then Mansfield, Stagg and others came out at his behest. Using his shrewd knowledge of form, he supplemented his promotional percentages with successful bets on the fights.

Soon the Sydney ex-docker was staying at the luxury hotel at Botany Bay where Jack Johnson and his female sparring partners had wined, dined, cavorted and sometimes trained before the fight with Tommy Burns in 1908. Goodwin's good times were more transient than Johnson's, but like his, greatly enjoyed. Sadly, his fighters sometimes suffered for the sake of Goodwin's wagers. Mansfield took a beating over the final rounds of a fight against Les O'Donald, urged on by

Goodwin. Unknown to Mansfield, Goodwin had bet a substantial amount on Mansfield lasting the distance.

While Summers, McCormick and the others fought in the southern hemisphere, many British boxers sailed west instead. British boxers versus American opposition were a perpetual draw in New York. The bill staged in Madison Square Garden on Tuesday, 27 January 1914 was typical.[12] Though the evening opened with an all-American ten-rounder of particular local interest – Gene Moriarty of Syracuse outpointing Johnny Reese of Brooklyn at what would now be super-featherweight – the two main bouts featured British fighters.

One was Sapper (Jack) O'Neill, a Gloucester lightweight with an aggressive reputation. (He served ten months with hard labour in 1925 for killing a man in a street fight.) O'Neill met the famous Italian-American Giuseppe Carrora, although only famous under his ring name, Johnny Dundee.[13] Dundee's other epithet, 'The Scotch Wop', should be forgotten. So should the 'Scotch' image his manager persuaded him to adopt – a top hat, a tartan kilt and a monocle. Dundee (b. 22 November 1893), fighting out of New York, embarked on his professional career in 1910 and, astonishingly, fought his last fight against Mickey Greb in December 1932! His ring record reads like a Who's Who of great featherweights and junior lightweights, including Benny Leonard, Pal Moore, Freddie Welsh, Terry McGovern, Lew Tendler and Tony Canzoneri.

The less stellar O'Neill was less skilful, less experienced, less swift than any of these but much bigger than Dundee. At a chaotic weigh-in, both

men were on and off the scales a couple of times. Dundee eventually recorded 8st 13¾lb/125¾lbs and O'Neill 9st 9lb/135lbs. As the New York State Athletic Commission insisted on a maximum discrepancy of ten pounds between opponents in the lighter weights, the contest survived by a margin of a few grams.

Dundee rarely knocked people out. He inflicted damage gradually. O'Neill survived ten rounds despite a swift right hook to the jaw dropping him to one knee in the second. In the last five rounds he merely survived. He back-pedalled and used his extra weight to cling and lean on the American. Experience in American rings came only at a price and the sapper bought his at the cost of two swollen eyes and a bloodied nose and ear. Dundee's newspaper win was unanimous.

The other British fighter that night was Owen Moran. His career had been going since 1901 and already totalled over 100 contests. He was beginning to wonder how many more gruelling fights he could take. (The 13 December fiasco when he had butted out against Joe Azevedo was possibly an exit strategy.) Moran was up against Young (Joe) Shugrue of Jersey City (b. 11 September 1894). Shugrue had lost to Johnny Dundee at the New Star Casino in New York five days before on 23 January 1914.[14] That was a conspicuously wearing ten-rounder, close to being 'the greatest staged in New York since the Frawley Law went into effect'; one where 'staid citizens found themselves shouting and dancing like schoolboys while [the fighters] stood toe to toe and swung their arms about as fast as they could'. Who, these days, would be taking another such fight a week later?

A fading fighter often tries to overwhelm in the first few rounds. This Moran wanted desperately to do, fiercely exchanging punches with Shugrue, who was quite as aggressive as he. Moran opened a cut over Shugrue's right eye in the first or, probably, reopened a cut inflicted in Shugrue's classic against Dundee. He avoided Shugrue's rushes but was still caught with effective body punches. These convinced him he must win early. In the third, he doubled his punch count, catching Shugrue to head and body from long and short range. Unfortunately, Shugrue was still there after the torrid three minutes and looking cool. In the fifth and sixth, Shugrue took over, Moran looking more and more desperate and going miserably back to his corner at the end of the sixth.

It ended in the seventh. Shugrue landed often to Moran's diaphragm, provoking spurious appeals from Moran that he was being punched low. When Moran lowered his guard to stop the damage, Shugrue clipped him brusquely to jaw and temple. When the bell rang, Moran threw his arms in the air and went not to his corner but to the ropes. Between big breaths, he addressed the crowd: 'Fourteen years is a long time to be in the ring, and I guess I have about reached the end.' (This uncannily pre-figured Roberto Duran's famous surrender – 'No mas' i.e. 'No more' – against Sugar Ray Leonard in New Orleans on 25 November 1980.) The boos that began at Moran's surrender died during his speech as listeners remembered what a doughty and even foolhardy scrapper Moran had been. After his declaration he was cheered all the way to the dressing room. The verdict was recorded as a

TKO. (Duran's rehabilitation was much less instant.)

The temporary absence of Britons who were fighting in the USA or Australia did not detract from the domestic fights of early 1914. Neither did the news from Nice that Carpentier had continued his one-man swathe through British boxers with a two-round dismissal of Pat O'Keefe of Canning Town (b. 17 March 1883) on 19 January 1914. Carpentier took 25 seconds blocking O'Keefe's punches and sizing up his man. In another 30 he had O'Keefe on the canvas and wondering about the hooks to jaw and ribs that had put him there for eight seconds. O'Keefe survived the round. Many unkindly pointed out that it was more than Bombardier Wells managed. It was a minor compensation. The French tiger pounced on the English goat immediately in the second and floored him again with a heavy left to the body. Foolishly, O'Keefe got up at two; was down again to a right uppercut for eight; masochistically got up and was definitively despatched by a Carpentier right hook to the jaw.

This kind of defeat ended the career of many a veteran middleweight. Pat O'Keefe was undeterred and quite intelligent enough to profit from adversity. A few weeks after he lay helpless as a French referee counted him out, he was in the ring at the NSC on 23 February 1914 to win the vacant British middleweight title against a younger, stronger opponent in Harry Reeve of Plaistow (b. 7 January 1893).[15] Reeve was 21 years old.

O'Keefe (11st 5lb/159lbs) was a lesser puncher than Reeve (11st 4½lb/158½lbs), but had mastered the art of slipping inside and delivering

punches to the body, which seriously weakened, gradually. Reeve had power in his right hand to put people away in one, could he land it cleanly on their chin. O'Keefe, aware of the danger, kept his chin tucked down on his chest. Reeve's rights thudded remorselessly into his left temple, his left ear and the left side of his neck, but not on that chin.

After 15 rounds, O'Keefe had piled up enough points to win. But one Reeve right could still render the entire patient stockpiling redundant. Cleverly, O'Keefe kept Reeve away whatever the Plaistow man did. No reversal took place and Referee Ayle confirmed O'Keefe as the new popular champion. As O'Keefe donned the Lonsdale Belt, he had done so on a bill featuring two former holders of the very belt he now held. One was Jim Sullivan, who had not lost it in the ring, but had fallen ill and was unable to defend it promptly enough for the NSC's satisfaction. Sullivan was, like O'Keefe, a sorry Carpentier victim – 29 February 1912, knocked out in the second round in Monte Carlo.

Sullivan was on the bill to meet Jack Harrison. Harrison had been champion himself when he outpointed Pat McEnroy over 20 rounds at the NSC on 20 May 1912. Harrison's reign lasted less than a year. It ended when Ted Kid Lewis ruthlessly exposed his limitations and knocked him out in three rounds, also at the NSC on 9 December 1912. Sullivan easily beat Harrison, putting him down five times. Harrison's seconds threw in a towel before the end of the fourth.

On 25 May 1914, the logical match between O'Keefe as champion and Sullivan as ex-champion took place at the NSC. O'Keefe outpointed

Sullivan over 20 rounds. All these match-ups received due attention, yet had Carpentier remained at the weight, none of the British domestic fighters would have sniffed either a European or world title. Carpentier's growth spurt had taken him quietly up the weight divisions. He was not a true heavyweight and never became one other than in name. His speed, his skill, his timing and his boxing brain had him rarely overmatched. He dealt with every fighter the British put up against him.

The British hoped for new talent in both the heavyweight and cruiserweight divisions. An interesting match was made at the NSC on 19 January 1914 at 12st 6lb/174lbs, a weight called cruiserweight in 1914. The division has been subject to confusing change during its history. It was initiated in the USA in 1903 to accommodate such fighters as Jack Root, who was, like Carpentier, too heavy for the middleweights and too light to compete fully at heavy. Fixed at the convenient American weight of 175lbs, it was termed, logically enough, light-heavyweight. When the British adopted it in 1913, naval matters were much in the headlines, so the term cruiserweight was adopted; a cruiser being powerful yet lighter and more manoeuvrable than a full battleship.

When the British Board of Boxing Control initiated a new belt in 1937, they borrowed the American nomenclature and called it light-heavyweight. Forty-odd years later in 1979, the World Boxing Council, recognising the growth in the average male over the 20th century, adopted a new cruiserweight division at 13st 13lb/195lbs and retained the light-heavyweight at 175lbs. By the early 21st

century, cruiser had swelled to a 200lb limit and heavyweight to 200lbs plus.

The new professional was Dick Smith.[16] Smith was from Woolwich and boasted an impressive amateur record as one-time successor to Billy Wells as heavyweight champion of the Army in India and reigning ABA heavyweight champion since 1912. He was a few weeks short of his 28th birthday (b. 10 February 1886) and had only just turned professional. He was ounces within the limit at the weigh-in.

He was facing a fighter from Tipperary, Denis Haugh, in the paid ranks since 1909 and only one and a half pounds lighter. The more skilful Smith was predicted a points win, providing he could last the 15 rounds. The contrast between the men promised an epic: classy ex-amateur v rough-hewn pro. An epic resulted.

After an even first round, Smith used his boxing finesse to win the next six, landing leads and crosses from a distance as well as short uppercuts and hooks, punching the Irishman with some ease. The scoring punches were as heavy as Smith could manage, yet after two-thirds of the fight Haugh was still there and looking quite unruffled. Smith had scarlet patches around his ribs and a swelling around his left eye to suggest that the traffic had not been all one way.

The last five rounds were thrilling as a tough and experienced Irishman gradually overwhelmed a weakening and even staggering Smith. Counter-punches from Smith could not stop him. Many members believed Haugh might have won by a knockout had this been a 20-rounder, but Smith's lead had been too big to be wiped out in 15. Referee Evans was in a minority

in thinking otherwise. He gave Haugh the verdict.

The decision was sufficiently contentious to demand a return. It took place at the NSC over the full 20 rounds on 9 March.[17] With the new British cruiserweight championship and a Lonsdale Belt at stake, it was expected to be as good and abrasive as the first match. At the afternoon weigh-in, Smith made 12st 4½lb/172½lbs and Haugh 12st 3½lb/171½lbs. The fight merely disappointed.

The broad-shouldered Haugh liked to attack and believed no boxer existed whom he could not knock out. As soon as the first bell sounded he was up off his stool and swinging punches. He did not add much nous to this commendable belligerence. His slowness of thought militated against him. His swings were easily avoided or parried or ridden. Potential openings passed by as Haugh ponderously worked out what he should do about them.

He had another dilemma. He damaged his left forearm early on and cracked a bone in it in the ninth. For the second half of the fight, he could swing and hook but not produce a simple straight left. Meanwhile, as Haugh rushed forward, Smith happily countered on the retreat, landing punches to the jaw that might have stopped a weaker man than Haugh. Haugh shrugged and ploughed on. The return was following the course of the first; Smith notching up a formidable points lead in the first half of the fight then tiring and going into survival mode for the last eight. Haugh knew what to do – catch Smith and finish him. Unfortunately for him and his many backers in the audience, he could not do it. Because of his injury and his laggardly thought pattern, he was condemned to continual frustration as Smith neutralised his every effort. Smith was left a clear points winner and holder of title and belt.

However disgruntled NSC patrons felt at the failure of the second fight to match the suspense of the first, they held a privileged and exclusive right to see official British title fights – and a good many other top contests. It was predictable that other entertainment venues would provide alternatives for those outside the lucky few. For example, the London Palladium, more associated with music and laughter than boxing, in February 1914 offered for three afternoon matinee performances (10, 12 and 13 February at 2.30pm) an extravagantly entitled 'Great Congress of Boxing Champions', priced modestly (seats from 2s. to 10s. 6d. and boxes at one guinea and two guineas).[18] At the 'Congress', audiences got an enterprising selection of international fighters strutting their stuff – punching bag or ball vigorously, and tamely each other. However ersatz compared with the real thing, this gave less-privileged Londoners a glimpse in the stripped muscled flesh of the men behind the names in the headlines; for example, Sam Langford, Frank Moran, Joe Jeanette, Kid McCoy, Willie Lewis, the Dixie Kid and Johnny Hughes. It is another example that white London audiences, like the Parisians, *would* pay to see black boxers.

At the Palladium as elsewhere the heavier men were the major attraction. Nevertheless, the lighter divisions in 1914 provided some stirring fights, including a notable one at the NSC on 26 January 1914. It had the suspense and action that was to be missing

from the cruiserweights in March. Two of the tiny gallant warriors who illuminated the summer of 1913 were back in action. Bill Ladbury, who had so noticeably thwarted Sid Smith at The Ring in June 1913, was matched over 20 rounds with a strong Welsh opponent in Percy Jones. The vacant British flyweight championship and a Lonsdale Belt were on offer. The quality of the fighters guaranteed these would be hard won.

Percy Jones was rated highly. *Boxing*'s 1914 annual reviewed 1913 and pronounced Jones 'the Find of the Year', one who 'bids fair to rival even the fame of Jim Driscoll', although the publication rated 'little Jimmy Wilde of Tylorstown' as best of all.[19] Ladbury v Jones promised much.[20] Jones had been trained by Driscoll and, like the master, tucked his chin safely behind his left shoulder and delivered left leads with weight and accuracy. Ladbury adopted a more open, square-on stance, but specialised in sustained two-handed onslaughts culminating in a deadly right – half swing, half chop – that had already anaesthetised many previous opponents, Sid Smith among them. The Ladbury–Jones clash was, said *The Times*, 'one of the prettiest fights which have ever been seen at the club'. It was not merely aesthetic, it had blood and thunder too – 'a tough, hard-hitting, game and hard battle, with the fortunes of war see-sawing from side to side', said *Boxing*.

Jones's initial victory was over the scales at the midday weigh-in. At first he was six ounces over the 8st/112lbs limit. A fully clothed jog around the streets of Covent Garden and a spell with a skipping rope brought him within the maximum. He lost some stamina along

with the perspiration. Some, it proved, but not all.

The first round was all collective caution. Jones shrank into a defensive crouch, absorbing some tentative flurries from Ladbury on his arms and gloves and ducking others. Occasionally he responded more positively, rocking Ladbury back with one straight left. Jones copied this in the second and added a few right crosses.

Ladbury was not deterred. At the cost of Jones's left darting into his face regularly, he landed a few heavy rights to Jones's body, punches that clearly hurt. In the fourth, as a Ladbury hook flew over Jones's lowered head, Jones struck back with a right hook of his own, and before Ladbury could regain either his breath or his balance, drove his unsteady opponent back, catching him with hooks, crosses, leads and especially uppercuts of his own. Ladbury, the fighter temporarily outfought, barely survived the round.

In long championship fights, early supremacy does not necessarily last. Jones opened the fifth as he had finished the fourth – on the attack. The crispest of right crosses had Ladbury weak-legged again. No one knew whether Ladbury was genuinely in trouble or acting. As Jones darted in again to finish the fight, he was sent reeling by a neat left hook meeting his chin at his anticipated moment of triumph. On their stools before the sixth, both men had plenty to think about. Jones found Ladbury easy to punch but a dangerous man to take for granted. Ladbury was meeting a Welsh skills merchant who did not lack a punch. Both men were due other surprises before the end.

The sixth was an edited highlight of the whole. Jones landed skilful blows close in and at a distance; Ladbury jolted him with an early uppercut. More often he rushed at Jones, swinging punches from all angles, many too wild to connect, and Jones picked him off with his left. One wild right swing caught Jones on the jaw, and it was Jones who had to grab, clinch and stagger through the round as Ladbury strove for a knockout. Jones survived and gave a three-minute exhibition of brilliant evasion in the seventh as he slowly brought his body back into coordination with his brain.

Both fighters recovered. With a full 12 rounds still to go, would the Ladbury power and strength yet prevail? Many thought so, especially during the ninth. Jones landed many punches. Ladbury absorbed them with barely a blink. At the end of the round, Ladbury brought up a right uppercut and caught Jones flush on the jaw. Jones did not fall but looked grateful to flop on his stool some seconds later. The pain included the nagging thought that, win or lose, he had a full 33 minutes of action still to endure against a stronger man. How he must have regretted that six-ounce miscalculation at the weigh-in.

Ladbury, sure that he could outlast Jones, attacked even more, profligate with his punches and directionally vague, still able to jolt the retreating Jones. But whenever Ladbury seemed destined to get on top, Jones would unleash an effective counter. In the furious 16th, a lunging Ladbury uppercut flew past Jones's face and left Ladbury open to a right cross from Jones that put him on the canvas for a count.

In a particularly thrilling 18th, Jones landed left after left to Ladbury's face yet took an even harder one himself.

When Jones switched to the body to make Ladbury gasp audibly, Ladbury produced a big left to the jaw from nowhere and it was Jones's turn to gulp.

In this see-saw action, long-term strategies were abandoned. On top in the 18th, Jones lost vigilance. As he attacked in the 19th, he was caught with a Ladbury right cross, costing him a count of eight, and hard pressed to survive the round. The 20th suggests Ladbury thought he still needed the knockout, and he went all out for it. He chased Jones around the ring, catching him frequently and winning the round easily, but not putting him down for the count. The referee awarded the verdict to Jones, although many others made Ladbury the victor. Sportingly, and accurately, Ladbury conceded, 'If the referee thought so, his is the only opinion which counts.' After so wildly fluctuating a contest, any verdict was likely to be controversial. Either man would have been a worthy recipient of belt and championship. (Jones confirmed his superiority in a return on 15 October 1915 in London with a technical knockout in the fifth round.)

No one could know on this night that these two men would be making sacrifices of a different order in the future. In June 1917, an exploding shell in a First World War trench in France killed Bill Ladbury, by then a lance corporal in the Royal West Kent Regiment.[21] His name was inscribed not on a Lonsdale Belt but on the memorial Menin Gate at Ypres, along with that of thousands of his equally unfortunate comrades. His conqueror, Percy Jones, was no luckier. A sergeant in the Royal Welch Fusiliers, he outlasted the war – barely. During 1916 he suffered a severe leg wound in France, an injury that led to many operations culminating in amputation. He was also severely affected by inhaling poison gas and contracting trench fever.[22] After the war he lingered on, a shadow of the fine athlete he had been, confined to a wheelchair, seen occasionally at ringsides and dying on Christmas Day 1922, one day before his 30th birthday.

In early 1914, the word France did not mean the killing ground where so many fine French and English sportsmen would lose their lives in a deadlier struggle than any had previously imagined. It was rather a country producing more and more excellent fighters, especially at the lighter weights. France paid Britain the sincerest flattery by taking up the British form of boxing and following it avidly. In barely half a decade, British patronisation and ridicule turned to grudging admiration for Gallic achievement. The French novelist Louis Hémon, who lived in England for a while, neatly caught the insufferable superiority of the British in his 1909 collection *Battling Malone* and other stories:

> One fine day they [the French] had suddenly grown tired of kicking each other in the face and had determined to learn the art of using their fists like men – of boxing, in short. All England had roared. A boxing Frenchman! It was the absurdist of paradoxes, a challenge to reason and common sense![23]

The triumphs of Georges Carpentier in English rings and abroad over British opponents had undermined such Anglo-Saxon complacency. Other fine

French boxers such as Charles Ledoux, Eugene Criqui and Robert Dastillon acquired many British admirers as they had proved *sans doute* to be as skilful and durable as their British counterparts.

Anyone who watched Charles Ledoux's technical win over Bill Beynon in December 1912 and believed Ledoux was just lucky, was certainly disabused of the illusion in Cardiff on 7 February 1914.[24] Beynon was not a great boxer, lacking the speed of hand and thought of the very best, yet a rugged, bustling bantamweight who could and did outlast and wear down better technicians than he. Vulnerable about the eyes, he boxed Ledoux at a distance. This suited Ledoux, who avoided Beynon's hooks and swings and picked the Welshman off with rights and lefts delivered bewilderingly off either foot. This was the scientific Ledoux. There was also the roughhouse Ledoux, who followed in with a forearm or an elbow whenever a referee lacked vigilance. He was warned eventually but had already inflicted legitimate and illegitimate damage.

Beynon adopted too open and too square a stance, allowing Ledoux to deliver a right over his guard into his vulnerable left eyebrow. It did not cut, but swellings above and below the eye robbed Beynon of any sight from that eye by the eighth. Beynon delivered a sweet left to the jaw in the fourth and hard rights in the fifth. Unfortunately for him, by the seventh there was no question about who would win the fight, only how long it would last. He took more damaging rights in the seventh and the ninth. He sank dolefully on to his stool at the end of the ninth, and his seconds, grasping that this would not be

his night, sympathetically retired him. Driscoll at ringside and the audience agreed, and sportingly cheered Ledoux to the exit.

The audience's magnanimity and Driscoll's desire to protect a gallant but outclassed boxer, preceded another happier return contest. Percy Jones was hardly out of the ring in 1913 – 24 fights, 24 wins. He met the durable Frenchman Eugene Criqui twice. The first, over 15 rounds, was in Liverpool on 12 February 1914, and produced a clear points win for Criqui on the referee's card at 73 points to 70, scored on the five-points-a-round maximum.[25] The referee's allocation did not accord with the impressions of anyone else. Jones was widely thought to have been robbed, cue for a return a. s. a. p.

It took place in Liverpool on 26 March 1914 over a full championship 20 rounds at 8st/112lbs for a £400 purse plus a £100 side stake, plus general European recognition of the winner as world flyweight champion. The title, and the anticipation of a wrong to be righted, caught the public fancy. On the day it was said there were more Welsh people in Liverpool than in Cardiff. Liverpool had a significant Welsh community. Many, like their English and French counterparts, were locked out of a heaving, stiflingly packed hall.

Driscoll had trained Jones to a fine peak. He was looking tauter and stronger. (Driscoll, much less cool than he had been in the ring, was up and down off his seat incessantly when one of his stable was in action, and he twitched and swayed as if giving and receiving every blow himself.) This night pupil did master proud.

From the first bell, Jones met Criqui's advancing onslaught head-on.

Criqui had one gear – fast forward. Jones with Driscoll-like lefts sent Criqui's head back faster than Criqui could reluctantly retreat and followed in with crisp punches. He walked through Criqui's counters as though through an ephemeral cloud of mayflies and delivered hurtful straight lefts. One, in the second, sent Criqui staggering sideways and down into a heap, a heap from which it took him nine seconds to rise. Another took him down again. Only the bell saved him the full count.

Criqui was made of hardy Gallic stuff and quite prepared to suffer to get back into the fight. In the meantime, he took many punches and clinched with growing desperation. The Bible (Acts 10:25) claimed it was more blessed to give than to receive. The text had a poignant meaning for pugilists.

Had Driscoll been Criqui's manager he would have pulled Criqui out of the fight halfway through. The French camp showed no such clemency despite Criqui's swollen and bloody face. Criqui had unnecessarily to demonstrate the concrete nature of his chin for the full 20 rounds. (His chin even stopped a German bullet in the trenches, as we will see.) Criqui's sacrificial performance in Liverpool left Jones the winner on points.

Boxing managers in the early 20th century varied from the paternal like Driscoll or Descamps, who felt their boxers' pains and pleasures as if they were their own, to the callous who had no more feeling for their protégées than for a carcass. Ted Kid Lewis, the British featherweight champion after beating Alec Lambert in late 1913, went on to acquire the European title when Paul Til of France was disqualified against him in the 12th round of a match at

Premierland on 2 February 1914.[26] His frustrating relationship with his father was echoed by the one with his early manager, Sam Shear. His fight to get out of Shear's clutches was conducted not in the ring but in the King's Bench Division over a three-day hearing from 18–20 February 1914.[27]

In the title fight Til lost to Lewis's speed and strength, and Referee Keen's xenophobic exasperation. Til did not understand English, especially when shouted at him. In the first and third rounds, this led to incidents more like a Georges Feydeau farce than a boxing match. Til liked to fight at close quarters. Whenever he moved close to Lewis, Keen vigorously and unnecessarily reprimanded him. The bewildered Til mimed his bafflement by looking appealingly at Keen, quizzically raising his shoulders and eyebrows, and spreading his gloves wide. He forgot that 'defend yourself at all times' means the same in any language. Lewis had not, so hooked and uppercut the hapless Til as the audience laughed unkindly at the comedy of the situation. Til was utterly unable to appease Keen, and after many reprimands, issued but certainly not understood, Til was disqualified for holding in the 12th. He had been hard done by, although most thought Lewis in any case an easy points winner.

The legal bout, Lewis v Shear, two weeks later was more evenly fought. Morton Lewis, his father's biographer, gives the case a mere sentence, and Harry Mullan, usually the sharpest of detectors of managerial sharp practice, does not mention the case at all in his chapter on Lewis in his *Heroes and Hard Men*. As the hearing exposed contemporary attitudes behind the scenes of boxing, this is a pity. Sam Shear was the plaintiff arguing that the Kid was contracted exclusively to his management for three years from 13 June 1912 and that he, Shear, had agreed to handle Lewis's career in return for 25 per cent of all Lewis's earnings. Lewis, he claimed, aided and abetted by his father Solomon Mendeloff and Harry Morris, a rival manager and Premierland proprietor, was now trying to get out of the Shear contract to sign with Morris. (This has to be true.)

Shear laid on his case with a trowel. He had been reluctant to sign Lewis, still a junior, but had succumbed to the aggressive pleading of his father Solomon. (Whatever hyperbole Shear was using here, it is difficult not to wince at the cynicism of old Solomon Mendeloff. Here is the father who preferred to send his son out of his workshop and out of his family home rather than have him box. The lad now seen as a potential cash cow, the father steps in again to try to secure a more profitable deal with a new manager. Fatherly concern indeed.)

The deal with Shear was struck in the summer of 1912, by which time Lewis had left the modest Judaean Athletic Club and had fought professionally (six fights in 1911 at The Ring, and 17 fights between January and June 1912 at Premierland). Shear claimed that it was his exertions on behalf of 'the boy' or 'the lad' that had led to the princely earnings of £750 and the Lonsdale Belt. Shear's past sacrifices (unspecified!) now entitled him to his fit and proper share of Lewis's present and future earnings. They should not go to Morris, who had done nothing.

Lewis and his father admitted they had signed a contract with Shear. They wished it annulled because at the time of signing the Kid was technically a junior. Furthermore, Shear had neglected his education and welfare duties towards his protégé. (From that day to this, the boxer who finds in practice that he has unwittingly signed a managerial contract on favourable terms to the manager has little recourse. One of the greatest ever light-heavyweights, Matthew Saad Muhammad, WBC world champion 1979–81, put it eloquently: 'You sweat, you work hard, you spill your blood and then they take away your money!')

As the hearing continued, so did the charges and counter-charges. Far from looking after the 'infant', Shear had taken him to gambling dens and brothels. Shear denied this. In public, at a music hall, Lewis had shouted at Shear and Mrs Shear, used foul language and thrown a wine glass at them. At the next day's hearing, in the witness box, Wally Pickard, straight man and sparring partner in music hall sketches to Lewis and other boxers, admitted he had seen the infamous slanging match but said that the Shears had also used foul language and had thrown a tumbler at Lewis!

On the second day, Solomon Mendeloff was in the witness box. He claimed that Shear had originally approached him (possible); that the Kid had received no money from Shear (unlikely); that as a father he had worried when Shear had deliberately kept the child away from his home (highly unlikely); that Shear had suggested Lewis get himself deliberately disqualified against Alec Lambert in the title match (just possible); and that not only had he warned his son about Shear's dishonesty (then why sign a contract with him?), but he had never even spoken to Morris (also highly unlikely). Other witnesses testified to Shear's slowness to pay debts and to the one-sided nature of his contracts that helped him cream off a commission even from a boxer's legitimate expenses. John Murray, the editor of *Boxing*, had little time for exploitative managers but admitted Shear was no worse than any other greed merchant.

In his summary of guidance for the jury, judge Mr Justice Avery conveyed a fastidious distaste for both parties and suggested the jurors ask themselves whether they could say yes to three propositions: Was the original contract for Lewis's education or instruction for his future benefit? Was the contract beneficent for him overall? Did Morris conspire or maliciously induce Lewis to break his contract? In his address, the judge added his own opinion that far from the infant benefiting from the contract, the real winner was Shear. He, after all, could force Lewis to fight anywhere even if his expenses might exceed his earnings from the fight. Furthermore, if some of the evidence was to be believed, Shear was the last man to be trusted with the welfare of a minor. Taking 25 per cent of gross receipts, instead of 25 per cent of net receipts after legitimate expenses had been deducted was unreasonable.

The jury must have taken a serious dislike to Lewis and his father and Morris, and thoroughly distrusted their evidence, for they decided to ignore all these reasonable judicial hints. They gave affirmative answers to all three questions and awarded £100 damages against Morris and £150 damages against Lewis. Gilbertian is the only word to describe the outcome. Having

consulted and cajoled the jury towards a verdict and getting a contrary one, Mr Justice Avery decided he should not have consulted them at all. Newly interpreting the infamous agreement between the Lewises and Shear, he declared it a trade contract and as such one that could not be binding upon a minor. The Kid and his father were *not* therefore liable as claimed. (A Shear counter-claim on a minor matter was allowed.)

In this sorry affair, the unethical behaviour of both parties was duly exposed to public view. The dirty linen was not to the sport's advantage. Shear's greed was transparent enough, but the role of Solomon Mendeloff, the father converted to his son's boxing only when he saw the chances of a meal ticket for himself, was equally dubious. (It later emerged that Solomon had originally pressed Morris's contract on his son in return for a £20 bribe for himself. Neither man had the youth's welfare at heart, only his earning potential.)

Lewis, free from Shear if not from his father, could now accept fights arranged by Morris or any other promoter. Rather than exploiting his status as British and European champion with serious defences, he chose rather to take two token challenges, winning them easily (14 March, knocking out Harry Berry in three rounds at Premierland; 18 March knocking out Ted Saunders in six rounds in Coventry). Then, to most people's surprise, he sailed to Australia before spring was out and subsequently found his way to Cuba, Canada and the USA. He would not fight again in Britain until Boxing Day 1919; a five-year hiatus that frustrated British fans, promoters and especially the boxers who wanted to challenge him. As many

pointed out, there was an ugly contrast between the flower of English youth volunteering or conscripted to fight in the war from 1914 onwards, and Lewis, able to pursue a glittering and richly rewarded career abroad, safe from a call-up.

Other British boxers pursued their careers domestically. The mightiest of atoms, Jimmy Wilde, spent 1914 doing exactly what he had done in 1913, taking on men to whom he gave weight, height and reach advantages and beating them, usually within the distance. Over the year he fought 20 times, winning them all, and knocking out or retiring his opponent 13 times. Often this was via his left hook, which seemed magically to concentrate all the power his seven-stone frame could muster into his left-hand knuckles with devastating effect. The men in the other corner were not nonentities.

He beat Alf Mansfield twice (27 April on points over 20 rounds in Leeds, and 28 September on a tenth-round retirement in West London Stadium), and Sid Smith (3 December on a ninth-round KO in Liverpool). He defeated the French (30 March, Eugene Husson, by a KO in the sixth at the NSC; and 16 April, Albert Bouzonnie, on a retirement in the sixth in Liverpool). The stubborn little Kid Nutter, who lost twice only on points over 15 rounds (3 January 1914 in the little lion's home den at Tonypandy, and 2 February 1914 at Birkenhead) did comparatively well. Nutter, killed in 1916, was another victim of the First World War.

For a glimpse of Wilde at his pre-war best, it must have been a real privilege to be in the NSC boxing theatre on the night of 11 May 1914.[28] Two delightful Anglo-French contests were held. The old club favourite, Joe Bowker, now 30 years old, the man who had distinguished himself, win or lose, against men such as Owen Moran, Pedlar Palmer and Jim Driscoll, was supposedly past his peak. Bowker thought differently. Matched against a robust Frenchman with acknowledged power in each hand in Robert Dastillon (8st 9¼lb/121¼lbs), Bowker (identical weight) proved his point. Dastillon was born in a Parisian suburb on 29 July 1894, making him almost 11 years the younger.

Bowker's speed of thought and deed were undiminished. Using his left, he kept the formidable Dastillon at arm's length. When Dastillon's profligate swinging punches came at him, Bowker made cool minor adjustments that had them safely grazing his chin or ruffling the hair on the top of his head. Meanwhile, Bowker, just like the Bowker of old, was in and out with short sharp lefts, many of them of Driscoll-like ramrod snap and power. He added clean rights by way of variation. Dastillon, a fighter with a rock-like chin and a steely ribcage, never retreated. Perhaps he remembered that his compatriot Charles Ledoux had also (29 January 1912) suffered total domination by Bowker, only to have the final say when Bowker's concentration had wavered momentarily and Ledoux had nailed him late on. Dastillon was not so lucky and lost on points. Some thought he lost every round. Dastillon's continuing strength brought him a ring career that lasted from 1911 to 1929.

It was a sign of Wilde's growing stature that he could take the NSC ring just after a masterly Bowker performance and impress even more. 'The most wonderful being the sport has ever produced,' said the reporter from *Boxing*. His opponent was Georges Gloria. He had fought twice with Georges Carpentier, once in Paris on 19 February 1909 when he knocked the young man out in the sixth. Carpentier went on maturing, then getting Gloria back to Lens on his home turf on 3 April 1910 had reversed the result with an eighth-round knockout. Carpentier had gained much weight and status since 1909, but Wilde was still facing a Gloria with a known knockout punch and one to whom he was conceding ten pounds.

In the third round Wilde damaged his right hand, a rare event considering how hard he punched. Gloria still found himself the target for thundering punches that might have dropped in from the roof for all he could anticipate them. Bowker's superiority was based on speed in and out, orthodoxy impressive but readily explainable. Wilde's dominance was more mystical. Even as he demonstrated it, spectators strove to comprehend it. His hands were down at thigh level as if a few ounces of leather might tire his relatively skinny arms if he brought them up to guard his chin. Gloria, like many another, suffered those gloves thudding painfully into his nose from unprecedented angles. In contrast to Bowker's dazzling footwork, buzzing around the ring like a fly on speed, Wilde's movements looked sluggish, his evasions economies of movement and energy. They made Gloria's powerful swings miss by a distance and threw him off balance. Then came Wilde's rejoinders, threaded accurately to their target by radar known only to Wilde himself. This was stoat and rabbit – nearer hypnotism than pugilism.

Boxing's enthusiasm for Wilde repeated the conclusion reached by *The Times* after Wilde's previous appearance at the NSC on 30 March 1914. Then he had knocked out Eugene Husson of France in the sixth round. Unhesitatingly, *The Times* had pronounced the Welshman 'certainly the cleverest boxer living'.[29] Husson, a tiny Frenchman, was even smaller than Wilde, 6st 3½lb/87½lbs to Wilde's 6st 10lb/94lbs. There was novelty in seeing Wilde, for once the larger man, stalking someone smaller than he around the NSC ring.[30]

Husson's sensible tactic was to punch Wilde very quickly indeed and accelerate even more speedily away ('like a parched pea on a frying pan'). For all its resemblance to a Tom and Jerry cartoon, the fight was not scripted to give Jerry a victory. Wilde remorselessly cut down the ring to trap Husson into a corner. No sooner was Husson in the corner than he fled again, elusive as ever. After nine or ten minutes of this back-pedalling, interspersed with some impertinent punches to Wilde's expressionless face, Husson slowed marginally to the merely supersonic.

Husson went down to a glancing blow in the fourth, perhaps for a breather. A short right in the fifth took him down for seven. The sixth saw Husson back on his bike but clipping Wilde twice, once to the body and once to the face. Wilde's revenge came before the end of the round. Apparently allowing Husson a convenient escape from a corner, Wilde feinted, and as Husson went for the illusory exit, drove a full-blooded left into Husson's solar plexus. Utterly winded, Husson stayed down. Wilde, the man never outpunched, had declined to be out-sped either.

For Bowker, Wilde, Jones and Lewis, the master plan was to continue their careers in their chosen moulds. For Bombardier Billy Wells, the dilemma was how to break the mould that had so far delighted, tantalised and dashed the hopes of his considerable following. Could he somehow find a new modus vivendi to deliver fully on his early promise? For the moment, his rehabilitation had been moderately impressive.

In ten days in January 1914, he had beaten Gunner Rawles in Belfast and Gaston Pigot in Cardiff. His London supporters, reading of his triumphs on the Celtic fringes, flocked to the Palladium to see whether this progress could be sustained in the West End spotlights. The date was 3 March 1914, and the opponent Bandsman Jack Blake, the East Anglian who had opened 1914 by beating the Dixie Kid.[31] The purse was £1,800 and Wells, ignoring NSC opinions, agreed to defend his British heavyweight title. It was not an even match. Blake was a middleweight.

The Palladium capacity was over 3,000, with every seat affording a reasonable view of the stage. Many of Wells's regular supporters found that richer members of the highly fashionable audience had snapped up the best of the five-guineas stall and dress circle seats. In attendance were peers of the realm such as Lord Lonsdale (cheered to his seat) and the arrogant Lord Ribblesdale (1854–1925), the Liberal Whip in the House of Lords (who disdainfully glowers at us in the brilliant John Singer Sergeant portrait of him in London's National Gallery); entrepreneurs such as the American Gordon Selfridge (1858–

1947), the presiding genius of the giant Oxford Street store opened in 1909; literary figures such as the playwright Sir Arthur Pinero (1855–1934); and a raft of sparkling Edwardian hostesses and actresses in glamorous gowns and jewellery set against the contrasting black and white of the dinner-jacketed men in the front rows and even crowded on the stage itself like hungry Emperor penguins in a blizzard. The boxing boom was still expanding.

The glitterati arriving in their carriages and motor cars inched their way through the heaving crowds in Argyll Street, Argyll Place and Great Marlborough Street. They were all part of the show. Less privileged men and women hung out of every available window and on the rooftops, cheering every celebrity as if they were stars arriving for the Oscars. (Although, the Oscar ceremony did not begin until 15 years later in 1929.) The police cleared paths to the front steps of the theatre for the arrivals. The boys in blue even resorted to the occasional use of the baton to keep proletarian enthusiasm in check. Good humour still prevailed. When a dray cart loaded with barrels arrived, it was greeted by a shout of 'make room for beer for the fighters!'

Inside the theatre, the presence of many women was noticeable – another aspect of the boxing boom. Whatever Parisian women could do, Londoners could match. They were Wells supporters to a woman; handsome vulnerability sexier than East Anglian ruggedness. When the two fighters appeared at 11pm, alike in their lilac robes of only slightly different hues, spotlighted in fierce arc lights, it was Wells who was given the warmer reception.

The raked stage created a slightly sloping ring, pleasant for the customers in the stalls, and one to which the fighters adjusted surprisingly well. Blake, from the first bell, gave Wells a warm reception of his own. He sped across the ring at the opening bell and approached at close quarters. Mindful of the tactics that had served Carpentier so well, he stayed close and peppered away with short hooks and jabs, colouring Wells's paler skin with scarlet patches. When Wells's guard came down, Blake clipped him high on the right cheek and half-closed his right eye.

Blake remained a middleweight tackling a heavyweight. His decision to crowd Wells was no surprise. Wells's initial response was perhaps to demonstrate that he *could* take punches to the midriff and survive, but he did not keep Blake away. He crouched, negating his superior height. He neglected his potent left jab and the driving right and failed to exploit his superior balance and footwork. Rather, head low, he produced some short body blows of his own, yet allowed Blake to win the first round with points-scoring body punches that left those blotches on Wells's torso.

When Wells persisted with the tactics in the second, was he trying to convince his critics or himself? Blake caught him with sharp left hooks and other short punches to the ribs. The punch count was now heavily in Blake's favour. However, shrewder observers noted that a Wells left to the temple and a right to the heart hurt Blake more than Blake was hurting Wells. One straight left, more reminiscent of the old Wells, connected painfully with Blake's nose before he could launch another rally. The trend was still in Blake's favour.

Wells had seemingly settled for winning hard. Blake breathed audibly in the third but hit Wells often with short body punches and even with uppercuts surging up under Wells's crossed arms guard. Blake also connected with long left leads to Wells's bruised right cheek. In eight minutes' fighting, Wells had taken more and Blake thrown more punches than either would normally have done in a full-length contest. Unfortunately for Blake, he had punched himself out. In the last minute of the third, the 13st 10lb/192lbs Wells dominated the 11st 12lb/166lbs Blake. Still in his crouch, Wells hit Blake with short sharp lefts and rights, added a few illegal chopping rabbit punches to the back of Blake's neck, and sent Blake back to his corner wan and groggy.

A minute's grace was insufficient for Blake to recover from this dramatic reverse. He came out for the fourth unsteadily and dangerously upright. Wells, with a determination so often eluding him, ruthlessly pounded Blake about the body, then reverted to his classic style, standing back, measuring the distance with a few tentative prods then delivering three straight punches to Blake's jaw. Blake went over backwards, as flat on the canvas as his county's landscape. His seconds tried, illegally, to revive him with a spray of water but he needed minutes rather than seconds to come round. His subsequent career will be examined later.

Wells had come through a stiff trial, and crowned his success with an impressive knockout, admittedly against a much lighter man. His Wells-can-take-it tactics for two and a half rounds also preserved his Wells-the-

enigma reputation. When the crowds in the street heard the result, they chanted, 'We want Wells!' Neither they nor Wells knew which Wells they would get next.

Among the wanters was the NSC. Wells was invited to return to the club to meet the Irish-American heavyweight James Coffey, dubbed 'The Dublin Giant'.[32] Only hyperbole and the lightness of contemporaries could have made the 13st 10lb/192lbs Coffey a real giant. He was exactly the same weight as Wells had been versus Blake. He knew Wells's style intimately, having accompanied Wells as sparring partner on the unfortunate New York trip of the summer of 1912. The NSC offered a purse of £1,000 – 45 per cent less than the one at the Palladium. As Wells's management quickly pointed out, if Wells were to lose and paid over his share of the side stakes, he would, after expenses, be out of pocket. Wells had no intentions of paying Coffey, who had a strong right hand, for the privilege of being knocked out by him. The offer was definite proof that the club, distinguished in membership and tradition, could no longer compete with commercial promoters who could hire vast arenas and offer boxers such as Wells much more generous purses.

Wells took another offer and met the Frenchman Albert Lurie, French champion until defeated by Georges Carpentier (who stopped him in the third round at Bordeaux on 29 June 1913). Lurie and Wells met, certainly for more money, at the Canterbury Music Hall on 2 April 1914.[33] Lurie had impressively knotted biceps and an upper torso like a mature oak tree. Unfortunately, he also moved with the speed and agility of a mature oak tree.

Wells stood off in the first, warily

guarding that vulnerable midriff. Lurie lumbered slowly towards him. Lurie tried to get inside. Wells moved away. Lurie launched a left. Wells trapped it illegally under his right arm and kept it there on the blind side of referee Baker. (Baker, an Australian, was the middleweight silver medallist who lost to gold medallist J. W. H. T. Douglas in the London Olympics of 1908, but boxing ability does not necessarily a good referee make.)

The stalemate continued for five rounds. Wells stayed out of the reach of Lurie's punches and hit Lurie from a distance. In the sixth the tactics had Lurie down for counts of nine, eight, six, and eight. In the seventh, Lurie sank on one knee and was disinclined to continue. The latest Wells revival did.

The British and the French heavyweight scenes were dominated by one name – Carpentier, the man who had demoted Lurie, Wells and Dick Rice (scheduled to meet Wells in Liverpool before the end of April). Carpentier in 1914 was still not having it all his own way. His year began with that impressive demolition of Pat O'Keefe in Nice. O'Keefe was a believer – after the fight he said, 'You can pick the five best British boxers – including me if you like – and Carpentier would beat the lot in less than five minutes!' It looked that way.

It looked that way until Saturday, 21 March 1914 when Carpentier met the talented Joe Jeannette over 15 rounds at the Luna Park in Paris.[34] There was strong interest in the fight in Britain. *The Times* gave a full half-column to a Saturday preview and two more half-columns to a report in the following Monday's paper. Nothing was made of the black v white aspect of the clash, supposedly so inflammatory, although *The Times* reassured its readers that Jeannette had 'more white blood than black in his veins'. This was of great comfort to all who read it, if not perhaps to Jeannette.

Inside or outside the black quadrille that Jeanette, Johnson, McVea and Langford performed across the world, Jeannette was an experienced and formidable adversary. He fought Johnson seven times – winning, drawing and losing once, with four no-decisions. He often fought in Paris to escape racist restrictions at home. Early in life he drove a coal truck, and many opponents found him about as easy to stop as a coal truck.

Carpentier v Jeannette was a thrilling encounter. Thrilling but very difficult to analyse as some thought Carpentier gallant and courageous but a clear loser. Others had him as a clear winner robbed by an inept referee. Accounts do not agree even on the details of the morning weigh-in. (Carpentier 12st 2lb/170lbs v Jeannette 13st 9lb/191lbs according to *The Times*; Carpentier 12st 1lb/169lbs v Jeannette 13st 2lb/184lbs according to *Boxing*; Carpentier 11st 11lb/165lbs according to his autobiography.) With such discrepancies over discernible statistics, it is impossible a century later to form any clear conclusion about the fight.

Carpentier was certainly much the lighter man. He moved around the ring, circling Jeannette, who commanded the centre. He launched long jabs and swings at Jeannette from a respectful distance, while Jeannette bustled forward to close and throw short hooks, jabs and uppercuts that made his extra power tell. Jeannette was adept at moving his head minimally to avoid the punches that had put so many Carpentier opponents on their backs. But he could not evade them all. A clean right caught him on the jaw in the first. Down went Jeannette and up went the Luna Park crowd in a noisy frenzy. The high-pitched screams of many women, dazzling in costume jewellery and purple, green, yellow and blue wigs, registered their delight at seeing their slim blond hero upright with his statuesque opponent down at his feet. The ecstasy lasted but three seconds, which was all it took for Jeannette to spring up and get in a heavy right uppercut of his own.

So it continued, each fighter claiming successes and sometimes punishment. Carpentier, swiftly in and out with left leads, took the fourth and probably the sixth. Jeannette, close in and angry at a Carpentier butt under his chin, landed two heavy right hooks to stagger Carpentier back to the ropes and followed in with right and left hooks to the ribs to win the seventh. Apart from occasional lapses like Carpentier's butt and Jeannette's attempts to grasp Carpentier with the left to punch him with the right, this was a clean contest. Referee Frantz Reichel was spared the task of separating the men in the eighth as they spent most of the round punching at close quarters and driving each other back and forth like two bulls testing each other's strength. Only at the end did Carpentier break off, and that was to land two swings to the head that stunned Jeannette just before the bell.

Despite the weight discrepancy, Carpentier showed he had trained hard and planned to last the full 15 rounds. He knew Jeannette capable of lasting a full 45. Carpentier slowed a little in the three rounds before the final one when both men staged a toe-to-toe finish. Carpentier always believed he had won and tearfully asserted so in his dressing room. Forty years later, in his autobiography, he was still claiming victory: 'I had command of the fight from the start and kept it throughout the whole of the fifteen round contest, which was a very testy one.'

Carpentier's view contradicts other facts. He took a severe uppercut in the 11th, another in the 12th that opened an ugly gash across his cheek, heavy punches around the body in the 13th and came out for the 15th showing signs of wear and tear in other cuts, abrasions and swellings. Jeannette, unmarked, delivered heavier and more effective punches. Carpentier's version of the reception of the verdict ('an indescribable tumult … in which the fittings and fixtures of Luna Park took a good deal of punishment') is not in accord with the British eyewitnesses present. ('And yet the most marvellous of the whole affair … was the comparatively quiet manner with which it was received,' *Boxing*; '"Vive Carpentier!" was shouted again and again by thousands, and "A bas l'arbitre" [Down with the ref] by a few,' *The Times*.)

Carpentier, unjust loser or gallant in defeat, was still the hero to his huge army of supporters, thousands of them outside the Luna Park ticketless. They waited for him until 1am and chaired him through the streets to his apartment. Outside the block they refused to disperse and chanted 'CAR-PEN-T-IER' until he waved to them from his window. The spectacle was worthier than the one he was involved in a few weeks later, more suitable for the pages of *Comic Cuts* than the *Sporting Life*.

A well-known English amateur boxer, George Mitchell, of the prominent Yorkshire brewing family, struck a bet with his friends that for £1,000 he could not only face Carpentier in the ring but last longer than the British heavyweight champion. (Carpentier knocked out Wells in 73 seconds.) The friends approached Carpentier and offered him 5,000 francs to face Mitchell privately before an invited audience of 150 and give the Englishman a chance to fulfil his boast. Carpentier was tickled, like most people, at an opportunity of earning 5,000 francs for a few minutes' work. He agreed.

The encounter took place in Paris on 14 April 1914.[35] Carpentier was not allowed to pull his punches. Carpentier, ever the total professional with an eagle eye for an opening, was as good as his word. He advanced on Mitchell with his right hand out. Mitchell, the gallant young English amateur, took this as an invitation to shake hands. As he went to grasp the hand, he was thumped in the ribs with the left and, as he doubled up, clipped on the chin with the supposedly friendly right. Boys were ill advised to play with men.

Still, the burly and strong Mitchell (14st/196lbs and 6ft 3in), floored by the first attack, did get up after nine. Carpentier knocked him down again three more times. Each time Mitchell dragged himself up. Seconds after Mitchell had won his bet, the referee stopped the show before Carpentier could administer another final punch. The clock showed 1 minute 35 seconds had elapsed. The merry company finished the night with a celebratory dinner at an excellent French restaurant,

the French waiters unfazed by the sight of a bruised Englishman, peering from a black and swollen left eye while calling for champagne in honour of a Frenchman who had just beaten him up.

Tragically, Mitchell, like many such privileged Oxbridge men, graduated and went straight into the army as a junior officer. In his case, his next visit to Europe, as for many of his generation, was final. He never returned to Britain but died, killed in France. Boxing, amateur and professional, just like every aspect of British society, would be grievously affected by the outbreak of the First World War in August 1914. Yet throughout May, June and July 1914, no one from the humble down-the-bill scrapper to the most affluent promoter gave it a thought.

The problem was still supposedly white men fighting black men in the ring. Bizarre inconsistencies continued. The Paris encounter between Carpentier and Jeannette was eagerly followed and reported in London. Jeannette was in London often. He would fight at Premierland on 4 May 1914 against the white Australian Colin Bell over 20 rounds with what result we shall see below. In the 10 February boxing jamboree at the Palladium, he boxed three exhibition rounds with (the white) Bink McKlosky. At that event, Sam Langford, the Dixie Kid and Jim Johnson – all black – had featured and been enthusiastically applauded.

The Dixie Kid often fought in British rings against white opponents, for example, the fight against Bandsman Blake at The Ring on 1 January 1914, and another against Bill Bristowe on 6 April 1914, also at The Ring, when he won by a second-round knockout. And that other great black fighter, Sam

Langford, had been mismatched with Petty Officer Curran over 20 rounds. That had been at Luna Park in Paris on 24 January 1914. Langford took seven seconds to knock out Curran, who was booed out of the hall. Two days later, Langford was an honoured guest at the NSC at Bettinson's benefit night and given an ovation for so resounding a victory over a white British fighter.[36] In Covent Garden, in a star turn he shared the ring with two black comedians. He could tell jokes and clown around but not fight there. Where was the consistency in these events?

On 16 March 1914, *The Times* began a series of articles on the theme 'The Revival of Boxing'.[37] Its anonymous correspondent heralded boxing's return to a truly national pastime over the preceding five years. He pointed to a fivefold increase in participants, amateur and professional; to crowds rivalling the Boat Race or Derby Day; to boxing's part in university and public-school life; to its rivalling soccer for popularity in the services. He also implied royal approval reminiscent of Regency days by pointing out that His Majesty King George V, that very afternoon, was attending a Life Guards boxing tournament. Thus boxing could claim 'the right of this essentially English sport to the regard of all sorts and conditions of Englishmen'. All sorts and conditions did not include a black skin.

The *Times* writer's general conclusion was, correctly, that 'the swift and scientific game of today' was far superior to the crude and corrupt prizefighting of the 18th and 19th centuries; superior in skill and morality alike:

No men live more austerely than the fashionable boxers of today;

the brightness of their looks; the fineness of their features, so vividly contrasting with the heavy aspect of the prize-ring heroes, prove that they subject themselves to a discipline that is spiritual as well as physical … Physically and morally the nation must profit from the revival of boxing.[38]

The physical and spiritual discipline of, say, Iron Hague, might be restricted to the pint and the pork pie, but most fighters did follow dedicated fitness regimes. The *Times* writer had reservations about their all-round tactics:

… with a few exceptions in the lighter divisions, our professional champions cannot hold their own against the intelligent foreigner; for many years past our best middle-weights and heavy-weights have been only too obviously outclassed by their American rivals, and, more recently, by French boxers who have adopted the American style of fighting … the French boxers decided that the American style was superior to the English, and that infighting is as indispensable a part of the modern game as out-fighting. The victories of Carpentier, Ledoux, Criqui, and other French boxers are a proof that they were wise in deciding that a system of offence and defence based on the 'straight left' is not sufficient nowadays.[39]

This was perceptive, as was the writer's wistful conclusion that the home countries produced large, tough second-row rugby forwards yet failed to find a genuine heavyweight boxer big enough and skilful enough to compete at world level. The author was not to know it would take another 85 years until 13 November 1999 when a boxer with some British credentials, Lennox Lewis, won a unified version of the world heavyweight championship. But then Lewis was black. Had he been around in 1914 he would have been prevented from meeting white rivals. The NSC adhered to the custom secretly agreed by Lord Lonsdale with the Home Office that fights between black fighters and white fighters were highly undesirable. As any divisional champion was only officially champion if he won the title and the Lonsdale Belt against an opponent chosen by the club, on the club premises, and refereed by a club official, how could any black fighter *ever* win a championship?

The members treated Langford as an honoured guest (when not fighting a white opponent), yet a more accurate picture of attitudes can be seen in what Ben Bennison, biographer and prominent member of the club, wrote in the *Daily Telegraph* in November 1922: 'In all my long experience I have known but very few negroes who, once they had beaten a white fighter of high degree, did not become insufferable.' It was all down to Jack Johnson again:

When Johnson first came to this country he was a modest, a tractable [!] negro; from the day he beat Tommy Burns … he was a menace not only to sport, but to law and order. The scandal of his fight with Jim Jeffries made it impossible for a white and black man ever to fight again for a world's title. [Or fight at the NSC.]

The exclusivity of title and belt jealously guarded by the NSC was not matched by their ability to muster an attractive purse to match the more affluent promoters. That NSC offer of £1,000 to Wells to meet Coffey at the club compared poorly with the £1,800 Wells got for beating Blake at the Palladium, and even worse with the £4,500 on the table at the Stadium, Liverpool to attract Carpentier and Gunboat Smith to fight for a light-heavyweight title.[40,41] Dick Burge at The Ring offered Carpentier £5,000 to fight at Blackfriars against Gunboat.[42] Burge was frank: 'There is much more money for boxing in London than in Paris.'

Wells accepted a lesser purse – £900 – to go to Liverpool on 30 April 1914 to meet Bandsman Dick Rice, a cruiserweight not expected to trouble him. Wells thought of this as a carefree outing. He played a round of golf on the morning of the fight.[43] He more than earned the money. Wells outboxed Rice as expected, but significantly failed to knock him out in the early rounds. Rice meanwhile landed some painful blows, some in the kidneys and others below the belt, not seen by the referee, even one that floored Wells in the seventh. A tiring and suffering Wells mauled his way to a narrow points victory over the full 20 rounds (£45 a distressing round).[44] The decision was not popular, especially as Wells had done little but lean and wrestle for the latter half of the fight. The only plus for a bruised and exhausted Wells were moral lessons that training was not to be skimped and no opponent taken for granted. He was notably fitter the next time he fought.

Days later, 4 May 1914, came a curious defiance of the secret ban on black v white contests. Premierland matched the white Australian Colin Bell in a heavyweight contest against the black American Joe Jeannette. Presumably, the authorities missed the negotiations and contract arrangements until it was embarrassingly late to do anything about it. Or perhaps the fight had a low enough profile to be tolerated as an experiment. The first is more likely, for how can a parallel case be explained?

On 30 April 1914, five days before the Bell v Jeannette fight took place, another London promoter, C. B. Cochran, signed up two prominent Americans – Gunboat Smith (white) and Sam Langford (black) – for a fight in London on 30 June 1914. Cochran was told by the Home Office, and by its willing emissary Lord Lonsdale, that the fight was to be banned:

> C. B. Cochran … explaining his position tonight, said that Lord Lonsdale had informed him that he believed there was a strong feeling at the Home Office against black and white contests. Cochran saw the Home Office authorities and learned that there was a distinct feeling against such contests because the question of a black and white contest becomes a matter for discussion, and this is considered against public policy, and is likely to do harm in the Empire.[45]

Cochran's later account (1945) confirms the substance of the *New York Times* report. He also shows that Lonsdale's influence behind the scenes saved Home Secretary McKenna from a possibly embarrassing lawsuit:

I had ascertained that there was nothing against the match from the police point of view, and also that *under the existing law the Government had no power whatever to stop such a meeting,* so I proceeded with my plans … [Italics added]

Cochran was summoned by telephone to breakfast with Lonsdale at the lord's London address and charmed out of his venture:

> The Home Office had decided that it would be highly prejudicial to our colonial interest at this time if a clash between a coloured man and a white took place in London, a clash which would involve a considerable amount of publicity and *reclame* [publicity]. Some way would certainly be found to prevent it … Lord Lonsdale gave me much confidential information of so decisive a character that I at once decided to call the match off on my own initiative.
>
> It was altogether a curious experience, and was rendered even more notable, in a different way, by the fact that it was the first time in my life I had ever drunk a fine Berncastler [*sic* – i.e. a Mosel wine from Bernkastel in Germany] with my breakfast, though there have been rare occasions on which a Rhine or Moselle has seemed to me more stimulating than tea or coffee.[46]

Thus did the contents of Lord Lonsdale's cellar save the British Empire.

The Times of London confirmed such official attitudes would continue in the future:

> The recent announcement that Sam Langford and Gunboat Smith will not meet in London … owing to the Home Office authorities, has been taken as a warning … that there is to be no more black and white boxing of consequence in this country. Even a return match between Jeannette and Colin Bell … would not be countenanced to the sorrow of all professional promoters, who know that such a contest would fill the largest hall in London.

The Times felt it obligatory to point to events four years before at Reno as a supposed object lesson, one 'which caused trouble wherever a coloured population has to be kept in hand by a few white men, [and] ought never to be forgotten'. The newspaper believed that modern communications made matters worse:

> In the days of the old prize ring news travelled so slowly that a black-and-white prize-fight was never the source of mutinous ambitions at the circumference of the Empire; today … information by telegram as to the chance of a contest of the kind is eagerly read by half-educated natives and the black man's victory is hailed as a proof that the hegemony of the white race is approaching its end.

Quite how news that Sam Langford had beaten a fellow American in London was going to provoke an Indian mutiny or a new Zulu war was obscure. Only the fears of the white writer are transparent. And they were so strong that he felt he had to warn Parisians that their general Gertrude Stein-like belief that a boxing match was a boxing match was a boxing match was mistaken:

> … it would not be surprising if public opinion in France was eventually aroused against such costly and much-discussed events. France also possesses an empire of dependencies with coloured inhabitants in which there has sometimes been talk of a 'Black Peril' and patriotic Frenchmen are beginning to remember these facts.[47]

The Premierland contest between Colin Bell and Joe Jeannette on 4 May 1914 passed off as peacefully as anyone could have wished. Even the slightly dubious verdict granted to Jeannette over 20 rounds provoked no colonial unrest.

Had Colin Bell (b. 6 October 1883), the reigning Australian heavyweight, walked unknown into one of the world's gymnasia, he would have been welcomed as the living answer to a trainer's prayers. He was reasonably tall yet thickset, and topped the scales stripped at 14st/196lbs with little excess fat or blubber. He was strong, with clearly defined muscles in the right places. Far from being a muscle-bound bodybuilder, fit only for modelling, he was a genuine athlete. He ran 100yds in even time, long-jumped over 23ft and cleared 6ft at the high jump. Unfortunately, he never quite delivered what his weigh-in appearances promised. He achieved an honourable draw against Sam Langford in Australia

(19 June 1913 over 15 rounds at Rockhampton, Queensland), but lost twice to Sam McVea (19 April 1913, knocked out in 16 rounds in Adelaide, and 26 December 1913 knocked out in two rounds in Sydney).

At Premierland he was at his best. He avoided Jeannette's heavier punches and scored freely with his left to head and body. Jeannette flagged after the early rounds. This was unsurprising, as he had fought two days before. Being the resilient man he was, he rallied in the last few rounds but most spectators assumed by then that he needed a knockout to win, a knockout he could not manage. 'Most' did not include referee Joe Palmer, who gave him a points victory over Bell anyway. The packed crowd disagreed and booed heartily. Empire risings did not follow.

Whatever happened or did not happen in London, the black v white issue coalesced, as usual, around the controversial figure of Jack Johnson. Johnson was still the holder of the world title. At the beginning of 1914 he was in exile from the USA, a convicted felon who could not go home again without being put into jail. He was leading an uneasy life, sometimes in Britain and sometimes in France, desperately seeking engagements to sustain his sybaritic lifestyle. For him, belts were not for tightening but for exploiting.

White racists all over the world would have been happy to see him deposed, in any fashion. Not that the racism was always conscious. For example, a journalist wrote in the 23 May 1914 issue of *Boxing* an article generally favourable to black boxers, yet demonstrating his naïve assumptions about human biology:

> … it has been scientifically and medically recognised that the higher a man's intellect, the more he is sensitive to pain. Here again we have some explanation of the greater physical endurance of the black man as compared with his white ditto.

Others, lacking such misguided certainties, would not mind Johnson losing his title – so long as it were in the ring, beaten squarely by a better boxer. Back in early November 1913, the embryo organisation formed in Paris with the express intention of controlling international boxing affairs, where Britain, the USA and Australia generally did their own thing with scant regard for others, met for the second time.[48] The organisation, which more in hope than reality dubbed itself the International Boxing Union, declared the world heavyweight championship vacant, because 'it considered that Jack Johnson is no longer qualified to claim the title'. The motivation was not racist as the Union also suggested, sensibly enough, that a match between Joe Jeannette and Sam Langford be arranged to decide the new champion.

By January 1914, *The Times* thought the French might have a point:

> There is no precedent for deposing an unbeaten champion in this summary style. None the less all those who have the best interests of the game at heart will agree with the majority of French judges in refusing to accept Johnson as holder of the world's heavy-weight championship.[49]

The Times could patronise but find nothing bad to say about Messrs Langford and Jeannette personally ('such well-conducted and unassuming negro fighters'). The paper was impaled upon its self-created dilemma. A white challenger could hardly depose a new black champion if black v white contests were forbidden. It fell back on the feeblest cliché: 'Yet it is absolutely certain that … public opinion would stop any black and white contest for the heavy weight championship, just as it put an end to the attempt to bring off a fight between Johnson and Wells in London.'

This was extremely disingenuous. *Some* members of the public (e.g. Meyer's congregation) might dislike the idea of black v white fights. *Others*, and enough others to have bought a million tickets had such an arena been available, would have been very happy to have seen Johnson, or Jeannette, or Langford fighting a British fighter such as Wells for the title in London. Public opinion had not stopped Johnson–Wells; the Home Office and the magistrates' court had. Furthermore, although some boxing historians put the ban down wholly to the misdemeanours of Johnson, the article in *The Times* makes it certain that none of the exemplary-behaved Jeannette, Langford, McVea trinity was acceptable either.

To the dismay of *The Times*, Johnson was still receiving offers. In January 1914, C. B. Cochran offered a purse of £6,000 – to be split £5,000 to the winner and £1,000 to the loser – for Johnson to meet Langford at Olympia on 30 June 1914 when the extra seating put in for the International Horse Show would conveniently extend capacity.[50] Even the NSC was prepared

to put up their biggest purse ever – £3,000, offer open until 1 March – for Johnson to meet Langford on club premises. So potentially attractive a fight permitted Bettinson to swallow his pride, wounded by Johnson's long-standing failure to return to the club after beating Burns. (The morality of negotiating with a felon escaping justice at home was conveniently forgotten in the excitement. And what might Lonsdale have said to the Home Office had the deal come off?) Johnson was less inclined to suppress old slights, and enjoyed rubbing it in. He wrote to Bettinson from Paris on 9 February 1914 with the bluntest response:

> I must say that the offer which you have made me is absolutely ridiculous to my thinking. I have defeated Langford, and not only that, Langford has been beaten four times in the last two years … and the only thing I can get out of the fight is money, because there will be no glory in defeating Langford as I have already done the trick … Mr C. B. Cochran, of the Olympia, London, has offered me £5,000. Why should I accept £3,000?[51]

The bravado is down to the slights Johnson felt he had received from NSC officials in the past. Since his enforced flight from the USA he had made appearances for much less than £3,000, although one can quite see the discrepancy between the club's £3,000 and Cochran's £5,000. The late 1913 wrestling and the music hall appearances in the British provinces brought as much rebuff and trouble as profit. In January 1914, the Stoke-on-

Trent magistrates closed the Hanley main hall rather than suffer a Johnson exhibition. The Wolverhampton Free Churches campaigned against his presence at the Wolverhampton Empire in February 1914. The Swansea Watch Committee objected to a projected appearance there, also in February.[52] Had the contract with Cochran for Olympia and Langford actually been signed, perhaps the Home Office would have vetoed it just like Langford and Smith.

Johnson landed a fight against a white opponent on 27 June 1914 at the Vélodrome d'Hiver in Paris. The opponent was a fellow American, the red-haired Frank Moran, owner-occupier of the patent sleep-dispenser 'Mary Ann'. The financial arrangements for the fight, with deals, double-deals, and the making and breaking of solemn promises, were a shambles. The fight was no better.

The promoter was Charlie McCarty (possibly McCarthy) of San Francisco, a one-time Coney Island showman. He promised $40,000, split 75:25 in Johnson's favour, but by the time of the fight, McCarty was no longer around.[53] The purse dwindled to a private agreement between the fighters to split the gate and the movie rights between them.[54] Bizarrely, it was announced that Georges Carpentier himself would trade dressing gown and shorts for tennis whites and referee the fight. Considering how few fights Johnson had had since July 1910 (two), surely few Parisians would risk their hard-earned francs on tickets? *Au contraire*, all fashionable Paris decided to be there as if this were the latest Diaghilev balletic extravaganza, 'The Ginger Beauty and the Black Beast'.[55]

27 June 1914, Paris: the passive and distant referee is Georges Carpentier as Moran and Johnson disappoint.

Prints & Photographs Division, Library of Congress, LC-USZ62-130084

Bathed in brilliant pink and green lights set up for the film cameras, the audience was a spectacle in its own right: rich Americans temporarily in Paris such as robber barons Gould and two Vanderbilts; affluent Frenchmen, including Rothschilds; politicians from the National Assembly; rajahs, princes and maharajahs; many ultra-glamorous women in haute couture. With a sprinkling of the more outré, such as Jeanne Bourgeois (better known as the chanteuse Mistinguett) and the music hall artiste and pornographer turned novelist Colette, the well-heeled multitude crowded into the converted cycle Vélodrome and paid over 181,000 francs (c. £7,240) for the privilege.

Moran, a devout Roman Catholic, sought a Papal benediction for his crusade, and many a candle was lit in Parisian churches in supplication. He needed divine assistance if Mary Ann were to penetrate Johnson's tight defences. Her best dates had been with ponderous boxers waiting patiently for her much-telegraphed delivery. Even a rusty Johnson would not tarry for her visit.

Johnson settled in the centre. Moran circled around him, throwing punches from a distance. Moran was cautious but tired of poking out feelers and having them caught contemptuously in mid-air by the unruffled Johnson. He reverted to swinging and hoping. Johnson calmly avoided the punches and uppercut Moran while he was still off balance. At least once Moran missed so badly he nearly fell out of the ring.

Moran's eyebrows, nose and mouth showed Johnson's counters could hurt. Nevertheless, having trained hard, he was not giving in easily. There was no let-up either in the abuse directed at Johnson from Moran's corner. Moran's

seconds, who included Willie Lewis, forgot that Corbett's insults at Reno in 1910 had inspired Johnson rather than Jeffries.

Johnson, feeling his 36 years, needed all the adrenaline that he could muster to get through 20 rounds. Carpentier gave him a severe wigging in the tenth when Moran obeyed a call to break and Johnson caught him flush on the nose with a short-arm jab. By the 20th, Johnson could hardly raise a smile let alone a jab.

Johnson haters in the audience howled at the punch on the break, and almost as loudly when a Moran left swing caught Johnson on the cheek. Unfortunately, it was more a loud slap than a punch and the cheers died when Johnson put his gloves together and ironically clapped the effort. The last three rounds were interminable. Johnson, desperately weary, smothered and clinched and leaned on Moran and somehow survived. Carpentier awarded Johnson the points victory.

Post-fight, both men licked their wounds without recompense. The long-lost promoter McCarty reappeared to serve an injunction to have the takings impounded by a court until he could lay his claim to part of the profits. Other accounts suggest Dan McKetrick, Moran's subsequent manager, frustrated at attempts to get Moran to sign with him exclusively, was the man who had the money impounded.[56] Either way, the money was lodged with the court and out of the reach of Johnson and Moran.

This was a tragedy, especially for the strapped Johnson, as the money disappeared into the maws of the court. It never emerged because all records of its whereabouts were lost in the turmoil of the First World War, now less than two months away.

A few hours after the Johnson–Moran fight, on 28 June 1914, a Serbian student, Gavrilo Princep, fired the starting pistol for the war so to speak. His shot killed Archduke Franz Ferdinand, heir to the Habsburg monarchy, and plunged all Europe into the diplomatic impasse that produced the Great War.

If the English journal *John Bull*, creation of the notorious fraudster Horatio Bottomley, can be believed (it often couldn't), Johnson made a private bargain with Moran on the day of the fight. Supposedly, Johnson agreed to share the purse – 60 per cent Johnson to 40 per cent Moran – providing Moran lost inside eight rounds. To support its story, the 18 July 1914 issue of *John Bull* reproduced a typescript document dated 27 June 1914 that states baldly:

> I hereby agree to devide [*sic*] of receipts of my contest with Frank Moran on June 27th on a basis of forty percent to Moran and sixty percent to me provided that Frank Moran loses inside of eight rounds.[57]

To this stark sentence is added, in what appears to be Johnson's hand, although only expert scrutiny of the now lost original could prove it, the cryptic note: 'Jack Johnson after fight must return this receipt [*sic*].'

It is difficult to take the document at face value. The errors are crude for a man like Johnson who prided himself on his literary pretensions. Also, what *point* could such a document have? An illegal fix was unenforceable in a court of law. No claims could be made on the basis of the paper. A fix has to

be verbal and secret to work. Johnson, like everyone else involved in this dodgy enterprise, had a vested interest in the action proceeding *after* eight rounds – the longer the fight, the more valuable the film rights. Furthermore, the contemporary report of the fight published in the *New York Times* of 28 June 1914 proffers a different 'agreement' altogether:

> Mortimer Schiff, sitting near The New York Times representative … said; 'Moran must have an agreement not to be knocked out or he never would have entered the ring. Johnson hits where he pleases and unless he has lost his punch utterly he can end it any minute'.
>
> The New York Times also learned today that the cinematographic people were considerably anxious, fearing that Johnson might lose his temper and knock out Moran, thus violating their understanding, but Johnson's good humor never wavered.

The *John Bull* feature makes it clear that the man who passed the dubious fix document to the magazine was Dan McKetrick, promoter and, at the time, Moran's manager; that is, a man with reason to damage Johnson and Moran. The glamour of fight night at the Vélodrome did not extend to the dubious goings-on behind the scense – whatever they were.

With the boxing boom in full swing in London, the English capital was as prestigious and glittering as Paris. The scene cried out for exploitation by a promoter/impresario who thought

on the grand scale and gambled on big promotions. There was one such: Charles Blake Cochran – later Sir Charles.[58] Cochran exuded theatricality and glamour and risk.

It was not always so. One of many children of a Brighton cigar and tea merchant, young Cochran was sent to a local grammar school in the 1880s but did not go on to a university. Instead he made an abortive attempt at a career as a music hall performer. He then tried his luck in the USA, lacking only money for the fare and the business capital. He made up the deficiencies with a 'loan' from his father's office; a loan for which neither father nor firm was consulted. He returned to London by 1899.

A pattern for his life was established – a bottomless supply of chutzpah and charm to make good any deficiencies in funds. He went bankrupt at least twice, yet few bankrupts can have been serenaded by his creditors with a chorus of 'For he's a jolly good fellow!' He died in an accident in 1951 when he was scalded in an extremely hot bath, an event cynics disbelieved on the grounds that the man had been in hot water all his life but always survived.

His entertaining autobiographical accounts are not reliable in detail. When he tells us that he promoted Fred Walsh at Olympia in 1913, we have to guess that he really means Freddie Welsh in 1914. His first love was theatre, and although his early American productions had some intellectual pretensions, for example, Ibsen and Rostand, he soon grasped that the theatrical might profitably include all sorts of presentations:

> I am – and I pride myself on it – a showman, and it is part of a

showman's business to sense the public taste, and, if he can, to forestall its demands … Actuated primarily by love of boxing, when I saw this interest growing by leaps and bounds it occurred to me that there was a good chance to step in as impresario, showman, or whatever you like to call me. At that time the National Sporting Club was the official home of the sport, but it was comparatively small … and it would soon find it impossible to stage championship contests for the gigantic stakes which were beginning to be asked for by the boxers and their managers.[59]

He turned to boxing in 1914 (not 1913 as he says) having dabbled in England in a real mélange of entertainments, including the deeply serious (a famous 700-strong production of Max Reinhardt's *The Miracle* at Olympia in December 1911 turned the arena into a cathedral lit with stained-glass windows, and the audience into a congregation).[60] Others were bizarre (magic with Harry Houdini; wrestling with Georges Hackenschmidt and Youssuf Ishmaeli the Terrible Turk; zoo animals at Olympia; freak shows and performing fleas). In the 1930s he enhanced his reputation with productions of plays by Noël Coward – intimate ones such as *Private Lives* of 1930 and monumental ones such as *Cavalcade* of 1931. After the Second World War, he staged the long-running ultra-English musical *Bless the Bride*.

A man with such catholic tastes and theatrical flair was bound to be drawn to boxing, the most dramatic of sports. A prominent ringsider at every major fight bill he put together, and a groupie before the term was invented, he was as happy to be seen with boxers as he was with actors. Adding an exotic air to contract negotiations with his full regalia of shiny bowler, glinting monocle and Savile Row suits, topped by his choleric red cheeks, his greedy eye permanently scanned the current company for attractive young ladies, actresses and dancers in particular.

On Monday, 11 May 1914, he attended the *Sporting Life* offices to have Colin Bell and Bombardier Billy Wells sign a contract for a 20-round fight at Olympia in June billed for the 'British Empire Heavyweight Championship'. The purse was £2,000 (£1,200 to the winner), modest enough in view of the ambitious bill, but Cochran's flamboyant get-ups concealed a hard nose for negotiations.[61] The boxers signed and departed for the NSC, where they watched that evening the Joe Bowker v Robert Dastillon fight. Bowker's heroics were conducted for a share of a £340 purse, Bettinson and the NSC being even more frugal than Cochran.

That same May night, the Drury Lane Theatre was in the middle of a Joseph Beecham season of music and ballet of the highest quality (Richard Strauss conducting his own operas; Feodor Chaliapin the great Russian bass as *Boris Godunov*; Tamara Karsavina, the wonderful Russian ballerina in Stravinsky's *Petrushka*) where the prices varied from 5s. to £1 10s. at the highest. It was people such as the cultured Drury Lane audience that Cochran wanted to lure to Olympia for Wells v Bell.

Most accounts suggest he succeeded. He sold 10,000 seats at prices from 5s. up to five guineas and took in about £6,500.[62] Cochran took a block in the centre of the U-shaped auditorium and split it into eight wedge-shaped sections of seats ranging from one to five guineas depending on their proximity to the action. At the next mezzanine level, a central seat cost one guinea, and places less close went by degrees from 10s. 6d. to 7s. 6d. to 5s. Above the mezzanine was the gallery with views ranging from the acceptably aerial to the ludicrously telescopic and priced accordingly at 10s. 6d., 7s. 6d. and 5s. For the elite, there was the royal box enclosure with seats at five, three and two guineas. On the night, standing room was sold until full. Could he have collected £1 for everyone collected in the streets around Olympia merely to hear the result, he might have topped £10,000.

Bell conceded about four inches to Wells's 6ft 3in, yet was three pounds heavier than Wells's 13st 7lb/189lbs because of his stockier frame. He was big-chested, lantern-jawed and had biceps that rippled ominously. Had Bell's loss to Joe Jeannette on 4 May 1914 left physical and psychological scars from which he had yet to recover? Was the Bombardier's rehabilitation complete, remembering his miserable surrenders in the past? Cochran exploited the questions and the unprecedented enthusiasm for the sport. Wells v Bell at Olympia on Saturday, 30 June 1914 became as big an occasion as British boxing ever offered.[63] Wells's supporters claimed that since the one-round fiasco against Carpentier (December 1913), Wells had fought more frequently and more successfully than ever – Rawles, Pigot, Blake and Lurie all despatched. He had beaten Bandsman Rice at the Liverpool Stadium, where as many favourites had fallen as at the nearby

Aintree racecourse, despite Wells's infamous morning round of golf.

Among Wells agnostics was *The Times*:

> On form Wells, even if he is properly prepared for this contest … has no chance whatever of winning.[64]

The newspaper referred to Wells as 'the neurotic English champion', ignoring the fact that Wells's neuroses had brought him so many supporters, including the women heavily represented at Olympia on the night:

> They graced that brilliant assembly by their charms, and imparted to the scene the aspect of a tourney in the days of chivalry.[65]

Cochran also exploited this angle, staging the entry of Wells, suddenly contender for the title of Chaucer's verray parfit gentil knight, as decorously and pageant-like as if Max Reinhardt were staging it:

> The contest was noteworthy, first, for the fact that the Rev. Everard Digby, the well-known sporting parson, acted as master of ceremonies, while many of the principal seats were occupied by fashionably dressed women. It was announced several days ago that a number of society women had bought tickets for the fight …
>
> There were women in every section of the immense audience, but seemed to be more in seats costing from 1 guinea to 5 guineas

than in those costing 5 shillings. They drove up in evening dress in their motor cars and they walked across the sanded floor of the great arena as calmly as if they were walking into the opera, and just held their skirts and evening cloaks up so as not to sweep the sand. A few of them sat in the circle seats immediately around the ring, where they could see every blow to the best advantage, and during nearly a couple of hours of boxing they looked on as unconcernedly as if listening to a sermon.[66]

Clearly the American reporter expected the society women to fulfil their stereotypes, refuse to walk over sand lest a grain stuck to their gowns or shoes, and to suffer a fit of the vapours when two fighters went into action in front of them. London ladies were made of sterner stuff. By 1914, roles previously allocated to gender did not necessarily apply. Bolder women left the boudoir for the ringside. Some donned the gloves and had a go themselves. As a sideshow to the Chantilly races in Paris in March 1914, about 400, mostly British, stable lads and jockeys formed the enthusiastic audience for a bout billed as the 'World *Female* Boxing Championship' between Mlle Carpentier (no relation) and Mlle Warner. After three furious rounds – in which both ladies were warned for over-enthusiasm – Mlle Carpentier knocked out a bruised and battered Mlle Warner in the fourth. The times they were a-changing.[67]

American women, like their British and French sisters, were attending boxing matches too. Within a few weeks of the Olympia fight, the American

journalist Djuna Barnes was sharing with the readers of the *New York World Magazine* of 23 August 1914 her impressions of a bill at Brown's Athletic Club on Long Island:

> … through a blue mist of tobacco smoke, gleam rows of human faces, and feminine laughter rings out in a shrill, piercing scale. I, a woman, join the others and watch the women come.
>
> They do not appear self-conscious, nor is there anything in their behavior to indicate that the situation is unusual … they finger their chatelaines [key-chains] and speak of the boxers' build. The men who make up the audience are opulent and portly; they smoke cigars; their hands, gesticulating, gleam with a flash of diamonds. The women are frail, slender-throated, swathed in the dainty trickery of silk and crepe.[68]

Ms Barnes's visit culminated in a (lightweight) ten-rounder between Phil Bloom and Young Gadwell. She admits her and the other women's interests were inevitably partly sexual:

> All the men are aware from the beginning that Bloom has the best of it; somehow they know the things that count in the game, and their interest is proportionate to their knowledge. But the woman's interest lies not in strength but in beauty. She is on the side of the boxer who has a certain trick of the head, a certain curve of the chin, a certain line from throat to brow.

The London women who swept into Cochran's expensive seats at Olympia hardly ignored the male beauty of Wells at his physical peak.

Billy was fit, splendidly fit, this time. On no single previous occasion had he ever looked so amazingly well. His skin was sherry coloured … He has never even approached such splendid condition … graceful, lithe, beautifully proportioned, the greyhound type. Handsome, classic ever in face and figure, he shaped both like the ideal boxer and the ideal runner, coupled with the hero of a romantic novel.

So wrote John Murray of *Boxing*. No doubt there were other males as well as females in the audience under Wells's spell and, like Murray, near to falling in love with him.

Wells, disrobing in his corner, had so affected audiences before, only to collapse when the real action began. Not this time, although Bell rushed at him from the very first bell, eager to use alacrity to break down Wells's defences. Bell aimed particularly to catch Wells in that much-discussed midriff. As Wells coolly jabbed, hooked, and uppercut in response, the Australian persisted. One man dedicated to attack; one man determined to counter; here was a recipe for three minutes of exciting action. It left the crowd breathless when the bell sounded.

The round was worth savouring as the only full one of the fight. Bell's vigour and intent surprised those who had seen him against Jeannette. Wells's new relish for a scrap and for taking body punches without folding like a penknife came as a pleasant surprise even to his doubters. Few observers noticed that Wells had improperly dispensed with bandages. Bell was getting the full force of big, clenched fists within lightly padded gloves – a dangerous and unforgiveable illegality.

Bell, a modest and gracious sporting opponent, admitted later that he had been handicapped by infected sinuses that had affected both his nose (and therefore breathing), and by an inflammation of the middle ear affecting his balance. He had a minor sinus operation before the fight but swore the doctor to secrecy. Bell was similarly guilty of a serious behind-the-scenes misdemeanour. He had, according to his doctor, 'very heroically injected more cocaine on his own account in order to relieve the pain from which he was suffering'! It is difficult to believe the ailments caused his defeat.

Bell hit Wells with punches every bit as substantial as those he had laid on Jeannette. Wells took blows to the kidney region and absorbed one torpedo left to the solar plexus that almost lifted him into the air. The new model Wells differed psychologically from the old as well as physically. Although a swift defeat by Bell would have ended his career ignominiously, the thought did not this time paralyse him. He lasted nine years as the British champion, and on this special Olympia night looked capable of beating anyone anywhere. The finish halfway through the second round was clinical. Bell stepped back from a clinch and was completely fooled by the neatest of Wells's combinations – a straight left to the nose followed by an impeccably timed right hook to the point of the chin that put Bell on the canvas for the best part of 20 seconds.

For all the British propensity to elevate a temporary success into a national feast day, this was a fine achievement. John Murray, still thinking of Wells as Adonis, and probably confusing Adonis with Achilles, called Wells that night 'a man who might quite possibly have been the greatest boxer who ever pulled off a shirt'. The hyperbole was ridiculous.

Wells received the plaudits, yet the supporting bout between Johnny Summers and reigning world welterweight champion Harry Stone of the USA, where the popular Londoner from Canning Town achieved a most honourable draw, was the more significant. The Summers v Stone purse was only £500 with a side stake of £250 – Cochran knew the heavies were the men to reward.

A week later, Cochran again had comparable crowds wending their way to Olympia to see a more important international fight. This was a greatly anticipated clash, with the world lightweight championship at stake, between the much-travelled Welshman Freddie Welsh and the man generally recognised as the champion, Willie Ritchie of California. According to Eugene Corri, Cochran lured Ritchie to London with a promise of £5,000, win, lose or draw.[69] This was worth Ritchie's embarking on the SS *Aquetania* and sailing for London. Welsh settled for very little just to get a chance at the title. Ritchie and Cochran admit that the man who put up the money in New York on Cochran's behalf was the notorious gambler and all-round fixer Arnold Rothstein. This is the same Arnold Rothstein who corrupted the

The glamorous clash between Welsh and Ritchie at Olympia on 7 July 1914 featured heavily in the British magazines and newspapers.
BoxRec

Willie Ritchie (1891–1975). The Californian lightweight sailed to London to challenge Freddie Welsh at Olympia.
Bain Collection, Prints & Photographs Division, Library of Congress, LC-DIG-ggbain-1669

Rothstein was a teetotaller and non-smoker. He appeared to be what I believe he was, a young man of a respectable Jewish family. I particularly noticed that his hands were beautiful. [p. 82]

I had not heard his name associated with crime. [p. 83]

A strange career, and there must to the end have been many casual acquaintances, like myself, who had no conception of this amazing man's double life. [p. 84]

The Cochrans received gifts, hospitality and other favours.

Rothstein could hardly have fixed the Olympia fight. The decision was in the sole hands of an upright referee in Eugene Corri. More likely, the Rothstein largesse was laid out in the hope of future involvement or to build a reputation for open-handed generosity – open-handed with money laundered from squalid undertakings.

All this was unknown to the carriage trade carrying well-favoured members of the audience to Olympia. There they would be mingling with the hoi polloi gathering from all quarters of London and from further afield in a splendidly cosmopolitan

1919 baseball World Series by paying some of the Chicago White Sox team to lose deliberately. (Rothstein was later shot during a poker game, leaving a safe full of evidence about his illegal dealings in gambling, drugs and assorted rackets – not of the squash or tennis variety.) The connection raises immediate questions about the legitimacy of the Welsh–Ritchie fight. Doubts are not allayed by Cochran's naïve comments in *Showman Looks On,* which perhaps should be retitled, *Showman Did Not Look On Closely Enough.*

… I did not know that Considine [a New York promoter] had induced his friend, Arnold Rothstein, to put up the money in my name. [p. 81]

assembly. It included many Americans, and hundreds of Welshmen who had poured in from trains from Cardiff all afternoon. There would have been yet more Welshmen had the fight taken place on a Saturday night to allow the Welsh miners to reach London without having to sacrifice a shift to do so. That was Welsh's proposal but was turned down by Cochran, happy with his metropolitan elite.

Before, during and after the fight, an impromptu Welsh choir sang the Welsh national anthem, 'Mae Hen Wlad Fy Nhadau', and other Welsh songs with fervour directly proportional to Welsh's successes in the ring. The master of ceremonies was the Reverend John Hervey Boudier, an Islington vicar, commissioned to add a certain class to the presentation. (Cochran's first choice, the Reverend Everard Digby, had withdrawn because of the disapproval of the Bishop of Stepney of his prominent appearance at Wells v Bell the previous week.) Boudier was popular with the Welsh contingent. He was a notably sporting curate in Cardiff in 1902–03, where he stimulated his flock to play cricket and football, and to box with muscular Christian gusto – more gusto than they showed for his temperance bar.

Willie Ritchie (b. 13 February 1891) rode into Olympia with an impressive recent record. He had knocked out Mexican Joe Rivers in San Francisco in the 11th round (4 July 1913); obtained a clear newspaper decision over Leach Cross over ten rounds in New York (10 November 1913); had two ten-round no-decision bouts in Milwaukee, winning one against Ad Wolgast (12 March 1914) and losing one against Charley White (26 May 1914); and

won another points decision over Tommy Murphy over 20 rounds in San Francisco (12 March 1914). He boasted over 50 professional bouts and was still only 23 years old.

In October 1970, when Willie Ritchie looked back on the Olympia fight, he was quite convinced he had won.[70] Ritchie's reminiscences probably conflate his loss at Olympia with an earlier encounter (30 November 1911 in Vernon, California) when he floored Welsh in the 11th and still lost on points over 20 rounds:

I thought I had outpointed him very easily because I landed the cleaner blows and all he did was to punch in close, whereas at long range I was hitting him clean punches … I knocked him down in the twelfth round, and he probably never forgot that. I hit him on the chin … The referee had Welsh ahead 1 point. I said to Eugene Corri, 'What's your decision?' He said, 'Welsh'. There has always been an unwritten law that unless a champion is beaten by a good margin he gets a draw. That's more or less an accepted condition in boxing, but of course in this case it was overlooked. Most referees wouldn't take the title away from a man on a very close score. They'd give him a draw so he wouldn't lose the title.

To this *cri de coeur* Heller adds a sympathetic footnote: '… referee Corri … scored the first 19 rounds even, awarding the twentieth and deciding round to Welsh, and with it the championship'. Ritchie was a man of integrity. His efforts in retirement

as a boxing administrator vehemently opposed to corruption and excluding gangsters from the Californian boxing scene were commendable. He believed unequivocally that he had beaten Welsh and in 1970 was still saying so.

But, and it is a big but, who can accurately recall events months later, let alone over 50 years later (the interval between fight and interview)? At the time of the fight, Ritchie said this, through tears of disappointment, to a *New York Times* reporter:

I am defeated but not humbled. A good sportsman always wants the best man to win. Welsh earned the decision. I know I disappointed my friends, but I could not get going right. The strong arc light over the ring was too dazzling and I could not measure the distance. I never fought before under such a glare and it affected my judgment. My friends cannot feel the defeat more keenly than I do.[71]

These are the words of a disappointed champion but hardly those of a man who thinks himself robbed. The strapline on the *New York Times* story was no more supportive:

'DECISION WAS NOT FAIR'
So Says Ritchie in Tears After Fight, though Few Question Referee Corri's Verdict.

The text told a similar story: 'No-one questioned that the verdict was fairly earned,' and 'At the end of the sixteenth round, Welsh had a clean lead. Emil Thiery, Ritchie's manager, told the American, he must get a knockout to win …' The English journal *Boxing* was equally convinced:

> Ritchie Wins Rounds 6, 11, and 18;
> Rounds 8, 13, 14, and 19 Even;
> Welsh Takes the Rest

and added:

THE WONDERFUL WELSH WIZARD WINS IN A WALK

Referee Corri's reminiscences about scoring the fight also contradict Ritchie's:

> In no one of the twenty rounds was there a wide margin in Welsh's favour. As a matter of fact, three of the rounds were Ritchie's, but only three. Seventeen rounds, with a fraction of advantage in each of them, made a substantial aggregate for Welsh, and it is just possible that he eased off a little during the three rounds in which Ritchie held the upper hand.[72]

Finally, the *New York Times* awarded round 12, in which Ritchie claimed retrospectively to have knocked Welsh down, to Welsh. No one mentions a knockdown and the New York paper says firmly, 'Neither man went to the floor.'

The sensible conclusion is that this was a contest of great skill, and that Welsh's victory was a highlight in the history of British boxing. Few British fighters spent so much time in American rings, fighting against boxers of widely differing styles, and rarely taking the favourite's corner. The experiences made Welsh a fighter who knew how to adapt to win, even if his

English and Welsh supporters rarely saw him. Apart from the notorious win by provocation over Driscoll in Cardiff in 1910 and the two fights against Matt Wells in 1911 and 1912, they could read about him but not see him.

Welsh was the ring student, brilliant at working out a new opponent and coping with whatever confronted him. This sharp intelligence was rigorously applied to his preparation, including then unfashionable considerations such as nutrition. He was unafraid to express his literary and social ideas, traits not necessarily appreciated by journalists with a taste for rough-hewn fighters with brains mainly in their fists and for whom lurid quotes could readily be invented. (In later decades, the intelligent and literary minded Gene Tunney had a similar cool effect on the boxing press.)

The weigh-in took place at Olympia at 2pm, the afternoon of the fight, a spectacle that drew a huge crowd in its own right. Welsh arrived from the Cardiff train one hour before and registered at 9st 11lb/137lbs, and Ritchie, up from his training headquarters in Brighton, at 9st 8¾lb. Welsh, the vegetarian but ever pragmatic, tucked into a large steak at a late lunch after the weigh-in. He wrote in early 1914 from the USA to Lord Lonsdale on behalf of the New York State Athletic Commission arguing for universal weigh-in procedures and that the time of the weigh-in and the precise poundage defining each weight class should be held in common everywhere. Lord Lonsdale's reply was published in the *New York Times*.[73] His lordship was fully in accord with an Anglo-American agreement – providing the USA adopted English practices!

Lonsdale pointed out that American champions imposed their own weigh-in rules once they held the title. (He ignored the fact that rules adopted in common by Britain, France, Australia and the USA would help the American Boxing Commission eliminate such anomalies.) He asserted, correctly, that he and the NSC were:

> … totally opposed to ringside weighing in, for we consider it dangerous to have boxers struggling to do a weight at which they were unfit to box, whereas by weighing six or eight hours before a contest … enables the medical officer to ascertain that a man is in a fit and proper condition to box.

Welsh's initiative foundered there. Cooperation on such vital matters between Britain and the USA went no further. As we shall see, discrepancies of practice led to an ugly future Olympia confrontation.

Eight hours later, Welsh and Ritchie received heroes' welcomes from the 10,000 packed into Olympia, Welsh miners and London cabbies mingling with a starry representative selection of peers, clergy, hostesses, actresses and celebrities such as John McCormack, the Irish tenor. The *Western Mail*, the Cardiff paper, claimed no English contest had ever assembled so many gentlemen in evening dress. Notes passed frantically from hand to hand in a frenzy of last-minute betting made Welsh the slight favourite. (His low share of the purse was an earnest of his determination to become the champion.) The cognoscenti also knew that Welsh and Ritchie had met in

California three years before on 30 November 1911, where Welsh had won and been the stronger at the finish. Fewer knew that Ritchie was a late substitute for Ad Wolgast and not fully prepared for Welsh.

At Olympia, there was a reversal of national styles, with Ritchie in a classic British-style upright stance and Welsh forgoing his slight height advantage in an American crouch, both gloves up in front of his face and elbows tucked in, leaving an opponent little to aim at as he bustled forward.

Ritchie, an aggressive fighter with power in both hands, especially in the right, expected Welsh to fight on the back foot, using all his defensive tactics to block and frustrate before looking to counter. Many of Welsh's opponents found their best efforts neutralised by gloves, arms and shoulders, or missing a moving target. This was disappointing enough, but more maddening was the insouciant smile playing on Welsh's lips. The smile, when it survived a clean hit, made an opponent doubt his own power and even sanity.

Welsh, ever the surprise packet, blocked and diverted Ritchie's best punches. But he did so while taking the fight to Ritchie, applying rapid lefts to his tanned features, supplementing them with left hooks off the jabs, stinging and discouraging his opponent. Both men clinched but broke impeccably on the referee's command. 'They obeyed me to the letter,' wrote Corri, who had recently forsaken his stool at fights and now sensibly patrolled the ring.

For three rounds Ritchie let Welsh feel the weight of his heavier punches. Welsh responded with bewildering hand speed, nifty footwork and a flexibility in ducking and swaying away from Ritchie's punches or neutralising their impact. Ritchie still inflicted a slight cut under Welsh's left eye and a graze on the bridge of his nose. In turn, he himself suffered a cut and bleeding mouth, and a mixture of bruises and swellings raised by those sharp lefts.

Ritchie was an expert at give and take – much adding to the classic nature of the contest – and he landed four excellent uppercuts in the fourth – three on Welsh and an accidental one on Corri who temporarily got *too* close. In the sixth he landed another after two heavy right swings to Welsh's head that came dangerously close to his chin. Exasperatingly, Welsh still smiled as he returned to his corner. Ritchie sped out again for the seventh, but Welsh finished off the round with two neat left jabs. He did it again in the 11th, even after a Ritchie left hook broke the skin by Welsh's right eye. Below the graze, the smile remained.

Urged on loudly by his seconds, Ritchie increased the pace in the 13th and 14th, landing at least two solid blows in each round, plus one below the belt in the 14th to bring a reprimand from Corri. Welsh defended with purpose, clinching when he had to and landing lefts when he could. He paced himself through a round to complete it with the last word. His plan was to do the same over the fight and stage a big finish. According to John Murray of *Boxing*, 'he came out like a giant refreshed for the 15th to hook home, jab and stab in, to swop upper-cuts and body blows, to exploit his great patent snap punch on coming out of a clinch, and to wind up the rd. with a really great left to the nose'.

Lesser fighters than Ritchie, landing excellent punches and seeing an opponent standing and smiling still, would have despaired. Despair was not a Ritchie attribute. On the contrary, yelled on by his corner and by the Americans in the crowd who had backed him heavily, he pursued Welsh all over the ring with two-fisted attacks, drawing blood from Welsh's nose. Despite that success, Welsh, aware of his points lead, made a Ritchie right swing miss by a foot and ran to his corner, bleeding and laughing.

Welsh controlled the last two rounds, forcing them into the pattern he wanted. He neatly measured off a round – one minute blocking Ritchie's frantic efforts to knock him out with a big right and snapping Ritchie's head back with painful lefts. In the second minute, he defended on the retreat, crouching and dodging, and modestly delivering parsimonious counters, more irritating than hurtful. In the final minute, he closed out a round with a flurry of big lefts, his full weight behind them, coupled with smarting left hooks into the puffy region around Ritchie's right cheekbone.

At the final bell, Welsh leaped into the air. He was too delirious with the emotions he had suppressed for an hour or more to see either Corri's move in his direction or the sporting handshake offered by Ritchie. He was the new champion and he knew it. So did his many supporters. Welsh was chaired from the ring and the arena and sung to his dressing room like a bard crowned at an eisteddfod. His own countrymen were embracing the prophet who spent most of his career in exile.

Such scenes would be repeated on the rare domestic occasions when a British fighter beat an American world champion. However, there is clinching evidence that the summer of 1914 represented a new high tide of fervour for boxing itself beyond domestic considerations. The next big – really big – London fight was between an American and a Frenchman. London was at least as involved as for Welsh v Ritchie: patriotism transcended.

The date was 16 July 1914; the venue Olympia. The promoter, trumping Cochran's ace, was Dick Burge. For the match, the management of the Liverpool Stadium had already offered £4,500, according to *The Times,* which later gleefully pronounced, 'London is the heaven in which boxing matches are made nowadays, and the air is full of rumours of great and joyous fights to come.'[74,75]

The foreign fighters now matched together had met the British champion Bombardier Billy Wells with disastrous results – disastrous for Wells that is. The American was Gunboat Smith, whose lanky and tough torso had taken the best Wells could muster on his unlucky New York visit, and had then knocked Wells out (14 March 1913). Official cancellation of the proposed Smith v Langford bout fostered increased British interest in Smith.

The French opponent was, of course, Georges Carpentier, who had knocked out Wells in Ghent (1 June 1913) and again in record time in London in December 1913. Given their impressive collateral form against Wells and the stylistic and physical contrast between them – boxer v roughhouse fighter; European sophisticate v American pioneering spirit; beauty v beast – Dick Burge's publicity script was already written. The fight promised to be 'great and joyous' indeed, and the tickets almost sold themselves.

Denzil Batchelor went further: '… the Carpentier–Gunboat Smith match … [was] the first glove fight to grip the public imagination as only such

spectacles as Coronations or Royal Funerals had gripped it in the past' and '… it was the first time that boxing had provoked a wave of mass hysteria in

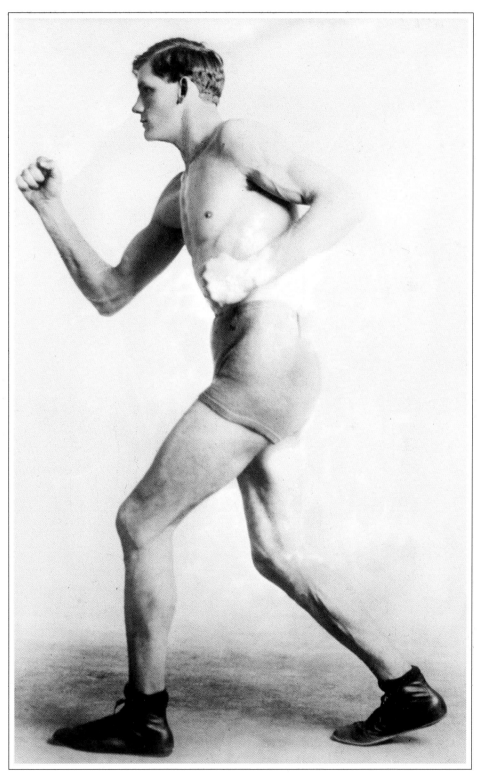

Gunboat Smith (1887–1974) was astonished when thousands of his British fans swamped Paddington station to greet him and his wife.

Bain Collection, Prints & Photographs Division, Library of Congress, LC-DIG-ggbain-11546

*Carpentier doffs his hat to
acknowledge the warmth and
fervour of his London reception.*
BnF

OUT

29

England'.[76] For once, Batchelor did not exaggerate.

Burge did not let the bout sell itself. Billboards and giant posters spread all over the London's West End. He attended meticulously to every detail of the promotion. The signing of the articles around the £5,000 purse and £500 side stakes at the *Sporting Life* offices by François Descamps, and their acceptance by the Smith camp by telegram *in absentia,* became an event in itself. So did the arrival of the fighters in London.

Smith stepped off the SS *Oceanic* in Plymouth at the end of May to prepare for the July fight. He travelled by train to Paddington station where he was astonished to receive the noisiest of welcomes. The station was swamped with thousands of well-wishers, eager to get a glimpse of him and his pretty young wife and cheering and chanting in counterpoint to a brass band playing 'The Star-Spangled Banner'. In a battery of flash photography, Smith gave an impromptu press conference, running through a gamut of clichéd answers to clichéd questions, including one about the number of women expected at Olympia. 'A prize-fight is a brutal display, and is no place for a woman, but a boxing contest is quite different.'

The quote was music to Burge's ears. He, like Cochran, turned down no revenue on grounds of gender. He wrote a letter to *The Times* full of assurances for women and their escorts: 'I will guarantee that any woman who desires to watch Smith and Carpentier box shall do so in as much comfort as if they were attending a concert or a theatre.'[77] Mr and Mrs Smith climbed into a hired car, the crowd pushed the vehicle for them and cheered it all the way to their

Charing Cross station, 14 July 1914: the arrival of Georges Carpentier.
BnF

hotel. The couple had raised the hype another two notches.

Carpentier was scheduled to arrive on 14 July, a delay that increased anticipation to the point of hysteria. When he arrived at Charing Cross station at 3.30pm on that day, neither the station nor Villiers Street, nor the Strand, nor the southern half of Trafalgar Square could be seen for

cheering crowds and waving tricolors. Traffic, motor or pedestrian, came to a complete standstill. *The Times* (15 July 1914) thought the unprecedented scene worth a full half-column, claiming: 'It is doubtful if such a scene of enthusiasm has any parallel in the annals of British sport.' The newspaper was correct.

The crowd swept up Carpentier and the ever-faithful François Descamps once they stepped from the train. Burge had arranged a landau hitched up to two white horses to trot them ceremonially around the corner to their hotel in Northumberland Avenue. Without mowing down thousands of Englishmen, Frenchmen and Americans clustered around the station forecourt, this was impossible. The American contingent was strong because many American sailors were already in town, the battleships *Missouri* and *Illinois* having already docked at Gravesend. Smith had served on the *Missouri* and the crew had taken shore leave specifically to support their former comrade.

The crowd found a way out of the impasse. Boxer and manager were hoisted up and carried shoulder-high to the carriage; the horses were unhitched and the brawnier fans pulled the vehicle through the cheering and chanting thousands to the hotel. The crowds then surrounded the building until Carpentier emerged on the balcony to wave in acknowledgement of chants of 'Carpentier! Carpentier!' Interminable choruses of 'La Marseillaise' then drowned out whoops of 'Smith! Smith!' and the singing of 'The Star-Spangled Banner'.

The Olympia event had caught the public imagination. It cemented boxing's rise to respectability. It even boasted royal approval. Burge sent a telegram to Buckingham Palace to King George V conveying the respects of the two fighters. A gracious reply was sent by the King's secretary: 'I am commanded to express his Majesty's thanks for the messages contained in your telegram on behalf of M. Georges Carpentier and Mr Edward Smith and for the sentiment to which it

gives expression.'[78] If the King himself commended pugilists, who then could turn up their noses?

Burge (and his publicity adviser, an American journalist called Frank Morley) had skilfully enhanced enthusiasm for the fight. Nevertheless, boxing's 1914 boom was a fact. Even the less magisterial tabloid *Times* of the 21st century would not give the many columns to the arrival of two foreign fighters, to previews of the fight, to the fight itself, and to the post-mortem, the way its ancestor of 1914 did.

Given the build-up and the 15,000-plus people crammed in on the night, it is a pity that the fight was nowhere near the quality of Welsh–Ritchie. The bill proclaimed the 'white' heavyweight championship was at stake. Ring drama and post-fight controversy had to compensate for lack of finesse.[79]

All London seemed to be there – 'from the white-shirted aristocrats on the floor to the Whitechapel costers in the highest galleries', wrote one American journalist also struck by the 'hundreds of richly gowned and titled women scattered about the immense arena'. The women were 'dainty, tiarad and bejewelled female goddesses … in rainbow chiffon' according to a British witness. Half Paris, most travelling Americans and a goodly minority of the US Navy were there too. The fight lasted but 15 minutes, the same time it took for Carpentier, in a grey silk robe, and Smith in a bright green one, to reach the ring and be formally introduced.

The action began slowly. Smith was not a fast mover, nor a speedy puncher. Carpentier was both but concerned to feel out his man early. He laid his head on Smith's chest or shoulder, comfortably closer than the zone threatened by

Smith's big swings. He picked up points with light jabs and hooks from a distance. They caused little damage. Smith adopted a scattergun approach and threw a miscellany of punches in the Frenchman's direction. One right drive and one left swing went well below legitimate French territory and strayed into the Mediterranean. Corri reprimanded him and Smith apologised, grudgingly. Carpentier, not seriously disturbed by the fouls, remained at a cautious distance, missing Smith by an embarrassing amount before the round ended. In his 1970 recollections, Smith remembered being hit and hurt in the first but no contemporary accounts confirm this. Corri later wrote that he scored the round even.

Carpentier got quietly on top in the second while respecting Smith's punching power. His body blows provoked grunts from Smith, audible to the first few rows of seats. Smith's head rocked when Carpentier landed uppercuts up under his guard. Smith looked quizzical, pushing out a left lead more as a range finder than an authentic jab, and took more body blows. Carpentier easily avoided the telegraphed right swing that followed.

Having failed to hurt Carpentier in the second, Smith tried again in the third. His left went inches low and Carpentier complained. Corri responded with another reprimand. Otherwise, Carpentier mostly avoided Smith's swinging punches. (Some still caught him about the body.) When he chose, Carpentier could clip and counter Smith with relative ease. An irritated Smith broke a clinch by forcing Carpentier's arm up behind his back. He got a short hook from Carpentier and another telling-off from Corri.

Gunboat rashly launches a punch at the fallen Carpentier on 16 July 1914 at Olympia. It will controversially get him disqualified.
BnF

In the fourth, Smith moved from slow and ponderous to moderate and hunted Carpentier down. The plan was to cut off the ring then catch Carpentier with one of his big punches. Some rights landed to the body; one missed so badly it almost toppled the sender through the ropes. Carpentier could not be complacent, as Smith's first clean straight left to his nose reminded him. At the end of the round, Gunboat swung another left and followed with a big right cross. Carpentier, beautifully balanced, swayed away from both, then caught Smith on the point of the jaw with an elegant right cross. Down went Smith on his bottom with a vacant look in his eyes. Corri leaned over him, tolling off the seconds.

The history of boxing comprises many such occasions when a single second has encapsulated the importance of lifetimes. Short counts, long counts, delayed counts, incomplete counts – they have all featured and been debated furiously. Dempsey v Tunney in 1927, the Liston v Ali rematch of 1965, Diego Corrales v Jose Luis Castillo of 2005 – a rich anthology of such particular seconds would make interesting reading. Smith v Carpentier would have an honourable place in the compilation.

As Corri brought his arm down for the ninth time, but before he pronounced the final 'ten and out', the bell rang for the end of the round. In the preliminary discussions, Corri, Carpentier and Smith all agreed that the count would depend *wholly* on the referee's actions. Towards the end of this count, Corri wrote later, the Gunboat was following Corri's actions carefully and preparing to get up. He did not get up because, it appeared, the bell had saved him. But it was *not* actually the end of the round. Sydney Hulls the timekeeper rang the bell. He had not coordinated his action with Corri's count and was indicating that ten had been reached, that Smith had been knocked out and that the action was over. This lack of communication between the officials was grossly unprofessional, however understandable. Hulls had called, 'He's out!' which only Corri could pronounce. Corri was correct to let Smith continue into the fifth.

The gods had still not finished their sport with this oddest of fights. Smith's strong powers of recuperation in the interval regained him his full wits. He attacked again from the start of the fifth. He took more of Carpentier's punches but landed rights about Carpentier's body, with one far too low for Corri's liking. Despite Smith's aggression, Carpentier looked the superior craftsman. Beauty was taming the beast and hurting him as well. Carpentier resumed his stool at the end of the round, having rounded off the three minutes of action with a clean left hook and short sharp left jabs to clinch another round on Corri's scorecard.

Internally, the Frenchman was less cool than his cultivated body language indicated. Early in the sixth, he threw Gunboat-style wild swings himself. Emerging from a clinch, he saw a chance to nail Smith with a right with all of his power concentrated into it. Once so launched, he was left helpless

when Smith disobligingly got out of the way, and the normally so elegant Carpentier was left ineptly sprawling under his own momentum. Rarely can such a miss have brought such rewards.

As Carpentier straddled the canvas – a contemporary photograph shows him tripod-like with his right knee and both gloves on the floor – Smith measured the distance to the back of Carpentier's neck with his left, then delivered a long stabbing right down to this limited target. He made contact pretty lightly, probably because he realised the consequences and began to pull the punch. Carpentier, quicker on the uptake, flopped down immediately on impact.

Corri, having given Smith four previous warnings for low blows and arm-twisting, had had enough. He promptly and correctly disqualified Smith for punching a man who was down. As many pointed out, Carpentier might also have been disqualified as Smith's blow had brought the excitable M. Descamps out of his seat and into the ring to protest. Five years later (1919) Corri wrote:

> M. Descamps immediately claimed a foul on behalf of Carpentier, and no other course remained open to me but to give Carpentier the fight.

This suggests that Corri was reacting not to the foul, but to Descamps's antics. He wrote also, nearer to the event (1915) an expanded version:

> It was contended that Descamps jumped into the ring before I had given my decision. That is not quite right. My mind was

instantly made up that Carpentier could have the fight on the foul if he claimed it … It is true that Descamps got into the ring before I formally gave the fight to Carpentier, but not before I had made up my mind so to act if Carpentier and his manager claimed the foul.

The accounts are not that incompatible yet reveal that Corri, rattled by the count fiasco, wrongly ignored Descamps's premature entry into the ring and pronounced the disqualification *after* Descamps's intervention. Carpentier could have fought on and won on points or stoppage had he so desired. The photographic evidence demonstrates that the disqualification was reasonable. Smith was on thin ice because of his earlier transgressions and went too far by punching a man on the floor.

That Carpentier may have played up the role of stricken warrior unjustly damaged, and that Smith regretted his action, are irrelevant. Carpentier did not bring his neck into contact with Smith's misguided blow and in no way provoked it. He claimed after that 'the real damage occurred owing to the contact of my nose and forehead with the boards, these being forced there by the sudden jar of the blow'. No one else saw such vivid consequences or such damage. The claim sounds rather like Carpentier excusing his reluctance to continue a fight he might well have won but only at some cost.

With publicity, interest and attendance at such a pitch, some sequel was inevitable. The pugnacious British weekly *John Bull*, alert to exploiting any trend, organised a campaign 'with a view to recovering for Great Britain the white Heavy-weight Championship of the World'. The magazine organised fights between British fighters to find this powerful white beast, elusive as a unicorn, and settled on a talented and self-confident middleweight, born in Preston, Lancashire. His name was originally Jacob Woodward, born 18 December 1892, who had adopted the ring name of Young Ahearn. He knocked out Sid Burns (a welterweight) in two rounds of 20 (15 June 1914 at Premierland), and Private Pete Braddock in eight (25 May 1914 at the NSC).

Conveniently forgetting that Young Ahearn had been mastered by Johnny Basham, a welterweight, in points over 15 rounds in Liverpool on 11 December 1913, the two knockouts were sufficient for the magazine to dub him 'John Bull's Boy'. Quite how John Bull's Boy, a middleweight of 5ft 8½in, would conquer the relative giants of the heavyweight world was forgotten. (Ahearn was in any case an unfortunate candidate for patriotic British hopes. Once war broke out he took himself off to the USA in September with his wife and father-in-law, subtracted three years from his birthdate and became known as 'The Brooklyn Dancing Master', fighting out of Brooklyn until his eventual retirement in 1924.)

John Bull put up a purse of £10,000 for Young Ahearn to meet Georges Carpentier on 17 August 1914 at the White City Stadium in London for that spurious 'white Heavy-Weight Championship of the World'. Carpentier was guaranteed £4,000, win or lose. He signed eagerly on the dotted line and was given £1,000 on account.

Carpentier was always willing to knock over an optimistic Brit in

minimal time for maximum returns. Yet however mercenary he was, or allowed Descamps to be in pre-fight negotiations, he was no mercenary in the other sense of the word. (*OED*: 'Hired soldier in foreign service'.) On the contrary, he was a strong French patriot, proud of his country and an intelligent man with a conscience, uncomfortably aware of the looming threat to France's very existence posed by a possible German invasion. In such dangerous times, he declined to stay abroad being feted and rewarded by foreigners.

On 4 August 1914, his British admirers gave him a farewell lunch at the Hotel Metropole – the hotel where he had been taken in glorious procession from Charing Cross station on his arrival for the fight against Smith. He stayed there as a base when fulfilling his lucrative engagements at English music halls. The day, a Tuesday, and a particularly fatal one, would be remembered for more than a sporting lunch. As all historians know, just as the three Western European superpowers, Great Britain, Germany and France, supposedly reached a new rapport, with only Russia giving cause for concern, they stumbled into a diplomatic stalemate that would lead to a mighty fight, damaging a whole generation and affecting their world irreparably.

On 1 August 1914, Germany declared war on Russia. On 2 August, Germany demanded free access through Belgium for her armies on the way to France, Russia's ally. On 3 August, Germany declared war on France. On 4 August, the very day of the lunch for Carpentier, Great Britain responded and declared war on Germany. On 10 August, Britain declared war on Austria-

Hungary as well. The First World War had begun and would not end until a formal armistice was declared at 5am on 11 November 1918.

That 1918 armistice was to bring cheering crowds out into the streets of London around the Hotel Metropole and packed in jubilant profusion around the corner in Trafalgar Square and elsewhere. Peace at last, but not before five and a half million military lives and perhaps another five million civilian lives had been lost directly or indirectly because of the war. The Spanish influenza epidemic of October 1918 to January 1919 added an unprecedented 21 million to these terrifying figures.

So many years on, we lack the historical imagination to grasp the true awfulness of these numbers. One could guess that one overwhelming contemporary emotional reaction would have been revulsion against *any* kind of fighting – even the relatively harmless and ritualistic conflict of two men in padded gloves punching each other in a roped enclosure. All the evidence suggests quite the contrary. For men in the trenches and on the decks of fighting ships absorbed in the obscene slaughter across the killing fields of France and Belgium and elsewhere in the world, boxing represented rather a striking and welcome emblem of normality in a surreal world. Others got their first taste for boxing by seeing it for the first time in the context of regimental leisure. In every regiment and on every fighting vessel, boxing became and remained extraordinarily popular. And combatants back in Blighty on leave were as eager to attend a big fight or a small hall bill as ever they had been in peacetime.

Endnotes:

1 *New York Times,* 11 January 1914.
2 *Boxing's Annual for 1914* p. 3.
3 *Punch,* 17 December 1913 p. 511.
4 Corri, E., *Thirty Years a Referee* (1915) p. 234.
5 Reports in *The Times,* 2 January 1914; *Boxing,* 10 January 1914.
6 *New York Times,* 4 January 1914; 'Gunboat Smith Packed Power' by John Jarrett in *Boxing News,* 11 April 1975; Heller, P., *In This Corner …! Forty World Champions Tell Their Stories* (London: Robson Books, 1985) pp. 30–45. [Gunboat Smith interview]
7 *Boxing,* 10 January 1914.
8 Greig, M., *Goin' the Distance: Canada's Boxing Heritage* (Toronto: Macmillan, Canada 1996) pp. 51–52.
9 *Boxing,* 24 January 1914.
10 *Boxing,* 31 January 1914; *The Times,* 26 January 1914.
11 For McCormick, see Odd, G., *Encyclopedia of Boxing* (London: Hamlyn, 1983) p. 73; McInnes. P., 'Tom Won British Title in Australia', in *Boxing News,* 15 August 1958; Odd, G., 'Private's Progress Stunned the World', in *Boxing News,* 11 July 1980.
12 *New York Times,* 28 January 1914.
13 Myler, P., *A Century of Boxing Greats: Inside the Ring with the Hundred Best Boxers* (London: Robson Books, 1999) pp. 92–94; obituary in *Boxing News,* 30 April 1965.
14 *New York Times,* 24 January 1914.
15 *Boxing,* 28 February 1914; *The Times,* 24 February 1914; ; Harding, J., *Lonsdale's Belt: Boxing's Most Coveted Prize* (Worthing: Pitch Publishing, 2016) p. 65.
16 See 'Smith was robbed by scandal of long count' by Gilbert Odd in *Boxing News,* 6 July 1979.
17 Not April 1914 as suggested in Harding, J., *Lonsdale's Belt,* p. 66. See *Boxing,* 14 March 1914; *The Times,* 10 March 1914.
18 Advertisement in *Boxing,* 14 February 1914.
19 *Boxing's Annual for 1914* p. 11.
20 *Boxing,* 31 January 1914; *The Times,* 27 January 1914.
21 Mullan, H., *Heroes and Hard Men: The Story of Britain's World Boxing Champions* (London: Stanley Paul, 1989) p. 35.
22 Mullan, H., *Heroes and Hard Men,* p. 38–39.
23 Quoted in Holt, R., *Sport and Society in Modern France* (Oxford: Macmillan, 1981) p. 143.
24 *Boxing,* 14 February 1914.
25 Card reproduced in *Boxing,* 21 February 1914.

26 *Boxing,* 7 February 1914.
27 *The Times,* 19, 20 and 21 February 1914. *The Times,* usually authoritative in legal matters, spells the plaintiff's name as Shears, although both Harding, J., *Lonsdale's Belt,* p. 36 and Lewis, M., *Ted Kid Lewis: His Life and Times* (London: Robson Books, 1990) p. 22ff opt for Shear.
28 *Boxing,* 16 May 1914.
29 *The Times,* 31 March 1914.
30 *Boxing,* 4 April 1914.
31 *The Times,* 4 March 1914; *Boxing,* 7 March 1914.
32 *The Times,* 20 April 1914.
33 *Boxing,* 11 April 1914; *The Times,* 3 April 1914.
34 *The Times,* 23 March 1914; *Boxing,* 28 March 1914; *Carpentier: By Himself* (London: Sportsman's Book Club, 1958) pp. 84–86.
35 *Carpentier: By Himself,* pp. 87–88; Kent, G., *Boxing's Strangest Fights* (London: Robson Books, 2000) pp. 91–92; *The Times,* 15 and 16 April 1914; *Boxing,* 25 April 1914.
36 *The Times,* 27 January 1914.
37 *The Times,* 16, 17 and 31 March, 11 April 1914.
38 *The Times,* 16 March 1914.
39 *The Times,* 17 March 1914.
40 *The Times,* 20 April 1914.
41 *The Times,* 6 April 1914.
42 *The Times,* 15 April 1914.
43 Shipley, S., *Bombardier Billy Wells: The Life and Trials of a Boxing Hero* (Tyne and Wear: Bewick Press, 1993) p. 96.
44 *The Times,* 1 May 1914.
45 *New York Times,* 2 May 1914.
46 Cochran, C. B., *Showman Looks On* (London, 1945) p. 298.
47 Quotations from *The Times,* 25 May 1914.
48 *The Times,* 7 November 1913.
49 *The Times,* 21 January 1914.
50 *The Times,* 30 January 1914.
51 *The Times,* 17 February 1914 carries the full text of the letter as released by Bettinson, as did *Boxing,* 21 February 1914.
52 *The Times,* 20 January, 22 January, 23 January 1914.
53 See 'Afterword' Odd, G., *Jack Johnson: In the Ring and Out* (London, Proteus, 1977) p. 197.
54 Roberts, R., *Papa Jack: Jack Johnson and the Era of White Hopes* (New York: Simon & Schuster, 1985) p. 192.
55 Reports appear in *The Times,* 29 June 1914; *Boxing,* 4 July 1914; Roberts, R., *Papa Jack: Jack Johnson and the Era of White Hopes* (New York: Simon & Schuster, 1985) p.

192; Odd, G., *Jack Johnson: In the Ring and Out* (London, Proteus, 1977) pp. 197–198; Ward, G., *Unforgivable Blackness: The Rise and Fall of Jack Johnson* (New York: Knopf, 2004) pp. 360–361; *New York Times,* 28 June 1914.
56 Ward, G., *Unforgivable Blackness* (New York: Knopf, 2004) pp. 362–363.
57 *John Bull,* 18 July 1914 but conveniently reproduced on p.230 of Gilbert Odd's, *Jack Johnson: In the Ring and Out.*
58 See Cochran's entry in the *Dictionary of National Biography* and two of his repetitive and chronologically confusing volumes of autobiography: *Cock-a-Doodle-Do* (London, 1941); *Showman Looks On* (London, 1945). He also wrote *Secrets of a Showman* (1925) and *I Had Almost Forgotten …* (1932).
59 C. B. Cochran: *Showman Looks On* (London, 1945) pp. 264–265.
60 Styan, J. L., *Max Reinhardt (Directors in Perspective Ser.)* (Cambridge: Cambridge University Press, 1982) pp. 86, 94–95.
61 *The Times,* 12 May 1914 and 25 May 1914.
62 *Boxing News,* 21 March 1951.
63 *Boxing,* 4 July 1914; *The Times,* 1 July 1914; Shipley, S., *Bombardier Billy Wells,* p. 100–107.
64 *The Times,* 25 May 1914.
65 *Health and Strength,* 4 July 1914 – quoted by Stan Shipley in *Bombardier Billy Wells.*
66 Both quotations from *the New York Times,* 1 July 1914.
67 *New York Times,* 6 March 1914.
68 Reprinted in Barnes, D., *New York* (Virago: London, 1990) pp. 168–173.
69 Corri, E., *Thirty Years a Referee,* p. 126.
70 Heller, P., *In This Corner …!,* pp. 19–29.
71 *New York Times,* 8 July 1914, pp. 121–122.
72 Corri, E., *Thirty Years a Referee,* pp. 121–122.
73 *New York Times* 12 March 1914.
74 *The Times,* 6 April 1914.
75 *The Times,* 20 April 1914.
76 Batchelor, D., *Big Fight: The Story of World Championship Boxing* (London: Sportsmans Book Club, 1955) p. 85 and p. 157.
77 *The Times,* 25 June 1914.
78 *New York Times,* 16 July 1914.
79 Details in *The Times,* 16 July, 17 July, 18 July 1914; *Boxing,* July 17, 25 1914; *New York Times,* 17 July 1914; *Boxing News,* 11 April 1975; Butler, J., *Kings of the Ring* (London, n.d. [1936]) pp. 52–59; Hurst, N., *Big Fight Thrills* (London, n.d. c.1969); Corri, E., *Thirty Years a Referee,* pp. 25–47; Corri, E., *Refereeing 1,000 Fights* (London, 1919) pp. 48–52; Heller, P., *In This Corner …!,* p. 43.

CHAPTER 11

WAR
AUGUST 1914–NOVEMBER 1918

In Which a Champion Falls and a Sport Helps Win a War

THE FIRST few months after the declaration of war were distinctly odd. Many believed the war would not last. All over by Christmas was a constant refrain. The optimism and flag-waving patriotic gatherings, singing jingoistic songs outside Buckingham Palace and in other public spaces such as Trafalgar Square and Whitehall, led many naïve and brave young men to join the forces immediately, impatient lest they missed out on the big adventure. No one of the appropriate age knew what war was really like.

The British Expeditionary Force (BEF), a mainly professional army, was the first to depart. By 24 August, they were outflanked at Mons. By the middle of November, they suffered such losses in the Battle of the Marne (1,700 killed, 11,300 wounded) and the First Battle of Ypres that the original army barely survived. At Ypres alone the British suffered 7,960 killed, 29,563 wounded and 17,873 missing.

Soon the authorities needed the heady volunteers to replace the original force. In a matter of months, recruiting offices became less and less particular. In August, a volunteer had to be 5ft 8in tall, a height few flyweights were likely to attain. By 11 October, 5ft 5in would

do, then by 5 November, diminutive men of 5ft 3in in their stockinged feet were being fitted out into the khaki uniforms originally designed for the Boer War and were sent off to France and Belgium.

Boxing inspired further height adjustments. The so-called Birkenhead Bantams – two Cheshire Battalions formed by a local MP in November 1914 to allow shorter men to join up – raised 2,200 recruits in four days and established a 5ft limit.[1]

Regardless of height, the raw recruits were, by the end of November 1914, joining a war where early mobility had become a static stalemate of barbed wire and trenches stretching thousands of miles from the Belgian coast to the borders of neutral Switzerland. The stalemate would last four very long years.

Statesmen had blundered into the conflict, but the government (led by a cabinet against conscription on principle) were forced into aggressive recruitment by the appalling losses and by urgent military requests from the front for more and more men. The country was in a serious war and wars lost risk everything. Admirable young men were overwhelmingly prepared to

risk their lives when every newspaper and authoritative figure urged them to do 'their duty'. For many the direct defence of home and hearth counted for less than the unselfish belief that they were crossing the Channel to save gallant little Belgium and their French friends from the big German bully.

Much less admirable was the number of well-fed and sedentary men, including newspaper columnists, of an age putting them comfortably beyond the limit of any likely call-up, whose bloodlust led them to campaign vigorously and stridently to put every young man into uniform regardless of circumstance.

No accusation of cowardice or treachery was too vulgar to be levied. The propagandists were aided and abetted by wives and daughters conducting the notorious white feathers campaign, targeted at young men not in uniform, sometimes at those who had already served, been wounded and been invalided out. People who detested sport, especially its professional manifestations, were heavy supporters of this offensive and hysterical campaign.

Association football, cricket and boxing bore the major brunt of the vilification. Professional football, with its fervent working-class following, was the perfect target for vocal members of the upper and middle classes to vent their anger at the proles who were, they believed, less patriotic than they should be.[2]

Typical of those within other sports was E. H. D. Sewell (1872–1947), successful amateur cricketer and a fervent supporter of rugby union football (then resolutely amateur). Just over a week after the declaration of war, the Rugby Football Union (RFU) sent out a circular telling all rugby players to sign on; all RFU games at every level were cancelled in the meantime.[3] Rugby football was, according to Sewell, an activity that 'above all games is one which develops the qualities which go to make good fighting men'. Soccer (professional), on the other hand, should 'remain the exercise of the munitions workers who suffer so much from varicose veins, weak knees, cod-eyed toes, fowl's livers and a general dislike for a man's duty'. His opinion of soccer *spectators* was beyond expression.

Other lofty voices echoed Sewell's views, if not in such pseudo-biological terms. For example, *The Times* published letters directing hostility at football in particular. One from A. F. Pollard, an academic at University College, stated:

… there is no excuse for diverting from the front thousands of athletes in order to feast the eyes of crowds of inactive spectators, who are either unfit to fight or else unfit to be fought for … every spectator who pays his gate money is contributing so much towards a German victory.

Another letter writer agreed:

Our flow of recruits of the best and most athletic type would be immensely accelerated if only the Football Association would show some patriotic spirit regardless of gate-money, and … put a stop to those spectacular displays of professional football that are such an irresistible attraction to our young athletes.[4]

Before long, the newspaper was editorialising on similar lines:

… it is high time that there should be an end of what is becoming a national scandal. The more football the better for those who need such recreation [i.e. industrial workers and those too old to serve]; but let it be a game and not a business.[5]

In other words, there should only be *amateur* football. Three days later, *The Times* published an article ('Football in War') suggesting that professional footballers were much less eager to sign on than they should be.[6] There was no more consistency in the paper's editorial offices than anywhere else. *The Times's* boxing correspondent, reporting a Wilde fight, was allowed to write:

If it be justifiable to watch any form of sport in war time then there can scarcely be anything so appropriate to our mood as a big fight such as that of last night at the National Sporting Club … Here are something of the ingredients of war – blood and sweat and struggle, the cunning

manoeuvring for blows and the taking of them cheerfully. This is a time when we are filled with admiration for sheer courage above all other qualities, and here is the courage of battle in miniature. Leaving on one side for a moment the skill of the boxers, their pluck and their fitness fill us with astonishment. To sit in a comfortable chair smoking a big cigar and then not to admire them, even in a certain sense to envy them, would argue something rather poor and mean in us.[7]

Boxing as vicarious enjoyment of war while relaxing with a cigar was certainly novel. Why so much nobler than watching soccer players from the terraces with a Woodbine in one's lips is more obscure.

Attitudes in cricket also indicated the strong amateur presence at the top of the game. By the end of August 1914, the season almost over, county cricket and most club games were halted. The MCC was slower off the mark than the RFU and originally allowed matches to continue: 'No good purpose can be served at the present moment by cancelling.' They were provoked, or shamed, into calling a halt by a famous letter to *The Sportsman* from that prodigious (sh)amateur W. G. Grace, disgusted 'that able-bodied men should be playing day by day and pleasure-seekers look on'.[8] Grace was joined by the *Daily Express*, which shrilly proclaimed, 'Men are still flocking to cricket matches, young able-bodied men with leisure and abundant health … If the nation does not wake up now, it will awaken only to dishonour and destruction.'[9] The future 1915 cricket season was not officially abandoned until January 1915.

Many high-profile cricketers joined up immediately. Indeed, at the traditional August Bank Holiday Roses match between Lancashire and Yorkshire at Old Trafford, both (amateur) captains left the game to re-join their regiments. At the Oval at the Surrey game, the Nottinghamshire captain A. W. Carr threw his wicket away to do the same. At Northampton, at the Northamptonshire v Leicestershire match, Mr A. Sharpe of Leicestershire was 'absent hurt' in the scorebook in a vital second innings when his side failed by only four runs to reach a winning target; in reality it was 'absent enlisted'. All four volunteers were gentlemen amateurs.

In the professional ranks, it was slightly different. Important professional cricketers such as Jack Hobbs (with a wife and four children to support), Sydney Barnes and Frank Woolley – players who would make any cricketing heroes' pantheon – did not sign on but pursued or supplemented their livelihoods in the Bradford League, founded as a professional league in 1903 and operating right through the war. Hobbs eventually enlisted in 1916. (The other major northern league, the Lancashire League, outlawed professionalism in 1916 as the war ground on and suspended all fixtures in 1917 and 1918.) To Lord (Martin) Hawke (1860–1938), Eton, Cambridge, Yorkshire and England amateur, the godfather of Yorkshire cricket, the failure of any cricketer to enlist was 'scandalous'. He was not alone.

In horse racing, the Jockey Club was pressured to halt meetings for the duration of the war. It declined to do so. In October 1914, as the casualties mounted up, it acted somewhat contrary to its usual inclinations and explained itself. Racing should continue, not for the sake of spectators, but in the interests of the whole bloodstock industry and its myriad employees (jockeys, trainers, stable lads, stewards, gatemen, caterers and groundsmen involved in the upkeep and raceday activities of every course).[10] This attitude was not popular with a puritan lobby that hated racing and gambling alike, yet many working-class people depended upon racing for their living. It was also argued that the bloodstock industry must continue to ensure a supply of horses to the cavalry. (Racing was, incidentally, a secondary source of employment for boxers in the summer months after the boxing season.)

The attitude of the racing industry was at the very heart of the dilemmas created for professional sport by the outbreak of war. Professional sportsmen, the fittest members of their generation, were obviously prime targets for recruitment. However, they depended upon their jobs for their livelihood and to support their families just as much as less high-profile professions.

It was easy to sneer at the spectators enjoying the feats of the professionals at football, cricket and racing and suggest they were all idle wastrels who should have been pounding the parade grounds, filling the trenches and ultimately lying dead in no-man's land. There were millions of factory workers, miners and dockers essential to keeping the country going while its soldiers fought on. Some supported large families and most people agreed that single men should serve first.

Some were too old or too unfit to fight. Others had already fought and been invalided out. Many others had joined the reserve, ready to serve in the case of an invasion or other emergency. Who was to say that workers and part-time soldiers were not entitled to their transient sporting pleasures at the end of the weekly grind?

As Stan Shipley accurately pointed out, those in uniform included the almost redundant cavalrymen, and civilians included invaluable workers slaving away on every shift there was. Later on, the part sport could play in both civilian and military morale was better understood. Significantly, on the outbreak of the Second World War in 1939, all theatres, cinemas and sporting arenas were closed immediately yet the ban lasted only about a week as wiser thinking prevailed. Film, entertainment and sport played important roles in sustaining wartime civilian morale in the 1940s.

In Liverpool, for example, throughout the Second World War, there were boxing bills averaging 37 shows a year (61 in 1942), sustained by boxers drawn from the ranks of essential workers such as merchant sailors, dockers, military personnel, plus servicemen on leave and those serving abroad, such as Czechs, Free French, Poles, Canadians and Americans.[11] Boxing still suffered criticism for continuing during the second conflict just as it did during the First World War.

In 1942, the *Daily Express* campaigned vigorously against continuance, especially of greyhound racing and boxing. The campaign provoked political responses. When a final eliminator for the British light-heavyweight championship between

Carpentier immediately enrolled in the French Army Corps. The war brought him medals, citations and enhanced status as a genuine French war hero.
Bain Collection, Prints & Photographs Division, Library of Congress, LC-DIG-ggbain-23457

Freddie Mills and Jock McAvoy took place at the Royal Albert Hall on 23 February 1942, the 4,500 tickets sold out immediately. Questions were asked in the House of Commons. Sir Stafford Cripps (1889–1952), evangelical Christian and the strongest advocate of austerity in all forms, was wartime Leader of the House. He proclaimed, 'We are not engaged in a war effort in which we can have as our motto "Business as Usual" or "Pleasure as Usual" … dog racing and boxing displays … are completely out of accord with the true spirit of determination of the people in this crisis in their history.' He was quite wrong, and quite ignorant of the considerable role sport could play in boosting national spirits.

Weeks before the Mills fight – won easily by Mills when McAvoy retired before the end of the first round with a back injury – England had beaten Scotland 3-0 at Wembley to the delight of a large crowd whose cash at the turnstiles finished up in Clementine Churchill's Aid to Russia Fund. Cripps's Labour colleague Herbert Morrison, serving as Home Secretary, was, unlike the affluent and privileged Cripps, from a working-class background. He had a more sensible view. As he declared in January 1942: 'We have taken the view that there must be, within reasonable limitation, recreation for the people. I do not think we had better too readily or extremely adopt the philosophy

or policy of progressive misery.' (Incidentally, Freddie Mills [1919–65], one of Britain's most popular fighters in the 1940s, broke another of service boxing's restrictions about clashes between ranks when he, as a flight sergeant in the RAF, an NCO, knocked out Pilot Officer Len Harvey for the British light-heavyweight title at White Hart Lane on 20 June 1942.)

Overlooked by professional sport's enemies during 1914–18 was another major element in the crowds attending wartime sporting events – soldiers in uniform. The temporarily invalided, the permanently disabled, those on leave, those in uniform and awaiting assignments all swelled the sporting crowds in the war years. A week of home leave was granted for every year spent in the trenches; more for officers who qualified after three months. Arnold Bennett's diary in 1917 recorded one officer able to breakfast in the trenches and dine at his London club in the evening. He was not the only one. In the serving ranks there was little hostility to the continuance of professional sport. On the front line there was rather an eager following of results and frequent discussion of teams, horses and boxers and their prospects.

As early as 7 August 1914, the first recruiting appeal appeared in *The Times*, under the name of Lord Kitchener, the middle-aged (64) Boer War hero, carrying the striking headline 'YOUR KING AND COUNTRY NEED YOU' backed up by 'A CALL TO ARMS' and a pungent personal plea:

An addition of 100,000 men to His Majesty's Regular Army is immediately necessary in the present grave National Emergency. Lord Kitchener is confident that this appeal will be at once responded to by all who have the safety of our Empire at heart.

(The better-known pictorial poster with the word 'BRITONS' above a striking Alfred Leete drawing of a heavily moustached Kitchener pointing alongside the eloquent words 'WANTS YOU' was issued in September 1914. There is some doubt about how widely it was distributed.)[12]

Many sporting newspapers and magazines during August 1914 carried a starker version of 'Your King and Country need you', adding an emotive paragraph:

Will you answer your Country's Call? Each day is fraught with the gravest possibilities, and at this very moment the Empire is engaged in the greatest war in the history of the world.

In this crisis your Country calls on all her young unmarried men to rally round the Flag and enlist in the ranks of her Army.

If every patriotic young man answers her call, England and her Empire will emerge stronger and more united than ever.[13]

Recruiting was remarkably effective with 500,000 responding in the first month and 100,000 every month for another 18 months. Professionals from all sports were among them. By December 1914, 186 county cricketers, including five England captains (all amateur), had joined up. Only 25 per cent of the men on the list were professionals.[14] The pages of *Boxing* in late 1914 reflect a professional sport racked with the controversies we have seen in football, cricket and racing, and trying to cope with the unprecedented wartime crisis. Boxers were particularly vulnerable to the accusation that they should be 'fighting' not for money but for their country.

As well as Kitchener's appeal, *Boxing* published many photographs of professional boxers in uniform. Its cover on 29 August 1914 depicted Dick Smith in khaki flanked by four Union Jacks, wielding a lethal-looking bayonet as he 'PREPARES FOR STERNER FIGHTING'. *Boxing* applauded enthusiastically each professional as he signed on – including Seaman Hayes, P. O. Curran, Dick Smith, Johnny Basham, Gunner Rawles and Dan

Voyles. This it would also do for French boxers who followed Carpentier's example, all commended by the magazine for joining the French forces.

The journal was soon forced to regularly record the melancholy news that Boxer A had been wounded or that Boxer B had been killed. Bandsman Blake, for example, was wounded almost immediately yet had *re-enlisted* before September was out. Because of the chaotic nature of wartime communications the 'information' was sometimes merely rumour and subsequently denied. In October, Charles Ledoux was 'severely wounded', a report contradicted in November. Ledoux was recorded 'dead' some nine times. Most embarrassing was the case of Eugene Stuber (b. 11 July 1887), the French heavyweight, that a magazine had previously suggested could have been a world title holder had 'nature afforded him just a few ounces more of brain'. *Boxing* put a portrait of Stuber on the cover of the 28 September issue and paid a fulsome tribute to him as gallant ally and martyr, the first French boxer and the first prominent participant in his sport killed in action. Only in November was it realised that Stuber was actually still alive. Indeed, he resumed his boxing career in 1918, boxed another six years and died in his seventies on 5 December 1959.

The Stuber episode was unfortunate but completely understandable because it could so easily have been true. The sober reality of the risks run by soldiers was demonstrated by middleweight Sergeant Pat McEnroy, now of the Irish Guards. McEnroy wrote a letter to *Boxing* describing his experiences under fire.[15] The letter was supplemented by the news that

McEnroy had received four wounds in calf and thigh and would be back in Blighty very soon. McEnroy on crutches was rapturously received at The Ring and at the NSC and returned to action in 1915 as soon as his wounds had healed. Welterweight Tom McCormick was another to send letters to *Boxing* describing life in the ranks – they ceased when he was killed on the Somme in the summer of 1916.

On 22 August 1914, the journal appealed for the formation of a boxers' battalion: 'Such a corps would at least be fully furnished with the basic essential of the soldier viz. the combative instinct. It is an easy proposition that the man who is habituated to hard knocks will make as good a Tommy as the best of them.' This could hardly be denied.

In September, *Boxing* could claim 'more professional boxers had gone to the front, in comparison to their numbers, than any other section of the community'.[16] In October, it launched an appeal fund to supply a pair of boxing gloves to every soldier who requested one. By December, the magazine could point rightly to boxing's efforts being quite as good as that of any other sport.[17] It calculated that 647 professional boxers had joined up and over 50 of their names had appeared on the casualty lists. It was a distinctly honourable record.

Boxing had inevitably to defend its continuation as recruitment fever flourished. The magazine believed their industry, like the others, should continue:

'But if the pursuit of racing should be a valuable method of displaying one's patriotism, what on earth can be the matter with the pursuit of football, cricket, boxing or any other sport?'

It was particularly incensed by the speeches of the elderly Lord Frederick Roberts (1832–1914), one of the 19th century's most decorated soldiers. Roberts had advocated conscription in the face of German aggression since *before* the war broke out. He pronounced the continuation of football a national disgrace. *Boxing* sarcastically defended its fellow sport and its spectators:

Does Lord Roberts suggest that they ought all to enlist – work hard at their trades all the week and then fly off on Saturday afternoon to deal the Germans a smashing blow, and then fly back again in time to respond to Monday morning's hooter?[18]

If professional boxing were to continue, then naturally some professional boxers would not be serving in the military for the time being. Bombardier Billy Wells, despite his rank, was one. He claimed that as husband and father with a mother and two young brothers also to support, he needed to be boxing because he had no employer to subsidise him in uniform. (His younger brother, who joined up early enough to be in the original BEF, did not survive even the second month of the war and was killed in action on 23 September 1914.) In the meantime (he would join up in May 1915), Wells pursued his career domestically, taking the slimmer pickings that wartime boxing could offer.

Others saw that a boxing career in Britain, were the war long to continue, would be less financially rewarding than it had been. One was Freddie Welsh. In mid-August, accompanied by his wife and daughter, Welsh

travelled in first-class comfort on the luxury liner *Olympic* bound for New York. Ever concerned about his public image, he authorised an article, 'WHY I LEFT SO HURRIEDLY!' in *Boxing* to explain and excuse himself.[19] He claimed a lucrative music hall tour worth $50,000 had been cancelled on him because of the war, and as all big-money fights had now died, he had to take up American offers, which 'I could not, in common fairness, refuse'. This sounded even more special pleading than Wells's claims. It certainly frustrated other boxers hungry to challenge for Welsh's Lonsdale Belt, now apparently out of their reach. We shall see how he fared.

Ted Kid Lewis spent the war years taking lucrative American fights.
BoxRec

A similar case was that of Ted Kid Lewis. From May to August 1914, Lewis fought in Sydney and Melbourne. His departure for London by early September and a request for a London manager to take over his resumed British career were rumoured. The rumours were false. At the critical moment, he and his entourage, including his Lonsdale Belt, had indeed embarked from Australia but were bound for San Francisco. He would stay in the USA until the war was over. The Kentish welterweight Arthur Evernden, fighting in Australia since August 1913, stayed put, and by the end of 1914 announced that he had emigrated permanently.

Lewis or Evernden would not be at the NSC in the near future. On the outbreak of war, there were doubts about the opening of the NSC for the 1914–15 season. In fact, it opened as usual on 19 October 1914 with a potentially interesting clash (see below). It felt obliged to do what it could for the war effort. It supplied seven ambulance cars for the Red Cross (cars said to have carried over 100,000 wounded back from the front by the end of 1915), and before 1914 was over launched a special NSC fund for the wounded. It held charitable events, concert evenings, services boxing tournaments, auctions and raffles, and justified its continuance with many contributions to war funds. Commercial promoters also had to find a formula acceptable to wartime.

An imaginative venture took place on Monday, 28 September 1914. The promoter, Jack Callaghan, a brave man in the straitened circumstances, launched the new West London Stadium on Church Street off the Edgware Road, close to Edgware Road station. He aimed to fill the stadium by charging reasonable prices. For the six-bout bill, top prices were three guineas for boxes, with stage seats at 20s. and 5s., plus reserved stall and circle seats at 5s. Cheaper seats in pit and gallery were only 2s. and 1s. Top of the bill was an attractive pairing of a fit and eager Alf Mansfield, the latest of a long line of Jewish East End flyweights and bantamweights, and the Welsh maestro, Jimmy Wilde. Wilde was also eager but the question was *how* eager? He let an indulgent holiday in Blackpool run over into his original schedule, leaving only eight days for serious training, further

curtailed by a two-day motor car trip. The remaining six days' training lacked sparring partners. His regular team had all signed on.

The two had met before in April at Leeds (27 April) when Mansfield, despite a severe weight-losing programme, took Wilde 20 rounds before losing on points. It was announced that after legitimate expenses, the West London takings would be going to the Prince of Wales's Relief Fund. They included £18 5s. raised by auctioning the winning gloves and a dozen silk handkerchiefs autographed by Wilde.

The fight lasted half the time of the first.[20] The highlight for many was to see the skills of Wilde for the first time. Master of the counter, Mansfield's determination to attack suited Wilde. At the first bell, Mansfield rushed out and swung a mighty punch, coolly avoided by Wilde, which took Mansfield clumsily down on to all fours. Hardly was he up than Wilde delivered a series of whipping uppercuts, short hooks and jabs to return him to the canvas.

Mansfield was clever but Wilde outclassed him continually. If he covered up and crouched, Wilde belaboured him in the ribs. If he stayed upright, gloves to the side of his head, Wilde jabbed him to the face. If he closed his gloves over the centre gap, Wilde hooked him to cheek and temple. *Boxing* called Wilde 'one of the few really great boxers of the world', and this night Mansfield agreed. Even when, in the third, Mansfield caught Wilde with some clever left leads, he suffered a sequence of straight lefts and rights to his own head.

As round followed round, Mansfield punched furiously but this was a night of Wilde at his subtly elusive best, taking

punches on his gloves and arms, or on a raised shoulder, or allowing them to miss him by a fraction. And back came the hurtful rejoinders, which Mansfield could do little to keep out. They left visible traces. Said *Boxing*'s eyewitness, 'Mansfield's face showed frequent and widespread signs of the punishment … and will probably note a plentiful lack of personal recognition to-day and tomorrow.' This was unkind, as was the suggestion that Mansfield's post-fight souvenirs included 'the winner's gloves … and an entirely newly assorted set of features'. Mansfield's bravery took him to the end of the tenth before his corner surrendered on his behalf. The seconds were wiser than he.

The main feature at the NSC opening night on 19 October 1914 was planned as a flyweight contest for the Lonsdale Belt, a matter in which Wilde had a considerable interest. It featured his compatriot Percy Jones, holder of the British title since his surprise victory over Bill Ladbury in January 1914, defending his title against the experienced Scot Tancy Lee of Leith (b. 8 February 1882).[21] Lee had beaten good men, including Johnny Best (retired in the 17th) and Bill Ladbury (stopped in the eighth). Jones and Lee, two clever boxers matched over 20 rounds for the 8st title and the Lonsdale Belt – an exciting prospect *on paper*.

In reality it was not. Jones struggled to keep within the flyweight limit at the best of times, and at the weigh-in was well over it. Frantic efforts, including running heavy-laden around the streets of Covent Garden and making three visits to the local Turkish baths, proved insufficient. To compensate disappointed members, Jones and Lee agreed to a catchweight contest instead.

The wasted Jones took 14 rounds of punishment before retiring. It was a fiasco that did no one any credit. Two months later, the diminutive Jones was a Welsh fusilier and enduring the dreadful wartime experiences that led eventually to his early death.

Meanwhile, Wilde was underlining his claims to be the undisputed leading flyweight. On 16 November 1914 at the NSC, he outpointed Joe Symonds of Plymouth (b. Hubert Toms or possibly Rupert Harvey, 28 December 1894), a serving sailor who had his own claims for recognition.

The wiry little Devonian had defeated, by a late stoppage, Percy Jones (again overweight) in Plymouth on 15 May 1914. Symonds also had two victories over Alf Mansfield (3 January 1913 and 3 March 1913). Wilde thought Symonds his most difficult opponent and many believe Symonds would have a greater reputation had he boxed more often in London rather than at his beloved Old Cosmo in Plymouth. There his opponents had to face the rugged Symonds and 6,000 raucous local fans. The Cosmo was another commercial venue determined to continue during the war, reopening in September 1914 after a complete redecoration.

Symonds, despite a 15-pound advantage and having trounced Smith, Jones and Ladbury, found weight and collateral form counted for nothing against a top form Wilde. He sensed it early for he punched Wilde low nearly a dozen times in the second and was fortunate not to be disqualified. Wilde let the bout go on specifically to punish Symonds for the fouls:

> … it may be remarked that Wilde
> not only won every rd., but never

once was reduced to the necessity of raising his gloves higher than his waist level in a posture of defence.[22]

Wilde next went to Liverpool and met Sid Smith on 3 December 1914. It took eight rounds to slow the Londoner down and another one to knock him out. Wilde took four domestic professional fights to sustain his professional career after the war had started, with ten to come in 1915 and 15 in 1916. The immediate next promised to be the most prestigious and lucrative – meeting Tancy Lee at the NSC on 25 January 1915 with the Lonsdale Belt and the official flyweight title on offer.

We shall soon see what happened then, but what about that other famous Welshman, Freddie Welsh, the man who spurned domestic action after the world title fight against Willie Ritchie and left for the USA to sustain his earnings unhampered by wartime deprivations? Just as he calculated whatever tactic would win him a fight and ruthlessly stuck to it, so would he conduct his American career. He had a powerful bargaining counter in the holding of the world lightweight championship, an asset recognised by American promoters such as Jim Coffroth, whose telegram offering Welsh $50,000 for three fights was waiting for him when he docked in New York.[23]

Welsh calculated that he could take ten-round no-decision bouts for handsome fees, lose in the opinion of newspaper journalists, and, providing he avoided being knocked out, would be richer and still champion. He would take no 20-round championship bout (for which few states gave the necessary legal blessing) putting his title genuinely

on the line unless he were paid at least $25,000.[24]

He first treated the Americans to a vaudeville act performed at Hammerstein's Victoria Theatre on 42nd Street at Seventh Avenue. The building was the less than successful creation of Oscar Hammerstein I (confusingly, Oscar Hammerstein II, famous for his musical collaborations with Richard Rodgers, was OH I's *grand*son). It was pulled down in 1915. Freddie's act, an unholy mixture of sparring, shadow-boxing, a mime of 'How I beat Willie Ritchie', and an offer to wrestle any man in the audience, did more for his future than the theatre's.

Having enhanced his profile, Welsh took *seven* more fights before 1914 was over, some days after another. He outpointed Matty Baldwin in Boston (27 October) over 12 rounds. On 2 November he was in Madison Square Garden for a stirring fight with the man whose ring performances echoed the feline nature of his nickname, the Michigan Wildcat – Ad Wolgast.[25] This was a piquant prospect: the unshowy and crafty Brit (9st 10lb/136lbs) using his skills to win but not necessarily to please, and the rough, tough American (9st 9½lb/135½lbs) determined to target Welsh's sardonic smile with a gloved fist. Wolgast was all aggression, assaulting Welsh about the body and taking the straight lefts and rights that Welsh landed on his nose. There was hidden provocation here as Wolgast had had plastic surgery on his nose and was vain about his new appearance. As expected, Wolgast used his strength and landed the heavier punches, Welsh was the more skilful. After close exchanges in the second, won by Wolgast, the champion decided to box at a safe if dull distance. He took a breather in the third and successively tied Wolgast up or sidestepped him. The tactic succeeded until the very end of the round when Welsh slipped momentarily and Wolgast caught him with a right uppercut that turned the smile into a grimace. A man with a lesser chin might have succumbed. Welsh did not. In a professional career of 167 fights, against all the leading lightweights of the day, he was actually knocked out only once.

He himself knew how to uppercut with venom. He launched one at Wolgast's chin in the fifth. It was intercepted by Wolgast's right arm held across his chest to defend from just such a possibility. It landed at an awkward angle and broke Wolgast's ulna a few inches above the wrist. The contest was over, although Wolgast struggled on one-handed for another three rounds before retiring. He was no artist but no one could accuse him of lacking bravery in the face of pain.

Welsh continued his lucrative series and nominally lost two of them. He met Charley White, a robust Jewish fighter who had been born in England (Liverpool, 25 March 1891) but subsequently became a local favourite in his adopted Chicago. The fight was at Milwaukee on 9 November (a mere week after the Wolgast match). White was no pushover. He beat many good men in his time, including Willie Ritchie, Ad Wolgast, Owen Moran and Matt Wells, and possessed a particularly effective left hook.

Welsh's biographer Andrew Gallimore refers to Welsh's 'victory' and says 'the challenger didn't win a round until the ninth' [of ten]. He is scathing about the newspaper decision in favour of White, which he attributes to the bias of local Chicago journalists. Under the ten-round no-decision system, such a travesty was always possible. However, the sober agency report carried in the *New York Times* suggests a 'fiercely fought' contest in which White was 'almost as fast as Welsh with his hands, and hit with more force' and that 'his [White's] stiff punching' and 'whirlwind finish … earned the decision by a small margin'.[26] Considering Welsh's commercial decision to face the hard-punching White a mere week after Wolgast, this version is at least possible.

Welsh's profitable pilgrimages continued with a visit on 19 November to Buffalo, where 10,000 people saw him justify a $5,000 guarantee by easily beating Jimmy Duffy. From there it was off to Boston for a ten-round struggle on 24 November against Fred Yelle (b. 8 August 1889), a local lightweight who had spent the last few months before the war boxing at the Stadium in Liverpool. Welsh won relatively easily but damaged a knuckle on his right hand. Stupidly and presumably over-greedy for the appearance fee, he went on to Syracuse, disguising the injury and outpointing Young Abe Brown over ten rounds on 26 November – two fights in three days.

Something was clearly wrong when, on 2 December 1914[27], Welsh faced Young Joe Shugrue (b. Jersey City, 11 September 1894), a man who had spent the summer of 1914 boxing in Australia where he lost to Ted Kid Lewis on points over 20 rounds (Sydney, 26 June 1914) yet knocked out the talented Hughie Mehegan in the 11th of 20 (Melbourne, 25 July 1914). One of a trio of sporting brothers, Shugrue

developed a detached retina over his next few fights and gave up boxing in November 1915. In December 1914 he was a stiff proposition for anyone.

In a packed Madison Square Garden, Shugrue and the ringsiders were astonished to see Welsh smiling as usual but spending most of the ten rounds working almost entirely with his left, his right held tight to his body and used rarely and tentatively. The knuckle cracked on Yelle and aggravated against Brown was now too painful to sustain a decent punch. Shugrue, short, thickset and with plenty of relish for a scrap, the rougher the better, took full advantage of the golden opportunity fate had handed him – the chance to share the ring with a taller but out-of-form and tired one-handed world champion. The afternoon weigh-in had both men at 9st 7½lb/133½lbs. A repeat performance in the evening at ringside put Shugrue at 9st 11½lb/137½lbs and Welsh at 9st 8¾lb/134¾lbs. Shugrue put his few pounds advantage to use in a belligerent eighth round to cancel out Welsh's best round, the seventh. He clinched his victory by newspaper decision with a final flourish, a ramrod right to Welsh's jaw at the end of the tenth.

So Welsh finished his late 1914 tour with two losses in seven fights, none of them putting his title at risk aside from the unlikely eventuality of getting knocked out. The *National Police Gazette* pronounced on the mini-series:

Hand Welsh forty-five per cent of the gross receipts and he doesn't care a rap who his opponent is or who the promoter selects to pit against him … Thus far it has helped fill his coffers with gold.[28]

The journal meant it as a compliment. Welsh travelled the eastern seaboard and elsewhere taking on all-comers week by week to sustain a lavish and fashionable New York address and the lifestyle to go with it. He exploited but did not create the ten-round no-decision situation. His hunger for cash trumped other serious considerations. No professional should be risking his health by fighting too often, taking new fights with no time to train or going into the ring carrying injuries. As well as two embarrassing losses, Welsh was guilty of all three.

He was desperate to cash in on every opportunity while they lasted. Who knew what would happen in the future? He made in excess of $50,000 in a matter of weeks but it cost him in other ways. He admitted privately, 'I'm horribly sick and tired of fighting, you don't know how I loathe it all.' The excess load had been self-inflicted and, sick and tired, he continued. Disillusionment did not stop him taking at least another 15 ten-round no-decision bouts in 1915.

Welsh probably felt vindicated when 16 days after his unfortunate outing against Shugrue, he heard the news from California. Two minor American lightweights – Eddie Moy (b. 1 January 1892) from Pennsylvania, once Welsh's sparring partner, and the Coloradan Red Watson (b. 8 December 1893) – drew a late-night 20-round bout at San Francisco. The referee declared the result at 11.35pm. Twenty-five minutes later, from midnight 19 December 1914, all bouts in California were restricted to a maximum four-round limit. The constraint lasted another decade and severely hampered West Coast boxing. Moy and Watson had

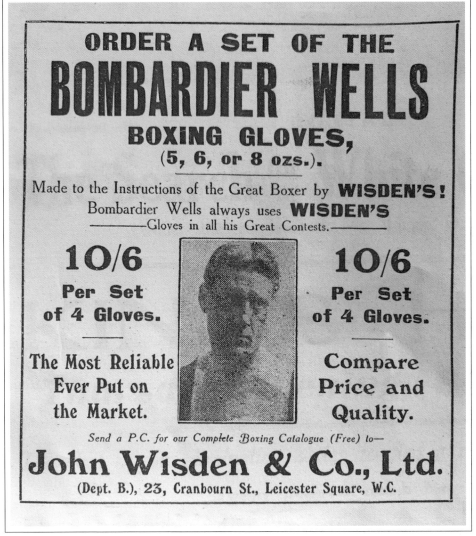

Billy Wells continued to box professionally in the early war years and enhanced his income with paid advertisements.
Boxing

just completed the last-ever 20-round fight in California. Another potential earning opportunity for top fighters in peacetime USA had been taken away.

Back in England, Jimmy Wilde knew that clinching the Lonsdale Belt in January 1915 would open rather than close doors. The holder of the belt would draw challengers and purse offers, if not on the pre-war scale. All he had to do was to beat Tancy Lee, a man admired but not thought to be Wilde's equal. Lee won the 1910 ABA bantamweight championship but being technically in breach of the stricter

than strict amateur rules, had the title taken away. The episode suggested Lee was also unlucky. Beat him and, even in wartime, Wilde would be making serious money.

Unwisely Wilde fulfilled the date against Lee after suffering a bout of influenza over Christmas and picking up a heavy cold a week before the clash. At the weigh-in, Lee was 7st 13½lb/111½lbs and Wilde 7st 11lb/109lbs; no great apparent discrepancy. This is seriously misleading as Lee had stripped and Wilde had stepped on the scales *fully clothed*.

Wilde's slim body weighed more like 6st 13½lb/97½lbs in reality, in other words he was giving away about a stone to a strong, heavy-punching opponent.

This may partly explain the unexpected result.[29] It neither excuses Wilde nor detracts from one of the best performances Lee ever delivered. On the night he matched Wilde for clever defences and outfought and out-thought the Welshman from the first bell. He hustled Wilde away from any range at which he felt comfortable and forced him back to the ropes or into a corner where space was at a premium. In those restricted quarters, he wrestled Wilde around, brushed aside or forced down Wilde's defences and delivered weakening body blows.

Lee followed these tactics for the first four rounds. He knew Wilde's reputation as a formidable boxer/puncher sustained in victories over men physically bigger. Lee kept a sense of discretion and left no easy openings. Against a man whose record then stood at 79 contests, 79 times undefeated, this was sensible. After 12 minutes of action he realised he was the superior and could boss Wilde physically without danger of being stopped himself. Undeterred by any of Wilde's punches he went on boring in, clinching, hugging, manoeuvring and mauling the Welshman back to the ropes where he wanted him. Wilde's counters were cleverly smothered.

In the 13th, Wilde traded blow for blow, to the delight of the packed audience, but it was a last-gasp effort. An exhausted and disappointed Wilde suffered nearly four more rounds of heavy punches before a towel came fluttering into the ring, thrown by his seconds who saw reasonably enough

that three more rounds of damaging hooks, jabs and uppercuts were superfluous and potentially dangerous. Tancy Lee clicked the Lonsdale Belt around his waist, the first Scot to win a British championship, and better off by £500. He would be cashing in further with appearances in the Holborn and the Camberwell Palace music halls during February.

The loss left Wilde out in the cold and having to fight all too regularly to rebuild his prospects. By January 1916 *Boxing* was particularly concerned about his hyper-productivity: 'The little man keeps busy – easily the busiest little boxer Great Britain has ever known … but it is to be doubted whether he will be able to stand the strain indefinitely.' Wise words. Wilde spent 1915 fighting in the provinces (Liverpool, Sheffield, Leeds, Bradford) and winning every one of the eight fights with knockouts and stoppages.

His return to the NSC was on 20 December 1915 against Sid Smith.[30] Having already knocked out Smith in nine rounds in Liverpool a year before (3 December 1914), he now went one better by stopping the faster, heavier Smith in the eighth. Smith began cautiously, his Liverpool experience in mind. It made no difference. Ducking, swaying and moving his head throughout, Wilde purposefully tracked Smith down and countered every punch thrown to stop him. Smith was down for eight in the second, down twice in the third, again in the fifth, four times in the seventh, and six times in the eighth – three times from sheer exhaustion. Only then was a halt called, mercy overtaking members' desire to see a masterly performance continue. A return against Lee was

obligatory. We shall see how Wilde fared in 1916–18.

A packed NSC and a famous boxer like Wilde in action made the wartime boxing scene in 1915 seem as familiar as in times of peace. In January, for example, although the Midlands lacked events because of the demands of war, there were bills to be seen in London at the NSC, the West London Stadium, Lambert's School of Arms, the Holborn Stadium and The Ring (offering evening and matinee bills with the tireless Dick Burge actively promoting refugee funds, recruitment and even soup kitchens). The St James' Hall in Newcastle continued, as did the Stadium in Liverpool. Abertillery in the Welsh valleys, the Victoria Club in Glasgow and the Old Cosmo in Plymouth all offered action, often from servicemen allowed to box, or at professional or semi-professional evenings where some worthy wartime charity received part of the funds. As the year went on, it became more difficult. Even so, by December 1915, boxing could still be seen at many old favourites, the Liverpool Stadium, St James' Hall, Newcastle and the Circle, Hull for example.

By November 1915, the NSC offered boxing bills adapted to wartime circumstances. The takings, after expenses, went to charity; for example, a refuge for blind sailors and soldiers. Three headline fights, one featuring Johnny Summers and one Alec Lambert, were padded out with a novices' heavyweight competition and exhibition spars (including a comic one with Wally Pickard). Members and guests coughed up prices from 10s. 6d. to three guineas and bought an expensive souvenir programme to swell the proceeds. The clearest sign that wartime was not peacetime was the announcement that *the ladies will once more be admitted*. Previously there had been no such a practice, although Mrs Wilde, wife, comforter and ubiquitous manager, was accommodated secretly at her boxer husband's request and her own insistence when Wilde was recovering from his beating from Tancy Lee. She had not been at ringside.

With so many men away, female guests brought in money, cash trumping gender prejudice. Just as eager for funds in December 1915, The Ring would sell up to 8,000 tickets (1s. to 10s.) for a police boxing tournament lasting at least three evenings. That money went to the Metropolitan Police Orphanage but the normal male monopoly at The Ring prevailed.

As 1915 wore on, sport was more and more restricted. (Professional football ceased after the FA Cup Final in 1915 as did county cricket, and though racing continued, the more glamorous and fashionable meetings such as Ascot and Goodwood were discreetly shelved.) Yet, for the moment, significant boxers with famous names were getting fights, in and out of uniform.

Bombardier Billy Wells, before and after his enlistment in May 1915, was one. He reigned officially as the British heavyweight champion and unofficially as the biggest box office draw in British boxing from 1911 to 1919. This was very creditable even if the war made for a lean period for serious challengers. Wells fought twice in February 1915, the second 12 days after the first.

On 12 February, he was down at the Old Cosmo in Plymouth facing Dan McGoldrick for a purse of £450. McGoldrick was a Scottish light-

heavyweight from Airdrie, a man never more than 12st/168lbs and some three to four inches shorter than Wells. A professional since 1907, he had a patchy record. He lost twice to Bandsman Rice, whom Wells had outpointed in Liverpool on 30 April 1914 after his notorious morning round of golf. McGoldrick outpointed a good American in Arthur Pelkey at the Old Cosmo over 20 rounds on 26 January 1915, but that was one of the sensitive Pelkey's losses after his dreadful experience against Luther McCarty. A win for Wells was practically preordained. McGoldrick's seconds accepted their man's fate by throwing in the towel at the end of the seventh.

On 24 February, it was Bandsman (actually now Sergeant) Rice's turn at the Grand Opera House in Belfast at prices from 2s. up to a relatively modest 20s.[31] The prices were generous yet failed to attract a full house. This is not surprising. The war was beginning to bite on the Home Front. By the end of 1915, food prices would be 45 per cent higher than before the war, straining many a household budget.[32] Had Wells's army of English fans fancied a trip to Northern Ireland to see him, it meant a sea voyage through waters where German U-boats were lurking. Those U-boats would be hampering many imports from now on. *Boxing* reduced itself to a meagre 12 pages from September 1915 because of the blockade's effect upon paper supplies.

The low attendance was a pity as there was plenty of excitement for as long as the bout lasted.[33] Rice, another shorter, lighter man who thought himself robbed by Wells in Liverpool, crawled tentatively out of his corner as if overwhelmed by the occasion and by

Wells's elegant presence. It was a mere feint. Suddenly, he leaped at Wells like a large carnivore determined to claw his victim before the champion settled his nerves. It was not classic but it very nearly worked.

Completely taken aback, Wells tried fending the attacker off with left leads and when that failed, turned his body away, meaning to save his ribs and midriff but taking blows to his kidneys instead. He opted passively to smother Rice's flailing punches, as well as the flying elbows, forearm smashes and suddenly shrugged shoulders. Rice wrested his arms free and gave him some more. Four successive digs to Wells's tender midriff folded Wells up and dropped him to his knees. With Rice hovering over him he sensibly stayed down for nine, getting up only when he had to.

After the humiliating first-round count and urgent advice from his corner, would Wells be overwhelmed by Rice's continued aggression, or would his classical left lead give him a chance to counter? For five turbulent rounds, the question remained open. After a third round in which a flying left from an airborne Rice closed the Bombardier's right eye, odds on a Rice victory shortened rapidly.

Only in the sixth did Rice's jump and swing tactic misfire. Just as he launched himself at Wells, his opponent produced a full-blooded left hook to Rice's rising chin. The meeting of two such forces had a satisfyingly dramatic effect, taking Rice even further up towards the roof, to a point in mid-air from which he turned over and fell so heavily on the ropes as to break the top one and to fall on his head on to the canvas. The count was a formality:

Wells by sixth-round knockout. The bare result hardly conveyed the reality. (Rice later blamed the broken rope for his demise. Others asserted correctly that he was rather saved further damage by it breaking his fall before it snapped.)

What survived Wells's Belfast venture were those saleable assets of Wells, his fluctuating skill, his vulnerability and his sheer unpredictability. People bought tickets to see what happened next like cinema serial fans returning the following week eager to see whether the heroine could be saved from the oncoming train. Dick Burge was the next promoter to exploit such a question.

He signed Wells and the 28-year-old American who had been Jack Johnson's last opponent before the war (27 June 1914, Paris). This was Frank Moran, the Pittsburgh Dentist and proud carrier of Mary Ann, his own portable anaesthetist. Moran and Wells met on 29 March 1915 over 20 rounds for a £700 purse at the London Opera House in Kingsway (not the Royal Opera House, Covent Garden as the BoxRec internet site has it).[34] Although prices reflected austerity and ranged from 2s. in the gallery to premium seats at £2 2s. and £1 11s. 6d., this was still the biggest domestic fight since the war began and one with plenty of appeal to what remained of the pre-war carriage trade. The 3,000 seats sold out immediately, a significant number to Wells's women fans, while 5,000 other people milled around Holborn on the night desperate to get inside. No one criticised the staging of the bout in the midst of war, and the naval and military uniforms throughout the house, worn by those standing in the aisles and seated on the stage alongside the ring,

suggested serving soldiers were eager to endorse the promotion. Anyone who planned to forget the war temporarily had to ignore the prominent row in the stalls occupied by wounded men.

The Times suggested correctly that attenders were being treated to a full anthology of Wells's assets and liabilities: '… the clever boxer, the sensation monger, the winner, and the hopelessly beaten'. Starting nervously with a mistimed assault, Wells left himself open to a big right that caught him on the right cheek and staggered him. Bemused, he half-moved and half-ran towards his corner. Moran was so taken aback by this reaction that he failed to press on for the first-round knockout he was close to achieving.

Wells in instant loser mode had survived, just. Out for the second round came another Wells, the clever commanding boxer. With a tighter defence and strong direct jabs to the squatter, slower Moran, this Wells, Billy Redivivus, gave a lesson in ring skills for the next eight and a half rounds. He was much the quicker, so much so that when Moran cumbrously telegraphed a big swing, a wag in the crowd shouted, 'Look out, Billy!' and both boxers paused and smiled. A few more seconds passed before the delayed punch was (unsuccessfully) launched. Meanwhile, Wells punished Moran round after round.

But there was another contrast between the two. Wells, now so much on top, was not relishing the contest; perhaps he never did. Moran, punched from pillar to post, was smiling, grinning and enjoying a scrap, as he did perpetually. His intransigence paid off. In the middle of the tenth round, his latest plethora of swings to and around

Wells included two crunching blows to Wells's body. As Wells bent forward, another connected with his jaw. Down he went and lucky to be up at nine. One more smacker from Mary Ann was sufficient. Flat on his face, he was counted out.

He was still British champion and remained so for seven years, ten months and three days, a worthy record finally taken away in the 1960s by Henry Cooper. The war helped many British champions to retain their title by reducing the number of contenders and limiting the number of possible fights. Welsh in the USA was recognised as lightweight champion; Basham domestically as welter.

Yet it was now easier to be a contender and win a Lonsdale Belt contest. Three fighters (Lee, Symonds and Wilde) won flyweight belts during the war; two (Curley Walker and Joe Fox) bantam belts; three (Llew Edwards, Charlie Hardcastle and Tancy Lee) featherweight belts; two (Pat O'Keefe and Bandsman Jack Blake) middleweight belts; and two (Dick Smith and Harry Reeve) light-heavy belts. The tendency of Lonsdale Belt holders to profit from its possession by boxing outside the NSC drew a formal statement from the club in March 1915 that belts could be won only at the NSC and should a champion lose under championship conditions elsewhere, the belt should be forfeited and returned to the NSC. In the cases of exiles such as Lewis and Welsh, this was a pious hope.

Whenever domestic champion Billy Wells tried to transcend the domestic scene against an international opponent he usually failed miserably. Well might Wally Pickard in his music hall turns gain laughs with his tribute to Wells:

'Look what I did to Colin Bell!' The line could as easily have been: 'Look what Carpentier, Palzer, Smith, Moran, etc. did to me!' Even Wells's most fervent supporters conceded that Billy had 'a weak spot'. *Boxing* obligingly defined it: 'Wells' weak spot is located in any part of his anatomy on which a really heavy blow may happen to land'– cruel but true.[35] Wells heeded the military call and re-enlisted. This did not affect his professional boxing career too seriously and he was able to take two more domestic fights in 1915 and four in 1916 as one of several soldier-boxers obtaining permission to appear in the ring. The British Army in particular saw that functioning sports stars in uniform were useful propaganda for recruitment. Wells's extraordinary popularity was unblemished even by the loss to Moran, and he was mobbed by fans when he turned out for a charity football match at the Everton ground in early May 1915. His commercial value dipped a little. His next contest on 31 May 1915 was at Dick Burge's South London proletarian boxing headquarters, The Ring – close geographically but some distance in internal décor and audience decorum from the London Opera House.

Pre-match publicity made much of his enlistment in the Welch Regiment and that his opponent, Sergeant Dick Smith, was a member of the Oxford and Buckinghamshire Light Infantry. Both soldiers were primarily army boxing instructors and indeed Smith trained hard in the military gymnasium at Portsmouth.

Dick Smith won the ABA heavyweight title in 1912 and 1913 but was never more than a light-heavyweight. When he turned professional he beat,

on 9 March 1914 at the second attempt, Dennis Haugh to clinch the Lonsdale Belt and the light-heavyweight title. Putting up a purse of £700, Burge matched the British heavyweight champion against the light-heavy champion – potentially a perfect fight for the NSC but one stolen by Burge's initiative. He got entertaining action for his outlay.[36]

With his superior height and weight (around 13 pounds) and reach (six inches), Wells was the betting favourite. Yet with his capricious record, who knew what might happen? Something unexpected, of course, and as if to give Wells's pre-fight nerves extra time to take effect, there were two pre-fight delays. One was an auction for the gloves, a venture that raised £31 10s. for wartime charities and took place as the boxers stood ready in the ring. The second was a crafty request by Smith to have his hands rebandaged at the last minute.

Neither interruption fazed Wells, who started confidently and staggered Smith with a left hook. Smith clutched at the top rope for support. Wells held off, suspecting Smith was foxing. Wells repeated the treatment in the third and again discreetly stood off and allowed Smith to recover. So far, so conventional, and even when Smith made a spirited rally in the fourth and Wells took a breather, no one believed Wells would lose. Wells reasserted his superiority in the sixth and shook Smith several times, although looking a trifle tired. He allowed Smith to take the seventh.

The unanticipated came in the eighth. Wells produced the punch of the fight, a straight left as good as any he had ever produced. Back went Smith's

head and back went Smith, pursued by a jabbing Wells. Suddenly Smith fought back and the two abandoned caution in a flurry of swings, hooks and uppercuts. Just as Wells threatened to overwhelm the smaller man, left and right hooks met his own chin and he toppled forward face-down on the canvas, motionless. Smith and his many fans leaped in delight and referee Dunning, watching from outside the ring, rushed through the ropes to complete the count.

Dunning was not a young man and he got tangled up with the ropes on his way in. Thus, the delayed count probably took 14 or 15 seconds. A bemused and stunned Wells was up at the supposed count of nine and barely able to defend himself when the bell rang. His seconds performed miracles of resuscitation during the break.

The ninth saw both men rushing towards each other and punching furiously as if there were only seconds left. So it proved. A Wells right caught Smith's jaw and it was his turn to totter. Wells followed up with short jabs and a final right to leave Smith in a heap in the corner. Smith, unluckier than Wells in the timing, got up at what he thought was nine but Dunning had already voiced 'ten' and waved *finis*. Wells had won again, and again shredded the nerves of his backers. He dominated the press coverage next day to Burge's delight and to the chagrin of the NSC.

The very same night, 31 May 1915, the NSC countered Burge's promotion with a British featherweight title fight for Ted Kid Lewis's old title.[37] Lewis's absence and his growth in weight out of the division meant he could not defend it. Lewis had taken his Lonsdale Belt on his travels and worse still mislaid it on a visit to Cuba.

The veteran Owen Moran, who returned from the USA just before war broke out, and the new Welsh featherweight, 23-year-old Llew Edwards (b. 22 October 1892) were invited to fight for the title and a replacement belt. Moran backed himself against the superior skills of Edwards but ran out first of stamina and then of patience. He alienated the crowd and referee Douglas (outside the ring) by dropping to his knees to take a breather in the seventh and for landing low blows in the eighth and ninth. When he unleashed another punch below Edwards's waist in the tenth, Douglas naturally disqualified him, a verdict volubly contested by Moran. He was visibly reaching the end, just as he had in the USA, and he finally called it a day on British soil on 21 August 1916 after another

disqualification against Billy Marchant at the Manchester Free Trade Hall. The abdication of his professional calling was less illustrious than his reigning years of glory. The Edwards fight was not a satisfying evening.

Alas, if the NSC members and management believed they had found a new hero in the ingenious Edwards, they were doomed to disappointment. Edwards fought 18 times in 1916 but all of them in Australia, where he settled for good. Apart from one post-war fight in Yorkshire in May 1920, once he won his belt he never fought in Britain again. His belt went with him.

Wells's 1915 position as a heavyweight champion, a regular soldier and a national icon was envied by the man who remained world heavyweight champion but a hunted exile from his native land – John 'Jack' Arthur Johnson. Johnson, after the financial fiasco of the fight against

Moran in June 1914, and with the German armies threatening to reach Paris, discreetly moved to London, a safer place but one without the possibility of a really big money fight. He took music hall engagements, spent money and got into minor scrapes with the law. One London magistrate, before whom Johnson appeared for causing an obstruction by leaving his luxury car in Leicester Square while being shaved in a barber's shop, spoke for many when he told Johnson, 'You and your motor cars take altogether too much room; there are others in London besides you!'[38] The fine was a pittance compared with his usual stage or ring earnings but these had seriously diminished.

One possibility emerged – a challenge from Jess Willard, the Pottawatomie [Kansas] Giant, suggested by Jack Curley, promoter of Johnson's fight against Fireman Flynn back in 1912. Willard, a self-proclaimed hater

Johnson on his back shading his eyes in the fateful round. Could he have got up? Many such questions were raised by the fight that lost him his precious title.

National Portrait Gallery, Smithsonian Institution

9 April 1915, the Oriental Park Racetrack, Havana, Cuba. Thousands of Cubans faced disappointment as Jack Johnson dominated all the early rounds against Jess Willard (1881–1968).

ORIENTAL PARK RACE TRACK
HAVANA CUBA

of boxing, was 6ft 6in and 18st/252lbs of grumpiness, with little skill but plenty of strength. He fancied he could beat Johnson.

No British or European venue was possible, and Johnson the felon would be arrested were he to enter the USA. Somewhere near the USA but not under its jurisdiction would be better. What inducements were on offer is obscure, but Johnson sailed from London bound for Buenos Aires believing he was en route for Juárez in Mexico to fight Willard.

Mexico was about as suitable a venue as war-torn Flanders. The country was riven between the northern Chihuahua territories (including Juárez), controlled by the revolutionary General Pancho Villa (in favour of the promotion as he stood to gain revenue from it) and the southern area controlled by Venustiano Carranza (a rival revolutionary who became President of Mexico in mid-1915). Juárez could not be reached without Johnson crossing the southern territories. Carranza, keen on good relations with the USA, declared he would hand Johnson over were the boxer to land in Carranza-controlled areas. So, Juárez was out. Johnson finished up on 15 February 1915 in Havana, Cuba and suggested the fight took place there.

The arrangements and the finances were as fraught as the politics. Johnson claimed a quid pro quo had been reached whereby:

> … if I permitted Willard to win, which would give him the title, much of the prejudice against me would be wiped out … and it would be easier to have the charges against me dropped, and I could again be with my folks.[39]

Like many of Johnson's later claims, this 'arrangement' has been doubted yet Johnson's most authoritative biographer, Geoffrey C. Ward in *Unforgivable Blackness: The Rise and Fall of Jack Johnson* p. 370, partly supports him:

> Curley apparently did promise to do his best to persuade the government to go easy on the champion, and there is documentary evidence that he followed through on that pledge. He may have further impressed the champion with talk of a potential ace … Secretary of State William Jennings Bryan was an old friend and former client …

One British boxer was in Cuba at the time and trained with Johnson in the weeks leading up to the fight. This was Ted Kid Lewis. Lewis also believed that a Johnson loss was arranged beforehand and always said so thereafter.

Johnson was not naïve enough to believe, loss or not, he could return to the USA as an absconded felon and be welcomed with open arms. However, perhaps he could *negotiate* a return on some basis of losing the title, surrendering himself voluntarily, pleading guilty and paying a heavy fine but escaping prison.

Money and mild corruption had, after all, smoothed his way *out* of the country into exile.

Randy Roberts in his excellent biography, *Papa Jack: Jack Johnson and the Era of White Hopes,* also points out that Chicago sportswriter Billy Birch, a man often in the know, reported rumours of a fix because Johnson was desperate for money and for a return to the USA:

By agreeing to lose, Johnson hoped to pocket more money and receive a reduced sentence when he returned to America.[40]

To relinquish his title while conscious of his advancing years, and reluctant to put in long training sessions to retain his fitness – he had just celebrated his 37th birthday – was no longer the great unthinkable. A return to home would, importantly, have meant seeing his aged mother for the first time since the trial.

> It was no easy decision. It meant the sacrifice of my heavy-weight title which I had striven years to obtain … On the other hand, there was held out the hope of returning home to those who were dear to me, and the possibility of finding leniency on the part of federal officials.[41]

Johnson arrogantly assumed that the clumsy Willard represented no threat and that his own strengths were bound to prevail. He had only to turn up to win. Therefore, a Willard victory was only possible if he, Johnson, decided to lie down.

A date was set then rearranged for Easter Sunday then rearranged again for Monday, 5 April to respect Christian sensibilities. Scheduled was a marathon 45-round fight on the Oriental Park Racetrack, 12 miles out of Havana, offering potential torture in the midday Cuban sun even for a young athlete, let alone for a veteran. Willard threatened to quit Cuba and go home at the first postponement but trained hard for potential rigours to come. Johnson, unless he put in secret hours out of sight, was more casual, spending time at the venue as a punter rather than athlete. He relied on his speed, skill and experience to outwit Willard (unless he did intend to lose).

Johnson and ring incidents were inseparable. This fight offered no less than three, much discussed then and ever after.[42] Cubans, including many Cuban women, were much taken with the fight. A local holiday was arranged to allow people to go. Several Americans sailed from Key West in Florida to be there.

Two platforms for film cameras and an elevated ring were constructed on the course, directly in front of the racecourse grandstand. In the stand, punters paying $15 could sit and watch the action. On the grassy slope of the enclosure leading down from the stand to the racecourse rails, $20 seats including 'ringside' were installed. $3 day seats were further away and available up to the last minute to anyone who came through the turnstiles opening at 7am. All attendees were subject to an additional $1 surcharge to cover the horse races staged after the fight.

Over 30,000 people paid up and another 5,000 watched for free from the hills surrounding the course. Come fight time, only two people were missing – Johnson and Willard. The crowd was kept waiting for another hour. This, the first of the incidents, was caused by Johnson, who refused to budge from his quarters until his promised $30,000 purse was delivered into his hands in crisp new notes. He feared another experience like Paris where he and Moran had jointly lost out.

He was very wise. Although advance tickets totalled $80,000 and the overall take was first announced as $110,000, by the evening, promoter

Curley was announcing that the figure was only $60,000, less than the expenses incurred, and that Willard would be lucky to get anything. Curley later left Cuba in a hurry, leaving many bad debts behind him. Johnson, cash in hand as requested, also left without settling his bills. The car renter who had provided his transport around the island was left suing vainly for the $640 bill still owed him.

The impatient crowd perked up when the fighters and their entourages made their delayed entry. Frustratingly, there was another pause. Johnson, in the lucky blue tights he had worn when beating Jeffries in 1910, was not leaving his corner unless his share of the film rights went up from 33⅓ per cent to 51 per cent. His last-minute blackmail was temporarily successful – a new agreement was signed in the ring. It ultimately failed because the full-length developed film never subsequently reached him.

At last the pair weighed in – Johnson at 16st 1lb/225lbs (at his peak he had been about 13st 10lb/192lbs, the extra mass more fat than muscle); Willard at 17st/238lbs (more muscle than fat). When the bell went it was still Willard the slow, cumbrous one, and the older Johnson the fitter, faster man.

Had this been a contest of 12 rounds, 15 rounds or even 20, all championship lengths at some time or another, there would have been one winner – Jack Johnson on points. He steamed out of his corner for the first, feinted a right cross and landed a solid left on Willard's jaw, followed by a stinging right uppercut. Willard was too slow to stop them, yet, more ominously for the smiling Johnson, barely reacted to their impact, absorbing them with all the emotions of a tightly stuffed

punch bag. Willard landed a couple of body blows during the round; Johnson smiled on contemptuously.

The third was even more one-sided. Willard missed with telegraphed swings and Johnson drove him back to the ropes with good clean punches to head and body. He was still landing well-directed punches when the bell rang. And he rounded out the fourth with another strong clip to Willard's jaw. Willard sustained at least superficial damage, bleeding at lip and cheek and red patches appearing on his torso. A Johnson left in the eighth opened a gash above his right eye. Johnson attacked in the sixth and seventh as if he wanted to finish the fight early. Willard did not go down, although he was pinned to the ropes as strong body blows penetrated his rudimentary guard.

Willard was immensely strong and, although normally a notoriously lazy trainer, had put in the necessary training hours on the road and in the gym, aware that he was in a marathon, not a six-round sprint. Despite Johnson's clear superiority, Willard landed the occasional body blow and leaned his full weight in the clinches to sap the lighter man of energy. Johnson, smiling and joking, ignored the body punches and pushed Willard off him with a flourish. There had to be some effect, even if it took time to show.

For the next 12 or 14 rounds, including a 14th where Johnson sent Willard's head back with four straight lefts and joked with ringsiders, and a 15th that Johnson rounded off with a flurry of rights and lefts to the head as Willard was caught on the ropes, it was still Johnson on top. He remained Willard's master throughout the 20th and 21st rounds.

But after more than an hour's action under the Cuban sun, the action slowed. It slowed because Johnson slowed. On the front foot throughout, he demonstrated Willard's inherent clumsiness; he landed punches of the kind that had knocked out good men in the past; he showed, considering his skimpy training, surprising lasting power. Yet, difficult for a modern fight follower to grasp, the fight was technically *not yet halfway through.* Over 21 rounds Johnson had taken several of Willard's heavy punches to the body. That body was telling him he could not continue for 24 more of the same. He was quite able to grasp what his body was saying.

This was the motivation behind the next incident. On his stool in the interval before the 22nd round, Johnson sent for Jack Curley to come to him. Curley, in the office counting the gate money, arrived at ringside at the end of the 25th. Johnson asked him to escort Lucille, his elegantly dressed wife sitting in a box seat and enjoying her husband's clear superiority, out of the arena. 'Tell my wife I'm tiring, and I wish you'd see her out.' This was not the message of a man who thought he could still win.

Lucille was even closer to the ring on her way out of the arena and became an eyewitness to the next incident, one of the most discussed happenings in boxing history, round 26. Johnson got wearily to his feet and moved slowly forward. After meaningless mauls and clinches and a few debilitating body blows, Johnson neared Willard's corner where Willard caught him unawares with a strong left lead. Johnson dropped his gloves and bent forward. Willard, with probably

the best punch he delivered in the entire fight if not in his entire career, sent in a long looping overhand right direct to Johnson's jaw. Down went Johnson on his back, not completely unconscious, but flat out and quite incapable of getting up again within ten seconds. He kept his gloves above his face, warding off the afternoon sun from his eyes. The referee Jack Welch counted to ten and raised Willard's right hand in victory. Johnson's controversial reign was over. There was no question about that.

There were plenty of questions about the ending. Had Johnson lost deliberately in return for a deal about his return to the USA? Afterwards – not immediately – he claimed he had. On 9 June, when the film from which he had hoped to profit failed to materialise, he sent an angry telegram to Curley claiming he had been promised $50,000 to lie down to Willard.[43] Later in 1916, in parlous financial straits, he sold a signed and sworn confession about the 'deliberate' loss to the boxing journalist (and later editor of *The Ring*) Nat Fleischer.[44] Other believers cite the circumstantial evidence of his shading his eyes with his gloves, hardly the action of a man out cold. The photograph of Johnson on his back, gloves to his eyes, became famous. Thousands of 10c postcards and $5 enlargements circulated in Cuba next day, although where the revenue from them went is another mystery.

No one can be sure a century and more on of the exact truth. One may only speculate on the most likely explanations. Johnson did not fight Willard in a manner suggesting he intended to lose. On the contrary, in many rounds he seemed to be

doing his best to knock Willard out. Had one of those formidable attacks floored Willard, Johnson would have remained champion. And if he really intended to lie down, why fight so hard for 25 rounds before doing so? It would have been easier to take a first-round punch, go down and plead he had been caught unluckily, prestige if not title intact. (So far as the gloves over the eyes are concerned, anyone temporarily blinded by the sun burning on the retina will know that self-preservation decrees an instinctive covering reaction even during half-consciousness. A dazzled boxer would be excessively vulnerable.)

Before the bout, Johnson's ambivalences about his reign and desire to return home if the consequences were not too severe, were completely understandable. Doubts faded when the bout began and Johnson saw how easy it was to belabour the clumsy Willard and how little hurt he himself was in the early exchanges. He could put this loutish cowboy out soon enough, and preserve his one great bargaining chip, the holding of the title, for another day. It was an arrogant assumption but not stupid.

Johnson's immediate post-fight comments were dignified and definitive: 'I have been beaten by a younger and a better man' and 'it was a clean knockout and the best man won. It was not a matter of luck.' *Boxing* was overwhelmed by his apparent sincerity: 'No single champion in the world's history of the ring ever faced his defeat, and the prospect of ruin which accompanied it, with either so good a grace, so high a heart, or in such a truly sporting spirit.'

Precious little grace came from the Cuban crowd, or from Willard, or from

Once he lost to Willard, Johnson could only trade on past memories, signing himself 'former Heavyweight champion'.
Collection of the Smithsonian National Museum of African American History and Culture

the American journalists, or from the crowds who mobbed Willard on his return to the USA. When Johnson hit the canvas there was uproar. Many Cubans present demonstrated an ethnic identification with whiteness by waving white flags, scarves, newspapers and handkerchiefs, chanted 'Kill the black bear', and shouted jubilantly at every Willard punch. White Cubans were all for Willard, and black Cubans too – their attitude based on Lucille's presence as the champion's white wife. Shrill screams from the women in the crowd added to the decibel count, all for Willard and against Johnson.

When the count was complete, both sexes howled jointly (*'Viva El Bianco!'*), danced, threw things in the air and surged ecstatically towards the ring to embrace the new white champion. Only local militia with blows from the flat side of their machetes kept them at bay.

Next day and subsequently, the newspapers could hardly contain their glee. Bat Masterson's words: 'The white race, after a hard pull for the last seven years, recovered the Heavyweight Championship of the world today at Oriental Park,' confirmed that Willard's victory signified more than a sporting success. For the *Washington Sun*, comically showing more prejudice than logic, Johnson's defeat demonstrated the unwisdom of blacks having 'connubial connections' with white women. The *New York Times* tried a po-faced editorial claiming that the result ('the quite reasonable rejoicing because a negro no longer holds the distinction of being the foremost and one unconquerable pugilist in the world') had been a very good thing for all reasonable people:

> The satisfaction over the victory of the white man was general and obvious. It will be felt throughout the country even by people who commonly pay no heed to pugilistic triumphs … The elevation of JOHNSON has not been of benefit to his race, his fall from the pinnacle will, we fancy, be looked on complacently by all intelligent colored folk.[45]

That Willard despised boxing and despised the crowds now wanting to laud him was forgotten in the regal procession back to his Havana hotel, led by a brass band, and later on his whistle-stop tour of the eastern states in the USA. Long into the night, the square outside his Havana hotel was full of chanting fans, pleading (unsuccessfully) for him to acknowledge them. He made two speeches in his time in Cuba – 14 words in total. ('I'll do my best April 5th' and 'If I could speak, I wouldn't be fighting.') He followed Freddie Welsh into a new engagement at Hammerstein's Victoria Theatre in New York the week after the fight where he had reluctantly to open his mouth as well as spar and punch. The $5,000 for the week was some consolation as he was still complaining eight months later that the Cuban venture had left him $3,352 out of pocket.

Massive crowds waved him off on the boat from Cuba. Massive crowds, trampling down barriers and restraining ropes, fought to glimpse his arrival at Key West, Florida. A special train with a decorated platform for the new champion to stand, wave and acknowledge his fans at every intermediate station, took him off to New York. After a few token appearances, the platform was empty. The champion preferred to keep to his special compartment, sending minions to announce to the assembled crowds at every station that he was 'resting' or 'sleeping'. He had his arm bandaged and put in a sling so no one would expect to shake his hand. He made two significant announcements to pressmen: he wouldn't be defending the title for at least 12 months; and he would never again fight a black. In practice he took just two 'fights': a six-round exhibition against Sailor Burke on 12 September 1916 and a ten-round no-decision bout (full rewards and little risk) against Frank Moran on 25 March 1916, against whom he was said to be fat, slow and clumsy. That is two semi-fights between his win over Johnson and his first formal defence over four years later. Dogs in mangers had rarely been more obstructive.

By the end of the year, *Boxing* underestimated Willard's year's earnings at $168,000, including 140 circus appearances at $1,200 a time ($168,000 alone), $26,000 for ghosted newspaper articles and $20,000 for the theatre appearances.[46] Even allowing for heavy expenses he cleared a six-figure income without setting foot in a ring at a time when thousands of families survived on a pittance. In June 1917 he invested hundreds of thousands of dollars in buying out the old Buffalo Bill's Wild West Show and the Sells Floto circus, investments which, unluckily for Willard, were subject to compulsory purchase orders when the USA entered the war and urgently needed a large supply of horses.

Jack Johnson, his defeated opponent, stayed a few days in Cuba, unable to follow Willard to the USA where arrest loomed. He travelled to the relative safety of England to take up music hall appearances in London and on provincial tours. It was not quite as safe as he had anticipated. Britain was a country at war, the newspapers full of casualty lists and depressing details about reversals in battle (60,000 men lost in May 1915; 85,000 in September–October). In every London railway station, trains back from the front decanted wounded soldiers, walking wounded and a melancholy remainder on stretchers and in wheelchairs.

Civilians did not escape deprivation. The home front suffered shortages and severe restrictions on comforting items such as food and drink. The London theatres and clubs continued, giving some sense of normality, but patrons had to find their way through blacked-out streets to attend. If the brave attendees did not trip on invisible obstacles, an explosive object from the sky might fall upon them.

By May, the Germans extended the range of their Zeppelin airship raiders, bombing parts of the Thames estuary during May 1915.[47] On 31 May 1915, the raiders reached London and dropped over 100 bombs and grenades on East London, the very heart of small hall boxing. There were four more raids in 1915, including one in October on the theatre district all around the NSC, and 17 people were killed in Wellington Street, a two-minute stroll away. Attending boxing was risky.

Jack Johnson was at risk. On his way home from a South London music hall to his rented accommodation on Haverstock Hill, he came near to being bombed by a Zeppelin. Characteristically, he believed the pilot was pursuing him personally. This was highly unlikely. His real enemies were in the Home Office. His provincial tour of music halls with his show *Seconds Out*, an entertainment featuring a turn from Lucille, left its usual trail of debts, quarrels and incidents. In January 1916, the Home Office issued an exclusion order under the Aliens Restriction Act. (When he knew he could no longer tour in the show, Johnson asked his fellow boxer Jimmy Wilde to take over his role. Wilde politely refused, sparing the theatre a spectacle akin to Norman Wisdom stepping in to a part previously played by Arnold Schwarzenegger.) Johnson and Lucille were deported to Spain on 2 March 1916. There his need for cash led him into other bizarre ventures, including self-proclaimed diplomacy between the Kaiser and the Russian Tsar, and a ludicrous 'fight' in Barcelona on 23 April 1916 with Arthur Cravan, the surrealist and Dada poet (1887–1917), an event quite as strange as any Dada happening. Johnson carried Cravan for five rounds and knocked him out in the sixth. He was in Spain until March 1919, when he went back to Cuba and, briefly, to Mexico.

Johnson never returned to Europe after 1919. He still bequeathed a graphic expression to the troops in the trenches. A deadly German shell that hit the ground and detonated fiercely in a cloud of black smoke was dubbed a 'Jack Johnson'. (Cruelly, another that sped through the air but then lay inert on impact was known as a 'Billy Wells'.)

The NSC, operating under wartime restrictions like every other London club, despite the blackout and air raids, continued its defiant existence. Even in 1917 after nearly four years of war, the membership figures, boosted by old members loyally continuing their membership, and by officers newly based in London or able easily to reach the capital and desperate to see some boxing, were surprisingly healthy:

Subscriptions (Town): 555 @ £6 6s. 0d. = £3,572 0s. 0d.

: 24 @ £3 3s. 0d. = £75 12s. 0d.

Subscriptions (Country): 290 @ £4 4s. 0d. = £1,218 0s. 0d.

: 27 @ £2 2s. 0d. = £56 14s. 0d.: 3 @ £1 1s. 0d. = £3 3s. 0d.

Entrance Fees: (Town): 68 @ £5 5s. 0d. = £357 0s. 0d.

(Country): 23 @ £2 2s. 0d. = £48 6s. 0d.[48]

The club could still put up a Lonsdale Belt and a title and draw a full house. On 18 October 1915 Tancy Lee defended his Lonsdale flyweight belt against Young (Joe) Symonds of Plymouth, Wilde's recent victim. The age gap looked significant.[49]

Lee eschewed the rushing tactics that had defeated Wilde, who was in the audience. He planted himself in the centre, allowing the speedy and younger Symonds to circle around the outside and consume extra energy. When Symonds attacked, Lee took his punches on gloves and forearms and countered frequently. By the seventh, Symonds, not relishing Lee's counters, speeded up even more to get away. Lee, thus encouraged, chased him to clinch the easy victory. Alas, Lee had been cleverly out-thought, Symonds's retreats taking Lee out of his comfort zone. By the 11th Lee was exhausted and went down in the 12th and in the 14th. Sharp left hooks from Symonds took him down another three times in the 16th. In came the towel and Symonds donned the belt. Wilde from the audience was quick to challenge the new champion and offer a £500 side stake to go with it.

Lee v Symonds was a connoisseur's contest, appreciated by the knowledgeable without seizing the public imagination. It was still better than the 22 November 1915 fight for the Lonsdale Belt and the bantamweight championship between Joe Fox of Leeds and the Northumbrian Jim Berry. Only in wartime would two less than top-flight men fight for such a title. It was said that four or five years previously Digger Stanley could have beaten both of them – simultaneously. (Fox had lost, on 16 September 1915,

to Digger in Liverpool.) Fox was a clear winner if substantially below his best, leaking openings that Berry was incapable of taking. Fox was the new champion but memories of Bowker, Beynon and Stanley cast a shadow over his achievement.

The Lonsdale Belt retained its prestige. Yet better-known fighters were not always willing to take the NSC's offers and fight for one. Sergeant Johnny Basham, a happy warrior in and out of his Royal Welch Fusiliers uniform, was a good example. Early in the war years, he met Johnny Summers at the NSC (14 December 1914), knocking him out in the ninth round of 20, and acquired the British welterweight title and Lonsdale Belt. Serving but given frequent leave to fight, he had an active 1915. Apart from fundraising spars and exhibitions, he took five fights, three in Liverpool and two in London. Only one was at Covent Garden.

In that one, 10 May 1915, Basham defended his Lonsdale Belt for a £550 purse and a £100-a-side side stake. It was the first Lonsdale Belt match-up between two serving soldiers.[50] Basham's opponent was Tom McCormick. As we saw, McCormick would not survive the war beyond 1916. He was the self-taught Irish Lancastrian who had lost to Matt Wells in Australia before the war.

Basham weighed 10st 5lb/145lbs and McCormick 10st 4½lb/144½lbs. McCormick came with an attacking reputation and looked more muscular than ever at the weight. The extra muscle, whatever it gave him in the way of power, did nothing for his speed. The much quicker Basham thwarted McCormick's attempts to close with him and kept him off with sharp rights.

There was going to be only one winner. In the meantime, McCormick ('slower than a funeral') suffered. Eventually, Basham floored him for three counts in the 13th and was about to do so again when referee Corri stopped the fight.

This fight for belt and title did not capture the public and the newspapers as did Basham's previous London outing, staged at the London Opera House before a heavily uniformed audience on 22 March 1915 against his old opponent Matt Wells. The purse was £500 and side stakes at £100 each.[51]

Wells, born in 1886, was about three years older than Basham and had been a professional since 1905. He looked what he was, a squat, hairy and rugged pro with strength and stamina. Three years before (26 December 1912) he put the promising Basham in his place at Swansea by knocking him out in the seventh of 15. Since then, Basham had rebuilt his career, being highly active in 1913 (16 fights) and 1914 (seven fights). The question was whether his smiling clean-limbed elegance could outwit the more utilitarian but clever Wells. The odds – 4/7 on Wells – suggested he could not.

Neither bookmakers nor punters were quite prepared for the exemplary showing Basham put up on the night: 'It was really a most brilliant bout, and one which was contested at top speed from start to finish.'[52] On the night, Wells was clever and fast. Ultimately, Basham was faster and cleverer by the narrowest of margins. Rounds were even or barely won by either man.

Wells remembered his decisive win at Swansea had come from a powerful body blow. He rushed Basham, closing in and hooking and uppercutting him while looking for another knockout. Basham, respecting Wells and his punching power, borrowed tactics from two of his famous co-patriots. He used the left lead of a Driscoll to stave off the rushes, and clinched, countered and blocked like Freddie Welsh when his opponent got inside. The approach served him well. Wells was still too smart and too strong to allow that to work all the time. He landed about a dozen good uppercuts over the course of the fight. Sometimes, in the fifth for example, he trapped Basham on the ropes or in a corner and punished him. And he caught Basham more than once with good punches on the exit from a clinch.

Basham knocked Wells down in the fourth for a few seconds but his victory came rather in the last four rounds when he retained his exemplary speed and slightly longer reach to stave off Wells. Ultimately, the Driscoll-style left notched him more points than the Welsh-style defences, but Basham had needed both to get Corri's favourable decision.

Even popular champions are liable to a comeuppance. Johnny Basham subsequently suffered two. The first was more embarrassing than serious. A fellow Royal Welch Fusilier was the poet and novelist Robert Graves (1895–1985), whose 1929 memoir *Goodbye to All That* was one of the most widely read of all the personal accounts of life in the trenches. Basham, in France behind the lines as a boxing instructor, offered to take on any of his fellow soldiers for three rounds one after the other. As each one proved no challenge, he began to showboat and ridicule his challengers. Graves, who had learned to box in his time at Charterhouse,

asked to have a go. Pretending to be the rawest of amateurs, he led with the right and feigned utter clumsiness. When Basham dropped his guard and offered his chin to this new beginner, Graves pounced and sent the pro reeling across the ring with a well-timed straight right. Basham, the good sport he was, then got down to a serious spar, using his own skill to make Graves his fellow soldier look even better.

He could put no such gloss on his Liverpool Stadium encounter with the Frenchman Albert Badoud on 21 October 1915 for the European welterweight title.[53] The two had met twice before, on 20 November 1913 (won comfortably on points by Basham over 15 rounds) and on 1 January 1914 (won easily on points by Basham over 20 rounds). Basham took Badoud (b. Geneva, 10 December 1893) as lightly as he initially took Graves. This was not wise.

A first round with relatively little action did nothing to disturb Basham's tranquillity. The second did. Badoud caught him with a left swing to the side of his face. Another left swing sent him reeling before the round was over. The third was even worse. Basham attacked, looking more like his old self and delivering a flurry of punches. Unfortunately, as he stepped back to admire his own cleverness, Badoud again caught him with a left swing to which Basham had no answer. It put the British champion down for a count of nine. Things were looking ominous. The fourth held no encouragement either. This time, Basham, with a cut below his right eye, was back on the floor for eight.

Basham always had powers of recovery. The next four rounds pleased

his corner, his fans and the punters who had taken the short odds on his victory. He settled into a better and easier routine, avoided the dangerous Badoud swing and piled up some points himself. But just as normality was being secured, came the ninth and last.

Badoud flew out of his corner and drew gasps from the crowd when another of his swings whistled past Basham's chin as he stepped back to avoid it. He should have done the same with the next one. Instead it took him down for eight, looking distinctly stunned. When he got up, groggily, Badoud hustled him into his own corner and caught him with a violent right that left him flat on the floor and counted out. Badoud happily danced around the ring, delighted to have upset the odds.

After his victory, one of the best of his career, Badoud headed not for a Paris potentially threatened by German forces but to a safe and so far neutral USA. He continued his career there with eight fights in 1916 and nine in 1917. He did not return to Paris until the war had ended. The French army was not for him.

Others felt the same about the military life. As the war continued, consuming more and more manpower, the fundraising and recruiting appeals became more desperate. It was impossible to attend a bill without hearing admonishing appeals to sign on or to be expected to bid at a fundraising auction for the gloves or some other item. On 29 November 1915 at the NSC, for example, before Willie Farrell beat Johnny Summers in a lively contest, there was an equally lively auction conducted by the Reverend Everard Digby, raising

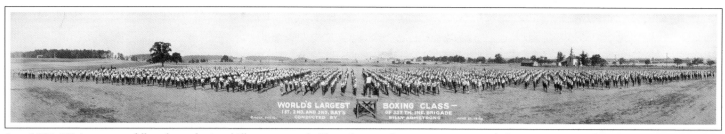

June 1918: US Army troops followed mass boxing drills on a vast scale. The military authorities were unwittingly fostering a postwar thirst for professional boxing.
Prints & Photographs Division, Library of Congress, 2007664557

£276 3s. Among the items sold were Emma and Peggy, a pair of French bulldogs; a signed cricket bat and a coloured print of the old Sayers v Heenan prizefight.[54]

The event was paralleled by one full of pathos at The Ring in late December when the unsuccessful but popular Camberwell lightweight Spud Murphy, permanently disabled by his war wounds, was brought into the ring and the MC appealed for 'a few coppers' to tide the victim over Christmas. £24 9s. 6d. in notes and silver were thrown into the ring. The middle classes had no monopoly on generosity.

Appeals to sign on were less effective after the enthusiasm of the early years. Dick Burge, always the patriot, refused to have boxers at The Ring unless they were in uniform but that was no solution to the general problem. Everyone, even the liberals and socialists originally opposed to compulsion, knew conscription would come.

On 5 January 1916, a Military Service Bill went through the House of Commons. From 10 February 1916, all single men aged 19 to 30 would be called up. Barely was the wax dry on the official seal than it was succeeded by a second act in May extending conscription to all men, married and single, aged 18 to 41.[55] From May 1916, the voluntary system was dead and compulsion was all. Even those

previously declared unfit were ordered to undergo a second medical with the unspoken message that it would be a deal harder to fail than the first.

Not every male citizen in the age group was prepared to be coerced. Some lay low or supplied themselves with false papers, probably fewer than the authorities believed, but draconian methods rooted out such malingerers. Boxing arenas were not sacrosanct. Added to the hazards of bombs and blackouts (sometimes ameliorated by staging boxing matinees in the afternoon) was the possibility of police and military raids on attendees. In early September 1916, The Ring at Blackfriars saw the authorities surround the building to check call-up papers and exemption certificates for anyone of call-up age. Many fled, some more nervous about the rough and ready treatment of individuals in the search than guilty of evasion. The chase through the streets of Southwark and over rooftops was more farce than serious military initiative.

The war was ubiquitous. In 1916 it was not going well. Pessimism about its long continuation was fully justified. The British had 38 divisions in France by January 1916, full of enthusiasm but not necessarily well trained. The summer of 1916 saw on 1 July the ill-judged attack of 13 British divisions upon the dugouts, barbed wire and

trenches of the formidable German defences at the Somme. As futile as a puny flyweight assaulting a super-heavyweight, the result was inevitable – 20,000 brave men killed and another 40,000 seriously wounded. 'The heaviest loss ever suffered in a single day by a British army or by any army in the First World War.'[56] By November, that casualty list was up to 420,000. 'After the Somme men decided that the war would go on for ever.'[57] In December 1916, Asquith's government fell and the pugnacious Welsh battler Lloyd George became the prime minister of a coalition government. Such disturbing events were the depressing background behind every domestic sporting event.

Prevailing gloom about events at home and abroad enhanced the desire of many to forget the war for a few hours and enjoy an evening's boxing. Attendance was certainly still possible. In January 1916, the Victoria Club, Glasgow announced it would stage no more boxing until the end of the war. This was an exception. In January 1916, the main London centres – the NSC, The Ring (matinees and evenings), West London Stadium – and other venues such as Hoxton Baths and Acton Baths were all putting on shows. And provincial cities, towns and villages staging boxing evenings included Newcastle, Coventry, Liverpool,

Bradford, Plymouth, Preston, Newport, West Bromwich and Barrow in Furness. The South Wales valleys retained their reputation as a centre for small hall boxing with shows at tiny places like Bargoed and Crumlin, whatever local Free Churchmen thought.)

Other sports were aggrieved at boxing's continuance. The Notes by the Editor of *Wisden* in the 1917 edition summed it up: 'People realised that with public boxing carried on to an extent never heard of before … there was something illogical, not to say absurd, in placing a ban on cricket.'

Occasional charity cricket matches featured celebrities but in total there was a mere eight days' play in 1917 and 17 in 1918.)[58]

After the night's boxing, a pleasure risked by many in and out of uniform, it was back to the all-pervasive war. Matters did not improve. The Whitsun and August bank holidays were cancelled in 1916 in recognition of the continuing grim news from the front. At Christmas 1916, London hotels cancelled all festive celebrations.

Meanwhile, casualties and disasters mounted up. From August to November 1916, newspapers printed lists after lists of the dead and wounded – 75,000 in August, 115,000 in September, 67,000 in October and 46,000 in November.[59] In roughly the same months in 1917 from April to November, losses never dropped below 20,000 *a week*. Every digit meant a loss or a hurt to some family.

In the summer of 1917, air raids from Zeppelins resumed, adding to the hazards of life at home. Then came the German Gotha biplane bombers, which in one single day killed 162 Londoners and injured 382, small totals compared to those fallen in

Europe but frightening and depressing for Londoners going about their daily business. By October 1917, they were suffering incendiaries as well.

The multiplicity of sacrifices at home and abroad did not seem to be producing results. On the contrary, the costly offensives failed to advance the Allied cause significantly. Just as the summer of 1916 had meant the failures on the Somme, so the attacks of 1917 – the Nivelle offensive of April–May, and the July–November attacks associated for ever with the dreaded name of Passchendaele – resulted in little advance and 200,000 to 400,000 casualties on each side. Even the declaration of April 1917 that the USA would be joining the Allied side failed to lift the prevailing pessimism. As late as September 1918, the newspaper magnate Lord Northcliffe was saying in private, 'None of us will live to see the end of the war.'[60]

With so sombre an outlook, boxing seemed like a small beacon of hope and normality. The fortunes of British boxers in exile and their opponents were written about and read widely. Freddie Welsh continued to take ten-round newspaper decision bouts all over North America, and even one 20-rounder (a points win over Charlie White in Colorado Springs on 4 September 1916). He fought 24 times in 1916, travelling hither and yon from Quebec to New York and Atlanta to Denver, making money but taking three fights in four days in September, three fights in four days in October and still another five days later. The toll was considerable and showed in his results. He won only once in 1917 (a 12-rounder points decision in St Louis on 17 April 1917 against the veteran Battling Nelson, once world lightweight champion).

Now nearing his 35th birthday and in serious decline, Nelson, the 'Durable Dane', was no longer so durable. He underwent plastic surgery in 1916 in a pathetic attempt to regain the favours of his ex-wife, and after losing to Welsh he never fought again. He died in 1954, indigent and insane, a sad reflection of the punishment he had taken in many a savage bout.

Welsh was risking a similar fate with his ludicrous production targets. He took five more fights apart from Nelson in 1917 and lost all five of them. Taking the hint that it was time for at least a fallow period, he enlisted in the US Army in September 1917. He would not be in a professional ring again until December 1920. Before enlisting, he launched on an epic trilogy against one of New York's young and best-loved fighters – Benjamin Leitner, b. 17 April 1896 in the East Village near 8th Street, and better known in ring history as Benny Leonard.[61] The fights were avidly followed in both countries despite the war.

Like other Jewish fighters from Orthodox homes, young Leonard adopted the new name to conceal his ring activities from his Yiddish-speaking parents, escapees from Russian pogroms and little aware of sporting activities in their new country. Regrettably, although Benny was to become a hero to his whole Jewish community and was greatly loved by everyone who saw him, his parents never fully reconciled themselves to his boxing career. His father was, however, a pragmatist, and when Benny brought home an early purse of $35 he said, 'You got that for one fight? Benny, when you going to fight again?'

For everyone else he was the New York equivalent of the East End heroes embodying London's Jewish people's hopes and aspirations (see Chapter 4). Budd Schulberg, the novelist and boxing writer, who worshipped Leonard, put it best:

> To see him climb into the ring sporting the six-pointed Jewish star on his fighting trunks was to anticipate sweet revenge for all the bloody noses, split lips, and mocking laughter at pale little Jewish boys who had run the neighborhood gauntlet.[62]

Jewish New York was out in force buying $16,000 of advance tickets when Freddie (still world lightweight champion despite the newspaper losses and narrow scrapes he had endured under the ten-round protective corset) met the new 'Ghetto Wizard' at Madison Square Garden on 31 March 1916.[63] The fight attracted more spectators than any previous lightweight bout under the ten-round limit. They made up as fashionable, mixed (many women) and responsive a crowd as a Broadway first night. Gratifyingly, Welsh notched $13,341 after the receipts were totted up. (Leonard got $4,258.) It was not all Welsh received.

Facing the young, fleet and hard-punching Leonard, Welsh's defensive skills were at a premium. He was as clever as ever but his powers and his speed were in decline. To the delight of the Manhattan audience cheering on Leonard with enthusiasm, Welsh deflected many of Leonard's best punches, but by no means all of them. Showers of blows, including those from Leonard's dangerous chopping right, came at him. Many got home. The champion was praised for his

elusiveness and his effective parries and smothers. Unfortunately for him, the cool and measured Leonard was always one step ahead with barely a scratch on him. Leonard's points advantage could be soon read on Welsh's face as clearly as if written on an English referee's scorecard. Welsh glided away from the dangerous Leonard right, only to be caught with the left instead.

In the fourth, Welsh's head was rocked back by left leads. His irritating smile looked particularly forced after a straight right thudded in after them. The fifth saw Welsh's nose cut and swollen from a ramrod left and a whipping left hook opened another cut under the left eye. A sorry-looking Welsh had to accept that the no-decision rule again left him champion but distinctly second best.

The two did not meet subsequently until 28 July 1916 at Washington Park, Brooklyn, a former baseball ground, again over ten rounds and again on the no-decision basis.[64] The 15,000 crowd hoped the restrictions would be irrelevant. Given the marked superiority

The much-loved Benny Leonard (1896–1947). 'The Ghetto Wizard' embodied the hopes and fears of the whole New York Jewish community.
BoxRec

of Leonard over Welsh in the first clash, surely there was every chance Leonard could win the world lightweight title by knocking out Welsh in ten rounds? They did not know that this was a very different Welsh.

Welsh trained rigorously and planned a different approach to the one that had gone awry in March. He came in at a trim 9st 9½lb/135½lbs. He took Leonard out of his stride by attacking from the start. He had sharpened up his defence and intercepted all of Leonard's dangerous punches with his arms and gloves. The only thing to bite him all evening was the host of bloodthirsty mosquitoes attracted by the ring lights and the half-bare boxers.

On this occasion, the reversal was complete – the old master making the relatively inexperienced Leonard look like a novice, albeit a novice who did not flinch when caught with good punches. The *New York Times* was particularly impressed:

> He [Leonard] was simply outclassed by a superior boxer, who was at the top of his form and gave an exhibition which was almost the quintessence of fistic skill. It was a beautiful exhibition to watch, and the crowd in the stands and the boxes was on its feet most of the time yelling like mad as the Briton drove the Harlem youth back under a storm of blows. [Benny had moved his family to the Jewish section of Harlem during 1916.]

Now was the perfect time to retire as winner and still champion. Welsh chose rather to re-join the peripatetic gravy train. Only after another 15 Canadian and American fights was he again to meet Leonard if not the mosquitoes – on 28 May 1917 over ten rounds in the large hall of the Manhattan Athletic Club. By then, Welsh was on the losing streak outlined above; Leonard on a winning one having beaten his last four opponents inside six, seven and nine rounds. He was still after Welsh's title and knew he had but ten rounds to put Welsh away.[65]

Welsh weighed in at 9st 10¾lb/136¾lbs. He had trained but not as hard as for the second bout. He was well aware of Leonard's progress yet assumed that even in dire straits he could survive passively on his defensive skills as he had done so many times before. Another newspaper loss he could take with equanimity.

Leonard, at 9st 7lb/133lbs, was in peak condition physically and had a master plan specifically to dominate Welsh. He attacked from the start, opening up Welsh's defence with well-timed direct punches or beating it down ruthlessly. When Welsh sought to clinch he weakened the Welshman with staccato body blows. This softening

process continued for eight rugged rounds and culminated in, for Welsh, the disastrous ninth round. So far Leonard had punched hard but craftily not quite as hard as he could. In the ninth he went all out.

A swinging right caught Welsh just behind his left ear. He staggered and half fell. Leonard, despite hysterical shouts from the audience and his corner, stayed cool and consummately professional. From just the right distance he belaboured Welsh with hard punches and stepped aside as Welsh staggered past him to go down on one knee in the corner. Getting up much too quickly, before the referee could start a count, Welsh rose only to get another hail of blows that left him down on both knees. Leonard knew just what to do. When Welsh got up again, he measured the distance and delivered another set of damaging punches culminating in a right to the jaw to take Welsh down in a heap. Welsh, whose chin was made of resilient stuff and who had only once been down before and had never been knocked out, dragged himself up but only with the assistance of the ropes. He

stayed upright by virtue of adopting a crucifixion posture, his arms entwined with the top rope. There he was helpless as Leonard, no sadist but doing what he had to do to be champion, sent Welsh's head dangerously back and fro with more heavy punches. In the 21st century, a stoppage would have been called immediately.

The referee was the retired lightweight Kid McPartland, who had retired in 1905 after being knocked out twice himself. He wanted to stop the one-sided onslaught, glanced at the Welsh corner to see whether surrender was contemplated but was as aware as anyone that a battered Welsh on his feet for another round and a half would still hold his precious title. After counting four, he stepped between the fighters and gently freed Welsh's arms from the top rope. The barely conscious Welsh staggered a few yards and collapsed again over the middle rope where he hung helpless. The fight and his long reign were over. Jubilant Leonard fans invaded the ring and chaired the new champion to his dressing room. On his stool in their wake, Welsh took about 15 minutes to recover then feebly argued that he had not actually been knocked out. He was still saying it months later. The gesture was futile. Defend and survive had not worked this time. It had been a fight too far.

Tragically, Welsh was not destined for a long, happy retirement. Apart from his luxurious lifestyle, he invested heavily in a 162-acre site at Summit, New Jersey, where he had an opulent home constructed with every known amenity, including billiard room and library, coupled with a health farm, swimming pool, gymnasium, golf course, tennis courts and lavish accommodation for

Leonard, world lightweight champion 1917-25, admired Gans, his historic predecessor (champion 1902–08).
BoxRec

paying guests. The enterprise cost him anything up to $200,000 in purchase, planning and building. It might have done very well in later times. American businessmen then were less gymnastically minded and by October 1918 the whole shooting match was on the market for $20,000 cash up front. There were no takers.

Welsh had trouble adjusting to a life outside the ring. He was in and out of court on various civil and criminal matters, including a fight in a Broadway restaurant with his manager Harry Pollok, whose ear he was accused of biting off. He put on weight, he drank, he gambled, he took a few desultory and meaningless fights years after the loss to Leonard. He went bankrupt. The health farm project was foreclosed in 1927, a year in which he also separated from his wife and family. There was a dreadful inevitability about his final demise, aged only 41, when he was found dead on 28 July 1928 in a cheap hotel room off Broadway having suffered a cardiac arrest. A month earlier he had been badly beaten up in a street fight. Somehow he was never able to apply the pragmatic and calculated approach that characterised his ring career to life itself.

If the mini-series between Welsh and Leonard was an epic, then the fights at welterweight between another Briton and another American born in Clinton, in upstate New York, were more like a travelling circus moving up and down eastern USA and on tour for six long years. It had the quarrels, the reconciliations, the strains, the stresses, the triumphs, the disappointments and the awareness of each other's virtues and foibles of a long-term marriage with the custody of the welterweight championship taking the place of a dispute about the children. The protagonists in this saga were our old friend Ted Kid Lewis and Jack Britton, an Irish-American born on 14 October 1885 as William J. Breslin.

Nearly a decade older than Lewis, Britton was a rugged old pro with scar tissue and cauliflower ears to prove it. He stopped fighting in 1927 only because the State Athletic Commission refused to allow him to go on beyond 41. The first time he met Lewis was about his 150th fight. He was clever. He had some of Welsh's defensive skills and a sound chin. He was not a knockout specialist but knocked out 30 opponents in his career (BoxRec), or possibly 28 (Hall of Fame, Canastota). At 5ft 8in, he was well matched to Lewis who was 5ft 7½in. He had always been a natural welterweight. Lewis had first looked to challenge Welsh in the USA at lightweight (an opportunity Welsh always declined) and grew to welter.

One has only to list the 20 encounters between Lewis and Britton to get the flavour of this unique sequence:

26 Mar 1915	No decision	10 rounds	New York
31 Aug 1915	Lewis on points & title	12 rounds	Boston
28 Sep 1915	Lewis on points	12 rounds	Boston
20 Jan 1916	No decision	10 rounds	Buffalo
15 Feb 1916	No decision	10 rounds	New York
24 Apr 1916	Britton on points	20 rounds	New Orleans*
17 Oct 1916	Britton on points	12 rounds	Boston
14 Nov 1916	Draw	12 rounds	Boston
26 Mar 1917	No decision	12 rounds	Cincinnati
19 May 1917	No decision	10 rounds	Toronto
6 Jun 1917	No decision	10 rounds	St Louis
14 Jun 1917	No decision	10 rounds	New York
25 Jun 1917	Lewis on points	20 rounds	Dayton*
6 Mar 1918	No decision	10 rounds	Atlanta
2 May 1918	Draw	10 rounds	Scranton
24 May 1918	No decision	6 rounds	New York
20 Jun 1918	No decision	6 rounds	New York
17 Mar 1919	Britton by KO in 9th	12 rounds	Canton*
28 Jul 1919	No decision	8 rounds	Jersey City
7 Feb 1921	Britton on points	15 rounds	New York

* World welterweight championship changing hands.

The pair therefore fought a total 224 rounds of boxing. What more could they ever have found out about each other?

Two decisive bouts out of the 20 are worth particular consideration. Their second meeting for the vacant welterweight title on 31 August 1915 in Boston, under the state provisions of Massachusetts, allowed the genuine on-the-spot decision, which their first meeting in New York, a spirited fight yet a feeler-out rather than an all-out contest, had not.

In Boston, the two shared a dressing room and felt each other out conversationally. Finding they had more in common than they had suspected, and having won mutual respect in the ring, the rivalry lasting through the six-year series almost became a friendship. Lewis was Jewish and Britton Catholic but their religious differences never became a factor. (Anti-Semitism did, bizarrely enough, crop up when Lewis met Charlie White, also Jewish, in New York [21 July 1915, newspaper decision to Lewis, ten rounds] before meeting Britton again. A misguided Irishman at ringside urged Lewis to 'murder the Jewish bum'. When he was informed that Lewis also was Jewish, he stalked out, prejudice intact, saying, 'Then fuck the both of them.')

The friendship did not preclude gamesmanship in the August 1915 fight.[66] Britton claimed Lewis's gloves were better than his own. Lewis, irritated, took his gloves off and offered them to Britton. Britton's corner then objected to Lewis's bandages. Adjustments were made. When the bell rang for the first round, Britton opted out – he would not fight so long as Lewis wore a gum shield.

Lewis was a pioneer in using the protective device later to become obligatory because a schoolboy friend in London, Philip Krause, dentist son of a dentist, developed a reusable one. American dentists were also experimenting in the field but the results had not reached Jack Britton. The referee agreed. Lewis should forego the novelty. Lewis, furious, took the offending article and flung it at Britton's feet. A melee between rival seconds began and was squashed.

The delays were designed to anger Lewis and put him off. They were effective insofar as he rushed out of his corner and attacked venomously but carelessly. A Britton right put him down almost immediately. This sobered him and eased him into cooler professional mode. He attacked fiercely, but in the spirit of revenge better served cold. In the penultimate round he put Britton down for six and finished the 12th the unanimous points victor, and new welterweight champion of the world.

Lewis, now champion, confirmed temporarily his superiority over Britton with a second victory a month later on 28 September 1915, also in Boston and also on points after 12 rounds. Britton did not accept this as final. With a neat symmetry rare in sport, he in turn regained the title on 24 April 1916 over 20 rounds in New Orleans, Louisiana, allowing proper decisions. He reaffirmed his victory over another 12 rounds back in Boston on 17 October 1916.

In normal circumstances, seven meetings would have been sufficient for anyone. These two gluttons were barely halfway through their moveable feast. Five more no-decision bouts followed before Lewis was able to gain another

points decision over 20 rounds on 25 June 1917 in Dayton, Ohio. That left Lewis in possession for another four no-decision bouts until Britton wrested the title back in the most decisive bout of them all, the 18th of the series.

Britton was no out-and-out puncher but the possessor of a clean and effective left jab that sufficed for decisions over most opponents, including the more versatile Lewis. On 17 March 1919 he excelled himself with an all-out attack inspired by his long wait to regain the title.[67] The match was scheduled for 12 rounds but Britton needed only six to penetrate Lewis's guard with a flurry of clean blows and put Lewis on the canvas three times. The bell aborted the third count yet Lewis never regained his equilibrium. In the ninth, after 2 minutes 10 seconds of one-way traffic, Britton administered a right swing from a distance that caught Lewis cleanly on the chin and knocked him out.

Shortage of potential contests was hardly a problem in 1917 and 1918 for American-based fighters, although the USA formally joined the European war on 6 April 1917. Lewis and Britton could always fight one another, and did, yet Lewis had 24 fights in 1917 and 13 in 1918 in addition to those with Britton. Britton, apart from his fights with Lewis, had 13 fights in 1917 and 19 in 1918.

One of Lewis's American fights, in the middle of the Britton series, was in the International Ball Park in Newark, New Jersey on 23 September 1918 against the man who had conquered Freddie Welsh, the great Benny Leonard. It was not a championship contest, being limited to eight rounds and a newspaper decision, despite Leonard being world lightweight champion and

Lewis world welterweight champion.[68] Predictably, neither risked losing his title by an unexpected knockout, although both inflicted visible damage on the other. The match was pronounced by the American press an honourable draw. Significantly, the fight drew takings of $31,024 and paid Leonard $7,772 and Lewis $6,980 (although Morton Lewis claimed his father got $10,000). No one in Britain was going to earn that much for a title match let alone for an enhanced exhibition.

In Britain, contests never died out but became increasingly difficult to make as the war dragged on. A contest at the NSC became more desirable, even for low purses, and the changing of hands of British titles and belts more likely. Keeping a belt permanently by defending it and qualifying for the £1-a-week pension from the age of 40 was also attractive.

Take, for example, four British fighters all born in 1894, all about 20 years old when the war began, and all gracing the domestic scene in the 1920s. All took NSC contests and fights involving the Lonsdale Belt during the war years. Joe Fox of Leeds, bantamweight and later featherweight, fought only three times in 1917 and once in 1918. He won the British bantamweight title and Lonsdale Belt on 22 November 1915 and defended them to win the belt outright. By the time he retired in 1925, he had fought at least 116 times – and many times more had it not been for the war.

Charlie Hardcastle from Barnsley, another experienced featherweight, had five fights in 1917 and three in 1918. Over his career from 1911 to 1923, he had nearly 80 fights. He acquired the Lonsdale Belt and the British featherweight title, vacated by Llew Edwards's defection, by knocking out Alf Wye in the first round of 20 at the NSC on 4 June 1917. He had a strong following despite his nickname 'The Barnsley Bombshell' looking particularly crass in 1914–18.

Joe Symonds of Plymouth, flyweight, was luckier in 1917 with 11 fights but got only three in 1918. He managed 140 over his industrious career from 1910 to 1924. He held the British flyweight title and the Lonsdale Belt from 18 October 1915 when a fading Tancy Lee, straining to make flyweight, tired and failed to complete the 16th round. Symonds's reign lasted only a few months. We shall see why.

Another bantam, Curley (Con) Walker of Lambeth won the British bantamweight title and Lonsdale Belt just before the war when Digger Stanley was disqualified against him (20 April 1914). He managed eight fights (two at the NSC) in 1917 and five (all at The Ring) in 1918. He would have 15 in post-war 1922 and 106 over his career from 1909–23.

The fluctuating nature of domestic fights for British fighters in and out of the Covent Garden headquarters showed these were not normal times. Happenings in the middleweight division were positively bizarre.

Older than Fox and the others, Pat O'Keefe (b. 1883), a very active middleweight before the war, having started his professional career at age 15, had no fights during 1917 and only one in 1918. A Londoner of Irish descent, he lost a middleweight title fight (pre-Lonsdale Belt) against Tom Thomas on points in May 1906. He boxed in the USA (three fights in 1907) and Australia (seven fights 1909–10).

When the Lonsdale middleweight belt was deemed vacated by Jack Harrison, the NSC invited O'Keefe and Harry Reeve, another Londoner (b. 7 January 1893 and better known in the 1920s), to contest the title on 23 February 1914. O'Keefe won on points over 20 rounds and defended twice against Jim Sullivan (25 May 1914 and 21 February 1916). In 1916 he was the reigning champion.

O'Keefe's fellow middleweight Bandsman Blake was younger (b. 1893 or possibly 1891 in Great Yarmouth) and a more taciturn and modest man than the genial O'Keefe and acquired plenty of military and ring experience. He looked tough beneath his mop of black hair and his caterpillar eyebrows, boasting the crudest of ring names 'The Yarmouth Ripper'. He remained a man whom unexpected circumstances could disturb, sometimes disastrously. He served in India like Bombardier Billy Wells, and also like Wells became an Indian Army boxing champion. In 1913 he fought often at The Ring, where Dick Burge rated him highly, and at the Liverpool Stadium. He was a natural middleweight and stood about 5ft 9½in. It made little sense to take him out of his comfort zone into the glamorous London Palladium on 3 March 1914 against the very much taller heavyweight Bombardier (Chapter 10). His defeat was inevitable.

He returned to home ground, so to speak, to fight American Joe Borrell a few weeks later at The Ring on 20 April 1914. Unlucky circumstances followed him.[69] Borrell (b. Giuseppe Borrelli in New York on 21 June 1892) adopted Philadelphia as his spiritual home and rarely left it apart from the brief visit to England and France in February to May 1914. He should not have bothered. Blake, cautious after the Wells bout, was not looking to trade. Neither was Borrell, although Blake was the chief offender. They hugged, clinched, pushed, wrestled and mauled. 'To describe either of them as boxers at last night's bout would be a gross libel on the sport,' said *Boxing*'s reporter. The noisy audience, at the end of the fourth, expressed their disgust so loudly that the timekeeper's bell was heard by Blake but by few others. Blake dropped his hands and moved to his corner.

Borrell, apparently in good faith, produced a left hook better than anything either man had produced in 12 minutes. Over and out went Blake. Referee Sydney Hulls indicated a Borrell win by knockout. Into the ring came Blake's angry seconds and other supporters demanding Borrell be disqualified. Hulls considered this, saw its merit and disqualified Borrell. Noisier turbulence and ring invasions followed. Hulls' next decision was to ask for the bell to start the fifth round and get the fight resumed. This idea foundered on the unfortunate circumstance that Blake was still lying on the canvas and had no intention of getting up. Hulls then pronounced the affair a 'No Contest'; probably the only time in ring history a bout was subject to four successive different decisions.

Blake was a reservist and one of the first to be called up to the BEF in August 1914. Before the month was out he was in real combat. Shot in the shoulder, he returned to Blighty. Once healed, he demonstrated bravery and resilience by returning to the front. He went on boxing and a year after his over-matched encounter with the Bombardier, he met, on 11 March 1915 at The Ring, Harry Reeve, the man

who took O'Keefe unsuccessfully to the distance at the NSC. He outpointed Reeve over 20 rounds, making a match with O'Keefe desirable whenever the two could get permission and the necessary leave. They met three times during the war: on 10 May 1915 at The Ring; and at the NSC on 22 May 1916 and 28 January 1918.

The Ring encounter rivalled Blake v Borrell for the unpredictable.[70] Blake, more confident than for some time and looking the decade younger than O'Keefe he was, bustled the Londoner and landed plenty of short punches. After 12 rounds, each won by Blake, Blake sat on his stool serenely and O'Keefe sagged gloomily. At this point, who should appear but Bombardier Billy Wells. The crowd cheered him to a front-row seat. On his way past the ring, Wells took the arm of his old mate O'Keefe and shook his hand.

This transformed the whole scene. O'Keefe, visibly inspired, got a new shot of energy. Blake, glimpsing the blond giant who had demolished him so comprehensively in 1914, was utterly thrown. He was still ruminating on the past when the 13th began. An O'Keefe left hook to the chin felled him for nine, a second for eight, and a third for the full ten.

When they met again a year later on 22 May 1916 at the NSC, O'Keefe was still British middleweight champion and outright owner of the belt by virtue of his win over Harry Reeve and successful defences against Nichol Simpson and (twice) Bermondsey's Jim Sullivan. (Simpson, a Tynesider, having lost his title chance and seeing the way the war was going, departed and spent 1917 and 1918 fighting in Australia and then the USA.) Remembering

Blake's superiority at Blackfriars before his mental aberration, most believed Blake would this time take O'Keefe's title away.

Blake entered the ring, a picture of sculptured health in contrast to O'Keefe, tired and haggard from taking off the pounds he had put on eating army rations. The betting was all on Blake. His backers felt their money practically in the bank when his high tempo kept O'Keefe at a safe distance, his hurtful right hooks sneaking under O'Keefe's guard and landing around his heart (an organ believed to be larger than most). O'Keefe's best hope was to lie low and land one really good punch to stop the bout. Easier said than done.

In the tenth, O'Keefe came very near with a right cross to the chin to stagger Blake, who clung as shamelessly to O'Keefe as he had to Borrell. It was the turning point of the fight. O'Keefe put Blake down again in the 17th for a long count, and also in the 19th with left and right hooks. Blake lay there motionless and one of his seconds believing him to be knocked out slid through the ropes to collect him. To everyone's surprise Blake got up again. For the rest of the fight, he survived by clinging and retreating, a beaten man. Then, to the astonishment of everyone, including Blake, referee J. H. Douglas awarded Blake the championship and the belt. He had missed the entry of Blake's second in the 19th, which should have led to instant disqualification and had given O'Keefe insufficient credit for overhauling Blake's early lead.

The demands of war kept both men busy in France for nearly two years before they could meet again at the NSC to settle the baffling question of who was the real champion.[71] When that day dawned – 28 January 1918 – much had happened in the meantime. Both had survived the war yet their experiences had damaged them as it had so many others. O'Keefe, the veteran, was now 35 years old, age and experience showing on his face, and was held in universal affection but was physically weaker than in 1916.

Blake, whose mental frailties had so let him down in the past, was suffering undiagnosed shell shock.

Air raids were particularly distressing. The evening of the fight was also the night of the biggest and closest air raid Covent Garden suffered. As Blake sat in his corner, the sounds of sirens, explosions and anti-aircraft guns resounded all around. Before the action he swore, 'If I get home safe tonight, I don't reckon I'll fight again.' It was less than ideal mental preparation.

In his anxiety to get the fight over with and return home in one piece, he endured a minute while each felt out the other, then impatiently rushed into close quarters with O'Keefe, a tactic calm reflection might have warned him to avoid. He grabbed O'Keefe's body with a prehensile left arm and hit him with short rights. O'Keefe, much more flexible, responded with a few painful jabs and body blows that got Blake breathing hard and coughing.

Despite the stern lecture given him on his stool during the interval, Blake foolishly and compulsively continued the same way in the second. O'Keefe saw no reason to allow Blake's suicide mission its full course. Driving Blake back into a corner, he produced an effective combination. A left to the solar plexus doubled up Blake, whose jaw met a follow-up left hook. As he fell, a right hook sped him on his way. He would not be getting up until his seconds carried him to his corner. O'Keefe was cheered and chaired out of the ring as Blake recovered on his stool. Both men half-fulfilled the vows they made before the fight. O'Keefe got his title back as he swore he would but retired without defending it. Blake was taken home unscathed, never to fight another major contest, taking only a few minor fights safely post-war in the 1920s.

One British fighter received more attention than any other during the war years, his fortunes representing a recurring and much discussed leitmotif. A boxer of undisputable world class and arguably the best Britain ever produced, this was the phenomenal Jimmy Wilde whom we last saw reeling in the NSC ring under the determined assaults of Tancy Lee. Less than 7st/98lbs, Wilde, the powerful mite, resumed his winning ways after that defeat and always drew crowds. He took fights regularly – he fought nine times in 1915 after losing to Lee; 16 times in 1916. Only his entry into the army limited his opportunities to two in 1917 and three in 1918. In 1916 he increased his ancillary earnings with guest appearances in one of C. B. Cochran's comedy revues at the Comedy Theatre, *Half Past Eight*.

For Wilde, 1916 was productive and impressive despite the fears expressed by *Boxing* that he was overdoing it. He met and beat the best fighters in his division. On 14 February 1916, he took a second fight against Joe Symonds, the man he had outpointed in November 1914. Though defeated by Wilde then, Symonds stole a march on Wilde by meeting and beating Tancy Lee at the NSC (18 October 1915). Symonds stopped Lee in the 16th and had the satisfaction of holding the flyweight championship and the Lonsdale Belt. His reign did not last long. Wilde took belt and title, dominating Symonds and punishing him to the extent that Symonds retired in the 12th. So far as the British were concerned that made Wilde the new world champion at the weight. Despite the obvious difficulties of crossing the wartime Atlantic, a good American boxer, Johnny Rosner, came to challenge him. This Jewish New Yorker was a tough and experienced campaigner, born 19 June 1894 and active from 1910 to 1923, although inevitably most of his bouts were of the ten-round no-decision kind. Courageous in and out of the ring, he braved the German U-boats and sailed into Liverpool to meet Wilde at the packed Liverpool Stadium on 24 April 1916 for a minor share of the purse ($2,000 Wilde, $1,400 Rosner) and a chance to call himself a world champion.[72]

He was taller than Wilde (5ft 6in) and both men made the 8st/112lbs limit fully dressed, Wilde estimated at 7st 2lb/100lbs and Rosner at 7st 5lb/103lbs. Rosner fought from a crouch and tried to belabour Wilde about the ribs with short swings. Wilde, more upright, used a long left jab to keep him away. Rosner had an additional handicap – a clash of heads in a sparring session had left him with a swollen and bruised left eye – and an additional asset in that he did not know when he was beaten. He needed all his bravery and stamina when a Wilde right in the third landed on the vulnerable eye and opened a deep and profusely bleeding cut. From then on Rosner could barely see Wilde or avoid his punches. He refused his manager's suggestion to retire. Rather, he chose to go on the attack, and regardless of how many times Wilde hit him, he went on swinging and advancing, punching through a blinding red curtain. This lasted another eight rounds until his trainer jumped between the ropes in the 11th to save him. *Boxing* thought the effort unprecedented: '... such a marvellous display of pluck and stamina never having been seen before within the Stadium walls'. The audience audibly endorsed that conclusion.

That left Wilde as a world champion and a British champion with unfinished business against the Scot who had mastered him back in January 1915. The long-expected return against Lee came at the NSC on 26 June 1916 for £500, and side stakes of £250.[73] A Lee finding the flyweight limit increasingly irksome, and a Wilde on top form made for a predictable result. *Boxing* thought Wilde's victory inevitable:

> For most people have long believed that the Tylorstown Terror is not only the greatest flyweight, but quite possibly the greatest bantam in the world, as he is assuredly the most wonderful boxer of all time.

Praise indeed and Lee conceded Wilde to be 'as crafty as a waggon-load of monkeys'. Wilde's win – it came with a stoppage in the 11th round – was predictable but no walkover. Tancy repeated the rough treatment, bullying Wilde to the ropes, leaning his weight upon him and pounding him about the ribs with the odd uppercut thrown in. For two rounds it seemed as though he might repeat his previous victory. Unfortunately for him this was a quite different Wilde, although a Wilde who had to work extremely hard to win.

When Wilde opened out in the third, some Welshmen in the audience so forgot themselves as to break the prevailing silence and perhaps their own trepidation by standing up and cheering. It disturbed NSC decorum but encouraged Wilde. In the fifth, Wilde closed out the round with hooks from right and left hands and a right uppercut that visibly hurt.

Lee, tiring a little, was by no means finished. Wilde elegantly avoided one rush in the seventh as Tancy almost fell through the ropes and laughed endearingly at his own folly. Others, especially in the eighth and ninth, succeeded. Wilde was cut over the left eye in the eighth and took heavy thumps to the body in the ninth.

In the tenth he decided to finish things before Lee landed any more. Jabbing succinctly to face and body to lower the Scotsman's guard, Wilde produced a forceful right to the jaw and clusters of punches. Down went Lee for nine, then for eight, then for another eight. A jabbing right to the jaw would have been the knockout punch had the bell not rung. The interval did not help. Lee took another count of six on his knee in the 11th. He struggled up only for a left and a right to spreadeagle him on the floor as referee Douglas waved the end. Wilde had the Lonsdale Belt that he would make his permanently, and the British flyweight championship that he would hold for seven years.

(Lee lost here but had consolations to come. Moving up to bantam then feather, he clinched his own Lonsdale Belt with wins at the NSC over Charlie Hardcastle [fourth-round KO on 5 November 1917]; over Joe Conn, to whom he conceded 17 years [17th-round KO on 21 October 1918] and

over Danny Morgan [by points over 20 rounds on 24 February 1919]. There were few more popular winners.)

Wilde continued his golden year, beating domestic and international opponents. On 31 July 1916, the NSC imaginatively promoted him to a wider public in an open-air contest at the National Athletic Ground, Kensal Rise, against Johnny Hughes of Bloomsbury. The spectators turned up in droves, many in uniform and saw Wilde at his best, knocking out Hughes in the tenth of 20.

Had the Trade Descriptions Act then existed, Wilde's next international challenger might have been found guilty of seriously misleading the public. This was Young Zulu Kid, a name suggesting a tall warrior of the Rorke's Drift variety taking time off from life on the veldt to invade the land of the imperial oppressors. Actually the Kid had been born Giuseppe Di Melfi on 27 April 1897 in Potenza in southern Italy, with no African connections whatever. He grew to a lofty 4ft 11in and was fighting out of Brooklyn, New York as an Italian-American. He weighed in on the day at 7st 12½lb/110½lbs. He was a serious and experienced opponent. (Over a career lasting from 1912–28 he had 137 fights, including eight against Rosner, Wilde's previous American invader. His meeting with Wilde was his 18th fight in 1916.)

Their fight took place at the Holborn Stadium on 18 December 1916, a major draw in the reopened and refurbished hall, and another sign that boxing was surviving the war and sometimes flourishing.[74] Wilde was the firmest of favourites as the more skilled of the two. Just as against Rosner, he found that for all his superiority he had to work very hard to win. The Kid had come to fight, armed with a fast right hook, exceptional stamina, and a clever defence, including an eccentric dip where he bent at the knee, taking himself downwards with a strictly perpendicular torso.

In the first round, Wilde retreated and picked the advancing Kid off with left counters, much to the pleasure of his supporters. In the second, Wilde rounded off some close encounters where the Kid had at least held his own, with a consummate combination of a left hook and three rights to the jaw. The Kid, on the brink of oblivion, was rescued by the bell and carried back to his corner by his seconds. The delight of everyone who had backed Wilde was patent but premature. The American came out for round three as fresh as if the fight were just beginning. He was not going to give in easily.

Wilde had the better of the next five rounds but had to suffer effective punching from the Zulu Kid, especially close in. The man's gameness and powers of endurance were remarkable – perhaps he could still outlast Wilde and take over. The seventh increased such possibilities. Four punches from Wilde were ducked deftly with that dip, then Young Zulu drove Wilde back across the ring and landed four body blows of his own. Wilde regained the initiative only to be caught again with three good punches just before the bell. He had to work even harder in the eighth and was caught around the body at the close.

The ninth was yet more ominous. With an excited crowd up on their feet, screaming encouragement to both men, the Kid seized the psychological moment, throwing and landing more punches than the champion, taking

some himself in the process. His stamina seemed endless and his continuing wish to force the pace admirable. But perhaps he had forgotten that both qualities were those Wilde had in abundance. The Welshman rarely ducked out of toe-to-toe punch-fests. The next two rounds proved it.

Young Zulu Kid began the tenth as if the ninth were still in full flow. Wilde wholeheartedly took on the challenge. Locked together and punching furiously, they lapped the ring until it was the Kid who broke off. Wilde could fight his own fight. He could fight the American's too, and was ultimately better at it. In the 11th he proved it. Out came the Kid, weakened by the tenth yet as game as ever and giving no quarter. It was not enough. An array of jabs and hooks, the last half dozen without reply, sent him staggering and finally down as the towel fluttered in from his corner. He had lost but no one who saw the fight ever forgot his contribution.

Wilde's other fight before the war ended was of major importance. As a serving soldier, he fought Joe Conn, a *featherweight*, two divisions above his own, in another open-air contest at Stamford Bridge, the Chelsea FC football ground. Wilde consistently declined to enlist and made a series of unsuccessful appeals against being conscripted. He was eventually called up against his inclinations. No longer a private citizen, Wilde could now box only with military approval.

The Conn fight took place on 31 August 1918, promoted by Jack Callaghan, the manager of the Holborn Stadium, in front of a supposedly disappointing crowd (about 8,000 according to one account). Callaghan

himself claimed 35,000 people had passed through the turnstiles and he was probably more correct. The disappointment was more in the vacancies among the expensive ringside seats, although not among the fans in the stand, who made a partly successful invasion of any privileged seats they saw empty.[75] Joe Conn was actually Joseph Cohen, a Jewish Cockney born in Bow on 13 March 1897. He, like Ted Kid Lewis, had launched his boxing career with six of his first seven fights at the Judaean Club in the East End. Now 21, he was a popular and experienced London favourite. When he finally retired in 1925, he had participated in 114 bouts.

In West London, the official weights were shrouded in secrecy, as Wilde's often were, but for 20 rounds Conn would have an advantage of 20 pounds – a huge discrepancy in size, strength and punching power. Conn decided that his best tactic was to operate defensively – allow Wilde to punch himself out and take over as he tired. It was a serious miscalculation. The man the *Sunday Times* dubbed 'Wilde the Invincible' suffered Conn's punches but took the fight to Conn, determined to knock out the heavier man as soon as he could. Given the physical discrepancies between them, that would need time and survival under the occasional Conn counter-attack, one of which inflicted a cut over Wilde's right eye and another that backed Wilde on to the ropes. Many rounds finished with a weary Wilde sinking gratefully on to his stool for a minute's rest even when he had had the better of the round.

Conn could postpone the end but not avert it. In the ninth, Wilde went fully on to the attack and Conn retreated. In the tenth, Conn's serious decline began. A Wilde uppercut shook him and when a right hook followed it in, Conn dropped to the floor for a count of nine. He was down for another *six* counts of eight before the round ended. He was down for another four counts in the 11th. It was surprising that he even came out for the 12th. It was only a gesture and the third time he went down referee J. T. Hulls intervened. Against the extraordinary Wilde, Conn's skill and his considerable physical advantages had ultimately counted for nothing.

Sergeant Wilde's ruthless punches had guaranteed £1,000 to the Eccentric Club Hostels for Limbless Sailors and Soldiers (7,000 of whom in blue hospital uniforms and on crutches attended, another clue that Callaghan's estimate was believable). Another 15 per cent of the takings went to other military charities. The Eccentric Club, the third under the title, was formed in 1890 in the Denman Street premises previously occupied by the Pelican Club. By the outbreak of the war it had moved to Ryder Street in the heart of St James's. Like the old Pelican, its members included boxing supporters such as Lord Lonsdale and Jack Callaghan. Like the NSC, it justified its continuing existence in wartime by charitable contributions – including £25,000 to the limbless.

The most bizarre part of the proceedings was what Wilde, or rather his wife, got out of it. She was at ringside to see his victory, if not in his dressing room to celebrate. She broke into another all-male sanctum as the sole woman at the Eccentric Club banquet the night of the fight. There were other unanticipated difficulties, in particular the rules of the Imperial Services Boxing Association about serving soldiers receiving purses for professional prizefights.

Originally, Wilde was expecting £2,850 and Conn £1,250 as offered by Callaghan. On the morning of the fight, Brigadier General Sir Richard Fitzpatrick (1878–1949) ordered Wilde not to accept the money. Either Wilde withdrew from the fight or fought without pay. As the charity funds depended upon the event, Wilde agreed to forego the cash and accept a special silver cup. He offered to swell the funds further by putting the cup up for auction along with his gloves in the event of victory.

The arrangement was not all it might seem. After the fight and his victory, his wife was discreetly presented with two packets of diamonds worth at least £2,000.[76] The gift was secretly engineered by Sir Bernard Oppenheimer (1866–1921), a South African diamond merchant and philanthropist, a member of the Eccentrics who had just opened a diamond works especially to train the war disabled in jewellery making. The device suited all parties and the Wildes got their cash by reselling the gems immediately; a slightly absurd proceeding in the best spirit of British compromise.

It was not sufficiently secret to avoid sarcastic mention a few weeks later in the columns of *Boxing* on 18 September 1918 that Wilde had been presented with a silver cup and 'a mysterious parcel of diamonds' and had pronounced, 'This is all I get.' As the magazine pointed out, at least one boxer who had volunteered for war service and had been gassed, three times wounded and sought a professional contest after a lengthy convalescence had been offered a munificent £15 for a 15-round title match – no gems for him, win, draw or lose. The relationship between professional boxing and the army remained most ambiguous.

The army, after the physical deficiencies of the troops shown up in the Crimean War of 1853–56, had sought solutions. An Army Gymnastic Staff was set up in 1860. James Yorke Scarlett, Adjutant General, wrote a long letter to *The Times* in May 1865 insisting on gymnastics for soldiers along with the necessary coercion: '… the attendances of men under 10 years' service is to be made compulsory'.[77] A print of 1866 showing the Headquarters Gymnasium at Aldershot shows that 'gymnastics' actually included fencing, single-stick combat and gloved boxing sparring in the open air.[78]

By the 1890s, under the auspices of a Colonel Fox, a man who had visited Sweden and seen Swedish gymnastic drills, more than 80 gymnasia were in operation.[79] The Aldershot site reopened in 1894 as the Cranbrook Gymnasium. Boxing was already so important and popular for recruits and serving soldiers that the Cranbrook Gymnasium included a new spectator gallery to accommodate boxing competitions. It was capacious enough to stage the Public Schools Boxing Championships in 1894, its first major venture but not the last.

The first Army Boxing Championships were held in 1893 outdoors in Aldershot and became an annual event. By 1910, regimental teams competed regularly in the championships held in London, clear recognition of the value placed on boxing as appropriate for serving soldiers.[80] In 1912 they were back at Aldershot, slightly preceded by the Navy and Army championships held at Portsmouth at the end of 1911. Boxing in the army was naturally segregated so far as rank was concerned. There were to be no opportunities for a disgruntled private to extract a painful revenge by beating up an unpopular sergeant major or knocking out a feeble platoon commander.

When the First World War broke out in August 1914, the army mistakenly dispersed the gymnastic staff back to regiments and had hurriedly to recall them. There were other factors than fitness and stamina. The war indicates the point when sport, popular in the ranks but unofficial, became more formally integrated into the military system.[81]

There were questions to be answered. Could sport make men so recently civilians into better soldiers? Surely the sporting virtues – bravery, controlled aggression, tolerance of adversity, subordination of the individual ego in favour of the team – would lend themselves readily to wartime conditions with the regiment and the platoon substituted for the team? Few would have gone quite so far as the 'Ex-Non-Com' in the *United Services Magazine* of 1910 (quoted by J. D. Campbell in his 'Training for Sport' article) that 'War [is] simply sport on a grand scale' but many would have accepted a watered-down version of the thesis.

It is not coincidental that those particular virtues were precisely the ones inculcated and justified by the public school cult of games. The thinking fitted beautifully with the belief that games induced character formation and moral discipline.[82] As most decision makers in the services,

from junior officers to the generals, were overwhelmingly drawn from public schoolboys, the forcible application of the philosophy to the other ranks was almost inevitable. By 1918 the General Staff had issued a guiding document on *The Training and Employment of Platoons*. It stated firmly:

> Too much attention cannot be paid to the part played by games in fostering the fighting spirit. They afford the platoon commander an unrivalled opportunity not only of teaching men to play for their side and work together in the spirit of self-sacrifice, but of gaining insight into their characters.[83]

The idea that sport, especially football and boxing, had helped win the war prevailed for many decades after 1918. In 1931, the Army Sports Control Board published a comprehensive little book, *Games and Sports in the Army*. In a fighting preface about the late war, General C. H. Harington confirmed, 'I am confident that "leather" played one of the greatest parts. Few have realised what we owe to the boxing glove and the football – the two greatest factors in restoring and upholding "moral" [*sic*].' (General 'Tim' Harington 1872–1940 was a much decorated soldier, educated at Cheltenham and Sandhurst.)

The quotation did *not* mean that the army was grateful to the professional boxers and footballers who had joined up. On the contrary, professional sport cut completely across the public school-engendered philosophy. It was supposedly *amateur* sport that had worked such military magic. In the boxing section of the

Games and Sports book, containing a potted history of army boxing and rules for its conduct, detestation of professional boxing is rife:

> The method of the referee in professional fights, which consisted of constant warnings and threats of appeals, had obviously failed to keep boxing clean, and the very strict refereeing adopted by the Services was the only suitable course. As the season progressed, the boxing became cleaner and cleaner. (p. 194)
>
> Money prizes were eliminated, and the boxing was carried out in the truest spirit of amateur sport. (p. 195)

On January 29th, 1918, there was a Committee Meeting in London, attended by the Navy, Army and Royal Air Force, and the Imperial Services Boxing Association was formed. On this day the question of money prizes was discussed at great length. The Army had seen the splendid spirit which the abolition of money prizes had introduced and pressed that this should be a rule of the Association. Colonel R. B. Campbell expressed the following views:– He admitted that the abolition of money prizes was at first very unpopular and a great deal of opposition was experienced from men in the ranks interested either directly or indirectly with professional boxing. But he had the support and approval of the Commander-in-Chief in France [General Douglas Haig], who was entirely opposed to money prizes and ordered that no boxing should take place if they were given. The professional was the chief difficulty. (pp.195–196)

Money prizes invariably led to unadulterated professionalism; they *undermine the character of the men who receive them … If money prizes are retained, boxing, instead of being one of the finest character-building sports, will become a byword for everything obnoxious.* [Italics added] (p. 196)

… it was decided to abolish money prizes entirely in Service boxing. This proved a red letter day in the history of Service boxing. (p. 196)

If these quotations do not sufficiently underline the heavily amateur and class bias on show, the instructions for conduct post-fight certainly do:

A habit that is often learnt by men taking part in low class boxing is to kiss their opponents when they shake hands on the declaration of the winner. This practice should be stopped at once, and any man attempting it should be reproved openly. (p. 214)

God knows what that might lead to – proletarian sex orgies in the ring?

The original custom of charging modest admission prices to spectators to army boxing tournaments to fund money prizes for soldiers from other ranks was common pre-war. It did not survive the influx of the amateur-minded organisers. One of them was (then) Major R. B. Campbell of the Army Gymnastic Staff, amateur boxer

and the very man making the eloquent appeal in July 1918 just quoted.[84] Campbell was a major influence behind the December 1916 decision by the inaugural conference of Superintendents of Physical and Bayonet Training that 'no money prizes should be given for any kind of "recreational training"'. The term 'recreational training' was a euphemism for boxing. After Campbell had lobbied the sympathetic General Haig, the decision was confirmed and applied specifically to boxing by regulation GRO No. 2059 in January 1917, followed by Training Pamphlet SS137 on Recreational Training in October 1917 ('Money prizes must not be given. They kill good sport, encourage selfishness, and destroy the spirit of individual sacrifice which games are intended to foster.')[85] Cash was replaced by medals, ribbons, cups and token gifts, and the boxing shifted from individual competition to *teams* – with the honour of the platoon, the regiment or the service substituted for any individual glory, a concept particularly fitting for the public-school ethos. (Even Campbell conceded that abolishing cash prizes was unpopular with the professionals in the ranks, but he and others were too committed to the amateur principle to be deterred.) An apparent paradox is that this man, so averse to professionalism, was a major recruiter of boxing professionals to the Army Physical and Bayonet Training Staff. In early 1915 the Army Gymnastic Staff acquired major responsibility for bayonet training across the army, mostly because of Campbell's expertise and enthusiasm.

He was instrumental in adding, for example, Bombardier Billy Wells, Jim Driscoll, Johnny Basham and Jimmy

Jim Driscoll's successes as Army Boxing Instructor drew gentle satire from W.D.Jordan in Boxing, 8 September 1915.

Wilde to his team.[86] He did so, not because he wanted them to box for him, although he was well aware of the publicity and prestige their fame brought. He wanted not performers but expert instructors to teach novices to stand up for themselves in one-to-one combat.

With the help of the pros, defences against bayonets, knives, clubs, rifle butts and fists could be devised and taught. His real passion, almost a vocation, was for the bayonet. He believed that speed of reaction, balance, aggression and perception of an attacker's weaknesses could all be learned in the boxing ring and readily transferred to bayonet drills. (Even the most hardened of NSC or Ring spectators might have blanched at the sight of Campbell and his assistant Driscoll, unprotected, having at one another with naked bayonets.[87] Driscoll and Campbell jointly authored an instructional booklet on bayonet fighting.)

Campbell was not naïve. He knew the bayonet was well-nigh obsolete even before 1914. He believed that the old-fashioned weapon could still induce bloodlust into the most pacific of squaddies. ('Get the bayonet into the hands of despondent troops and you can make them tigers within hours.')[88] 'What makes the grass grow?' he exhorted. 'BLOOD!' was the expected reply. 'What is the spirit of the bayonet?' 'TO KILL!' By March 1916, Campbell and 51 other instructors were in France behind the lines spreading the gospel of the bayonet.

Apart from raising the soldiers' testosterone to murderous levels, could sport contribute to enhancing soldiers' leisure out of the line? As the distinguished military historian Richard Holmes reminds us, at the beginning of the war about 16 per cent of the army were in non-combatant units, and by 1918 a full 33 per cent.[89] Add in the combatants standing down from the front line to rest areas on a temporary rota basis, unit by unit, and that meant many men with much spare time. Spare time invited boredom – the scourge of army life – and soon enough disaffection. It made sense to organise sport to fill that time; sport on a regimental basis. Even the most unsporting general could see that games and play were healthier than the booze and the brothel.

As any gathering of British males near an empty space leads to a casual kickabout with a football, many spontaneous games had taken place behind the lines. (In the so-called Christmas truce of 1914, such games had famously taken place *between* the

lines with *German* participation, much to the disgust of the top brass.) It made sense as the war went on to put such games on a better organised basis.

Where this was impossible because the potential pitches belonged to unsympathetic French farmers, or were utterly waterlogged or frozen, what better than to put on boxing in a barn or in the open-air space available instead? Minimal equipment, minimal space and plenty of enthusiasm made for easily initiated and successful competitions. Not only did the boxing arouse enthusiasm in its participants, but the spectators became quite as involved as the boxers.

The newspapers and journals carried accounts of many such wartime tournaments. In September 1915, *Boxing*, for example, carried the results of a two-day 1st Loyal North Lancs regimental show 'behind the line, somewhere'. The event constituted an 8st/112lbs competition and two 9st/126lbs competitions, all finishing with semi-finals and a final. They were followed by four four-round fights. All the participants were privates and corporals and presumably amateurs. The climax of the show, a featherweight ten-rounder between Bob Donati of Scotland and Cyclone Thompson of Bermondsey (disqualified in the eighth) was between *professionals* who were undoubtedly paid and who were watched by 1,300 spectators.[90] For all the propaganda for amateurism, professionalism was not so easily eliminated. All most spectators wanted was a good scrap – the protagonists' status was irrelevant.

In collaboration with the YMCA, Captain Temple Clarke of the Advanced Horse Transport Depot at Abbeville

(in Picardie on the Somme) promoted several similar tournaments – one top fight, good supporting fights and two-minute-round fights for novices. The events drew houses handsome enough to guarantee payment for the fighters plus a contribution to the company's games fund.[91]

Only after the order against money prizes was issued, did amateurism prevail. This was why Wilde had been denied his purse for the Stamford Bridge fight. A *Times* correspondent in an article 'BOXING IN THE BEF/ THE FUTURE OF A BRITISH SPORT' thoroughly approved:

[Boxing] has come into permanent existence in every unit of the BEF ... It is now an irresistible attraction ... The number of tournaments must be legion ... [up] to the big affairs of three days, which draw all the officers and men from miles around. It is exhilarating to attend one of these larger gatherings. The onlookers, usually trench-worn troops, forget their weariness. The lassitude, born of inaction or overwork, drops from them as if by magic and in a twinkling of an eye they regain their old eager fighting spirit.[92]

Ring action transcended its context, even the ever-threatening sound of shelling and the unusual venues:

Anything and everything constitutes a ring, even to four men as corner-posts, each holding up his section of the rope. In church rooms, Y.M.C.A huts, mairies [town halls], circuses, hotels de ville, cow-sheds, and barns rings have been erected, with anything solid, from barrack tables to sandbags, for a platform. Even a shell crater [has] been borrowed …

The correspondent does justice to these remarkable authentic wartime scenes. (His newspaper a month later carried another romantic description of a bout where 'the room [was] lit by four acetylene lamps; on tiers of benches and boxes sit hundreds of khaki-clad men'.)[93] However, he goes seriously astray in predicting that these extraordinary scenes at an extraordinary time would lead to a peacetime where professionalism would wither away and amateur participation would be all:

The amateur spirit of the universities and the public schools has laid hold upon the Army. Men box now, either for boxing's sake or to win a point

or two towards the team … Will this athletic spirit continue after the war? The young man who has once tasted the joy of physical fitness and the fierce delights of … the ring will not be content to be one of 30,000 spectators … When spectators become players, there will be no demand for highly specialized professionals, still less for the promoter, whose interest in sport is circumscribed by the revenue it affords. There will be thousands of boxing clubs … needed in England when the men come home. And with … no promoters searching for travesties of 'white hopes' temptations to professionalism will vanish.

It is easy now to find such prophecies ludicrous, but even at the time the logical flaws in the argument were patent. In the army and also on board ships and at early aerodromes, recruits had been encouraged to spar, to get into

a ring and fight, or to roar on others who were better at fighting than they.

Many had never been near a boxing hall, never seen a fight on film at their local fleapit. Suddenly, an exciting sport, in abbreviated form, was being encouraged officially and widely discussed; subtleties, tactics and rewards demonstrated daily. In their eagerness to tap boxing for its contribution to the fighting qualities of the British male, and for its aid in usefully filling leisure time and boosting regimental morale, the military authorities fostered an appetite for watching boxing and boosted a demand to see the sport at its best. That meant an appetite not for amateurism and joining amateur boxing clubs but for seeing the real masters of the sport – the professionals fighting over an extended number of rounds. The privileged place of boxing in the services during the First World War led in the first full year of peace in 1919 to the biggest boost in professional boxing in Britain there has ever been.

Endnotes:

1 *The Times,* 6 December 1914.

2 Veitch, C., 'Football, the Nation and the First World War' in *Journal of Contemporary History* Vol. 20 No. 3, July 1985.

3 Birley, D., 'Sportsmen and the Deadly Game' pp. 288–310 in *British Journal of Sports History* Vol. 3 No. 2, 1986; [an article with many other useful comments on the war].

4 Both quotations from *The Times,* 7 November 1914.

5 *The Times,* 25 November 1914.

6 *The Times,* 28 November 1914.

7 *The Times,* 26 January 1915.

8 Birley, D., *A Social History of English Cricket* (London: Aurum Press, 2000) pp. 206–207.

9 Quoted by Leo McKinstry in 'The Summer Before the Deluge of War', *The Cricketer* Summer 2014.

10 Birley, D., 'Sportsmen and the Deadly Game' pp. 294–295.

11 Taylor, M., 'Leisure and Entertainment' in *The Great World War 1914–45* Vol. 2 *The People's Experience* (London: Harper Collins, 2001) pp. 371–394.

12 Hiley, N., '"Kitchener Wants YOU" and "Daddy What Did YOU Do in the Great War?": the Myth of British Recruiting Posters.' *Imperial Museum Review* No. 11 pp. 40–58.

13 *Boxing,* 15 August 1914.

14 *The Times,* 11 December 1914.

15 *Boxing,* 3 October 1914.

16 *Boxing,* 16 September 1914.

17 *Boxing,* 26 December 1914.

18 *Boxing,* 12 September 1914.

19 *Boxing,* 29 August 1914.

20 *Boxing,* 3 October 1914.

21 Harding, J., *Lonsdale's Belt: Boxing's Most Coveted Prize* (Worthing: Pitch Publishing, 2016) pp. 53–54.

22 Mullan, H., *Heroes and Hard Men: The Story of Britain's World Boxing Champions* (London: Stanley Paul, 1989) pp.44–47; *Boxing,* 21 November 1914.

23 Gallimore, A., *Occupation Prizefighter: The Freddie Welsh Story* (Bridgend: seren Books, 2006) p. 229. [Mr Gallimore's book contributes other useful details to what follows.]

24 Gallimore, A., *Occupation Prizefighter,* p. 230.

25 *New York Times,* 3 November 1914.

26 *New York Times,* 10 November 1914.

27 *New York Times,* 3 December 1914.

28 Quoted by Gallimore, A., *Occupation Prizefighter,* p. 237.

29 *The Times,* 26 January 1915; *Boxing,* 30 January and 6 February 1915; film in the National Archive.

30 *Boxing,* 22 December 1915.

31 Poster reproduced in Shipley, S., *Bombardier Billy Wells: The Life and Trials of a Boxing Hero* (Tyne and Wear: Bewick Press, 1993) p. 115.

32 White, J., *Zeppelin Nights: London in the First World War* (London: The Bodley Head, 2014) p. 118.

33 Shipley, S., *Bombardier Billy Wells,* p. 114–116; *Boxing,* 6 March 1915.

34 *The Times,* 30 March 1915; *New York Times,* 30 March 1915; *Boxing,* 31 March 1915; Shipley, S., *Bombardier Billy Wells,* pp. 118–122.

35 *Boxing,* 31 March 1915.

36 *The Times,* 1 June 1915; *Boxing,* 2 June 1915; Shipley, S., *Bombardier Billy Wells,* pp. 124–127.

37 *Boxing,* 2 June 1915; *The Times,* 1 June 1915.

38 *New York Times,* 14 October 1914.

39 Johnson, J., *Jack Johnson is a Dandy: An Autobiography* (New York: Chelsea House, 1968) p. 101.

40 Roberts, R., *Papa Jack: Jack Johnson and the Era of White Hopes* (New York: Simon & Schuster, 1985) p. 200.

41 Johnson, J., *Jack Johnson is a Dandy,* p.101.

42 Film extracts on YouTube; *Boxing,* 14 April 1915 and 'How Willard Won' by Bat Masterson in *Boxing,* 21 April 1915; *The Times,* 6 April 1915; *New York Times,* 6 April 1915; Snelling, O.F., 'Did Jack Johnson Quit?' in *The Ringside Book of Boxing* (London, Robson Books, 1991) pp. 28–44; and every standard boxing history and Johnson biography.

43 Telegram in full in Ward, G., *Unforgivable Blackness: The Rise and Fall of Jack Johnson* (New York: Knopf, 2004) p. 386.

44 Roberts, R., *Papa Jack,* p. 203.

45 *New York Times,* 6 April 1915.

46 *Boxing* 5 January 1916

47 White, J., *Zeppelin Nights,* pp. 125–128.

48 National Archives: File BT31/15196/35292.

49 *Boxing,* 20 October 1915.

50 *Boxing,* 12 May 1915; *The Times,* 11 May 1915.

51 *The Times,* 23 March 1915; Roderick, A., *Johnny! The Story of the Happy Warrior* (Newport: Heron Press, 1990) pp. 57–60.

52 *Boxing,* 21 March 1915.

53 *Boxing,* 27 October 1915.

54 *Boxing,* 1 December 1915.

55 White, J., *Zeppelin Nights,* p. 157.

56 Taylor, A. J. P., *The First World War: An Illustrated History* (Harmondsworth: Penguin, 1966) p. 136.

57 Taylor, A. J. P., *The First World War,* p. 140.

58 Taylor, M., 'Leisure and Entertainment' in *The Great World War 1914–45.*

59 White, J., *Zeppelin Nights,* p. 167.

60 Taylor, A. J. P., *The First World War,* p. 211.

61 Blady, K., *The Jewish Boxers Hall of Fame* (New York: Shapolsky Books, 1988) Chapter 13, pp. 109–127.

62 See 'The Great Benny Leonard' in Schulberg, B., *Sparring with Hemingway and Other Legends of the Fight Game* (London: Robson Books, 1997) pp. 53–63.

63 *New York Times,* 1 April 1916; Gallimore, A., *Occupation Prizefighter,* pp. 272–273.

64 *Boxing,* 16 August 1916; *New York Times,* 29 July 1916; Gallimore, A., *Occupation Prizefighter,* pp. 283–286; Butler, J., Kings of the Ring (London, n.d. [1936]) pp. 187–189.

65 *New York Times,* 29 May 1917; *Boxing,* 27 June 1917 and 25 July 1917; 'How Welsh Lost World Title – In No-Decision Contest', *Boxing News,* 7 August 1959.

66 Lewis, M., *Ted Kid Lewis: His Life and Times* (London: Robson Books, 1990) pp. 76–77.

67 *New York Times,* 18 March 1919.

68 *Boxing,* 16 October 1918.

69 *Boxing,* 25 April 1914; 'The band played on but poor Jack was flat on his back' by Gilbert Odd in *Boxing News,* 29 June 1979.

70 'The old-timer who blazed a title trail' by Gilbert Odd in *Boxing News,* 30 May 1980.

71 *Boxing,* 30 January 1918.

72 *Boxing,* 26 April 1916.

73 *Boxing,* 28 June 1916.

74 *Boxing,* 20 December 1916.

75 *Sunday Times,* 1 September 1918; *Boxing,* 4 September 1918; *The Times,* 2 September 1918; *Illustrated Sporting and Dramatic News,* 7 September 1918.

76 Wilde, J., *Fighting Was My Business* (London, Robson Books,1998) p. 140.

77 *The Times,* 11 May 1865.

78 Oldfield, E. A. L., *History of the Army Physical Training Corps* (Aldershot: Gale and Polden, 1955) opp. p. 6.

79 Campbell, J. D., '"Training for Sport is Training for War": Sport and the Transformation of the British Army, 1840–1914' in *International Journal of the History of Sport* Vol. 17, Issue 4, 2000, pp. 21–58.

80 Brereton, J. M., *The British Soldier: A Social History from 1661 to the Present Day* (London: Bodley Head, 1986) p. 109.

81 Riedi, E. & Mason, T., ' "Leather" and the Fighting Spirit: Sport in the British Army in World War I' in the *Canadian Journal of History* Vol. 41 No. 3, Winter 2006, p. 486.

82 Riedi, E., & Mason, T., ' "Leather" and the Fighting Spirit, p. 496.

83 Campbell, J. D., *'The Army Isn't All Work': Physical Culture and the Evolution of the British Army 1860–1920* (Farnham, Surrey: Ashgate, 2012) p. 175.

84 A helpful biography explaining Campbell and his attitudes is Gray, J. G., *Prophet in Plimsolls: An Account of the Life of Colonel Ronald B. Campbell* (Edinburgh: Edina Press, 1978).

85 Quotation and details from Mason, T. & and Riedi, E., *Sport and the Military: The British Armed Forces 1880–1960* (Cambridge: Cambridge University Press, 2010). [A first-class account of many relevant themes in military sport.]

86 Campbell, J. D., *'The Army Isn't All Work',* p. 167.

87 Gray, J. G., *Prophet in Plimsolls,* pp. 24–25.

88 Campbell, J. D., *'The Army Isn't All Work',* p. 157.

89 Holmes, R., *Tommy: The British Soldier on the Western Front* (London: Harper Collins, 2004).

90 *Boxing,* 29 September 1915.

91 Temple Clarke, A. O., *Transport and Sport in the Great War Period* (London: Garden City Press, 1938) pp. 174–177) quoted by Mason, T & Riedi, E., *Sport and the Military,* pp. 87–88.

92 *The Times,* 19 April 1917.

93 *The Times,* 30 May 1917.

CHAPTER 12

FOR KING AND COUNTRY
DECEMBER 1918

In Which the Amateur Spirit Flourishes

AT 5AM on the 11th day of the 11th month (11 November 1918), Germany and the Allied powers signed a formal armistice to bring the First World War to an unexpected end. Adding to the symbolic symmetry, the 11th hour of the day (11am instead of the actual 5am) was agreed as the emblematic moment when the guns that terrified men on the Western Front for five long years would be silenced. The news set off hysterical celebrations; cheering, dancing and even fornicating in the streets.

Every local community followed the initial frenzy with commemorative festivals, street parties, victory carnivals and parades, and later with unveiling of war memorials to their dead. Among the public activities was an event unique to boxing. Announced on 1 November, even before major aspects of the armistice were finally resolved, was an imaginative festival of military boxing.[1]

Taking place on Wednesday and Thursday, 11 and 12 December 1918, in the Royal Albert Hall was a British Empire and American Services Boxing Tournament in the presence of King George V, proceeds going to the Prisoners of War Fund. Here was formal recognition of the prestige

boxing now enjoyed in the services and with the general public. Far from reminiscent of the bloody violence of war, boxing had become an upholder of peacetime decency and moral virtue, symbol of a better world too long forgotten. (There was a similar upsurge in public interest in boxing and other sports in the aftermath of the Second World War during the 1945–50 period when ex-servicemen packed every sporting hall and arena quite as enthusiastically as they dumped their uniforms and donned their demob suits.) Whatever constituted 'normalcy', in President Calvin Coolidge's famous phrase, by 1918 two men in padded gloves punching each other in a ring had become part of it.

Annually in November at the Royal Albert Hall, there is to this day a Festival of Remembrance on the Saturday before Remembrance Sunday. The Sunday's ceremonial at the Cenotaph in Whitehall (with 111 seconds' silence commemorating the 11th hour of the 11th day of the 11th month) is preceded by a moving ritual at the Albert Hall where millions of dead servicemen are honoured by a cascade of poppy petals falling silently from the roof, each petal a representative of a life lost in war.

Both events are devised to stimulate the imagination of later generations too young to remember yet fortunate to survive because of the sacrifice of those who did not.

In December 1918, collective memories needed no refreshing. Every person in the building, in or out of military uniform, scarred in some way mentally or physically by the Great War, needed less to remember than temporarily to forget. For two days of boxing, personal circumstances could be put aside and every individual subsumed in the collective identification with his country's team.

An organisational stroke of genius was the team formula. No matter how illustrious a boxer, his victories won points for his team towards the trophy donated by the King. Individually he received only a mini replica as a member of the overall winning team, or an enamel medallion as a member of the runners-up, or a small souvenir as a general participant. The only individual medals were gold and silver for the finalists at each weight. The team trophy, unveiled at a Trocadero luncheon, was a handsome shield of a luxurious Edwardian design incorporating laurel leaves, a striking fist and a fancy Latin tag: 'NON MANIBUS SOLUM SED CORDE' (Not by hands alone, but by heart). It emphasised the elevated prevailing spirit. *The Times* termed it modestly 'the greatest event that has ever happened in the history of boxing'.

Nine teams were involved: three British (Royal Navy and Marines, Army, Royal Air Force); four from the British Empire (Canada, Australia, New Zealand, South Africa); and two American (US Army, US Navy). Hands, hearts and patriotism were all incorporated.

Despite the team emphasis, the quality of individuals stoked excitement. The British Army team was a good example: heavyweight, Company Sergeant Major Instructor W. T. Wells; welterweight, Sgt Inst J. Basham; bantamweight, Sgt Inst J. W. Wilde! The US Army team was as illustrious: heavyweight, Sgt E. McGoorty; light-heavyweight, Pte Mike O'Dowd; middleweight, Pte Augie Ratner; featherweight, Pte Eddie Coulon; bantamweight, Pte Joe Lynch; flyweight, Pte K. O. Brown. Here was an assembly of professional boxing talent beyond the resources of the most munificent commercial promoter to assemble. Yet it was professionalism with a deliberate difference.

Commander C. Walcott of the Royal Navy declared at the Trocadero lunch that he was 'not against professionalism, but we did want to have clean professionalism, and it was their object to show that could be obtained'. *The Times* agreed:

Those responsible for the arranging of the event may be said to have taken the sport and boldly tubbed it, and scrubbed it, and turned it out as wholesome as it is possible to make it. They have purged it of almost every vice that has been associated with it since the day of the 'Corinthian' and the amazingly plucky, yet too often, degrading knuckle fights.

The hygienic desire to 'scrub and rub' led to rules inspired by *amateur* boxing. Bouts were of three rounds only. A bout in which a man was outclassed would be rapidly stopped. Points could be awarded to plucky losers. No clinching would be allowed. Bizarrely, all counts would be silent on the highly dubious grounds that professionals were wont to listen for 'eight' and struggle up in a dazed condition vulnerable to another blow. (Logically, surely a man on the canvas who received no guidance about the count would be *more* inclined to get up groggy, having failed to use the full recovery period?) The knockout was made more difficult by the adoption of heavier, softer gloves 'so close a resemblance to pillows', said *Boxing* sarcastically.

The context was a time when rigorous barriers existed between amateurs and professionals across the whole panoply of British sport from rowing and boxing to rugby and soccer. The services' addiction to amateur philosophies produced the wartime edict against money prizes. The uniqueness of the Albert Hall 1918 event was that it, like services boxing, brought together sportsmen for whom boxing apartheid was the norm (with the limited exception of pre-war NSC exhibitions at a private members' club). The words of Commander Walcott or a well-meaning *Times* reporter were already sounding dated, as if the efforts of the NSC and Cochran and others since 1909 to make boxing the acme of respectability had gone for nothing. Many, then and later, believed the acceptance of money to participate in sport was corrupting. Two days of boxing, practically by royal appointment, thoroughly undermined the idea that professional boxers did not know how to behave.

The two days comprised two afternoon and two evening sessions at 2.30pm and 7.30pm, with about 15 bouts to be seen in each. Considering the quality fare, prices were modest: 2s. to £2 on Wednesday and 2s. to £5 on Thursday. Five hundred seats at 5s. were reserved for the exclusive use of officers. More democratically, other ranks, provided they were in uniform or had been recently discharged, were allowed in at half price. Inside, for 10,000 spectators, proceedings were run with military precision and panache. Military bands and pipers from the Scots Guards played in the intervals and accompanied fighters to the ring in the centre of the arena.

No matter how hard the organisers strove to present boxing at its politest, when dedicated fighters took the ring determined to win, plenty of the sport's raw power and excitement was bound to break through. Straight left leads could give added pleasure when contrasted with crude swings and wallops.

One of the first bouts on Wednesday afternoon was a tidy lightweight contest featuring Sergeant Instructor J. Miller of the British Army, who used his amateur experience to outpoint Sergeant R. C. Miller of the US Navy, both men respectfully applauded for skill in attack and defence. It was followed by the brief appearance of Seaman H. C. Greb of the US Navy, better known to boxing history as Harry Greb, the Pittsburgh Windmill. He was born in Pittsburgh on 6 June 1894 to a Dutch-American couple (hence 'Windmill') on a streetcar on the way to the maternity hospital, when Greb decided on his premature bare-fist debut. (The Pittsburgh Threshing Machine might have been a better choice – windmills did not zoom angrily across the ring at you.)

It was rumoured that Greb was Jewish and had reversed the name Berg to disguise his true ancestry. This was pure fiction. Other fictions abounded about his career. The facts were quite as lurid. His black, well-oiled hair, immaculately plastered to his skull with the straightest of partings, was the neatest thing about him. His modus vivendi was much more outlandish.[2]

Greb ruthlessly demolished his Albert Hall opponent, a South African Corporal Baker, in short but hardly good order. To the displeasure of the audience, no niceties were on show. Rather, in the few minutes it took to floor poor Baker, the gamut of Greb illegalities was demonstrated: the thumb in the eye; the roughing-up with the heel of the glove; the round-arm swings that landed with the mass force of a gloveful of wet concrete; the treading on the toes; the hold and hit on the referee's blind side. Baker's sole consolation was that in later years better men than he would also be getting the Greb treatment: Gene Tunney (nose broken in the only defeat of Tunney's career); Gunboat Smith (knocked out before he had registered fully the start of round one); Mickey Walker (thumbed in the eye and hooked ruthlessly from that side when he could not see).

Frank Moody (b. 27 August 1900) the Welsh middleweight from Pontypridd, (later Lonsdale Belt holder at light-heavyweight) was unlucky enough to be knocked out in the sixth round by Greb in Connecticut in 1924. He found that Greb had not mellowed over the intervening six years.

> It was like fighting a dozen men or an octopus with gloves on. Midway through the first round Greb butted me under the chin and as my head went back he gave me the laces of his left glove. He finished the stroke by jabbing his thumb into my right eye.

Did Greb smuggle into his Albert Hall dressing room any London chorus girls to help him sweat through an amorous pre-bout workout? This practice he indulged throughout his career. In 1918 he had been married about a year and had recently become a father. His marital vows restrained his sexual proclivities no more than Queensberry Rules his ring conduct.

Considerable interest was taken in the heavyweight class, especially in a swarthy ruffled-haired Englishman representing the Royal Air Force. Born in Wickham, near Southampton on 4 April 1892 and thus aged 26, an excellent age for a heavyweight, this was Joe Beckett. He would have been better known by 1918 but for the interruption of the war. There was nothing precious or fancy about him. He had knocked out opponents and been knocked about himself in fairground boxing booths since the age of 12.

His parents were fairground travellers who ran a booth with a touring circus. His father died before Joe was born, leaving his mother, him and his elder brother to survive as best they could. Like Greb, he was born on wheels but in a caravan, not a tram.[3]

Beckett's movements, in attack or defence, were slow verging on ponderous. He had, though, a left hook of speed and power, unmatched in British heavyweight boxing until the rise of Henry Cooper in the 1950s and 60s. What Beckett lacked in height and reach at 5ft 9in, he compensated for in burly compactness.

He first appeared professionally at the NSC on 20 April 1914, although he had previously been the loser there in a final for novice middleweights. Since then, most of his bouts had been in the services with the limited exceptions of four other fights: losing by a seventh-round knockout to Harry Reeve at The Ring, Blackfriars on 21 December 1914; beating Porky Flynn in a ninth-round knockout at the NSC on 17 June 1917; losing to Frank Goddard by an eighth-round knockout at the NSC on 17 December 1917; and losing to Dick Smith on points over 20 rounds at the NSC on 25 February 1918. The last bout had let Dick Smith regain the vacant British light-heavyweight title and own a Lonsdale Belt. It left Beckett with an unimpressive record.

Beckett's afternoon bout matched him against the taller (6ft 5in) and heavier (14st 4lb/200lbs) Chief Master-at-Arms of the US Navy Joe Cox. Cox, from St Louis, Missouri (b. c.1893) had once been a 'white hope' despite an equally inconsistent record. He had lost to Fireman Flynn (second-round KO, 29 June 1911) and Jim Coffey (third-round KO, 15 March 1917) but had defeated some 'names' (Jess Willard, who retired in the fifth, 9 October

1911; Luther McCarty by sixth-round KO, 6 December 1911; Arthur Pelkey by ninth-round KO, 9 August 1915). It was the lesser Cox who turned up at the Albert Hall. Ill-matched in size and style, the out-of-sorts Cox and the surly Beckett exhausted themselves and their audience with minimal action for three rounds. Beckett was awarded the victory for having glowered the more menacingly. Beckett could scowl as well as he could punch and Cox was given a half point for surviving both.

At the end of the afternoon, ponderousness was replaced by artistry of the highest order. In one corner was Joe Lynch of the US Army, known as the Californian Peach, a title more botanically suggestive than accurate for a tough Irish-American born in New York on 30 November 1898. He rarely fought outside the East Coast in his 1915–26 career. A natural bantamweight, he looked relatively insubstantial. This was distinctly misleading as he was as insubstantial as a miniature carved from mahogany. In an age of talented bantamweights, many fighters had rushed out of their corners expecting to demolish the frailer Lynch in one go. The slender 5ft 7in Lynch stopped them dead in their tracks with the neatest of left jabs then sobered them considerably with a straight hard right with all his 8st 6lb/118lbs behind it. At times in his career he fought two and three times a week and was never knocked out or even knocked down in 157 contests.

Lynch was not necessarily the solid, gold-plated, guaranteed team points winner the US Army expected. The reason was in the other corner. Even shorter at 5ft 2in, even paler, even apparently frailer and certainly lighter having made 8st 2lb/114lbs fully

clothed was the Welsh phenomenon Jimmy Wilde in his military billing as Sergeant Instructor J. Wilde of the British Army.

Inhibited by the unfamiliar rules (he spent barely a few months as an amateur before joining the paid ranks), Lynch found himself out-Lynched. Poker-faced Wilde was on top form. He picked Lynch off from a distance, one painful left to the nose after another sent from unaccustomed angles and returning to rest, apparently harmlessly, alongside Wilde's left thigh. When that wounding left was at rest, right leads and crosses hit home instead. Lynch strove desperately to recover the initiative in the second and the third rounds and get on the front foot to drive Wilde backwards. Wilde was an easy winner and cheered by the whole house all the way back to the dressing rooms.

However gratifying the win for the home forces, the matching of two consummate professionals such as Lynch and Wilde over an abbreviated nine minutes of action showed the artificiality of the tournament. What gave professional boxing its edge was to see men such as these testing each other to the limit over a championship distance and leaving ringsiders limp and exhausted along with them. The quality of the Albert Hall fare was fine but it was a series of hors d'oeuvres stretched out to a full meal.

Tasters are still better than bare larders. No lack of appetite could be detected as the afternoon crowd exited to the street, many eagerly joining the queues at every entrance for the evening session, anticipating another 15 bouts on the card.

No evening fights matched Wilde–Lynch for quality, and the audience was

firmly reminded that the American team was there as honoured guests and entitled to proper appreciation ('Applaud when applause is merited and, above all things, remember that the first principle of British sport is a fair field and no favour!') It responded by applauding the three American winners – featherweights Seaman F. Chaney and Private Eddie Coulon, and middleweight Sergeant Augie Ratner – as warmly from the stalls and boxes as from the galleries up in the roof where rows of American personnel cheered with gusto.

Eddie Coulon, not to be confused with the Canadian flyweight/bantam Johnny Coulon, was born in New Orleans on 20 August 1895. He had plenty of 'names' on his record, including Pete Herman (two draws and a loss) and Pal Moore (two wins and a draw). Ratner, a New Yorker of some flamboyance, had taken professional fights since 1915 and would be back in London five years later to outpoint one of Britain's greatest ever fighters Ted Kid Lewis at The Ring, Blackfriars over 20 rounds in 1923. In 1918 he was not quite the finished product but quite clever enough to beat his US Navy opponent, Chief Yeoman Wallack. Ratner was not to know that another British fighter, welterweight Sergeant Johnny Basham, successful against Sergeant J. Attwood of Canada that very afternoon, would be meeting him at the NSC over 20 rounds in June 1919 as we shall see.

At the end of the first day, the team table had the British Army at the top, tied with the Royal Air Force on 21pts, with the Royal Navy and Marines in third (19½pts) and the US Navy (17½pts) and US Army (16pts) trailing. Canada and Australia were also on

Company Sergeant W.T.Wells wins a team point for the British Army against Leading Seaman Powell of the Royal Navy.
BnF

16pts each. The scores reflect less innate British superiority than the formula adopted, which suited the British teams particularly with their amateur and services experiences. American knockout power was neutralised by the softer gloves. The British public did not allow this fact to dampen their enthusiasm.

To the public, the personalities on show were irresistible. Bouts, tactics and fighters were discussed endlessly in the hall and in the streets. More and more people decided they had to be there for the final session on the Thursday. Hours before the afternoon session started there were massive crowds at every entrance. Desperate not to be locked out, one determined contingent forced the doors on the east side and poured in. In a vain attempt to drive them out again, a band of stewards, with military support, turned the fire hoses on the intruders. Gallons of water were no deterrent to men who had been facing German guns. About 300 hardy souls, readily identifiable in the sodden suits and uniforms in which they sat and gradually dried out in the aisles and in all available spaces, saw the climax of the competition for free.

The high excitement provoked by the invasion infected the audience, and in turn the protagonists. The afternoon bouts fizzed accordingly. The audience and especially the Royal Marines found a hero in Sergeant W. Ring, a light-heavyweight put in to face the all-action Harry Greb. Ring, no scientist he, decided he could counter Greb's worst – Harry's worst being certainly worse than most – by throwing punches as hard and as often as he possibly could. Greb's answer was to punch just as often, just as wildly and

with total disregard for anything else. Greb 'swung so wildly in the second round that the lamps above his head were in greater danger than Ring', said *The Times*.

It was not Greb's way to do what most professionals would when confronted with a wildly punching amateur – stand off and use skill and experience coolly to tame him. As a result, Greb neglected the defensive basics. Ring with his eccentric mixture of pluck and luck got home with a surprising number of punches and was given the verdict. Greb had no rounds left to reassert himself. Fighting three times in three rounds against three opponents over three sessions, although gruelling enough, is inherently different from nine continuous rounds against one determined opponent.

Speed and scientific skills were more prevalent in the other afternoon bouts. In the light-heavyweight class, Sergeant Harold Rolph of Canada had a huge 14-pound advantage over his American opponent, a natural middleweight. But the middleweight was Private Mike O'Dowd, an Irish-American from Minnesota and the slipperiest of middleweights, sometimes dubbed the St Paul Phantom. He was also aggressive, justifying his other nickname, the St Paul Cyclone. O'Dowd was resuming a successful professional career begun in 1913 while still a teenager. Born 5 April 1895, he had 115 fights, nearly half (52) of them no-decision bouts. The list of his opponents reads like a who's who of world-class middleweights: Mike Gibbons, Ted Kid Lewis, Augie Ratner, Harry Greb, Jack Britton and many others.

Just over a year before O'Dowd's Albert Hall appearance, the then

reigning world middleweight champion, New Yorker Al McCoy (b. 23 October 1894), had complacently agreed to one of those no-decision bouts in his own Brooklyn backyard against the coming man, O'Dowd. Newspaper decisions served for betting purposes but not for the winning and losing of titles. The McCoy/O'Dowd bout took place on 14 November

Eddie McGoorty (1889–1929), the Wisconsin middleweight. One of many American professionals to grace the King's Trophy military tournament in London.

1917. For three rounds O'Dowd the Phantom glided away and quietly assessed McCoy's southpaw style and vulnerabilities. O'Dowd the Cyclone took over in the fourth. Down went McCoy four times in the fourth, and once in the fifth when the bell rescued him as he tottered to his feet. In the sixth, O'Dowd clinched matters with a dazzling combination – right drive to the waistline, left hook to the jaw – leaving McCoy to be counted out. Mike O'Dowd was the new and unexpected world champion.

Rolph was not a bad fighter, although he lost fights in British rings after the war to Eddie McGoorty (10 February 1919), Boy McCormick (28 April 1919) and Harry Reeve (22 September 1919). His strong weight advantage could not cancel out O'Dowd's class. Rolph was competitive for two rounds and was given an ovation for surviving the third when O'Dowd cut loose and had him on the brink of a stoppage at the final bell. O'Dowd was the middleweight even light-heavyweights feared.

A genuine light-heavyweight in Company Sergeant Major Instructor Dick Smith of the British Army was the division's veteran champion. Before the war he moved up a division in the amateurs to win the ABA heavyweight title in 1912 and 1913. He was less successful when he tried to do the same as a professional. Earlier in the year (25 February 1918) he had used his repertory of skills, especially his accurate left jab, to outpoint the new prospect Joe Beckett over 20 rounds at the NSC. That had been a lighter and slimmer Beckett competing at the lesser weight. In later years, when Beckett had filled out, he twice knocked out Smith when they were matched as heavyweights (5 March 1920 in the fifth, Albert Hall; and 14 March 1923 in the 17th, Holland Park).

In the services tournament Smith was in his natural light-heavy division and comfortably put more points on the board for the British Army. Following Smith came appearances by two genuine heavyweights – Sergeant Joe Beckett for the Royal Air Force and Company Sergeant Major Instructor Billy Wells for the British Army. Beckett walked through the best punches of Canadian Sergeant Borthwick with barely a wince, cut off the ring and floored the Canadian with ease. Wells met a heavily tattooed Royal Navy boxer, Leading Seaman Powell. Wells was slow and ponderous, as if he had left his boxing abilities on the parade ground along with his old rank of Bombardier. He won, just, but the warmth of his reception from all parts of the house owed more to nostalgia and his charisma than to anything he did in the ring that afternoon. The two wins put Wells and Beckett on course to meet one another in either the semi-final or final bout in the evening, a prospect that excited much animated discussion about their relative form and status in the post-war future of British heavyweight boxing.

Meanwhile, an unlucky Australian, bantamweight Private Evans, was escorted to the ring for his third series bout. In the other corner was the practically unbeatable Jimmy Wilde. And this was a Wilde at the top of his form. Evans endured that maddening left thudding into his nose perpetually to get somewhere in Wilde's vicinity to deliver a few punches of his own.

The Royal Albert Hall, venue for many boxing contests over the years, hosted the 1918 tournament.
Prints & Photographs Division, Library of Congress, LC-DIG-stereo-1s22417

Pal Moore, seen here with his wife, fought Jimmy Wilde under the amateur rules of the tournament and created the demand for a full scale professional return.
Bain Collection, Prints & Photographs Division, Library of Congress, LC-DIG-ggbain-29251

Evans's nose and cheeks soon showed colourful evidence of his ordeal. However, when did an Australian sportsman ever give in easily? To loud audience reactions, Evans stuck it out a full three rounds, bobbing back and forth as Wilde punched him again and again yet refusing to go horizontal. Evans was still punching back at the end, contriving to give the impression that he was actually enjoying himself. He was the hero of the afternoon. (The Royal Navy and Marines team was less

of a force in the bantam division than expected because Stoker Joe Hervey failed to make the weight. The humble stoker was better known in boxing as the highly experienced Devonian Young Joe Symonds.)

Credit (and a good loser's half-point) went to Evans's compatriot Private Tierney in a welterweight semi-final. The inexperienced Tierney was also up against a major Welsh obstacle in the form of the British welterweight champion, Johnny Basham. Basham,

with the evening's final on his mind, won economically, but the outclassed Tierney made sure it was a real fight. He came to the ring sporting a plaster over his left eye. Basham immediately targeted the plaster with a right cross only to have Tierney duck, grin and chop him with an overarm right. Basham avoided most of Tierney's punches for the rest of the bout.

Commercial promoters could only groan enviously as the line-up for the evening's finals and semi-finals emerged

– Augie Ratner, Mike O'Dowd, K. O. Brown from the USA; domestic draws such as Johnny Basham, Dick Smith, Billy Wells, Joe Beckett and Jimmy Wilde; each man accustomed to topping a bill in his own right. 'Never was there such a constellation of boxing "stars",' said *The Times,* and 'the greatest night of boxing the country has ever witnessed is about to begin'. By 7.30pm there were thousands inside the hall, grateful for the privilege, and thousands out in the street. Strengthened security kept them separate this time. With the heightened anticipation, the wonder is that the evening was not an anticlimax.

To the delight of the Americans and all the neutrals who loved to see a good little 'un beat a rather good big 'un, Mike O'Dowd used his full stock of skill, speed and power to outsmart the heavier veteran Dick Smith for three rounds. Smith, a man of courage and stamina and the possessor of a clean crisp left, found O'Dowd slipping his leads and punishing him about the ribs. If Smith lowered his arms to cover his body, O'Dowd switched to neat right and left hooks to the head and was out of reach again before Smith could do anything about it. His right eye closing by the minute, Smith survived the three rounds but the whole house knew what the verdict would be. Even after his outing against Smith, O'Dowd had enough reserves left to outpoint Sergeant W. Ring of the Royal Navy in the final in the same session.

The house was as confident about the projected result of the next bout, the bantamweight final, which was expected to be *the* fight of the evening. A genuine and skilful bantamweight in Pal Moore of the US Navy faced the little man who could wear three wet overcoats and still make the bantam limit, the well-nigh unbeatable Sergeant J. Wilde of the British Army. Over the next nine minutes of the bout, preceded by a huge ovation for both men, the house's confidence was fully justified. Moore's weight advantage was nothing Wilde had not conquered on similar occasions. Although Moore's extra strength might begin to tell by the third, few could match Wilde's speed and concentrated power. Or the famous left hand delivered from all points of the compass at angles known only to the Welshman.

The two men acted out their projected roles. For two rounds, Moore tried vainly to work out Wilde's unorthodoxy and as the price of his education took many clean strikes from that tightly clenched left glove. Wilde's left was in and out like lightning but had plenty of power behind it; a solid amalgam of leather and knuckle. In the third, Moore succeeded in throwing more punches than previously but they were interrupted by subtle touches of Wilde's gloves and arms or missed completely.

Judge then the astonished silence, succeeded by a fusillade of boos and protests, when Moore was pronounced the winner! The three servicemen operating as ringside judges had seen a different contest from everyone else. This needs no formal explanation. It is in the nature of any sport where the subjective rules the statistical that even experienced judges will sometimes differ. In the Royal Albert Hall that night perhaps 99 per cent of the spectators saw Wilde as the clear winner; two out of three judges did not. High emotions and senses of injustice made no difference.

They *might* have made a difference as the house showed no inclination to let the show continue. The catalyst for peace was Wilde's second Jim Driscoll, known as the most emotional of men. (Remember how hard he took the abject failure of Bombardier Billy Wells against Carpentier at the NSC in 1913.) He strode to the centre of the ring, gestured the house to silence, and declared, 'On behalf of the British Army Team, I wish to say that I am satisfied with the judges' decision.' It was a sporting gesture worthy of the occasion and restored good order.

Before and after the Wilde/Moore decision, there was plenty of action in the other divisions. K. O. Brown clinched the flyweight points for the US Navy with a narrow but uncontroversial win over Cook's Mate G. Stephens of the Royal Navy. The other top American, Augie Ratner, sustained his form to win at middleweight against Sergeant Instructor Fullerton of the British Army.

Interspersed between the lighter courses were the prime beef bouts of the heavyweight division, an attractive mini-tournament in its own right. Only four men were left to contest the semi-finals and final – Joe Beckett (RAF), Billy Wells (British Army), Eddie McGoorty (US Army) and the much less known Australian Corporal Stephenson who, unlike the more famous three, had received an afternoon bye because his expected opponent had fallen sick.

The bye was an insufficient advantage. In the first semi-final, Stephenson was prepared to trade punch for punch with Joe Beckett, although Beckett's punches were the harder. Beckett sapped Stephenson's resistance with hooks to the body. By the second, the Australian was crouching and covering as best he could as Beckett became more resolute. Stephenson lasted the second with a few wobbles and the referee spared him in the third with a stoppage.

Beckett was in the final and eagerly watched his two potential opponents in the other semi. So did everyone else. Could Billy Wells shake off the ring rust of the previous day? Could he outwit a lighter but clever man in Wisconsin middleweight McGoorty? McGoorty (b. 31 July 1889) held the world middleweight title from 1912–13 but was obviously no real heavyweight. He was only in the division because he could no longer make middleweight without amputation. Neither was he still the slick fighter who had so impressed against O'Keefe at the NSC seven years before. He was rather a veteran with receding temples and an incipient spare tyre around his waist. Wits dubbed him the Wisconsin Whale. Training gradually became more arduous and took too much time. What he had not lost was his relish for a real scrap in the ring any more than his open-handed generosity out of it. He was given the warmest of receptions. Shorter than Wells at 5ft 10in, he still had a long reach (6ft 1in) and a left hook that had ended many a bout early.

At every venue in London, there was a noisy and affectionate welcome for Wells, both the tentative and self-doubting Wells, and the smiling confident one. Happily for the British team it was the latter Wells who took the ring. The Wells left did not paw the air tentatively but shot out, straight and powerful, keeping McGoorty at a respectful distance. Wells moved as

nimbly as McGoorty, in and out and also laterally. Whenever McGoorty looked to close, Wells had already done damage and moved away. McGoorty's left retained plenty of its old power but he could not land it. Wells could and did land his own and added powerful straight rights and crisp crosses. The impressed judges gave Wells the points. This set up the perfect final bout: the older British heavyweight champion Wells against Beckett the young pretender. All it lacked was context. The team placings had already been decided. The RAF, even if Beckett won, could only finish in third place.

(For the record, the final tally was British Army 50pts; with the US Army on 39pts, having moved up the table on the second day from fifth to second but well behind the British Army, more experienced at this kind of contest. Nevertheless, of the eight finals fought, the British Army won three but so did the US Army. The next three places were almost impossible to separate – Royal Navy 32½pts; RAF 32½pts; US Navy 32pts. Further behind were Australia 28pts; Canada 18pts; New Zealand 14½pts and South Africa 10½pts.)

Supporters of Wells and supporters of Beckett failed to consider the bout as now unimportant. The merits and demerits of each fighter had been discussed in every barracks, on every ship and in every living room. Here would be proof positive of who was better. Or would it?

Wells came to the ring determined to show he was still number one. He believed he could repeat the form and the tactics used so successfully against McGoorty. Beckett, comfortable with his own form and fitness, believed he

could slip Wells's famous left and pepper him around the ribs and the famously vulnerable midriff. If Carpentier could do it, so could he.

The result was a win for the Army. *The Times* agreed with the judges: 'Wells is even better than he was against McGoorty … Beckett playing for the body the whole of the time, never looks like winning.' But it wouldn't be the sport of boxing if everyone thought similarly. *Boxing*, having pronounced, 'Beautiful Billy was *the* disappointment of the whole tourney,' suggested Wells was 'lucky' to get a win over Beckett as Beckett, to the magazine's satisfaction, had won the first and second rounds with aggression and superior fitness.

Wells's victory was by no means as controversial as the Wilde defeat that very evening, although both results cast a shadow on the self-congratulatory glow surrounding the closing ceremonial. King George V did not make his anticipated appearance but that was no royal snub. The King returned to London on 11 December following a sombre tour of the battlefields and war cemeteries of Belgium and northern France to prepare for a state visit on Boxing Day by President Woodrow Wilson. In his place was Prince Albert (who later succeeded his father and his brother and became King George VI). The prince, dressed in a Royal Air Force uniform, watched the closing bouts from the royal box. He participated fully in the pageantry that closed the show.

The flag-draped ropes were lowered and the ring platform filled with the embracing boxers who had spent the four sessions knocking lumps off each other. No kisses were observed. The prince presented his father's shield to the captain of the British Army team, shook hands and presented medals to every finalist. Surrounded by the competitors, many showing cuts and bruises along with their commemorative ribbons, the prince emphasised the approval of boxing mutely implied by his participation:

The King asks me to say how very sorry he is not to be present tonight at this exceptional Tournament and to congratulate the members of the various teams on the splendid display, and on the sporting spirit in which the contests have been won and lost.

Especially do we welcome the officers and men of the United States Navy and Army, who with perfect co-operation and good will have adopted our rules for boxing, to which they are not accustomed. They have given us a fine performance this evening in winning five finals and being the runners-up in two other contests.

The King heartily congratulates the organizers on their efforts to encourage sport for the sake of sport. No one more than His Majesty appreciates how valuable a part manly games and sporting instincts play in maintaining the character of the English-speaking race.

I am proud to have been deputed to present this trophy and medals, and I warmly congratulate the winning team on a memorable achievement.

Although Prince Albert found public speaking an ordeal then and later (as the 2010 feature film *The King's Speech* emphasised), his words clearly conveyed the message that for the residents of Buckingham Palace boxing was making an honourable and valued contribution to British society. (What did the Reverend Frederick Brotherton Meyer up in Regent's Park make of that?)

The boxers and the prince stood to attention in the centre of the arena as the military band and the full-throated and fervent male voices in the audience gave rousing renderings of 'The Star-Spangled Banner' and 'Land of Hope and Glory'. Perhaps, as the words rang out, one or two like Billy Wells may have silently pondered how his and others' activities, recently declared a threat to public order and outlawed on at least three occasions, had somehow been transmogrified into a phenomenon helpful in saving the nation?

There was a coda to the tournament, a formal luncheon at the Savoy Hotel for organisers and competitors next day (13 December). The lasting camaraderie of the event had rival boxers swapping gossip, jokes, autographs and drinks as willingly as they had exchanged punches. Wells complimented McGoorty. McGoorty reciprocated. Wilde and Lynch sat together, drank together and posed for photographs together. One of the judges responsible for the Wilde/Moore uproar, a Canadian Captain L. H. Warn, very indiscreetly toured the room telling all and sundry that he personally had marked Wilde the winner of every round and 'almost fell out of my chair in astonishment' at the verdict. The other two judges (one from the Royal Navy and one from the British Army) wisely kept their counsel and ate their luncheon. Had they been less honourable men, they might have been suspected of being in the pay of bookmakers wanting a hot favourite nobbled or of commercial promoters eager to boost a future profitable rematch.

This unique tournament made the sport even more respectable and fashionable. There was a further by-product. By matching experienced professionals within the artificial limits of amateur rules, for team points alone and restricted to a mere nine minutes of action, the military organisers had stimulated interest in further questions. What would happen were Moore and Wilde, or Billy Wells and Joe Beckett to be rematched over full championship distances under *professional* rules? Even stupid promoters could take broad hints. C. B. Cochran, for example, the man who had brought such glamour to pre-war boxing, was not stupid.

In the last few days of 1918 there were two news releases from Cochran's office. One announced that he had acquired a long lease on premises in Holborn and would stage boxing promotions at this central location (a few hundred yards from the NSC). The other promised a £5,000 purse for a Wilde/Moore return and £7,500 for Carpentier for a London rematch with Wells. This gave the general impression that, as far as boxing was concerned, 1919 would be proceeding as if the long hiatus of the war had never happened.

Endnotes:

1   *The Times,* 2 November 1918. Details in this chapter are gathered from November and December 1918 issues of *The Times*; December 1918 issues of *Boxing*; December 1918 issues of *Mirror of Life and Boxing World*; National Archives File HO144/1502/369532.

2   See Geoff Poundes, 'The Legendary Harry Greb' in *Boxing Monthly,* February 1991. Light on dates but full of colourful detail is Fair, J. R., *Give Him to the Angels: The Story of Harry Greb* (Chichester: Summersdale, 1997).

3   'Don't be hard on Joe Beckett' by Gilbert Odd in *Boxing News,* 12 August 1977.

CHAPTER 13
COCHRAN'S EXTRAVAGANZAS
1919 (PART ONE)

In Which Boxing Comes into its Kingdom

THE UNIQUE mixture of thanksgiving, celebration, relief and mutual admiration of the successful Anglo-American tournament of late 1918 could not obliterate all prejudices. The camaraderie demonstrated as English and American boxers fought each other then stood arm in arm in token of enduring friendship was mildly misleading. After all, who were the allies who had stood together in the Flanders trenches for four and a half years? Surely, the British and the *French*. An Anglo-French boxing tournament would have been quite as fitting a celebration of peace.

Many a long-standing British prejudice about the French (fostered during the Hundred Years War and boosted by the expansionist ambitions of Louis XIV in the 17th century and of Napoleon in the late 18th and early 19th) had been dispelled during the First World War by the keen domestic awareness that although the British suffered grievously, the French suffered a lot more.

The modern historian Niall Ferguson discusses the casualty figures of the First World War in his revisionist history *The Pity of War*.[1] He suggests a 'best estimate' for total casualties

(including deaths, prisoners of war and wounded) as 2,556,014 for Britain, 324,170 for the USA and 3,844,300 for France. If one takes the French figure as some kind of ghastly 'norm', the British suffered only 66 per cent as many losses, and the Americans about 8 per cent. Put another way, Britain's French allies suffered 12 times more casualties than their transatlantic comrades. This is quite some discrepancy.

Unsurprisingly, the British Tommy who welcomed the late American intervention in the war (27 American divisions in France by July 1918), still felt that in the long attritional years before, it had been the French and the British who had withstood the full impact of the German western assaults and sacrificed so mightily. The American contribution was thought too little, too late, and late American victories too easily won. The American press, conscious of their patriotic duty to boost a European war still unpopular in American isolationist quarters, tended to write up a minor skirmish as the Battle of Gettysburg refought. The British remained cynical about successful American manoeuvres for years to come.

Correspondingly, the Americans thought of the British with a mixture

of pity and condescension. A once mighty nation, an imperial power that had splashed the colour pink all over the atlases of the world, had been pauperised by the necessities of war. Only American dollars and American materiel and American intervention had tipped the balance in the Allies' favour. Only American goodwill and post-war handouts could restore Europe in peacetime. A British soldier – and by extension a British boxer or golfer or athlete or tennis player – was no longer the equal of a good red-blooded American.[2] The Brits were no longer winners but whiners. And, as with all mutual prejudices, anecdotal evidence was sufficient to support the thesis.

Boxing was now a highly prestigious part of the panoply of British sport and an entertainment as attractive as any other. Blessed with royal approval; earning widespread press coverage and public fascination sufficient to make a Bob Arum or a Frank Warren of later times green with envy; praised by the military authorities for stimulating courage, morale and patriotism; and sought out eagerly by celebrities as likely to be seen at ringside as in a theatre or opera first night stall; surely boxing's dubious past was truly dead and buried? In actuality boxing was *still* illegal. Were the full letter of the law to be applied, no meaningful boxing would be allowed. That was true in 1910 and 1911. It was true in 1919 and remains so in the 21st century. Its legal status, unlike its public standing, had not changed over the war years.

Boxing was a good example of the British art of compromise. A significant percentage of the population believed boxing should be banned on an assortment of ethical, religious and moral grounds. A rather larger percentage, including some rich and powerful people, believed boxing in its modern form should flourish. Its followers were not nostalgic for the bare-knuckle, fight-to-a-finish brutality of Regency and mid-Victorian prizefighting and were content to see those practices disappear along with bear-baiting and cock-throwing. The wearing of gloves; the ten-second knockout; the pre-determined distance of a fight; firm refereeing and the tight controls over behaviour operating within venues such as the NSC and Olympia; all these were widely approved and had turned the sport into a spectacle at which men and women of social standing were happy to be seen.

What was the alternative? Had boxing enthusiasts pressed Parliament to make professional boxing unchallengeably legal, such legislation would have been so complex as to occupy a busy legislature for thousands of hours better spent on debating more important issues. (In the spring of 1925 Commander Kenworthy, a Conservative backbencher who loved the sport, assembled a bill to make the sport legal and operating under a board of control. Lord Lonsdale dissuaded him. Lonsdale

knew better than anyone the potential slipperiness of the authorities when a major fight was planned and preferred an ambiguous legal vacuum in which he could still wield his personal and unofficial influence.)[3]

Had boxing's enemies published a bill to ban boxing, a similar plethora of debate, amendment and committee-bound futility would have ensued. A ban would engender illegal secret fights, free from the sensible controls operating within the sport and open to widespread corruption by betting interests. In other words, exactly the opposite effect to the intentions of the ban. Ban boxing as it did and does exist, and a corrupt version would flourish.

Many in boxing in early 1919 knew that the sport was technically illegal, however popular and widely practised. Buried away in his enthusiastic preview to the King's Trophy published by *The Times* on 11 December 1918, the first day of the tournament, the special correspondent quietly admitted it:

The truth is that the naval and military authorities of this country are realizing what good, healthy boxing means to the youth of the nation. Lectures on anatomy, demonstrations by experts like Driscoll and Wilde – these are part of the propaganda. *It may not be generally known that boxing is illegal*; the efforts that are now being made to elevate it may bring about the legalizing of the sport.[4] [Italics added]

At the Savoy Hotel lunch, which formally completed the King's Trophy festivities, the speech by Colonel R. H. Campbell DSO of the Gordon

Highlanders was equally indiscreet. He spoke of having emotional reactions to two incidents. The first was the surrender of the German fleet, which he had observed from the deck of *Queen Elizabeth*. The second was to see world champion boxers ('nothing finer in this world'), contesting for 'a piece of enamel and their honour'. He went on:

'This wonderful spirit should be kept up. Boxing *must be legalized*, because the authorities recognize that it is a great national asset.'[5] [Italics added]

It was no time for complacency. Barely had 1919 got under way when news came that the National Sporting Club of Paris and the French commercial promoters had been informed by the prefect of police that boxing was deemed illegal and was temporarily banned there.[6] (The ban in Paris did not last, but what could be done in Paris, and had been done in New York [see below], might be done in London too.)

In the summer of 1919, at Bridlington, the Humberside seaside resort, the holiday crowds were treated to a contest, openly called a prizefight, between two feuding local tradesmen at £100 a side, with admission charged at 6s. or 12s. with deckchair. Though 'the police had many misgivings before allowing it to proceed', proceed it did for a full 80 seconds when one of the warring merchants, aged 42, put the other down twice and the referee stopped the fun. So unlawful an occasion was tolerated by the police purely because of boxing's contemporary popularity.[7]

Boxing post-war had defenders in prestigious quarters. Evidence comes in two English publications that graced many an aristocratic breakfast table. *The Times* in February 1919 reminded readers of the exalted status of boxing by 1914, and of its wartime ubiquity:

The interest in boxing has been increased by the war. It was a national pastime in 1914, and, although it has had to give way to more serious fighting for more than four years, it is already showing signs of an activity even more marked than it was in the boom which had been temporarily closed ...

There was never a more popular sport in the Army, during the past four years, than boxing. For all boxing competitions held in France the entries were enormous and the crowds of spectators invariably too numerous for the accommodation at the disposal of the promoters ... There was boxing everywhere. Tournaments were held in the fields, and on many occasions in the squares of shattered villages in roughly improvised rings ...

Boxing is an international art, which appeals to all classes. It is popular in both Services, at the universities, and at both the public and preparatory schools.[8]

During 1919 there were many quality fights in Britain and abroad, and so many column inches devoted to reports and previews that it is difficult to think of a comparable year, before or since, when the sport so monopolised public attention. The hiatus caused by the war created a hunger for fistic action greater than for four lean years put together. Every serviceman had been encouraged to box and to support boxing. Such support did not wither in times of peace.

In 1919, another prestigious journal, the *Illustrated London News,* also detected a new enthusiasm, stemming from boxing's contribution during the war, and its new civilian status. In the 29 March 1919 issue, one of its regular columnists wrote an article on 'The Popularity of Boxing': 'Boxing is once more a national game,' he thought, and had to be defended against its critics:

Fortunately, the war has put an end to the efforts of the 'wowser' (a pleasant Australian name for the professional kill-joy) to suppress even the latter day form of fisticuffs, which taxes the mind as much as the body, and is the most searching and exhilarating of exercises. Seeing that the nation in arms made boxing its favourite diversion – in training camps, in billets, and even in the fighting zone – to the amazement of our gallant French comrades – we can be sure the 'unco'guid' will never succeed in suppressing it.

... we need not grudge the money spent on bringing really hard, skilful experts into the four-square arena under the white flare of pugilistic publicity. It is part of the young boxer's training to watch boxing *in excelsis* – to see the subtle bewildering art of Jimmy Wilde (a law to himself), or the rough virile onslaught of a Beckett or a Goddard, or the debonair ruthlessness of Basham and Carpentier, or the classic conventions of defence and offence expounded by the Welsh disciples of the incomparable Jem Driscoll. I take my own son to see these contests so that he may

learn to put a keener edge on his boxing. Up with boxing, then, and down with the long-haired, lacklustre enemies of a traditional English sport![9]

The *Illustrated London News* believed its readership had fully absorbed so ringing an endorsement. In early December 1919 it printed a generous preview and extensive pictorial coverage of a top heavyweight bout in London. The headline told all:

A SPORT THAT INTERESTS ALL SOCIETY: THE GREAT BOXING MATCH

And the caption underlined the imprimatur of the *haut monde*:

Boxing as a sport has risen greatly in public estimation of late years, owing, no doubt, to its having proved so valuable an exercise, both physically and morally, for soldiers and sailors during the war. *Now all Society is interested in it.*[10] [Italics added]

As the weekly's sports coverage had previously rarely strayed beyond Wimbledon tennis, the Henley Regatta and the racing calendar, things had certainly changed. The journal's new stance was in striking contrast to its firm pronouncement on prizefighting in September 1845 that 'the practice of pugilism has been one revolting to mankind, degrading to all the honourable and honest feelings of human nature'.

The Times was every bit as ready to herald boxing, fully fledged young commercial cuckoo flown from the NSC nest. In an article titled 'The Revival of Boxing: a study in psychology' printed in April 1919, the paper blamed the past failings of boxing on that most convenient of ill-focused general targets, the crowd:

> Although the sport has always had a large and devoted following, it has had to combat an enormous amount of prejudice from those who could not bring themselves to see more in it than the primitive love of fighting or the cruel exploitation of brute force pandering to a neurotic craving for sensation and excitement.[11]

My thrill is your neurotic craving presumably. The amateur psychologist writing the article analysed the typical (?) NSC audience and divided it into five categories: the experts who 'understand and appreciate every movement of the boxers'; the sportsmen 'who are attracted by the competitive element, be it in the ring or in any other sphere of sport'; the curious 'who imagine that the gloved blows are far more painful than they really are'; the lowest type 'who … revels in a "slogging" match when blood flows'; and the parasites of the ring 'who care only for the victory of the man upon whom they are betting'. The neatness of the classification conceals the probability that most men present would have embodied a mixture of three or more of the writer's supposedly separable attributes.

So far as the inherent violence of the ring was concerned, the writer had perhaps not seen the neatly ironic cartoon carried by *Punch* on New Year's Day 1919. It showed a conversation between two different types at ringside:

Enthusiastic Civilian – 'Well, how are you enjoying yourself, Mate?'

Mons Veteran [!] – 'Middlin'' *Enthusiastic Civilian* – 'Oh, you've got to get used to IT. Of course at first it seems a bit brutal.'[12]

The Times journalist felt able to pronounce patronisingly on women, known at the NSC in peacetime only by their absence. Their motives varied:

> To a healthy minded woman the spectacle of a boxing contest could produce nothing but admiration and appreciation of determination, courage, and strength: to a decadent woman it could appeal to a primitive love of cruelty and fighting instinct.

In any case:

> Few women … would ever be sufficiently interested to study the finer points of the game, and consequently little is to be gained by encouraging their attendance.

Quite how audiences for boxing, male or female, were to be improved morally was left to the imagination. (Somehow it is difficult to see a Cochran steward asking the holder of a 15 guinea ticket: 'Excuse me, Madam, are you here because you're healthy-minded or are you merely decadent?') Nevertheless, the article confirms that by 1919, boxing, amateur and professional, was highly regarded in the best of social quarters:

> The recent Royal patronage given to boxing by the Prince of Wales

[later King Edward VIII] and Prince Albert [later King George VI] will, of course, do much to give the status to the sport which it requires and deserves, owing not only to its position as a sport, but to the important part it has played in the making of character and physique in our fighting forces.

There was nothing wrong either with big purses or big fights:

> The public insist upon seeing pastmasters of boxing if they pay to see boxing at all. To be a pastmaster a man must study

C.B. Cochran, the theatre impresario, brilliantly exploited the new hunger for big, glamorous fights in London.
The Print Collector/Print Collector/Getty Images

for years, train for years, live cleanly, and fight his way up the roughest road to success, which any profession in the world offers. It is only when he gets to the very top that he can command 'big money' and he may be beaten any day and his value decrease … The boxer's career is the shortest career of any highly-paid profession in the world and the hardest, and so long as the public wants to see first-class boxing the labourer is worthy of his hire.[13]

The enhanced status of the sport and the rewards top professionals expected were certainly understood by C. B. Cochran in his taking of the Holborn lease at the end of 1918. On the day that the signing was announced he also declared, as we saw, the £7,500 purse to get Wells and Carpentier together again, and the £5,000 for a Wilde and Moore rematch.

The new site – on the north side of High Holborn between High Holborn and Eagle Street – had undergone many a transmogrification since its opening in May 1867 as the New Royal Amphitheatre.[14] Horse shows, comic operas, novelties, ice skating, circuses, ballets, pantomimes and black and white minstrel shows had come and gone, as had new owners and new titles – the Holborn Amphitheatre, National Theatre of Novelties, Newsome's Circus, the Grand Central Skating Rink, the Royal Connaught Theatre, the Alcazar, the Holborn Theatre and the Holborn Central Hall included. Few impresarios would have leased a site with so chequered a record. And only Cochran would have put the handsome but stage-shy Bombardier Billy Wells

(as 'a sentinel of great physique') into an exotic musical called *Afgar* alongside the glamorous Alice Delysia.[15]

Cochran's plan was to stage regular Holborn bills at reasonable prices, for example, for Billy Fry v Raymond Vittet in February 1919, seats at 11s. 6d. and £1 4s., with a few premium ringside seats at £2 7s. Similar prices were charged for Tommy Noble v Eugene Criqui in April 1919, with additional cheaper accommodation at 5s. 9d. and 8s. 6d.[16] Cochran hoped to add substantial profits from enhanced prices for top fights; fights unmissable even at a premium. It was a gamble.

Cochran counted on further profits rolling in after a big fight from the showing of film of the action to audiences excluded from the venue by the scarcity or high prices of tickets or by the constraints of geography or transport. The prestigious clash between Jimmy Wilde and Joe Lynch (31 March 1919 at the NSC) was served up cinematically ten days later at the Association Hall, Manchester for a three-day run under the title 'Did Jimmy Wilde beat Joe Lynch?', a question seemingly already answered 'yes, because the referee said so', but the film was shown on a continuous basis from 2pm to 10pm every day, 10–12 April, at 'Popular Prices'.[17]

Those revenues were destined for the coffers of the NSC, not Cochran's pockets. The club, even more than Cochran, needed money if it was to regain its pre-war prestige as the headquarters of British boxing and co-exist with commercial promoters such as Cochran. The ambition was in practice beyond them. John Harding, in his entertaining history of *Lonsdale's Belt*, neatly summarises the inevitable result:

The Club's monopoly of the Lonsdale Belts would prove insufficient to prevent its grip on championship contests slipping. In fact, where three divisions were concerned – middle, welter and heavyweight – the belts rapidly lost any significance whatsoever. Between the years 1919 and 1924, there were to be twenty-two championship contests involving the three weights, only five of which were for a belt and only two of which would take place inside Covent Garden.[18]

The club's most prominent historian, Guy Deghy, is even more brutal:

When the dust of war had cleared away, the actual, dire and bitter fact became evident that the National Sporting Club had completed its task in the honourable service of British boxing, and was now obviously redundant.[19]

British boxing itself was anything but redundant, but it had outgrown the cosy home in Covent Garden where paternal care had protected it in return for exclusive privileges. Just as, say, the Beatles would go from the Cavern Club in Liverpool ultimately to fill Shea Stadium, so top boxing could no longer be contained in tiny premises for the few.

For boxing, the year 1919 was as good a year as any, past or present. The war terminated the lives of many boxers, such as Bill Ladbury (killed in action in 1917), interrupted or ruined the careers of many more and provided the motive for others, such as

Freddie Welsh and Ted Kid Lewis, to stay abroad glove-fighting for dollars in preference to risking their lives for an army pittance. Well aware of the propaganda value of the professional boxers who had served their country during the war, the British Army was quick to demobilise its best-known boxing instructors. Before January 1919 ended, Billy Wells, Johnny Basham, Pat O'Keefe, Jimmy Wilde and Jim Driscoll had all been honourably discharged from the ranks.[20]

Indeed, the handsome and popular welterweight Johnny Basham – still billed as Sergeant – was back into action immediately. He won a 15-rounder on points at the NSC on 27 January 1919 for a purse of £550 and assorted side stakes, against another serviceman, Private Eddie Shevlin of the US Navy (a contest clearly inspired by the success of the Albert Hall programme).[21] Already, on 4 January 1919, Basham had won comfortably in Liverpool against George Kid Plested of Birmingham.[22] Plested, a strong puncher, had his limitations demonstrated by the classy Basham, who outpunched as well as out-thought him. The Midlander had so exasperated the referee by his holding, smothering and grabbing that the official disqualified him in the 12th.

Shevlin, a Bostonian whose quiff of hair swayed a disconcerting fraction of a second slower than his head, was a much worthier opponent, a clean and skilful puncher and notoriously tough. The verdict went to Basham for his speed, which allowed him to take risks and pile up points. His unorthodox right leads left him open yet Shevlin was not quick enough to counter. Shevlin still suggested that over a full 20 rounds he might slow Basham enough

to dominate the last five and sneak the verdict. Basham, confident he could do over 20 what he had already done over 15, agreed to a return on St Patrick's Night, 17 March 1919, at the NSC.[23]

In the return, Basham's sole concession was to open more cautiously and to attack less flamboyantly than he had in January. In strategic terms this made sense. Shevlin, a thinking boxer with a granite chin, had learned a lot from the first encounter. Once in close, he drove short, sharp punches to Basham's ribs, flurries returned with interest by the Welshman. Both men had successes: Basham a lightning combination of right-left-right to Shevlin's head in the third, and a right hook opening a slight cut above Shevlin's eye in the second. Shevlin, in turn, delivered a heavy right to the body in the fourth before Basham had barely left his stool, and another clean right uppercut to the jaw in the fifth.

Encouraged, Shevlin adopted similar tactics in both the ninth and tenth rounds – rushing across and hitting Basham before the Welshman could leave the corner. Basham countered vigorously, yet even the crispest of rights to the jaw in the 11th stopped Shevlin for barely a second. By the end of the 14th, Basham had been cut slightly on both brows and was beginning to wonder whether he could ever really hurt Shevlin, whose chin had absorbed jabs, hooks and clips to little apparent effect.

Yet there were few more irrepressible fighters around in 1919 than little Johnny Basham. He calculated that hitting Shevlin more often than Shevlin hit him might not bring him a knockout but would mean a safe win on points. Over the last five rounds, where Shevlin

had been predicted to be at his best, and was, Basham showed what a champion he was by outdoing him in attack and defence alike. As *Boxing* put it, 'the longer the bout lasted the more certain became Basham's prospect of victory'.

Basham's reputation, enhanced by this second victory over a dangerous opponent, was sustained when Shevlin stayed in London to meet other British opponents. On the afternoon of 14 April 1919, Shevlin was at The Ring, Blackfriars to meet Fred Newberry of Limehouse.[24] Over 20 rounds, Shevlin's ability to absorb an opponent's best punches and to use his superior strength told, as they had not against Basham. Newberry, skilful but weaker, lasted the distance for a points defeat.

On 19 May 1919, Shevlin (10st 4½lb/144½lbs) returned to the NSC to face Eddie Beattie of Kilsyth (10st 4lb/144lbs) with a £650 purse at stake.[25] Beattie had his moments and his bravery and doggedness were much admired. Shevlin earned a comfortable points victory over 15 rounds, loudly applauded by the members. Beattie was also cheered, more in the spirit of sympathy for his swollen and cut face, evidence of the power and frequency of the American's punches.

Attractive fights were also staged in the lighter divisions in February 1919 at the NSC and at the Blackfriars Ring. The first, on the afternoon of Monday, 3 February 1919, was at Blackfriars, another Anglo-American clash inspired by the Albert Hall tournament.[26] Private Joe Lynch of the US Army was matched over a championship 20 rounds with the reigning British bantamweight champion Tommy Noble. The match was made at a generous 8st 8lb, yet Noble, by indiscipline or by unsporting design, refused to weigh in, choosing to pay a £25 fine rather than to disclose his actual weight (much to the disgust of the packed audience). Lynch generously agreed to fight anyway, having comfortably made the limit.

The weight squabble affected the innocent Lynch more than the ignoble Noble. Noble commanded the centre of the ring. Lynch tentatively circled around him, cautiously trying to land left leads and getting caught in the face with left and right counters. Most spectators put Lynch's slow start down to apprehension about Noble's unexpected weight and possibly enhanced power. They forgot Lynch was a wily old craftsman quite prepared to concede initial advantage as he worked out opponents' styles.

The change came in the sixth when Lynch's lefts became visibly sharper and more effective. When Noble rushed in to counter or to hold and smother, Lynch's rights found their mark too. Noble, a skilful boxer at his best, adopted a tedious punch-then-hold pattern to the displeasure of crowd and referee. Lynch piled up points and was justifiably awarded victory after the 20th. He had done what he could to entertain. Noble's last-round rally could not obliterate memories of his shabby weight ploy and his negativity. The referee, much criticised for his failure to remain in the ring to stop Noble's holding by physically separating the pair ('he jumped in and out again like a man being sniped at in the front line trenches'), had at least awarded the verdict correctly.[27]

The NSC presented a unique experience for a fighter when a championship and a Lonsdale Belt were on offer. On 24 February 1919, for the British featherweight championship, a Lonsdale Belt and a moderate purse (£450) the Scot Tancy Lee met Danny Morgan of Tirphil, a Welshman who replaced the original challenger, the injured Billy Fry of Tylorstown.

If Lee won for a third time the belt would be his own property. Lee, popular with members, was the 37-year-old veteran. Many had been in the house in January 1915 when he had famously defeated the suffering Jimmy Wilde in a weight division Lee could no longer accommodate. It would be a fitting swansong to beat Morgan (18 years younger than he), especially as Morgan had got a narrow hometown decision against him in Cardiff the year before (5 January 1918). The Cardiff fight had been at catchweight and Lee had only half-trained.

To growing disappointment, a championship performance from Lee (8st 13¼lb/125¼lbs) failed to materialise. Instead of the audience wallowing in the nostalgic pleasure of urging a favourite home, round by round, the more astringent experience was to see a confident young challenger putting the stocky Scot firmly in his place. Morgan (8st 13¾lb/125¾lbs) had reach and height advantages but was unexpectedly willing to fight the good fight at close quarters. He blocked Lee's short hooks and uppercuts, and landed choice hooks and uppercuts himself. By the fifth round, Morgan's inside work built him a useful points lead. In the following rounds he opened out his full repertoire, punishing Lee in the clinches but also landing straight incisive punches from a distance.

Lee was not entirely out of it. He clipped Morgan's face and jaw with solid left hooks and uppercuts in the fifth, and with a powerful left jab in the seventh. He strayed into illegalities with head and elbow on the blind side of the referee but he opened a small cut close to Morgan's right eye in the ninth with a clean punch. *Boxing* suggested Morgan established even more physical and psychological supremacy in the 11th:

… quite Morgan's best rd. to date. Getting and keeping away from the Scot's deliberate advance, he made full use of his greater speed and of his youth. Knowing that Tancy could not afford to gallop, Danny slipped him almost contemptuously at times, shooting out his longer arms in the face and body in back-handers and jabs, and whipping in long lefts or rights to face and body and forcing a close rally. Even in the first of these close exchanges he got home heavily with short right hooks to the chin, and it was plain that Tancy was commencing to tire. A full-armed right from Morgan went astray, and Lee got in to jab and uppercut, but Danny got most of his own back with two sharp lefts to the face just before the gong.

Lee was getting visibly wearier by now …

Although Lee was indeed weary, he was a tough and combative little champion. Sensing the coveted belt was being peeled away from his waist, he rallied in the 13th and, handicapped as he was by a closing left eye, took that and the 14th. Morgan meanwhile rested in these rounds in the knowledge that he had plenty of stamina in hand. As *Boxing* saw it, the 15th was also Morgan's:

Lee fought hard, but had the worst of the exchanges, both at long and close range. Tancy was persistent, but age and weariness were telling their tale, and he had to take more than he gave, even of uppercuts and body jolts, while at long range he was both outreached and outboxed.

The Times agreed:

> At all the finer points of the game, however, he [TL] appeared to be distinctly second best.

As did the *Mirror of Life and Boxing World*:

> … Morgan, to our way of thinking, held a distinct lead when hostilities ceased …

It was so recognised by every witness except one. With the Lee camp and the members, whose warm sentiments about Tancy had led them to risk heavy wagers upon him, all praying for a miracle, the miracle came. Not a last-minute knockout (generally assumed to be the only hope left), rather, referee J. H. Douglas awarding an unlikely points victory to Tancy – an exhausted half-conscious Tancy slumped in disappointment in his corner.[28]

Not for the first, and certainly not for the last time, boxing had suffered an unjust and shocking decision. In every sport depending upon subjective assessment, inexplicable results are always a possibility. Such uncertainties ultimately add to a sport's fascination rather than distract.

The persistence of radiant optimism over practical disappointment is personified by the devoted followers of unsuccessful soccer teams, and even more so by those who believed Bombardier Billy Wells would one day match his talent with a performance on the big day. How often had his fans arrived in hope and gone home mulling over his latest failure? His name on the bill guaranteed attendance from his loyal followers and perhaps from masochists eager to see their gloomiest predictions fulfilled. The contrast between Wells's looks and his nervous ring performances was the subject of a cruel jibe in *Boxing* in July:

> Rumours had been floating around that Beautiful Billy had discovered that the society of Film Operators, Film Heroes, Film Villains, and Film Beauties was ever so much more agreeable than that of rude and boisterous pugilists.[29]

Two British films featuring Wells as actor, *The Great Game* (December 1918) and *The Silver Lining* (November 1919) were launched in the post-war period and perhaps, like Corbett before him and Dempsey after him, he found acting, even with stage fright, a less painful profession than boxing.[30] C. B. Cochran was well aware of Wells's drawing power and of the interest stimulated by his beating of Joe Beckett – as rude and boisterous a pugilist as any – in the Albert Hall tournament. Could Wells do it again over 20 championship rounds?

Cochran, with his new Holborn Stadium to fill, offered Wells the opportunity to top the bill at the Stadium on 27 February 1919 and answer that question. Initially, Wells wanted another crack at Carpentier and a £1,000 purse for the privilege. Cochran, an optimist but no cockeyed one, had visions of another first-round fiasco and told Wells bluntly to rehabilitate himself before he could be rematched with Carpentier. For a more modest £600, he should beat British rivals such as Frank Goddard or Arthur Townley or Joe Beckett. Only then could he hope for a third encounter and big payday with the Frenchman.

Wells chose Beckett. Beckett agreed, providing he got a purse equal to that of Wells.[31] So, for an outlay of £1,200 plus a mere £30 for preliminaries, Cochran secured an event that brought in £3,344 in ticket sales. A highly profitable match was on.[32] The Holborn venue, with so many fewer seats than Olympia, could stage such top fights but only at top prices.

Beckett, the one-time booth fighter, was not blessed with a vivid imagination nor apparently cursed with self-doubt. He was an unsmiling, tumble-haired, stocky (5ft 10¾in), swarthy, crouching fighter who would walk through an opponent's elegant leads and ambush the man's ribcage with his short jabs and hooks, especially his left hook, to hurtful effect. What you saw with Beckett was supposedly what you got; street fighter over pugilistic academician.

He was the perfect complement to his more famous opponent. The taller, blonder, handsomer Wells cultivated an upright stance and a long left lead, supposedly heroic attributes. Wells was a commanding and authoritative controller of the ring and its vicissitudes at one moment, and an apprehensive misfit at others. In the walk to the ring in Holborn, it was the nervy

Wells who looked apprehensive, and Beckett particularly determined. Appearances can mislead. The seemingly impermeable and muscular Joe, who could have matched English Kennel Club standards in the bulldog class, was actually quite as inconsistent and brittle as Billy, and every bit as likely to descend into a moody stasis. As Eugene Corri once pointed out, it meant Beckett usually won the bouts he was expected to lose and lost the bouts he was expected to win.[33]

The quality of the clash matched neither the extensive publicity nor the intense noise generated by the packed crowd (1,250 on the ring level and another 320 in the gallery).[34] The drama did. At the first bell, Beckett rushed across the ring and bustled into Wells, who was arranging himself into a classical boxer's pose, left arm and left foot forward. Wells went down on his bottom, more embarrassed than seriously hurt, but needing a count of seven to recover his equilibrium if not his dignity. 'Oh, Billy!' called a sympathetic Carpentier from a ringside seat. Dressed in his French aviator's tunic, his gallantry awards gleaming on his chest, Georges, the war hero, had every reason to support Wells, an opponent whom he knew he could beat, and who would contribute more to a sell-out match than Beckett. This is not to attribute Carpentier's affection for Wells to French cynicism. There was considerable mutual respect and liking between these two honourable sportsmen that lasted their lifetimes.

Beckett, suspecting Wells was foxing, stood off after the count, rather than risk a damaging Wells counter. His caution did not last long and he resumed his onslaught on Wells's body. Wells, always uncomfortable at close

quarters, tucked his solar plexus away from Beckett in a low crouch. This was futile. He was caught on his lowered right temple by a fierce left hook that toppled him over sideways for a longer count of nine. One round and two knockdowns were about as bad as Wells's camp's worst fears.

Wells in the second looked more comfortable as if his nightmare, a knockout in the first, had been averted. His jab began to operate, as did his better-balanced footwork. Beckett refused to keep a respectful distance and successfully landed hooks, jabs and uppercuts in close.

A severe talking-to in his corner brought out an even better Wells in the third. He kept Beckett away with clean strong lefts. He sidestepped with impressive alacrity when Beckett closed in. But there were danger signs. Beckett barely blinked under his bushy eyebrows when Wells landed, and patiently cut off the ring to punish Wells with harder and hurtful punches.

Only in the first minute of the fifth did Wells give a sign that he might yet win. An early Beckett rush was halted with a joltingly strong left, and Wells followed with a neat left and right combination to Beckett's permanent six o'clock shadow. Wells's supporters brightened up – 'Give him another!' yelled a French voice (Carpentier's). Promise did not come to fruition. Rather, Beckett advanced remorselessly, catching the retreating Wells with two powerful left hooks. The weakening Wells went down for a short count, and then for a slightly longer one.

With ample time left, Beckett moved in. Under a flurry of left and right hooks to the body, and an ugly swinging right to the point of his jaw,

Wells stopped, shook and sank to the canvas where he was counted out. Carpentier visited Wells in his dressing room to console him, but Wells's chances of a rematch were dead.[35] Neither a rival's sympathy nor the continuing affection of his loyal fans could revive him as a serious contender.

The Holborn result had clear consequences. Britain had a new heavyweight champion in Joe Beckett. He had convincingly beaten the reigning champion in the ring over a championship distance. The NSC had other ideas, behaving as if it were still 1910 and as if nothing could happen in boxing except upon their say-so. They had had no chance of staging Wells v Beckett and refused their approval to an event out of their control, especially one staged by Cochran. Before the war, their chosen flyweight champion and Lonsdale Belt holder Sid Smith had lost to Bill Ladbury (2 June 1913) at The Ring. They had insisted on Smith's belt being returned and had arranged a rival title bout at the club.

Similarly, this time, instead of simply recognising Beckett, they declared the heavyweight title vacant and arranged a new title fight on 26 May 1919 at the club between two other contenders – Frank Goddard 'The Fighting Farmer' and Jack Curphey. This was unjust and a snide attempt to spoil Cochran's future plans.

Cochran, like Carpentier, would have preferred a Wells victory because of Wells's commercial drawing power. Instead he accepted reality and dished the NSC by signing up Beckett and Frank Goddard for an Olympia promotion on 17 June 1919. Should Curphey now beat Goddard at the NSC in May, Goddard's big day out in June at

Olympia would be thoroughly devalued. On the other hand, if Goddard *did* beat Curphey at the NSC, two British reigning heavyweight champions, one official and one unofficial in Goddard and Beckett, would meet in June with the winner bound for an even more lucrative fight with Georges Carpentier before the year was out. Neither bout would be within the financial reach of the cash-straitened NSC.

The darker sides of boxing were not wholly banished by its wartime prestige. The ritualistic gentility of an NSC presentation or the social pretensions of a Cochran first night was all very well. Boxing, like any real sport, could generate high passions in ring and hall alike. Sometimes these passions spilled into violence and disorder. No matter how morally reprehensible, the occasional incident could be expected. (Over the centuries, boxing has probably a cleaner record on crowd behaviour than, say, association football.)

One such blemish occurred at The Ring, Blackfriars in February 1919. An unsatisfactory fight between Dick Moss of Leeds and a London favourite, Con Houghton of Hackney, went nine rounds of a scheduled 20 when Joe Palmer the referee, having repeatedly warned Moss for holding, lost patience and disqualified him.[36] An enraged Moss supporter (or perhaps a disgruntled punter who had taken the longer odds against him) sprang into the ring and hit Palmer over the head with a shiny object. He was arrested and, at the magistrates' court next day, was identified as middle-class commission agent Edward Joyce. As with soccer violence, rioters and thugs did not necessarily come out of the ranks of the lumpen proletariat. The

shiny object was displayed in court – it was a revolver. Little imagination is required to see the danger of an angry fan with a firearm in a crowded and closely confined space.

Though a former chapel, The Ring was prone to dissent expressed in uneccclesiastical form. Moss Deyong, the veteran referee, recorded in his autobiography that unpopular decisions there regularly provoked a gastronomic cascade of bottles, saveloys and pease puddings into the ring.[37] In 1914, Deyong awarded a minor bantamweight (George Clark) a narrow points verdict over the greatest of local heroes, Sid Smith. As a result he was pelted from the balcony with spanners, pliers and tyre levers. (A Blackfriars custom was to allow taxi drivers into the balcony after nine o'clock. Rather than risk leaving the tools of the trade out in their parked cabs, the taxi drivers brought their bags in with them. Professional accessories could also be missiles.)

A problem, not specific to boxing, but particularly damaging to boxers, is the false belief of an ageing veteran that he has at least one more success within him. Anyone with a basic knowledge of the sport will name both historical and modern examples. The greater the fighter, the greater the temptation for unscrupulous moneymen to get one more big promotion out of him. And the greater the fighter, the greater is the temptation to believe in his own immortality.

Three boxers whom most would place at the top of an all-time rankings list – Sugar Ray Robinson, Joe Louis and Muhammad Ali – all went to the ring too late and too often and were unnecessarily damaged physically and mentally. The phenomenon is an ugly

cut on the face of boxing. The sport could not save its bravest and best from their own and others' folly.

Such disfigurement did not creep in in modern multi-million-dollar times. Take the 1919 experiences of another all-time great, Peerless Jim Driscoll. Driscoll, before the First World War, had embodied personally all the Edwardian sporting virtues. With Driscoll there were the insouciance of the lifted dark eyebrows, the vivacious bob of the ruffled hair as the head moved stylishly and precisely out of range of an oncoming punch, and the intricate footwork that moved him in and out and side to side like an impeccably programmed machine.

Outside the ring, there were the generosity of spirit, the open-handedness to charitable causes or to fellow human beings down on their luck, the fierce pride in his country and his craft, and the strong competitive urge that never transgressed the bounds of good sportsmanship. (His famous or infamous loss to Freddie Welsh by disqualification was generally excused as the response of an honest fighter provoked beyond endurance by sly and underhand tactics.) He was, said *Boxing*, 'the greatest of all living sportsmen and the truest good fellow'.[38]

Many said Driscoll should have retired before he met Owen Moran in that long-delayed fight in January 1913 when aged 33. Admittedly Driscoll's subsequent beneficiaries had been bookmakers as often as Catholic charities and there were no reasons beyond past and present profligacy for him to re-enter the professional ring. Driscoll spent the war years as instructor and trainer. He had not faced a serious opponent in the ring for the best part of six years. He was 38 years old. He needed the money.

His re-emergence took place in the less than glamorous Hoxton Baths on Monday afternoon, 10 March 1919. He looked a real picture – 'tanned and healthy', said *The Times*; 'his whole appearance suggestive of fitness', said *Mirror of Life*.[39] Guy Deghy in his history of the NSC, *Noble and Manly*, was premature in describing Driscoll as 'old and battered'.[40] Admittedly some sub-editor at *The Times* undermined its reporter's compliments by adding the headline 'OLD-TIME BOXERS'.

It is true that Driscoll's opponent was indeed an old-timer – 42-year-old Pedlar Palmer, veteran of veterans, born 19 November 1876 (!), who won the British bantamweight championship back in November 1895 and began his professional career in 1891. The perky Cockney, who had delighted NSC members with his 'box o' tricks', had also had a hiatus in his career when

detained at His Majesty's pleasure for five years' penal servitude after killing a man on a train in April 1907. The man, considerably bigger and heavier than he, had spoken insultingly to Palmer but died as a result of Palmer punching him on the jaw. As Palmer knocked out only five opponents in 65 fights when trying, the fatal blow was a freakish accident. Nevertheless, a professional boxer who killed a man out of the ring was hardly going to be treated sympathetically.

Palmer's tricks, the ducking and swaying, the bewildering lateral movements, were all dependent upon speed. A slow Palmer was a sitting target, especially for a man as skilled as Driscoll. With some compassionate voices in the Hoxton crowd pleading with Driscoll not to cause Palmer unnecessary damage, the Welshman did what he had to do. Out-thought and outclassed, Palmer soaked up the famous Driscoll left for two rounds, went down for several counts in the

third and was rescued by referee Eugene Corri in the fourth as he tottered on legs refusing any more to do what his brain told them. Driscoll looked like a champion restored, but in truth had participated in little more than a one-sided exhibition.

Palmer, exemplifying against Driscoll the boxer who had gone to the ring at least once too often, presented another common boxers' failing – the capacity to get into trouble outside the ring. In July 1919, a few months after his drubbing at Hoxton, he was lying in a hospital bed recovering from knife wounds inflicted in an East End public house by a father angry at the Pedlar's attempts to charm his daughter with his out-of-the-ring wiles.[41]

The Palmer/Driscoll match was an event that should not have taken place. However, in the ring with them, metaphorically, was a grim spectre. That was the ghostly memory of Palmer's famous contemporary, another British bantamweight champion, George 'Digger' Stanley. Three days before the Hoxton fiasco, the corpse of the Romany Stanley, first ever holder of a Lonsdale Belt, was found in a bedsitter in Fulham. After a hip dislocation, he moved only on crutches and declined terminally from poverty, starvation and self-neglect.

(Palmer's later years were no more in accordance with the dignity of his championship status than Stanley's and included his being formally charged with attempted suicide in the early 1930s after being found in the nick of time with his head in a gas oven. Had it been allowed, Palmer would have fought on pushing a Zimmer frame.)

Palmer, Driscoll and Stanley earned substantial sums from boxing.

10 March 1919, Hoxton Baths: Jim Driscoll floors 42-year-old Pedlar Palmer in the third. Palmer was rescued by the referee in the fourth.
BnF

Pittances compared with the pay-per-view and casino promotions of the 21st century, yet far beyond the dreams of the miners, travellers and dockers of their own times. They were but minor players in the Frivolous Spenders League compared with, say, Mike Tyson, who splurged many millions of ring dollars in orgies of conspicuous consumption in the late 20th century. Hardly was the ink dry on Tyson's signature on the contract offered him by promoter Don King on Tyson's release from prison after serving a sentence for a rape conviction in March 1995, before he had spent $3 million on a Las Vegas estate, plus unspecified amounts on five BMWs, and $200,000 on Versace outfits.[42]

Having famously tested his gold teeth on Evander Holyfield's ear in a rematch in 1997, by the time he met Julius Francis in January 2000, he was said to be fighting on only because he was millions of dollars in debt again; the Don King Prisoner Aid Fund spent on such necessities as motorcycles, cocaine, pet tigers and a trillion mobile phone calls. He was declared bankrupt in 2003 despite having earned over $300 million. In late 2013, he was the star of an HBO one-man show *Mike Tyson: Undisputed Truth,* directed by Spike Lee, enacted live upon Broadway and other stages. The 'truth' included the very real episodes of his frightful childhood but also ridicule of his battered ex-wife and his rape victim, tragedies turned into self-justifying stand-up.

For the moment, the resumption of the great Driscoll's career was inevitable. A new date was arranged for 31 May 1919.[43] Deep in the Welsh valleys at Mountain Ash, the renascent Driscoll met another Welshman, the promising Francis Young Rossi of Cardiff, in a match made at 9st/126lbs and over 20 rounds. This is misleading as the Driscoll camp negotiated a limit of two minutes per round, guaranteeing he would be spared a full 60 minutes of action. Notwithstanding the proviso, 6,000 locals packed the Mountain Ash Pavilion, where the cheapest seats cost 6s. 9d., to see Rossi try to outhustle Driscoll: young cub versus old lion 16 years his elder. Driscoll trained hard, scaling 8st 9lb/121lbs with some ease, an effort Rossi believed would favour him over the later rounds. Cheekily Rossi pretended not to know whom he was fighting: 'Who is Jim Driscoll anyway?' After the fight he answered his own question – 'A better man than I am!'

The fight, attended by all the London boxing writers, was better than anticipated. One boxing correspondent, Charles Rose, pronounced it the greatest fight he had seen in years, and most mention the sheer speed of the action. Rossi used his hand speed to catch the Old Master whenever and however he could, and Driscoll twisted and ducked out of awkward corners and landed crisp punches to head and torso. Even the 20th round was no tired huddle indulged by two weary men ticking away the remaining seconds. Instead, both men advanced and retreated in turn, so absorbed in the task in hand that they failed to hear the bell and had to be separated when the two minutes were up.

Rounds seven and eight, according to *Boxing*, served as a paradigm for the whole fluctuating fight:

RD.7. – The speed was remarkable, some of the exchanges falling so fast that it was only with difficulty the eye could follow them. Driscoll brought cheers by his clever ducking, and once Rossi nearly went through the ropes as a result of a quick side step. Towards the finish, however, Rossi piled up a few points with left-hand leads and shaded Jim.

RD.8. – Rossi, encouraged by his success in the former rd., attempted to cut out the pace. His attempts at close quarters were cleverly blocked, however, Jim, meanwhile scoring with some snappy little uppercuts at close quarters which earned him a shade of points.

By the end, most spectators assumed that the pre-match favourite Driscoll had won more rounds than Rossi and was entitled to the victory. The *Mirror of Life and Boxing World* agreed: '… we were certainly of the opinion that Driscoll had won by a clear margin, and we, like others, were amazed when the decision was announced as a draw' (7 June 1919); and also (14 June 1919) '… at the finish I [J. Frank Bradley, boxing reporter and editor] made Driscoll no fewer than nine points ahead of Rossi'. *Boxing* suggested Dan Whelligan, the referee, who had prematurely and embarrassingly predicted a Driscoll knockout before being appointed as referee, was so determined to credit Rossi with every possible point to prove his own integrity that he had overdone it.

If Driscoll had won, and won clearly, he was entitled to the victory. The fighting draw featured a fit and

Charles Ledoux (right) in his day job. He carved up many British fighters.
BnF

skilful veteran holding his own with a brilliant young challenger. There is still a vast difference between sustaining ring action for two minutes, rather than a full three. As any amateur knows, it is the third minute of a round when the lungs begin to burn, the legs to stiffen and the arms feel the gloves have turned into lumps of iron dragging down one's guard. Meanwhile, one's opponent appears to get stronger and his hits more painful.

The draw against Rossi – if draw it were – fostered the illusion that the 1919 Driscoll was the 1910 Driscoll reborn. More objective thinking would have dispelled such self-deception. Driscoll's next match-up was the subject of hard-headed thought, but only within the entourage of his opponent, the tough Frenchman Charles Ledoux. The clash was announced for September, subsequently postponed to 20 October 1919, when it took place at the NSC.[44]

The Ledoux camp refused two-minute rounds and the desire of the Driscoll team to fight 15 rounds rather than 20. Only the weight stipulation theoretically favoured both men – a non-standard 8st 11lb/123lbs against the usual bantamweight limit of 8st 6lb/118lbs. Driscoll still discarded his shirt and socks to meet the requirement. All the other contractual obligations, apart from the venue, the NSC where Driscoll was much loved, favoured Ledoux. The canny François Descamps, Carpentier's lifelong mentor, was managing Ledoux and negotiated conditions fully favourable to the younger man. Driscoll's advisers were less perspicacious.

The French obtained what they could out of every negotiation. They harboured deep suspicions about the perfidies of Albion in boxing in the light of recent events. On 10 April 1919 there had been some particularly dubious decisions at a well-publicised Anglo-French night at Cochran's Holborn Stadium.[45] A top-of-the-bill match, between Eugene Criqui of France and

Tommy Noble of Bermondsey for £500 and the European bantamweight championship, ended dramatically. Noble, born 4 March 1897, was tall but well-proportioned and had long elegant legs. His fighting style was uglier than his suave and handsome mien, just like his shabby weight ploy against Joe Lynch a few months earlier.[46]

Noble served in the Army Service Corps and was spared full combat. He did plenty of fighting in Civvy Street, beginning with the boyhood scraps of a Bermondsey upbringing. His professional record included two losses to Jimmy Wilde (knocked out in the 11th at New Cross, 24 January 1916, and in the 15th in Liverpool, 9 September 1916) and proceeded at a rate of two fights a month for most years. It culminated on 25 November 1918 with a 20-round points victory at the NSC over Joe Symonds of Plymouth. That significant win brought him a Lonsdale Belt and the British bantamweight title. (This was the high point of Noble's career. From 1920 to 1925 he fought

Eugene Criqui (1893–1977), Parisian bantamweight and French war hero. His jaw was rebuilt after he failed to duck a German bullet.
BoxRec

in the USA and Canada, usually unsuccessfully.)

The thin and pale Criqui, whom we last saw in action against Percy Jones in 1914 (Chapter 10), had been in French uniform and in the midst of some of the hottest action on the Western Front. He was seriously wounded and invalided out of the French Army as a war hero in 1915. A bullet seriously damaging his lips, gums, teeth and jaw had exited through the back of his neck a few millimetres away from his spinal cord. His presence in a post-war ring was a minor miracle wrought by French surgical skill. Among his war souvenirs was a new jaw reconstructed around a silver plate because of the shattering of the original jawbone. Only with a special protective shield worn in his mouth was he able to box at all. Despite this fearful handicap, he had a successful boxing career in the 1920s, not retiring until 1928, then living almost 50 happy years after that.

Little could faze this brave and resourceful man, but even he was astonished at the licence Noble was granted by the out-of-the-ring referee to punch to the kidneys, press his forearm against Criqui's throat and rub the laces of his glove into his face. The final betrayal of the entente cordiale came in the 19th when a low Noble punch caught a nerve in the joint between hip and thigh, temporarily paralysing the whole leg. Criqui dropped to the floor and the referee, instead of granting him a legitimate period of recovery, began a count. Criqui struggled up at six, only for Noble, who was prowling behind him out of his sight, to smite him down again with two clubbing rights. The referee obligingly counted him out. Even the strongest Francophobes in

the house felt Criqui hard done by. (A return on 27 June 1919 under a stricter referee in Paris was drawn.)

Injustice to the French was the keynote that Holborn evening. French lightweight Georges Pepin was awarded a painful points verdict over Ernie Rice of Hounslow, but only after another incompetent referee had declared open season on Pepin's kidneys and lower abdomen. Furthermore, Pepin's compatriot and fellow lightweight Raymond Vittet was harshly disqualified in the third round of an ill-tempered bout against Bob Marriott (British amateur lightweight champion in 1912 and 1914 and recently turned professional). Marriott tried illegally to assert his physical strength in a clinch by wrestling Vittet to the ground. As Vittet struggled to get his arms free, his elbow struck the side of Marriott's jaw and the referee disqualified him.

So the Anglo-French night in Holborn, designed to increase international understanding, contained three dubious results – an English victory based on fouls, a French victory at the cost of a multitude of painful fouls and an English victory on a non-foul. No wonder the French camp were determined to concede nothing when Ledoux met Driscoll in October 1919.

That October evening, the NSC theatre rang to a rousing reception for Driscoll. Several late bets were placed upon him when he stripped off his robe to show a firm torso fine-honed for the occasion – another reason for doubting Deghy's words 'old and haggard' were anywhere near the truth. Ledoux was another French patriot who had enlisted in the French Army as soon as the war began. He was greatly respected in Britain for both his pre-

war appearances in the ring and for his exemplary war record. He too was warmly received, although many in the audience sympathetically murmured that for boxing skill he would never be in Driscoll's class. Even his manager François Descamps conceded that.[47] 'Charles could never win by boxing,' he said. 'But,' he added, 'he can win by his strength. For fifteen rounds Driscoll will be very good, very clever; he will then be winning, but after that, twenty-seven will beat forty.'

Had he not been a successful boxing manager, Descamps could have sustained a career as a soothsayer. His prophecy was deadly accurate. Ledoux began cautiously, staying out of reach of Driscoll's counters, reluctant to make the 'Old Man's' task easy by opening up fully. Meanwhile, Driscoll's cool left flicked in and out of Ledoux's face with all the accuracy of old, if not with quite its old power.

As the early rounds went by, some of the old Driscoll forcefulness returned to that left. According to Peggy Bettinson, 'It was wonderful to behold. It shot out like lightning; it stabbed and stung in a way that would have caused any man less sensitive and courageous than Ledoux to have imagined that he was up against all the fighters that ever were.'[48]

Other observers confirm this is no great exaggeration. Looking back 17 years later, Ben Bennison, boxing reporter and historian, described it as 'the greatest fight I ever saw in my wanderings at home and abroad'.[49] Bennison asserts the superiority of Driscoll as round succeeded round:

Driscoll, carriage perfect, feet twinkling, eyes clear, planted blows as he pleased, stabbing with

– his right ear bled, as did a cut above his right eye, and an ominous bruise swelled on his cheekbone. Too good a sportsman to resort to fouls and too full of French élan to think of retreating, Ledoux continued to attack.

By the tenth, as yet another round slipped by with the young man being clipped, cuffed and jolted for his effrontery, the bookmakers in the audience were offering the longest odds against Ledoux, hoping to attract French guests with more francs than sense. There were no takers.

In the summer, Ledoux beat the British bantamweight champion Tommy Noble in Paris with a tenth-round knockout on 31 July 1919.[50] He looked notably tired at that point even with ten potential rounds to go. By October he had trained to last 20 rounds in all contingencies. This was just as well, as the punishing Driscoll tutorial continued for the next four and a half rounds. During those rounds, Driscoll hit him with lefts and rights mercilessly, and as he sat on his stool to recover, shouts of 'Bravo, Driscoll' assaulted Ledoux's already reddened ears.

During the 14th, Driscoll feinted with his deadly left and landed an explosive right uppercut to the point of Ledoux's jaw, a perfect knockout punch, perfectly delivered. Unfortunately for Anglo-Welsh hopes, Ledoux declined to fall down. He merely blinked. As even the restrained NSC members gasped, it was Driscoll's turn to look disconcerted. He had outclassed his opponent for about 50 pulsating minutes. He had caught him with hundreds of damaging punches. He had administered a superlative *coup de grâce* yet the Frenchman was still there and still coming forward.

La Vie au Grand Air *published action pictures of the NSC clash of 20 October 1919 between Driscoll and Ledoux. The magazine had Ledoux comment generously on the day Driscoll's resources ran out: 'I had the honour of beating the incomparable Jim Driscoll on the 20th of October in London. My opponent was beaten more by age than by me. 1. I look for an opening to attack but this is difficult. 2. Driscoll scores points: his blows do not bother me. 3. I slip down, not from a blow, and I get up immediately. 4. At the end of the 10th round, I have produced my effort and I have ground down the grand old Driscoll when seconds throw in the sponge at the beginning of the 16th round. It is with a full heart that I go to hug my honest and brave opponent.'*
BnF

his left, countering with his right, slipping and skipping punches as if it were all childishly easy.

Plan B succeeded Ledoux's passivity in the early minutes soon enough. He stormed towards Driscoll, determined to slow him down. His hooks and drives aimed at Driscoll's ribs were intercepted with precision or avoided with minimal movement. His face showed evidence of Driscoll's stinging leads and counters

This was the most significant moment of the fight; the moment of truth. There are many sporting parallels. The competitor in a marathon runs 23 of the 26 miles of the race yet is struck suddenly with physical and psychological agony as surely as if they have run into a solid glass wall. For boxers, a whole career is not unlike a marathon. The boxer who goes on too long will, sooner or later, be struck by a similar lapse: tank empty, vigour dissipated, hopes gone, a 'shot' fighter in the grim parlance of the ring. On 20 October 1919 in the 14th round, the reborn Driscoll had run finally into the wall of reality.

The 15th round proved it. Ledoux moved forward, swinging punches, and landed a heavy right cross on Driscoll's chin. Severely shaken, Driscoll survived by avoidance and retreat until the very last seconds of the round. Desperately close to his corner and a much needed minute's rest, Driscoll's concentration wavered for an instant; an instant just long enough for Ledoux to catch him with a wicked left piledriver to the solar plexus, a punch to drive the wind from Driscoll and double him up helplessly. The bell spared Driscoll the count, yet neither the break nor the frantic efforts of his seconds could undo in 60 seconds what two heavy punches and decades of action had done.

The bell rang and Driscoll got up off his stool. Before Ledoux could complete the destruction, the towel fluttered in from Driscoll's corner. An unsteady and tearful Driscoll seemed at that moment to be acting out Oscar Wilde's tale, *The Picture of Dorian Gray*, turning from handsome hero into an old, corrupted and punished portrait of himself. He was bundled off to his dressing room by his grieving seconds.

Bennison the journalist and Peggy Bettinson visited him, slumped inconsolably on the dressing room massage table. Eventually they persuaded him to greet his supporters in the bar. Bennison records the conversation:

'Jim,' I said, 'don't hurry away. You are wanted.'

'Who are they [wanting me]?'

'Everybody,' I assured him.

'To tell me that I am a damned old fool, I suppose. Not on your life! [Bettinson among others had earlier urged him to retire]. Jim Driscoll finished long ago, and I should have known it. I have let the Club down. I'm sorry.'

But Driscoll was not allowed to hide himself, for Mr 'Peggy' Bettinson dragooned him into the smoke room, which was crowded by distinguished sportsmen.

'Gentlemen,' rapped 'Peggy', as he took the arm of Driscoll, 'you have seen the greatest fight ever.'

'But, Guv'nor,' excused Driscoll.

'To hell, Jim,' snapped Bettinson.[51]

In this clubby atmosphere, playing out the script when an old, trusted house retainer is forced into a penurious retirement, the assembled company knew what to do. The hat passed around was filled with over £2,000 for Driscoll to take away. No one will ever know whether the sum adequately compensated the proud Driscoll, not for the bruises received from Ledoux, but for the hurt he had suffered inside. Driscoll was not the first and certainly not the last professional to have difficulty in finding a post-ring role to match the glamour and income of his sporting career. At least he was a man much loved and admired within his Cardiff community; a state of affairs that persisted until his early death and beyond.

No such consolations were available to the man who had grasped the world heavyweight championship title in Sydney, Australia in December 1908, and relinquished it on his back in the Cuban sunshine in April 1915. Since losing his title to Jess Willard, Jack Johnson was a lost and lonely figure wanted only by his creditors and the US authorities. The charges he had gone into exile to avoid stood. The CIA kept him under surveillance as he wandered around neutral countries, taking exhibition matches against gimmicky opponents who would have been unworthy of carrying his gloves a few years before.

Still barred from Britain since February 1916 under the Aliens Restriction Act, Johnson spent most of the war living on his wits, pawnbrokers supplementing what he could earn from pathetic fit-ups like the surrealistic spectacle acted out with Arthur Cravan on 29 April 1916.

In March 1919, when Driscoll began his ill-fated comeback against Pedlar Palmer at Hoxton Baths, Jack Johnson and Lucille were embarking on a boat back to Cuba; their ultimate destination Mexico.[52] The current hostility between Mexico and the USA was to Johnson's advantage. He was outside the jurisdiction of the

American authorities but near enough geographically to conduct negotiations about potentially lucrative encounters on Mexican soil against, say, Gunboat Smith or Porky Flynn. It was the perfect perch from which to needle and provoke white American public opinion, as only he knew how, on the embarrassing subject of race relations.

One money-making scheme launched during this Mexican sojourn was a land-buying scheme to benefit American blacks. In return for an investment in the Jack Johnson Land Company, black Americans could exchange their inferior status at home for a place in the land-owning classes in Mexico:

Colored People: You are lynched, tortured, mobbed, persecuted and discriminated against in the 'boasted' land of liberty; own a home in Mexico where one is as good as another, and it is not your color that counts, but simply you.

So said an advertisement for the company published in a socialist newspaper.[53] Only a remarkably naïve and trusting black American citizen would have sent his life savings to Mexico to the free-spending Johnson supposedly to invest on his behalf.

In practice, the money-spinning bouts against high-ranking American heavyweights rarely materialised and were substituted for over-hyped farces against local and other nonentities; opponents such as Marty Cutler and Tom Cowler, barely worthy of featuring in a trivia quiz.

Too late to see his mother again (she died in March 1918), Johnson's long exile ended in July 1920 when he crossed the border from Mexico to the USA and surrendered to the authorities. After serving a year in Kansas at Leavenworth prison as Federal Prisoner 15461, he was released as a free man and was home at last. Taking 11 meaningless fights throughout the 1920s to scrape up much needed cash, he eventually retired from the ring in 1931. He died, rather as he had lived, by crashing a fast car on his way to attend the second world heavyweight contest between his first black successor Joe Louis and Billy Conn on 19 June 1946. (Only when Louis knocked out James J. Braddock in eight rounds in Chicago on 22 June 1937, did the white monopoly on world heavyweight fights post-Johnson end. With Joe Louis and his successors, the championship became rather a black monopoly with the exception of the Rocky Marciano reign from 1952–55. The black monopoly was one of merit, not discrimination. The white monopoly on British titles went on rather longer.)

Johnson's life in and out of the ring epitomises the ugly nature of race relations in the USA. He had sometimes (i.e. when it suited his present purpose) contrasted his treatment in the USA unfavourably with his treatment in London. All was not necessarily sweetness and light between black and white in the communities around the many boxing halls of post-war Britain. For example, in the heart of London's East End, and adjacent to many boxing venues, there was an ugly riot stimulated by racial intolerance at the end of May 1919 and a court case in which Johnson's name was evoked.

A Limehouse lodging house, where up to 100 sailors of mainly Jamaican origin lived, was attacked by an angry mob of local whites. John Martin, one of the Jamaicans, was put on trial for shooting and wounding one of the mob. Various witnesses at the trial outlined the context:

If there was one thing more than another that white seamen resented it was black sailors associating with white women …

A police-inspector said … The trouble started through black men speaking to white girls. The whites wanted to clear the blacks out of Limehouse.

In summing up the Common Sergeant pointed out that there was no evidence that the defendant went about with white girls.

On the basis of flimsy evidence, and what might be called an anti-Jack-Johnson defence, the unfortunate Martin was found not guilty and discharged.[54]

The year 1919 was an extraordinary one for boxing, and for the heavyweight division at home and abroad in particular, yet the spring and summer delivered memorable encounters at lighter weights. Jimmy Wilde featured in two of them. The first was in the theatre of the NSC on 31 March 1919.[55] It featured Wilde and Joe Lynch, the American who had beaten Tommy Noble at Blackfriars in February. The Wilde–Lynch match was given an additional significance in boxing history as the subject of the regularly reproduced oil painting by W. Howard Robinson.

Truthfully, Robinson was not much of a painter and the figures in the ring

A painting by William Howard Robinson (1864–c.1940): A Welsh Victory at the National Sporting Club 31 March 1919. *Jimmy Wilde beats Joe Lynch (USA) on points. The Prince of Wales (later King Edward VIII) shakes hands with Wilde. Others in the ring are (l to r) Arthur Gutteridge; Jim Driscoll; Eddie McGoorty; Lynch; A. T. Bettinson; Don Williams (crouching); Lord Lonsdale.*

look more like Madame Tussaud's waxworks than human beings. Nevertheless, the canvas records for later generations a significant occasion when Edward, Prince of Wales (the future King Edward VIII), his head at the oddest of angles, shakes hands with the diminutive Wilde, attended by his seconds (including Jim Driscoll) and watched by Lynch (attended by his seconds including Eddie McGoorty). The two dignitaries in tailcoats and gleaming white dress-fronts are Peggy Bettinson and Lord Lonsdale. The audience comprises a virtual gallery of boxing celebrities.

That Lonsdale is rendered on a giant scale owes more to the artist's insecurity with perspective than to the device of medieval painters of relating size of figure to theological importance. One hopes so as the tiny spectator in military uniform, barely glimpsed between Bettinson and Lonsdale, is Prince Albert (the modest and retiring brother who became King George VI after his brother Edward's notorious abdication in 1936). Framed by the plush stage curtains and the ornamental railings of the balconies, a selection of po-faced celebrities stand like a paralysed male voice choir.

For all its imperfections, the painting commemorates, in permanent form, how the sport and the NSC had achieved public acceptance. Less than two decades before, both had been on trial in the Central Criminal Court and their existence threatened. NSC proceedings could now be graced with the presence of two future kings of England, one of them personally congratulating a fighter in the ring.

The fight was more animated than the painting. The meeting was stimulated by the three-round bout won by Wilde over Lynch at the Royal Albert Hall tournament in late 1918. When Lynch had later beaten Noble in February 1919, Noble had been positively secretive, preferring to pay a £25 forfeit rather than disclose his actual weight. Perhaps Lynch had learned the advantages of mystery, as it is difficult to know what Wilde and Lynch weighed at the NSC in their rematch – 8st 6lb/118lbs had been the limit agreed.

Observations by experienced journalists suggest substantial differences between the two men. Wilde conceded reach, height (possibly six inches) and weight (possibly 14–18 pounds). At a midday weigh-in Lynch was 8st 4½lb/116½lbs. Wilde was so comfortably within 7st 4lb/102lbs that he had not stripped fully.

Importantly, this was an older, slower Wilde whom the war years had not enhanced. He was slower and marginally less damaging a puncher than he had been. When he doffed his grey dressing gown (and Lynch a US Army greatcoat), Wilde's swarthy frame looked frail beside the whiter-skinned American. He was soon enfolded within his opponent's clinches like a slim pinky-brown frankfurter enclosed in a large white bun. Lynch eagerly clinched, leaned on Wilde and thumped away at Wilde's kidneys with one glove, while clutching with the other arm. Referee J. H. Douglas reprimanded these offences but spoke too sharply and unfairly to Lynch when a round-arm swing connected with Wilde's soft kidney region. Wilde had unwisely turned his torso towards his opponent.

Wilde's characteristic stance, one glove down along his thigh, seemingly invited punches to his unguarded chin, punches he avoided economically with those short, evasive movements of upper body and neck. Lynch held his gloves higher, if unorthodoxly wide, content to back-pedal and await an opening, while ducking, sometimes to knee level. He liked to end a passage of fisticuffs with crisp, heavy counters, or otherwise smother. The variable approaches made for a lively encounter, but one difficult accurately to score.

The men's long-term strategies were also at odds. Wilde planned to attack as long as stamina allowed, accumulating points for lighter punches landed, where once he looked to knock men out early. Lynch was content to wait and see. He weakened the impact of an opponent's punches by riding with them. Then he looked to use superior weight and power to take over in the later rounds.

For nine rounds the Wilde strategy worked well. He racked up points, although Lynch landed punches to head and body that would have left a younger Wilde untouched. Only Douglas could know what penalties Lynch's holding cost him in points earlier on. The tide turned in the tenth when Wilde's punches were weaker and more circumspect. Three successive rights to the jaw from Lynch brought Wilde's left glove up to the side of his face to prevent a repetition.

In the 11th, Wilde found his left leads mere stimuli for two-handed assaults from an eager Lynch. Wilde had lost none of his old guile and suggested throughout the 12th that he had plenty of stamina in hand and could still outmuscle the American. Lynch was not convinced. He absorbed Wilde's opening flurry in the 13th easily and repaid it with interest. Now Wilde was definitely on the retreat and used every last bit of ringcraft to survive.

Qualities that separate the great from the good showed in Wilde's rally in the 14th. A surprised Lynch began the round as aggressively as he had finished the 13th. Wilde, looking like a master but one operating from a scarcely remembered pre-war boxing manual, rallied to stop Lynch mid-flow. He forced Lynch back, swinging to head and body. When Lynch ducked low, he waited patiently and clipped him with a sharp uppercut as Lynch came up. This was the old Wilde revived.

Lynch, no shrinking violet, weathered the Wilde rally and reasserted himself. Wilde had to back off, block, swerve and duck to stay on his feet. It was a tired and weakened Wilde who came out for the 15th and last round. Unlike Driscoll, Wilde had insisted on a non-championship 15 rounds, even though the NSC manager Bettinson cheekily billed the fight as one for the 'World Bantamweight Championship'.

Lynch sensed that he must knock Wilde out to win. Wilde sensed that if he survived the last three minutes, the verdict, after his early lead, would be his. With Wilde clinching and smothering to keep out of trouble, these were three desperately exciting minutes as Lynch went all out to stop him.

He hooked Wilde twice with his left. He sent Wilde staggering sideways with a right cross. He landed a lethal right hook to Wilde's left cheekbone. The ferocious punches landed millimetres away from the point of maximum effect. Wilde collapsed but only after the bell and only on to the stool Driscoll slipped under his buttocks. It was on his stool, drained and in a pool of sweat, that Wilde was personally congratulated by the Prince of Wales, who grasped his gloved hand as it hung down helplessly by his side. (The standing pose in the painting is pure artistic licence.) Many members believed Lynch had done enough to win but appearances can lie. It is easy to see the fresher of two men as the victor but Wilde had triumphed over another much stronger, heavier and younger opponent.

Wilde was back in action on 16 May 1919 at Cochran's Holborn Stadium over 20 rounds against Alf Mansfield.[56] Few expected Mansfield, much bigger than Wilde at 8st 4lb/116lbs, to win, despite his record as a tough scrapper who never went easily. There were vacant ringside seats, unlike the cheap seats and standing areas, which were packed with eager Cockneys and Welsh exiles.

Wilde hit precisely and hurtfully, mostly deflecting and marginalising Mansfield's leads and counters. Often Mansfield put in a whirl of punches to drive Wilde to the ropes. Wilde broke off and retreated. Mansfield left out his gum shield to convey his lack of fear of Wilde's punching power. He regretted its absence soon enough.

Mansfield took many hard punches in the sixth and was tiring by the ninth. Yet he still refused to be intimidated by Wilde's growing belligerence. He succumbed finally in the 13th. Wilde caught him early with a right to the chin that felled him. He waited on one knee for nine before getting up. Wilde caught him again with the right and again he waited for nine before getting up. Wilde repeated the punch for Mansfield to go over on his back, still showing every intention to resume.

He was pre-empted by his corner, who threw in a towel. Mansfield deserved every decibel of the applause he was given. In this May contest with Wilde he had shown skill, heart and obstinacy quite out of the ordinary.

Wilde's fellow Welshman, the smiling welterweight Johnny Basham, was back on 16 June 1919 at the NSC against the man who had held the welterweight championship of the USA, Augie Ratner.[57] The match was made at 11st/154lbs, with a £1,200 purse at stake, although Ratner came into the ring with a seven-pound advantage over Basham. (He ended his career in 1926 as a middleweight.) Ratner, the Jewish New Yorker born on the Lower East Side on 20 May 1894, had a power advantage, but in charisma and warmth of personality he matched Basham fully. Ratner and his blonde Bronx partner provided plenty of copy for journalists at their hotel and training camp as they lived up to the clichéd image of Americans abroad with some dedication.

His vivacious companion became Mrs Ratner during the trip. They held a lavish wedding reception at the Berkeley Hotel. Having laid out handsomely for food and champagne, Augie refused to invest more of his hard-earned ring earnings in a full morning dress outfit for either ceremony or reception. When he tipsily escorted his bride on to the dance floor for the first waltz, a few overzealous hotel attendants escorted them off again as improperly dressed. Understandably, the new Mrs Ratner, fluent in Brooklynese, loudly invited the staff to perform an anatomically impossible manoeuvre, and Augie was only just restrained from demonstrating his punching power on the spot.

In the NSC ring more dignity prevailed. Ratner crouched slightly, hands held high, eager to land vicious right and left swings over the top of Basham's more perfunctory guard. Basham was a true pupil of the school of Driscoll with an upright stance, a classic left jab and excellent speed. Yet where Basham could usually rely on his leads to outpoint lesser opponents, Ratner had a sound defence and was adept at taking punches on his gloves and forearms, or of melting away backwards or sideways to leave a rash opponent hitting the air and open to his counters.

Ratner was the harder puncher, but it was Basham who landed more despite Ratner's defensive skills. Basham refused to fade under Ratner's power, yet he was visibly shaken by a right cross in the third, and twice in the tenth by heavy Ratner punches. His own punches did not bother Ratner unduly, but gave Basham the edge on points.

Basham performed strongly over the last third, leaving Ratner apparently needing a knockout. In the 20th, Ratner went all out desperately. He and his corner believed he was too far behind to win any other way. He failed, so it was a surprise when the referee pronounced the fight an honourable draw. Both men took the decision as sportingly as they performed over the hour of action.

Two weeks later, two tough bantamweights contested a championship title and a Lonsdale Belt at the NSC on 30 June 1919 with a £450 purse on offer (strikingly less than for Basham/Ratner).[58] They were Walter Ross of Glasgow and the Bermondsey favourite Tommy Noble. Noble's ugly performance against Criqui at Holborn

had won him £500 but devalued him in the eyes of those who saw it. His fouls were not the niceties of ringcraft appreciated at the club. Any repetition would be greeted by protests from the more knowledgeable and observant members.

He was meeting Ross on a Monday night, having met Criqui again over 20 gruelling rounds in Paris the previous Friday (result, a draw) – pugilistic productivity or managerial exploitation unthinkable in more recent times. Noble was hardly at his sharpest three days later. The Glaswegian had no sympathy. Noble was taller and had a reach advantage. He could not keep the stronger Ross away over a full 20 rounds.

So long as the fight was at a distance, Noble scored valuable points. Ross still rushed Noble back to the ropes and pummelled him with short hooks, close-quarter jabs and uppercuts. Noble's defensive skills diverted many of these, but not all. He took body blows and grabbed and held to avoid others. This brought noisy displeasure and repeated reprimands from the referee.

Occasionally, Noble fought back off the ropes and threw his own hooks and uppercuts. Ross usually avoided them. Remorselessly, Ross wore Noble down, round by round. During the tenth Noble's corner retired him. The belt and the purse went back to Scotland and Ross was given a warm send-off by the members.

Though skilful boxers such as Wilde, Basham and Ross had countless admirers, there is no doubt that the 'Iron Law of Boxing' (that mass avoirdupois equals big box office takings) prevailed in 1919 as in other times. The public appeared in abundance when two big men knocked each other about. Wild excitement prevailed even if the affair lasted a matter of minutes. Heavyweight boxing resumed in Britain on 26 May 1919, with that 'official' contrived NSC match for the British heavyweight championship, a Lonsdale Belt and a purse of £1,200 between Jack Curphey and Frank Goddard.[59]

As we saw, Goddard was matched with Joe Beckett for a June date at Olympia under Cochran's auspices, a prospect thoroughly enhanced by Beckett's victory over the reigning champion Billy Wells. A Curphey victory at the NSC would devalue the Olympia event, a result the NSC would view with equanimity. The risk, for the NSC, was a Goddard victory, which would further enhance Cochran's promotion. Goddard was a 4/1 favourite to beat Curphey.

For the privileged members this was the most significant night since the pre-war fights of 1914. The boxing theatre was filled to the brim. A generous purse by the club's standards had attracted two big men to fight. Two young heavyweights were making their club debuts, appropriately for maximum post-war euphoria, two ex-guardsmen. Goddard served in the Royal Horse Guards, Curphey in the Grenadier Guards.

His regiment taught Goddard how to stand tall on parade, how to ride and how to march meticulously. Unfortunately, it did not teach him how to box. In the ring he was an overgrown schoolboy with only vague ideas of how to stop anyone hitting him. This, a serious disadvantage for a professional boxer, was compensated for by a chin as hard as a guardsman's metal breastplate. He could take a punch to the face without blinking; and had a punch of his own of percussive force. He never learned how to punch correctly (which probably spared him a future manslaughter charge). He never learned a methodical defence. Had he learned both he might have been a world champion.

Goddard was, short term, eager to learn, yet not a quick study. Long term, his concentration wandered to his real interests – his assorted canaries, rabbits, ponies and dogs. They occupied his attention to the exclusion of opponents. He turned up to training with an ugly and aggressive bull terrier on a leash. Many thought the large-jawed, flat-nosed, furrow-browed Goddard and his pet looked remarkably alike and shared similar IQs.[60]

Fifty-five years before Muhammad Ali's 'rope-a-dope' tactic against George Foreman in Zaire in 1974, Goddard believed he could beat the more skilful Curphey by having Curphey hit him until he tired. Then he could hit Curphey hard enough to stop him. It was not a plan in which many would have put their faith, but Goddard, unburdened by doubt, had supreme confidence in it.

In the first round, Goddard ponderously offered some left leads. Curphey countered with a right and a left to the jaw that were loudly applauded by the audience but shrugged off nonchalantly by Goddard. Curphey repeated the treatment in the second, so effectively that even the placid Goddard had the grace to stagger before the bell rescued him. In three minutes Curphey landed fully a dozen rights to Goddard's freely available chin.

In the third, Goddard responded to the frantic pleading of his corner and deigned to clinch and cover up as he regained some of his senses. In the fourth and fifth, he landed short arm punches himself, although Curphey continued to land as Goddard bustled in. Goddard's remarkable strength told as the fight continued. Curphey's ribs reddened, and his nose, recipient of a cruel uppercut, bled. Curphey rallied in the eighth but with a distracted air about him – the despair of a man who had far outpunched his opponent statistically but conspicuously failed to stop him.

Physically and mentally weakened by the ninth, Curphey wilted. Even the generally unaware Goddard recognised this and put him down for two counts of eight and delivered a follow-up left that felled him for another seven. Curphey survived, but no matter how frantically his seconds tried to revive him, the end was near. Goddard's next attack felled him again in the tenth. Ted Broadribb his second pre-empted the referee by frantically waving a towel from the ring apron. The referee obliged and stopped the bout in Goddard's favour.

Goddard's British title now came with the NSC imprimatur and a Lonsdale Belt. The trappings were scorned by Joe Beckett and C. B. Cochran. They were still ecstatic at how the Goddard win at the club had further enhanced the Beckett/Goddard Olympia date – 17 June 1919.[61] Goddard's win had not changed the general view that Beckett was the real champion – and now he could confirm it.

There were plenty of rival attractions in June 1919. José Collins was packing them in at Daly's to see her in *The Maid of the Mountains*. *Chu Chin Chow* ran and ran at His Majesty's

Theatre. The Diaghilev ballet was back in town offering Tamara Karsavina and Leonide Massine at the Alhambra. Yet the hottest ticket that June night was for Beckett v Goddard.

The hot and hard-pressed Olympia audience, patiently waiting for 9pm and the entry of the two gladiators, was a spectacle itself. Lounge suits for gentlemen and evening dresses for ladies were de rigueur, and dinner jackets and gowns in the ringside section. The pattern was varied kaleidoscopically with the browns and blues of the uniforms of the serving armed forces, including a special enclosure for war-wounded. Further sartorial highlights came from the decorative hats, toppers, summer dresses and formal attire worn by the jolly parties coming straight to the arena from the Ascot racecourse.

As celebrities taking their seats were recognised, they were cheered accordingly. This was true for those from the sporting sphere such as Carpentier and Descamps; for royalty such as the young princes; for war heroes such as Admiral (later Earl) Beatty, commander of the British battlecruisers at the Battle of Jutland; for the war wounded in their wheelchairs; and for newsworthy celebrities such as the intrepid English airmen Alcock and Brown, who had made the first flight across the Atlantic from Newfoundland to Ireland three days before and had been feted in London all day. In retrospect, such preliminary pleasures were particularly welcome as the fistic action lasted less than five and a half minutes.

At the first bell, Goddard walked out naively holding out both gloves to 'touch gloves', a gesture already performed under the referee's auspices. Beckett, who would have been entirely within the rules had he punched Goddard, hesitated, then responded in kind. Goddard swung wild punches mingled with more effective chops and hooks, eager to close in on Beckett and bear down on him from his four-inch height advantage. Beckett had prepared carefully with a wide selection of tall sparring partners and operated a skilful defence. He took most of Goddard's blows on his gloves and forearms, and punished Goddard's openness with left hooks to cheek, jaw and temple. Some of Goddard's punches got through, including a smart right that made Beckett's nose bleed. Goddard and he both bled from the mouth early on.

For Beckett, pain was gain. He used Goddard's first-round flurries to calculate what he had to offer. Apart from brute strength and hard clumsy hitting, this did not amount to much. In the second round, he rushed Goddard to the ropes, both men punching in close. Before they parted, he exploited Goddard's vulnerability to lefts over the top of a lowered guard after Goddard had thrown a right. One left hook caught Goddard on the point of the jaw and sent him down for almost a full count. He was up at about nine but had not recovered. With lowered arms, he was the easiest target. Beckett coolly paused and closed the gap between his glove and Goddard's exposed jaw with a fiery right that dropped Goddard to the canvas and out to the world.

The vast crowd, appreciative of the action, however brief, cheered Beckett's victory noisily. They continued as Beckett was presented with a commemorative gold cup and a sparkling belt was placed around his waist. (Cochran as showman could out-Lonsdale Lonsdale and the NSC when he felt so inclined.) To get the event on, he had been forced to pay Goddard £2,000 and Beckett £2,500. He still made a decent profit from a gate of £8,001 7s., with film and programme rights on top.[62] He could anticipate even greater returns from further heavyweight follies yet to be arranged.

Meanwhile, on the other side of the Atlantic, the hunger for a genuine world heavyweight championship fight on American soil, built up over four long and eventful years ever since Jess Willard's unexpected win over Jack Johnson in April 1915, was about to be satisfied. The date was 4 July 1919. The place was Toledo, Ohio. The protagonists were the long idle champion Willard and a new young contender named Jack Dempsey. Together they ensured the date and the place would be permanently enshrined in boxing history.

Endnotes:

1 Ferguson, N., *The Pity of War* (Harmondsworth: Allen Lane, the Penguin Press, 1998) Chapter 10.

2 This and other points are made in Graves, R. & Hodge, A., *The Long Weekend: A Social History of Great Britain 1918–1939* (Readers Union, 1941 edition) p. 36.

3 Harding, J., *Lonsdale's Belt: Boxing's Most Coveted Prize* (Worthing: Pitch Publishing, 2016) p.108.

4 *The Times,* 11 December 1918.

5 *The Times,* 14 December 1918.

6 *The Times,* 6 January 1919.

7 Details of the 'prize-fight' reported in *The Times,* 16 June 1919.

8 Extracts from 'Boxing. Old and New Methods' in *The Times,* 8 February 1919.

9 'The Popularity of Boxing' by E.B. Osborn in *Illustrated London News,* 27 March 1919, p. 440.

10 *Illustrated London News,* 6 December 1919. The match, as we shall see, was between Georges Carpentier and Joe Beckett.

11 *The Times,* 22 April 1919.

12 *Punch,* 1 January 1919, p. 10.

13 *The Times,* revival article, 22 April 1919.

14 Mander, R. & Mitchenson, J., *The Lost Theatres of London* (London: Hart-Davis, 1968) pp. 144–167.

15 *Mirror of Life,* 22 February 1919.

16 Details drawn from *Boxing,* 19 March and 9 April 1919.

17 *Boxing,* 9 April 1919.

18 Harding, J., *Lonsdale's Belt,* p. 75.

19 Deghy G., *Noble and Manly: The History of the National Sporting Club* (Hutchinson, 1956) p. 195.

20 *The Times,* 31 January 1919.

21 *The Times,* 28 January 1919.

22 *The Times,* 6 January 1919.

23 *The Times,* 18 March 1919; *Boxing,* 19 March 1919; Roderick, A., *Johnny! The Story of the Happy Warrior* (Newport: Heron Press, 1990) pp. 69–74.

24 *The Times,* 15 April 1919.

25 *The Times,* 20 May 1919.

26 *The Times,* 4 February 1919; *Mirror of Life,* 8 February 1919.

27 *Mirror of Life,* 15 February 1919.

28 Reports in *The Times,* 25 February 1919; *Mirror of Life,* 1 March 1919; *Boxing,* 26 February 1919.

29 *Boxing,* 2 July 1919.

30 Shipley, S., *Bombardier Billy Wells: The Life and Trials of a Boxing Hero* (Tyne and Wear: Bewick Press, 1993) p. 150.

31 Cochran, C. B., *Secrets of a Showman* (London: Heinemann) p. 286.

32 Cochran, C. B., *Secrets of a Showman,* p. 287.

33 Corri, E., *Fifty Years in the Ring* (London: Hutchinson, 1933) p. 37.

34 Shipley, S., *Bombardier Billy Wells,* p. 150.

35 Details of the fight gleaned from *Boxing,* 5 March 1919; *The Times,* 28 February 1919; and Chapter IX 'Joe Beckett and Bombardier Wells' in Lynch, B., *Knuckles and Gloves* (London: Collins, 1922) pp. 170–175.

36 *Mirror of Life and Boxing World,* 22 February 1919.

37 Deyong, M., *Everybody Boo!* (London: Stanley Paul, 1951) p. 13 and pp. 41–42.

38 *Boxing,* 4 June 1919.

39 *The Times,* 11 March 1919; *Mirror of Life and Boxing World,* 22 March 1919.

40 Deghy G., *Noble and Manly,* p. 119.

41 *The Times,* 8 July 1919.

42 Heller, P., *Tyson: In and Out of the Ring* (London: Robson Books, 1996) pp. 314–315.

43 Reports in *The Times,* 2 June 1919; *Boxing,* 4 June 1919.

44 Fight reports in *The Times,* 21 October 1919 and *Mirror of Life,* 25 October 1919. There is film of the fight in the National Film Archive but only of rounds one to seven.

45 *Boxing,* 16 April 1919.

46 'Bermondsey's World Champ' by Gilbert Odd in *Boxing News,* 8 April 1977.

47 Deghy G., *Noble and Manly,* p. 187.

48 Deghy G., *Noble and Manly,* p. 187.

49 Bennison, B., *Giants on Parade: Some Sporting Reminiscences* (London: Rich & Cowan, 1936) p. 35.

50 *The Times,* 2 August 1919.

51 Bennison, B., *Giants on Parade,* pp. 37–38.

52 Roberts, R., P*apa Jack: Jack Johnson and the Era of White Hopes* (New York: Simon & Schuster, 1985) pp. 210–211; Ward, G., *Unforgivable Blackness: The Rise and Fall of Jack Johnson* (New York: Knopf, 2004) pp. 395–398.

53 Quoted in Roberts, R., *Papa Jack,* p. 212.

54 *The Times,* 1 July 1919.

55 Reports in *The Times,* 1 April 1919; *Boxing,* 2 April 1919; *Mirror of Life and Boxing World,* 5 April and 12 April 1919.

56 *Boxing,* 21 May 1919; Lynch, B., *Knuckles and Gloves,* pp. 199–200.

57 *The Times,* 17 June 1919; Roderick , A., *Johnny!* p. 74.

58 *The Times,* 1 July 1919.

59 *The Times,* 27 May 1919; *Mirror of Life and Boxing World,* 31 May 1919.

60 'The Real Frank Goddard' by Harry Reeve in *Boxing,* 4 June 1919.

61 *The Times,* 18 June 1919; *Boxing,* 18 June 1919; *Mirror of Life and Boxing World,* 21 June 1919; Corri, E., *Fifty Years in the Ring,* pp. 214–215.

62 Cochran, C. B., *Secrets of a Showman,* pp. 294–295.

CHAPTER 14

TORTURE IN TOLEDO
1919 (PART TWO)

In Which a New American Hero Comes Out of the West

JACK DEMPSEY (b. 24 June 1895, d. 31 May 1983) became one of the most iconic figures in American sport. The New York restaurant he ran on Broadway until 1974 was a place of pilgrimage for boxing fans from all over the world. They came to wonder at the dapper and avuncular man, handsome and sexy in a rugged way, with a smile and a word for friend and stranger alike; a gracious host to the end of his squat fingertips. His very presence exuded kindness and bonhomie. When he died there was an outpouring of national grief as Americans from coast to coast mourned the loss of a hero and the symbolic passing of a fondly recalled sporting era. Included on a bronze memorial plaque on his gravestone was an appropriate tribute – 'a gentleman and a gentle man'. Nearly a century on from some of his greatest fights, this is how the man is still regarded. In Patrick Myler's words, 'one of the world's most instantly recognised and best-loved personalities'.[1]

Somehow, this man was the same Dempsey who came storming out of western obscurity, and out of his Toledo corner, to attack Willard with a remorselessly cruel ruthlessness that made Harry Greb look like a pacifist. The young and the old Dempseys shared a birth certificate, but little else. The metamorphosis of the pitiless and savage young fighter into warm genial celebrity is an enigma. The integrity of the older Dempsey is not in question yet we cannot fully comprehend the explosive impact of young Dempsey upon his sport and his nation if we allow the image of the mellow 87-year-old to blind us to the uncouth reality of the youth.

As an example of the cliché that fighters have to be hungry to reach the top, Dempsey will do very well. He was hungry. He was angry. Life gave young Dempsey ample reasons to be both hungry and angry.[2]

He was born in Manassa, source of his crass nickname 'The Manassa Mauler', chosen originally by Damon Runyon for alliteration not accuracy. (Dempsey might batter you to the floor but anything so cuddly as a maul would be unlikely. A modern tabloid would prefer 'The Manassassin' or 'The Manassa Assassin'.)

Manassa was an early settlement in the San Luis Valley of Colorado, still a frontier state in the 1890s, offering frontier hardships and frontier morals. It was an environment in which only fighters survived. Dempsey's mother Celia was both fighter and survivor, undergoing 11 births without the advantages of modern obstetrics, suffering the deaths of two children in infancy and three in adulthood before her own. Two sons died in violent circumstances. Bruce was stabbed to death while selling newspapers on the street (with rivals jostling for a favourite pitch, newspaper selling was originally a hazardous undertaking). Johnny, long a drug addict, ended his unsatisfactory life by shooting his wife and then himself. According to her most famous son, Celia was small and wiry but prepared to get physical herself should circumstances require it:

Finding that my mother had a silver dollar, she [a gypsy fortune teller] borrowed it to put under her tongue 'to help the spell'. Before the spell could be helped, the silver dollar disappeared. My mother, nobody's fool, demanded her coin back. The gypsy didn't move, so my furious little mother put her hands around the gypsy's throat and threatened to choke her either standing up or upside down, unless the money was returned. It was – fast![3]

Unlike her son, Celia did not mellow, even on her deathbed in her late eighties:

She was a true fact-facer, my mother, and her answer [to a polite enquiry about her feelings] summed up her life-long philosophy. 'Dr. Pendleton,' she replied, 'you know very well I'm dying. If you ask me how I feel again I'll get out of this bed and punch you in the nose.'[4]

Celia's ninth child was christened William Harrison Dempsey. Only later did he adopt 'Jack' as a ring name to evoke the pioneer days of American boxing and the successes of the veteran Irish-American middleweight Jack Dempsey (world middleweight champion 1884–91). The new 'Jack Dempsey' took the name second-hand

Jack Dempsey (1895–1983), the benign Broadway restaurateur in 1953 (with his third wife Deanna) bore little resemblance to the savage world heavyweight champion of 1919.
BoxRec

(actually third – or fourth-hand as two of his brothers fought professionally under the pseudonym). He was the one to bring it universal recognition.

The gritty determination of mother and son was not a quality shared by husband and father Hyrum Dempsey, who spent or drank away any money the family got (precious little). Hyrum combined fecklessness with wildly optimistic ambitions that he never had the application to fulfil. He was a father to his brood in only a genetic sense, and as a result of his wanderlust, the family left Virginia and travelled from place to rudimentary place all over Utah and Colorado, finding out as they went the difference between the dream of the riches the west supposedly had to offer and the grim realities of the frontier jungle.

Hyrum was attracted initially by the stirring words of a Mormon missionary preaching the wonders of Salt Lake City to the youth of Virginia. Both he and Celia became Mormon converts, although predictably she stuck to the faith in coming years and he found its tenets too rigorous to accommodate his fondness for drink and infidelity.

To understand the young 'Jack' Dempsey is to empathise with the daily difficulties and humiliations suffered by a boy made to grow up too soon. When the head of the family fails or deserts like Hyrum, the children become breadwinners and scavengers for the basics of existence. Normal childish pursuits and education are sacrificed. Later, Dempsey used part of his unprecedentedly large purses to subsidise his relatives, even the feckless ones – a generosity begun even while his returns from boxing were miserably small.

He worked at least part-time in menial jobs from the age of eight, boxing like his brothers from the age of ten, and striking out, uneducated, unsophisticated, vulnerable and alone, to make his way in the world at 16. Even as a boy he was snubbed and humiliated by the fall-out from the family's poverty. Most accounts of his life include the distressing and frightening episode when a zealous ticket collector threatened to dump him off a train in the middle of nowhere, because his mother lacked the pitifully few coins necessary for his half-fare.

When you have humped beetroots, shined shoes, mined coal and waited on table, all before you begin to shave, it might be thought that there was not much left to find out about life at the bottom. Far from it – Dempsey's years from 16 to 19 were even grimmer.

Not for him even the discomfort of inferior class travel by stagecoach or train. To get to another state where employment was rumoured to be easier or opportunities to box might exist, he travelled by train alright, but only by clinging on to the undercarriage centimetres from the track speeding dangerously beneath him. This suicidally perilous venture, where to doze was death, could only be escaped by climbing on to the roof or into a freight car when the train halted.

That brought fresh jeopardy in human form from two directions. Firstly, the railroad guards, sometimes armed and always carrying wooden cudgels or truncheons, and on board under orders to clear the train of low-life characters like Dempsey. Secondly, there were fellow freeloaders who saw a young addition to their ranks less in terms of comradely feeling than as a target for violence, robbery or sexual assault. At 16 years old, physically attractive and with a curious high-pitched voice about which he remained embarrassed for the rest of his life, no wonder Dempsey learned to fight.

Apart from life- and virtue-defending brawls, fighting was an activity where the teenager could pick up the odd dollar. Not surely on a promoter's bill in custom-built boxing rings with a referee, but rather in bare-knuckle punch-ups, speedily improvised among the sawdust and spittoons of smoky barrooms and saloons. In cahoots with the barman, the teenage Dempsey would fight any local drinker who fancied his chances against the young stranger with the funny voice. A purse fund was collected, bets were struck and the fight begun. In this context, Queensberry Rules were as remote to the combat as hygiene regulations to the saloon. Win, by any means, fair or foul, and you ate. Lose, and you crawled off to lick your wounds and starved until the next time. All that his brothers had taught him when he was only 12 – how to pickle your skin with brine or bull's urine to toughen your face and your fists; how to chew on pine resin to strengthen the jawbone; how to get the other feller before he assuredly got you – these were life skills not to be gleaned in the writings of Joseph Smith the Mormon prophet or practised by the Angel Moroni.

Gradually, Dempsey's pugilistic career moved out of the bars and into slightly more conventional contests. His new ring name was Kid Blackie, a reflection of his raven hair, swarthy complexion and his youth. He was now 19, the year 1914. Over the next few years there would be recorded

fights and unrecorded fights all over Colorado, Nevada and Utah, many still obscure and even the more prominent known only because of the devoted researches of Toby Smith, author of *Kid Blackie: Jack Dempsey's Colorado Days* (Wayfarer Press, 1987), which retraced Kid Blackie's encounters as well as modern circumstances permitted.

For Dempsey, the learning process continued, especially into what that most lurid of modern promoters, Don King, called 'trickeration'; that is, anything you can get away with. Do unto others what they will do unto you given half a chance. Kid Blackie was well versed in sharp practice in the ring in the hardest school. He rarely complained if an opponent reciprocated in kind. That was to be expected.

Some opponents recur during this period. There was the heavier and stronger heavyweight, Johnny Sudenberg, with whom he shared two ten-round draws (31 May 1915 in Goldfield, Nevada; 13 June 1915 in Tonopah, Nevada), quite possibly split by pre-arrangement to boost interest in their third meeting, which took place on 1 February 1916 at Ely, Nevada. Dempsey walked 50 miles across the scorching Nevada desert to get to one of the draws. In the decider, lacking so arduous a ring walk, Dempsey knocked out Sudenberg in the second.

Trickeration was involved in a fight with George Copelin, whom Kid Blackie knocked out in the seventh round in Cripple Creek, Colorado on 19 November 1915 after hearty exchanges. The knockout was genuine enough but Kid Blackie was appearing as his own brother Bernie aka 'Jack Dempsey'. This was a typical ploy in the unregulated match-ups of the day

when ringers and fixes were common. The swap was unsubtle, as his brother was 20 years older than he. Dempsey thereafter stuck to being the new Jack Dempsey and made the name genuinely his own. The morality of the deception was less impressive.

There was also suspicion about Dempsey's first fight with Fireman Jim Flynn in Murray, Utah on 13 February 1917. Flynn caught Dempsey with a punch in the first ten seconds of round one and Dempsey stayed down for about 30 seconds, a result that surprised Flynn and the bookmakers equally. Rumour, and some later accounts, have it that Dempsey had more need of undercover readies than a modest purse and another step up the ladder to the heavyweight title. He took the loss and the cash.

He denied it thereafter, but a fix is not inherently unlikely given the prevailing moral climate. A much-syndicated sportswriter of the 1930s, Joe Williams, named the reward as a much-needed $300, and although Williams's column was published in Dempsey's time of greater affluence, Dempsey declined to sue or force a retraction.

By the end of 1918, Dempsey's ring record was genuinely impressive, full of legitimate gold-plated wins. During 1918, he had 21 fights, losing only one (to Willie Meehan in San Francisco on 13 September over four rounds; 'I got careless') and having two no-decision bouts against Billy Miske over ten rounds (3 May in Minnesota) and six rounds (28 November in Philadelphia). Most were knockout victories over fighters of some note, many in the first round when their demise followed very quickly upon Dempsey charging with controlled fury out of his corner. Down went Fireman Jim Flynn on 14 February, Fort Sheridan, Illinois; Arthur Pelkey on 29 May, Denver, Colorado; Dan 'Porky' Flynn on 6 July, Atlanta, Georgia; and Carl Morris on 16 December, New Orleans, Louisiana. No Dempsey Christmas charity was extended either to Gunboat Smith in Buffalo, New York on 30 December, knocking him out in the second round. (Note too that Fireman Flynn, who had supposedly knocked him out cold in 1917, could not live with him a year later.)

Early on, Dempsey suffered promoters and managers dedicated only to exploiting him. First came Hardy Downer and Buck Weaver, part-time promoters offering occasional possibilities for a bill-filling fight, and even a fellow boxer Andy Malloy, who twice shared a Colorado ring with him (7 October 1915 in a no-decision bout at Durango, and knocked out by Dempsey in the third at Montrose, 23 October 1915). Molloy offered to find other opponents but soon lost interest. By 1916, Dempsey was on the books of a Jack Price, based in Salt Lake City.

Price took him on an abortive trip to New York City to extend Dempsey's name to the East Coast, to find him better opponents and to make the acquaintance of boxing journalists powerful enough to make or break a fighter. (Money conventionally changed hands to obtain such 'endorsements'.) The trip was minimally successful by bringing him to the attention of the young Nat Fleischer and the flourishing Damon Runyon and getting him more opponents. More disastrously, Price, naïve rather than dishonest, was deceived into relinquishing Dempsey's contract to the notorious John 'The Barber' Reisler, a man who could shave a boxer's earnings and trim his contract as ruthlessly as his nickname suggests. Under Reisler's auspices, Dempsey was matched with the tough and experienced John Lester Johnson (14 July 1916). The newspaper decision ten-rounder went against him and the fight cost him three broken ribs. Just as painfully, his loser's earnings were lost to Reisler's purse-shearing accountancy.

Unsurprisingly, Dempsey decided to escape the harshness of the city and the ruthless clutches of Reisler by clinging, broken ribs notwithstanding, to the undercarriages of freight trains going west until he was back in Salt Lake City. (Reisler was not to be so easily evaded and was a sinister and litigious presence in Dempsey's career for years to come.)

Dempsey, declaring himself manager-free, accepted an approach from Fred 'Windy' Windsor, a minor promoter with Californian connections. As the Californian statutes restricted prizefights to four-round no-decision bouts, Dempsey throughout 1917 rushed out from the first bell and knocked an opponent out early or at least impressed the newspaper decision-makers as the likely winner. A canny operator who could keep him at bay had a good chance of sharing a decision. He met the savvy Willie Meehan four times during 1917, losing one (28 March, Emeryville), winning one (25 July, Emeryville) and drawing two (10 August and 7 September, both in San Francisco). Mixed results at four-round contests could not advance his career to championship standard. He needed more guidance than Windy could give him. He needed a fairy godfather.

Anyone less like a central casting fairy godfather than John Leo McKernan, better known as Doc Kearns, is difficult to imagine. But this loud, unscrupulous, flashy, amoral, astute and roguish man, who had been in his time a welterweight, a baseball player, a gold prospector, a saloon-keeper, a bouncer, a taxi driver, a gambler and a failed manufacturer, came to Dempsey bearing gifts, gifts that would send them together to the top. Although he was even more careless with Dempsey's money than with his own, the two men formed an unbeatable partnership.

To Dempsey's mental strength and will, Kearns added the extrovert flamboyance and chutzpah to get them out of the stickiest situation with cheek when all else failed. To Dempsey's willingness to work, he added a disciplined and efficient training routine. To Dempsey's clubbing right, he added an accurate and deadly left hook. Dempsey's taste for paid sex he shared, but he knew when to enforce celibacy. When the parasitic John the Barber reappeared, Kearns paid him a cool $5,000 to get lost again.

Kearns's skill in negotiating and matchmaking lay behind Dempsey's notable ring successes during 1918. So did his willingness to stuff the boxing reporters' typewriters with gold, whiskey and various perquisites and sexual favours to ensure Dempsey's name was rarely out of the headlines. Such venal practices were not invented by Kearns but grew out of the misguided legislation that made newspapers responsible for decisions.

Gangsters and other high rollers bet frequently on boxing. Promoters offered large purses for top fights.

Results depended not on a neutral referee but on lowly paid reporters at ringside. It did not take an economic guru to see that here was a monetary free market that could be slanted by the secret transformation of funds into the pockets of the opinion-formers.

Damon Runyon, for example, became a very rich man when his colourful short stories were converted into Hollywood movies, beginning with Frank Capra's *Lady for a Day* in 1933. (The royalties from *Guys and Dolls*, the Broadway and Hollywood adaptations of another Runyon story, came posthumously and benefited only his widow.) Before hitting the literary jackpot, he lined his pockets with 'subsidies' diverted from fighters' purses to ensure favourable mentions in his syndicated columns or to declare verdicts purely in the interests of wagers made by himself and his underworld friends. He further used gangster connections to cream off a share of the modest earnings of many promising young fighters unable to get a fight unless some hoodlum okayed it.[5]

He was not alone. Neither was Kearns, who was copying the boost-by-bribe strategy used extensively by Tex Rickard for all his major promotions. Tex Rickard had signed Jess Willard in January 1919 to defend his title whenever a suitable challenger could be found.

Dempsey, under Kearns's guidance, and with his remarkable 1918 successes, proved himself worthy of a title challenge by 1919. He had no compassion for lesser fry (Big Jack Hickey, Kid Harris, Kid Henry, Eddie Smith and Tony Drake), all of whom he despatched in successive first-round knockouts in 1919 in warm-up fights

Dempsey and Jack 'Doc' Kearns (1882–1963), his manager, mentor, partner, trainer and friend before their litigious falling-out.
Prints & Photographs Division, Library of Congress, LC-DIG-hec-43969

before the big, big date against Willard on 4 July 1919 at Toledo, Ohio. Without Kearns greasing some palms, it might never have happened.

Toledo was just as famous, or perhaps infamous. Dempsey, in his years of want, met an incredible assortment of oddballs, no-goods, thugs, sex workers, thieves, con men, gun-toting gangsters, punters and down-and-outs. When 4

July dawned, it seemed all of them had travelled to Toledo for the fight and the entire mosquito population of the USA along with them. The two-legged parasites outmatched even the six-legged winged bloodsuckers in bleeding the punters of their cash. Mighty bets were struck. Lucrative concessions for the supplies of ice cream, of sandwiches, of beer, of lemonade and of other creature comforts within the arena were traded to the highest bidder. Even the rights to see Willard and Dempsey train (25 cents-a-time) brought in cash.

Toledo was accessible to travellers from east and west alike. Trains from every direction brought in more and more people on the day, adding to early birds who monopolised accommodation from hotel beds to barns, billiard tables and ditches. The town's population almost doubled.

Baking heat boosted the sale of hats and parasols, but the optimists who had invested in the rights to sell flimsier comestibles were doomed to disappointment. The ice cream melted, the sandwiches fried and curled, the beer boiled and the lemonade bought only by a minority of punters blissfully unaware that the former lightweight champion, Battling Nelson, a man of notoriously unhygienic habits, had taken his biannual bath in the tub of lemonade mixture.

The hurriedly constructed (six weeks from scratch) wooden, octagonal arena also had its disadvantages. The sun brought the resin to the surface of the rough wooden benches so that more than the fighting action glued many spectators to their seats – and they left with the splinters to prove it. If they had chosen to leave simultaneously, say in case of fire, the crush in the solitary exit would have been fatal. Rickard ensured no one got in without a ticket – his or her safety inside was a minor consideration. Having reaped $452,225 from the 19,650 spectators, he figured the sum did not include life insurance.

The excitement and tension surrounding the clash between Dempsey and the reigning heavyweight champion Willard, and the crowds

prepared to suffer every privation to glimpse it, suggest great support for both men, as does the small army of journalists there to report the fight. In fact, both boxers were deeply *un*popular. Where had they been when their male contemporaries had sailed for Europe to fight 'Over There'? Despite their supreme fitness and fighting qualities, attributes bringing them so many dollars, how did Willard and Dempsey compare with the doughboys who had donned uniforms and risked their lives in a European war for a pittance?

Since 1915, when Willard's popularity soared because of his regaining the title from the much-hated Johnson, he made one title defence in four years, and that a mediocre no-decision ten-rounder against Frank Moran at Madison Square Garden on 25 March 1916. Apart from a six-round exhibition against Sailor Burke in Bridgeport, Connecticut on 12 September 1916, that was his total ring career as champion. Lucrative engagements in low-budget film serials and Wild West shows, where his size and his cowboy pretensions disguised his acting deficiencies, were much preferable to professional boxing, which he cordially disliked. Two weeks before the Dempsey fight, Willard appeared in the premiere of *The Challenge of Chance*, a cowboy melodrama of no cinematic virtue whatever. No Oscars were awarded.

Unconcerned about his public image so long as the dollars flowed in, Willard had refused even to participate in exhibitions for the troops. There had also been an unfortunate occasion when Harry Houdini the escapologist had invited Willard up on stage, having spotted him in his audience. Willard stormed out of the theatre after telling Houdini into which orifice the magician might next disappear.

Jess Willard (1881–1968), 'The Pottawatomie Giant' from Kansas. Physically commanding (6ft 6½ins/1.98m), he was ruthlessly attacked by the smaller Dempsey in Toledo, Ohio on 4 July 1919.
Bain Collection, Prints & Photographs Division, Library of Congress, LC-USZ62-60661

In normal circumstances, the reign of an unpopular champion means support for a gallant challenger. Unfortunately, the Dempsey who was to be so deified in the future was, in July 1919, in the words of the leading sportswriter Paul Gallico, 'one of the most unpopular and despised champions that ever climbed into a ring'.[6]

He was just as vulnerable to the failed-to-fight-when-it-really-mattered charge as Willard, a matter that would dog Dempsey for some years to come, an accusation to which we will have to return later. The much-read Grantland Rice, reactionary dean of American sportswriters and resolute defender of the so-called amateur spirit, took exception in the *New York Tribune* to the discrepancy between a prizefight for huge rewards between two professional non-combatants before hundreds of ringside pressmen and battles in France fought by thousands of well-nigh amateur soldiers and recorded for posterity by a handful of war correspondents many a mile from trench-side. Many Americans agreed with Rice.[7]

The crowds packed into the wooden arena to see the fight, although certainly not the social elite that Cochran was pulling in in London, were there because they anticipated a thrilling piece of action. For the first time in the USA, a small but significant section of seats was reserved by Rickard for women spectators and divided off by barbed wire. Whether the wire protected women from assault by men enflamed by the testosterone on display in the ring, or protected men from women enflamed by male musculature in action, is not known.

Another precedent was set by Ethel Barrymore, first of many film actresses subsequently to be seen at ringside. She spurned a seat in the 'safe' zone.

Of whichever gender, spectators expected action and from Dempsey in particular. Even Grantland Rice, looking back in the 1950s, conceded that was what Dempsey in his pomp provided:

> He was keen and lithe, almost as fast as Cobb [i.e. Ty Cobb (1880–1961), the super-aggressive baseball player who stole bases ruthlessly in milliseconds]. It was his speed, speed of hand as well as foot that made him such a dangerous opponent.
>
> Dempsey was the oddest mixture of humanity I've known. In the ring he was a killer – a superhuman wild man. His teeth were frequently bared and his complete intent was an opponent's destruction. He was a fighter – one who used every trick to wreck the other fighter.[8]

An irritating delay was caused by Major Drexel Biddle's troupe of marines marching around the ring and tearing up the canvas. Dempsey, hands heavily bandaged, in white trunks, with a white towel draped casually across his shoulders took the ring, self-absorbed, and stared grimly at the replacement canvas. He remained like that for some minutes until Willard, in blue shorts and black robe, deigned to join him. Doffing the robe, Willard, his back to Dempsey, raised his fists to the crowd, showing to Dempsey, at least half-intentionally, the size and musculature of his torso. The glimpse made Dempsey fully aware of the task in front of him. 'I thought I was going to get sick to my stomach … and I said to myself, this guy's liable to kill me.'

Dempsey was two pounds under 14 stones – 13st 12lb/194lbs, or so he claimed later, and was officially 187lbs – and a fraction over six feet – 6ft 0¾in. The giant human wall in front of him was 6ft 6½in and, having weighed 16st 6lb/230lbs at his formidable peak, was now even heavier at 17st 7lb/245lbs. The arms stretched so triumphantly spanned an awesome 83 inches.

The physical advantages were all Willard's, the mental all Dempsey's. Willard ultimately did not want to be in this ring, or any ring, other than a circus one where no one hit him and he could profitably ride a horse for $1,000 a day. Dempsey was where he had dreamed of being for most of his young life and loved to hit and hurt people. Willard never forgot that Bull Young had died at his hands, and worried about future tragedies. Dempsey's instant response to his own first reaction ('This guy's liable to kill me'), was 'but not if I kill him first'. All the hurts and humiliations of his treatment by the world made him angry, and anger controlled and consolidated into those fast and punishing fists was a more formidable weapon than anything Willard had in his armoury. (Much the same cause and effect could be seen in the frightening spectacle of the young Mike Tyson in the 1980s knocking out ever bigger men in record time on his way to the heavyweight championship.)

At Toledo, the events of the next three minutes (because of further incompetence, actually two minutes and fifty seconds) still shock, even as glimpsed in the grainy extant film where black-and-white shadows act out deeds that need high definition Technicolor digital images to do their awfulness full justice.[9]

As the bell, disabled during the replacement of the wrecked canvas, failed to sound, proceedings began with a whistle ten seconds late. Willard expected Dempsey to rush out of his corner and try to overwhelm him in the first minute, as Dempsey had so many heavyweight hopefuls. Willard was ready to stop him in his tracks with a straight left, thus taking advantage of his own giant reach, and planned to follow up with a clubbing right: fight over. Willard did not believe a further plan would be necessary.

Dempsey was angry and eager, but never so stupid as to do what his opponent expected. Moving slowly, gloves well up, and moving his head around elusively, Dempsey approached his so much taller opponent cautiously. Three times Willard poked out his left, the first glancing harmlessly off Dempsey's forehead and the next two feeble range-finders that connected with nothing. The leads told Dempsey all he wanted to know and exposed that giant torso to fast and ferocious body punches. Before Willard could grasp what was happening, a sickening right under the heart and a left hook to his side brought his guard down and his head forward just where Dempsey wanted it. Lefts and rights, culminating in Dempsey's newly perfected left hook, with all his strength and aggression behind them, smacked into the sides of Willard's jaw and temple. Like a tall chimney undermined, Willard slowly collapsed, suffering further damaging punches before he reached the floor.

Willard takes a right from Dempsey (white shorts) with a left uppercut clearly ready to follow.
Prints & Photographs Division, Library of Congress, LC-USZ62-41454

Dempsey was no observer of niceties. Just as he punched a man on his way down, he was ruthlessly ready to punch him as many times as he could get away with while his victim was still getting up. He lurked behind the slowly rising Willard to repeat the attack. He punched Willard to the head, to the jaw, illegally to the back of the neck and head and the kidneys, sending him back to the canvas. Every time the courageous Willard hauled himself off the floor, with or without the assistance of the ropes, Dempsey duplicated the onslaught. Willard had to suffer pain and humiliation for every slight Dempsey experienced in his hard life. Quite why Willard refused to quit is unknown, but as an undistinguished champion, he deserves the highest possible commendation for the courage he showed in this 'Massacre in the Sun', the lurid term coined later for a Dempsey autobiography.

Dempsey's relish in the bloody destruction of Willard survives 40 years later in that *Massacre in the Sun* autobiography (p. 83) of 1959. (His 1977 account is more austere.) In his own ghosted but presumably dictated words of 1959:

> I straightened up instantly and hit him with a left hook on his cheekbone and temple. It busted his eye open and down he went, shaking the ring like an earthquake.
>
> There was awful hollering and screaming and confusion. I felt like I wanted to get down there on the deck on top of him and beat him some more. One punch wasn't enough. But then he started to get up. I stood right over him and beat him to the canvas again. And again. And again. And again. And again. And again … I couldn't miss. Wherever I hit him, he lumped up or bled. It was a slaughter.

Referee Ollie Pecord failed to stop this grim spectacle as Dempsey floored Willard seven times in the first round, or to restrain Dempsey from the more blatant illegalities.

Willard got up himself, one way or another, six times, and at the seventh count at the end of the round his seconds pulled him up from where he sat helplessly on the seat of his trunks, swollen, bleeding and bemused. Pecord lacked compassion and also competence. He stood over the seated champion and counted up to ten. Had he looked at the timekeeper or had his full wits about him he would have known that, in lieu of the bell, the whistle had been blown to end the abbreviated round two seconds *before* the completion of the full

count. Willard was not knocked out but saved by the whistle.

For the moment, few people realised the event was not over. Dempsey left the ring and threaded his way through the excited crowd back to the dressing room. Willard on his stool regained what was left of his senses. Ironically, Willard's well-known parsimony cost him the fleeting opportunity of an unorthodox victory. He declined to pay for a top-class team in his corner, so no one there claimed a win on the valid basis that the one-minute interval had elapsed and Dempsey had left the ring.

Willard did not know what he was missing. Neither did Dempsey. The wily Kearns, who climbed into the ring and swiftly escorted Dempsey away as if proceedings were all over, had, unknown to Dempsey, invested $10,000 of Dempsey's purse at 10/1 that Dempsey would win by knockout in the first round, a bet two seconds short of fulfilment. Kearns, like Don King decades later, supported laissez-faire philosophies, especially with his fighters' money.

Willard's third-rate seconds pushed him back out for a delayed second round to face more punishment. Pecord allowed it. For another cruel six minutes, Willard stumbled, clinched and leaned and occasionally poked an optimistic paw in the general direction of Dempsey. Dempsey did not knock him down again but hit him time and again as if there were something left to prove. Even sadists among the spectators were relieved when Willard's seconds greeted the ringing of the repaired bell for the fourth round, not by pushing out the tottering Willard, but by throwing in a bloodstained

towel. The new heavyweight champion was challenger Jack Dempsey.

The sad ex-champion, slumped on his stool, had every reason for declining to continue. Beneath the swollen and bleeding flesh on his face, Willard had suffered a cheekbone fractured in 13 places, six of his teeth forcibly removed and the right side of his jaw broken. Some accounts add broken ribs and a fractured skull.

To this day, there are unanswered questions about the Toledo drama. How did Dempsey contrive to cause such damage to Willard in the first round with its seven knockdowns, yet fail either to knock him out or even over in the next two rounds? Noticeably, Willard suffered no such damage at the hands of any other fighter, although he was knocked out in the eighth round by the hard-hitting Argentinian Luis Angel Firpo four years after his encounter with

Willard shrinks away desperately as Dempsey attacks from behind.
BoxRec

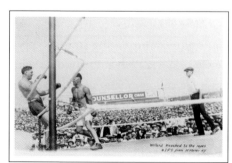

The ropes offer no respite.
BoxRec

Willard slumped in the corner after suffering a cruelly sustained battering.
Topical Press Agency/Hulton Archive/Getty Images

Dempsey (12 July 1923, Jersey City). He had also faced men with notable punching ability in Jack Johnson, Frank Moran, Arthur Pelkey, Luther McCarty and Gunboat Smith without serious mishap. His bones were not fragile. Furthermore, in gruelling encounters, Dempsey inflicted no parallel damage on anyone. Bill Brennan suffered a broken bone when knocked down and out by Dempsey in the sixth round (25 February 1918, Milwaukee, Wisconsin). The bone was in Brennan's ankle. Dempsey had certainly not punched his ankle.

The explanation offered by some, and believed by many, was that Dempsey's gloves had been 'loaded'; that is, packed with some foreign body to have maximum illegal impact. Attention focused particularly on Dempsey's hand bandages inside his gloves. Had they been soaked in some hardening substance like plaster of Paris, turning the fist into the equivalent of a heavily massed bludgeon? Years after the two men became estranged, Dempsey's long-standing manager claimed water had been poured on to Dempsey's bandaged hands (neither unlikely nor illegal), and that he (Kearns) sprinkled powdered plaster of Paris, disguised as talcum powder, on the bandages so that they would go rock hard inside the gloves. In January 1964, the American weekly *Sports Illustrated* published an article, 'He Didn't Know the Gloves Were Loaded', incorporating this posthumous claim by Kearns from his posthumous memoirs. There is every reason to doubt the story.

The only way plaster of Paris could have such an effect – think of old-fashioned casts to keep broken limbs rigid – is if gauze bandages were soaked in a congealing plaster mixture, wrapped around the hand and allowing time thoroughly to dry into a rigid block. The formidable, dried mass cannot be removed unless chiselled or sawn off. Excellent photographs from Toledo (see, for example, the one reproduced in the picture section between pages 158 and 159 of Roger Khan's *A Flame of Pure Fire*), show Dempsey's well-wrapped left hand in bandages and tape and nothing like a cast. In any case, plaster powder merely sprinkled on wet bandages would disintegrate immediately and

be no more lethal than a brushing of talcum powder. Even though Willard's seconds were pretty feeble, one of them, Walter Monahan, was in Dempsey's dressing room to observe the taping of Dempsey's hands, standard practice for any fight. The gloves were added only in the ring – in front of thousands of witnesses.

Then, had the mythical plastering survived the fight, when could Dempsey remove it? The moment a new champion has his gloves held aloft in victory, pressmen, well-wishers, parasites and hangers-on surround him. Even Willard's enemy Houdini would be hard-pressed to remove a rigid plaster cast in such a melee. (A modern example of the illegal use of plaster of Paris in South Africa in 2008 was rumbled when the trainer of super-bantamweight Edward Mpofu had difficulty removing his man's gloves. Mpofu was forced to flee the ring and the arena before his bandages could be properly inspected. He was arrested outside the East London arena. His unlucky opponent had to go to hospital.)[10] It is also true that a Dempsey legal suit extracted a retraction and financial compensation from *Sports Illustrated*.

There is another explanation. If Dempsey had some foreign body in his gloved hand during the devastating first round, and jettisoned it at the end of the round, that would explain the unprecedented damage in the first and why it was not repeated in the second and third. There are Toledo photographs in which some dark, cigar-like object appears temporarily on the ring apron. Ferdie Pacheco in *The 12 Greatest Rounds of Boxing* (pp. 18–19) records a private showing in March 1963 of an 8mm reel of film

of the fight, which disclosed Dempsey dropping a 'spike' on to the apron, only for it to be spirited away under a hat by an unidentified ringside spectator.

Unfortunately, this is not quite conclusive. The man who showed Pacheco the film was the very Doc Kearns who had to be privy to the illegality. Kearns's record suggests him quite capable of giving Dempsey an advantage, fair or foul, but just as capable of lying about it (e.g. his plaster of Paris 'confession'), once alienated from Dempsey. But did he have the technical skill to amend a film sufficiently convincingly, frame by frame, to fool half a dozen experienced boxing reporters? The stricken Willard believed on reflection that something more than Dempsey's fists had inflicted his facial damage. The film was not found in Kearns's effects when he died a few months after the private showing and has not shown up since, doctored or not (no pun intended). Until it does, and can be examined forensically, the evidence is purely circumstantial.

Another New York sportswriter, Jimmy Breslin, wrote confidently in 1991 that Dempsey had concealed some lead piping in his palms and that two of Al Capone's henchmen had obstructed the view of Willard's second, sent to observe the bandaging, whom Breslin calls Moynahan (*sic*).[11] Capone and Runyon had bets on a Dempsey one-round finish. Breslin gives no sources for his claims (although he was privy to private conversations with many old-time fighters and writers), and lead piping and spikes are not unalike. It is true that the Toledo photographs just might conceal a metal object in the left palm.

Would Kearns have hesitated to take an illegal advantage? No. Would Dempsey? Perhaps the later mellower Dempsey, but possibly not the ruthless young Dempsey. The latter was the product of a savage dog-eat-dog society and his philosophy was to do what you had to do. Two of his wives were physically terrified of him. In May 1917, his first wife, the prostitute Maxine Cates, of whom we will hear much more, testified that he had dislocated her jaw with a punch; and Paul Gallico records that his ill-fated marriage with a Hollywood actress, Estelle Taylor, was torn to shreds by his wild rages.[12] It was his widow and fourth wife, who married him in 1958 when he was in his avuncular sixties, who devised the gravestone epithet to Dempsey as 'a gentle man'. She never met the younger, more savage Dempsey, although the choice of words suggests she was aware of his earlier reputation and wanted to refute it from personal experience.

The inspired ring violence that brought such success and ultimately popularity was not easily sated. Gallico records Dempsey's cruel practical jokes on those around him, some of whom suffered painful injuries from a knee in the testicles or dangerous kidney punches. Even Roger Kahn, his biographer, who much admired him, was honest enough to record the darker rumours that the young man in his extremities of early poverty had not hesitated to go pimping his prostitute wife, spending time in brothels straightening out the rougher clientele and taking raw recruits to the trade and, so to speak, introducing them to their future duties. Another veteran boxing writer, Herbert G. Goldman wrote unambiguously:

His first wife, Maxine Cates, was a prostitute, and Jack later did his best to portray her as a callous whore who laughed at her young, lovesick husband and repeatedly threatened to go back to her old trade. The truth, however, was that Dempsey was her pimp, and that Maxine was afraid of him. Jack married her in the fall of 1916, after he'd turned 21, not because he loved her but to avoid prosecution under the Mann Act, a federal law which prohibited bringing a woman across state lines 'for immoral purposes'. This law had been used to 'get' world heavyweight champion Jack Johnson a few years earlier; but it also threatened Dempsey.[13]

It is not a pretty picture, but such was Dempsey's world. One of his most admirable qualities is how he lived it down in later life.

He announced the day after the Willard fight that he would not defend his title against any black fighters, in case the USA suffered another Jack Johnson. (His account of training in *Massacre in the Sun* [p. 26] admits that, post Johnson's Reno win in 1910, his father and his brothers talked regularly of 'white supremacy' and that he drew black faces as targets on his punching bag to inspire him.) He joined campaigns in the 1930s and 1940s to keep boxing whiter than white by finding a pale-skinned challenger to take the title away from the black Joe Louis (world heavyweight champion 1937–41, 1951). Fat chance![14]

Dempsey's life had many more vicissitudes before he matured into the kindly Broadway restaurateur and liberally minded Democrat. To help him on that journey, the sportswriters of the day, almost before the blood had dried on Willard's face, were hailing the new American hero as a model of clean living and an affable and sociable delight. Years would pass before they were right retrospectively.

Whether Britain could produce a challenger to Dempsey was not yet known, if unlikely. Nevertheless, in the lighter weights, there were British fighters of the highest class despite the serious disruption of the war. As we have seen, before 1919 was out, Jimmy Wilde, Johnny Basham, Matt Wells and Ted Kid Lewis were back in domestic rings and demonstrating conclusively that their careers were far from over.

Less than two weeks after Dempsey's Toledo blood-letting, on 17 July 1919 at an Olympia packed to the brim, there was a match-up of more immediate interest to many British fans than Willard v Dempsey.[15] This was the return of Pal Moore, the American who had supposedly outpointed Jimmy Wilde over three rounds at the Royal Albert Hall tournament and was now back to face Wilde over a full 20. A future date against Pete Herman, world bantamweight champion, was on offer for the winner.

The Wilde v Moore match was made at 8st 4lb/116lbs, a serious challenge to Moore, a naturally bulkier fighter. This second meeting was a delightful prospect for connoisseur and ordinary fan alike, and in the context of a sport buoyed up by its unprecedented popularity in 1919, offered a sumptuous spectacle people would pay almost any amount to see. (As Cochran well knew.)

The purse was settled at £5,000, 60 per cent to the winner, with side stakes of £500-a-side. Compared to the prestige of a victory in front of as distinguished an audience as could be assembled, even these amounts seemed trivial. The fullest of houses, including more women than ever, was an extravaganza in its own right. It applauded each new celebrity arrival as fervently as victories on the undercard. The many Americans cheered, whooped and stamped as General Pershing, lately commander of all American troops in France, was ushered to his seat. The Welsh contingent sang 'Land of My Fathers' whenever a daffodil, a leek or a Welsh dragon were sighted.

When Wilde entered the ring and accidentally if symbolically occupied Moore's allocated corner where the Stars and Stripes fluttered, another rousing chorus resounded. The whole audience, full of post-war euphoria, rose, cheered and sang an impromptu version of 'For They Are Jolly Good Fellows' when the two princes, Edward, Prince of Wales, and Prince Albert, walked to their ringside seats. Boxing by royal appointment was a truly national sport.

Even experienced professionals such as Moore and Wilde could have been forgiven had the intense atmosphere engendered physical tension and brought a torpid, anticlimactic fight. Instead, as *The Times* admiringly put it:

The largest crowd on record at Olympia witnessed one of the greatest exhibitions of boxing and dogged pluck that has ever been seen.

The man who put on the great exhibition and showed the dogged pluck was William James Wilde, a pocket-sized Prince of Wales in his own right. Moore was approximately a stone heavier than Wilde, with all the extra muscle power and natural strength that implies. Every clinch and every lean-on brought that extra bulk to bear upon Wilde's slender arms. Every Moore punch came with perhaps 15 per cent more power behind it. Over 20 rounds these factors were critical. The expert consensus was that Wilde's speed and skill should be uppermost for two-thirds of the fight, but he would tire in the last third, when Moore would take over and possibly win by knockout.

Wilde had other ideas. He began as if he intended to put Moore on the canvas early and definitively and have his post-fight shower before Moore's power came into consideration. From the first bell he was aggressive and stunningly effective, getting off punches with aplomb. While Moore was still blinking from the painful impact of the Wilde left thudding into his nose, Wilde stepped in close to clip him with hooks to head and body and to uppercut him up inside his two-fisted guard. When Moore tried counters, they disappeared into the cigar smoke-filled air or slapped harmlessly around Wilde's sides.

Moore tended, as referee Corri picked up often, to punch open-gloved or with the side of the hand. The resounding slaps were heard above the din of the crowd and cheered lustily by the American contingent. More noisy than effective, their limited impact did little to deter Wilde's belligerence.

For ten rounds the Welsh onslaught continued, varied only by deliberate Wilde retreats, drawing Moore forward and showing that Wilde could counter quite as hurtfully as he could lead. Wilde kept his weight on his right foot, even when advancing with the left, and when he did go back it was accompanied by an economical sway from the waist, making an opponent miss by a well-calculated centimetre.[16] Then came the counter-punch with speed, and with all the power generated by the lightning switch of weight from back foot to front foot. This was parry and thrust like a fencer with a foil, and just as quick. An opponent who can hurt you when going forward or back is most boxers' idea of a nightmare proposition.

After 30 minutes, Moore looked unsteady and even desperate. Caught by several punches in the 11th, he resorted to grasping the top rope with one hand and using leverage to swing wildly with the other like a half-pivot blow. Corri and the crowd reprimanded him in unison, yet the one way Moore could get back into the fight was to turn it into a brawl.

Moore's double strength – the physical endurance to take sustained punishment and the psychological fortitude to refuse to know when he was beaten – kept him going. He had successes himself, catching Wilde in the 13th and cutting his lip in the 14th. The 15th was a thriller. Moore advanced and Wilde refused to give ground, both men throwing flurries of punches at the bell and beyond, as cheers and counter-cheers drowned out the timekeeper's efforts to indicate three minutes were up.

Wilde's brilliant skills and fighting heart, packed into a diminutive frame, were never better demonstrated than in the last quarter of this fight. He sank on his stool at the end of every round, looking utterly spent, yet as soon as the bell rang for the next, he bounded back into action, taking anything Moore could inflict. Moore's head, perhaps accidentally, opened a deep cut in his nose in the 16th, a painful and distressing wound that bled alarmingly for the rest of the fight. Nevertheless, every time Moore sought to apply his extra weight and strength, Wilde did his best to outpunch and outlast him.

Bleeding and tiring as he was, Wilde could have relied discreetly on his long points lead and kept a safe distance between him and the bustling Moore. Wilde was not that kind of champion. Rather, he seemed to realise that here he was, a legendary talent, in front of an audience and an opponent worthy of him, living up to the legend. No one in the arena that night ever forgot it in the future.

Moore had the best of the 17th. Wilde still closed the round with hooks to Moore's jaw with both hands, and it was Moore's turn to suffer. Moore was just as strong and as tough as everyone predicted. Yet even being 14 pounds heavier than his opponent, it was Moore who had to perform miracles to last out the 20 rounds. In the 18th, 19th and 20th, it was the bleeding Welshman punching and dancing triumphantly, and the American tottering to the finish, lucky to stay on his feet, as every Welshman in the house sang Wilde on to victory. When Corri raised Wilde's arm in victory, so many hats, caps, umbrellas, walking sticks and even chairs were thrown into the air, that it looked like a wild climax to a graduation ceremony.

Wilde's feat inspired *The Times* enthusiastically to endorse him and his sport in a full editorial 'In Praise of Boxing':

That the popularity of boxing was increased enormously by the war may be accounted as a war benefit. There is no sport in the world which demands cleaner living. There is no more natural sport. Success at boxing depends on the man himself. Low cunning will not help him, but a quick, clear brain, a hard body, and perfect training will carry a man a long way. Weight is not everything, as the incomparable WILDE showed at Olympia when he gave MOORE, his plucky opponent, nearly a stone in weight and gained a victory which will live as long as the great victories of TOM CRIBB, MENDOZA, and the mighty BELCHER.[17]

Here was further confirmation of boxing's journey from social menace to establishment darling in record time. The achievements of Wilde and Moore still came at a price to both men. The next time Pal Moore fought in Britain was against the resilient little Frenchman, Eugene Criqui. Moore had been scheduled to fight Charles Ledoux, but Ledoux had withdrawn after several tough fights in the latter half of 1919: v Tommy Noble (won by tenth-round knockout, 31 July, Paris); v Driscoll (20 October, London) won on Driscoll's retirement after the 15th; v Walter Ross (13 December, Paris) won on Ross's retirement in the 12th.

Moore and Criqui met on a poorly attended Boxing Day bill, 26 December 1919 at the Royal Albert Hall, London. Moore was victorious but under peculiar circumstances.[18] Early in the fight, he dissipated his natural power with too many open-gloved punches, and Criqui did what Wilde had done, picked Moore off with the left and landed damaging right hooks and crosses. So matters went until the 14th round.

To the dismay of the few spectators well placed to see, Criqui collapsed out of a clinch and on to the canvas, clutching his genitals and protesting to referee Eugene Corri about a low blow. Corri, like most of the audience, had not seen the offence, and ordered Criqui to box on or lose. As Criqui continued protesting, Moore whipped around his blind side and hit him with another sickening body blow. This weird reprise of what had happened to Criqui against Noble back in April provoked a storm of booing from the crowd when Moore was given the victory.

(Criqui could have been forgiven a persecution complex about British promotions. He was doomed to shabby treatment whenever he fought in a British ring. One hour before a fight with the Leeds bantamweight Joe Fox in May 1922, he vomited profusely and believed his coffee had been deliberately poisoned. He stopped Fox in the 12th but said that he had been at the very end of his tether and desperate not to continue.

Even Criqui's knockout victory over Walter Ross at Holborn on 18 September 1919 was controversial.[19] He knocked Ross down at the end of the 14th, and Ross was counted out. In fact, the bell preceded the tenth second. Ross was in no state to start the 15th, despite a minute's rest on his stool. Criqui came over to Ross's corner as a sporting victor commiserating with a beaten opponent and was told by the referee to box on. He had the distasteful task of obediently and redundantly knocking Ross out with one right-hand punch.

Ross's supporters, unaware of the true circumstances, booed Criqui vigorously as a final count proceeded.)

Moore was the victor in the Boxing Day match against Criqui, but not worthily. He neither looked, nor was, the same fighter who had put up the epic performance against Wilde three months before. Of Wilde, the other Olympia hero, *The Times*'s sports department took a more sanguine view of his future than the paper's leader quoted above. Hearing that Wilde, for financial reasons, would visit the USA for a series of no-decision contests preceding further championship fights, the newspaper urged him rather to retire: '... it would be advisable for the great little Welshman to take pause and seriously consider the question of retiring from the Ring'.[20]

Wilde, possibly not a *Times* reader, did not take the advice. In Milwaukee on 6 December 1919, he met a New York bantamweight called Jack Sharkey (not the Jack Sharkey who became world heavyweight champion in 1932–33, but one of half a dozen Jack Sharkeys operating in the USA before the Second World War). In practice, he might have conceded that *The Times* had a point.[21]

This Sharkey (known as 'Little Jackie') was really New York Italian Giovanni Cervati (b. 20 June 1887). He and Wilde drew over 7,000 spectators, although the match was on the ten-round maximum, no-decision basis. Wilde gave away at least seven pounds to the stronger Sharkey (Wilde 7st 9lb/107lbs; Sharkey 8st 2lb/114lbs). Wales is a time zone and thousands of miles away from Wisconsin, but the real weakener affecting Wilde was the hard, hard fight against Pal Moore in July. Sharkey easily convinced the ringside pressmen he had

out-thought and outfought Wilde in every round. In the sixth, Wilde had the humiliating experience of having Sharkey drop his guard, inviting Wilde to hit him on his exposed chin. Wilde landed two punches on Sharkey's jaw, only for Sharkey to smile with blithe indifference. This was treatment that Wilde was more used to administering than receiving. The Wisconsin crowd enthusiastically applauded Sharkey for his 'victory', but it was over a shadow of the real Wilde.

There are too many complicating factors to reach any very definite conclusion about the relative standards of the sport in the three main boxing countries – Great Britain, France and the USA – in 1919. All could point to negative influences hampering the natural development of fighters. The French and the British mourned thousands of youths buried in the fields of Flanders and elsewhere, unable ever to glove up again. American boxing had suffered from the operations of the Frawley Law, limiting every contest to a constricted 'exhibition', and from the machinations of unsympathetic state governors and city mayors determined to retain the puritan vote by keeping boxing out of their fiefdoms, as if it were an infectious disease.

Common sense and the record books suggest that the USA, after the Great War particularly, produced more champions and had the greater strength in depth. Nevertheless, the European nations never failed to produce several outstanding fighters, such as Jim Driscoll, Jimmy Wilde, Ted Kid Lewis, Charles Ledoux, Eugene Criqui and Georges Carpentier, all of whom were to take their rightful places in the American boxing pantheon, the

International Boxing Hall of Fame at Canastota, New York State.

Meanwhile, Britain and France dreamed of producing a contender who might get his foreign hands on that most glittering, lucrative and seemingly perennially American prize of all – the world heavyweight championship. Such ambitions were exploited by promoters such as C. B. Cochran or Tex Rickard, who did not need to dream dreams themselves to turn fancies into genuine pounds, dollars or francs. Selling fights was, ultimately, a matter of selling dreams. In the latter half of 1919, there was a selling of dreams so optimistic they were nocturnal chimera, likely to disappear in the cold light of day.

Too few people took notice of the fate of the alchemist Bombardier Billy Wells, a proven expert in turning the false gold of expectation into the lead of despair in a matter of seconds. Cochran, even after Wells's defeat by Beckett in February, had Wells on his bills because he still drew crowds, but refused him over-generous purses or to match him again against Beckett or Carpentier without a programme of rehabilitation against lesser fry. Wells's biographer quotes a stanza from *Health and Efficiency* (February 1920), which summarises Wells's perennial appeal neatly:

> Our hope he flatters to destroy,
> Our confidence to kill;
> And yet we'll never fail to love
> Our own Bombardier Bill.[22]

The sentiments are more accurate than the scansion.

Wells had two contests in late 1919 on Cochran bills at the Holborn Stadium. The first, against the outclassed Jack Curphey (17 October),

Joe Beckett (1892–1965), the Southampton booth fighter, was British heavyweight champion from 1919–23. His politics brought him attention from the secret services.
Topical Press Agency/Getty Images

had Curphey counted out in the second. The next, against Arthur Townley of Birkenhead, was on 20 November, watched predominantly by 'the people who declare that they have lost all faith in Wells – but persist in turning up every time he fights'; people who 'proclaimed loudly their belief that Wells was quivering with nervousness while waiting in his corner'.[23] Townley was not a good enough fighter to pounce on Wells before he got over his stage fright, although he inflicted a cut over Wells's right eye that roused the Londoner a little. Alas, not enough. Wells's supporters escaped their first dread (that Billy would be knocked out before the reverberations of the first bell had died away), but now had to face their second (that Billy, superior in most meaningful departments, would fail to assert his superiority and put his opponent away satisfactorily). So it proved.

Wells put Townley down for counts of nine in the second, the third, the sixth, and twice more in the eighth; in between, he continued to stand off and prod at Townley as if the Lancashire man were a trick punching bag that might explode if hit too often. When Townley's seconds threw in their towels and sponges in the ninth – and looked as if they might throw in the spit-bucket as well – compassion ruled and the fight was stopped. Some thought the gesture was to spare Wells further embarrassment rather than save Townley from further punishment.

The search for a European challenger for Dempsey was still on but Wells was unlikely any more to figure in it. But there was Georges Carpentier. Even before he had fought anyone after the war, he received an inadequate offer to meet Dempsey. Meanwhile, his appetite for despatching British boxers, as if revenge for Crécy and Agincourt was uppermost in his memory, had not been slaked by his war experiences. He proved it in Paris on 19 July 1919 at the Cirque de Paris against Dick Smith, with a European cruiserweight championship on offer.[24] Smith, the highly popular Londoner, had only turned professional aged 27, after pre-war successes in the Amateur Boxing Association finals. He was not, however, a genuine heavyweight, lacking real weight and power to go with his skills. The significant victory on his record, the one over Joe Beckett (25 February 1918 at the NSC on points over 20 rounds), was achieved by boxing on the retreat and picking up points as the more ponderous Beckett tired of chasing him. Smith never knocked out a heavyweight opponent.

A patriotic Englishman, he was in uniform before the first month of the war was over and featured on the cover of *Boxing* on 29 August 1914, wielding a bayonet and recruiting by example. As a member of the so-called Sportsman's Battalion, he, unlike Carpentier, took eight fights during the war years. He also, for once, outweighed an opponent by about 2½lbs: Carpentier 12st 3⅓lb/171⅓lbs, and Smith a fraction under 12st 6lb/174lbs.

Despite his years out of the ring, Carpentier had the power that Smith lacked, and floored Smith for nine in the third and the fifth. Smith, always game, rallied in the seventh and eighth.

4 December 1919, Holborn: Beckett's less than glorious showing against Carpentier lasted 74 seconds.
National Museum of Australia http://collectionsearch.nma.gov.au/object/153558

9 June 1920, Olympia: Johnny Basham (l) and Ted Kid Lewis (r) launch one of the most compelling series of fights in British boxing (1920–21). Could Basham's superior skills keep Lewis's strength and aggression at bay for 20 rounds?

The Ring Magazine via Getty Images

Carpentier decided he had had enough of a workout and delivered explosive uppercuts, followed by two choice left hooks, leaving Smith out cold before the end of the eighth.

News from Paris of Carpentier's decisive victory made the match-up between Carpentier and Joe Beckett a hotter ticket than ever, and boosted Beckett's final outing before meeting Carpentier in December 1919. This was against the American with a strong British following, Eddie McGoorty, at Olympia on 2 September 1919, as the main attraction of a strong Cochran promotion.[25] Supporting contests included another heavyweight fight, Fred Fulton (USA) against Arthur Townley, won by Fulton on a first-round knockout; and a welterweight contest between Johnny Basham and François Charles of France (like Carpentier, recently a French war hero and a holder of the Croix de Guerre). Charles attacked with élan and bewildering speed, and it needed all Basham's skills to keep him at bay in the early rounds. Basham characteristically smiled his way through to a points victory, although the smile was a little forced when Charles put him down for a count of seven in the seventh.

Eddie McGoorty followed Beckett into the ring to a warm reception, though in truth he was beyond his best, carrying more flesh around his waist than in his prime, his once instant reactions slowed by the lifting of too many pint pots. Born 1 August 1889, he first used his fists for cash aged eight, when his pugnacious father employed him as a bouncer at the family hotel. He was a full professional boxer from the age of 15, glorying in and mostly living up to his nickname as 'The Oshkosh Terror'.[26]

Now self-managed and self-trained, his preparation schedule featured more carrots than sticks. Even overweight, he conceded about a stone to the fully trained Beckett. (Admittedly Beckett, even when training seriously, preferred passive sparring partners who allowed themselves to be hit without retaliating.)

The fight was good value. Beckett was as aggressive as expected. Like most fighters, he looked better on the attack than in defence. Given his edge in brawn, his best hope was to advance, swinging and hooking, and cancel out McGoorty's edge in skill. Often, McGoorty stuck out a skilful jab but failed to keep Beckett away, taking some serious hooks to his well-covered ribs and to the side of his head. Even in the fifth, when McGoorty's weaving and side stepping, reminiscent of the old McGoorty who could have avoided Beckett in a telephone box, made Beckett look raw and clumsy. By the eighth and ninth, McGoorty clinched and held and leaned on Beckett for a breather, and to tire Beckett in turn. Beckett declined to be weakened,

especially with Carpentier on his future agenda.

In the 12th round, a Beckett right cross put McGoorty down for a count of seven and raised an ugly bruise on his left cheek. McGoorty's less than ascetic lifestyle sapped his stamina, but his old courage and willpower were intact. He got up and fought back valiantly, despite being floored again in the last seconds of the 13th. In the next three rounds, Beckett went all out to finish him. McGoorty avoided many of Beckett's hardest punches and remained upright. Only in the 17th did Beckett put him down with a right for a long count, and when McGoorty got up, still unsteady, produced a ruthless flurry of punches to send the American back to the canvas to be counted out.

Beckett's victory, impressive as it was, was widely praised in the British press. It led to the popular question that if Beckett could beat Britain's finest (Wells and Goddard), and a top American (McGoorty), could he then do what so many had failed to do, beat Carpentier and meet Dempsey for the world title? This was to forget that the punter who bets on collateral form in boxing is usually broke. Nevertheless, as an extraordinary climax to an altogether extraordinary year of boxing, the prospect was overwhelming. Cochran lost no time in making the match – Joe Beckett v Georges Carpentier to take place on 4 December 1919 at Holborn.

The Times rightly saw that this was an event that extended boxing's normal hinterland:

> … there has been a steady increase in the interest taken in the match, not only by those who have boxed themselves, or who watch boxing

habitually, but also by a very large number of people whose only knowledge of the pugilistic art has been derived from pictures in the daily Press, on the screen, and from descriptive articles. For every person who will see the great fight tonight there will be thousands today who will be discussing chances of the two men. The most unexpected people may be heard talking gravely in public places of hooks and uppercuts, infighting and foot-work, as if they had spent a life-time in the study of pugilism … Even elderly and highly respectable 'charladies' may be heard airing their views on 'that there Carpentier' … whenever and wherever two or three men have collected together during the last few days, sooner or later the topic of the fight has arisen, and 'Who do you think will win on Thursday?' has been the common greeting of the 'bread winners' and season-ticket holders during their journey City wards each morning.[27]

Public interest, from charlady to commuter, was genuinely intense. The unavailability of Olympia for the fight on 4 December 1919, and the switch to Cochran's Holborn Stadium, meant that only a select number could be accommodated. When a demand so exceeds a supply, as the densest of economics students knows, the result is a huge rise in prices. Of this Cochran made a virtue. Ringside seats were offered at ten guineas a time for those lucky enough to get their hands on one. As one writer pointed out, his seat cost him ten times what it had cost him to see six and a half hours of Wagner's *Parsifal* at Bayreuth, with a lot less laughs. The black market price for Holborn was more like 25 guineas.

Every member of the glitterati wanted to be there, and many of the literati too. Intellectual journals hardly known for their regular coverage of the pugilistic world vied with each other to send a more distinguished writer than the next. There was Arnold Bennett reporting the fight for the *New Statesman* as 'The Prize Fight', 13 December 1919, and George Bernard Shaw writing 'The Great Fight' for *The Nation*, 13 December 1919. Shaw's was reprinted in June 1921 as a separate pamphlet. (It is a pity the *Psychic Times* did not contact the shades of William Hazlitt to send in his opinion.) The literary giants were joined by sufficient other people of mark to get *Boxing World* very excited:

> … there were celebrities of the social, of sport, of politics, of the stage and of the learned professions. There were aristocrats of the bluest blood, officials of the highest rank, celebrated actors, famous men of letters, distinguished doctors, eminent authors, noted painters, illustrious lawyers and conspicuous men-about-town. A few ladies were present – three or four in evening dress.[28]

The Times correspondent directly contradicts the last sentence, insisting 'there were many ladies present, more than have ever attended a fight before in this country'.

The audience also struck Arnold Bennett:…

I cannot recall whether the Prince [of Wales] and Mr Cochran wore smoking-jackets or swallow-tails. Opinion was divided as to the sartorial proprieties. Some star actors and some millionaires wore smoking jackets; some star-actors and some millionaires wore swallow-tails. The millionaires were richly represented … women were certainly too few; some had sought to atone for the paucity by emulating the attire of the gladiators in the ring. They made futile spots of sex on ten guineas worth of plush …[29]

The Prince of Wales took a front-row seat an hour before the contest and was cheered to ringside, where he made an impromptu speech. He was given a rousing chorus of 'For He's a Jolly Good Fellow'. Like everyone else unless they arrived hours early, the royal party was escorted by scores of police and stewards through the vast crowds packing every street around the stadium, all determined to see someone or something before or after, if they could not see the fight. Arnold Bennett is a good witness:

> All the streets of the vicinity were full of people abroad for the event. They were all aware of the result … [yet] They all stood or moved in attitudes of amaze [*sic*], watching with rapt faces the long lines of departing motors. You perceived that the English race was profoundly interested and moved, and that nothing less than winning the greatest war could have interested and moved it more profoundly. This emotion was no product of

a Press campaign, but the Press campaign was a correct symptom of it. It was as genuine as British fundamental decency.[30]

Boxing World's editor confirmed the extraordinary atmosphere: 'I have never seen anything like the interest, excitement and enthusiasm which last week's battle created.'[31]

It seems indisputable that the meeting between Carpentier and Beckett, to which so many hundreds of column inches were devoted before and after the event, was a genuine cultural phenomenon, climax of the overwhelming interest boxing was engendering throughout 1919. Quite beyond the sporting press, readers of, for example, the *Illustrated London News*, were thought to be eager recipients of the more arcane pieces of information, such as the men's full statistics:

> The two men are of almost equal age, Beckett being 25 years and 7 months old, and Carpentier 25 years and 10 months. A few days before the meeting their respective measurements are given as follows: Weight – B., 13st. 2lb; C., 12st. 2lb. Height – B. 5ft. 10in.; C. 5ft. 9½in. Reach – B. 71½in.; C., 69 in. Chest – B., 42½ in.; C., 40¼in. Waist – B., 31in.; C., 29¾in. Thigh – B., 24in.; C., 22½in. Calf – B., 15¾in.; C., 15¾in. Neck – B., 16½in.; C., 15½in. Biceps – B., 15½in.; C., 12in. Fore-arm – B. 13in.; C., 11in. Thus, Beckett had the advantage in weight and strength, while Carpentier relied on his science and speed of footwork …[32]

The physical advantages were indeed all in Beckett's favour. A modern reader will be greatly struck by how small these men were in contrast to the behemoths of the 21st century. For example, Lennox Lewis, British holder in the 1992–2004 period of various IBF, WBC and WBA world heavyweight championship titles, was 6ft 4¾in tall and weighed about 17st 11lb/249lbs. His final opponent, Ukrainian Vitali Klitschko, was 6ft 7in tall and weighed 17st 5lb/243lbs. Nicolay Valuev of Russia, WBA champion 2005–06, dwarfed even Lewis and Klitschko at 7ft 2in tall and tipped the scales at a phenomenal 22st 12¾lb/320¾lbs.

To anyone familiar with the nature of sport and with the history of boxing in particular, the first thought about the Beckett v Carpentier contest is its clear vulnerability to the First Law of Pugonomics – The more a contest is hyped, the more the punter will be disappointed. (The Second Law is – The longer the column inches devoted to previews, the shorter the meaningful action.) For their ten guineas, the ringsiders got a fashion parade, but little else. The story of the fight is so easily told, *The Nation* and the *New Statesman* were fortunate in employing distinguished literary wordsmiths who could conjure plenty out of very little.

Beckett, in a nondescript brown dressing gown, sidled first into the ring and doffed his robe to show an immaculately sculptured torso rippling beneath his swarthy skin. Some easily impressed punters doubled their bets on him at the sight. He coolly nodded his short black forelock in acknowledgement of his warm reception and scowled beneath his prominent brow at the incoming Carpentier.

Carpentier, in contrast, made a definite and calculated entrance. Clad in a handsome grey gown of Japanese silk, he contrived to look more at home than Beckett and more regal than the Prince of Wales. Waving and nodding to his friends and supporters as nonchalantly as a debonair *flâneur* sauntering down a Parisian boulevard, he ignored Beckett. He contrived to suggest that he was the star in a new romantic movie and that the stark blue arc lights shining on the ring, and the cameramen precariously balanced along the balcony, were for him alone. Arnold Bennett could not get over how little like the traditional pugilist Carpentier looked:

> [He] … stood out astonishingly from all the rest … He might have been a barrister, a poet, a musician, a Foreign Office attaché, a Fellow of All Souls; but not a boxer. He had an air of intellectual or artistic distinction. And long contact with the very physical world of pugilism had not apparently affected his features in the slightest degree.

The Times correspondent concurred:

> Carpentier, fair and pale … was beautifully trained. A more beautiful man has seldom if ever been seen in a ring.

Rare is a fictional story where Beauty fails to win against the Beast. Actuality in this case was no different. At 9.45pm the bell rang, the men touched gloves and the real action began. Began, that is, for Carpentier. After a few feints, Carpentier rocked Beckett's head back with an impeccably timed left lead delivered straight over the top of Beckett's slightly lazy guard. Coming out of an inconclusive clinch, Carpentier did it again.

Beckett launched but failed to land a left uppercut, and before he could bring his gloves back into an adequate defensive position, Carpentier drove a perfect straight right to the jaw with all his weight behind it. Insensible to the world around him, including Carpentier, Beckett collapsed forward, half-tangling with Carpentier's lower limbs. The Frenchman extracted himself smartly and allowed the comatose Beckett to fall face down on to the canvas. From outside the ring, the referee B. J. Angle and the timekeeper Joe Palmer coordinated on a count of ten and out. The great fight was over.

So stunned was Beckett's corner at the speed of the execution that Carpentier himself, rather than Beckett's seconds, carried Beckett ('a crumpled, inert mess', *The Times*) back to his stool to recover. While poor Beckett was attended to, Carpentier was kissed in the ring by Descamps, and kissed even more passionately by some stunning Mesdemoiselles, who were lifted to the ropes for the purpose. He blew his own kisses to the crowd in general, then leaned over the ropes to shake hands with the Prince of Wales, who stood up out of his ringside seat to congratulate him. The entire fistic action had lasted one minute 14 seconds, giving Beckett the very dubious distinction of lasting one second more against the Orchid Man than his old rival Bombardier Billy, whose last effort had lasted a mere one minute 13 seconds. The extra second no way contradicted *The Ring's* later dismissal of Beckett as 'The Glass-Jawed Champion of England'.

This great fight, or anti-fight, whose very brevity made it a spark of glory rather than a blaze, was the climax of one of the most significant years British boxing ever experienced. The importance did not escape the great novelist the *New Statesman* had sent along. As he concluded:

> Was the show worthy of the talents and the time lavished in its preparation and accomplishment, worthy of the tradition, of the prowess, of the fostering newspapers, of Mr Cochran? It was. Was it a moral show? It was – as moral as an Inter-University Rugger match. Was it an aesthetic show? It was. Did it uplift? It did. Did it degrade? It did not. Was it offensive? No. Ought the noble art to continue? It ought. I had been deeply interested.
>
> ARNOLD BENNETT

The boxing year 1919 actually closed instead, with a downbeat tailpiece at the Royal Albert Hall, appropriately on Boxing Day.[33] Many potential customers spending their Christmases in hearthside comfort chose not to make their way there on 26 December, especially as London suffered hailstorms and heavy rain.

The bill was not uninteresting, and it was announced that part of the proceeds would be going to charity. (In the event, it was the unlucky promoters, the Barry brothers, who could have done with a charitable contribution to alleviate the heavy losses they took on the evening.)

Carpentier gave a sparring exhibition with his partner Jules Lenaers, so that those of his fans unable to afford a premium Holborn Stadium seat, or who had invested yet blinked at the wrong moment, could see him in more sustained, if artificial action. There were also three genuine fights. One was the unfortunate encounter between Pal Moore and Eugene Criqui described earlier.

The second was a welterweight contest between Johnny Griffiths (USA) and François Charles of France, a two-round maul with an unexpected early finish in the third when Charles took a short jab to the stomach and was counted out.

The third was another welterweight match that, like the evening, promised more than it could deliver. In one corner ready to fight was Matt Wells, a veteran of a decade of fighting, who had just celebrated his 32nd birthday.

Many Boxing Days ago (26 December 1912), Wells had been down in Swansea, knocking out the happy Welshman Johnny Basham, three years his junior, in the seventh. They met again during the war (22 March 1915) and Basham had narrowly outpointed Wells over 15 rounds. A decider had recently taken place (13 November 1919) on a Cochran bill at the Holborn Stadium and a thoroughly bruising contest it had been – British welterweight champion (Basham) against a former British lightweight champion (Wells), and plenty of blood spilled.[34]

Basham clinched often to neutralise Wells's more powerful punches. Wells, frustrated by Basham's holdings of his arms close in, made artistic and illegal use of his own hard head, rubbing Basham's collarbone raw and cutting his forehead with an old-fashioned goat butt in the 18th. More conventional and legitimate damage was caused by hard punching from both protagonists – Basham's ear bled profusely from round one onwards, and Wells's nose and face freely from the 12th to the close. The decision on points went overwhelmingly to Basham. The disappointed Londoners in the audience who booed the verdict were being unjust.

They had certainly missed the Walworth champion ever since the second of the Basham fights in March 1915, after which their man had been absent from British rings in favour of the USA. There, Matt Wells pursued his boxing career vigorously. He had 27 American fights during 1915, 1916 and 1917, and returned to London for only one warm-up fight (20 October 1919), beating Kid Carter on points over 20 rounds, before meeting Basham for the third time.

Wells's new opponent on the Boxing Day bill could claim no better record than Wells of sharing the miseries of wartime Britain with his loyal supporters. On the other stool, ready to give combat, was none other than Ted Kid Lewis. He had been lured back to Britain only by a more generous deal than the promoters could afford ('$25,000 purse, $15 grand to the winner').[35] An authentic gold cup was included. The balance sheet was calculated on filling the Albert Hall, at prices from £1 1s. to £9 9s. Banks of empty seats therefore made for heavy losses.

After knocking out Ted Saunders in Coventry in the sixth round on 18 March 1914, Lewis had left Britain for Australia, where he had five fights in the summer of 1914. He was therefore in Australia when the European nations abandoned diplomacy and stumbled into the military adventure that became the First World War. From there, he chose to go, not back to Britain, but to the neutral USA. He stayed for the next five years, only returning in November 1919 to train for the Wells match. His fights in exile included that epic 20-match series with Jack Britton extensively covered in the British press. Lewis fought 21 times in 1915, 19 times in 1916, 29 times in 1917, 17 times in 1918 and 11 times in 1919, all in the USA, apart from one in Cuba and five in Canada.

As many pointed out, then and subsequently, there was an ugly contrast to be drawn between the professional boxers who served in the armed forces during the 1914–18 period in whatever capacity, and others who, despite being the fittest and finest fighters of their generation, chose to pick up regular purses by exiling themselves from their nations. Others did the real fighting in uniform for a pittance.

So far as the Albert Hall contest between Matt Wells and Ted Kid Lewis is concerned, surely the sparse attendance was due to a silent question posed by the absentees: Where were you two when we needed you? (They were friends and Wells had sometimes acted as Lewis's second in American rings.) In any other circumstances, the clash would have packed out an arena in the most inclement weather imaginable. Significantly, the sparring exhibition by Carpentier, the authentic war hero, was described by *The Times* as 'perhaps the *most popular* event of the evening' [Italics added].

The prevailing December chill infiltrated the fight, cool from the start when Wells, seven years older than Lewis, adopted a negative strategy to neutralise Lewis's speed and power. He

bored in, head down, eager to clinch, hold on and lean on Lewis, all to tire Lewis and sap his punches. The tactics were in vain. As Wells wormed in, Lewis jabbed and hooked him ruthlessly at close quarters or stood off and jabbed him fiercely from a distance. Wells was chastised twice over – verbally by the referee J. T. Hulls, especially for hitting and holding simultaneously, and physically by Lewis, who might have preferred to have knocked his old friend out early, rather than to continue the one-sided punishment. By the end of the third round, Wells was a sorry sight, bleeding profusely from a cut over his right eye, and from an ugly split in his lip.

Hulls had to be mindful that Wells was famous for winning fights by refusing to give in when on the wrong end of an opponent's punches. Many a time had he phlegmatically soaked up blows, and, in the later rounds of a long fight, outlasted and outwitted talented fighters unable to match his bruised defiance. This was not one of those occasions, and Lewis was not one to be outdone.

By the 12th, Wells was an ugly sight, and from all parts of the hall came appeals to the referee to stop the one-sided proceedings. Even Wells agreed when Hulls stepped between the two and called, 'Sufficient!' Wells's flesh had proved all too mortal, but his spirit and his dry wit remained intact. He smiled a bloody grin at Hulls and Lewis, and said, 'That's the word I've been trying to think of for the last nine rounds.' Even had he thought it, he was too much the warrior ever to utter it.

Wells's love of boxing persisted after his formal retirement, aged 36, in 1922 and he remained a significant

presence in amateur boxing for many years. He coached at the Lynn Athletic Club in Walworth, where he had begun his own amateur career, as well as for Dulwich College, Guy's Hospital and the Metropolitan Police. He handed on the benefits of his own experiences to many hundreds of younger boxers, including the twin brothers, Henry and George Cooper. It is sad to record that he damaged his own considerable reputation as a result of a dubious decision he gave as a referee in March 1933 in the same Albert Hall ring where he had had to give Lewis best.

Briefly, the unsavoury episode began when a German boxer well known to British audiences, Walter Neusel, clearly overhauled the British boxer Don McCorkindale, in a 12-round fight for a comfortable points win. Alas, Wells awarded McCorkindale an undeserved draw. Worse, the unexpected result enabled several professional gamblers to operate a betting coup. A British Boxing Board of Control inquiry followed, where Wells gave feeble answers to legitimate questions. (For example, he said he doubted both boxers had been genuinely trying to win. This drew the obvious rejoinder – why then had he not either warned them or declared a no-contest? His claim, that as an old boxer he could not bear to turn two professionals out of the ring, carried no conviction. Most old boxers would have considered it an insult to their whole careers to be accomplices in a phoney fight and would probably have physically thrown the men out in disgust.) Unsurprisingly, the Board found Wells guilty of an illegitimate decision and suspended his referee's licence.

Wells's quality, of not knowing when he was beaten, now operated to his considerable disadvantage when he sued the Board. In court, he gave as poor a performance as he had at the Board inquiry, giving rise to the further suspicion that he had been part of the criminal conspiracy to pervert the result of the fight, and that his suit had been brought in cahoots with the guilty ones. If so, his fellow conspirators left him with the heavy costs when the court inevitably found for the Board. Wells was rendered broke and bankrupt, with a once mighty reputation for integrity in tatters.

As 1919, British boxing's *annus mirabilis* closed, there were reasons to look beyond its warm memories to future possibilities. The sport was an unexpectedly popular, glamorous and respected cultural phenomenon. So surprising a development, and the new social context in which it had taken place, were extremely welcome. There were still signs that any new board of control in Britain would need plenty of parenting skills to keep the ugly caterpillar turned colourful butterfly out of future trouble.

What took place in administrative boardrooms and committee discussions, or in the carpeted splendour of cigar-smoking promoters' offices, was of relative indifference to the general public. What the public cared about were good fights that could be widely discussed in anticipation and recalled with relish. As we have seen, matches such as Beckett v Carpentier, or Wilde v Moore, or Driscoll v Ledoux, transcended the normal confines of the sport and became subjects of national interest commanding hundreds of column inches.

It requires a strong historical imagination in the indifferent 21st century to grasp how important boxing seemed in 1919. One tiny detail may help. The night of the Beckett v Carpentier match, an aeroplane was flown over London with the sole purpose of showing coloured lights in the night sky as a coded signal of the result for the benefit of the thousands thronging the pavements of the West End eager for news. Simultaneously, crowds estimated as 20,000 strong were packing the boulevards of Paris, awaiting the firing of huge rockets similarly coded to give the result. When the rockets exploded, filling the French sky with red sparks symbolising a Carpentier victory, the crowds stood still and sang 'La Marseillaise'. This was hardly *la guerre* but it was certainly *magnifique*.

Small wonder then, that prospects of the next dream match – Carpentier v new world/New World champion Jack Dempsey – filled the newspaper columns. Cochran offered Dempsey $185,000 to fight Carpentier in London; a Paris promoter offered Dempsey $250,000 and an unspecified percentage of the gate to fight Carpentier in Paris; New Orleans mustered a more modest $150,000; Cochran went up to $300,000; other American cities offered $350,000 to stage the match; Doc Kearns asked the Paris Wonderland for a minimum $250,000; the Paris Wonderland guaranteed Dempsey 1,200,000 francs plus another 250,000 francs from the film rights.

The authenticity of the stories, or their lack of it, is unimportant. They appeared throughout December 1919 and over the next year and a half, as each and every bait and its nuances were duly recorded. What mattered was that if the match were ever to be made, it would be the richest, the most important and the most widely covered fight boxing had ever known.

1   Myler, P., *A Century of Boxing Greats: Inside the Ring with the Hundred Best Boxers* (London: Robson Books, 1999) p. 84.

2   Full details of Dempsey's early difficult life can be gleaned from several sources, including two autobiographies: Dempsey, J. with Considine, B. & Slocum, B., *Massacre in the Sun* (London: World Distributors, 1963); Dempsey, J. with Piatelli, B., *Dempsey: The Autobiography of Jack Dempsey* (London: W. H. Allen, 1977); and two excellent if contrasting biographies: Roberts, R., *Jack Dempsey: The Manassa Mauler* (New York: Grove Press, 1980); Kahn, R., *A Flame of Pure Fire: Jack Dempsey and the Roaring '20s* (New York: Harcourt, Brace and Co., 1999).

3   Dempsey, J. with Piatelli, B., *Dempsey,* p. 7.

4   Dempsey, J. with Considine, B. & Slocum, B., *Massacre in the Sun,* p. 16.

5   Cavanaugh, J., *Tunney: Boxing's Brainiest Champ and His Upset of the Great Jack Dempsey* (New York: Random House, 2006) p. 115.

6   Gallico, P., *Farewell to Sport* (London: Sportspages, 1988) p. 14.

7   Roberts, R., *Jack Dempsey,* pp. 58–59.

8   See Heinz, W. C. & Ward, W., *The Book of Boxing* (New York: Sports Illustrated Classics, 1999) p. 298.

9   This account is mainly based on the film but there are valuable details to be gleaned from *The Times,* 5 July 1919; *New York Times* 5 & 6 July 1919; *Boxing,* 10 July 1919; *The Ring,* May 1945; Pacheco, F., *The 12 Greatest Rounds of Boxing: The Untold Stories* (London: Robson Books, 2004); Beadle, B., *Boxing's Mister President: The Story of the World Heavyweight Championship* (Dagenham: Wat Tyler Books, 1997); and all the biographies of Dempsey listed above. Every standard history of boxing includes the fight.

10 *Boxing News,* 3 October 2008.

11 Breslin, J., *Damon Runyon: A Life* (London: Hodder & Stoughton, 1992) pp. 192–193.

12 Gallico, P., *Farewell to Sport,* p. 29.

13 Goldman, H. G., 'Dempsey, Anyone?' *International Boxing Digest,* August 2000.

14 Mead, C., *Champion Joe Louis: A Biography* (London: Robson Books, 1993) p. 168.

15 Not at the NSC as *The British Boxing Board of Control Yearbook 2000* suggests. The fight was reported in *The Times,* 18 July 1919 as well as in, e.g. *Boxing* and *Mirror of Life*, all as taking place at Olympia.

16 Carpenter, H., *Masters of Boxing* (London: Heinemann, 1964) p. 25.

17 *The Times,* 19 July 1919.

18 *The Times,* 27 December 1919.

19 *The Times,* 19 September 1919.

20 *The Times,* 28 July 1919.

21 *The Times,* 8 December 1919.

22 Quoted by Shipley, S., *Bombardier Billy Wells: The Life and Trials of a Boxing Hero* (Tyne and Wear: Bewick Press, 1993) p. 159.

23 *The Times,* 21 November 1919.

24 *The Times,* 21 July 1919.

25 *The Times,* 3 September 1919.

26 See Pete Ehrmann: 'Eddie McGoorty: The Idol of Oshkosh' in *The Ring,* September 2000.

27 *The Times,* 3 December 1919.

28 *Boxing World, Mirror of Life and Sporting World,* 13 December 1919.

29 *New Statesman,* 13 December 1919.

30 *New Statesman,* 13 December 1919.

31 *Boxing World, Mirror of Life and Sporting Observer,* 13 December 1919.

32 *Illustrated London News,* 6 December 1919.

33 *The Times,* 27 December 1919, although only in late editions. See also Lewis, M., *Ted Kid Lewis: His Life and Times* (London: Robson Books, 1990) pp. 138–40.

34 *The Times,* 14 November 1919; Roderick, A., *Johnny! The Story of the Happy Warrior* (Newport: Heron Press, 1990) p. 76.

35 Lewis, M., *Ted Kid Lewis,* p. 136.

CHAPTER 15

MARKING TIME
1920

In Which Mighty Plans Are Made

THE *PUNCH Almanack* opened 1920's New Year with a pastoral drawing. Mr Punch, a tidily dressed farmer in wellington boots, opens his arms and smiles at the new dawn, yet he leads a ponderous shire horse pulling a plough for another dejected farmer who plods miserably behind, cutting through earth too unyielding for him. A curly-headed androgynous mite labelled '1920' rides on the horse, yet he/she can travel only as fast as the lumbering horse will allow.

After boxing's wonderful 1919, the sport's participants should have looked forward to the New Year with enthusiasm and optimism. Rather there was a sense of anticlimax, of marking time and of the sport lumbering along like the horse, obstructed by circumstances beyond the control of individuals.

New Year's night at the Holborn Stadium, for example, had a decidedly utilitarian look, of a management filling in a popular holiday date with token events, not matches demanding to be made. Curley Walker was a Bermondsey bantamweight near the end of his career (b. 4 February 1894). Turning professional in 1912, his moderate record eventually comprised

55 wins (12 KOs), 41 losses (six KOs) and ten draws. He retired in 1923. His opponent was Leon Poutet, a Frenchman, five years younger (b. 26 October 1899 in Marseilles) and better known as Eugene Criqui's sparring partner than for the 11 fights of his abbreviated professional career – three wins (one KO), five defeats (two KOs) and three draws. The light-punching Walker pursued the Frenchman in desultory fashion, and Poutet eked out a boring draw over 15 tiresome rounds.

The supporting bout was equally dull. Guardsman Charlie Penwill (b. 30 November 1895), a Devonian heavyweight who fought professionally from 1912 to 1929, was a journeyman with a slightly better career record – 52 wins (21 KOs), 38 defeats (17 KOs) and seven draws. (Had it not been for the serious interruption of the war, the careers of boxers such as Penwill and Walker *might* have been more impressive.)

Penwill also was up against French opposition. In the other corner was Paul Journée (b. 19 April 1893), who came from a village south-east of Paris, looked better than he fought and rarely let a contest go the distance, usually by

losing – seven wins (six KOs), 28 defeats (20 KOs) and one draw. To cynics, he was Paul Journéeman. He lost twice to Bombardier Billy Wells during 1920. At Holborn against Penwill, the bored referee in the 13th round spared Journée, or possibly himself.

(Journée's purses were modest yet he shrewdly acquired a portion of a 20 per cent share in the tragic figure of Primo Carnera (1906–67). This giant Italian heavyweight of the 1930s was infamously heralded, exploited and robbed by a sordid army of unscrupulous

Paul Journée (1893–19??), the tall (6ft 4ins/1.93m) Parisian heavyweight.
BnF

owners, crooked promoters and parasitic gangsters. Journée's investment in Carnera netted him 250,000 francs; rather more than he earned with his fists and much more than poor abused Carnera finished with.)

The first Monday night of the year at Covent Garden's NSC on 5 January did not sparkle either. The jollity of the annual pantomimes, *Cinderella* at Drury Lane and *Dick Whittington* at The Lyceum, contrasted strongly with the miserable boxing fare. This included Fred Jones, a mediocre featherweight from Rushden. Jones had limited successes in early 1920 but ran into serious opposition. His year culminated in a beating by a young inexperienced Scot, 'Hamilton' Johnny Brown (b. 1 January 1901), after which Jones retired with a record of seven wins (five KOs) and six defeats (two KOs). Jones at the January NSC outing outpointed Tommy Gardner from Smethwick over 15 rounds. Gardner had no better a career record – ten wins (five KOs) and ten defeats (four KOs). Jones v Gardner was no classic.

Memories of great featherweight fights before the war, such as the 1910 battles between Driscoll and Robson, were bitterly recalled by the NSC members on Monday, 26 January as they watched and suffered the first British title contest of 1920. Up for the British featherweight title were Mike Honeyman (b. 11 November 1896 in Woolwich) and Bill Marchant (b. 26 December 1890), one of four Salford boxing brothers. The pair had met before at the NSC on 13 October 1919 for a forgettable contest over 15 rounds won by Honeyman on points.

That October match was to find the best two British featherweights out of four possibilities – Honeyman, Marchant, Londoner Joe Conn and Welshman Francis Rossi. Conn's and Rossi's contributions had been dire. Their match (6 October 1919) had been so passive that they had been thrown out of the ring in the 17th round by referee J. H. Douglas for not trying and were afterwards suspended. The second meeting between Honeyman and Marchant was making the best of an already poor job.

The fight matched the low expectations.[1] The shorter Marchant (5ft 5in) was more aggressive and stronger. Honeyman used his extra height and defensive skills to neutralise him and to throw feeble counters. Referee Douglas gave the decision to Honeyman but he was not alone in finding the bout 'tedious to a degree'. One distinguished spectator agreed as he left, bored after ten rounds. He was Jim Driscoll, well aware of what standards featherweight champions could and should attain.

The NSC officials (Bettinson in particular) had worked hard to promote a satisfying championship club evening but failed. Yet suddenly commercial promoters and managers were having no better a time themselves. Poor Cochran in particular must have felt like the mournful farmer in the *Punch* drawing, trying desperately to carve an honest furrow through the soil of multiple deceptive negotiations and seeing firm and binding agreements dissolve as if written in mud. Only the glittering prize of an eventual lucrative meeting between Jack Dempsey and Georges Carpentier kept his hand to the plough.

Back in December 1919, Cochran was confident he had signed Carpentier for a 1920 fight against Dempsey for a £35,000 purse, split 60:40, winner:loser.[2] Kearns supposedly confirmed Cochran's offer would come first. The fight would certainly be at Olympia on 7 June. No such details would actually transpire.

Cochran spent most of January 1920 in the USA. From Chicago on 4 January to weeks in New York, he tried to get meaningful signatures on binding documents.[3] He was participating in a pugilistic poker game with hard-faced participants well used to taking issues down to the last card and more than capable of stringing him along. In the 18 months between early 1920 and July 1921 when, miraculously, all-round agreement was reached and the fight actually took place, the deals, double-deals and spurious contracts were multifarious. By that time Cochran was out of contention.

Cochran was up against the bargaining skills of the two managers, François Descamps and Doc Kearns. Descamps's famously paternal care for Carpentier was coupled with a tiger-like defence of Carpentier's and his own interests. Kearns was capable of all sorts of double-dealing to line his own pockets, and he defended Dempsey's interests vigorously, providing they did not impair his own. (In 1926 he brought three spurious lawsuits against Dempsey after they parted permanently.) A manager careless with his charge's assets was predatory with everyone else's.

Beyond the camps of the two fighters were eager promoters looking for a large piece of the action – Tex Rickard, for example. After Rickard's spectacular promotion of the Gans–Nelson epic of 1906, which had put

Goldfield, Nevada on the map and Goldfield's gold into Rickard's pockets, he flirted with several swindles and more legitimate schemes, home and abroad (Argentinian cattle ranching and touring circuses included). He never relinquished his interest in fight promotion, having a fat finger in both the Johnson–Jeffries and the Dempsey–Willard financial pies.

By 1920, Rickard returned to New York City and, with the financial backing of John Nichols Ringling (1866–1936), was running Madison Square Garden. Under him it became a venue not just for boxing but for any spectacle he could sell to a gullible public. John Nichols Ringling was the most famous of the seven brothers who became synonymous with circus. By 1929 they owned every circus in the USA. Controlling lions, tigers, elephants and clowns was no more exotic or troublesome than negotiating with Rickard in his late prime, so Cochran was entering a lion's cage in doing so.

Another player was the sometime boxing promoter, sometime theatre producer, and permanent gambler William Aloysius Brady (1863–1950).[4] Like Rickard and Cochran, Brady won and lost fortunes at regular intervals, and like Cochran would go for any theatrical or boxing promotion that took his fancy. He made fortunes from staging melodramas on Broadway and touring sentimental weepies around the country.

Boxing fans knew him better as the manager who had signed up James J. Corbett and led the handsome young fellow to the 1892 victory over John L. Sullivan. Among Brady's promotional gimmicks then was a commissioned poster showing Corbett in the intimate company of Queen Victoria, Gladstone, the Kaiser and the Russian Tsar. Corbett had never been near any of them. Brady also acquired James J. Jeffries, one-time sparring partner to Corbett, and took him to the world heavyweight championship in turn. (Jeffries was a retired undefeated champion until he was persuaded to return against his nemesis Jack Johnson.)

The Californian promoter James Coffroth (1872–1943), outbid by Tex Rickard for the Johnson/Jeffries promotion, also hovered. He sent a message, duly reported in the New York sports pages, that he had obtained Kearns's signature for Dempsey to meet Carpentier in Tijuana over 45 rounds for a purse of £80,000 and that his agent was in France securing agreement from Carpentier to such a deal.[5] These details too proved spurious.

Even more bizarrely, William Fox (1879–1952) of the Fox Film Corporation claimed, with Hollywood hyperbole, an agreement to a Labor Day clash between Dempsey and Carpentier worth $300,000 to Dempsey and $250,000 to Carpentier, plus $200,000 profits to split between them, and another $40,000 for the American Red Cross. These unlikely sums were based, said Fox, on building an arena in the New York area plus incidental promotional expenses for a mere $150,000 and then selling seats as follows: 200 at $1,000; 500 at $500; 5,000 at $100; and 15,000 at $10, producing a projected gate of a cool $1,100,000.[6] The arithmetic also sounds awry.

Confusion upon confusion! Fox, Coffroth, Brady, Rickard, Kearns, Descamps, Dempsey, Carpentier – small wonder that Cochran sailed back to London before the end of January no nearer a definitive deal than he had been in 1919.

Promoters and managers in 1920 believed that boxers had become greedy, perverse and less tractable than their pre-war counterparts. Gone were the days when they obligingly signed on the dotted line when told to do so, or waited, cap in hand, at the tradesman's entrance for an audience graciously granted by the money man.

Take Joe Beckett, the current British heavyweight champion. Here was the uneducated product of travelling fairground folk taking on all-comers at boxing booths from the age of 12 and for whom a book was a foreign object. Stories circulated freely about his unsophisticated views. (Reporter: 'Have you ever been to Switzerland?' Beckett: 'No. There ain't no Swedish heavyweights.')[7] How could such a man understand the legal and financial subtleties of a contract without the paternal guidance of a good manager? What he needed was to leave matters to those who properly understood them. Boxers like Beckett did not necessarily conform to such mistaken managerial expectations.

Beckett was a loose cannon, often at odds with authority, yet with plenty of native wit. Speeding through Brentford in an unregistered car brought him a £1 fine with costs at the magistrates' court.[8] Not for Joe the humble apology and the paying of a modest fine representing a tiny fraction of his ring income. He argued forcefully that he had just bought the car and had no time to register it. He added that he needed it because of a rail strike and was only travelling because he had promised to box an exhibition for war widows' and orphans' funds.

Watched by Kearns, Dempsey and Descamps, Carpentier signs for the fight of the century – it would not happen quickly.
Bain collection, Prints & Photographs Division, Library of Congress, LC-DIG-ggbain-50391

Whatever he lacked in education, his sob story made up for in ingenuity.

He wriggled out of another court case the following month when sued by his manager, Bernard Mortimer, for the return of a loan of nearly £4,000, including training expenses. Mortimer sought an order to prevent Beckett boxing without his specific permission. Mortimer lost the suit.[9] Beckett's version must have been persuasive. The verdict also shows that boxers could take contractual claims to law and be supported against their so-called betters.

Jack Dempsey, ultimate target of Cochran's wooing, was also at odds with authority, in particular with the military. He was the target for waspish comment about his war record. The American Legion, still going strong today, was founded in 1919 by servicemen returning from European First World War battlefields. Then as now, it vigorously promoted and defended the welfare and interests of veterans. Many members strongly felt that Dempsey's fighting for money was immoral, while many of his weaker brethren were risking their lives abroad.

John S. Smith, chairman of the New Jersey Athletic Commission, for example, pronounced that 'in support of the American Legion I wish to state that Jack Dempsey is not good enough for the State of New Jersey' and was against Dempsey boxing anywhere in the state.[10]

Similar resolutions were passed in Cleveland and Indianapolis. *Home Sector*, an ex-soldiers' magazine, printed a virulent editorial comparing the non-combatant Dempsey with his potential opponent war hero Carpentier, much to Dempsey's detriment. Meanwhile,

Dempsey's well-intentioned wartime recruiting drive in a Pennsylvania dockyard backfired when his patent leather shoes showed beneath the overalls.
Bettmann/GettyImages

wounded soldiers in a federal hospital on Staten Island sent a hostile questionnaire to Dempsey posing loaded questions about his wartime activities and asking the champion 'to tell how much money he earned in the prize ring while the American boys in France were busy fighting and dying'.[11] The *New York Times* joined the bandwagon with a snide editorial stance:

… Dempsey, six feet one of strength, in the glowing splendor of his youth, a man fashioned by nature as an athlete and a warrior – Dempsey did not go to the war, while weak-armed, strong-hearted clerks reeled under pack and rifle; while middle-aged men with families volunteered … Dempsey did not go to France to do battle for forty-eight states, but is ready now to go for four hundred thousand dollars.[12]

Disturbed by threats to the earning power of his charge, Jack Kearns issued an open letter outlining Dempsey's need to support his family in the war and the many dollars Dempsey had raised for the war funds.[13] All this was true but hostile publicity is a powerful stimulus to political action. Sure enough, by February, Dempsey was indicted to appear on charges of unreasonably avoiding the draft. The result of that hearing we will see later.

The protracted negotiations about the fight were looking more farcical than meaningful. British journals did not hesitate to point that out. *Punch* took the appropriately satirical line twice in January 1920. It published a cartoon showing a group of street urchins under a railway bridge with two squaring up

to each other. Action could not start without one of them acting the embryo promoter/manager and negotiating an appropriate fee in marbles: 'Look 'ere! 'Fore my man fights he wants two potties, three glassies an' a blood-alley; an' I wants a packet o' fags for meself.'[14]

A week later a comic article dealt with the financial negotiations surrounding other championships such as the World's Halma Championship, the Ladies' Patience Championship, and the World's Cokernut (*sic*) Shying Championship. Disputes apparently included rival claims from the Home for Stray Cats and the Fund in Aid of Distressed Spinsters.[15] Elsewhere, the issue solemnly declared, 'It is reported on good authority that Mr C. B. COCHRAN will visit America daily until the signature of DEMPSEY'S manager is obtained.'

Despite the anticlimactic nature of early 1920 and the ludicrous mating dances around the projected Dempsey v Carpentier bout, some events pleased and some pre-war patterns repeated themselves. Visits made by ambitious British fighters such as Matt Wells, Billy Wells, Owen Moran, Ted Kid Lewis and Freddie Welsh to the rings of the USA before and during the war inspired others to do the same. Despite the misgivings of his truest supporters, Jimmy Wilde sailed across the Atlantic and from December 1919 until the end of May 1920 fought exclusively in American and Canadian rings. He was not always at his best as we saw with the 6 December 1919 meeting with Jack Sharkey in Milwaukee (Chapter 14).

In St Louis, Missouri on 8 January 1920, he met local champion Babe (Johnny) Asher, seven pounds heavier and very much less experienced than

he, and despite his obvious superiority in class, failed to knock Asher out even when landing clean punches to the jaw.[16] Puzzled ringsiders concluded that Wilde was not the merciless finisher his reputation suggested. They forgot that 27-year-old Wilde was engaging in about his 135th fight and was no longer able to pull out his best every time.

The real Wilde was not on show until 29 January 1920 when, now fully acclimatised to American conditions and physically fitter at 7st 10½lb/108½lbs, he demolished Mike Ertle (b. 4 October 1898) in Milwaukee in the third.[17] Ertle (not to be confused with his brother Johnny) held his own for two rounds but succumbed to a perfect Wilde combination in the third. Wilde drew down Ertle's guard with a right feint to the body, and the moment Ertle's descending left glove left his jaw exposed, Wilde whipped the right over to the chin. Ertle fell over backwards and needed 30 seconds' attention from his seconds before gaining consciousness. Less was said about Wilde's lost punching power after that. He had eight more fights on his tour and, although he lost none of them, in only half did he knock his opponent out. Perhaps he had indeed been going on too long.

Another European sojourner in the lucrative green fields of the USA was Georges Carpentier, anxious to pick up a few dollars towards his marital funds after getting married in Paris on 8 March 1920. Although the ceremony was secret, vast crowds turned up. He was Europe's biggest draw yet he needed to boost his reputation in the USA were he to justify an enhanced share of the purse in a future clash with Dempsey. Instead of a honeymoon, five days after the ceremony the couple stepped on to the *Savoie,* a French ocean liner, and sailed for New York.

The more naïve fan might have thought that the obvious way to boost Carpentier's fighting image in the USA was for him to go there and destroy a few good American fighters the way he had mercilessly carved his way through every British contender. Members of Carpentier's entourage, especially Descamps, saw that as distinctly dangerous. Suppose, like Bombardier Billy, he were to flatter only to deceive and finish flat on his back after a wild thump from some overambitious American heavyweight? That would kill any fabulous payday with Dempsey.

No, the plan for Carpentier, once the newlyweds recovered from their Atlantic seasickness, was to boost him without risk. All the Frenchman had to face initially were American pressmen full of questions at press conferences, and film cameras at the New Jersey studios where he starred as the French secret service agent and boxer Henri D'Alour in a 1920 silent epic called *The Wonder Man.* For minimal acting and carefully controlled boxing sequences against a non-boxer, Carpentier picked up a modest $45,000. After that there was a luxury tour of about 40 towns giving four-round exhibitions with his regular sparring partner Jules Lanaers.[18] They then toured with the Sells Floto Circus along with the elephants for two months. Here he followed in the large footsteps of Dempsey, who capped his 1919 Toledo title-winning fight not with a speedy defence but a lucrative tour with the pachyderm heavyweights of the Sells Floto ring.[19]

Dempsey's heavyweight title was also an admission ticket to places such

as 'Pickfair', the luxurious 22-room mansion in Los Angeles built by Mary Pickford and Douglas Fairbanks and now venue for glamorous parties with readily available Hollywood actresses. Celebrity and newly won riches could do for a sportsman what had once been restricted to the socially distinguished. A 'Pickfair' party was a more salubrious and sexier place to be than a sweaty gym or a lowly brothel.

Whatever the American jaunt did or did not do for Carpentier's prestige as a fighter, it added almost $100,000 to his pocket. He was no slouch at the life of a bon viveur himself. 'I was certainly popular with the women,' he wrote later, although he always knew when to ease off and get fighting fit again.

Carpentier's American adventures, in and out of the circus, like Wilde's boxing tour, appeared relatively novel. Too many domestic events in Britain looked a stale repetition of what had gone before. Nothing in 1920 was more futile than that hardy perennial, the relaunching of Bombardier Billy Wells. What anticlimaxes his defeats by Carpentier and Beckett had been; mortifying nights when passionate patriotic hopes and the fervour of his gratifyingly loyal fans had collided dismally with reality.

It was as if the memory bank had been wiped clean when 1920 began and fair Billy was back in action. First was the 27 January date against Harry Reeve of Plaistow at the Canterbury Music Hall.[20] Reeve (b. 7 January 1893), whose career lasted 24 years from 1910–34, was roughly six years younger than Wells, considerably shorter (5ft 8in) and a hard-working boxer always up for a fight – if not always for training or temperance. Being a

light-heavy himself, he was expected to take the fight to Wells, especially as he was quite vocal pre-fight about his determination to prove himself better than the ex-champion.

Harry had not had a happy war. A private in the military police, he served in the notoriously squalid base camp at Étaples near Boulogne. On 9 September 1917, he fired into a rebellious crowd of angry soldiers and killed a Gordon Highlander and a French woman onlooker. The act provoked a full mutiny, one quelled by ruthless action and punishments, including penal servitude and an execution. Reeve was court martialled and imprisoned for a year. Back in action on release, shrapnel seriously damaged his leg. Only in January 1919 was he able to box again, with mixed results. And a mere eight days before the Wells fight, he lost to Dick Rice on points over 20 rounds at The Ring. With a new sense of discretion, unsurprising after his experiences, he stood off and fought at a distance, a tactic that suited Wells admirably.

Occasionally Reeve made Wells grunt with short punches to the body. More often he smothered Wells's right with his own left and raised ugly red welts along Wells's body with his laces. Such marks were irritating but did not hamper Wells seriously. By the third round, Wells realised there was no serious danger and that Reeve could be kept away with an occasional left jab.

Complacently, Wells intended to continue passively for a 20-round points victory, but willing to accept any presents that came his way. A convenient one, gift-wrapped and irresistible, arrived in the fourth. A weak lead and a dropped guard left

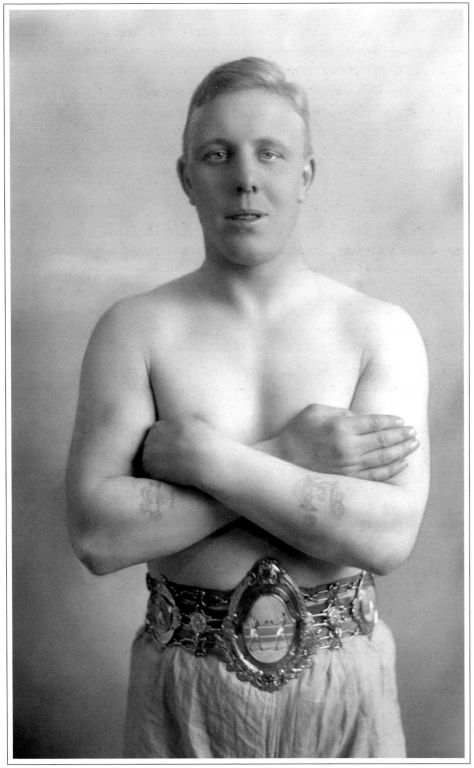

Harry Reeve (1873–1958). The Plaistow heavyweight endured a fraught war, wounded and court martialled for shooting at a crowd, killing a civilian.

PA Images/Alamy Stock Photo

black fighter lost (light-heavy Harold 'Rocky' Knight b. c.1899) and another won (featherweight Sam Minto, a Barbadian living in London b. c.1894). No disturbances ensued. Indeed Minto was a presence in British rings from 1912 to 1934. Knight, another Barbadian Englishman, moved into the heavies and travelled, taking contests from Boston to Budapest. He became the subject of the perfect trivia question by losing on points over eight rounds in Cologne on 4 October 1924 to a young and inexperienced German called Max Schmeling (b. 28 September 1905). Knight was around until 1931.

Wells would not be around in the 1930s when the mighty Schmeling became world famous for his fights against Joe Louis, but meanwhile went on beating hand-picked opponents. The next was Paul Journée, the largely unsuccessful French heavyweight credited with that scrappy victory over Charlie Penwill at Holborn. On 17 March 1920 at the Royal Albert Hall, Wells met Journée, supposedly over a full 20 rounds, but some records have this down as of *two*-minute rounds. Wells's stamina was hardly being tested. What *was* being tested was whether Wells's drawing power retained its pre-war strength. *The Times* confirmed it was intact:

> The mere fact that Wells was to appear was a sufficient reason for the presence of a great crowd [including many glamorous women]. Win, lose, or draw, Wells is a sure magnet for a stream of gold into the promoter's pocket.[21]

Reeve wide open. Wells stepped back half a pace to increase his power then drove a neat right straight to Reeve's chin. Flat on his face, an inert Reeve

was counted out and Billy's career was supposedly back on track.

Interestingly, the bill included two black v white contests in which one

Wells was older than Journée but more skilled, more experienced, heavier, taller, faster and with a longer reach. Only in appetite for a contest did Journée exceed him. His willingness to continue in the face of heavy punishment retained minimal interest as the contest dragged on. Wells showed, round after abbreviated round, his inability to despatch an inferior boxer unless he fell over cooperatively when jabbed to the face. At no time did he punch Journée about the body.[22]

Even in the final round, the 13th, Journée got up five times from the canvas before a sixth knockdown finished him off as much by aggregation as by the final right swing.

C. B. Cochran was not impressed by Wells's powers of execution, but he saw the attraction of a full paying audience. He speedily signed Wells up to come to the Holborn Stadium and meet, at enhanced prices, another heavyweight whose drawing power exceeded his waning punches – Eddie McGoorty, a man first in the ring in 1900. The American had been a lithe, skilful and successful middleweight before the war. By 1920 he was a podgy heavyweight going through the motions and picking up purses to pay his alcohol bill. Posted to France by the US Army late in the war, he had battled with magnums of French champagne in Paris rather than with Germans in the trenches. The drinking continued post-war. Having knocked out Harry Reeve at the NSC in May 1919, he celebrated so well he left his winner's cheque on the dressing room floor. When sobriety and cheque were temporarily restored to him a few days later, he had no recollection of cheque or fight.

Wells and McGoorty had met over three rounds on an amateur basis at the King's Trophy in December 1919,

Wells winning on points in a bout that proved very little. The real question was whether either fighter could deliver a genuine performance over a full 20 rounds. The fight at Holborn on 8 April 1920 depended on which man could more nearly match his past prowess on the night.[23]

Against Journée, Wells had laboured mightily to beat a lesser man. McGoorty had just (4 March 1920 at Holborn) met the tough and ponderous Frank Goddard in a fight with an unsurprising conclusion.[24] Goddard moved cumbrously forward, looking to nail McGoorty with one of his slow big punches, relying on his own legendary capacity to take plenty for the sake of delivering one. Big, strong and young, he had prepared for a long fight. McGoorty in this late phase was thoroughly unprepared and looking to use his old skills to outwit the mountain in front of him.

For four rounds, it was all McGoorty, making Goddard miss embarrassingly and moving in and out to clip his opponent firmly to the jaw with rights and lefts. Unfortunately, McGoorty's failure to train adequately had him slowing visibly like a child's toy with a depleting battery. This was just what Goddard needed. He landed more and more while McGoorty's counters looked like tickles. By the 12th, McGoorty could barely hold his arms up and Goddard made free play with attacking punches. Twice in the round McGoorty wearily subsided to the floor, once for a count of nine and once a second before the bell sounded. No one believed he would last the 13th and he did not. Although McGoorty tried to keep away, Goddard lumbered after him and one more right to the chin finished it.

Form suggested that Wells would beat the latter-day McGoorty, providing McGoorty did not catch him early with one of his favourite left hooks, and providing Wells did not suffer a paralysing bout of big-occasion nerves. On the night, there were a few surprises.

First, the McGoorty who turned up was a fitter version of the man who had succumbed to Goddard. Second, the fight was genuinely exciting, to which both fighters brought something new.[25] Wells outboxed McGoorty from the start. Using all his advantages in reach and height (five inches), Wells was quicker to the punch, confident and aggressive, and tested McGoorty's defensive ploys beyond their limits. His old failings showed when he had openings and did not follow up immediately. Under the onslaught, McGoorty wilted but by a judicious mixture of holding and covering survived.

By the eighth, McGoorty was still there and finding reserves of energy no one believed he still had. Suddenly he began to fight back. Despite seven and a half rounds of punishment, and despite appearing to be on his last legs, he took the fight to Wells. The one-way traffic went into reverse. Now it was Wells going backwards and McGoorty winning rounds. McGoorty dominated the 11th and in the 12th was on the verge of knocking Wells out.

Wells, sensing that McGoorty's extraordinary recovery must have finite limits, dug deep himself, showing an unaccustomed determination to outlast the man presently outlasting him. Holding his own in the 13th, he dominated the 14th. A powerful left hook sank painfully into McGoorty, who went down for nine, needing every second to recover. The hurt American looked vulnerable throughout the 15th, a man awaiting a final dismissal. It came in the 16th when Wells, knowing there was now no danger, delivered left and right hooks to McGoorty's undefended jaw for a clean knockout.

In the excitement reigning in the Holborn Stadium through the see-sawing fortunes of both fighters, it was easy to forget that McGoorty should already have retired and that Wells almost lost a fight he should easily have won. C. B. Cochran, undeterred, heavily boosted a return contest between the supposedly rehabilitated Bombardier Billy ('today a vastly better man than any one of us has really believed', said *Boxing* helpfully) and the surly champion, Joe Beckett.

Beckett's record in early 1920, outside his difficulties with magistrates and litigious managers, is easily told. After his ignominious demise against Carpentier in December 1919, he had no fights until March 1920. On 5 March 1920 he met the veteran Dick Smith at the Royal Albert Hall in five rounds of stirring action.[26] Smith, ex-amateur champion and the better boxer, was Beckett's master at a distance. With Beckett on the end of his leads he could hurt and visibly damage the shorter man. For reasons known only to himself, he began with two rounds in which he went toe to toe with Beckett, exchanging punches with alacrity but ultimately weakening when Beckett's punches proved the weightier. When he went back to his regular style, he was too weak to keep the bustling and stronger Beckett permanently away from him. In close, Beckett pummelled Smith to the body and hooked and uppercut him about the jaw and head. In the fourth, despite a strong left that

stopped Beckett temporarily, Smith paid the price. Beckett's retaliation was a series of uppercuts that took Smith backwards into a tangle with the ropes and ultimately to the floor. Up at nine, he was seriously stunned and barely able to last the round. In the fifth Beckett repeated the treatment and Smith failed to beat an early count.

Beckett, after the fights against Carpentier and Smith, was clearly vulnerable to punches from a good boxer, but knew how to finish a fight once it was going his way. Wells, after the fight with McGoorty, was clearly vulnerable even to inferior fighters, and never predictable. With all the prospects of a classic British triumph or a classic British fiasco, Wells v Beckett II, or perhaps technically II½, had 20,000 people, including many women, packing out Olympia on 10 May 1920.[27]

Wells began aggressively with long-range punches, landing most of them and to the right places. Beckett, showing the defensive frailties that had cost him dearly against Carpentier, bustled in clumsily, leaving himself open. Beckett threw punches with the profligacy of a man seeding a lawn and landed accurately perhaps two out of every ten. Unfortunately for Wells, his own consistently targeted punches had little serious effect, while Beckett's heavier occasionals hurt.

Beckett's crouch exaggerated the difference in height between them, yet Wells's height and reach counted for little when Beckett's sporadic battering caused him such discomfort. There was a symbolic exchange towards the end of the first. Beckett charged crudely in, arms swinging, clearly inviting a sharp counter. Wells delivered a smart right uppercut and a curt left hook, both to

Beckett's jaw. That should have been that. It was not. Beckett wobbled but marched in, irritated not deterred.

Similarly in the second, Wells rocked Beckett's head back with a left and landed a right hook to his ribs. Neither halted Beckett, punching as wildly yet as fiercely as ever. Wells was dropped to his knees by a left uppercut and took nine seconds of the count to get up again, looking woebegone. A large ice bag held to his temple by his seconds in the interval helped little.

Out came Beckett for the third, swinging away crudely in his eagerness. Wells's counters had no significant effect on his swarthy opponent. A heavy left and a heavy right staggered Wells, and a final left brought Wells's weary arms down, exposing his chin to a driving right. Over he went with some force, banging the back of his head on the boards and lying deaf to the voice of the referee counting him out.

Unkindly, it was pointed out that after Wells's first loss to Beckett he claimed he had taken Beckett too casually and trained insufficiently. This time he had trained very hard, only to find himself beaten in even shorter order. It was time to call it a day on his career.

Beckett cashed in on his latest win with a lucrative advertising contract for a magic potion called Sargol. Sargol was widely advertised in, for example, the *Sunday Times* of 16 May 1920, endorsed by Beckett, who was now 'The Lion of the Ring', credited with 'Clever boxing, Great Strength, Fine Physique and … Terrific Lightning-like Punches', and the 'Coming Champion of the World'. How could a mere mortal like Wells have beaten a Beckett subject to such a metamorphosis? Gallons of Sargol could hardly post facto have restored Wells's career this time.

If Beckett needed the assistance of Sargol, the world heavyweight champion Jack Dempsey needed Sargol and every magic chemical presently available for his latest contest against the US authorities on a charge of draft dodging heard in June 1920 in a San Francisco courtroom.[28] Under the requirements of the war, which the USA entered formally in April 1917, the government resorted to a military draft to raise troops to send to Europe. It was amended in 1918 to exempt two categories of men: those working in industries essential to the war effort and those supporting a family. Dempsey was placed in the second category.

Sensibly, at Kearns's urging, Dempsey put no faith in patent drugs, rather in hiring a first-class expensive lawyer Gavin McNab, a legal eagle who had just (March 1920) extracted Mary Pickford from her first marriage to a violent and drunken actor to allow her to marry her lover Douglas Fairbanks. It probably cost Dempsey a cool $75,000 up front but was worth every cent if it kept him out of jail and notching further ring earnings. (If the roaring '20s roared for anyone, they certainly roared for Dempsey. During that decade there were only five one million-dollar gates for fights. Dempsey participated in all five of them. He would not have done that from a prison cell.)

The trial began on Tuesday, 8 June before Judge Maurice T. Dooling and an all-male jury of agents, stockbrokers, wholesalers and merchants. Only one of their number (a wholesaler of dry goods) had ever seen Dempsey fight. Jury attitudes were unpredictable, unlike those of the court spectators,

many wearing prominent American Legion buttons in their lapels.

Cleverly, McNab ensured that prominent in the room would be Dempsey's separated parents, the white-haired Hiram and Celia, temporarily reunited to defend their son, the man whose claim to be a non-combatant rested upon his need to box to support them during the war, as well as to support Maxine his estranged wife, his widowed sister (also present in the courtroom) and her two children. McNab knew how to use silent images of persuasion.

Kearns secretly played his own part by supplying, quite improperly, free food, booze and accommodation to pressmen attending the trial. McNab's handsome fee and the hospitality money were raised from Rickard and Ringling by Kearns, all three men anxious to keep Dempsey, their potential cash cow, out of clink.

The first day's hearing was devoted to a detailed examination of Dempsey's original service questionnaire. Relative minor errors and financial inconsistencies were pointed out. Apparently, the real filler of the form had been Kearns. Dempsey had filled in a few gaps and signed on the dotted line. This did not look too helpful to Dempsey's case but McNab and Kearns ensured that evening that the complaisant reporters enjoying their complimentary cheer were heavily briefed on the fact that a draftee did not need to be the *only* source of support for those dependent upon him, merely the *main* support. With the open-handedness characteristic of Dempsey in mind, this was almost certainly true and on its basis he had been granted 4A status. On the main charge he

was innocent, although Kearns hardly went out of his way in the form filling, helpfully to allow Uncle Sam to take over his protégée and main source of income.

Being innocent and being declared innocent in a court of law in a hostile environment are two different things, as both McNab and the chief prosecutor Colonel Charles W. Thomas, assistant US attorney, well knew. If, on the second day, some less salubrious aspects of Dempsey and his private life could be highlighted, then perhaps 12 good men could be persuaded to condemn one amoral/immoral one. Here, the prosecution believed they held the trump card by calling as a witness Maxine Dempsey, sometime wife, full-time sex worker and good-time girl to whom her husband had been violent and on whose behalf he had pimped likely clients.

Maxine had already made public attempts to damage Dempsey's reputation. Six months before, she wrote to the *San Francisco Chronicle* (23 January 1920) calling into question Dempsey's claim to have supported her. She suggested her 'fees' had supported *him*, and that she possessed 23 of his letters to her which 'proved' he and Kearns had jointly conspired to get a favourable draft rating. However, at a formal meeting in February 1920 with Thomas, she retracted her claims, saying she had lied in a fit of temporary jealousy. Maxine's equivocation might have made a cautious prosecutor hesitate but the infamous letters were actually of 'a salacious nature'. A frank discussion between an admitted prostitute and a famous heavyweight champion, both comfortable with the language of the bar and the brothel, about their sexual preferences and practices – it is difficult to think of better fodder for a tabloid editor, or, more importantly, for a prosecution looking to bring the man down. If Thomas could have extracts from the letters read in court or have Maxine disclose their fruitier contents, Dempsey was as good as banged up already. (Had not Jack Johnson, one of Dempsey's predecessors, been irreparably damaged in court and convicted by evidence of sexual impropriety?)

On the second day, some of Maxine's fellow sex-workers and two madams in whose brothels she had resided were called to the stand. Nothing in the evidence cast doubt as to Maxine's chosen source of income or suggested marriage had made much difference to her lifestyle. Inevitably, the answers cast her in as unfavourable a light as Dempsey.

On the other hand, a Dr Fife testified to having been called to a brothel to treat a woman with a dislocated jaw. She (Maxine by implication) claimed then that falling downstairs had done the damage. Perhaps it had been from a punch (from Dempsey by implication) but she had been too afraid to say so. That was not a detail calculated to give the jury a favourable impression of the powerful man slumped in a chair in the front of the courtroom.

No appearances were more closely scrutinised than the entrance of the star witness – Maxine. Walking with poise and certainty, dressed in a smart and revealing black dress, she crossed the courtroom floor within a few feet of her ex-husband, barely deigning to look at him, and took the witness chair like a model arranging herself for a glamour photograph. This elegant impression, in strong contrast to the grubby details heard about her, was barely dented when she admitted she had been known under several aliases. For example, she had been 'Bobby Stewart', a prominent servicer of clients in a Cairo, Illinois brothel.

The legality of her testimony was questioned. Prosecutor Thomas waved Dempsey's questionnaire in front of her and demanded, 'Do you recognise the signature?' McNab was on his feet immediately, arguing that any answer would require testimony relating to the period from 9 October 1916 to 4 February 1919 when Maxine and Dempsey had been man and wife. Private matters, including confidential letters one to another, were privileged by the marriage. No spouse could testify against the other. Ninety minutes of legal disputation followed. Eventually, Judge Dooling admitted he was unsure whether a subsequent divorce invalidated the confidentiality but promised to rule on the matter next day.

This approach temporarily thwarted Thomas's next attempt to introduce the notorious letters as containing evidence of Dempsey's illegitimate attempts to avoid service, surely 'a higher doctrine than so-called spousal privilege'. The judge was not to be intimidated and reiterated his promise to rule on the letters next day. His promise gave small comfort to the prosecution's supplementary tactics, making it clear that the case was to be strictly a legal one, not as a trial of morals:

The only question is whether or not Dempsey evaded the draft, not whether he has violated the white slave law or any other question of morals. Because Jack Dempsey happens to be a prizefighter and because the newspapers have played up his case he is not going to get any different sort of trial than if he were plain John Doe, charged with the same offence.

That was bad news for the prosecution, although they still hoped the letters *would* be permitted next day, in which case more sordid goings-on could still be introduced along with matters strictly germane to the draft charge.

The third day's hearing was as dramatic as any spectator could have wished. It began with Judge Dooling's cool and careful decision on the letters. They were inadmissible and could not be cited as evidence of Dempsey's conduct on the main charge. Nevertheless, the now divorced Mrs Dempsey was at liberty, within the judge's careful supervision, to testify against her ex-husband. This was the cue for Maxine, in another modish low-cut black dress, to repeat her catwalk-like parade to the front.

Helped by prosecutor Thomas, she recounted her travels and travails during 1917 and 1918 and how she made her money – 'I worked in houses' – unblushingly making it clear that 'houses' meant brothels. Her frankness took the *San Francisco Chronicle* reporter aback: 'So eager was she to dwell on the sordid details of her life in one city after another that she ran ahead of the questions …' She talked of Dempsey's violence towards her: 'Dempsey made me support him … And when I didn't do it good he knocked me down.' She explained that the infamous dislocated jaw had indeed come from a punch from Jack. (At this point, Dempsey looked quite ready to get out of his chair and punch her again.) She emphasised that his payments to her were minimal ('Dempsey was cheap') and totalled no more than $900 over the period from January 1917 up to November 1918 when they formally separated.

There was plenty here to make the champion look less than an upright citizen in the eyes of the jury. Thomas wanted further to convince them that Dempsey was guilty of draft evasion. To this end, despite the judge's general ruling, he sought to have one particular letter read out in court. Judge Dooling read it himself, allowed the defence to read it, and then coolly pronounced, 'I will not permit Maxine Dempsey to testify to anything regarding that letter.' The sending of moneys and the delivery of blows were not privileged communications; a private marital letter was.

Worse was to follow for the prosecution. Three Western Union employees from the Salt Lake City office testified that more, and more generous, payments from Jack had been collected by Maxine, and that she had been a more frequent recipient at their office than Jack's mother. They also recalled some of Maxine's less guarded remarks. On the receipt of $200 from Jack just after the Fulton fight, she had said, 'Fulton must have hit Jack hard to jar him loose from $200.' More damagingly, she had said on another occasion, 'Jack always sends plenty of money when he has it.' Once she had been sent two payments in two days and admitted, 'I needed it. I lost the first lot playing craps.'

Maxine's stunning appearance and her forthright account of matters many women would have glossed over, lent her words conviction. But this had been under the benign leading and sympathetic questions of prosecutor Thomas. Her vague testimony about the money she had or had not received from Dempsey had been less convincing, especially as the Western Union men had contradicted it. And now she had to face a hostile cross-examination from McNab, one of the sharpest forensic minds around.

He soon proved that the sums sent by Dempsey to Maxine were nearer to $2,000 than $900. The more he pressed her on details, the vaguer she became. The total became something she 'guessed … was about $900', but could give no dates or amounts to support the guess.

As the afternoon continued, McNab had other questions for her about the infamous letters and what she had chosen to do with them. Maxine's confident volubility of the morning was replaced by increasing aphasia ('I don't remember!') and by temporary deafness ('I couldn't hear the question'). Her answers became ever more nebulous and unconvincing ('I'm not swearing to anything!'), even bizarre. She claimed she had threatened to publish the letters not for personal gain or out of pique but out of patriotic duty: 'I just wanted to help the government.' Sure.

McNab pointed out how a news item stating that Dempsey would be getting $250,000 to fight Georges Carpentier coincided with the particular patriotic duty that had led Maxine to contact the *San Francisco Chronicle*. The item inspired her to say to fellow inmates at the 'house' that she was going to make sure she got $40,000

of it herself. McNab let listeners draw their own conclusions as to the correct interpretation of the workings of Maxine's conscience. There is no doubt about who was well ahead on points at the end of this third day.

The fourth day was much less dramatic and just as favourable to the defence. McNab was temporarily absent, having gone off to deal with an embarrassing appeal hearing in the Pickford divorce case – some celebrity clients being clearly more important than others. He had his assistant John Preston put Celia Dempsey on the stand ('a little, white-haired, wrinkled woman with hands gnarled by hard work and shoulders bent by years' – loaded phrasing that shows at least one journalist responding to Kearns's generosity).

Preston gently led her through questions about the financial support Dempsey had provided for her and the rest of the family ever since he became an adult. 'How could you have managed in the years in question, ma'm, 1917 and 1918, if Jack hadn't sent you money?' 'I couldn't have managed. We wouldn't have had anything at all.' Jack had supported her with some $37,000 in those years. Celia recounted a succession of family tragedies – the poor health of two of her other sons refused for enlistment on medical grounds; the murder of young Bruce; the deficiencies of Hiram as breadwinner ('crippled with rheumatism and inclined at times of absent-mindedness and melancholy' – the drink and the infidelities were tactfully not mentioned). The generosity of her famous son's financial support for this demure lady seemed clear. It is notable that it was the demure Celia who presented herself, rather than the feisty lady capable of threatening violence when crossed.

Demure Celia, the reticent mother-in-law, added further details about Maxine's deficiencies as a wife. Jack's purse from the Willard fight had helped to install Celia in a new $20,000 luxury house but domestic bliss there had not been. 'She had been restless and dissatisfied for a long time. She used to say that life in Salt Lake was too slow … "I'd rather go back to my old life and smoke hop than stay in any show place like this," she said once.'

Under cross-examination Celia stuck to every detail of her testimony. On the adjournment of the case until after the weekend, the prospects for Dempsey and Kearns looked much rosier than on the first day when the infamous questionnaire had been dissected.

Sunday's paper puffed the Monday appearance of the champion himself who 'will bare story of long struggle', and of a defence that 'has many witnesses to produce when case reopens'. Kearns's hospitality dollars were paying off. Only directly from the defence could the *Chronicle* have known that 'Lodging-house keepers and others [are] to be called to offer testimony in contradiction of her statements that Dempsey ill-treated her and to corroborate the story that her greed for money was the real reason behind her sudden desire to "show up" her former husband.' Not so much 'Doc' Kearns as 'Spin Doc' Kearns.

The inspired predictions proved perfectly correct when Monday's hearing featured Dempsey on the stand in person. Considering how alien the environment and how much the man would have preferred to let his fists speak for him, he was an impressive witness, speaking in rough terms with a forthrightness that carried conviction. Led by the returned McNab, he refuted the main planks of the prosecution case with firm statements, coherently expressed.

He had never failed to support Maxine. He had never struck Maxine. She had never worked as a prostitute when they had been man and wife. He had been disgusted when she left him and resumed her 'professional' life. His earnings in the ring had been necessary to support his parents and family through their vicissitudes. Not only had he, for example, supported his sister, he had paid all the medical bills for her wounded husband when the man had returned from service in the war in Europe.

Furthermore, Dempsey had been committed fully to the war effort and had personally raised no less than $331,500, including $197,000 for the Army and Navy War Activities Fund; $73,500 for the Salvation Army; and $26,000 for the Knights of Columbus War Relief Fund by his charitable appearances.

Back in November 1918, one of Kearns's inspired publicity stunts had badly misfired. Kearns engaged a photographer when Dempsey visited the Sun Shipyard in Chester, Pennsylvania to boost recruitment. A widely published photograph showed Jack in worker's cap and striped overalls, holding a rivet gun and smiling at the camera. The highly polished patent leather shoes, more suitable for ballroom than dockyard, peeping out below the trousers, had undermined the image of the horny-handed worker. The phoney detail was much commented on by Dempsey's enemies in the press and had undoubtedly contributed to the enduring 'slacker' taunts. McNab laid the blame where it was due: 'Kearns putting out photos of Jack in a work apron was stupid, just stupid. And putting the apron on him in the shipyard when he was wearing patent leather shoes was stupider still. I thought boxing managers were supposed to be smart.' In the witness box, Dempsey added that his shipyard visit, actually made under the orders of the Department of Labor, had recruited 300–400 workers for the yard. As he said, 'I thought I was doing my country some good.'

Finally, he declared that he *had* tried to enlist in the navy in September 1918 and been frustrated by the suspension of navy enlistments. A naval lieutenant sailed back especially to confirm the claim later in the day. Other witnesses gave further details about payments made, support contributed and the unreliability of some of Maxine's statements. Prosecutor Thomas huffed and puffed but failed to lay a punch on Dempsey in his cross-examination.

Had the judge been a referee he might have stopped the contest at the end of the day. Instead, the proceedings went into the Tuesday morning but for a very short time. Both sides eschewed their right to final summaries and the judge sent the jury off to consider its verdict with his words in their ears: 'The question is … whether or not Jack Dempsey sought to evade military service by falsely answering certain points in the questionnaire, and whether or not, if false statements were made, these were made wilfully and knowingly. Other points are merely auxiliary to this principal issue.'

The jury was back within about seven minutes. Dempsey was acquitted of all charges. The government had spent an estimated $80,000 for nothing. Only *Punch* over in Britain felt Dempsey still had a charge to face; not draft – but Cochran-dodging.

It would be easy to record the Dempsey result as a vindication of unbiased American justice. However, the very same front page announcing Dempsey's innocence carried two other reports.[29] The first was a statement from an agent in San Diego that he and others expected to arrest Jack Johnson when the Mexican authorities deported him across the border to southern California. In Mexico he had 'danced with white women'. The other report came from Minnesota. At Duluth, three 22-year-old blacks, arrested with five others on a suspected rape charge, had been wrested from the police station and hanged by a 5,000-strong white lynch mob. Unbiased American justice had not been their lot.

As we have seen so often, boxing endured an ambiguous relationship with the law on both sides of the Atlantic. However, 1920 was the year when New York State initiated a reform to abandon the legal limbo and to free professional boxing from the contrived restrictions that had ruled for almost a decade; for example, the ban on a decision at the end of a fight, and the ten-round limit. There were simple remedies. The passing of legislation to activate those remedies was anything but simple. Given the tortuous nature of New York State politics, it could hardly have been otherwise.[30]

The 1920 change came after the political turbulence of the 1914–19 period. Substantial Republican gains in upstate New York in the November 1914 elections meant a power shift. The new Republican Governor Charles S. Whitman exercised his patronage to replace the serving three-man Athletic Commission with his own nominees. The Commission controlled New York boxing after the passing of the Frawley Law in July 1911. That had legalised the sport, but only within limitations imposed by that law (e.g. ten rounds maximum and no decisions). Whitman granted each nominee a $3,000 fee each and levied a 7½ per cent tax on takings to finance it. He took new premises in Albany for Commission offices (an inconvenient distance from New York City where most boxing actually took place). He nominated Fred A. Wenck, a newspaper editor, and one-time amateur boxer, as commission chairman. This was a big mistake.

Wenck had plenty of ideas about boxing and, like many, worried about the decline in New York boxing since the passing of the 1911 law. Fewer bouts took place and clubs offered two nights a month where once they had offered at least one every week. Wenck 'felt that the fans had tired of the same boxers and the same matches'. He believed, correctly, that a sporting match needed a decision rendered by the referee there and then.

Wenck's enthusiasm was matched neither by his political skills nor by his integrity. A new company running Madison Square Garden applied for a licence to stage fights. Wenck turned them down twice. An appeal against Wenck disclosed that not only did he hold personal grudges against some of the company's directors, with one of whom he had exchanged public fisticuffs, but he had requested a $1,000 bribe to grant the licence. Wenck was heard to say, 'A lot of people are making money from the boxing game and I'm going to get mine.'[31]

Under cross-examination, Wenck's aggression and his financial manoeuvres were laid bare. A director of the holding company at Madison Square Garden, Harry M. Polock, said that Wenck had called him a thief and had hit him. Wenck, he asserted, had kicked him so severely that he was laid up in bed for two days. Another witness, Michael E. Collins, one-time manager of heavyweight Fred Fulton, testified about the match between Fulton and Al Reich at the Metropolitan Opera House, New York on 28 April 1916 when Fulton stopped Reich in the ninth of ten rounds. According to Collins, Wenck had, quite improperly, *promoted* the bout. Wenck's answers under hostile questioning revealed an embarrassing ignorance of the very Frawley Law he was supposedly upholding and administering.

Wenck's performance was embarrassing for him. It was personally and politically embarrassing for the governor who had appointed him. Wenck was duly sacked in March 1917 for his incompetence, his corrupt activities unmentioned but hanging like a cloud over him and boxing.

Some weeks before, two of the Wenck-appointed commissioners were at ringside in the German Hall, Albany on 30 January 1917 when two junior Albany fighters, Stephen T. 'Young' McDonald and William Toddy Hicks met. The match was an unimportant preliminary preceded by McDonald's father's attempting to dissuade his son from facing Hicks, another novice but one rumoured to have a big punch. McDonald went ahead, and with his father sitting in the front row, took a right-hand punch to the heart in the first round and died. The two apathetic commissioners callously allowed the rest of the bill to proceed. The evening brought ignominy to the governor by proxy. The exposure of the crooked Wenck's doings shortly after, served to make the governor sympathetic to the abolition of boxing. That could be done simply by the passing of a short act to repeal the 1911 Frawley Law.

Sometimes known as the Malone Act, Chap. 555 of the Laws of New York was legalised then approved by the governor on 18 May 1917. The Frawley Law was dead. Boxing in New York had lost the corset restricting it but providing conditional legality. The Malone Act passed by 94 votes to 42 in the Assembly and by 26 to 20 in the Senate, a result made possible by inbuilt Republican majorities. One Democratic senator spoke belligerently against abolition. He was Senator James ('Jimmy') Walker, of whom we shall hear later, but for all his colourful eloquence and cheerful insults aimed at the bill's proponents, the new Act stood.

Its provisions were binding. From 15 November 1917, 'the state athletic commission shall not issue any new license … to conduct, hold or give boxing and sparring matches or exhibitions'. New York State, which had been, despite the Frawley Law, a major venue for boxing promotions was now somewhere where boxing was absolutely illegal. Even boxing on the dubious private club membership basis was no longer allowed. Boxing was still permitted in 23 states but two major centres (New York and Chicago) were not among them. The new Act

damaged New York and the whole prospects of American boxing.

The First World War damaged every participant in one way or another. Boxers joined up and were wounded. Some joined up and were killed. Others, like Dempsey, did not join up and permanently suffered the 'slacker' charge. For spectators, the fights on offer were meagre and some of the best boxers, just like Carpentier, were engaged in more crucial forms of fighting. It was deeply ironic, therefore, that two unintended consequences of the First World War were the enhancement of the general reputation of boxing and the boosting of its supposed usefulness for military purposes.

From the outbreak of war, boxers and boxing played an honourable part in recruiting soldiers. Hardly a newspaper or journal refrained from publishing photographs of well-known boxers ditching the gloves and bayoneting a mock punch bag with murderous intent. If X can do it, so can YOU! As the war continued, regimental boxing sustained morale and staved off boredom for thousands of troops miles away from Civvy Street. So successful was the ploy that many generals and admirals believed boxing, above all other sports, produced fighting spirit in raw recruits, instilling controlled aggression and self-reliance at times of physical danger. This made sense, although *The Times* in London was surely exaggerating on 15 June 1920 when it bought the whole R. B. Campbell thesis and published an article entitled 'Boxing and the Bayonet: A Lesson of the War'. According to the anonymous correspondent:

Few people realise how boxing … proved to *be one of the greatest*

factors in the winning of the war for this country and her allies. [Italics added]

Furthermore, the principles of boxing practically governed the use of the bayonet. Quickness, footwork, a hard punch delivered straight from the right shoulder with all the force and weight of the body behind it, a fine parry, and a trained comprehension of the vulnerable points at which only a blow became deadly were identical and vital both to boxing and bayonet training … boxing became an essential part of the training of the Army. The better boxer the recruit became the finer 'show' he gave in the bayonet lessons …

Even if they did not buy the dubious thesis that the boxing-inspired bayonet trumped a machine gun or a tank, many in the US military were alarmed by the prospect that American boxing might die, poisoned by toxic civic legislation like the Malone Act and by morally misguided public opinion.

From 1918 on, many sought to rescue boxing from the outer darkness into which the Malone Act had placed it. The campaign continued during 1919, gathering pace as boxing clubs, promoters and others saw the advantages of the restoration of boxing as a legal and commercial activity and the services pleaded its utility. This unlikely alliance between monetary and martial forces made for powerful propaganda.

Local jealousies were also aroused when New York's neighbouring state New Jersey took an initiative. In New Jersey, it had been a serious misdemeanour for 'any two or more persons to fight together or commit or attempt to commit assaults and batteries upon each other' or for others to aid or abet them. As of 5 March 1918, the state legislature surprisingly adopted a new bill (the Hurley Boxing Law) to legalise boxing in New Jersey within severe limits – eight rounds maximum; no decisions; eight-ounce glove minimums; pre-fight medical examinations. Nevertheless, here were fights permitted conditionally where there had previously been none other than underground. Again the motivation was partly military. In the New Jersey Senate, which voted 11 to 4 for change, two senators 'urged the passage of the Bill, declaring that boxing could not be considered a brutal sport *in these days of war,* but that on the contrary it was useful for young men'.[32] [Italics added]

How soon would New York, jealous of its neighbour, feel bound to repeal the anti-boxing law of 1917 and pass legislation at least to restore boxing to its previous status, or go even further to acknowledge its post-war prestige?

One determined to make it happen was the maverick New York senator who had spoken so eloquently in the 1917 debates, when he had called the abolitionists 'long-haired men and short-haired women', epithets calculated to insult every gender and sexual persuasion. He was James J. Walker (1881–1946), known universally as Jimmy, and one of the most colourful personalities that even American politics ever threw up. (In the 1930s, his happy-go-lucky attitude to money from corrupt sources caught up with him and he resigned the Mayoralty of New York before he could be sacked. In 1920 he was a force to be reckoned with.)

Son of an Irish immigrant lumberyard owner prominent in Tammany Hall politics, Jimmy did his father's bidding and studied law with a political career in mind. Soon bored, he turned to writing lyrics for Tin Pan Alley hits and struck gold with the sentimental favourite 'Will You Love Me in December as You Do in May?' Tin Pan Alley was then centred on West 28th Street between Broadway and Sixth. Walker, with royalties and fees pouring in, threw himself enthusiastically into Broadway nightlife. In 1912 he married a vaudeville singer, although fidelity was never his thing. Fidelity, however, to his father's ambitions reasserted itself, and he became successively state assemblyman (1909), state senator (1914) and Mayor of New York (1925) without tempering his popular tastes or his flamboyance. More likely seen at racetrack or casino than in the mayoral office, he turned his natural eloquence and his popular touch to a cause if it appealed to him. Sunday sport, Sunday cinema, legalised boxing, anti-Prohibition – anything puritan-minded Republicans were against, Walker was for.

As Minority Leader in the Senate at Albany, Walker supported every attempt to legalise boxing and pushed for a bill of his own. It foundered in the assembly and died in committee in April 1919. He was not easily deterred. Sensing the military-inspired opinions in favour of boxing, he reintroduced his bill in February 1920. It provided for 15-round fights going to a decision (by two judges with a referee's casting vote in case of disagreement); a controlling commission of three; and an independent licensing committee.[33] With a strong nod to military needs,

he also introduced an amendment to permit boxing in state armouries.

Some of the bill's supporters also inclined to emphasise military advantages. Colonel Ward suggested the sport was as essential as rifles because 'Uncle Sam's fighters [had carried] boxing gloves on their backs as part of their equipment on hikes in France'. Two people from the Army, Navy and Civilian Board of Boxing joined in. Major Anthony Drexel Biddle, its president, whose troupe ruined the Dempsey/Willard canvas in Toledo in July 1919, claimed optimistically that the new licensing system would bring all corrupt managers, fighters and promoters to heel. His fellow board member, Gutzon Borgium, pounding the table with his fist as if it were an obdurate opponent of boxing, declared boxing a thoroughly wholesome sport desired by the majority and one in which military control would work wonders: 'If the Army and Navy Board had [had] control over the Dempsey–Willard bout at Toledo last year, it would not have gone three rounds and there would have been no possibility of the indecent spectacle which developed.'

The bill's opponents raised fears about unintended consequences. Canon Chase of Brooklyn suggested the 15-rounds clause and instant decisions would make boxing 'a brutalizing spectacle and an object for renewed activities by the gambling element of the metropolis'. (As boxing in New York in the 1920s to 1940s fell notoriously under the control of organised crime, the canon had more of a point than he knew.) George West of the New York Civic League argued the agitation was merely a guise to swell the pockets of film magnates by permitting the staging

Major Anthony Drexel Biddle (1874–1948), the rich Philadelphian evangelist and boxing campaigner.
Bain Collection, Prints & Photographs Division, Library of Congress, LC-DIG-ggbain-27288

touch that enhanced his political popularity.)[34]

The objectors were now in the minority. Walker's bill was favourably reported upon by the Senate Judiciary Committee on 9 March 1920 by 9 to 2 and passed by the Senate on 24 March 1920 by 31 to 19. In the early hours of Sunday morning, 25 April 1920, the Assembly passed the bill by 91 to 46. To become law, the bill still had to be endorsed by the Governor of New York, Al Smith. This was not a foregone conclusion. Politics is a complicated business, especially when votes are in question.

Alfred Emanuel ('Al') Smith (1873–1944), representative of Tammany Hall and a devout Roman Catholic member of the Irish-American New York City community, had little in common with the flamboyant Walker. Not opposed to boxing in principle, he was disinclined to risk his personal reputation by endorsing a measure so disliked by many religious groupings. His election as governor in 1919 was based on spreading his appeal beyond the confines of the Irish Catholics of New York City. He intended to be re-elected. He also had hopes of nomination by the 1924 Democratic Convention as the Democratic Presidential candidate. These were not ambitions to be enhanced by unnecessarily alienating influential supporters.

Walker visited Smith on Friday, 20 May 1920 hoping to use his personal charm to persuade Smith to sign off the bill. He was only partially successful. Smith agreed to sign the bill on Monday *providing* a hundred clergymen endorsed it. The catch was that they had to be *Protestant* clergymen – not Catholic priests (who would vote for

and filming of the lucrative Dempsey–Carpentier bout. (Interestingly, Walker himself was *not* in favour of the Dempsey–Carpentier contest on democratic grounds: 'The fight has not been licensed in this State yet, and I hope it won't be, for the good of the sport. I am against large purses, and always have been. It is not fair to the little fellows. They cannot pay the price of admission, and are therefore against it.' A good example of the common

Smith anyway), and not rabbis (who would support the bill for the sake of the darling of the Jewish community, Benny Leonard 'The Ghetto Wizard'). It is doubtful whether Walker, presently indulging in an open extra-marital affair with an actress a quarter of a century younger than he, even *knew* ten Protestant clergymen let alone have a hundred of them support his bill.

Fortunately, although Walker could hardly do the business, he knew a man who could – Major Anthony Drexel Biddle (1874–1948). In addition to his efforts on behalf of army, navy and civilian boxing, the evangelical and very wealthy major was an important

publisher, a lecturer, a founder of what he called 'Athletic Christianity' and, crucially, the founder of an international network of impeccably Protestant bible schools – schools that had recently obtained half a million dollars from him. It was easy for him to call in some favours and have over 600 telegrams and letters sent from Protestant ministers to Al Smith supporting the Walker Bill. Smith kept his word and signed the bill, putting a gloss on it as best he could:

> The stress of the times demands healthy and wholesome amusement for the men of the State, and when an amusement can

be afforded under such rigid restrictions and control by the State itself as this bill provides, no possible harm can, and on the other hand, a great amount of good will results from its enactment.[35]

The great amount of goodwill did not extend directly to Smith. The man they called the Happy Warrior lost his position as governor in the 2 November 1920 state elections to Republican Nathan L. Miller by 1,334,540 votes to Smith's 1,260,335. As Walker's one-time hit half-predicted, the voters would not love Smith in the winter the way they had in May. No one can say

Alfred E. 'Al' Smith (1873–1944) 'The Happy Warrior' campaigning alongside his wife Catherine. As New York Governor he helped boxing but suffered a political backlash as a result.

Bain Collection, Prints & Photographs Division, Library of Congress, LC-DIG-ggbain-27477

how many marginal voters the Walker Bill alienated but it must have been an electoral factor. The bill was now law – Chap. 912 of the Laws of New York 1920 – effective as of 24 May 1920.

In 30 clauses over more than seven detailed pages, it laid down comprehensive instructions over many vital matters: for example, the State Boxing Commission of three, its salaries, expenses and its comprehensive powers:

> The commission shall have and hereby is vested with the sole direction, management, control and jurisdiction over all … boxing and sparring matches or exhibitions to be conducted, held or given within the state of New York, and no such boxing or sparring match or exhibition shall be conducted, held or given within the state except in accordance with the provisions of this act.

A widespread licensing system controlled participants:

> All corporations, physicians, referees, judges, timekeepers, professional boxers, their managers, trainers and seconds shall be licensed by the … license committee, and no … corporation or person shall be permitted to participate, either directly or indirectly, in any such boxing or sparring match or exhibition, or the holding thereof, unless such corporation or persons shall have first procured a license from the said license committee.

The new regulations are strong evidence of what was *not* done consistently previously. The new Act demanded safe and suitable venues, the presence of an experienced physician (at the promoter's expense), a medical before a contestant entered the ring and minimum ages for professional fighters (over 18) and spectators (over 16). Licences might be revoked for abuses, owners of venues must not have financial interests in any fighter competing on their premises, only light-heavies and heavies might face opponents more than 18 pounds heavier than themselves and the official weight classes were to be those presently prevailing with the Army, Navy and Civilian Board and the International Sporting Club (New York).

Every requirement was likely to be supported by anyone who genuinely loved boxing, if not by those voters who abandoned Smith six months after his signing of the bill. Even more crucial were the orders laid down in Clause 12 about the conduct of fights:

> No boxing or sparring match or exhibition shall be of more than fifteen rounds in length, such rounds to be no more than three minutes each; and no boxer shall be allowed to participate in more than fifteen rounds within twelve consecutive hours. The commission may in respect to any bout … limit the number of rounds of a bout within the maximum of fifteen rounds.
>
> … there shall be in attendance a duly licensed referee, who shall direct and control … [He] shall have power in his discretion to declare forfeited any prize, remuneration or purse, or part thereof, belonging to the contestants or one of them, if in his judgement, such contestant or contestants are not honestly competing … Each contestant shall wear, during such contest, gloves weighing not less than five ounces, if such contestant be a light weight or in a class of less weight, and six ounces if such contestant be in a class heavier than the light weight class.

Amendments were made in future years but in general the Walker Act consolidated the foundations for modern boxing for the USA. As such it was extremely successful. After its passing, New York boxing speedily regained its previously prominent place.

Because the Act was an official initiative, the State of New York committed $40,000 of public funds to help set up the controlling commission. (Expenses in future years would be met from the compulsory licensing fees.)

How would the NSC in London have reacted had they been promised public funds provided they were willing to relinquish their pre-war monopoly over official championships in favour of a new controlling body out of their control? They had always shown fierce independence and very few people were aware of Lord Lonsdale's backdoor deals with the Home Office. As in the USA, the military authorities had smiled upon boxing during the war and had helped to advance the sport's prestige as a contributor of all the military virtues.

Back in 1914 there had been close cooperation between the NSC and the Imperial Services Boxing Association over many boxing matters. Many NSC bills during the war had featured boxers appearing under their military titles (Sergeant Johnny Basham, Bandsman Blake, etc.) and seen the boxing theatre thrown open as much to servicemen on leave as to members. Less well known was that the NSC had *back in 1914* already established in theory a new Boxing Board of Control supposedly to serve as a national governing body for professional boxing – 'to encourage boxing in general, to raise the standards of pro-boxing, to control and regulate the sport and to act as a central board of control'.[36] The 1914 meeting had actually asked the military representatives present to press the Home Office for formal recognition of boxing.

Just how independent the new body was intended to be may be questioned. It was designed to have *ten* members who were actually members of the NSC and four representatives from the military. In any case, this new board, formed so discreetly as to be practically invisible, was put into storage for the duration of the war. Even the minutes of the initial meeting, which took place on 5 February 1914, were not actually confirmed until another meeting on 4 February *1918*.[37] The NSC formally announced the board's existence in June 1918.

Much had happened in the war years since that first gathering. As we saw, the military showed militant initiatives in imposing *amateur* rules upon professional boxers in fights within and without the military context and banned money prizes in internal competitions. The most enthusiastic of the military boxing administrators showed ambitions to take over the whole conduct of boxing in the future. The 4 February 1918 meeting expressed

particular concern about the tendency – 'some of the Army representatives had advocated some very drastic measures' (the Navy was only mildly in agreement). It was not long before even the most enthusiastic army men saw that professional boxing would go its own way after the war and it would be futile to oppose it or attempt a takeover. By the end of April, the Board 'had heard that Imperial Services Boxing Association declined the invitation to join' and the services representatives had resigned.[38] It appears that the order that Wilde was to receive no money for his fight with Conn four months later was issued with a certain spirit of revenge for military ambitions thwarted.

There were other thorny questions for any new board seeking to control all boxing. Had not the NSC proved a distinctly poor relation to the commercial promoters in the staging of big fights? Critics of NSC pretensions could point, for example, to the futile club claim that Bombardier Billy Wells was still the official British champion and that his two humiliating defeats by Joe Beckett could be ignored because they had not taken place on the Covent Garden premises. The NSC, whatever it chose to call itself, looked distinctly anachronistic.

In strong contrast to the New York commission, it had no legal or official backing. It could exert moral pressure at best unless commercial promoters, managers and the like voluntarily joined in with the new board and accepted its authority and its decisions. The new organisation might want to do for boxing what the MCC did for cricket, or the Jockey Club for horse racing, but, as the *Boxing World, Mirror of Life and Sporting Observer* put it:

… until the Board of Control has the unanimous and whole-hearted support of all lovers and followers of boxing, promoters, boxers and everybody connected directly or indirectly with the game, its powers will be limited and its authority and rulings of little or no use in keeping the game as it ought to be kept.[39]

Furthermore, was the new body, designed 'to encourage boxing in general', prepared to interfere if the interests of amateur or services boxing were at odds with that of *professional* boxing, clearly the new board's main concern? There was already a fully functioning Amateur Boxing Association and administrative bodies for services boxing. (Only in May 1928 was a reconstituted and relaunched British Board of Boxing Control brought into existence to play a proper administrating role for British professional boxing.)

In 1920, what about economics? The NSC could no longer hold fights of the first magnitude because it could not offer attractive purses. Mediocre rewards drew run-of-the-mill fighters engaged in run-of-the-mill fights. The club was caught in a vicious circle, its income suffering accordingly.[40]

There was an air of desperation about the NSC's initiative launched in spring 1920. The club took a lease on premises near Shepherd's Bush, a Holland Park hall that had previously been the Holland Park Ice Rink. The idea was to stage NSC fights there, but to attract the general public to pay for and see them. Entrance fees for the opening night on 31 May 1920 were designed to lure in fans eager to see international clashes like those previously restricted to the Anglo-French or Anglo-American nights at the NSC exclusively for members and guests, yet still keep away the lower orders who might appear at, say, The Ring at Blackfriars.[41]

The perennial desire of NSC officials to achieve respectability at all costs was not entirely misplaced. At The Ring in November 1920, a controversial decision in a flyweight bout between Bert Ware and George Langham led to the referee being given a good kicking by disappointed punters.[42]

Prices at Holland Park started at a minimum of one guinea plus tax. The coal miners would a few months later be going on strike in a vain attempt to gain an extra two shillings per daily shift. How many workers then could have afforded a minimum of a whole guinea for one event?[43] As might have been anticipated, the hall was barely half-full, the venture falling between the desire to maximise revenue and the fear that overemotional rebellious toughs might get *too* involved and wreck the evening.

For their money, the limited audience was offered two major bouts with two British champions against foreign opposition. British bantamweight champion Jim Higgins from Hamilton, Scotland (b. 25 October 1897), who had gained the British title at the NSC on 23 February 1920 by knocking out Welshman Harold Jones of Ferndale, had been regarded as lucky to get a shot at the vacant title. Outboxed by the Welshman, losing the first ten rounds and taking a count of seven in the fourth, Higgins had pulled out a driving right to Jones's jaw in the 13th that sent Jones down for eight. When Jones rose groggily,

Higgins nailed him again with another right for nine. Jones got up again but could do no more than cover up in a corner as Higgins lambasted him until referee Douglas spared him. The new, unexpected champion two months later acquired the British Empire title as well with an uneventful points victory at the NSC on 26 April 1920 over Australian Vince Blackburn (b. 4 August 1895).

At Holland Park, Higgins was hardly a major attraction, only as good as NSC officials could presently muster. He was out-starred even by his seconds – Jim Driscoll and Tancy Lee – who accompanied him to the ring. It would have been better had they accompanied him *in* the ring.

His opponent, also weighing in at 8st 6lb/118lbs, was the extremely tough and experienced Charles Ledoux, born 27 October 1892 and thus still only 27. Over a career that lasted until 1926, Ledoux had about 135 fights with the impressive record of 97 victories, 23 defeats, five draws and nine no-decisions. How dangerous the so-called Little Apache could be was proved by his knockout record – 81 of 97 wins, 83.5 per cent, eminently respectable even compared with later heavyweight knockout specialists such as Rocky Marciano (87.8 per cent) and George Foreman (84 per cent). Ledoux was knocked out himself a mere three times. He, of course, had been the man whom Driscoll had early outpointed in October 1919 only to be ruthlessly outlasted and forced to retire by the Frenchman's teak-like resistance.

Higgins's best hope, instilled by Driscoll in training, was to stay away and pile up points with his skills (limited but better than Ledoux's). Higgins's greatest assets did not include

discipline and restraint but were rather aggression and fearlessness. Ledoux was never wanting in either quality.

The first three rounds were fought at close quarters and both claimed their successes. Higgins's approach came particularly into question when a Ledoux short right hook took him down for nine in the third. Higgins was undeterred and in the next three rounds still closed and freely exchanged hooks and uppercuts on equal terms with the Frenchman. Indeed, in the eighth he came close to putting Ledoux down, and in the tenth forced Ledoux to put a glove on the canvas to save himself in what today would have counted as a knockdown. At the end of the tenth, Higgins returned to his corner much applauded and looking like a man who could pull off a real surprise.

It was not to be. The toll of vigorous exchanges with a stronger man caught up with him and he weakly took too many punches about the body. A left hook, less fierce than many he had already taken, clipped his jaw and down he went, sadly out for the full count in the 11th; a rather forlorn anticlimax in seconds to the hopes slowly building in the previous 30 minutes.

Higgins's fellow Briton, Mike Honeyman, was no more successful in a 9st/126lbs match against Arthur Wyns (a thoroughly appropriate name for a fighter). Wyns, a Belgian born in Brussels on 1 March 1893, looked to cut a Carpentier-like swathe through British featherweights. At 5ft 3½in of bristling aggression under a crop of brownish hair flattened on top and with the biceps of a lightweight, he was no pushover. He had knocked out Francis Rossi of Wales in April and would stop Joe Conn in the 14th on 26 July 1920.

Wyns first boxed professionally in 1911 and retired in 1926 with a record only slightly less successful than Ledoux – 61 victories (46 KOs), 22 defeats (eight KOs) and seven draws. He conceded a little height and a little weight (8st 12lb/124lbs to Honeyman's 8st 13½lb/125½lbs). As in the Higgins/Ledoux match, the Englishman's best hope lay in fighting at a distance. Unlike Higgins, Honeyman stuck to his plan and by the end of the ninth had built a substantial lead with light-scoring left leads. He then retreated before the Belgian's late fightback. When Wyns's counters connected they looked ominously effective.

Like Higgins, Honeyman had flattered only to disappoint. The change came in the tenth. A misplaced lead from Honeyman allowed Wyns to catch him with a fast-travelling left swing to the jaw followed by a similar right. Down went Honeyman, distinctly stunned. Unsteadily back on his feet, a volley of Belgian punches put him firmly back down. The new pattern was up, down; up, down; up, down; up, down; up, down. At the fifth down the referee halted proceedings and declared Wyns the winner by stoppage. Evening result: Europe 2 Britain 0, and the NSC no nearer to solving its post-war difficulties via the Notting Hill initiative.

The commercial promotion staged on 16 July 1920 at the Royal Albert Hall was hardly innovative, heavily dependent upon nostalgia rather than reality. Top of the bill was the man who began his boxing career in 1900 and became world famous for losing the championship to Jack Johnson in 1908. This was the enterprising Tommy Burns, born 17 June 1881 and now a few weeks past his 39th birthday.

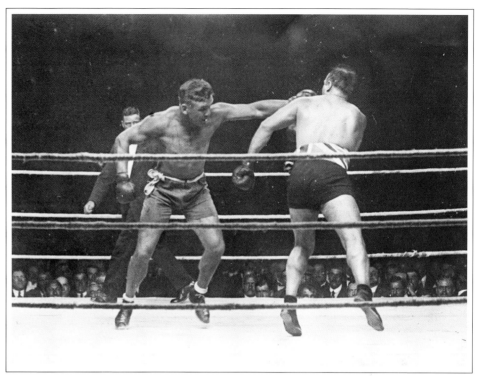

16 July 1920, Royal Albert Hall: Beckett attacks an ageing Tommy Burns, who has shamelessly tied a Union Jack around his waist.
BnF

One says enterprising because Burns's entrepreneurial activities had for many years supplanted his boxing. Since that dubious six-rounder against Arthur Pelkey on 2 April 1913 (see Chapter 9) he had fought twice. The first was on 26 January 1914 against Battling Brandt, an undistinguished San Franciscan heavyweight in his very first fight. Brandt was knocked out in four of ten and went on to be 'outclassed in every round' of 12 against his only other name opponent, Battling Levinsky, in Columbus, Ohio on 26 September 1916. Burns's second fight was nearly *five* years later on 19 September 1918 in Canada when he knocked out in four Bob Bracken of Vancouver, a *middleweight* with a mediocre record of two wins, five defeats and one draw. Burns's formbook, two mini-fights in seven years, was underwhelming.

His opponent for the Royal Albert Hall show was Joe Beckett, who had his own blemished record, especially the first-round knockout at the hands of Georges Carpentier on 14 December 1919, which lingered in the memory longer than Beckett's 1920 wins over Dick Smith and Bombardier Billy Wells. At stake was the Empire heavyweight title.[44]

The press, before and after, predictably focused on the only vaguely interesting theme – youth versus age. It was no real contest. Burns pushing 40, looked it, and Beckett, 13 years younger, was unafraid of the one-time world champion's reputation, and disinclined to be over-respectful. In skilful footwork and elusiveness, Burns was still the better, but in strength of punch, aggression and stamina, there was one man in it and that was not Burns.

Beckett advanced immediately to his opponent, brushing aside or ignoring Burns's leads, and delivering heavy blows to his body just above the Union Jack tied around the Canadian's waist. (On earlier occasions, Burns had worn the Stars and Stripes. He was a shameless chameleon pretending to be a local favourite wherever he was.) 'You won't strike your own flag will you, boy?' joked Burns. Beckett was unpatriotically happy to do just that.

Burns took a succession of right uppercuts in the second. In the fourth, some of Burns's evasive skills made the over-eager Beckett miss clumsily, but Burns could not follow up or counter. In the fifth, Burns's speedy start to the round soon slowed, his stamina running out as the effects of Beckett's body punching caught up with him. His right eye swelling, he suffered a heavy right cross just before the bell.

There was warm applause for Burns as he came out for the sixth. He was the popular choice over the morose and scowling Beckett. Yet it was applause based on nostalgia and sympathy for his courage under the rough handling he was receiving. No one believed he could turn things around. He made Beckett miss, sometimes humiliatingly, but all too often Beckett hurt him with clusters of heavy punches.

The seventh saw the conclusion. Peering out of a half-closed right eye and bleeding at the mouth, Burns pretended he was fresh and ready to take over. Neither crowd nor Beckett was fooled. A flurry of heavy hooks to head and body took him down for eight, a mini-rest insufficient to need. Another left and right toppled him face down. Although he got up, just, he was in no condition to defend himself and his seconds pre-empted the referee by throwing in the sponge. The man who had never lost by knockout was spared

that in this, his last fight. Youth had definitely been served, if not boxing.

In Britain, the failure of the NSC's optimistic jamboree at Holland Park at the end of May and the Royal Albert Hall July mismatch between Beckett and Burns were in strong contrast to the scene in New York. In Manhattan, on Saturday, 18 September 1920, the irrepressible Tex Rickard was profiting from the recently passed Walker legislation. He celebrated the return of professional boxing to the city and the state after its three-year hiatus with an attractive bill at a renovated Madison Square Garden. When Rickard announced his plans in July he emphasised that the boxing 'will be promoted at popular prices'. His four-bout card included innovations such as a 15-round contest and, wonder of wonders, decisions announced immediately after each fight.[45]

Three years of pent-up demand brought the punters out in force – 12,000 of them. The less affluent queued for hours for the cheaper unreserved seats in the freshly painted balconies – now in a patriotic red, white and blue. On high they could gaze down on the ring in the centre and at the regimented rows of highly polished chairs allocated to richer holders of reserved seats at ring level. Below, on the first level, the overhanging boxes were similarly decorated. The $18,000 spent by Rickard on décor was supplemented by the services of handsome, white-gloved stewards, who politely inspected tickets and escorted the more privileged spectators, including many glamorously gowned women, to their seats. (An unacknowledged tribute to Cochran's London operations perhaps.) Adding gaiety to the excited anticipation was

a band of black musicians playing popular minstrel numbers.

If the *New York Times* is accurate, the boxing fare was up to the occasion: 'Never an idle moment was experienced from the time the opening six rounder started … until the gong clanged on the last round of the stellar attraction.' That opener was between two Brooklyn residents, Sammy Nable (8st 5lb/117lbs) and Robert Hansen, who had started as a flyweight and still only scaled a bare 8st/112lbs. Hansen, proper name Hanssen and sometimes incorrectly spelled Hanson, was a Danish immigrant born in Copenhagen. Nable was American. They had met recently in Hartford, Connecticut (28 June 1920) over ten rounds, and would have a third encounter the following year (24 June 1921) over 12 rounds in Queens. Nable was the points winner on all three occasions, using his extra weight, power and speed to impress, although Hansen was always competitive. What made this their second bout historic was that it ended in the first official decision pronounced in a New York ring for 20 years.

Scarce is the bill that fails to produce controversy. This was not one of them. The row came after a ten-rounder featuring another Dane, Pete Hartley (b. 3 April 1897) who weighed 9st 10¼lb/136¼lbs, and whose real name was Peter Eisenhardt. The posters adopted his ring name, the tediously predictable 'The Durable Dane'. Not many long-lasting Norsemen came sailing out of the Bronx. By the end of his raiding career in 1930 he had fought 189 bouts.

His Californian opponent (b. 8 September 1898 in Oregon) was lightweight Joe Benjamin (9st

9lb/135lbs), also crassly dubbed as the 'Sheik of San Joachin'. They provided two-fisted action from start to finish accompanied by wild applause from the crowd and the drumming of feet on Rickard's new floor. Enthusiastic approval turned to noisy disagreement when the two judges, William Muldoon and Charley Thorley, gave the points verdict to the more experienced Benjamin. Deafening boos and shouts went on for some time but many ringside spectators thought the decision fair.

The excitement did not slacken when new principals climbed into the ring that Benjamin and Hartley had barely left. They were Tommy Noble, the British featherweight champion, who scaled 9st 0¾lb/126¾lbs, and a fighter from Baltimore, Andy 'Young' Chaney (real name Andrew Kwasnik), who was a mere half-pound heavier. Anglo-American clashes were a formula as popular in New York as in London. (Noble, a long way from his native Bermondsey, became more popular in the USA than in Britain, where his ethical lapses were widely known. Rickard gave him another big Madison Square Garden date on 8 October with a local favourite, Jewish New Yorker Johnny Murray, real name Herman Sloves, and aka 'The Bronx Bonecrusher'. Noble won on points over 15 rounds and was presented by Rickard with a diamond belt as a souvenir. Few diamonds were offered in Bermondsey.)

When Chaney quit the ring after a 14-year career, he had won 51 (15 KOs), lost 26 (seven KOs) and drawn nine, a misleading tally overall because he spent the last four years from 1924–28 as an 'opponent', a fighter guaranteed to put up a reasonable show and lose. In 1920 he was on the up, a tough, strong and experienced prospect holding decisions over some notable boxers – Johnny Lynch (3 May 1915), Pete Herman (8 May 1918) and twice over Johnny Kilbane (29 December 1919 and 2 June 1920). He already held a newspaper decision over Noble on 7 June 1920 in Jersey City and was looking now to have his superiority confirmed on the spot.

Chaney began with an aggressive two-fisted attack and sustained it for ten rounds. Noble took many a fearsome body blow that would have floored a weaker man. Although he flagged visibly towards the end, he responded with many counters of his own. At the end there was no disagreement about the points or the verdict awarded to Chaney. Both fighters were given a standing ovation for a fight that would have graced any period.

Top of the bill, and no anticlimax despite the bruising Chaney/Noble and Benjamin/Hartley encounters, was a 15-rounder between Johnny Dundee (b. 22 November 1893) and Joe Welling (b. 9 January 1891). Dundee was 9st 5½lb/131½lbs and 5ft 4½in, and Welling heavier and taller at 9st 10½lb/136½lbs and 5ft 8in. On paper, the match gave credence to criticism levelled in the Albany debates about the Walker Bill – that the same old fighters were meeting again and again. Dundee and Welling had met six times before over the 1917–20 period. Over six, eight, ten and 12 rounds, one had been drawn, three won by Welling the Jewish Chicagoan, two by Dundee the Italian New Yorker. But all these had been *newspaper decisions*. Now as the fighters met for the seventh time, a genuine result over a full distance loomed.

Welling, with his superior reach, kept Dundee away with long lefts, mixed with hard right crosses to Dundee's jaw. Another driving right to the solar plexus in the second lifted Dundee up on his toes. Dundee, who had trained hard anticipating a long fight, eschewed his usual dancing, bouncing style. He could not afford to take such risks and win.

Fortunately for Dundee, Welling had gone off at a pace he could not ultimately sustain and took a breather in rounds seven to ten. As he eased off, Dundee ducked under the leads that had earlier kept him away and ruthlessly hooked and uppercut Welling to the face.

In the last third Welling reverted to his early tactics, if not with quite the vigour with which he had begun. He forced Dundee to retreat and dictated the pace of the fight. Dundee was left alternating backward steps with desperate rushes at Welling, more wild than effective. His brave persistence as he lost the closing rounds was admired but the decision went against him.

The excitement was not quite over. Two gentlemen in elegant suits were introduced into the Madison Square Garden ring and to the crowd; and, some said, to each other for the very first time. They stood comfortably alongside one another, chatted amiably and posed for press photographs either side of Tex Rickard. They were Jack Dempsey and Georges Carpentier, who were greeted with more rousing cheers and foot stamping than the fighters had received; acclaim so loud it endangered Rickard's new décor. The warmth and the noise left no doubt that could they finally be brought to fight and not a person present would forego a ticket. In the ring with them was Rickard, a man whose antennae could sense a profit a continent away let alone one under his nose. The evening operated in a new legal context for boxing and set the scene for greater things to come – Dempsey v Carpentier in particular.

Where? When? Under whose auspices? The details remained obstinately undecided. Only one thing was abundantly clear – C. B. Cochran would not be involved. In mid-September, Cochran wrote a definitive letter to the British sporting press announcing his withdrawal from all boxing interests forthwith.[46] He formally withdrew his £50,000 offer to Dempsey for a fight with Carpentier. He was closing the Holborn Stadium for the time being until its future was decided. Current negotiations for two major fights in which he was involved – a fight between Jimmy Wilde and the American Pete Herman originally scheduled for 27 September, and a projected heavyweight rumble between Joe Beckett and the American Frank Moran – would now be handled by other parties. He went on:

I have not minded paying the boxers well: and I have not minded putting up such extra things as belts, gold watches and other inducements; the patrons of my boxing shows have received every attention in the matter of comfort and convenience, and they have known they could rely on getting value for money so far as it lay in my power to give it them. [Unsaid: Don't blame me for Wells and Beckett succumbing so miserably!]

But in the face of the disappointments I have experienced – I need not go into details – I feel that the time has come when, as a showman, I can no longer risk breaking faith with the public, and I am giving up the promotion of boxing entertainments henceforth. The failure of Herman to fulfil his engagement to meet Wilde (notification of which I received today) has been the last straw. 'I am fed up!'

Poor Cochran had been doubly put upon. In the run-up to the fight with Frank Moran, Beckett, having signed for £2,300, demanded another £1,000 and when refused claimed he would fight for £2,300 but only if Cochran were not the promoter. Beckett had received more for his fights against Wells and Burns but failed to realise that was because they were bigger draws than he. 'I do not regard Beckett as a first-rate boxer – a world-beater – and he has disappointed me more often than any other member of the fraternity,' said Cochran.[47]

On top of the Beckett irritation came the last-minute postponement from Herman when the fight against Wilde was in its final preparations. No wonder Cochran thought that the 'last straw' and was terminally 'fed up'.

With Cochran out of the picture, Beckett v Moran and Wilde v Herman would be taking place as we shall see. What made the prospects of Dempsey v Carpentier more likely even post-Cochran was that they took warm-up fights before 1920 was out.

On Tuesday, 12 October 1920 in front of over 15,000 people in the Jersey City baseball stadium, Carpentier made his American *fighting* debut as opposed to his previous publicity junket. He left for the USA in late August and acclimatised himself to American conditions, training hard at a New Jersey training camp, ensuring himself hearty and familiar French cuisine at a private home nearby. At stake was the world light-heavyweight championship held by Battling Levinsky since October 1916.

Levinsky, Carpentier's opponent, was born on 10 June 1891 into the Philadelphian Jewish community as Barney (Beryl) or Bernard Lebrowitz.[48] He started his ring career in 1906 pseudonymously, calling himself 'Barney Williams' originally to disguise his ring career from his Orthodox parents. After early successes, he changed both his manager and his name to one more ethnically suggestive in 1913 with parental blessing. Under his new manager (Dan Morgan) and his new identity, Levinsky's career flourished, culminating in five 1916 fights against old opponent Jack Dillon, the so-called Hoosier Bearcat (b. 2 February 1891 in Frankfort, Indiana), then holder of the light-heavyweight title. Dillon, strong and experienced like Levinsky himself, went anywhere and fought anyone, including heavyweights. He beat Gunboat Smith, Frank Moran and Fireman Jim Flynn (whom he knocked out in four).

Levinsky's persistence got him recognised as Dillon's successor. In the 1916 series, they met in New York (28 March over ten rounds, newspaper verdict Dillon); in Kansas City (25 April over 15 rounds, points Dillon); in Baltimore (13 July over ten rounds, newspaper verdict Levinsky); in Memphis (12 September over eight rounds, newspaper verdict draw); and finally in Boston (24 October over 12 rounds, where the heavier Levinsky was thought to have won almost every round for a points victory). After this epic series, more like some marathon travelling repertory than a title fight, Levinsky was generally recognised as the champion, the first Jewish light-heavyweight title holder. He continued his long career fighting on an industrial scale. From 1910 until his second and final retirement in 1929, Levinsky fought officially nearly 300 times, and probably another 100 lost to the records as he started aged 15. He once took three fights – one in Brooklyn, one in Manhattan and one in Waterbury, Connecticut – all on the same New Year's Day 1915.

Georges Carpentier was facing an experienced and skilful but careworn operator; one more likely to eke out an evasive victory than a knockout. Levinsky's blond hair, blue eyes and handsome features remained. Only close up could his scar tissue and cauliflower ears be detected. Carpentier needed an impressive and swift end to the fight. Everyone knew that Dempsey had knocked out Levinsky in Philadelphia on 6 November 1918 in two and a half rounds. Carpentier needed to be just as quick and ruthless to boost a match with Dempsey.

The fight was moderately dramatic, though less startling than the prelude outside the stadium.[49] Vast crowds from New Jersey and in ferries from New York flocked to the arena, intending to pay the $3.50 general admission. When those areas filled, the next-priced accommodation meant an outlay of $5.50, a sum many would not or could not pay. A distant gratis

view from the roof of an adjacent scrap iron works was preferable. About 200 people scaled the roof, more than the structure could bear, and it collapsed, throwing 50 of them on to jagged pieces of scrap below. Fifteen were seriously injured, many more cut and bruised. All were lucky to escape with their lives. Carpentier does not mention the incident in his reminiscences, more concerned about his night's earnings and the potential mega-day with Dempsey: 'The gate would amount to approximately 200,000 dollars and my purse was to be about 425,000 francs at the rate of fifteen to the dollar.' Possibly the fighters were unaware of the dire happening outside until the next day or later. Carpentier, or perhaps Descamps, was also discreet about his weight.

The *New York Times* ringside reporter recorded Levinsky as officially 12st 7lb/175lbs and Carpentier as 12st 2½lb/170½lbs. This has to be an exaggeration. It still shows Carpentier, heavyweight contender, as *lighter* than the light-heavyweight champion. The French camp concealed how light he really was. Carpentier conceded, 'I weighed almost 12 stone,' (i.e. at least eight to nine pounds lighter than Levinsky). But that was in his 1950s autobiography when it no longer mattered. With Dempsey on the agenda, the relative sizes of heavyweight champion and challenger were better veiled.

Preliminaries over, Carpentier discarded his natty grey silk dressing gown with the black trim and did his best to out-Dempsey Dempsey, rushing from his corner and swinging punches furiously. This was not the skilful and clinical Carpentier known to Europeans and it took Levinsky by

surprise. Two counters from Levinsky, a right uppercut and a left to the body, failed to halt the oncoming Carpentier. Levinsky went into rapid retreat. Carpentier – or his ghostwriter – wrote many years later that Levinsky seemed so set on evasion that he (Carpentier) mocked him by standing still, gloves on hips and staring across the ring. Contemporary accounts suggest rather that Carpentier tried to draw Levinsky forward with a few tentative left leads designed to produce opportunities for counters, a Carpentier speciality. Another Carpentier rush at the end of the round caught Levinsky with left and right hooks. Levinsky sank on to his stool looking decidedly shaken.

He was perturbed, especially when Carpentier continued in the second what he had begun in the first. When Levinsky refused to be drawn, Carpentier drove him to a corner and delivered a flurry of wild punches and then a well-timed right to the jaw. Down went Levinsky on one knee for a count of eight. He got back to his feet, only to receive another mini-storm of punches and another count from the referee. The bell prevented Carpentier finishing the job.

Outmatched, Battling Levinsky did more in the third to justify his nickname, recovering his senses and boxing well on the retreat, picking off Carpentier with left jabs. Carpentier was quiescent, knowing his time would come.

It came in the fourth after a minute. Carpentier drove the American back against the ropes and followed him when he slid along them to a corner. There he switched his punches to the body to lower Levinsky's guard, and as soon as he saw Levinsky's jaw, struck it with a big right. Down went Levinsky in a heap, half in and half out of the ring and groping unsuccessfully for the lowest rope to drag himself up. He was still groping when referee Ertle completed the count. His manager and seconds carried Levinsky back to his corner, where he received five minutes' treatment on his stool before leaving the ring unassisted. Carpentier rejoiced in the resounding cheers he received from the crowd and threaded his way through throngs of well-wishers and back-slappers, carefully nursing the rose the Broadway actress and French patriot Alice Delysia had tossed him to commemorate his victory. Despite his rather erratic performance, he had gained more American supporters.

On this damp and dank night, his fellow Frenchman and one of Carpentier's sparring partners, welterweight Marcel Thomas (10st 9½lb/149½lbs) had much less to celebrate, escaping a knockout but suffering a six-round heavy beating in one of the preliminaries. His opponent, a fraction lighter at 10st 7lb/147lbs and hander out of punishment was our old friend Ted Kid Lewis. Lewis hoped to challenge Carpentier himself and was never averse to picking up a purse, especially in the USA where he had spent his war, living up to the complimentary adjectives thrust on him by British newspapers.

This latest American visit was an autumn sojourn from his post-war resumption of a British career launched with the Boxing Day 1919 clash with Matt Wells. After his defeat of Wells, as a mature 26-year-old, he had happily used his significant physical strength and robust fighting style to demolish several British fighters inside

the distance from January to April 1920. Warming up in Manchester (13 January) and Mountain Ash (28 February) by knocking out, in one round each, two Welshmen in Frank Moody (b. 27 August 1900) and Jerry Shea (b. 12 August 1892), he stopped Gus Platts in his Sheffield backyard (4 March) when his opponent's seconds threw in the towel in the 18th.

C. B. Cochran soon signed Lewis for a London appearance at the Holborn Stadium against Johnny Bee from Birkenhead, supposedly with the British middleweight title on the line (an impertinent gesture to the ailing NSC). Intimidated neither by the occasion nor his opponent, Lewis put Bee down twice for nine in the first, down for short counts in the second and third, then knocked him out cold in the fourth. His swathe through the best Britain could offer continued in April with two encounters with Kid Doyle from the Tyne and Wear area. On 5 April at the Liverpool Stadium, he knocked Doyle out in the 11th round, and on 30 April showed the patrons of the Holborn Stadium just how he had done it by knocking Doyle out in the fifth.

Lewis's dramatic re-entry to British boxing was the answer to a hungry promoter's prayers, providing he could be matched with a quality opponent in a major arena. The solution was obvious. Book Olympia for Wednesday, 9 June, put up a handsome purse (£3,000 for the winner; £2,000 for the loser), add three welterweight titles to the spoils (British, European and Empire); and invite one of Britain's most popular and skilful boxers, Johnny Basham (holder of the titles and the Lonsdale Belt) to use all his ring ingenuity to defend

his titles against the rougher, tougher challenger. (As Lewis had enrolled in the US Army in October 1918, thus automatically becoming an American citizen, there was speculation whether a victory over Basham would qualify him to hold the titles. However, Lewis claimed to have been naïve about the enrolment and no formal objection to his authentic British nationality was ever lodged. His so belated donning of a uniform, any uniform, went some way to mollify those critics on both sides of the Atlantic who disapproved of his non-military fighting in the USA throughout the war. Others were not convinced – it is difficult otherwise to explain why so attractive a match did not actually fill every seat in the arena.) As with all great matches, the contrasts between the contestants were thoroughly intriguing – invention v power; smiling nonchalance v poker-faced sobriety; Wales v England; and perhaps a much-loved hero against one highly respected for his prowess but around whom lingered suspicions of absence during his country's greatest need. The consensus among journalists was that the 30-year-old Basham would win on points, *providing* Lewis did not overpower him and knock him out. The other common view was that this could not fail to be a great and historic fight worthy of a major niche in the sport's annals.[50] It was.

From the first Basham had no difficulty in thrusting out smart left leads into Lewis's face. His hand speed and his accuracy were admirable. Lewis was by no means deficient in skill, if less finely honed than Basham, and landed lefts of his own. They carried more potency than Basham's and in a busy round, coupled with some short-arm swings to Basham's body, they left the champion looking a little uncomfortable. Just before the bell Basham landed a swinging left over Lewis's guard but took in turn a left from Lewis that opened a small cut on his cheek. Basham's seconds, mopping his cheek, had much to think about. Although their man had boxed beautifully and stayed his cool and joking self under assault, could he withstand Lewis's power to the end and win?

The second round suggested Basham might still answer that question with a yes. Lewis rushed in close and landed a few body punches. Basham squirmed away, delivered a few quiet jokes, then landed a profusion of lefts and the occasional right to Lewis's face. If not even, the round belonged to Basham.

In the third, Basham was again winner on the punch count. Two left leads to Lewis's face were taken on that unblinking mask with equanimity. In response, a Lewis left thudded into the cut cheek of Basham, increasing the damage, and was followed by a right to the jaw that nearly floored the Welshman. Champions like Basham are rarely made out of less than champions' material. Basham's well-nigh immediate response showed it. Recovering his balance, he clipped Lewis with five neat lefts to the face and rounded off the three minutes with a left and right combination much appreciated by his supporters in the crowd. Unfortunately, of two of Lewis's uglier but effective punches, one had reopened the cut on the cheek and the other had inflicted a deeper one on Basham's lower lip. He went bleeding back to his corner.

A factor of great significance had already emerged. It would feature heavily in the reports and in the memories of eyewitnesses – the skill and courage of the indomitable Johnny Basham, incapable of surrender, fighting on as his blood poured out in quantities to cover him, Lewis and the canvas in an ugly red tide. Modern sensitivities would have demanded a halt to the fight, possibly in the fourth or fifth as Basham's blood continued to trickle from both wounds unstoppably, and most definitely in the sixth when Lewis caught the damaged lip again and trickle turned into a pulsing flow. That specific blow had driven the lip on to a tooth and created an even more squalid exhibition for the next few rounds.

A ringside doctor, who could only advise not stop the contest, suggested a halt, as did Basham's manager. Basham himself was adamant he could continue and win. His obstinacy prevailed in the seventh, surprising Lewis by his continuing speed and obduracy. Lewis eased off a little, less from compassion than to husband his own resources after the furious pace of the early rounds. He knew his eventual victory was inevitable. In the break, Basham's corner again suggested throwing in the towel. Basham adamantly refused to allow them to do so. His misguided intransigence took him through the eighth as well. In one clinch, Lewis suggested to Basham that he would be advised to stop there and then. The bleeding mouth split into a grin and Basham politely declined. Lewis, who could hardly do other, resumed with a full-out attack. Astonishingly, Basham kept punching even after Lewis connected with two more powerful weakening blows to his wounded face.

Against all sense, out he came for the ninth as well. It went much like the eighth except that the closing attack from Lewis, almost as red as Basham by now, staggered Basham and left him hanging on desperately at the end. To his tearful rage, his seconds threw their towels into the ring and the referee, too late, stopped the fight in Lewis's favour. There could have been no other result. It was still a result that raised other questions: Without the unlucky bloody wounds, would Basham's brilliant boxing and inexhaustible courage have brought him a points victory? If Lewis could not knock out a stricken and weakened Basham, how would he fare against a fully fit one? Such questions were inevitable as was a return match to settle them.

It took place in the Royal Albert Hall on 19 November 1920 and was every bit as good as the first, although noticeably not packing out the arena.[51] It still drew a large crowd to what was J. Arnold Wilson's first promotion. (Wilson had been Cochran's assistant at Holborn and was now ready to promote in his own right.) Another 20 rounds had each man demonstrating again all the qualities he had shown in the June clash.

Since then, Lewis had returned to the USA as we saw to beat Marcel Thomas so easily on the Carpentier bill (12 October 1920). He had also (23 September 1920), at the same venue, taken on Mike O'Dowd, the world *middleweight* champion, in a 12-rounder governed by newspaper decision. O'Dowd weighed in at 11st 4lb/158lbs and Lewis at 11st 1lb/155lbs, a relatively insignificant difference. These bald figures do not disclose that Lewis stepped on the scale *in his street clothes* and was giving away about 11 pounds to a man strong enough and heavy enough to dominate a whole division higher than his own. It was a good recipe for a thrashing and that is exactly what Lewis received.[52] Two early rounds (first and third) were fairly even. In all others, Lewis was outboxed and had O'Dowd swarming all over him, trying desperately to knock him out. He came very near to doing so. A bloodied and battered Lewis survived only by a combination of retreat, cover-up and clinch in the face of an unrelenting storm of punches to his head and torso. It was a loss of unusually decisive newspaper decisions in a fight Lewis should never have taken.

Would this heavy, silly loss and the sustained punishment hamper him against the brilliant Basham, who had taken no fights since the Lewis one in June, preferring to repair his wounds, his bruises and his morale for the return?

From the start there were echoes of the first fight. Lewis advanced slowly, feet firmly planted on the canvas, ready to deliver meaningful heavy punches from his powerful arms and shoulders. Basham had not forgotten the stamina-sapping course of the 20 rounds to come, but still came dancing out of his corner on his toes, making play with lightning lefts, as straight and neat as the parting in his hair. After the first few rounds he became more and more accurate, landing often, then dancing and whirling away out of reach as soon as Lewis countered. Some of Lewis's counters got home, although most were evaded or smothered. Basham's lighter blows piled up points.

In the fifth and sixth, Lewis leaned on and clinched, calculating that his superior strength would slow this irritating, smiling Welsh wasp buzzing around and stinging him. Referee Eugene Corri broke up such clinches and insisted on continuous action. Even in the sixth, when Lewis's left glove burst, Corri would allow a replacement only at the end of the round.

The new left glove featured heavily in the ninth when Lewis delivered a serious left hook to Basham's face. Basham's lip began to bleed to the dismay of his many supporters, remembering all too clearly the June mishap. They were being unduly despondent. The wound did not affect the Welshman's confident demeanour and the seconds patched it up effectively.

Untroubled, Basham began the tenth as stylishly as ever. He absorbed Lewis's attacks, smothering the punches with ease and peppering away with both hands in strict contrast to his weakened responses in June. In the 11th and 12th he stuck to his plan. He opened the rounds with swift scoring punches to Lewis's head and body then used all his boxing intelligence to evade, deflect and defend Lewis's advances.

In these rounds, Lewis's punches grew wilder but he was no less determined than Basham. His seconds boosted him on his stool before the 13th – a bag of ice to the back of his head and an illegal swig of champagne. Even so, it was more his patient persistence that paid off, rather than stimulants. In the 13th, after more of Basham's pretty thrusts upon him, Lewis loosed a brutal right swing. Had it landed on Basham's chin, even that happy warrior might have fallen. Instead, because Basham was moving forward it landed on the left side of his head, missing his temple but badly splitting his left ear.

Here were all the fears of one camp and the hopes of the other instantly revived, along with the happy/unhappy and bloody memories of June. Basham was well ahead, but stricken – could he sustain that lead for another seven rounds? And could Lewis use his strength and his own skills to overwhelm Basham's guile?

Basham stayed cool even as Lewis stalked him around the ring, landing further rights over his left leads, each landing painfully on that damaged ear. Remorselessly Lewis began to reduce the lead as Basham slowed. Lewis took the 15th when Basham was half-pushed, half-punched down a few seconds before the bell, and he targeted the ear throughout the 16th. He switched his rights to Basham's body in the 17th and 18th but had to take more of those maddening lefts to do so.

At the end of the 18th, shrewd observers thought a grandstand finish over the last two rounds might just earn Lewis a points victory or at worst a draw. Basham was showing obvious damage to his ear and also his mouth and an eye, but none to his smile or his bounciness. His clever feints and counters, though slower, had not ceased. Could he go on in the same vein, he would win.

Boxing's continuing capacity to surprise brought a climax in round 19. In a momentary lapse of concentration or from sheer fatigue, Basham failed to do what he had automatically done hundreds of times in big fights. He moved from a clinch with his gloves slightly lowered. Lewis specialised in turning the marginal to his advantage. A right swing over Basham's left glove powered into his chin and left him sitting dazed on the seat of his pants. The Welshman struggled up at nine

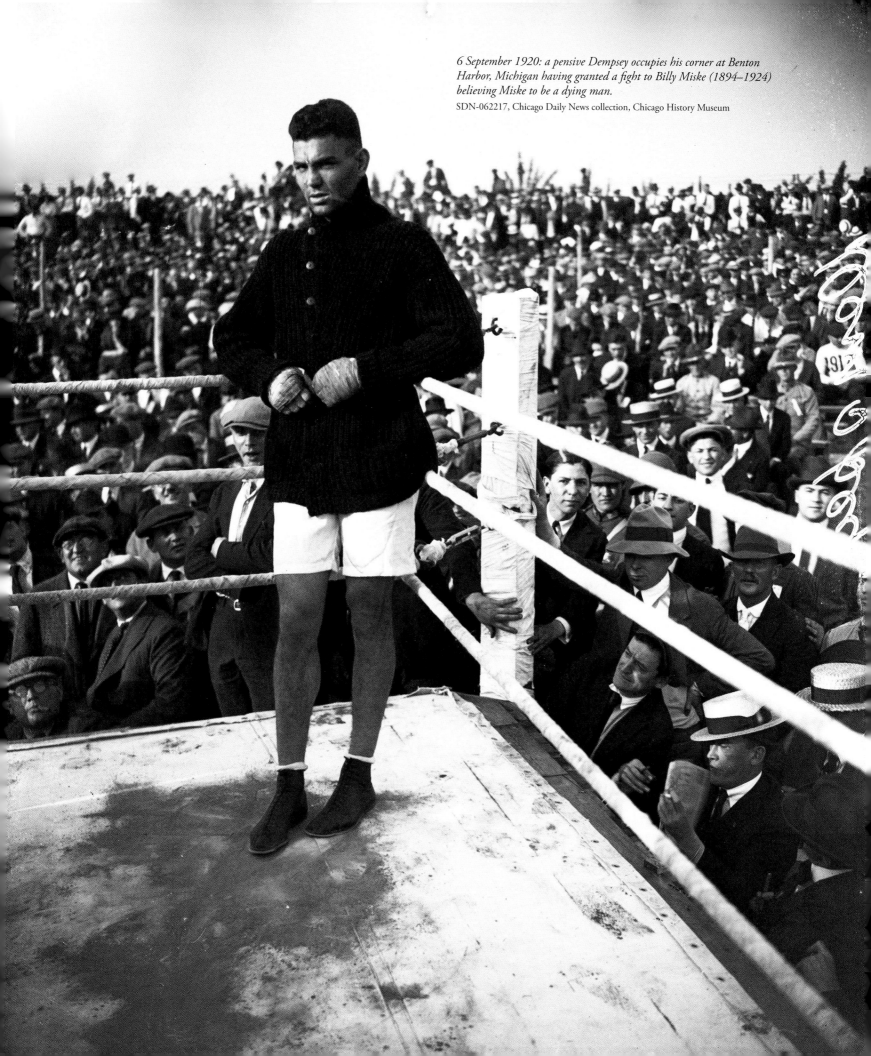

Miske hangs on the ropes, stopped in the third round.
SDN-062260, Chicago Daily News collection, Chicago History Museum

but barely knew where he was. Lewis obligingly reminded him with punches that took him backwards to the ropes. Basham punched back by instinct rather than calculation only to take another swinging right to the jaw accompanied by a left as he fell again, this time to his knees. He got up, still ready to fight on, only to find, unheard in the uproar, that the timekeeper had already called the final ten.

To say Basham was unlucky would be unjust to Lewis who had, after all, twice beaten him inside the distance. Further evidence of Lewis's ultimate superiority is that a year later (14 October 1921), he completed a trilogy of wins by making Basham – 'the

greatest man I ever fought' – retire after 12 rounds. Sadly, a misguided fourth match also took place eight years on in 13 December 1929 when Basham, pushing 40, was foolish enough to come out of retirement and suffer three rounds of one-sided punishment before the referee spared him. It is the first two fights of the series that people would remember.

And yet, as always, it was the heavyweights who captivated the general public. Carpentier had fought on American soil to prove himself a worthy challenger. How could Dempsey prove himself the authentic champion? Appearances in the law court were no substitute for defeating challengers in

the ring; neither was swanning about Hollywood with starlets. Dempsey was at one with Kearns and Rickard in excluding any black contenders, partly from personal inclination and partly from commercial apathy. The prospect was elegantly summarised by Rickard: 'A black heavyweight champion would not be worth a bucket of warm piss.' Good white contenders were as rare as ever.

Kearns was the prime mover in arranging a fight for Labor Day (6 September 1920) against Billy Miske at Benton Harbor, Michigan where ten-round restrictions and newspaper decisions prevailed. Supposedly Dempsey's title was on the line but Miske would have to knock him out to acquire it. Meanwhile, there was $55,000 for Dempsey and $25,000 for Miske. The men had met twice back in 1918 (3 May and 28 November) in two tedious mauls over ten rounds and six rounds respectively, awarded meaningless newspaper decisions as a draw and as a marginal Dempsey win. Miske was known as the 'St Paul Thunderbolt' – against Dempsey he had so far barely rumbled.

Neither was the Labor Day match promising. Behind the scenes were three factors not known to the public. Miske had been diagnosed with Bright's Disease (a serious inflammation of the kidneys) and pleaded with Dempsey for the return to help his family and to pay heavy medical expenses. Dempsey later said Miske was dying.[53] This is a little melodramatic. Miske did die on 1 January 1924 but fought another 23 times after losing to Dempsey. The second factor was Rickard, who had contributed money to Dempsey's legal expenses in the draft-dodging case and taken on the Madison Square Garden venture with Dempsey in mind. He was well aware that Dempsey's financial treatment by Kearns left much to be desired. As Kearns was trying to woo Dempsey to keep away from Rickard, so Rickard visited Benton Harbor in disguise, trying to woo Dempsey away from Kearns.[54]

The third unknown was that the notorious Al Capone, gangster and gambler, visited Dempsey in his dressing room and waved a huge roll of bills in front of him asking him to fight in one of Capone's private clubs.[55] Dempsey wisely turned the offer down, for who knows what future requests might have come from the mobster once he had his hooks into Dempsey? Had Capone's visit been known, wild rumours about a fix would have spread among the betting fraternity and cast doubts on the bout's authenticity. In the event, the fight was utterly predictable. Dempsey landed some powerful combinations in the first, knocked Miske down with one of his left hooks in the second, and with a succession of rights knocked him out after about a minute of the third.

Dempsey's next test, under the auspices of Tex Rickard at Madison Square Garden, was scheduled for 14 December 1920 and financially promising. On paper it did not look too taxing. His opponent was Bill Brennan, who had previously met Dempsey on 25 February 1918 in the middle of Dempsey's impressive rise to the title. 'Brennan', that Irish-sounding surname, was misleading. Bill's original name was Wilhelm Schenck, born 23 June 1893 in Chicago of German parentage, and now fighting out of Louisville, Kentucky. He claimed that he lost in

1918 to Dempsey only because a broken ankle forced him to retire. In truth, the ankle damage had come in the sixth after a knockdown and he had *already* been floored five times, including four times in a one-sided second round. Dempsey saw him this time as no major threat even if Brennan was rumoured to have joined the Capone circus Dempsey had spurned in Michigan.

Dempsey still spent his days in training vigorously. He was less abstemious nocturnally when the manifold attractions of Manhattan, its bars, its speakeasies and its nightclubs beckoned. Some believe that a glamorous brunette who often accompanied him on the late-night social whirl was on the Capone payroll but this is unproven.

Either way, the fight against Brennan turned into a bigger test than he had anticipated and became 'one of the most vicious and closely contested heavyweight bouts ever seen' according to one major account.[56]

The stifling new Garden was packed with people – 15,000 say some, 14,000 says another and almost 17,000 says yet another. In this heated arena, Brennan, 'K. O. Bill', proved a handful. He weighed in at 14st 1lb/197lbs compared to Dempsey's 13st 6¼lb/188¼lbs, so Dempsey conceded nearly nine pounds despite being marginally heavier than when he fought Miske. In green trunks designed to keep up the Irish pretensions, Brennan walked to the ring to cheers. Dempsey entered to jeers. He had not been forgiven on the slacker charge by many present, whatever the San Franciscan court said. Dempsey was philosophical about the reception, less about the message from Brennan in the

second in the form of a vicious right uppercut that sent him back on his heels and wobbling. Brennan looked as surprised as Dempsey, who clung on and survived the round. Had Brennan stood off and added a few more long rights, Dempsey's career might have tumbled there and then.

Dempsey's other career, as celluloid hero of tat such as *Daredevil Jack*, was also endangered when a swinging left hook from Brennan in the tenth round caught his right ear and split it severely. Dempsey felt 'suddenly the whole side of my head was warm with my blood'. Brennan calculatedly landed more punches there in the 11th. (To British observers it was an ugly reminder of Basham's fate in London.)

At the beginning of the 12th, Dempsey glowered menacingly across at Brennan, whom he feared had already left him with that characteristic badge of a pro fighter, a cauliflower ear. Since his mingling with film actresses, Dempsey was more aware of his personal appearance than he had been in the Kid Blackie days. (He underwent plastic surgery on his flattened nose in 1924.) If he did nothing about Brennan here and now, worse damage to his rugged features might follow. He shook off the effects of the early uppercut and switched his attack to Brennan's body, coupled with illegal rabbit punches to the back of his neck. The tactic was very effective. Having led Brennan to expect a visit from his famous left hook, Dempsey caught him just under the heart with a powerful right hook. When Brennan folded over in pain, Dempsey let the left hook go and buried it deep into Brennan's right side. Brennan, an agonised look on his face, dropped to his hands and knees.

He made a futile attempt at rising on the count of seven and was still getting unsteadily to his feet when referee Haukop called ten. Dempsey, eager to finish Brennan off definitively, hovered above him ready to do just that, but was restrained by Haukop and waved off to his jubilant corner. The victory was not by the referee's stoppage but by knockout. With the film rights added, the final punches earned Dempsey $100,000.

A tragic sequence to the fight has to be added. Brennan, like Miske (who knocked Brennan out in four in Omaha on 7 November 1923), would not survive more than a few subsequent years. He purchased a New York speakeasy, using much of the $35,000 he earned from the Dempsey fight. He threw two hoodlums out of the premises when they suggested forcefully that he come to them for his supplies of beer. In the early hours of 15 June 1924, he went to the door to receive two visitors. One pulled out a gun and shot him dead. Dempsey's reaction to this dreadful event, much paralleled in Prohibition USA, beautifully encapsulate his dual nature. On hearing the news he sent a sympathetic telegram to Brennan's widow. Reminiscing in the 1950s to one of his ghostwriters, his epitaph for the man who in his eyes had deliberately tried to maim him (as if Dempsey would have done differently) was considerably more callous: 'Bill bought the wrong beer.'

The way was now supposedly clear for that dream clash: Carpentier the European war hero versus Dempsey, the unpopular champion and draft dodger absent from the fields of war. Both men had cleared the hurdles of warm-up fights without disaster. Losses to Levinsky or Miske or Brennan would have taken the edge off the big attraction. Tex Rickard, the one man who knew how to think big when big was needed, was to slice through the tangled knot of contract negotiations by using two weapons: borrowed money and self-generated cheek. This was no easy accomplishment.

Rickard's rival Kearns mopped his brow with relief after the narrow squeak against Brennan. Having a champ who did little but lucrative and safe personal appearances and went to the ring only to defend his title for maximal purses against hopeless contenders as infrequently as he was allowed, would suit Kearns fine.

The exception was if some mighty new promotion guaranteed him and Dempsey unprecedented returns for a night's work. Kearns had offered a $200,000 guarantee to Descamps for Carpentier to share in just such an event, money Kearns did not have and could not deliver. Neither did he have an arena fit to stage it. He was better at spending money regardless of its true ownership than accumulating to invest.[57]

Logically, Kearns would have reached an accommodation with his disliked but canny rival Tex Rickard and combined forces to bring the match to fruition. Kearns did not do straightforward. Instead, he paid two Cuban waiters to dress up as visiting millionaires and lunch with him at the Hotel Claridge in New York where Rickard was a lunchtime customer. He introduced the stooges to Rickard as Cubans who had guaranteed $500,000 to stage Dempsey/Carpentier in Havana. The poker-playing, figure-juggling Rickard had in his chequered international career come across every scam ever invented. He was supposed to have been fooled and panicked into a counter-offer. One finds this hard to believe. His counter-offer was to guarantee $300,000 to Dempsey plus 25 per cent of the film rights; $200,000 to Carpentier plus 25 per cent of the film rights. He personally would stage the fight in a suitably large arena in the New York area and make the proceeds top a million dollars. It seems rather that Rickard had outmanoeuvred and outwitted Kearns.

There were still snags. Rickard had no funds at his disposal either. He could not pay money up front to seal the contracts with the rival parties. Neither did he have the wherewithal to build a stadium sufficiently large to accommodate the number of spectators necessary to guarantee a mammoth gate. He was not deterred. He was a lot smarter than Kearns at creative solutions to difficult problems.

So was the man presently operating in New York as sports promoter and ticket tout, Michael Strauss Jacobs (1880–1953), better known as Mike Jacobs.[58] Jacobs was famously to monopolise New York and world championship boxing in the 1930s and 1940s. Since his boyhood, Jacobs had hustled a small fortune ($1,000 aged 16) by obtaining tickets to popular events (boxing, basketball, baseball, concerts, plays, musicals, revues) and selling them through an army of scalpers to an eager public at prices far exceeding that on the printed tickets. He and Rickard, jointly sensitive to the magical operations of the laws of supply and demand, had previously had lucrative mutual dealings.

He was the perfect partner in the present dilemma. Jacobs came up with

$200,000 in cash; in exchange Rickard came up with $200,000 worth of gold-embossed, elegantly engraved premium tickets for the fight, beautifully designed and executed and ready for Jacobs to sell at beautifully enhanced prices. According to Roger Kahn, the (nominal) prices were $50 ringside, $40 and $30 for the inner circle, $25 outer circle, $15 ordinary reserved seats, and $5.50 for general admission. To have any sense of contemporary value these prices would have to be multiplied by at least a factor of 20 – not a cheap day out or a working man's dream. What the Jacobs multiplier added to the sums in practice is anyone's guess.

What is known is that the official gate cleared $1,789,238, a sum no recipient complained about.

Once Rickard realised what a major promotion this could be, he increased the planned capacity of his stadium from 50,000 to 90,000. A behind-the-scenes deal with Frank Hague, Democratic Mayor of Jersey City and ace political fixer, brought a free donation of a tract of New Jersey marshland immediately adjacent to New York City, known as Boyle's Thirty Acres. There Rickard reassembled the crew who had operated so successfully in Toledo in July 1919 and got them to build another round wooden arena especially to house

Dempsey v Carpentier and the affluent and fashionable hordes eager to see it.

Logically the natural home for the clash would have been Rickard's Madison Square Garden, and if that indoor arena were too small, then an open-air New York ball park such as the New York Giants' Polo Grounds with a potential capacity for boxing of 80,000. This did not happen because of that power shift up in Albany with the new Republican Governor Nathan Miller now in office in place of the Democrat Al Smith.

Miller was opposed to major fights in New York State despite the recently passed liberalising legislation signed

Sir Oswald Mosley seen here on one of his notorious marches through the Jewish East End recruited two prominent boxers to his party to their ultimate embarrassment.

Jewish Chronicle/Heritage Images/Getty Images

off by Smith. If the fight went ahead regardless he would press actively for the Act's repeal. Rickard, his future Garden bouts in mind, knew when to fight but also when not to. Boyle's Thirty Acres was easily accessible from the metropolitan area yet had no potential legal complications. New Jersey it was, leaving Rickard free to do what he did best – build interest in the fight, emphasising every comparison that could reasonably be drawn, and others that were ridiculous. The clause in New Jersey legislation restricting the length of bouts was no hazard – no one believed a Dempsey–Carpentier bout *would* last a distance.

Dempsey v Carpentier; slacker v war hero; beast v beauty; boxer v slugger; tough v gentleman; Yank v Frog; villain v hero; the fight of the century; the most meaningful continental collision since 1776; the biggest duel in New Jersey since Aaron Burr shot Alexander Hamilton; no comparison was too far-fetched and no hyperbole too tasteless. In London, there was great support for the ever-popular Carpentier yet wistful regrets for what might have been had the British produced a genuine challenger for the title.

A generation would pass before that happy event. Cold reality was underlined in the Royal Albert Hall on 10 December 1920 in emphatic fashion.[59] The hall was packed with 10,000 people focused on the brightly illuminated ring in the centre and peering breathlessly through a blue pall of cigar and cigarette smoke. They had come to see Joe Beckett attempt, almost a year to the day since his instant demise against Carpentier, to rehabilitate his career and to confirm in the ring his boasts outside it. He intended to prove

he was still a serious challenger against Carpentier for his European title. He also planned to go off to the USA to seek a fight against Dempsey. Great as always are future paper fights, but first Beckett had to defeat the man on the stool in the other corner – Frank Moran, who had brought his beloved Mary Ann along with him.

The physical advantages were all with Moran, the taller blond giant (6ft 1½in). He towered comfortably over the swarthy, dark-haired Beckett (5ft 9in), outreached him by five and a half inches and outweighed him by possibly 14 pounds. Beckett had argued correctly that he was the better boxer and that he moved more speedily. This should enable him to avoid Mary Ann and regularly pick off the cumbersome Moran. He must not close and clinch and allow the strong American to deliver short, sharp blows inside. This had been emphasised to Beckett by his experienced second – Jim Driscoll – and by the evening's guest of honour – the man of the moment, Carpentier. Carpentier was cheered more loudly than either boxer and looked to be helpful. Carpentier left his seat at the end of the first round, leaned over Beckett and re-emphasised the correct tactics before the second round began.

Regrettably, Beckett's ears were closed to all entreaties. In close, he uppercut and hooked Moran to face and jaw. This was superficially encouraging yet had as little effect on Moran as if he had been one of those distinguished rocky profiles on Mount Rushmore attacked by a pea-shooter. The disparity between the uppercuts and Moran's short jabs, which visibly hurt Beckett, was wide, about as wide as the distance between Beckett and Moran's wilder

punches when the two men were apart. Moran was reprimanded twice, once for swinging his forearm into Beckett's face and once in the second round for holding Beckett with one arm to bring Mary Ann into action from somewhere near Australia.

The offence brought a severe lecture from referee Joe Palmer. A guilty Moran proffered a handshake to Beckett, who perfunctorily accepted it and immediately landed another four good punches to the jaw of the oblivious Moran. This was Beckett's last useful contribution to a disappointingly abbreviated fight. Unblinking, Moran caught Beckett with a short right hook to the jaw that had the Englishman clutching for support on the only thing within reach, Moran's left arm. Moran's right was still free and thudded into the side of Beckett's head three times before clinically finishing the fight and the evening with a powerful uppercut. Over went Beckett on to his back, with Moran tripping over his legs and going down on all fours himself. Moran was up straightaway. Beckett was not. It took him eight to roll over and get to his hands and knees. Ten came and went. Moran tried to help him up but Beckett's seconds pushed him aside and carried Beckett to his corner. He was still inert, along with any chances the British ever had for a serious challenge to Dempsey. It was all down to France now.

Sad to record, there was a melancholy postscript after the completion of the fighting careers of two of the prominent British fighters featured in this chapter – Ted Kid Lewis and Joe Beckett. Depressingly in later years they both fell among fascists, the one embarrassingly and the other dangerously.

Much was down to the personal magnetism of one of the most dynamic yet flawed politicians of the inter-war years – the baronet Sir Oswald Mosley (1896–1980).[60] Mosley, previously a Conservative, served in the Labour government of 1929–31 until exasperated by the timidity of Ramsay MacDonald (1866–1937) and his cabinet who stayed wedded to financial orthodoxy as mass unemployment soared. Breaking away in February 1931, Mosley founded the New Party to propagate his own ideas. Fatally attracted by the emerging right-wing movements on the Continent associated with Benito Mussolini in Italy and Adolf Hitler in Germany, the New Party had fascistic elements within it. All too soon it adopted symbols such as fasces, paramilitary trappings such as black-shirted uniforms, and troupes of biff-boys up for a street fight or aggressively squashing dissent at rallies and meetings. As early as 1932 it turned itself into the British Union of Fascists (BUF).

When Mosley, at a cocktail party, met Ted Kid Lewis, he personally recruited him to the fold. Lewis had attributes useful to Mosley. He could use his formidable fists and he could train others how to fight. Mosley appointed Lewis on the spot as his 'physical youth training instructor to the New Party'.[61] (In private, though not to Lewis, Mosley admitted his thugs would look better to the British public if they could be disguised as the products of healthy sports clubs.) Lewis was conveniently naïve and, best of all, Jewish – the perfect antidote to common accusations that Mosley and his New Party were, like their Continental counterparts, anti-Semitic.

Mosley persuaded Ted Kid Lewis to stand for Parliament. It was Lewis's most humiliating defeat.
Central Press/Hulton Archive/Getty Images

Lewis in his new role trained recruits and enrolled anything from ten to 50 brawny East Enders to 'steward' meetings at £10 a time with expenses, an attractive proposition to anyone on the breadline who did not mind thumping a few communists and socialists. Mosley had another role for him also. At a Café Royal dinner given in his honour, Lewis was announced as the New Party candidate for the Whitechapel constituency at the October 1931 General Election.

The scheme was to exploit Lewis's personal popularity, his ethnicity in a strongly Jewish area, his local connections and his glittering name as possibly Britain's best-ever boxer. It misfired pathetically and he finished bottom of the poll of 23,689 votes with a miniscule 154 (even communist Harry Pollitt got 17 times as many). The venture damaged only Lewis and his reputation. His usefulness over and the party daily more anti-Semitic, he was 'frozen out' during the change from New Party to the BUF.[62] In his filial biography, Morton Lewis gives a highly colourful version of Lewis's split with Mosley.[63] He writes that as a 14-year-old, he accompanied his father to Mosley's office where Mosley, flanked by two brown-shirted bodyguards, was asked by Lewis, 'Are you anti-Jewish?' and replied 'Yes'. Lewis slapped Mosley to the floor, where Mosley prudently remained, and then Lewis knocked out cold the two guards in turn. After leaving the building, Lewis returned almost immediately and knocked out two other guards on the door.

Perhaps a row did take place but the account as written is full of improbabilities. Why would Lewis have to ask such a question? Even his wife and his relatives told him of the dangers of associating with the anti-Semitic Mosley. Would Lewis really take a child along when he expected trouble? Why would Mosley be so passive? Mosley was an accomplished boxer ('with a formidable straight left') and a notable fencer (Public Schools Fencing champion) and was notoriously short-fused, having frequently fought fellow pupils at Winchester and Sandhurst at minor provocations. A retired world welterweight champion was tough opposition but even his enemies agree that Mosley, whatever his faults, was physically courageous. Cowardly passivity on the floor as a result of a slap? Hardly. And those *brown* shirts? The Nazis in Germany wore brown shirts; their British imitators wore *black* so as not to look like a British branch of the Hitler Youth. Four hefty goons all knocked out clean with a single punch each? That sounds more like children's fiction than sober reality.

Mosley's malign influence, unlike Lewis's brief swim in these murky waters, continued. He replaced Lewis as chief enforcer with a British heavyweight champion who retired a decade before after another one-round knockout by Georges Carpentier (1 October 1923 at Olympia): Joe Beckett. Unlike Lewis, Beckett believed in fascist philosophies, at least at an unsophisticated level, and willingly supervised rallies, distributed literature, parroted fascist slogans and believed in Mosley as Supreme Leader.

For most of the 1930s this was distasteful but relatively harmless. Once the Second World War had broken out with Nazi Germany, such activities became unpatriotic and, said the authorities, subversive and traitorous. Under Defence Regulation 18B(1A) amended in May 1940, offenders could be detained. In May and June 1940, many BUF members and sympathisers were rounded up. Mosley was held in Brixton Prison for the next 18 months and under house arrest from November 1943 onwards.

His minion Joe Beckett was also subject to the 18B regulation. He and his wife Margaret were detained on 30 May 1940 as members of the BUF.[64] They were secretly interviewed by a Home Office Advisory Committee at an Ascot hotel on 29 October 1940 under the formidable chairmanship of Norman Birkett (1893–1962), later Lord Birkett and a prominent figure at the notorious Nuremberg Trials of Nazi war criminals. Birkett's forensic skills were superfluous to need in this context. He and his three fellow panel members swiftly recognised that the rather pathetic couple in front of them were hardly dangers to the realm,

and their activities had extended little beyond silly talk in pubs and the unwise display of fascist badges. Margaret in particular was 'of sound mind although she is considerably below the average standard of intelligence'. Beckett displayed some unthinking anti-Semitism:

Q. (Sir Arthur Hazlerigg) Are you a person who dislikes Jews very much?

A. (Beckett) Of course, they did not treat me too good when I was in the boxing game.

Q. You did not treat them 'too good' when you had the chance.

A. I never got the chance.

Q. (Birkett) Speaking generally, I think my colleague meant not merely your personal opinion of Jews but generally what was your general attitude to Jews?

A. I have met some good Jews but in the boxing game you do not get the good Jew.

Although Beckett's answers if published would have offended many in the boxing community, they were hardly in the sinister Hitler and Goebbels league. Birkett could reserve his ammunition for Nuremberg.

There was nothing in Joe's or Margaret's testimony to suggest they were in any way unpatriotic or plotting for a German victory. The panel suspended their detention as from 21 November 1940 with the proviso that they reported monthly to a police station for the duration of the war. It had all been a bit of a storm in a spit bucket.

Endnotes:

1 *Boxing World, Mirror of Life and Sporting Observer,* 7 February 1920.
2 *New York Times,* 6 December 1919.
3 *New York Times,* 5 January 1920.
4 See Brady entry in the *American National Biography,* on-line version.
5 *The Times,* 6 January 1920.
6 *The Times,* 25 February 1920.
7 Corri, E., *Fifty Years in the Ring* (London: Hutchinson, 1933) p. 46.
8 *Boxing World, Mirror of Life and Sporting Observer,* 17 January 1920.
9 *Boxing World, Mirror of Life and Sporting Observer,* 14 and 28 February 1920.
10 *New York Times,* 14 January 1920.
11 *New York Times,* 26 January 1920.
12 *New York Times,* 26 January 1920.
13 *New York Times,* 15 January 1920.
14 *Punch,* 21 January 1920.
15 *Punch,* 28 January 1920.
16 *New York Times,* 9 January 1920.
17 *New York Times,* 30 January 1920.
18 See details in *Carpentier: By Himself* (London: Sportsman's Book Club, 1958) Chapter XIII.
19 Roberts, R., *Jack Dempsey: The Manassa Mauler* (New York: Grove Press, 1980) pp. 68–69.
20 *Boxing World, Mirror of Life and Sporting Observer,* 31 January 1920; Shipley, S., *Bombardier Billy Wells: The Life and Trials of a Boxing Hero* (Tyne and Wear: Bewick Press, 1993) pp.158–160.
21 *The Times,* 18 March 1920.
22 *Boxing World, Mirror of Life and Sporting Observer,* 27 March 1920.
23 *The Times,* 9 April 1920.
24 *Boxing World, Mirror of Life and Sporting Observer,* 13 March 1920.
25 *The Times,* 9 April 1920; *Boxing World, Mirror of Life and Sporting Observer,* 17 April 1920.
26 *Boxing World, Mirror of Life and Sporting Observer,* 19 March 1920; *Sunday Times,* 7 March 1920.

27 *The Times,* 11 May 1920; *Boxing World, Mirror of Life and Sporting Observer,* 22 May 1920.
28 *San Francisco Chronicle,* 9, 10, 11, 12, 13, 15 and 16 June 1920; Roberts, R., *Jack Dempsey,* pp. 77–87; Kahn, R., *A Flame of Pure Fire: Jack Dempsey and the Roaring '20s* (New York: Harcourt, Brace and Co., 1999) pp. 142–166.
29 *San Francisco Chronicle,* 16 June 1920.
30 Details drawn partly from Reiss, S., 'In the Ring and Out' in *Sport in America: New Historical Perspectives,* edited Donald Spivey, Westport 1985.
31 *New York Times,* 30 and 31 January 1917.
32 *New York Times,* 28 February 1918.
33 *New York Times,* 18 February 1920.
34 *New York Times,* 28 November 1920.
35 *New York Times,* 25 May 1920 – quoted by Reiss, S., 'In the Ring and Out'.
36 Harding, J., *Lonsdale's Belt: Boxing's Most Coveted Prize* (Worthing: Pitch Publishing, 2016) p. 72.
37 British Boxing Board of Control Minutes No.1.
38 Minute Book No. 1 entry for 30 April 1918.
39 *Boxing World, Mirror of Life and Sporting Observer,* 17th April 1920.
40 Deghy G., *Noble and Manly: The History of the National Sporting Club* (Hutchinson, 1956) pp. 194–195.
41 *Boxing World, Mirror of Life and Sporting Chronicle,* 5 June 1920.
42 *Boxing World, Mirror of Life and Sporting Observer,* 13 November 1920.
43 *The Times,* 15 October 1920.
44 Reports in *Boxing World, Mirror of Life and Sporting Observer,* 24 July 1920; *The Times,* 17 July 1920; fight film in *Boxers* 48: Tommy Burns.
45 *New York Times,* 18 September 1920.
46 *Boxing World, Mirror of Life and Sporting Observer,* 18 September 1920.
47 *Sunday Times,* 12 September 1920.

48 Blady, K., *The Jewish Boxers Hall of Fame* (New York: Shapolsky Books, 1988) pp. 98–103.
49 *Carpentier: By Himself,* pp. 130–133; *New York Times,* 13 October 1920.
50 *The Times,* 10 June 1920; *Boxing World, Mirror of Life and Sporting Observer,* 19 June 1920; Roderick, A., *Johnny! The Story of the Happy Warrior* (Newport: Heron Press, 1990) pp. 83–91; Lewis, M., *Ted Kid Lewis: His Life and Times* (London: Robson Books, 1990) pp. 143–144.
51 *The Times,* 20 November 1920; *Boxing World, Mirror of Life and Sporting Observer,* 27 November 1920.
52 *New York Times,* 24 September 1920.
53 Dempsey, J. with Considine, B. & Slocum, B., *Massacre in the Sun* (London: World Distributors, 1963) p. 101.
54 Kahn, R., *A Flame of Pure Fire,* pp. 208–209.
55 Kahn, R., *A Flame of Pure Fire,* pp. 208.
56 *New York Times,* 15 December 1920.
57 For details of Kearns's and Rickard's actions pre-fight see Kahn, R., *A Flame of Pure Fire,* pp. 231–242 and Roberts, R., *Jack Dempsey,* pp. 104–109.
58 See the Jacobs entry in the *American National Biography* online version.
59 *The Times,* 11 December 1920; *New York Times,* 11 December 1920: *Boxing World, Mirror of Life and Sporting Observer,* 18 December 1920; documentary film 'The Great Fight' in the BFI collection.
60 Skidelsky, R., *Oswald Mosley* (London: Macmillan, 1975).
61 Lewis, M., *Ted Kid Lewis,* p. 224.
62 Skidelsky, R., *Oswald Mosley,* p. 321.
63 Lewis, M., *Ted Kid Lewis,* pp. 227–228.
64 National Archives files HO144/21840 June 1943 (Joe) and HO144/21839 (Ruth Margaret).

CHAPTER 16
ANTICIPATION RULES!
JANUARY TO JUNE 1921

In Which Many Illusions Are Shattered

FOR ALL the European and American anticipation for the meeting between Dempsey and Carpentier, other domestic shows engaged full attention. None more so than the bill widely advertised for the Royal Albert Hall for Thursday, 13 January 1921 under the joint auspices of American boxing promoter Reuben 'Rube' Welch and a London syndicate led by Leon Pollock. Welch stepped into the promoting vacuum created by Cochran's withdrawal and promised an attractive evening's boxing. Few knew that if one shook hands with Welch, it was advisable to count one's fingers afterwards.

The main supporting bout was Battling Levinsky (so recently defeated by Carpentier in New Jersey) v Bombardier Billy Wells. Most engaging was the top of the bill pairing – Jimmy Wilde v Pete Herman. This was the very fight that fell through in 1920 much to Cochran's disgust and led to his renouncing of boxing promotion.

Welch promised more than he could deliver – *deliberately*. When he stepped off the *New York* in Southampton in October 1920, he claimed to have the signatures of many top American boxers on contracts, duly endorsed by the New York State Boxing Commission, requiring them to box against British boxers in British rings. His stable supposedly included Dempsey (who would 'probably' fight Joe Beckett). However, he genuinely contracted both Battling Levinsky and Pete Herman for the Albert Hall event. At the last moment, Levinsky withdrew from the Wells bout, turning up with his arm in a sling. This disgusted the Wells fans who, emboldened about Billy's prospects after Levinsky's recent defeat by their favourite Frenchman, had paid handsomely to see it (minimum price £3 10s.).

That left the bill-topper, Wilde v Herman, as the sole event carrying British hopes. Pete 'Kid' Herman (b. 12 February 1896 in New Orleans as Peter Gulotta) had been world bantamweight champion since January 1917. He was a brilliantly skilled boxer who punched his weight and punched it accurately, especially at close quarters. Just as Wells's supporters were boosted by Levinsky's recent loss to Carpentier, so Wilde's followers were buoyed by hearing that Herman, in Madison Square Garden on 22 December 1920, barely three weeks before, suffered an unexpected off-night and lost his world title on points to Joe Lynch, the Irish New Yorker, by a decisively wide margin. Wilde had already beaten Joe Lynch in London at the end of March 1919.

Some conspiracy theorists claimed darkly that Herman lost deliberately to Lynch, his inferior. Lynch earned $7,000 out of the occasion. Herman earned $30,980. The result placed Herman's world title out of the reach of Wilde in London. Herman, cynics said, surrendered the title knowing he could meet Lynch again any time and regain it. (The only circumstantial evidence supporting this 'plot' is that Herman easily reclaimed his title against Lynch at Ebbet's Field, Brooklyn on 25 July 1921 on points over 15 rounds, an event so marred by crowd turbulence in and out of the stadium as to get the promoter's licence removed.)

That December 1920 night in Manhattan had seen wild scenes as Lynch, the favourite son of Irish New Yorkers, claimed the title, donning a gold-and-diamond-studded championship belt donated by Tex Rickard, while Herman slumped morosely on his stool. Next day, Herman sailed for England to meet Wilde. Even a victorious Wilde could not now add Herman's old title to his own world flyweight championship. Yet surely Herman's Manhattan debacle enhanced Wilde's prospects of beating the heavier man? How much heavier turned on a bizarre set of quite unanticipated circumstances, almost as dramatic as the fight itself.

The mood of the Albert Hall audience was not one of sweet tolerance. Levinsky's last-minute withdrawal stirred anger all round. And after a few boring preliminaries, came a substitute 20-round heavyweight bout between Erminio Spalla of Italy (b. 7 July 1897) and a so-called American billed ominously as Wild Bert Kenny. Kenny was actually Canadian. There was little wrong with Spalla, who built a very reasonable career – 41 wins (30 KOs), 19 losses (six KOs), three draws, three no-decisions – and helped to put Italian boxing on the map. He would hold the European heavyweight title from 1923–26. He is probably the only boxer to double as a professional operatic tenor.

Kenny had little to sing about. Largely unsuccessful – 16 wins (eight KOs), 40 losses, four draws – his method was to advance on an opponent, while crouching as low to the canvas as gravity would allow, looking like a large fat attacking crab. When it saw an opening, the crab would leap dementedly towards his opponent swinging wildly. The strategy did not endear itself to a disaffected audience or the referee. Kenny was disqualified in the sixth, one of the nine disqualifications he received during his eccentric career, and booed.

More displeasure came with vociferous protests from the upper reaches of the hall from those who had paid good money and realised they would see nothing of Wilde/Herman because the imported arc lamps over the ring enhancing exposures for the film cameras blotted out their view of the action. A riot threatened until Lord Lonsdale took the centre of the ring and promised changes to the lighting before the fight took place.

This was not the only delay. As the audience waited, less than patiently, and 11 o'clock came and went, Wilde was sitting in his dressing room and refusing to come out. He had agreed to a 20-round fight at a maximum of 8st 6lb/118lbs, weigh-in to be conducted at ringside at 10pm prior to the fight. Even for £8,000, which is what Wilde claimed to be earning, this fight was a high-risk and ill-advised proposition. Wilde had not fought for seven months. He had decided provisionally to retire until tempted by Welch's offer and had rarely exceeded 7st 2lb/100lbs at any fight, no matter how many nutritious dishes 'Lisbeth had put on the table to tempt him. Taking on a strong-punching bantamweight and conceding ten pounds was a foolhardy if self-inflicted handicap.

It soon emerged that the situation was even worse – Herman had weighed in at just under 8st 6lb *at 2 o'clock that afternoon* and spent the intervening hours packing in more calories. He claimed to be following the terms of his contract to the letter and had no intention of stepping on the scales again and disclosing his present weight. (Actually he did do so secretly and scaled 8st 7½lb/119½lbs.) Wilde claimed his own weight that night was about 7st 1lb, so a difference between the men of about 20 pounds. In the past, Wilde had famously knocked out men much heavier than he – but that was in the past. This was a recipe for a heavy beating. Wilde stayed resolutely in his dressing room and the audience grew more restive.

His resolve to stay there was undermined by his strongly deferential sense of social class. Waiting at the ringside were aristocrats such as Lord Lonsdale and a royal in the Prince of Wales (later Edward VIII). The prince responded to the warmth of the crowd's greeting by making a self-deprecating little speech from the ring, wishing both fighters well and covering up the delay. At the prince's bidding, Lonsdale went to Wilde's dressing room to find out what the problem was. Lonsdale reminded Wilde how many people and how many distinguished people were waiting upon his appearance and escorted him to meet the prince at ringside. The match was late but on. As, post-Levinsky, it was the *only* major fight of the evening, Wilde's change of heart probably saved the Albert Hall's fixtures and fittings.

Wilde's more fervent admirers believe that he was only beaten by Herman's illegitimately acquired weight advantage. Alas, it is more likely that Wilde was fundamentally defeated by three factors. First was his foolhardy decision to take the money for a fight against a man conspicuously heavier and stronger. This was true even if Herman had been 8st 6lb at a 10pm weigh-in. Second, the Wilde who climbed reluctantly through the ropes to please his betters was a shadow of Wilde in his prime (seven months of golf and snooker following his American-Canadian venture of early 1920 were no substitute for regular training and fighting). Herman had 15 serious fights during 1920. Third,

Wilde was seriously distracted by the preliminary goings-on and disputations in and out of his dressing room that night. He was not in a mental state to give of his best. He said to the prince, 'I'll do my best, Your Highness, but I don't think so much of my chance after all this bother.'

That Wilde was a shadow of his former self was clear to at least two experienced boxing writers. Said J. Frank Bradley of *Boxing World*:

When I saw Jimmy get home with both hands, straight, well-judged and perfectly timed, flush hits, and noticed that Herman was apparently unhurt, I realised that Wilde's hitting power of six or seven years ago had departed, and without that, no man of Wilde's poundage can possibly concede a stone in weight to a useful opponent.

An editorial in *Boxing* was even more brutal:

He was beaten because he was no longer the man for whom the match with Herman had been made, because he was no better than a bad imitation of that man. Far too much stress has been laid on the weight he was conceding. He conceded fully as much to Joe Lynch …

And, as the magazine's reporter felt:

… in all ring history there had been no falling off so complete and so rapid … Not only was Wilde a long distance removed from the Wilde of a few years back: he was almost as far removed from the Wilde of a few months, nay, of a few weeks back. The Jimmy we saw at Mr Bettinson's benefit last December 22 had four or five times as much 'zip' and 'go' in him as the Jimmy who climbed through the ropes at the Albert Hall last Thursday night.

The fight was as one-sided as the accounts suggest yet no one who saw it would ever forget the one quality Wilde had not lost – his grit.

In the first round, the strikingly pale Wilde attacked immediately, throwing punches with abandon and ignoring defence or evasion. Pete Herman, of rather Mediterranean complexion, was coolness personified, unruffled by any of the Wilde punches that penetrated his defences – few did – and quietly sized Wilde up. Towards the end of the round he poked out a tentative range-finding left to Wilde's chin and followed it in with a strong right cross. Wilde was staggered, as were knowledgeable spectators. No one could remember Wilde previously caught by such a telegraphed and predictable delivery. Here were two depressing and unprecedented signs – Wilde landing punches that had little effect upon the recipient, and Wilde taking a punch that once would hardly reach his neighbourhood.

Worse followed in the second. Where the old speedy Wilde could lead with his right and get away with it, the slower Wilde could not. At the end of the round he tried it and got the fiercest of right crosses to his chin, a punch that wobbled him at the knees. He went shakily back to his corner for a severe talking to by his seconds.

The wigging did some good. Wilde had lost his uncanny power and his speed of punch. He had not lost his skill or his knowledge of how to box. Throwing off the effects of Herman's right cross, he boxed Herman cleverly for the next four rounds, landing often with his left and giving the American no easy openings. From the more distant reaches of the hall, it appeared that the worst was behind him and he was quietly getting on top. Those with more privileged and closer views saw his punches land often and prettily, but saw that they did not hurt Herman. Herman's rarer counters had more weight (those extra pounds) and venom. He was cautioned twice for hitting Wilde low – the last thing the lighter man needed.

It went from bad to worse. In the seventh, Wilde's jaw met a staggering left hook from Herman and he suffered a punishing 30 seconds as blows rained in on him from all angles. He survived both and courageously sought to fight back, sending out plenty of punches, most of which Herman blocked or easily evaded. Wilde's ability to fight back when threatened was one of his striking qualities. It carried him through the eighth and ninth. In the ninth, he took another punch hard enough to make him stumble, yet even Herman admired the skill with which he escaped from a corner out of another flurry. Wilde supporters breathed again, more in relief than hope.

Spurious hopes reignited in the 12th when Wilde attacked, landing lefts and rights through and over Herman's usually effective defence. It looked good, though the wisdom of mixing it with the stronger Herman was questionable. Wilde took the points for the round. Herman was unruffled; a man happy to bide his time.

Wilde had done everything a man could reasonably do against a heavier and stronger man catching him often. He may even have led on points. He had sustained miracles of recovery and valour. Not even Wilde, at his less than best, could sustain that for another eight rounds.

The inevitable conclusion began in the 15th. The steadily weakening Wilde, still fighting with every morsel of vigour he had left, made desperate attacks on Herman, who responded with uppercuts and hooks, two of them staggering Wilde seriously. In the 16th, Wilde was even more vulnerable to heavy punches and doing everything but fall down. He punched on, yet he was a pale imitation of his former self and doomed to defeat. Everyone present knew it, including Wilde. Because of his exemplary reputation of defeating big and powerful opponents, he was allowed to emerge for the 17th and further unnecessary punishment. What further had Herman or Wilde to prove? The extended beating Wilde received was a significant factor in his development of Alzheimer's in later years.

Many called for a merciful stoppage. Wilde, dazed and weary, took everything the aggressive Herman handed out. A left lead went between Wilde's gloves, unusually elevated in front of his face, followed by a right that sent him crashing through the ropes and banging his head on the ring apron. On autopilot, he was up at seven and back through the ropes for more. A left and two rights sent him through the ropes again for another count. Barely had the referee pronounced

four than Wilde hauled himself back upright, a pathetic and vulnerable target for Herman to knock back down. Surrender still evaded Wilde's dazed mind and he struggled back up. Only then did enlightenment dawn.

Referee Smith waved Herman away and practically carried the Welshman to his corner. Wilde was assisted from the ring. In the circumstances, he should have been carried away on a hero's shield.

The solution to the abiding mystery about the staggered weigh-ins and Herman's supposed duplicity is disclosed in Minute Book No. 1 of the British Boxing Board of Control. In the midst of C. B. Cochran's withdrawal from boxing in September 1920, prompted by Herman's late withdrawal, Cochran wrote to the Board enquiring whether they could bring pressure to bear on Herman to come as originally promised. Apart from the disinclination of many board members strongly associated with the NSC to help so commercial a promoter as Cochran, the Board recognised, in the absence of international agreements and coordination, its own impotence:

> It is somewhat difficult to understand what effective action the Board could take at present, at any rate, with an American boxer who is not in this Country & has apparently no intention of coming here.

The Board had never associated with Cochran, nor he with them, and they had never been privy to details of Cochran's contracts. Primly they declared:

… in so far as promoters are responsible … they have only themselves to thank for any difficulties or disappointments they may meet with.

So there!

The Board could not ignore the fight, however, especially if Wilde beat Herman and claimed the world bantamweight title. Two days before the fight, they decided after a narrow vote (6 to 4) to issue a statement that 'as they have not sufficient official information as to the conditions under which Herman fought Lynch in America – they cannot at present give a decision [on Wilde's possible claim]. They agreed to write to New York enquiring about the validity of Lynch's victory over Herman.

The Board had a further dilemma in the weeks following the fight when Wilde's manager, Ted Lewis, sent them a letter. In it he registered the Wilde camp's complaint that Herman had failed his contractual obligations to weigh in at 8st 6lb/118lbs at ringside. Wilde, against his manager's advice, had 'under great pressure' consented to box. The Board's noncommittal response was that Wilde had consented to the irregularities and made no personal appeal to them.

In February, the Board discussed the affair further. More interesting details emerged from Ted Lewis. At the meeting on 8 February it was claimed that the Albert Hall overall purse had been £11,000 – £7,000 for the winner and £4,000 plus £250 for Wilde. More important was the disclosure that *there were actually two contracts* – one signed by Herman in the USA and a second one signed by Wilde in Britain.

For this highly irregular and indeed illegal procedure, Rube Welch was obviously responsible. Conveniently, the elusive Rube was now in Paris and uncontactable.

Details trickle out in subsequent meetings of the Board over the next five months of further Welch duplicities. On 19 April, the Board digested the contents of the New York Commission's reply to its query about the Lynch/Herman contest. Yes, said New York, Lynch had won fairly and all championship conditions had been met – Lynch was genuinely the world champion at the weight. That was predictable. What was much less palatable for the Board was to be told that things were clearly run better in New York than in London, because Herman would not have been 'mulcted' of his legitimate share of the Albert Hall purse had the fight been in the USA!

This is symptomatic of the serious difficulties the early Board faced continually in trying to bring order to a sport where so many fighters and promoters did their own thing. So major a fight as Herman/Wilde took place with the Board impotently unaware of crucial details about the arrangements. They could investigate only retrospectively. They invited Herman's manager, Mr Goldman, to attend their 28 June 1921 meeting.

Goldman attended and had other interesting claims. He signed a contract in New York with Welch, guaranteeing Herman $35,000 (including $5,000 expenses) *win, lose or draw*, to be paid before the fight.

The Board disapproved of any such arrangements where the result made no difference to the rewards. Back in February 1919, they had censured

Ernie Rice of Hounslow (1896–1979) shows off his rippling muscles and his lightweight Lonsdale Belt. He was rarely given his due.
Popperfoto/Getty Images

Ernie Rice for agreeing to split a purse equally with an opponent. The underlying principle was that each fighter should have every incentive to fight to win. The Board's rule stated specifically:

No member shall enter into a contract with any boxer or boxers for a contest under the terms of which the loser may receive an amount equal to or greater than the winner.

There was worse to follow.

Goldman said that when he had arrived in England, Rube Welch had taken him to one side and persuaded him to agree to a revised sum of $24,000 on the grounds that the event was not going to pay as much as anticipated. Goldman accepted reluctantly and was given two sterling payments of £180 and £50, leaving approximately £4,500 to be paid on the day of the fight. When that day dawned, Welch was surprisingly elusive for most of the day but *after the banks were closed* [!] wrote a cheque to Goldman for the full £4,500. Paid in next day, it bounced. Welch had been out of reach ever since, so the proper fee was still unpaid.

Goldman then turned to the weight issue. Herman's contract with Welch signed in the USA had stipulated a weigh-in at 2pm at a maximum of 8st 6lb/118lbs. Mention of an agreement with Wilde for a ringside weigh-in was there none. If Welch had signed a different agreement with Wilde on Herman's behalf that was quite without Herman's and Morgan's knowledge or approval.

The revelations left much to be investigated. After a few weeks' correspondence and invitations to others to bear witness, the Board met again on 21 July 1921. They had before them much corroborating evidence – from the press (the *Sunday Sportsman* for example printed one of the Welch contracts); from Wilde's manager Ted Lewis, who produced Wilde's articles of agreement; and from H. M. Herbert, the accountant to the English syndicate helping to promote the fight. Goldman had clearly been telling the truth – there had been two differing agreements not known mutually to the fighters. Herman had properly fulfilled every detail of his contracted obligations. Herman had never been paid properly. Testimony was lacking only from the man at the centre of the trouble – Mr Reuben Welch. He had been summoned to appear and explain yet for some reason had not even replied. Really? All the Board could do was to issue a statement outlining their conclusions and send a copy of their proceedings to New York. It was a sorry tale and the damage to Wilde and Herman irreparable.

It would be some years before the Board acquired real power. In the meantime it would be criticised and mocked whatever it did. When it declined to endorse a match-up between Johnny Basham and Gus Platts on 31 May 1921 for the European middleweight title, *Boxing World* thought the Board 'ridiculous' and added:

> As at present constituted the British Board of Control is a pretty useless body. It is neither impartial nor representative, and its power, if it has any, is very limited. It does not control boxing in this country, and never will as long as it is what it is.

The magazine was accurate about the Board's impotence. It was unfair over the Basham/Platts decision. Both Basham and Platts lost convincingly to Ted Kid Lewis at welterweight. Lewis was to fight Jack Bloomfield on 27 June 1921 for the British middleweight championship and a Lonsdale Belt. This raised the odd possibility that Lewis might be British champion while an inferior British fighter in Basham or Platts, both of whom he had defeated, would be European champion, generally recognised as a superior title. That is exactly what did happen. Lewis beat Jack Bloomfield at Holland Park, under NSC auspices, and acquired the British title and the Lonsdale Belt on 27 June 1921. Basham was already European middleweight champion (31 May 1921), unrecognised by the NSC and the Board. Only pedants cared much about the anomaly, but anomaly it was and the Board was entitled to point it out.

Meanwhile, internationally speaking, the big fight between Jack Dempsey and Georges Carpentier still seemed remote. Cynicism that it would ever take place was more common than optimism. *Boxing World, Mirror of Life and Sporting Observer* warned its readers not to allow pessimism to take over. In the 12 February 1921 issue, an editorial stated: 'The proposed Dempsey–Carpentier fight may be regarded over here as about as dead as it could be, but Tex Rickard and others concerned are apparently persuading themselves that there is still hope of the affair materialising.'

By 12 March, the journal was gloomier and downgraded the possibilities.

'Our Notebook' by J. Frank Bradley pronounced, 'I do not believe that Dempsey and Carpentier will ever meet in the ring.' As late as 16 April 1921, the magazine was certain that the match was off:

> Ever since the Dempsey–Carpentier match was mooted I [Bradley, again] have expressed my opinion and conviction that they would never meet in the ring, and now the Sports

News Association has sent from Paris a telegram saying that Carpentier has applied to the New York Bank for the return of his 50,000 dollars deposit for the match, and has agreed to fight Frank Moran at the Royal Albert Hall on the eve of the Derby in June. The agreement with Dempsey stipulated that the venue of the contest should be fixed by April 1st, and as this was not done, the agreement was automatically cancelled and the match collapsed.

In fact there was still hope, although the readers of *Punch*'s issue of 20 December 1920 were expected to resign themselves to a very long delay indeed. According to a two-page prediction called 'Our Heavy-Waits', written by the humorist 'Patlander', the negotiations would include helpful interventions from Henry Ford, the Reverend Billy Sunday, Lloyd George and the White House. They would culminate in a 'Great Fight' in Geneva on 4 July 1960 (*sic*) with the following result:

The fight for the Heavyweight Championship of the World, held under the auspices of the League of Nations, took place yesterday before a gigantic crowd. DEMPSEY, who now wears a flowing white beard, was wheeled into the ring in a bath-chair. CARPENTIER, now wholly bald, appeared on crutches and was seconded by two trained nurses and his youngest grandson. Both champions were assisted to their feet by their supporters, shook hands and

immediately clinched. In this clinch they remained throughout the entire round, fast asleep. At the opening of the second round they attempted to clinch again, but missed each other, overbalanced and went to the mat. Neither could be persuaded to get up, and consequently both were counted out.

British pessimists did not realise the perennially active Rickard was still receiving meaningful offers of sites to stage his fight (Cumberland, Maryland and Fallen, Nevada made substantial offers during March 1921). He made large profits at Madison Square Garden, cashing in on the new permissive boxing legislation. In his first six months 270,076 customers had paid to see Rickard's professional boxing. (Even amateur bills had drawn nearly 24,000.) He cheerfully paid $186,916 in taxes on his boxing evenings so the revenue and profits were obviously substantial.

In Britain all was not so well. Match-ups, fights, champions, despite the euphoria of 1919, were all looked on as relatively mediocre *compared to those of the pre-war period*. They may have been inferior but there were cogent reasons for this.

The natural succession of fighters was severely interrupted by the demands of the war. For five years, men who might have donned gloves professionally had donned uniforms instead. Young professionals beginning first-class ring careers lost vital years of natural development. Pros such as Carpentier seamlessly resuming careers in 1919 where they had left off in 1914 were rare. Others never recovered, quite apart from those injured physically or

mentally by their war experiences. Death and injuries reduced a generation's pool of candidates. British boxing from c.1909 up to the fateful 1914 boasted more competent professional boxers in action than at any time before or since.

Ultimately these factors are susceptible to statistical analysis. There is another consideration beyond numbers. We are all susceptible to nostalgia about the past and the heroes of our childhood and early youth. Somehow, we feel, the world was simpler and better then. Followers of sport, and sports writers, are particularly prone to a déjà vu that never was, and likely to use myths of the past to condemn the present.

Consider then someone born, say, in the late 1890s or early 1900s. For such a person to look back at the 1909–14 period from the perspective of the early 1920s was to look back across an immense gulf created by the hiatus of the First World War and to look back at a remembered world quite beyond recapture in reality. Part of that lost world were giants of the ring such as Driscoll, Wells and Welsh, brilliant fighting representatives of a society supposedly of stability and certainty.

No one who has read this far will be unaware of the strife and social tensions that underlay those illusions. Nevertheless, in comparison with the pre-war generation, post-war champions such as Mike Honeyman, Walter Rossi or Danny Morgan were thought adequate at best.

Predictably given a grudging treatment in the press was the boxer who won the British championship and the Lonsdale Belt in the glamorous lightweight division in the spring of 1921 and went on to clinch the European title a month later. He was not stylish enough for those remembering his pre-war predecessors. This was Ernie Rice of Hounslow, a particular sufferer from the past-was-better syndrome.

Rice, born in Hull on 17 November 1896, settled in the London suburb of Hounslow as a child and pursued a long career from c.1912 to 1930, starting in boxing booths, proceeding to The Ring, Blackfriars and graduating eventually to the NSC. With dark hair closely greased to his skull, prominent ears and a long sharp nose, which over his ring years got flatter and wider, he was a picture of the professional pugilist, more functional than glamorous. His body was compact and muscular, with the shoulders and biceps of a welterweight. His boxing style was equally utilitarian.

His breakthrough to national prominence came when his successes at Blackfriars brought an NSC invitation to contest for the British lightweight title recently vacated by Bob Marriott. His fellow invitee was his near contemporary Ben Callicott (b. 4 March 1895), stalwart of the Old Cosmo[politan] Gym, Plymouth.

The title contest took place at the NSC on 11 April 1921. Rice at 9st 8½lb/134½lbs had only a pound over Callicott yet looked stronger and more robust. He *was* stronger and more robust yet slower, less stylish and less accurate. Callicott set the pace, the orthodox boxer with a graceful probing left and clean right counters, using nifty footwork to circle the relatively stationary Rice. Rice advanced slowly from a crouch with a hedgehog-like defence, gloves crossed in front of his face and elbows tight in, defending his ribs, though those ribs could hardly be seen under his formidable pectoral and abdominal muscles. This was Callicott the fencer with a foil circling a tank.

For four rounds Callicott flitted around, picking off Rice with lefts and rights but making no real dents in the armour plating. Too often he landed merely on the crossed guard. Sometimes Rice let go with a swing. His punches were rarely straight and missed or connected with sides and kidneys. Callicott was too speedy to be caught properly by anything so crude – yet. Rice was not out to impress but was craftily biding his time.

By the fifth and sixth, Callicott slowed a little. A few powerful swings from Rice caught him glancing blows, others missing by a distance. Rice was never able to follow up an initial success when Callicott sped away. In the few clinches, Rice's strength showed, so Callicott fastidiously extricated himself from them. Callicott was warned about the power of the left hook that had felled many of Rice's Blackfriars opponents. His caution was wise. The seventh showed why.

Callicott launched more probing lefts, above and below Rice's guard, and countered with rights when Rice responded. Rice had the grace to stagger when the rights went home. The stagger was bluff. When he went in to finish Rice off, he met a short, sharp right just under the heart. Callicott stopped, seriously shaken, and Rice landed a critical left hook to the jaw. Callicott stood upright as his brain took seconds to register he had no strength left to keep him vertical. He collapsed to the canvas and failed to beat the count. The belt and the championship were Rice's. The belt was clipped around Rice's waist as Callicott, on his stool and still dazed, recovered gradually.

Barely a month later on 9 May 1921, Rice was back at the NSC for an even bigger date – a 20-round bout for the European lightweight championship against Georges Papin of France. Papin (b. 1887 and now 34), a tangle-haired Parisian veteran, lacked Rice's punch power. In a professional career lasting from 1910–23 he knocked out only seven of his opponents. He was cleverer than Rice and had easily outpointed him at Holborn on 10 April 1919 over 15 rounds. Two years on, he had slowed a little yet retained most of his old skills. The real transformation over the two-year interval was in Rice, no more refined than before, but who had found new ways to win. It was an intriguing rematch.

At the weigh-in, Rice made 9st 8¾lb/134¾lbs and Papin 9st 8¼lb/134¼lbs. From the first, both men were confident. Papin believed he could freely attack a man he had already beaten, and Rice knew one punch might reverse the 1919 result. Only Rice's faith was rewarded. When he landed a left to the jaw, Papin clinched. At close quarters was where Rice liked to be and he made it count.

Papin, quite as game as Rice, for four rounds took several of Rice's left hooks to his jaw and to the side of his face as the area around his right eye bruised and swelled alarmingly. By the fifth there could be only one result. Rice continued to catch Papin, who resisted futilely. Under more damaging lefts in the sixth and seventh, he went down three times in each for counts of eight. More left hooks floored him for nine in the eighth, and twice more for nine in the ninth.

Many thought that if Rice had modified his swinging style and punched straight from the shoulder he could have gone home early. This was not Ernie's inclination – why change a winning formula? In the tenth, Papin took two more long counts and was spared another when his second threw in a sponge and the referee responded. As *Boxing* put it quaintly:

> His seconds … came to the conclusion at which everyone else had long arrived, viz. that Georges Papin did not stand the chance of a snowball in an oven.

Rice's treatment in the boxing press was ungenerous. He was a man of limited skills who made himself into a British and European champion by rigorous training and developing physical and mental strength. Sometimes dedication trumps glamour but not to the journalists of his day. *Boxing World*, for example, said:

> … he's some distance removed from a classy lightweight and apparently not the terrific hitter his followers credit him with being.

and

> … they [Rice and Callicott] are not of the class as such men as Freddie Welsh and Matt Wells were when they stood out as the leaders of the lightweight division.

Boxing was no kinder:

> … you would not describe him as a champion boxer to go into ecstasies over …

and

> He will never develop into one of the Rare Old Masters … and it is to be most devoutly hoped that he will never seek to develop himself in this direction.

The magazine also reported on a group of observers who watched Rice in training:

> Their considered opinion, so they told us, was that Rice was easily the worst light-wt. champion England has ever had.

The Times was no more complimentary:

> Rice has served a hard apprenticeship … and no one will grudge him his belated success, but it would be absurd to regard him as anything more than a national champion in lean years.

and

> Rice still is nothing out of the ordinary as a boxer …

'Berkeley' of the *Daily Mail* was one of the few prepared to give him more credit:

> Rice is one of the toughest customers I have ever seen in a ring … there is nothing fancy or extra-ornamental about Rice. He believes in strength of punch rather than cleverness and his long succession of victories proves that his comprehension of things is the correct one. He has a remarkable defence. It is not pretty, but it is wonderfully effective, and his hooks with the left are devastating. I expect great things of Rice, with ordinary luck.

Had Rice won his titles in 1914 before the war started, he would surely have had a better press.

Rice had ambitions to fight the outstanding Benny Leonard in the USA for the world title. He visited the USA in autumn 1921 and took a fight in Milwaukee (24 September 1921) v the hometown favourite Richie Mitchell (b. 14 July 1895). Mitchell had boxed professionally only from 1919. On 14 January 1921, Leonard had stopped him in the sixth round of a world lightweight championship bout at Madison Square Garden but not before Mitchell had floored the champion. Mitchell held newspaper decisions over good men, Johnny Kilbane (1 January 1916) and Freddie Welsh (16 January 1917) among them. He had also drawn (newspaper decision) with Welsh on 7 April 1918 at Milwaukee.

After four even rounds, Mitchell retired with a broken arm, a result enhancing Rice's reputation and clinching him a bout against one of the most unlikely American fighters ever to pull on gloves. Had Sailor Bill Friedman (b. 18 June 1899 in Brooklyn) not existed, Damon Runyon would probably have invented him.

Born into the Brooklyn Jewish community and settling in Philadelphia, Friedman worked for Max 'Boo Boo' Hoff (1872–1941), a boxing manager whose interests included bootlegging, gambling, drug dealing and fight fixing. Just like Abe Attell (whose retirement activities included nefarious errands for

Hoff and who was arrested in Times Square in May 1921 for his part in the baseball scandal of 1919), Friedman's grasp of the legitimate was hazy. As a boxer (manager Hoff) he was suspended for a year for using loaded gloves. Out of the ring he dealt in drugs and illicit liquor and served as a bouncer in a Hoff gambling saloon where he kept order with fist and nightstick. His thuggery brought him a 1922 murder conviction and a 14-year sentence (sentence spirited away by a Hoff pet lawyer).

On 28 October 1921, the Sailor (9st 13lb/139lbs) was at Madison Square Garden to meet Rice (9st 11lb/137lbs) over 12 rounds. Rice lost in the seventh round because of a serious cut eye, perhaps legitimately inflicted, although with Friedman and Hoff around who could be certain? In front of 9,000 people, some drifting away as the contest dragged on, Rice was genuinely unlucky. He was credited for his 'un-English' qualities – willingness to mix it under attack. In the second, a Friedman right opened an ugly cut on Rice's left eye, a cut that bled so profusely as to rob Rice of his vision. For five rounds Rice sheltered behind his crossed arms and peered myopically at Friedman, who happily continued to punch him. In each pause, Charlie Harvey, Rice's manager, mopped desperately at the cut with a redder and redder towel, which he threw into the ring in the middle of the seventh, accepting the inevitable.

Friedman was not normally a puncher, with unloaded gloves at least, yet Rice, who had sailed to the USA with such confidence, was never quite the same after this bitter experience. He surrendered his British and European titles to another nautical fighter, Seaman James 'Nobby' Hall of Peebles

(b. 15 October 1892) in Liverpool a year later (18 September 1922). Rice failed three more times to win back the British title, once in 1923 and twice in 1926.

In contrast to Rice, the stylish British fighter who lost that epic series against Ted Kid Lewis in 1920 received very favourable press treatment when he resumed his winning ways in 1921. This was Johnny Basham. Despite his losses to Lewis, no one downgraded him in favour of some pre-war hero. Aesthetics were still prized above effectiveness.

On 31 May 1921, at the Royal Albert Hall, Basham acquired the European and British middleweight championships with a mercurial one-sided points victory over 20 rounds against Gus Platts of Sheffield (b. 24 October 1891). The stolid blond Platts was 'mere putty' in the hands of the Welshman notable for 'brilliant footwork' and 'brilliant hitting'. Basham's 'brilliance and speed have often provided the subject of a panegyric by sporting writers, but last night … he excelled himself'. Basham would win no major contests after beating Platts but he was given his full due in 1921.

British coverage of the Dempsey/Carpentier dream match was less percipient. The British journals, unaware of the successful deals Tex Rickard was reaching with Mike Jacobs over finance and with the New Jersey authorities over a site, were gloomily agnostic. They failed to grasp Rickard's speed and determination once the wherewithal was within his grasp. Rome was not built in a day but had Texus Rickardus been in charge, the Colosseum (begun under Vespasian, emperor AD69–79 and completed under Titus, emperor AD79–81) would have been up in weeks. Work in New Jersey

began at the end of April with two mighty steam shovels levelling the site.

In June on the swampy ground close to Jersey City, in place of the detritus from the old Montgomery Oval once home to the now defunct Jersey City baseball team, arose a vast wooden amphitheatre closely resembling the structure erected in Toledo to accommodate the 1919 Dempsey v Willard slaughter. (Today, an Idaho State Historical Marker plaque on the Bay View Retirees golf course commemorates the Toledo site of Rickard's first wooden superstructure. That one had cost $100,000 to construct and after the fight was sold to a wrecking company for $25,000. Good business.)

The Boyle's Thirty Acres (actually 34 acres) project, from the ruthless clearing of 60,000 cubic yards of soil to the sawing of planks and supports from two and a quarter million feet of timber at an on-site saw mill, paid no attention to the industrial safety of the construction crews. No one was killed and no one seriously injured but that was more luck than precaution. Permanent stability was not intended – on the day, waves of excitement in the crowd provoked alarming swaying of the outer bleachers. Late in life, Dempsey believed the seating took merely a week. This is probably a faulty memory of an 84-year-old as there were last-minute bangings and sawings and stencilling of numbers early in the morning of the fight. Sixty tons of nails took some hammering and over 90,000 numbers took some painting. The timescale was still extremely impressive.

The size and scope of the planned arena varied according to when and to whom Rickard spoke. It was to be 50

Preparing Boyle's Thirty Acres site in New Jersey was a massive project.
BnF

feet high (9 April, Rickard at a press conference), or 35 feet high and 400 feet across (end of April, Rickard to Jersey City Building Commission). The transport possibilities were permanent. Three railway companies: the Brooklyn Rapid Transit Subway, the Interborough Rapid Transit and the Hudson 'tubes', served the area, as did trolleys, streetcars and ferries. Every transport authority promised maximum services. No one would struggle to be there on the day.

Shrewdly, Rickard tailored capacity to ticket demand. His spruce planks, kept up by pine pillars, could eventually accommodate nearly 92,000 bottoms. He pronounced on 22 June that the arena would be finished by the end of the week and that he had sold $850,000 worth of tickets, despite a temporary scare when a gang of skilled forgers was caught with ultra-sophisticated copies of the gilded $50 pasteboard tickets.

The announcement was optimistic. A carpenters' strike stopped work for a day and Rickard coughed up to settle the strike, paying 200 carpenters Sunday overtime to save his schedule. The advance sales of $850,000 were unaffected. Over the next few days, the figure reached $1,300,000, not including the 8,000 tickets at $5.50 to be sold at the arena only on the day of the fight for walk-up attenders. The gross take eventually totalled $1,789,238.

The $850,000 figure was particularly significant because the original contracts signed with Dempsey and Carpentier by Cochran, Rickard and Brady included a clause guaranteeing $300,000 for Dempsey and $200,000 for Carpentier. When Rickard took over he substituted a promise to pay Dempsey 36 per cent of the receipts and Carpentier 24 per cent, with a crafty proviso that if the advance sales reached $850,000 he could revert to the $300,000/$200,000 split. Had the percentages prevailed, Dempsey would

have received $644,126 and Carpentier $429,417! Rickard, financial maestro/gambler/miracle worker, was on the verge of his greatest triumph.

On the day, the audience assembled under two giant billboards proclaiming to them and to the world's cameras, 'THIS FIGHT IS BEING HELD ON BOYLE'S 30 ACRES' and 'THE LARGEST ARENA IN THE WORLD'. A third billboard to proclaim 'RICKARD – WORLD'S SHREWDEST OPERATOR' would have stated the obvious.

Rickard proficiently manipulated the publicity, which turned into an unprecedented international ballyhoo. Once the long-promised, long-hindered clash was on, the sportswriters of the world, aided and abetted by social and political commentators, devoted millions of words to the prospects of both men and to every ancillary detail about their and Rickard's preparations. The *New York Times* of Tuesday, 28 June 1921, for example, having covered on its front page the futile last-minute efforts of religious and social reformers to put a legal stop to the fight, then devoted a whole page to *11* separate stories about it in the sports section – stories about tickets, bets, training sessions, foreign interest, etc. This was not untypical and the paper followed with another *12* stories on 29 June and no less than *26* on 30 June.

Given the perfect contrast between Dempsey and Carpentier, their celebrity or notoriety, their appearances, their styles, their war records, their nationalities and their fight results, wide coverage was inevitable. For all the hype there was a genuine international thirst to know more about each man.

Carpentier's Long Island training camp was usually off limits.
Prints & Photographs Division, Library of Congress, LC-USZ62-88719

This extended to avid curiosity about their deeds in their training camps – Dempsey in the New Jersey farm set up by Freddie Welsh and later in Jersey City. Arriving in the city on 16 May he was treated like visiting royalty. He attended two formal lunches, three dinners, a midnight supper and several local receptions. Had such hospitality continued, he would have weighed in on the big day at 300lbs plus. The only sour note in the bonhomie was a formal invitation from the Atlantic City Post of the American Legion to train in their city. It was issued to *Carpentier* and pointedly *not* to Dempsey. The slacker charge was not forgotten.

Carpentier, the war hero, arrived in the USA in mid-May and was installed at a farm at fashionable Manhasset on Long Island. Enquiries about Dempsey's preparedness and training were more easily settled than Carpentier's. Dempsey's camp was open in daytime to anyone who cared to pay a dollar to see him work out and spar. Thousands did. It was closed at night, not to keep the crowds out, rather to keep Dempsey *in* and, in Kearns's words, 'away from the dames at night'. No such welcome and no paid admission were provided over on Long Island.

The Carpentier camp, under its commandant François Descamps, resembled a military post where secrecy was all. A barbed-wire fence and a tall board stockade denied access, even casual glimpses. A police guard with a trained dog patrolled the fringes looking almost as formidable as Descamps who, bizarrely clad in purple sweater and red slippers, was as ready to sink his teeth into the uninvited as was the dog. Reporters were allowed only on special press days when what they could see had been skilfully prearranged by the manager. Other witnesses perched in trees and peered hopefully through binoculars and telescopes. In the last few days, Nassau County deputy sheriffs and two armed guards added to the defences.

At the Levinsky fight in October 1920, the Carpentier team boosted his actual weight, claiming him to be 12st 2½lb/170½lbs when he was not. ('Why, he's kinda small, isn't he?' said Dempsey.) Dempsey was much the heavier man. The closer experienced observers watched the stripped Carpentier in training, the more obvious the discrepancy. In the controlled circumstances of official sparring sessions, Carpentier could demonstrate speed and skill and deflect criticism of his lack of poundage.

Even then the official sessions had farcical elements. On Thursday, 26 May, a so-called press day, reporters turned up to be faced by the padlocked gate and given a second-hand account that, out of their sight in the barn, Carpentier had sparred two rounds each with Allentown Joe Gans (1896–1953) – a middleweight – and Joe Jeannette (1879–1958), a veteran heavyweight just short of his 42nd birthday. Only when the frustrated writers returned next day for another 'press day', were they allowed to see Carpentier for real.

After the padlock was removed at 3pm on the Friday, a select group was privileged to enter to see Georges himself, who claimed, after a long run, to weigh 12st 3½lb/171½lbs. He sparred ('waltzed through' said one) two rounds with Gans. Then he shared the ring for one round with Henri Marcat ('Marco'), a substantially built sparring partner who doubled as the camp's chef. This was meant to demonstrate how Georges could wrestle around a big opponent; that is, Dempsey. Whatever culinary skills Dempsey lacked, out of the kitchen a gloved Marco was no Dempsey.

The spectacle was unimpressive. Even Descamps realised a better public show and more favourable press coverage were urgent. The following Wednesday (1 June 1921) another band of critics was admitted to see Georges demonstrate his speed with heavily padded gloves, 'pillows', in two three-minute rounds, first against Joe Jeannette and then against Jack Red Goldberg, a Panamanian middleweight who gratifyingly lurched and staggered when hit by Carpentier's puffed right. Obligingly, the *New York Times* correspondent boosted the Frenchman's prospects as the 'proud possessor of a right hand which will probably cause considerable trouble for Jack Dempsey'.

Carpentier trained in the barn, surrounded by agricultural detritus.
BnF

This was hinting at the truth, that Carpentier needed to knock Dempsey out to win. However, Dempsey had to knock Carpentier out to win himself. With the transfer of the fight from New York State to New Jersey came the inconvenient fact that the revised Jersey regulations, like the old Frawley Law, allowed no points decisions. The clause was tacitly ignored because no one believed the fight would go the distance whoever won. Twelve full rounds and the champion retained his title on the no-decision basis.

On 1 June, the same day as the Carpentier sparring session, there was an ugly reminder that the emotional tide of public interest and the blanket coverage for the big fight were only for a contest between a white man and a white man. In Tulsa, a young black was accused of assaulting a white lift girl. Rumours spread that he was to be sprung from jail and lynched. A group of blacks formed a protective circle around the jail. They were outnumbered and outmanoeuvred by an armed white mob burning down the 30 city blocks lived in mainly by blacks and shooting down any black fleeing the blaze. There were 68 blacks killed, hundreds injured and a substantial part of the city destroyed. It can readily be imagined how the shadow of the incident would have hovered over Boyle's Thirty Acres in July had either Dempsey or Carpentier been black. Like the rest of American society, heavyweight championship boxing, post-Jack Johnson, remained for now a white man's world.

The tight-lipped silence prevailing in the Carpentier camp created a vacuum that journalists rushed to fill. As facts were hard to come by, rumours and wild speculations would do. Supposedly French expertise had Carpentier polishing a one-two combination, feinted left and thrusting right, from a fancy manoeuvre in fencing invented in 1547. The idea also spread, which Descamps did nothing to deny, that Carpentier was secretly practising a 'Frog' (*sic*) punch, a powerful leaping right that would knock out Dempsey in a moment. That moment would come after Dempsey had been distracted by Descamps's powers of hypnosis – evil stares that only special goggles could block. Dempsey apparently insisted Descamps wore such a safety device if he were allowed at ringside. Perhaps mystic Gallic powers were operating behind that padlocked gate. And Carpentier needed some such – he admitted in the 1950s that he had *lost* weight in the USA's hot and humid weather:

> On the day of the fight I tipped the scales at only twelve stone, *even a trifle under*, though I believe the official figure was put at twelve stone six. [Italics added.]

Descamps ensured the true figure did not appear. On another occasion when Carpentier was sparring with Paul Journée, both men fell to the canvas. Descamps refused to let any photographer leave the camp until their exposed plates of a recumbent Carpentier had been improperly confiscated.

The news from the Dempsey camp was more reliable because of newsmen's easy access to the camp and to the champion and his manager. This had its inconveniences. On 6 June, a sparring clash left Dempsey with a cut above his left eye. It was not serious, despite stitches and a three-day ban on sparring. It received press coverage across the world and one can imagine the jitters from Kearns and Rickard at a potential postponement of July's mega-date. Descamps in Long Island

Dempsey and Kearns sit grumpily together.
Prints & Photographs Division, Library of Congress, LC-USZ62-60697

isolation would never have allowed such a mishap to leak out. Neither would he have permitted rumours to spread of any rift between himself and Carpentier, whereas a supposed quarrel between Kearns and Dempsey was openly discussed in the press. (In later years they would indeed split their partnership acrimoniously.)

As the big day got closer, coverage increased exponentially with global wordage soaring from thousands to millions and column inches doubling and tripling. As 700 writers would be attending (compared with the 400 reporting Dempsey v Willard in Toledo), the despatches and previews had to justify the paying of so many journalists to be there and the funding of their expenses. In the last week of June, a visiting alien would have thought the fight more ubiquitous than international politics. In Paris, international diplomacy and the threat

of another war were eliminated in conversations in favour of talk about the fight. As far away as Buenos Aires, newspapers were full of fight talk.

The event *was* a genuinely international affair. For example, Saturday, 2 July 1921 was a particularly important day in British sport – last day of the international Henley rowing regatta; third day of the England v Australia third Test at Headingley; the Men's Final at Wimbledon – yet on the day *The Times* felt it could only list these major domestic events below two other headlines: DAY OF WORLD SPORT and THE GREAT FIGHT IN AMERICA.

Just as the *New York Times* on 28 June carried a dozen stories about the fight, so on the same day *The Times* in London acquainted its readers with every relevant and some irrelevant facts about the promotion: 96,000 people would be there; thousands had booked

out the New York hotels; all other traffic was suspended for the day; special trains would come from all the great American cities as well as from Canada; 1,000 policemen assisted by 400 firemen would form a cordon 300 yards away from the stadium keeping anyone other than genuine ticket-holders away from the entrances; 600 stewards and another 200 policemen would usher people to their assigned seats (and ensure no one snuck into a more expensive section, or sexually harassed the 5,000 and more women who were expected). Other promoters made predictions; only Rickard fulfilled them. He had spent $250,000 on his new arena – it was worth every cent.

In the last four or five days, the focus concentrated on the boxers and their prospects. Like the betting where Dempsey was at least 3/1 on, opinion heavily leaned towards the champion. Despite general confidence in the Dempsey camp there were still jitters. On 27 June, contrary to the previous announcement that Dempsey would be having a rest day, the gates were suddenly locked in the Descamps fashion, and Dempsey took a five-mile jog, shadow-boxed, skipped rope, punched the bag, and sparred two rounds each with Larry Williams and Eddie O'Hara (sparring partners conspicuously lighter than himself). Reports of Carpentier's speed filtered into the champion's consciousness and he was doing something to counter it. That he was practising to disable Carpentier's dangerous right by punching the Frenchman on the elbow, as one commentator suggested, is more dubious.

In strict secrecy Carpentier pursued a similar programme – a morning session with roadwork, a half hour in the gym and a speed-work spar with Charles Ledoux, the French bantamweight and famously conqueror of Driscoll, followed by an afternoon session of gym work and six rounds of sparring, two rounds each with Paul Sampson (heavy), Chris Arnold (light-heavy) and Joe Jeannette (heavy). Details were second-hand, enhanced by little nuggets that Jeannette had been severely tested with a close-quarter right uppercut and that Arnold was astonished by Carpentier's punching power – 'believe me, he's got a kick in both hands that hurts worse than a belaying pin in the hands of a first mate' – a quotation good enough to have been coined by Descamps, and perhaps was. It was more colourful than Carpentier's trainer Gus Wilson stone-walling, 'We cannot comment on Georges' sparring.'

Other unlikely sources promoted last-minute interest. The fashionable Manhattan store Saks and Co., advertising luxurious men's silk and mohair suits, published the wares under the headline 'The World's Greatest Sporting Event Takes Place Saturday', implying that was where all best-dressed men would be and that a Saks suit for attendees was obligatory. Rickard's one-time partner William A. Brady countered the idea that Carpentier was an outsider: 'He [Dempsey] meets the fastest, brainiest, trickiest, hardest hitting boxer he has ever met in his career.'

Carpentier was not quite that, yet he was a clever and dedicated professional, good at sizing up opponents and sensing weaknesses. He had shown Europeans his ability to adapt, fighting

Fans paid to watch Dempsey skip rope.
Prints & Photographs Division, Library of Congress, LC-USZ62-60706

out of a defensive crouch in one fight and boxing in an upright English style in another. Beneath his blond longish hair (trimmed short for the title fight), his handsome face, white and pale and barely tanned by the Long Island sunshine that failed to penetrate the famous barn, and his slim, elegant frame, made him look like a classical marble sculpture. Not rooted to a pedestal, he was quick on his feet and quick to the punch. He had beaten men such as Beckett and Wells with well-timed blows. Had he the wherewithal to keep Dempsey away then knock the tough American out? He was something of the irresistible hero, and an elegant and gentlemanly one.

Dempsey in the ring was no gentleman. No one questioned his strength and power. He had put on about seven pounds, mostly muscle, since his ruthless victory over Willard.

He stood in a corner before a fight, a dark scowl on his leathery dark-tanned face, sprouting a few days' stubble, and impatiently pawing the ground like a bull while waiting for the first bell; more Murderous Jack than his celluloid alter ego Daredevil Jack. The stationary menace became a charging, snarling attacker with bared teeth once the round commenced, dedicated merely to a swift victory using jabs, hooks, chops and rabbit punches to achieve it. If illegalities such as standing over a fallen opponent ready to strike him from behind before he was properly upright were necessary, or to chop him into submission, that is what he would do. Stringing along a loser for the sake of the film cameras or mollifying the purchasers of expensive seats by delaying a knockout were alien to his philosophy.

The rushes fooled some into believing that Dempsey was raw.

This was to overlook his genuine talents. He was a lot harder to hit than it appeared. His head was no static target, his chin tucked safely down behind his shoulder. His powerful arms neutralised another man's punches at source. A cruel opponent but never crude, he justified the odds on him.

A few doubts remained. Even the toughest of heavyweights can be knocked out if caught by a good punch on the point of the chin (Tyson, Lewis, Louis, Charles, etc. all suffered knockouts in their careers). Also, significant physical attributes are ineffective unless accompanied by the right mental attitude. Would Dempsey's ring walk reinforce his consciousness of his unpopularity compared to Carpentier? Many columns commented that most of the 5,000 women present would be for Carpentier, and even a majority of men. Dempsey was believed the likely victor yet that thought was frequently accompanied by the sentiment 'but I hope Carpentier wins'. Carpentier 'will enter the ring with more good wishes than any foreigner ever carried in a bout on this side of the Atlantic'.

The *New York Times* unsympathetically reminded Dempsey (on the very morning of the fight) of the 'acquittal that cleared him legally without restoring the loss of prestige that his absence from the real conflict entailed'. This was a follow-up to another damning reference the previous Sunday (26 June) to the infamous press photograph from the dockyard. Dempsey would have been better off from 6 April 1917 to 11 November 1918, suggested the paper, wielding a real machine gun instead of a pneumatic rivet gun.

Such comments did hurt Dempsey. Many years later (1977) in his last autobiography, ghosted by his step-daughter, Barbara Piattelli Dempsey, he recorded the abuse he received from the audience assembled in Rickard's great saucer:

I climbed into the ring and disrobed to a chorus of cheers mingled with jeers and cries of 'Slacker! Get outta there, ya bum!' It was worse when they saw the American flag sewn on the waist of my white trunks. Several hostile ringsiders threatened to rip the trunks off me. I tried to ignore them. I was in the ring to fight.

Neither could he rely on moral support from previous heavyweight champions. Three of the fighters who had once held the title, Tommy Burns, Jim Jeffries and Jess Willard, with less than convincing excuses, had all turned down Rickard's invitation to be introduced in the ring and to wish Dempsey well.

The published statistics were some consolation for Dempsey, almost all in the champion's favour. Age: D 26; C 27. Weight: D 192lbs; C 170lbs – although the poundage was a guess (i.e. D 13st 10lb; C 12st 2lb). The ring announcements gave Dempsey as 188lbs (13st 6lb) and Carpentier as 172lbs (12st 4lb), perhaps with Descamps's foot on the scale, but a considerable discrepancy. Height: D 6ft 1in; C 5ft 11in. Reach: D 74in; C 73in. Chest (normal): D 42in; C 41in. Chest (expanded): D 46in; C 43¼in. Waist: D 33in; C 31in. Neck: D 16½in; C 16¾in. Biceps: D 16¼in; C 14½ins. Calves: D 15¼in; C 16¾in.

Two other pieces of data were as Dempsey wanted them. The ring, brought over from Madison Square Garden and placed on a five-foot-high solid steel platform to be seen clearly by everyone in the great throng, was only 18 feet square. A full 24 feet would have given the Frenchman ampler space to avoid Dempsey's rushing attacks. Kearns and others anticipated that Carpentier would fight Dempsey at long range. Surprisingly, the Carpentier camp raised no objection to the size of the ring.

Debate about the gloves took an unanticipated turn. They had to be a minimum of eight ounces to comply with New Jersey legislation. In view of Dempsey's power, this might have been thought to soften the impact of his savage attacks and favour the Frenchman.

In fact, Carpentier was just as keen to have lighter gloves to enhance his own blows. Dempsey, Carpentier and Rickard publicly agreed to the eight-ounce limit, but secretly arranged that the eight-ounce stuffing in both pairs would be manipulated so as to have five ounces around the wrists and a mere three ounces along the knuckles and the business end of the fist. This failed to happen because Rickard got cold feet when opponents of the fight went to court to prove that the event was an illegal prizefight by focusing on details such as the legality of the gloves. He arranged it that only two ounces of stuffing remained in the wrist area and that six ounces covered the knuckles.

By 2 July 1921 at 3pm all such manipulations and speculations were superfluous; only the course of the most anticipated fight in history mattered.

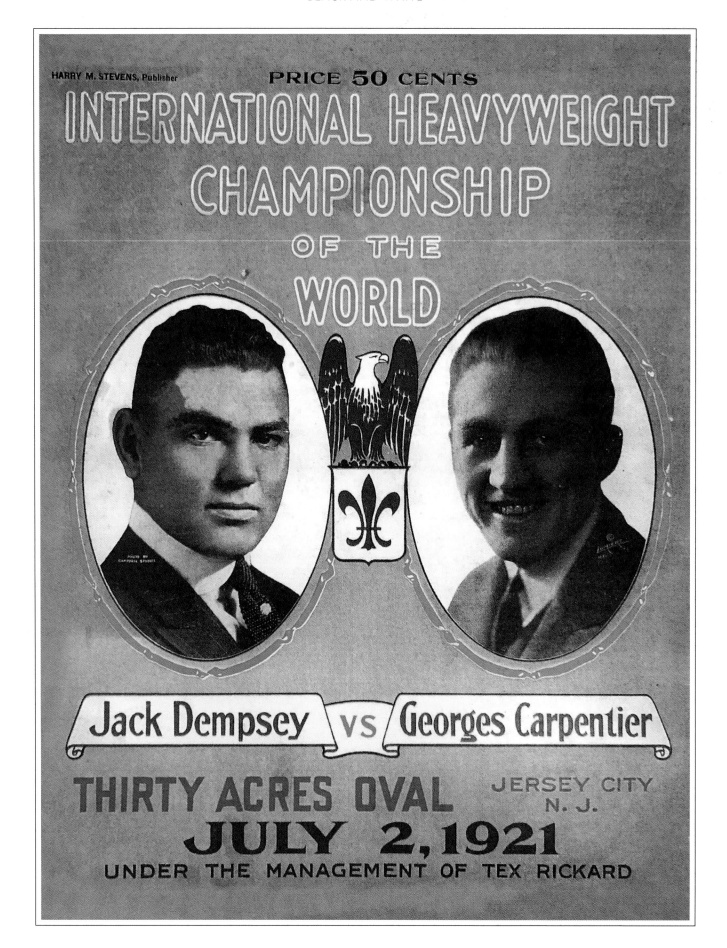

CHAPTER 17

THE FIGHT OF THE CENTURY
3.16PM SATURDAY, 2 JULY 1921

'For the greatest single day in the ancient history of an ancient sport has come at last, a day that has caught the imagination of more people, from crowded centers to the remote off-lying places of existence than any single contest since the world's dim dawn.'

– Grantland Rice quoted by Roger Kahn

GRANTLAND RICE, quoted here, was prone to hyperbole. But on this occasion he was pretty accurate. The global audience for this event was genuinely unprecedented. First let us see what actually happened in Rickard's huge saucer on that special Saturday.

It cost $5.50 in the cheapest sections, sold only on the day from automobiles parked outside the ropes and the police cordon sanitaire surrounding the arena. Some enthusiasts spent the night standing in queues or lying on the ground to guarantee they got in. The first arrival started queuing at 8pm on Friday and he was joined first by a trickle and then by a consistent stream of people finding their way by every possible conveyance. He was at the head of hundreds by 1am and soon enough of thousands.

At 8am, policemen, firemen and stewards were allowed in to rehearse their duties and to conduct a search of the premises. The day before, 20,000 sightseers toured Rickard's wooden miracle to marvel at its size and ingenuity. Rickard made sure no one hid under the seats to sneak a free view on the day. The few who had were ejected.

The gates opened at 9am on Saturday. The luckier holders of more expensive tickets, sold in advance, could take their time, but anticipating delays at the last minute caused by vast crowds arriving together, many came early. All the seats were nearly full by lunchtime. It was a long wait until 3pm, the time promised for the main event.

The vast wooden venue filled from the outer reaches downwards as holders of the $5.50 tickets climbed the winding staircases to the top of the banking. There was of course no roof, even over the ring at the centre, so the weather on the day assumed major importance. A tropical downpour would abort the whole mega-operation. Rickard's prayers or luck prevailed. The morning began with grey, lowering clouds and there was a light shower just after 1pm but no others. The whole metropolitan area that day suffered a hot and oppressive atmosphere with maximum humidity – the kind where shirts, suits and dresses cling wetly and papers go limp, sodden and useless. A thick suffocating haze of cigar smoke hung in the air above the spectators. The wooden seats had been soaked with water to lessen the danger of a match or a cigar butt sparking a conflagration.

Until 12.50pm and the first preliminary bout, there was nothing to do but chat, eat the overpriced sandwiches and drink. (Thanks to the Volstead Act of 1919, the drinks were soft and the assembled multitude sober.) Another diversion was to spot the great, the good and the notorious as they were escorted to their places. No more distinguished a sporting audience seemed ever to have been assembled.

There were about 100 politicians (the Senate and the House of Representatives had adjourned early to facilitate attendance in New Jersey). Foreign embassies and consulates emptied as representatives of countries such as Spain, Romania, the Netherlands and

Ticket security was meticulous.
Bain collection, Prints & Photographs Division, Library of Congress, LC-DIG-ggbain-32675

Russia took up their tickets. Old Money vied with New Money and for every Robber Baron there was a member of the real Social Elite. Rickard, the very soul of the Self-Made Man and a real social snob, had in the days preceding the fight published lists of Who's Who? and, moreover, Who's Coming? He personally ushered some to their seats and sycophantically claimed that 'escorting Mr Rockefeller was the very greatest moment of my life'.

Hollywood and Broadway royalty such as George M. Cohan, Douglas Fairbanks Jnr, Tom Mix and Al Jolson trooped in with their entourages, as did businessmen such as Henry Ford and railway magnate George H. Gould. One person in the crowd was representative of many. Henry Payne Whitney (1872–1930) was there. Although a businessman, he had sporting pretensions, having been part of both the US polo team (which trounced the English team in 1909) and an America's Cup yacht crew. He bred horses, winning the Kentucky Derby twice and the Belmont Stakes four times. He inherited $36 million and married into the equally well-endowed Vanderbilt family, in case his original fortune were insufficient. Affording his $50 ticket will not have been painful, even if it placed him democratically in the same section as crooks such as Arnold Rothstein and Max Hoff.

Rickard from 12.50pm supplied six preliminary bouts, mostly bantam and feather, of eight rounds each. He announced that these would not proceed beyond 2.40pm and would not delay the main bout at 3pm. As always, more people responded to the later ones as the audience increased. Rickard cleverly held one of the two heavyweight clashes over, not because of time but because he hoped to divert the multitude from making for the exits simultaneously at the end of the big bout. (Billy Miske v Jack Renault, a Dempsey sparring partner, was the one fight deferred. The unfortunate pair, draped in towels and waiting at ringside, were sent back to their dressing room at 2.45pm. When they did fight it was with the depressing background of thousands of retreating and exiting backs.)

The clash that finished at 2.40pm, lightly regarded by those impatient to see Dempsey and Carpentier emerge, became important in retrospect. In it, Gene Tunney, the Fighting Marine, (b. 25 May 1897) was 'unimpressive' and 'comparatively slow and wild' in stopping an even cruder Soldier Jones of Canada in the seventh of the eight rounds. Tunney, after this victory, sat in the crowd and carefully studied Dempsey and Carpentier in action. The scrutiny was effective – later in the 1920s he would be meeting both men and beating them. He would take on Dempsey, winning each time in two of the most famous and controversial fights in ring history and became world heavyweight champion himself from 1926–28. No one in the 1921 crowd anticipated that.

The two most important protagonists of the day made their own ways to Boyle's Thirty Acres. For Carpentier, the day began on Long Island with a morning jog. At 9.30am he returned to camp and read the newspapers over a light breakfast. (Those papers gave flatteringly extensive previews of the afternoon's fight. None boosted his morale by predicting his success.) He changed into an elegant light-grey suit, silk shirt and colourful tie and embarked with his entourage on the *Lone Star* yacht conveying them in comfort from Port Washington to Jersey City as they ate a pleasant light lunch on board. A car with a motorcycle escort then took them to the arena by

2pm. Confusion reigned when the car arrived at the wrong place – there were 18 entrances – and he needed a guide to take him to the correct one and his dressing room. His dressing room was separated from the champion's by a full section of the seating, so that the two made their way to the ring down different aisles. The best news was that a light breeze was now blowing and alleviating the Turkish bath atmosphere previously enveloping the stadium.

Dempsey, already based in Jersey City, had a much shorter journey. He slept overnight at the luxurious home of William C. Heppenheimer, a local banker, hoping thereby to avoid the press and well-wishers. Once he had breakfasted on his boiled eggs, tea and toast, news of his presence leaked out and his quiet stroll in the surrounding streets was abandoned when fans mobbed him. Holed up in the mansion, he played pool and listened to jazz records to kill time until his steak lunch. His car collected him at 2.35pm. In a curious coincidence, he also was taken to an incorrect entrance and was intercepted on his way to Carpentier's dressing room. He was escorted back outside and around the corner to the proper entrance to get to his own quarters and prepare.

In the 21st century, many boxers feel obliged to insult and demean an opponent, so it is notable that Dempsey and Carpentier, on the verge of the biggest fight in history and under relentless scrutiny, had no difficulty in thoroughly respecting one another and observing all the usual courtesies before, during and after the event. They were no less formidable opponents because of it. Neither did they feel it necessary to participate in a ring walk

one degree down from a coronation or the coming of the Messiah. The entrances of both men bordered on the distinctly anticlimactic.

The master of ceremonies was the florid-complexioned Joe Humphreys (1872–1936), the doyen of ring announcers (he was eventually inducted into boxing's Hall of Fame in 1997 in posthumous recognition of his services to the sport). He was a handsome fellow with a very loud singing and booming speaking voice. He owed his start in boxing to his Tammany Hall connections. He normally quelled a crowd to silence by raising a commanding right hand and calling, 'Quiet, please, quiet!' In this unprecedented assembly, he shouted into a hand device linked to three giant Magnavox megaphones and urged the vast crowd to sit down. This was a waste of decibels.

If anyone in the lower rows stood up to see better or merely carried away with excitement, all the people behind were bound to follow suit or have their view blocked. While Humphreys glowered at the recalcitrant standees, a small party of Dempsey supporters, 'Friends in Jersey City', struggled into the ring bearing a huge floral horseshoe in which roses, carnations and gladioli spelled out the word SUCCESS. They were accompanied by a scrum of cameras, tripods and photographers.

This was a serious distraction, as down in one of the aisles at 2.56pm police and officials were struggling through latecomers to clear a path for the challenger. There stood Carpentier, accompanied by his seconds – Descamps, Gus Wilson, Ledoux and Journée – and clad in his beautiful grey silk robe with deep

The crowd waited patiently to get in.
Prints & Photographs Division, Library of Congress, LC-DIG-npcc-21979

blue trimmings, waiting to walk to the ring. Though not everyone could see him, news spread through the arena. He was greeted with a huge roar and many stood up on their seats and waved their straw hats and their bonnets to speed him into the ring. He reached his corner while the floral tribute was still being photographed. A brass band struck up 'La Marseillaise' and all attention was on him as he went to every side of the ring, clasping his hands and waving. This was no stage-managed entrance, rather an unprompted outpouring of American enthusiasm for the foreigner recognised as a hero and an ally. Some in the crowd wore the Stars and Stripes and a tricolor to summarise the ambiguity of their feelings.

Before Carpentier's broad smile could subside, a grim-faced Dempsey strode down the other aisle, followed by his seconds – Kearns, Teddy Hayes and his brother Bernard. Clad in white trunks with a red, white and blue ribbon in place of a belt, a small American flag sewn to them, and a maroon sweater carelessly thrown over his shoulders, this was a man who meant business. The business was to beat the man in the opposite corner as swiftly and as effectively as he could. Many cheered him but, as we know from his reminiscences, the acclaim was not universal and he was hurt internally by the insults. That did not stop him walking over to Carpentier's corner and shaking hands – ruthless he might be but never petty. (The pair would shake hands again formally in mid-ring for the benefit of photographers.) Dempsey would soon suffer another reminder of whom the crowd favoured before his fists could speak for him.

Ringside seats were more substantial than the bleachers.
Bain Collection, Prints & Photographs Division, Library of Congress, LC-DIG-ggbain-32692

First came tedious ring introductions: the city mayor; the state governor; three boxing commissioners; Bill Brennan, the perpetual challenger; Harry Ertle, the white-shirted and flannelled referee; and the blue serge-suited, cigar-waving organising genius, Tex Rickard. That took a good ten minutes then Joe Humphreys, redder by the minute, was back on his sound system introducing the fighters. Dempsey was the one 'on whom every red-blooded American pins his hopes this day'. This got a mollifying cheer, yet if it mollified Dempsey it hardly

did so in contrast to the moment when Georges Carpentier was described as 'the heavyweight champion of the Old World, the idol of his people, and a soldier of France'. These words produced so frantic a standing ovation of waving, stamping and shouting as to put the upper reaches of the arena in danger of collapse. No wonder Dempsey glowered and scowled.

A fat Frenchman in scruffy cap and sweater and carrying a pink striped towel waddled across the ring as Dempsey's hands were being bandaged. This was Descamps, who believed that heavy

adhesive tape on Dempsey's knuckles had contributed to the ugly damage done to Jess Willard in Toledo and was making sure Dempsey had nothing other than soft gauze bandages under his gloves this time. He snatched the roll of tape away and cried, 'Non! Non!' At such close quarters, perhaps the Dempsey glower rivalled Descamps's infamous evil hypnotic stare, but Descamps got his way not because of his mystic powers but because that was what the contract stipulated. Dempsey's hands were soft bandaged while Descamps watched. Dempsey's stubble

The view from the ring. Distant seats needed optical aids.
Bain collection, Prints & Photographs Division, Library of Congress, LC-DIG-ggbain-32667 & LC-DIG-ggbain-32696

Carpentier remained impressively relaxed.
BoxRec

bristled as never before. Carpentier sat, patiently waiting.

A plump lad in white shorts and shirt paraded a placard with Round One printed upon it, and, at last, at 3.16pm the bell rang and the fight of the century began. Almost to a man, the boxing writers were agreed. Dempsey would rampage out of his corner and attack Carpentier the way he had destroyed all those eager contenders on his climb to the Willard fight. Carpentier, the lighter but speedier man, would avoid Dempsey's bustling attacks, using the ring and his skill to keep the fight at a distance. The writers' predictions were all wrong.

From the bell, Carpentier went straight at Dempsey, closing with him and landing a left, followed with a left and right to the head and a right uppercut to Dempsey's jaw. They did not have much effect but did they necessarily comprise the foolhardy tactics some inquests judged them? *Boxing*, for example, declared that Carpentier had here 'made his first mistake, the one that led him to early and decisive defeat'. *The Times* magisterially concluded, 'If he ever had any chance of winning, Carpentier threw it away, by imagining he could swop punches with Dempsey.' Other

All eyes on the ring.
Bain Collection, Prints & Photographs Division, Library of Congress, LC-DIG-ggbain-32689

later accounts confirm this (Trevor Wignall: 'he should not have fought, but boxed') or suggest that Carpentier should have kept Dempsey cautiously at a distance and survived for ten rounds and a no-decision, leading possibly to a lucrative return. Carpentier did not agree:

> It has been said that in adopting this [forward] tactic I showed … great imprudence. I don't agree. The fact is that I had no alternative; I certainly had no interest in a war of attrition with a powerful fellow like Dempsey.

Carpentier was an intelligent man. He knew he had only one chance of beating Dempsey – by catching him off guard with a knockout punch to the jaw. In his initial onslaught he had two thoughts in mind: by pulling his punches in this first onslaught, he could make Dempsey think he was no real puncher and give himself a chance for a full-blooded punch later; and by attacking so promptly and unexpectedly, he tested Dempsey's defence and found out how strong at close quarters Dempsey *really* was.

There was never a serious possibility of weakening Dempsey by picking him off at a distance.

Not a blow would remain uncaptured.
Prints & Photographs Division, Library of Congress, LC-USZ62-93074

Dempsey was also a thinking fighter. Aware of Carpentier's record of knocking out heavyweights, he did not go springing out of his corner to be caught by a sucker punch. Rather, he tucked his chin out of danger, let Carpentier close in and clinched. Realising his superior weight and strength allowed him to wrestle Carpentier around at will, he fought back and made Carpentier retreat with a left jab.

As Carpentier withdrew, Dempsey followed, punching with both hands and driving Carpentier to the ropes. One punch caught Carpentier's nose and made it bleed. Though painful, this was no more than the Frenchman would expect in any major fight. More damaging and confirming Carpentier's need to get Dempsey out early if he were to have any chance of winning, were the heavy short-arm body punches thudding into his abdomen, leaving visible blotches and lowering his guard. Carpentier caught Dempsey with one right to the head but took a more powerful one himself. The interval could not come soon enough. The minute's grace was inadequate despite all Descamps's frantic sponging.

The second round was the most significant of the whole event. Carpentier smiled and discreetly retreated as if his lesson had been learned and he was prepared to concede ground to the ever-more confident Dempsey. He was foxing. Dempsey plunged forward eagerly, punching hard just like in the first. He landed a few times on the retreating target. Suddenly, Carpentier sidestepped and coolly delivered a full right with most of his limited poundage behind it. It went over Dempsey's outstretched arm and

smacked into the side of his jaw. It was the very twin of the punches (with four-ounce gloves) that had flattened Billy Wells and Joe Beckett. Unfortunately for the Frenchman, it did not meet the point of the jawbone but spread his eight-ounce glove between jaw and left cheekbone, dissipating its full effect.

Lucky ticket holders were packed into the vast arena [air view].
BoxRec

Dempsey later denied it had bothered him at all but many ringside witnesses confirmed that it stopped him dramatically in his tracks – 'he [Dempsey] avoided the ko. only by a hair's breadth', said *New York World*; 'Dempsey was shaken by a punch to the jaw,' said the *New York Tribune*; 'It landed flush on the champion's jaw. It staggered him. It rocked him from the top of his black thatch to his heels. He was groggy, and if ever Dempsey has been in danger of being stripped of his sceptre it was at that moment,' declared the *New York Times*, which added also, 'Dempsey was shaken from head to heel. His eyes were glazed.'

It provoked a further response. As the punch went home, the crowd erupted in a second outburst in favour of Carpentier, the sentimental favourite. That certainly impacted on Dempsey, who scowled and bared his teeth at being again slighted in favour of a foreigner. Someone was going to

pay for the punch and for the insults. That would be the handsome Adonis in front of him.

Worse still for Carpentier, the impact of his punch had sprained his right wrist and fractured the metacarpal bone of his right thumb. Had that right hand collided with Dempsey's jaw a centimetre lower, then perhaps the great fight might have ended there and everyone would be endorsing the cleverness of Carpentier's strategy. Instead, he was the one more damaged. The Frenchman, with a broken and badly swollen hand, was in the midst of a fight for which there was now only one likely outcome. That outcome was not going to be a Carpentier win.

Dempsey shook his head, snarled and attacked. Every time Carpentier grabbed his arms, Dempsey wrestled free and punched on. The notorious Dempsey left hook landed into Carpentier's ribs, slowing the Frenchman further, and over his guard into the side of the face, inflicting a cut over the eye. Carpentier went courageously on punching with left and damaged right. Neither kept Dempsey away.

The third was mostly Dempsey. He sensed Carpentier was suffering when the Frenchman used his right. He stalked and punished Carpentier with fierce punches, many leaving visible marks on Carpentier's body and reopening the cut over his eye. Carpentier could only clinch. These embraces Dempsey threw off with ease but meanwhile punched fiercely to body and head and rabbit-punched to the back of the neck before he wrestled Carpentier away. Carpentier's heroism had survived wartime battlefields. Excruciatingly painful as it must have been, he struck Dempsey around the

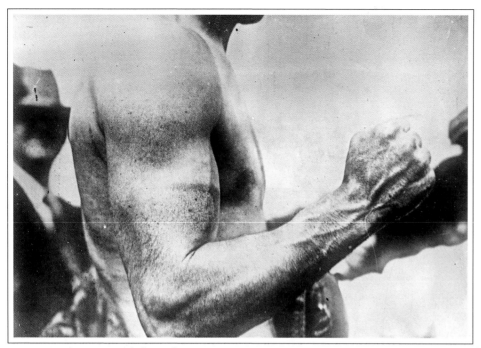

Dempsey's right arm carried plenty of power.
BnF

jaw twice with his damaged right hand. The blows were less effective than the original surprise right on which he had set such store and just provoked more savage responses from Dempsey. Carpentier grasped that he was going to lose but he was determined to go down fighting to the last. Near the end of this torrid round, Dempsey connected with an uppercut and a weakened Carpentier gratefully snatched a rest on his stool at the bell.

With a rampant Dempsey and an ailing and bleeding Carpentier, everyone sensed how the fourth would end. It took a mere one minute and 16 seconds. Carpentier looped his gloves around Dempsey's arms trying to clinch and hamper, or merely retreated, circling the ring backwards. Dempsey stalked him, his right poised for a *coup de grâce*. Dempsey's right was dubbed by some American sportswriters 'Iron Mike', the nickname more familiar to modern readers ignorant of its true origins because it was adopted by the troubled soul Mike Tyson as his self-anointed alter ego. (Dempsey's 'Iron Mike', like Moran's 'Mary Ann', also had a precedent neither was aware of. In bare-fist times, Tom Sayers's right hand had been dubbed 'The Auctioneer' – when the hammer came down, proceedings were over.)

Dempsey's Iron Mike, in the form of a hook to the jaw, now stretched Carpentier out on the canvas. Referee Ertle began to count. At about seven, Carpentier sunk even further. Ertle had reached nine when Carpentier astonished everyone by springing back up with alacrity. The speed of his ascent was misleading as he was still unsteady on his feet. Dempsey would not be denied. In close after a left hook, he followed in with a driving right just below Carpentier's heart. Calculated to extinguish all hopes of recovery, it took Carpentier down into an untidy heap, lying on his right side like a drowned man just hauled on to the shore. Never completely unconscious, he made an effort to rise by raising his left arm and his left leg vainly into the air, followed by a perfunctory push at the canvas with both gloves, only to fall back as Ertle completed the final ten.

It was nearly 3.27pm. The big match with its ten minutes 16 seconds of action was over. The victor helped pick the victim up and assisted Descamps to half carry and half escort the exhausted Carpentier to his corner. From his own corner, Dempsey, smiling at last, waved to the audience applauding his utterly convincing victory.

Questions immediately arise. How could a fight of such abbreviated and one-sided action seem so important? How could so obviously ill-matched a contest ever receive the accolade of the so-called fight of the century? To answer those questions, we must remember two things. First, it is in the very nature of sport that eagerly awaited events will sometimes disappoint. Just as some lightly anticipated clash between two unfancied and mediocre boxers may turn into an absolute classic, so two brilliant fighters with skill and experience may meet and produce a mediocre dud. Could we anticipate what will happen, the glorious unpredictability of sport would disappear – the very attribute that draws us in again and again. Stay away and we miss that most memorable of days when the unfancied titch with the slingshot downs the mighty champion of the Philistines.

Equally important is that Dempsey v Carpentier was not just a fight but an unprecedented public event and a worldwide phenomenon. In July 1921, boxing appeared the most important thing in the world. In the forward press section at ringside were some

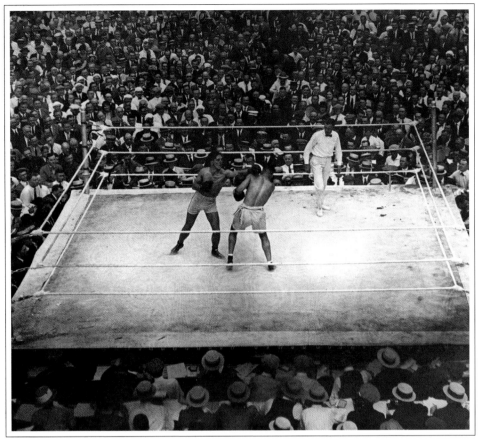

Carpentier clips Dempsey's head with a left lead.
George Rinhart/Corbis via Getty Image

Dempsey hunts down a weakening Carpentier.
Bettmann/GettyImages

200 journalists whose word-by-word reports were carried by telegraph all over the world – to London, to Tokyo, to Copenhagen, to Toronto, to Buenos Aires, and to Manila, for example. Just behind were another 500 scribes with less instant deadlines but who were reporting the event for millions of people who expected to read of every detail.

High up in a precarious wooden basket on a 30-foot steel spindly column towering above the arena was a group of film cameramen with five heavy cameras, including two slow-motion ones, recording every movement of the fighters and the spectators. High above them, and dangerously raising Rickard's blood pressure, were four aeroplanes, two of which flew directly over the stadium, in contradiction of the express orders of the promoter and the Jersey authorities, to allow their occupants to take spectacular aerial pictures. (Rickard's fears were not unreasonable – a photographer's plane had recently crashed near the US Tennis Open, and he had nightmare visions of a plane plunging into his 90,000 spectators and causing unimaginable casualties.)

This incomparable media extravaganza was not confined to the packed wooden saucer. Back in Manhattan, some 10,000 spectators surrounded the *New York Times* offices, drawn by the special coverage offered during the fight. On three sides of the building, giant amplifiers carried blow-by-blow details directly by wireless telephone to those within 100 feet of the building. For any unable to hear because of the city noise, or out of earshot, large bulletin boards supplemented the commentary with written descriptions in giant type. By fight time, the street

The Fight of the Century nears its end. Referee Harry Ertle counts as Carpentier lies helpless.
PhotoQuest/Getty Images

viewers and listeners, jam-packed together, had spread from Broadway to Seventh Avenue and all the way from 42nd Street to 44th, stopping the traffic and worrying shopkeepers fearful of their plate glass.

The newspaper also excelled itself next day (the Sunday) where the *13 opening news pages* carried full reports in thousands of words on the three and a bit rounds of action, and *over 70* supplementary stories about incidents, personalities and sidelights relating somehow to the event and its impact. Can one imagine any serious paper of record in the 21st century giving all its front and all prime news pages to a *boxing* match?

A clue to just how extraordinary the public interest was in Dempsey v Carpentier, is to contrast it to the coverage of the English soccer team's victory in the 1966 World Cup. On the Monday following the English victory, the only one ever, *The Times* confined the report to three and a half columns of one of the sports pages where it had to share the coverage with two yachting stories, polo, the Curtis Cup women's golf, and a Britain v Europe men's golf match. The only front-page reference was a short report about the German team's return to Bonn.

In 1921, thousands of miles away from Boyle's Thirty Acres, Europe was avid for news. Paris was bound to be obsessed with the prospects of France's favourite son. Because of the time difference, news was not expected until

The victorious Dempsey salutes the crowd including those whom he knew had wanted him to lose.
PhotoQuest/Getty Images

All over the world crowds gathered to hear what was happening at the clash between Dempsey and Carpentier in New Jersey. Here fans stop the New York traffic.

Historic Collection/Alamy Stock Photo

mid-evening. By then, up to a million people had gathered on every boulevard and blocked every wide public space such as the Place de la Concorde. Not a restaurant or bar place remained vacant as the Parisians prepared to celebrate Carpentier's victory.

The news would be conveyed from a multitude of sources: bulletin boards, sirens, aeroplanes dropping flares, and coded light signals. Curiously, the first cable to reach the City of Lights, with the stark message 'Dempsey Wins', came via London to the *Daily Mail*'s Paris Office just before 8.30pm European time. By 9pm the disappointing news had spread throughout the French capital by every mechanical means as well as word of mouth and confirmed by the very flood of over 20 evening editions of the newspapers reaching the streets. The streets and the restaurants gloomily emptied and the crowds sullenly and almost silently melted away. It was as near a national mourning as any sporting event is likely to provoke.

In London, in the streets of the West End and the City, and in the high streets of most of the suburbs, hopeful expectation turned to disappointment for the many thousands craning their necks to look upwards after sense was made of the initial confusion when a profusion of contradictory signals was received. Rockets and aeroplanes appeared in the metropolitan skies but some showed red for a Dempsey win

Mr and Mrs Carpentier ruefully examine the right thumb damaged in the punch that almost brought a shock Dempsey defeat.
BoxRec

and others green. The *Daily Mail* was the speediest and most authoritative – first (8.22pm) to receive first-hand news at its office by cable, and first to launch an aeroplane (as early as 8.38pm). Its aeroplane dropped a white Very light to identify itself, followed by red flares to indicate a Dempsey victory.

The newspaper's technical superiority and speed of action reflected the importance that its proprietor, press lord Alfred Harmsworth, Lord Northcliffe (1865–1922), placed on providing the news he sensed the public wanted. Sometimes called the father of modern journalism (at a time when newspapers were the only source of news), he knew that on 2 July 1921 there was but one hot topic: What has happened in New Jersey? His instinctive grasp that readers were more interested

in sporting news than verbatim reports of political speeches was vindicated. Northcliffe was also the proprietor of *The Times*, where Monday's paper reflected the interest of the classes, as well as the *Daily Mail*'s masses, by devoting 51¾ inches of its main news pages to its report of the fight under the headline 'Dempsey The Champion'.

There was provision on that Saturday evening for those not out on the streets looking up to the skies. Cinemas projected the 'Dempsey Wins' message on their screens in the middle of feature films, although not everyone might have appreciated a moving love scene being supplemented in this way. Theatre audiences were treated to announcements from the stage, although possibly not in the middle of a Shakespearean soliloquy.

NSC members mobbed the club's ticker tape machine. An affluent group of fans hired the Royal Opera House for the evening and sat absorbing fight bulletins as they came in.

In the next decade, even more people attended big fights than had crowded into Rickard's structure on 2 July 1921. The first Dempsey v Tunney clash in Philadelphia in September 1926 brought in an estimated 135,000 (if this is an exaggeration, even the federal tax records show over 120,000) and they paid $1,895,733 for the privilege. The rematch in Chicago drew 104,943 and produced a gate of $2,658,660. Nevertheless, the 1921 event featuring Dempsey and Carpentier set so many precedents in sport and the media that it seems reasonable to award it its usual title of 'Fight of the Century'.

Relatively unnoticed in the press scramble to get the news out by telegraph as soon as possible were two men at ringside, Major Andrew White and J. O. Smith, using radio microphones to transmit a wireless broadcast, the very first blow-by-blow live commentary on a championship boxing match. (Not until 24 January 1927 would Britain follow suit.) The words of White and Smith carried barely 100 miles beyond their seats, yet this was a development pregnant with meaning. Just as the fight of the century was carried in mostly traditional fashion retrospectively to the millions only by the black-and-white of film or the black-and-white of newsprint, so the 'Black and White' era of boxing was coming to a close. It would be succeeded by the immediacy of the commentaries of the Radio Age and by the end of the 1930s by the visions of the early Television Age. But that is another story …